Politics and Literature
in Shanghai

STUDIES ON EAST ASIA

Editorial Board
Shaun Breslin, University of Newcastle upon Tyne
Gordon Daniels, University of Sheffield
Delia Davin, University of Leeds
Reinhard Drifte, University of Newcastle upon Tyne
Park Jin, University of Newcastle upon Tyne
Don Starr, University of Durham

Chairman of the Board Reinhard Drifte

POLITICS AND LITERATURE IN SHANGHAI:
THE CHINESE LEAGUE OF LEFT-WING WRITERS, 1930–1936

Wang-chi Wong
Department of Translation
Chinese University of Hong Kong

STUDIES ON EAST ASIA

MANCHESTER
UNIVERSITY PRESS
Manchester and New York

distributed exclusively in the USA and Canada
by St. Martin's Press

First published in 1991 in Great Britain by
Manchester University Press, Oxford Road, Manchester M13 9PL, England
and Room 400, 175 Fifth Avenue, New York, NY 10010, USA

Distributed exclusively in the USA and Canada by
St. Martin's Press, 175 Fifth Avenue, New York, NY 10010, USA

Editorial responsibility rests with the East Asia Centre, University of Newcastle upon Tyne, England, which promotes publications on the individual countries and culture of East Asia, as well as on the region as a whole.

All rights reserved. No part of this publication may be reproduced, stored in a retrieval system or transmitted, in any form or by any means, electronic, mechanical, photocopying, recording or otherwise, without the prior permission of the Publishers

British Library Cataloguing in Publication Data
Wong, Wang-chi
 Politics and literature in Shanghai : the Chinese League
 of left-wing writers, 1930–1936. – (Studies on East Asia).
 1. China. Intellectual life, 1919–1938
 I. Title II. Series
 951.04

Library of Congress Cataloging in Publication Data
Wong, Wang-chi,
 Politics and literature in Shanghai : the Chinese League of Left-Wing writers, 1930–1936/Wang-chi Wong
  p.   cm.—(Studies on East Asia)
 Includes bibliographical references and index.
 ISBN 0–7190–2924–4
 1. Chung-kou tso i tso chia lien meng—History. 2. Chinese literature—China—Shanghai—History and criticism. 3. Chinese literature—20th century—History and criticism. 4. Chinese literature—Political aspects—China—Shanghai. I. Title.
II. Series: Studies on East Asia (Manchester, England)
PL1011,W65 1991
895.1'09951132'09043—dc20   90–25519
                                                                                                CIP

ISBN 0–7190–2924–4

Printed in Great Britain
by Billing & Sons Limited, Worcester

Contents

Foreword by David E Pollard — 1

Acknowledgements — 3

Introduction — 5

Chapter One — 9
The Pre-League Period: Debate on Revolutionary Literature (1927-1929)

Chapter Two — 39
The Road to the Establishment of a United Front (1929-1930)

Chapter Three — 59
The Left League: Its Formation, Membership and Structure

Chapter Four — 87
Years of Achievement - The Left League 1930-1933 (I)

Chapter Five — 120
Years of Achievement - The Left League 1930-1933 (II)

Chapter Six — 152
The Waning Years - The Left League 1934-1935

Chapter Seven — 177
Dissolution and Polemic (1935-1936)

Conclusion — 213

Bibliography — 224

Index — 250

Foreword

The League of Left-wing Writers has to figure largely in any history of modern Chinese literature by virtue of the fact that having got off to a relatively liberal start, the trend of the literature was increasingly leftward, and from 1930 to 1936, the years in which it existed, the League led the trend. It led the trend not because its members published the most or the best literature of the time, but because it dominated discussion of literature and society in the periodical press, so moulding views which informed the next wave of literature.

Before the formation of the League and attendant on its dissolution, some of the noisiest and not the politest of the debates were conducted by left-wingers among themselves, but this was not necessarily harmful to the cause; the frays attracted spectators, who might have thought one side wrongheaded, but that still left the winners on the left. While the League was active, internal feuding was damped down and hostility directed outwards, apparently victoriously, if victory is won by endurance and weight of numbers: the rival ideologues were never so strident, and fell silent first. Both in its polemics and in its propaganda, the League undoubtedly achieved its aims of promoting the class struggle and arousing interest in proletarian literature.

So much is generally known, but a great deal about the workings of the League has been obscure, due partly to the fact that it had to operate secretly and partly to deliberate obfuscation. The obfuscation arose because communist historians, who were of course in the best position to tell the tale were first required to represent the operations of the League as an unqualified success, as it was led by the Communist Party, but then to declare a succession of its leading lights black sheep when they fell from favour, a process which culminated in the condemnation of Zhou Yang, the man in charge of the League in its later years, as a 'bourgeois revisionist'. Added to these complications have been questions raised about the arrest of the Five Martyrs of the League executed in 1931 (were they betrayed?), and the relationship between the communist leaders of the League and Lu Xun, whose prestige made him necessary as an ally but whose prickly temper made him an uncomfortable bedfellow.

The rehabilitation of the old guard after 1976 released a flood of memoirs intended to put the record straight, but inevitably also to show the individual authors in a good light. The result was to further cloud as much as to clarify certain issues. It has been Dr Wong's task to sieve the wheat from all this collected chaff and reconstruct what happened where that can be ascertained, and assess the balance of probability where it cannot. He has been remarkably thorough in the first respect and shown very sound judgment in the second. In other words, he has put forward as complete and reliable a picture as may presently be obtained.

The Chinese League of Left-wing Writers

Dr Wong's book may be profitably read as the detailed history of one communist front organisation among many, or more particularly by students of modern Chinese literature as an answer to a number of puzzling questions surrounding some of the most forceful personalities of the day.

D E Pollard
Professor of Chinese in the University of London

Acknowledgements

The present book is a revised version of my PhD dissertation at the School of Oriental and African Studies, University of London. In the process of writing, I was helped in one way or another by so many people that it is impossible to acknowledge them all. I am particularly grateful to Professor David E Pollard, my supervisor, without whose guidance, advice and assistance, this study could not have been accomplished. His valuable comments and suggestions corrected many of my mistakes. I am especially grateful for his willingness to write a foreword, which adds so much pride to this book. I am also heavily indebted to Dr Siu-kit Wong, my teacher at the Department of Chinese, University of Hong Kong, Drs Nigel Bedford and Gregory Lee, two of my best friends in London, who read the manuscript, providing illuminating suggestions and saving me from many errors in English. Needless to say, I alone am responsible for any mistakes that remain.

Special thanks should go to, among others, Mrs Man-yee Fung and Mrs Kit-ling Kiu, Professor Ling-yeong Chiu and Professor Ping-leung Chan, my former teachers in the Department of Chinese, University of Hong Kong, for their constant encouragement in the process of writing. I must also thank my several schoolmates in the University, Mr Sai-shing Yung, Dr Ching-kiu Chan, Dr Kwok-kou Chan, Dr Kang-kwong Luke and Dr Wing-on Yeung for their immense help and interest.

For friends and scholars in Shanghai, I would like particularly to thank Mr Tang Tao, Mr Wang Xiyan, Mr Wang Xiaoming, Mr Hu Congjing and Mr Ding Jingtang for hospitality and help during my stay there. I am also grateful to Dr Zhou Yushan of the Institute of International Relations, Taipei. His thorough research on the Left League has provided me with useful information and suggestions.

In the west, there are two pioneering works in the study of the Left League, Dr Neale Hunter's 'The League of Left-wing Writers, Shanghai, 1930-1936' (Unpublished PhD dissertation, Australian National University, 1973) and Dr Anthony Kane's 'The League of Left-wing Writers and Chinese literary policy' (Unpublished PhD dissertation, University of Michigan, 1982). I would like to thank them for providing some illuminating ideas and useful information.

I must also express my gratitude to Dr David Goodman and Dr Ian Neary, of the East Asia Centre, University of Newcastle upon Tyne for their kind inclusion of the book in the series *Studies on East Asia*. Their encouragement and help have greatly eased the hard work of revision. I should also thank Mrs Margaret Levy of the centre and Miss Celia Ashcroft of Manchester University Press for the help in various ways which makes the publication of the present book possible.

I wish to thank the Association of Commonwealth Universities for the Commonwealth Scholarship, and the Central Research Fund of the University of London which enabled me to do research in London and Shanghai.

Lastly, I wish to thank all members of my family and in particular my wife, Anita, who has shared with me the hardships of a student's life, and my three sons, Tsun-ting, Wai-ting and Ho-ting, who have always been able to cheer me up at times of frustration.

Introduction

1927 was one of the most important years in modern Chinese history, especially in the history of the Chinese Communist Party (CCP). It marked the end of the first united front with the Guomindang (GMD, the Nationalist Party). At its formation in 1921, the young Communist Party, comprising a few dozen intellectuals with no experience in politics, stood no chance in the fight against China's two evils, feudalism and imperialism. Collaboration with the bourgeois party, the GMD, seemed a natural and acceptable course of action, as the latter's large membership constituted the strongest force in the revolution, and the bourgeoisie, after all, was the only class then fully aware of revolutionary ideas.[1] The Communist International (Comintern) in Moscow, to which the CCP turned for guidance, had also been in favour of a united front. As early as September 1921, Maring (H Sneevliet), the secretary of the National and Colonial Committee of the Comintern, met Dr Sun Yat-sen at Guilin. It was reported that Maring proposed a collaboration with the GMD.[2] Though the plan failed, it seemed that Dr Sun was very much impressed by the New Economic Policy of the Soviet Union. GMD delegates were sent to attend the Congress of the Toilers of the East (the Eastern People's Congress) in Moscow in January 1922. There, the Soviet delegate, Safarov, commended the achievements of the GMD and declared that 'in colonial and semi-colonial countries the first phase of the revolutionary movement must inevitably be a national-democratic movement'.[3] The first united front was finally realised in 1923 when the GMD was reorganised and took in Communist members.

During this first collaboration, the Communist Party grew rapidly. With only fifty-seven members at the First Congress in 1921, it had 57,693 members in 1927, plus some 35,000 members of the Youth Corps.[4] But this did not mean that the collaboration was smooth and stable. After Sun Yat-sen's death on 12 March 1925, the hostility of many GMD members towards the Communists became apparent. Liao Zhongkai, the Finance Minister and an ardent supporter of the united front, was assassinated in August. In November, about ten important GMD members met in Beijing and formed the group which was later known as the Western Hill Group (*Xishanpai*). They demanded the immediate expulsion of the Communists. Several months later, the March 20th Incident - or the Gunboat Zhongshan Incident (*Zhongshanjian shijian*) - took place in Guangzhou. Jiang Jieshi claimed that the gunboat manned by Communist officers planned to kidnap him, and declared martial law.[5] Although the incident did not immediately lead to serious hostilities, it became clear to the Communists that Jiang was not a reliable ally. Then early on the morning of 12 April 1927, Jiang staged a coup against the Communists in Shanghai. Large numbers of Communists were arrested and shot. Similar action was taken in other parts of the country. On 18 April, Jiang formed a new national government in Nanjing and the first united front was completely shattered.

The impact of the 'purge' on the Communists was strong. The leadership changed: Chen Duxiu, CCP founder and chief secretary since its formation, was replaced by Qu Qiubai. Qu, reacting to Chen's so-called 'capitulationist' policy, initiated, under Comintern direction, a 'putschist' line. Desperately trying to regain lost ground, he ordered CCP members in different places to stage uprisings, but they were easily crushed by the GMD. Even worse, within a year, party membership had fallen to less than one-fifth of the level before the coup.[6]

The 1927 coup also had its impact in the literary field. The left-wingers, defeated in politics, took refuge in literature. They launched a large scale revolutionary literary movement in Shanghai, and within a few years, left-wing literature became the dominant element in the literary arena. Thus 1927 has been regarded as a turning point not only in the political history, but also in the literary history of modern China. In fact, the ten years following 1927 are commonly known as the 'Left League Decade' (*Zuolian shinian*).[7] The Left League (*Zuolian*), or in full, the Chinese League of Left-wing Writers (*Zhongguo zuoyi zuojia lianmeng*), was a literary organisation formed on 2 March 1930 under the direction and control of the CCP, after a polemic among the left-wingers had been brought to an end. In the first half of the thirties, the Left League fought a number of lively battles against pro-government and even apolitical writers, regarded by the Left as obstacles to their revolution. 1936, the year in which the League was dissolved, marked the end of this era as the Communists called for another collaboration with the GMD against Japanese aggression.

During the Left League Decade, the CCP's political and military survival was threatened. Jiang Jieshi, firmly established at Nanjing, was determined to wipe out Communism in China and launched five large scale campaigns against the Communists in remote areas of Jiangxi until they were driven out of the so-called Soviet areas and forced on to the Long March in 1934. In Shanghai, the base of the Left League, the situation was even more serious. 'White terror' threatened the life of every left-winger. The propagation of their ideas was difficult owing to strict censorship and the banning of their publications. Internally, the left-wingers themselves were troubled with intra-Party conflict. Within the same period, the Communist Party is said to have been ruled by three left-deviationist lines, under Qu Qiubai (from August 1927 to June 1928), Li Lisan (from 1929 to September 1930) and Wang Ming (alias Chen Shaoyu) (from 1931-1936).[8] Literary activities were directly or indirectly affected by party policy, resulting in some serious mistakes. Further, the base of the Left League was not solid. Thus, in its final years, the League itself was badly hit by factionalism, ending the Left League Decade with another polemic.

However, it was not an easy time for the Nationalists either. Having won a telling victory over the Communists in 1927, they still faced other internal enemies. Warlords like Li Zongren, Li Jichen, Yen Xishan and Feng Yuxiang,

Introduction

in different parts of the country, posed great threats to the newly established regime. In the early thirties, large scale battles took place. Though Jiang finally emerged the victor, the damage was huge. It was reported that three hundred thousand men were killed in a single battle in 1931.[9] Such wars also damaged the nation's economy. Military expenses in 1928 was $210 million; that of 1930 was $310 million, a fifty percent increase.[10] To meet these expenses, government bonds had to be issued, a total of $520 million in 1928-1930.[11] The situation was made more acute with the worldwide economic slump in 1930.

This period also saw the Japanese invasion of China. In 1931, there was the Mukden, or September 18th, Incident, when the Japanese invaded the northeast of China, and took more than a million square kilometres of land in four months. Then, in January 1932, the infamous Shanghai battle erupted. In neither case did Jiang take serious and positive action against the Japanese. He adopted a policy of 'pacification first, then resistance' (*xian annei, hou rangwai*) believing that the Communists must be wiped out before China could fight a successful external war. This inevitably aroused anti-GMD feelings among the people.

Throughout the thirties, Communists continued to pose a serious threat to the nationalist government. Although badly hit by the coup, they gradually regained some strength outside the cities. With the expansion of the Red Army, Party membership began to grow again.[12] A large Soviet area was built up in southeast China, greatly threatening the Nationalist regime. The first four campaigns launched against them ended in failure on the part of the GMD, resulting in heavy casualties and economic strain.

In Shanghai, the Left League and other leftist cultural groups tried every means available to propagate Marxist theories and attack the authorities. Often, left-wingers sought refuge in the foreign concession areas. One fatal weakness on the part of the Nationalists was that they could not build up any sort of literature or literary movement of their own to counter the influence of the left in the literary circle. On the other hand, the left was able to secure the services of Lu Xun, one of those writers who were dismayed at the coup of Jiang Jieshi. Lu Xun's contribution to the left in the thirties was invaluable. His name alone stood out as a great symbol. A famous writer and the 'mentor of the youth' (*qingnian daoshi*), he was able to attract around him a group of young fighters. This alone made him such an important member of the left-wing literary movement.

However, since so much importance had been attached to him, Lu Xun could constitute a strong divisive force if alienated. Consequently, the solidarity of the organisation and the development of the left-wing literary movement depended very much on his relationship with other cadres of the Left League. Unfortunately there was no solid base for a genuine personal friendship. Before the formation of the Left League, there was a heated debate between him and other left-wing writers, while in its final years, he was very much discontented with the deeds of some of the most important members of the organisation.

Hence, the period covered in this study can be properly described as volatile. Both the Communists and the nationalists were confronted with internal and external foes and problems, as was the entire nation. It was in this chaotic situation, in the Shanghai, 'paradise of adventurers',[13] that left-wing literature emerged and grew.

Notes to the Introduction

1. Jacques Guillermaz, *A history of the Chinese Communist Party, 1921-1949* (Translated by Anne Destenay) (London: Methuen & Co, 1972), p 68.
2. Wang Jianmin, *A draft history of the Chinese Communist Party (Zhongguo gongzhandang shigao)* (Taibei: Zhongwen tushu gongyingshe, Sept 1974), pp 93-4.
3. Jacques Guillermaz, *A history of the Chinese Communist Party*, p 70.
4. *Ibid*, p 83.
5. For an account of the incident, see James P Harrison, *The long march to power: A history of the Chinese Communist Party, 1921-72* (New York: Praeger Publishers, 1972), pp 76-82.
6. *Ibid*, p 83.
7. For example, see Wang Yao, *A draft history of modern Chinese literature (Xinwenxue shigao)* (Shanghai: Shanghai wenyi chubanshe, November 1982 reprint), pp 162-216.
8. Mao Zedong, 'Resolution on certain questions in the history of our Party', *Selected works of Mao Tse-tung* (Beijing: Foreign Language Press, 1965), Vol III, pp 183-8.
9. Wang Yunsheng, 'Observing the tides for ten years' (*guanchao shinian*), *Guowen zhoubao* Vol XI No 1 (1 January 1934), pp 1-13.
10. Wang Yuanqi, *A history of modern China (Zhongguo xiandaishi)* (Henan: Henan renmin chubanshe, July 1982) Vol I, p 277.
11. *Ibid*.
12. James P Harrison, *The long march to power*, p 148.
13. G E Miller, *Shanghai, the paradise of adventurers* (New York: Orsay Publishing House, 1937).

Chapter One

The Pre-League Period: Debate on Revolutionary Literature (1927-1929)

The years from 1927 to 1929 are generally taken as the 'pre-League Period' of the Left League decade, as the Chinese League of Left-wing Writers was not formed until March 1930. Nevertheless, this short period was no less important than the six League years. In Shanghai, there was a heated debate over the issue of revolutionary literature among the left-wingers who were driven to literary activities after the political setback caused by Jiang Jieshi's coup in April 1927. This revolutionary literary movement provided the basis for the formation of the Left League and other left-wing literary movements in the thirties.

Three groups were involved in the polemic on revolutionary literature; the ultra-left, who ardently advocated and supported revolutionary literature; the left, in basic agreement with revolutionary literature but not satisfied with the means proposed and the ideas expressed by the first group; and the right, who opposed revolutionary literature on principle. The first group was made up of members of the Creation (*Chuangzaoshe*) and Sun Societies (*Taiyangshe*), the second was headed by Lu Xun and Mao Dun, representatives of the Thread-of-talk group (*Yusipai*) and the Literary Research Association (*Wenxue yanjiuhui*) and the last group was mainly the Crescentists (*Xinyuepai*), with Liang Shiqiu as the key theoretician. The polemic was three-cornered: fierce arguments took place between the first two groups as well as between those two and the third.

Soon after the debate began, in early 1928, there was an argument among the ultra-leftists themselves over the question of leadership in the revolutionary literary movement. Li Chuli, prominent in the last stage of the Creation Society, labelled as the first voice in the advocacy of revolutionary literature the article 'Revolution and literature' (*Geming yu wenxue*), published in April 1926 by Guo Moruo, a founder of the Society.[1] This idea was unacceptable to Qian Xingcun of the Sun Society, who believed that Jiang Guangci was at least two years ahead of Guo in advocating revolutionary literature, because as early as August 1924, Jiang had published an article 'Proletarian revolution and culture' (*Wuchan jieji geming yu wenhua*).[2] This dispute reflected clearly the sectarianism of the ultra-leftists, who tried to take all merit for their own groups.

It is difficult to give a general definition of revolutionary literature. The new literature created shortly after the May Fourth Incident can be regarded as 'revolutionary' in a broad sense as it aimed at the destruction of the old order and the promotion of radical change. In terms of form, the use of the new vernacular (*xinbaihua*) was an emancipation from classical Chinese (*wenyan*). But obviously, this was not the kind of revolutionary literature demanded by the self-proclaimed revolutionary writers of 1927. They wanted a revolutionary literature in Marxist terms. An acceptable definition would be as follows:

> Revolutionary literature must consciously endeavour to 'raise the consciousness' of its audience - that is, it must promote and increase the audience's understanding of socio-historic reality according to the perspective of class struggle and the stages of historical development all societies pass through on their way to communism.[3]

By this definition, works from the May Fourth period were excluded from the category of revolutionary literature, since class consciousness was not distinct then and the Communist Party was formed only two years later. Not until 1922-23, was there the first advocacy of the kind of revolutionary literature to fit a Marxist definition.

In 1922, the Chinese Socialist Youth Corps (*Zhongguo shehuizhuyi qingniantuan*) held its first general meeting. Its members included Deng Zhongxia, Yun Daiying, Shen Zemin and Xiao Chunu, who became important members of the CCP. The corps passed a resolution in the general meeting calling for members to take part in various literary activities and proletarianise literature and art.[4] In December 1923, Deng Zhongxia published in its official organ *Zhongguo qingnian* (*Chinese youth*) an article called 'Proffered to the new poets' (*Gongxianyu xinshiren zhiqian*). In the article, he expressed his disgust at those poets who took no notice of social problems. He discussed the effect of literature in driving people to revolution:

> We admit that men are sentient beings. We admit that revolutions are economic and political struggles in the face of oppression. But it is necessary to move people's sentiment first if we want to awaken their revolutionary consciousness and inspire them so that they have the courage for revolution. You may use speeches or treatises to move their sentiment. But the most effective means is literature.[5]

He also urged writers to participate in revolutionary activities and write on actual life in society.

Deng's close associate, Yun Daiying expressed a similar idea in a short essay called 'Literature and revolution' (*Wenxue yu geming*). He believed that taking part in revolution was a prerequisite for writing revolutionary literature. To him, as literature was a product of the noble and sacred feelings of mankind, one had to have revolutionary feelings before creating revolutionary literature; and as one could acquire revolutionary feelings only by participating in revolution, one had to become a revolutionary first. He did not mean that all revolutionaries could be revolutionary writers. 'Among these revolutionaries, there will be someone who has abundant feelings and he will certainly create revolutionary literature.'[6]

Shen Zemin, younger brother of the famous writer Mao Dun, also pioneered the promotion of revolutionary literature. On 15 December 1923, a week before Deng Zhongxia published 'Proffered to the new poets', he had already called for writers to 'go among the people' (*dao minjian qu*).[7] In another essay, 'Literature and revolutionary literature' (*Wenxue yu geming de wenxue*), he argued that a great change was approaching and the whole structure of society was shattering.

The Pre-League Period

The world's proletarians had awakened. A revolutionary writer, being their spokesman, should use literature as a means to express the desires, sufferings and wishes of the oppressed. More important, he was able to bring out the issue of proletarian consciousness. He believed that someone with only revolutionary ideas could not create revolutionary literature. Unless one had joined a workers' strike, been thrown into prison or chased by police, or had worked hard and been ill-treated by employers, one could never understand the proletarian subconsciousness and could never be qualified to write revolutionary literature.[8]

Although *Zhongguo qingnian* was a very important publication in advocating revolutionary literature, it was largely neglected because the few essays it contained sparked off no large scale movement. The issue of revolutionary literature was taken up again and turned into a widespread movement basically because of the work of Jiang Guangci of the Sun Society and Guo Moruo of the Creation Society.

Jiang Guangci was also a member of the Chinese Socialist Youth Corps, having joined in the winter of 1920. In 1922, he became a member of the CCP. From 1921 to 1924, he studied at the Oriental University of Moscow. Upon his return, he lectured on Marxist sociology at the CCP-run Shanghai University.[9] In 1924, he published his first book of poetry, *New Dreams* (*Xinmeng*), which has been regarded by many as the first fruit of the revolutionary literature. In the poems, Jiang Guangci called for a world revolution and the awakening of the proletariat. He also demanded the downfall of imperialism and an end to civil wars between warlords. His first piece of fiction, 'The young tramp' (*Shaonian piaopozhe*), published in 1926, was described by Qian Xingcun as a piece of 'proletarian revolutionary literature' and 'a genuine record of the germination period of proletarian revolutionary literature'.[10] His subsequent works, such as 'On the River Yalu' (*Yalujiang shang*) and 'Des Sans-culottes' (*Duankudang*), are important, though maybe not good, specimens of revolutionary literature.[11]

However, he did not seem to put much emphasis on theory. As late as 1928 he still insisted that 'what we demand from writers are literary and revolutionary creations, not those empty and elusive treatises which can be written by anybody'.[12] On the other hand, the contribution of the Creation Society in the theoretical field was much greater. The different attitudes of the two groups towards theory constituted a major source of conflict between them.

Initially, the Creationists advocated 'art for art's sake' introducing to China the work of such Western romantics as Goethe, Whitman, Byron and Shelley. They denounced in particular so-called 'artistic utilitarianism' and for this reason, a pen-battle erupted between the Society and the Literary Research Association. But soon there were signs of change. In the May 1923 issue of *Chuangzao zhoubao* (*Creation weekly*), the two leading figures of the Society, Guo Moruo and Yu Dafu, published two articles considered by some critics as 'preludes to the later revolutionary literary movement'.[13] In the short essay 'Our new literary movement' (*Women de wenxue xinyundong*), Guo condemned the militarists, politicians and capitalists of China, stating unequivocally:

We are against the evil dragon of capitalism.
Our movement must develop in literature the proletarian spirit and expose human nature in its nakedness.[14]

On the other hand, Yu Dafu mentioned in his article 'Class struggle in literature' (*Wenxueshang de jieji douzheng*) that the class struggle of twentieth century literature very much resembled the actual class struggle in society. He quoted from the Communist Manifesto and appealed to proletarians and the oppressed to unite in an effort to realise their ideals.[15]

Although the title of Guo Moruo's article strongly hinted that he aimed to start a new literary movement, obviously he did not have revolutionary literature in mind. In the essay, he stated that the motto they believed in was: 'The kind of literature identical to the Huanghe and Yangzi!' He went on to explain:

> The river systems of the Huanghe and Yangzi Jiang are the two great masterpieces suggested to us by nature. Receiving rain and dew from the sky, absorbing running water from the ground, dissolving all external substances in themselves, making them all their own blood, they roll on and on, rolling out of all themselves. Any stones blocking them will be destroyed! Any unreasonable dams will be destroyed! Brace up the entire blood and energy, brace up all of the spirits, flow into the eternal sea of peace.[16]

Stripped of symbolism, Guo's words meant to demand from literature a true and complete expression, or outflow of the 'self' (*ziwo*). Though he exhibited a rebellious attitude, it was merely a result of this demand, as what he called for was destruction of those who hindered and obstructed the expression of the self.

Similarly, Yu Dafu's 'class struggle' had nothing to do with the proletarian class struggle against the bourgeoisie. The following lines clearly reveal Yu's interpretation of the expression:

> The materials taken up by them are mostly reflections of class struggles. For instance, the drama 'Die Bürger von Calais' by Georg Kaiser shows the struggle between justice and cruelty. The tragedy 'Ein Geschlecht' by Fritz von Unruh shows the struggle between mother and son. Walter Hasenclever's 'Der Sohn' shows the struggle between father and son.[17]

Here, Yu interpreted class struggle in its broadest sense as anything rebellious and against tradition. This definition is not Marxist but nihilist.[18] Further, most of the writers praised in the article, such as Baudelaire, Verlaine, Rolland, Duhamel, Barthel and Werfel, cannot be regarded as Marxists and did not advocate the kind of literature acceptable to Chinese revolutionary writers.

Guo Moruo himself believed his conversion to Marxism came with his translation in April 1924, of the Japanese Marxist Kawakami Hajime's book *Social organization and social revolution* (*Shakai soshiki to shakai kakumei*).[19] He wrote to another founder of the Creation Society, Cheng Fangwu, 'it clarified my past muddled thinking. From then on, I changed my direction to Marxism'.[20]

The Pre-League Period

Changes in society were also very important. Advocates of revolutionary literature in 1927 almost unanimously saw the May Thirtieth events as the main cause of the revolutionary literary movement. On 30 May 1925, in the Shanghai International Settlement, British police fired on demonstrators protesting against the arrest and killing of agitators in strikes that had been going on since April at Japanese-owned cotton mills. A general strike of merchants, factory workers and students followed. Not until September did all factories resume operation. This so-called May Thirtieth Movement spread quickly to other cities, like Hankou, Nanjing and Chongqing. Most famous was the great Hong Kong-Guangzhou Strike which ran for sixteen months from June 1925 to October 1926, the longest in Chinese history. Working class activity was unprecedented. According to a report by the General Union of Shanghai, over 156,000 joined the strike between 5 May and 13 June.[21] This nationwide movement of Chinese workers, was taken as an awakening of proletarian consciousness. Seeing the immense power of the working class, left-wingers came to believe that a new revolutionary age had dawned. The literary scene, as one element of the superstructure, had to change accordingly. Revolutionary literature seemed the answer. Qian Xingcun's words were typical:

> After the May Thirtieth Incident, the class positions in China suddenly underwent a great change. The class power of workers and peasants was shown up gradually. At this time, the long awaited fourth class literature began to rise.[22]

May Thirtieth also had great impact on the Communist Party which increased its membership tenfold in six months, from 1,000 in May to 10,000 in November 1925. In the next eight months it tripled to 30,000 (July 1926) and doubled again to 58,000 by early April 1927.[23] It was possibly for this reason that so much importance was attached to the incident.

Many revolutionary writers were eye-witnesses of the May Thirtieth events; some of them participated, leading strikes and demonstrations. In early 1926, all the most important Creationists found themselves gathered in Guangzhou. Guo Moruo's 'Revolution and literature', widely accepted as having sparked off the revolutionary literary movement, was written and published in this 'cradle of revolution'. It was after the 'Party purge' of the nationalists in April 1927 that writers, taking refuge in the concession areas, brought the issue to Shanghai.

In this first article, Guo mechanically divided literature into two categories: the revolutionary and the counter-revolutionary, asserting that in revolutions, there were always two opposing classes, the oppressing and the oppressed:

> At such a time, each class will of course have its own spokesman, and what you say depends on what class you side with. If you take the side of the oppressing class, you are certainly counter-revolutionary. If you side with the oppressed class, you will support revolution. When you are counter-revolutionary, the kind of literature you produce or appreciate will definitely be counter-revolutionary literature, one which speaks for the oppressing class.

> This kind of literature does not correspond to revolution and will be despised and disowned by revolutionaries. But if you are sympathetic with revolution, the works you create or appreciate will be revolutionary literature, speaking in the name of the oppressed class.[24]

Guo argued that revolutionary literature was the vanguard of revolution and would bring a golden age of literature. By contrast, counter-revolutionary literature was worthless. 'What is literature is always revolutionary, and there is only one kind of genuine literature: revolutionary literature.'

There may have been no systematic planning beforehand, but 'Revolutionary literature and its perenniality' (*Geming wenxue yu tade yongyuanxing*) by another prominent member, Cheng Fangwu, which appeared straight after Guo's article naturally led others to think that the Creation Society, which had advocated 'art for art's sake', had shifted to promoting revolutionary literature. Meanwhile, Lu Xun, who had had a poor opinion of the behaviour of the Creationists,[25] expressed a wish to cooperate with them. On 7 November 1926, he wrote to Xu Guangping:

> In fact, I have one more ambition. I hope that upon my arrival in Guangzhou, I can carry on with my fight against the 'gentlemen' ... Secondly, [I would like to] unite with the Creation Society in a front to attack the old society.[26]

Similarly, it seemed that at this stage, the Creationists also welcomed an alliance with Lu Xun. According to Guo Moruo, it was he who recommended Lu Xun to Sun Yat-sen University,[27] but upon the latter's arrival, most of the Creationists, except Cheng Fangwu, had already left Guangzhou. It was then that Cheng published the provocative 'Complete our literary movement'. In the article, Cheng complained that the literary movement had been badly damaged by those writers who sought only 'fun' (*quwei*) and treasured 'leisure, leisure and leisure'. A number of well-known writers were criticised by name, among them Lu Xun, who was attacked for killing time collecting and copying old fiction.[28]

Lu Xun did not seem to be too annoyed at the time. While he was in Guangzhou, he often visited the Creation Society. In his private letters, he described this Society as one of the three groups which continued to contribute to the literary arena, and even said that 'relations with the Creation Society seem to be very good'.[29] Then on 20 February, he received a letter from Cheng Fangwu, inviting him to issue a proclamation.[30] 'The proclamation from the Chinese writers to the British intellectuals and general public' (*Zhongguo wenxuejia duiyu Yingguo zhishifenzi ji yiban minzhong xuanyan*) can be regarded as the first cooperation between Lu Xun and the Creation Society, because all other signatories were members of the Society. Together they appealed to the British public for joint action with the Chinese against the invasion of China by British and other imperialists.[31]

Lu Xun made his first utterance on revolutionary literature on 8 April 1927 in an address to the Huangpu Military Academy, less than a week before Jiang

The Pre-League Period

Jieshi took action against the Communists. Although the speech was entitled 'Literature of a revolutionary period' (*Geming shidai de wenxue*), Lu decried the importance of literature, saying that it would only be taken up by the weakest, most useless people while the strong would continue to kill without saying anything or paying attention to what others said. To him, the remedy for China was a successful revolution, rather than literature of any sort. 'A poem could not have frightened away Sun Chuanfang, but a cannon shell scared him away.'[32]

As for the question of revolution and literature, he suggested a three-stage relationship. In the first stage, before the outbreak of revolution, there was a literature of discontent against inequalities in society. In the second stage, when revolution was under way, there was silence only, as people would be actively engaged and could have no time for literature. In the third stage, when a successful revolution was over, two kinds of literature would appear, one eulogising the revolution and the other bemoaning the past. But the writing of these two kinds of literature would not last long. After that, there would possibly be a 'people's literature' (*pingmin wenxue*).[33]

For these reasons, Lu Xun could not accept other people's (including Guo's) assertion that literature played a big part in revolution. To him, it was revolution that played a large part in literature. But he did not mean to deny the existence of revolutionary literature:

> For revolution, we need revolutionaries, but revolutionary literature can wait, for only when revolutionaries start writing can there be revolutionary literature.[34]

Lu Xun did not believe that revolutionary literature already existed in China, nor was it likely that this literature would soon appear. This cautious attitude was possibly born of his disillusionment upon arrival in Guangzhou. At first, he was delighted and happy to be there, saying that people were more lively there than elsewhere.[35] But it did not take long for him to find out that Guangzhou was no different from other places. Just like the red banners with characters written in white paint, it was 'white within red'. He warned that Guangzhou, the cradle of revolution, could also be the cradle of counter-revolution.[36]

But it is wrong to say that Lu Xun's address to the Huangpu Military Academy 'would probably have touched off a fiery debate in Guangzhou' had there not been the Party purge of Jiang Jieshi several days later.[37] After the purge, in October, Lu Xun wrote on the issue of revolutionary literature again. The ideas given expression in the speech were repeated:

> I believe the basic question is whether the writer is a 'revolutionary'. If yes, it is revolutionary literature, no matter what topic is written on and what materials are used. What comes out from the pipe is water; from the vein, blood... There is no revolution when revolutionary writers appear in large numbers.[38]

These ideas were not condemned by the revolutionary writers in 1928. In fact, relations between Lu Xun and his later antagonists in the revolutionary literary polemic were at their best when Lu Xun went to Shanghai after the coup.

The Chinese League of Left-wing Writers

Lu Xun and Guo Moruo arrived in Shanghai in October 1927. In view of the political defeat, Guo wanted to do something in the literary field. Zheng Boqi recalled that he proposed to Guo an alliance with Lu Xun. Zheng, with Jiang Guangci and Duan Keqing, visited Lu Xun on 9 November 1927 to discuss the issue. Lu 'gladly agreed' and suggested reviving the *Chuangzao zhoubao*.[39] On 3 December, an advertisement announcing the revival of the weekly appeared in *Shishi xinbao* (*Current affairs news*). The four editors listed were all members of the Creation Society, Cheng Fangwu, Zheng Boqi, Duan Keqing and Wang Duqing. Lu Xun's name was first in the list of special contributors, among those of Guo Moruo (pseud Mai Ke'ang) and Feng Naichao. The advertisement also said that the weekly would come out on the first day of 1928.[40]

It did not appear as announced. Instead, in *Chuangzao yuekan* which came out that day, there was another notice, saying that the weekly would be published on the following Sunday. A long list of special contributors, thirty in all, was given, including almost all those involved in the revolutionary literary polemic. Lu Xun was again first, followed by Jiang Guangci who soon founded the Sun Society. Others of this group in the list were Yang Cunren and Meng Chao. The young Creationists, including Li Chuli, Feng Naichao and Peng Kang, were also there among the old ones, Guo Moruo and Cheng Fangwu.[41]

Had *Chuangzao zhoubao* come out as planned, there might have been great cooperation among writers in Shanghai but this cooperation never materialised. In the second printing of the above-mentioned issue of *Chuangzao yuekan*, the advertisement was replaced by an 'Urgent notice of the change of *Chuangzao zhoubao* to *Wenhua pipan* [*Critique of culture*]'.[42]

Obviously, someone within the Creation Society opposed cooperation. Lu Xun was completely in the dark and later complained that he simply did not know why the plan to revive *Chuangzao zhoubao* was dropped and why he became a target of attack. Most people blamed Cheng Fangwu and other young Creationists. While it was true that they opposed cooperation with Lu Xun, Guo Moruo should be the first to be blamed for not consulting and seeking the consent of Cheng Fangwu beforehand. Guo said in retrospect:

> At the time when I laid the plan [of cooperating with Lu Xun], Fangwu had already gone to Japan. I thought he would accept the plan. In order to speed up the progress, I did not ask for his opinion beforehand.[43]

It was Zheng Boqi who introduced Li Chuli, Feng Naichao, Peng Kang and Zhu Jingwo to Cheng Fangwu. Except for Zhu who studied in Tokyo Imperial University, these 'young Creationists' (*Chuangzaoshe xiaohuoji*), as well as Zheng Boqi, all studied at Kyoto Imperial University and had discussed the promotion of proletarian literature. Now back in Shanghai, Zheng told Cheng Fangwu about this. Cheng went to Japan to meet them.[44] Thus, two plans, one with Lu Xun and one with the young radicals, were being pursued at once.

At the end of 1927, these young radicals returned to Shanghai. It is difficult to establish with certainty what happened immediately afterwards because different people told different stories. Feng Naichao recalled in 1978 that he did not know there was such a plan and that he was not against it.[45] This is not convincing as his name appeared in the list of contributors, together with that of Lu Xun; and the idea of changing *Chuangzao zhoubao* to *Wenhua pipan* was certainly formulated after their return from Japan. Guo Moruo supplied a different version:

> The two plans could not go hand in hand. The Japanese fire met the Shanghai water. At the beginning, there was deadlock. I suggested waiting until Fangwu's return before making any decision. A telegram was sent to him and he returned from Japan soon after. He strongly opposed the revival of *Chuangzao zhoubao*, saying that its mission was over. He supported the suggestion of the returned friends of publishing a militant monthly called *Kangliu* [*Opposing stream*] (this title was not adopted but changed to *Wenhua pipan*). As for the cooperation with Lu Xun, everyone was indifferent.[46]

Here, Guo Moruo claimed that he insisted on collaboration with Lu Xun. He suggested that there was a hot quarrel over the issue, but Zheng Boqi pointed out that Guo Moruo agreed to the plan of the newcomers even before their return:

> All of them [the young Creationists] were ready to quit school and come back. Fangwu wrote us a letter, telling us this news. We were all very happy and anxious to see their arrival. Moruo and I also agreed to Fangwu's new plan. The previous plan of collaboration [with Lu Xun] was then dropped.[47]

Zheng even said that Guo Moruo secretly met the newcomers and they agreed on the future work.[74]

Thus Guo Moruo's attitude is open to question. Did he support the newcomers' plan or that of cooperation with Lu Xun? The recollections of the people involved have to be assessed with caution as they were written long after the incident and details might have been forgotten. Moreover, there might be deliberate distortions - no one would now publicly admit to having shunned Lu Xun. Judging from later developments, that an urgent notice appeared in such a short time, that *Wenhua pipan* was able to come out on 15 January 1928, and that Guo continued to support the activities of the Creation Society, we may surmise that the friction within the Society could not have been great. Guo might not have wanted to drop the plan to cooperate with Lu Xun, but he was certainly not against the returned students.

This development alienated not only Lu Xun, but a group of young writers who were among the special contributors and who finally formed the Sun Society. According to Yang Cunren, a founder of the society, the idea of publishing *Taiyang yuekan* arose as early as June 1927 when Jiang Guangci, Qian Xingcun, Meng Chao and Yang himself were in Wuhan. The magazine's name and content had already been decided too. 'The failure of the Creation Society's plan strengthened our drive to publish our own magazine', Yang recalled. They did not intend to set up an organisation then, but after they were attacked by Creationists felt the need to form an association to put up a better fight.[48] Nevertheless, Jiang Guangci had long been unable to get on with the young Creationists. Jiang was arrogant, and the young writers at the Creation Society publishing house did not hide their contempt for him.[49]

It is therefore not surprising that Jiang's article 'Modern Chinese literature and social life' (*Xiandai Zhongguo wenxue yu shehui shenghuo*) in the first issue of *Taiyang yuekan* which came out on 1 January 1928 was harshly criticised by the young Creationists. Here, Jiang claimed that the pace of revolution was too fast for writers to keep up with. When a writer tried to describe social life in literature, a certain thought process was involved. But with the speed of social change, however quick a writer's pen was, new changes occurred before he could finish describing former changes. This was why 'our literature cannot but be backward'.[50] This idea was challenged by Li Chuli in his article 'How to create revolutionary literature' (*Zenyangdi jianshe geming wenxue*). Li believed that literature was backward due to the petit bourgeois ideology of writers, rather than the fast pace of revolution. He accused Jiang of having a woman's kind heart. 'His attempt to transport all souls in the literary world to the paradise of "revolutionary literature"' by asking the pace of revolution to slow down was not only unnecessary, but impossible.[51]

However, a closer look at their articles will show that the above difference was not so great as to cause an open dispute between the two groups. After all, Jiang did not say that ideology was not important, and Li accepted that the pace of revolution was fast. There was yet another point of dispute between the two which has often been overlooked by critics.

In his article, Jiang Guangci commended 'a group of new writers who emerged from the tide of revolution':

> They themselves are revolution - they have participated in revolutionary movements, they abound with revolutionary moods. They do not separate themselves from revolution... In other words, they have a close relationship with revolution.[52]

Jiang did not name these new writers but everyone would know that he was referring to the members of the Sun Society. Jiang himself, plus Qian Xingcun, Meng Chao and Yang Cunren, had all been eyewitnesses as well as participants in previous revolutionary activities. Doubtless, they took great pride in this. In another paragraph, he revealed his low opinion of revolutionary theory:

> What we demand from writers are literary and revolutionary creations, not those empty and elusive treatises which could be written by anybody.[53]

Jiang said that although some writers had put out some vigorous political treatises, they were not qualified to be writers.

These words were taken by members of the Creation Society as a malicious attack. The young critics of the society were inexperienced in revolutionary activity having been in Japan when the May Thirtieth, the Northern Expedition and Jiang Jieshi's coup took place in China. To overcome this inadequacy, the young Creationists put less weight on actual revolutionary activity and stressed instead the importance of theory. This was a result of the influence of Fukumotoism with which they were acquainted during their stay in Japan.

Fukumotoism was the political theory of the young Fukumoto Kazuo which became the dominant theory among Japanese Communists until its liquidation by the Comintern in 1927.[54] It arose at first as an opposing force to Yamakawaism, the theory of Yamakawa Hitoshi, then the leading member of the JCP. Seeing the lack of mass political consciousness, Yamakawa believed that there was no way to form an advanced political party and called for the dissolution of the Party and the establishment of a common front of worker and peasant organisations. Thus it was necessary to make concessions to the rightist elements. Fukumoto, however, held an entirely different viewpoint. Tatsuo Arima has summed up his basic ideas:

> Fukumoto argued that Yamakawaism was eclectic and that it neglected to emphasise the revolutionary element with Marxism. The gist of Fukumoto's argument, now called Fukumotoism, was that the Japanese Communist Party should separate the genuine Marxists from the fellow travellers and social democrats and then crystallise them into a well-organised party. Hence, the well-known 'Break away before we unite'. He saw that 'for the time being, the struggle is to be limited to the realm of theoretical struggle'.[55]

Thus the two main points of Fukumotoism were 'break away first before unite' (*fenli jiehe*) and 'theoretical struggle' (*lilun douzheng*). This latter point marked the greatest difference between the young Creationists and the Sun group.

In the foreword to *Wenhua pipan*, Cheng Fangwu declared that the new journal would devote itself to revolutionary theories.[56] The concluding line of Li Chuli's article 'How to create revolutionary literature' read 'let this essay of mine be the beginning of a "theoretical struggle"'.[57] This expression, in quotation marks, was taken from Fukumotoism. In another article by Li Chuli, 'Reply to an open letter' (*Yifeng gongkaixin de huida*), this 'theoretical struggle' appeared eight times, all in quotation marks. These essays, together with others by the young critics of the Creation Society, all stressed the importance of revolutionary theories. Obviously Jiang Guangci's argument in 'Modern Chinese literature and social life', that theoretical treatises were not needed, was unacceptable to the Creationists.

But Jiang Guangci was supported by other members of the Sun Society. Qian Xingcun said:

> You critics! Please do not ever forget that behind theories, there is a term called 'action'. Please do not ever forget that it is not necessary to have a sound revolutionary theory before there are revolutionary actions... You can find revolutionary actions in actual working experiences. Sometimes, this can even correct revolutionary theories.[58]

The quarrel between the two revolutionary groups, the Creation and Sun Societies took place in early 1928. Apart from the issue of theory, sectarianism was an important cause. Each group praised and defended people of the same camp but found fault with articles written by members of the opposing camp. As seen earlier, they tried to grasp the leadership of the revolutionary literary movement by insisting that the first article on the issue was written by one of their group. More than once, the Sun group accused the Creationists of trying to monopolise the literary circle and the revolutionary literary movement. The 'Editor's note' in the March issue of *Taiyang yuekan* was most provocative:

> The Sun Society is not a literary group monopolised by returned students. It is not the private property of a few people, and it is not a literary organisation which on the one hand shouts loudly for working class literature while on the other exposes its philosophy of hero-worship by its actions and in its literature.[59]

This was unbearable to the Creationists, mostly returned students from Japan. Li Chuli in an open reply denied that the Creation Society wanted to monopolise the movement. 'As all of us aim at promoting revolutionary literature, there should not be such a distinction between returned students and those who are not returned students.' Li dismissed the 'Editor's note' as 'senseless demagogy and an unsolemn declaration", and "a stain on the Sun Society that cannot be washed away'. However, in this open letter, Li stressed that they regarded the Sun group as comrades and claimed that he had not been malicious in the quarrel.[60] Soon, after a series of meetings between the groups, the debate came to an end.

According to Yang Cunren's detailed account of the first meeting, it was the members of the Creation Society who called for it.[61] The date was not given but it was certainly after April 1928 because at the meeting, Cheng Fangwu had to defend his article 'The necessity of total criticism' (*Quanbu pipan zhi biyao*), sharply criticised in the April issue of *Taiyang yuekan*.[62] The meeting was at the office of the Creation Society. Most of its members were present, including Cheng Fangwu, Zheng Boqi, Wang Duqing, Zhang Ziping, Hua Han (Yang Hansheng), Li Yimeng and Gong Binglu. On the other hand, only the 'Big Three' of the Sun Society, Jiang Guangci, Qian Xingcun and Yang Cunren, attended. They were harshly criticised by the Creationists, yet it was finally agreed that a weekly joint meeting would be held.[63]

This act of solidarity between the two revolutionary groups was spontaneous. Some of the Creationists and all of the Sun group were CCP members, but it was not a Party meeting. The chairman of the meeting, Cheng Fangwu, was not a member then and no Party representative was present. After the meetings, the quarrel between the two groups ended and they united to attack Lu Xun.

It has been noted that Lu Xun's discussion on revolutionary literature in 1927 had not excited comment from revolutionary writers. In January 1928, when Feng Naichao began the assault in the article 'Art and social life' (*Yishu yu shehui shenghuo*), nothing was said on Lu Xun's theory. Instead, he was accused along with other writers, of being backward and out of step with changes in society. To Feng, since Lu Xun often yearned for the past, he could, in the end, only reflect in his writings the sorrow of those who fell behind the social changes taking place. Feng said:

> the old fellow Lu Xun - if I were to put it poetically - often sits upstairs in a dark wine shop, looking at life outside the window through befuddled eyes.[64]

The expressions 'old fellow' (*laosheng*) and 'befuddled eyes' (*zuiyan*) enraged Lu Xun most and were taken up in a number of subsequent essays.

In the article, Feng Naichao also criticised other established writers, including Ye Shengtao, Yu Dafu and Zhang Ziping. Again this was a result of the influence of Fukumotoism, and the 'break away before unite' theory. Because the theory said that fellow travellers and others had to be separated from genuine Marxists, the young Creationists hastened to attack those who were not, in their eyes, genuine Marxists. That was why Lu Xun and other established writers came under fire.

Cheng Fangwu's most famous article 'From literary revolution to revolutionary literature' (*Cong wenxue geming dao geming wenxue*), published in early February, was even more militant. Often referred to as the battle cry of the radicals,[65] it claimed that capitalism had already reached its last days. The world was divided into two opposing camps, the capitalists and fascists on one side and the united front of workers and peasants on the other. At this critical moment, Cheng said:

> Nobody is allowed to stand at the middle. Come to this side, or go to the other!
>
> Don't just follow. Don't be left behind. Join this historical process of social changes consciously.[66]

This was more dogmatic than Guo Moruo's mechanical division of literature into revolutionary and counter-revolutionary. Obviously, to these revolutionary writers, Lu Xun was a symbol of backwardness and hence should be criticised.

Lu Xun was the only writer among those attacked to respond to these assaults. In 'Befuddled woolliness' (*Zuiyanzhong de menglong*), he accused the Creationists of being befuddled. They could not see that the 'art of weapons' (*wuqi de yishu*), the mightiest of all arts, was held by 'the other side'. Their 'weapon of art' (*yishu de wuqi*) was powerless.[67] Here Lu Xun was repeating the ideas expressed in the speech to the Huangpu Military Academy. He could not help mocking the deeds and behaviour of so-called revolutionary writers:

> Unfortunately they were a bit late. The year before last, the Creation Society called for share-capitals, last year they engaged lawyers, and only this year have they raised the banner of 'revolutionary literature'. Now the resurrected critic Cheng Fangwu has finally stopped defending the 'palace of art' in order to 'win over the masses' and to 'guarantee the final victory' to revolutionary writers.[68]

Lu Xun mocked the Creationists for their overnight change from advocating romantic literature to revolutionary literature. Pointing out the confusion in their ideas, he mentioned Li Chuli's article 'How to create revolutionary literature' which said that proletarian literature could be created by writers of any class, providing that they had acquired proletarian consciousness. Yet at the same time, Li talked a lot about the class background of writers and even asked what class Lu Xun belonged to. This was taken up by Lu Xun and it was easy for him to demonstrate that Li Chuli was by no means a good theoretician.

After publication of this 'Befuddled woolliness' the Creationists concentrated their fire on Lu Xun. In a single issue of *Wenhua pipan*, there were four long articles attacking him. *Chuangzao yuekan*, the other publication of the Creation Society, joined in. After Li Chuli had called Lu Xun's article 'the wild dance of our Chinese Don Quixote', Lu was given the title 'Don Lu Xun', one who had no political thoughts and was blind to the realities of social change.[69] In some articles, Lu Xun was accused of being a humanitarian, a running dog of the ruling class, a faithful watchdog and the best spokesman of the bourgeoisie, fighting against the proletariat. Du Quan's article 'The feudal remnant of the literary front: Criticisms of Lu Xun's "My attitude, tolerance and age"' (*Wenyi zhanxianshangde fengjian yunie: Piping Lu Xun de "wode taidu qiliang he nianji"*) was the harshest of all. Lu Xun was labelled a feudal remnant, a frustrated fascist and a double counter-revolutionary.[70] Du Quan's identity was established with certainty only recently: it was the pseudonym of Guo Moruo.[71]

Meanwhile, Lu Xun was also attacked by the Sun group. Even before the appearance of 'Befuddled woolliness', Qian Xingcun had already published his famous 'The era of Ah Q that has passed away' (*Siqule de A Q shidai*). At the very beginning of the article, Qian said that Lu Xun's works were in no way representations of the times. To Qian, the ideas expressed were those of the late Qing period. Great social changes such as the May Thirtieth, the great Hong Kong strike, the Shanghai insurrections, had brought about the rise of proletarian consciousness and the 'literary movement of the fourth class'. Lu Xun had lagged behind and all he could do was lament past glory. 'We do not want this kind of work!' Qian said. He even alleged that Ah Q, the most famous character of Lu Xun's short stories, had died. The peasants of China were not as naïve as Ah Q. They were well organised and had considerable knowledge of politics. They even participated in political struggles against landlords.[72]

Qian's over-optimistic attitude was influenced by the Communist Party line. After its formation, the Sun Society developed close relations with the CCP. Members of the Party's Central Committee, such as Qu Qiubai, Yang Pao'an, Luo Qiyuan and Gao Yuhan, were also members of the Sun Society. In fact, the Society had been designed as a literary organisation of the CCP. There was even a party group in the Society as almost all its members had joined the Communist Party. Qu Qiubai, then chief secretary of the Party, directed the affairs of the Society.[73] It was almost inevitable that the Sun group should have been seriously affected by Party policies.

The Pre-League Period

In Mao Zedong's analysis of Party history, the CCP under Qu Qiubai held a leftist line of putschism from August 1927 to June 1928.[74] Qu, with Comintern theoreticians behind him, did not agree that the coup of April 1927 was a defeat for the CCP. Instead, he saw an upsurge in the revolution and so called for a general intensification of revolutionary policy. Moreover, he claimed there was 'no demarcation between the democratic and the socialist revolutions'. After the coup, Qu alleged, the national bourgeoisie became 'an absolute counter-revolutionary force' and the petit bourgeoisie 'an obstruction to revolution'. He therefore demanded the destruction not only of the landlord class, but of the entire bourgeoisie.[75] In a reaction to Chen Duxiu's 'capitulationist' policies, he initiated radical agrarian policies and a series of insurrections. From August 1927, uprisings broke out, later collectively known as the Autumn Harvest Uprisings. Defeat in these uprisings brought further setbacks to the Party. In June 1928, during its Sixth Congress, Qu Qiubai was criticised and replaced.

During this putschist period Lu Xun was under fire in Shanghai. The impact of Party policy on revolutionary writers can easily be felt. Often, revolutionary writers, as with Party documents, claimed that the revolutionary movement was developing and rising, and argued that the bourgeoisie and the petit bourgeoisie should be wiped out altogether.[76] Their militant attitude can be seen as a reflection of the Party's insurrection policy too.

Influenced by both Japanese ultra-left Fukumotoism and a putschist Party line, revolutionary writers in Shanghai brought Lu Xun under cross-fire. One reader of *Yusi* called this 'an organised and united onslaught'.[77] Lu's own words presented the picture most clearly:

> Now there are many gentlemen and revolutionary writers accusing me overtly or covertly of being revolutionary or non-revolutionary.[78]
>
> From the year before last [1928], there have been numerous attacks on me. In every magazine, it is quite certain that the name of Lu Xun is there.[79]

To the radicals, two things about Lu Xun were unacceptable; his being blind to social changes and his hostility to revolutionary literature.

To discern whether Lu Xun was blind to social changes, it is necessary to know what was in the minds of his opponents. Qian Xingcun pointed out that those social changes included such mass movements as the May Thirtieth, the great strike of Hong Kong and the insurrections of Shanghai which brought about a gradual manifestation of the class power of workers and peasants.[80]

It is unfair to say that Lu Xun was blind to all these events. From his writing, it can be seen that he always paid attention to social problems and hoped to find the means to solve them. His taking up literature as a career because he saw it as a way to save people's souls amply proves this.[81] His participation in the 'Beijing Women's Normal College Affairs', supporting the students in their fight against the autocratic and feudalistic principal and her unreasonable rules, earned him the reputation of 'Mentor of youth'. As for the May Thirtieth Movement, fourteen days after the massacre, on 13 June 1925, he wrote to Xu Guangping, 'in my opinion, the student movements are far better this year'.[82] Besides donating money, he wrote several essays supporting the movement. He attacked the warlord regimes and the March Eighteenth Massacre. Such articles as 'Flowerless roses' (*Wuhuade quangui*) and 'In commemoration of Miss Liu Hezhen' (*Jinian Liu Hezhen jun*) are famous.[83] By 1927, he began to drop Nietzschean ideas and put greater emphasis on the masses. In February that year, he cursed those who 'took themselves as the centre but never agreed to take the masses as the principal body'.[84] On 25 October, he declared that the masses were above the intellectuals: those intellectuals who were sympathetic to and supported the peasants were progressive and good while those who oppressed them were reactionary and bad.[85]

For a short time, Lu Xun was as overjoyed as the revolutionary writers were over the 'successes' in revolution. He had written an article celebrating the recovery of Shanghai and Nanjing by the Northern Expedition Army.[86] But optimism vanished with Jiang Jieshi's coup d'état. He witnessed the massacres in Guangzhou which took place three days after the one in Shanghai. Lu Xun recalled, 'I was frightened. I had never had such a frightening experience before', and 'in my whole life, I had never before seen such a massacre'.[87] His faith in the young people was completely gone:

> I always believed in evolution, thinking that the future would definitely be better than today, young people would be better than the old. But then I realised that I was wrong. ... When I was in Guangzhou, I witnessed how all the same young people were divided into two camps, informing and helping the government to arrest! My thinking was shattered![88]

Apart from feeling that his faith in the young had been smashed, he also saw no hope in the Chinese revolution:

> Revolution, counter-revolution, non-revolution. Revolutionaries are killed by counter-revolutionaries. Counter-revolutionaries are killed by revolutionaries. Non-revolutionaries may be taken as counter-revolutionaries and killed by revolutionaries, or taken as revolutionaries and killed by counter-revolutionaries, or taken as nothing and killed either by revolutionaries or counter-revolutionaries. Revolution, re-revolution, re-re-revolution, re-re...[89]

To be more exact, what really disappointed Lu Xun was the GMD. He was very much disgusted with the brutal arrests and killings carried out by the GMD on the pretext of 'party purge' and 'suppressing the red' (*taoche*):

> One day, even the wearing of ragged clothes will be prohibited, for those who do so will be taken for Communists.[90]

> We must avoid coming close to red thinking or writing as well as to thinking and writing that may in future appear to be red. For instance, to attack the traditional ethical code or to use the vernacular is running the risk of being red, since the Communists

despise all old things while the use of the vernacular started in *Xinqingnian* [*New Youth*]. *Xinqingnian* was edited by Chen Duxiu.[91]

On the other hand, he did not seem to have a clear understanding of the Communist Party, although its members were sent to see him. He once said:

> In Xiamian, I knew only in general terms the Communist Party. Only after coming here [Guangzhou] did I realize that there was a distinction between the CP [Communist Party] and the CY [Communist Youth]. I did not know until recently that among non-Communists, there are several this and that Y groups.[92]

Thus it seemed natural for him to be pessimistic about the future of China. More than five months after the coup, he wrote in a letter to Tai Jingnong, 'What I see before me is still darkness'.[93] In other places, he said:

> The game of blood has just started. The actors are again young people and they all look complacent. At present, I cannot see the ending of this play.[94]
>
> What will come after the feeling of fear has gone? I do not know. I am afraid it will be nothing good.[95]
>
> As for me, I feel that China is now in an age in which she is marching to a great age. But this so-called 'greatness' does not necessarily mean that you can be saved; you may be killed by it.[96]

In these circumstances, Lu Xun had to accept the charge of being pessimistic, dispirited and unable to see the 'bright' side of the Chinese revolution. He did not view the developments in revolution in the same way as the radicals did. To him the 1927 coup had brought a setback to revolution and hence there could be no revolutionary upsurge. For this reason he could not agree that a revolutionary literary movement would soon be successful in China.

Lu Xun's first discussion on revolutionary literature in a speech at the Huangpu Military Academy has been dealt with. In it he decried the importance of literature, urging people to take practical action. Revolutionary literature had no place in his three-stage theory of the relationship between literature and revolution as he did not think that it existed in China then. But this did not mean that he was totally against revolutionary literature since, as has been seen, he maintained that it could be created by revolutionaries. This was typical of his attitude. In April 1928, he expressed a more positive attitude:

> Since revolutions are constantly taking place, there must be revolutionary literature. The people of quite a number of nations in the world are awakening. Although many of them are still suffering, some of them are in power. Naturally there is people's literature - or to speak more specifically, literature of the fourth class.[97]

While still claiming that literature had no power to turn the world upside down, he approved of Upton Sinclair's words 'All art is propaganda', often cited by the radicals in the polemic.[98] Then in early 1930, in articles rebuking Liang Shiqiu, Lu Xun defended the idea that literature had a class nature and argued the need to create proletarian literature.[99] Soon he was writing 'the only literary movement in China today is the proletarian revolutionary literary movement'.[100]

Throughout the polemic, Lu Xun made no attack on revolutionary literature itself. But he did not spare its advocates. In his eyes, those self-proclaimed revolutionary writers were not genuine fighters. They were afraid of darkness, and did not have the courage to face reality.[101] 'There were only empty cries but no achievements'.[102] He believed that the radicals were too rash in putting up the signboard of revolutionary literature without paying attention to the quality of their writing. Their works were 'the products of petit bourgeois concepts, some were even warlord-minded'. As those revolutionary writers just used slogans and watchwords,[103] their writing was worse than news reports.[104] Lu Xun asserted that content and technique were most important:

> But I believe that we should first look for rich contents and skilful techniques. There is no hurry to put up the signboard... To my mind, though all literature is propaganda, not all propaganda is literature. In addition to catchwords, slogans, notices, telegrams and textbooks, etc, revolution needs literature simply because it is literature.[105]

Thus it is fair to say that Lu Xun held the revolutionary literary movement of China in low esteem. But elsewhere in his writing he affirmed that 'the present transient phenomenon in China cannot by any means be regarded as disproof of the rise of proletarian literature'.[106]

He believed that one shortcoming of the radicals was their inability to master literary theory. In August 1928, he revealed his wish of 'having some earnest people to translate some books about historical materialism which contained accepted ideas'.[107] Later he elaborated on this theme:

> I then came to the belief that there were too few theories for reference, and this made people muddled. The dissection and chewing of the enemies are ineluctable at the present stage. But if there is a book on anatomy or cookery to follow, we should be clearer about the structure of the body and produce something more delicious.[108]

Lu Xun was one of the earnest ones to provide the book of anatomy. From the second half of 1928, he worked hard for two years, translating books on Marxism-Leninism, mainly from Japanese. Thus there was truth in Lu Xun's saying that he owed a debt of gratitude to the revolutionary writers as they forced him to read some scientific literary criticism.[109]

During the polemic, Lu Xun was unable to use this knowledge in the discussion on revolutionary literature. In August 1928, he admitted that he could not make a fair judgment on revolutionary literature as he was a layman in historical materialism.[110] Harriet Mills's observation is correct:

> Through all the clamour, Lu Hsün [Lu Xun] remained aloof. He wrote very little and refused to become involved in discussion of theoretical points about which he felt both he and the leftists knew

little. His often sarcastic comments served both to rebut the charges levied against him and to ridicule the fanciful and arrogant illusions of the young radicals.[111]

Throughout the polemic, Lu Xun did not argue in theoretical terms. He did not quote from such figures as Karl Marx, Engels or Bukharin. Most of the time he was pointing out or mocking the mistakes and shallowness of his opponents. His comments were on what he had observed, rather than from what he had read. This had an advantage over his opponents as he could relate the movement to the actual situation in China. Lu Xun showed himself aware of this weakness of his opponents when he said in retrospect:

> They had not analysed in detail Chinese society before they mechanically adopted the methods which were workable only under Soviet rule.[112]

From August 1928 the attack on Lu Xun abated. About this time the first open article by a CCP member, Feng Xuefeng, was published, criticising the Creation Society's sectarianism and the radicals' attack on Lu Xun. In his article, 'Revolution and the intellectual class' (*Geming yu zhishi jieji*), Feng, under the pseudonym Hua Shi, stressed that there was no need to despise intellectuals during the course of a revolution, although at most they could only be the followers, rather than the main force of a revolution. In Feng's opinion, Lu Xun was ahead of other intellectuals in realising the values of revolution. During the May Fourth and May Thirtieth eras, 'among the intellectuals, the one who did the best was Lu Xun'. His criticism of the national character and the feudal tradition was a valuable contribution to revolution. Further, Lu Xun had never slandered revolution. Feng correctly pointed out that Lu Xun attacked only the movement of revolutionary literature, not revolutionary literature itself. There was no reason why he should be under fire. Feng Xuefeng considered this a mistake on the part of the Creationists who had never given up their sectarianism. It was dangerous to continue these attacks and he urged the radicals to stop immediately before any harm was done.[113]

Many regard Feng's article as a CCP attempt to conciliate Lu Xun since attacks on Lu Xun quietened down some time in October, and Feng Xuefeng's article had appeared on 25 September 1928.[114] Unfortunately this was a mere coincidence. At the end of the article, Feng Xuefeng stated that he finished this essay in May 1928. From evidence available now, there was no CCP activity to stop the polemic at this early stage. Most recollections say that it was not until the autumn of 1928 or even 1929 that the CCP intervened. In fact, many articles condemning Lu Xun were published after May 1928. If the CCP was behind the article, this should not have happened. Moreover, the article appeared in the journal *Wugui lieche* (*Trackless Train*), published and edited by non-CCP figures like Dai Wangshu, Du Heng and Shi Zhecun. It was unlikely that a CCP instruction to end the polemic would have been published here.

Further, if the CCP aimed to conciliate Lu Xun, it was bad tactics to have someone who had not been involved in the polemic write the article. Lu Xun would not have appreciated the good will. Moreover, the content was not very conciliatory. Feng Xuefeng himself later reported that Lu Xun was not pleased with it, saying that it might have been written by a member of the Creation Society. Feng also admitted, years later, that he had made two serious mistakes in the article: being too arrogant and taking Lu Xun as a fellow-traveller only.[115] If it was CCP policy to have the article written, Feng would not have committed such 'mistakes', or he would not have called them mistakes. Several decades later, he made it clear that he did not write the article at the Party's behest:

> There were serious mistakes in the article 'Revolution and the intellectual class', which was written in May or June [May 1928] and published in July or August [25 September 1928]. It was based on my own shallow and wrong viewpoints. I had not discussed it with anyone. No one asked me to write it.[116]

With the exception of the parties involved, however, people seemed happy with the article. It was regarded, even in the early thirties, as the best and fairest appraisal of the polemic.[117] Most important of all, Rou Shi, then close to Lu Xun and an old schoolmate of Feng Xuefeng, after reading the article, urged Lu Xun to meet Feng.[118] The latter soon secured Lu Xun's confidence and friendship, which enabled him to act as a mediator afterwards. In this sense, the article 'Revolution and the intellectual class' can be regarded as significant in paving the way for the unification of left-wing writers.

Meanwhile, Lu Xun continued to attack the radicals verbally, but there was little response, for they were then busy attacking another writer, Mao Dun.

Mao Dun had joined the CCP in 1921 and throughout the twenties, was very politically active. In 1924, he lectured at the CCP-run Shanghai University and during the May Thirtieth Incident he helped to organise strikes in Shanghai. After the incident, he finished an article called 'On proletarian art' (*Lun wuchanjieji yishu*) which was regarded by some as 'the most important of Mao Dun's contributions to the theory of proletarian art'.[119] In the article, Mao Dun pointed out that proletarian art did not end with a description of proletarian life. It should be a kind of art centred on the proletarian spirit which was collectivist, anti-patriarchal and non-religious.[120] Then in 1926, during the first united front period, like Guo Moruo and other Communists, he went to Guangzhou and for a time, he was Mao Zedong's secretary in the Central Propaganda of the GMD. Before the coup of Jiang Jieshi, he taught in the Central Military and Political School of the Northern Expedition Army in Wuhan. In July 1927, he had to flee for his life after the Wuhan GMD left-wing government fell.

In fact, in early 1928, Mao Dun was already involved in the revolutionary literary controversy. Upon reading the first issue of *Taiyang yuekan*, Mao Dun, using the pen-name Fang Bi, wrote the article 'Welcome the Sun' (*Huanying taiyang*), which, on the one hand expressed support for the new magazine and on the other, criticised Jiang Guangci's excessive emphasis on a writer's revolutionary experiences. In this way, Mao Dun asserted, Jiang was in effect forcing revolutionary literature onto a monotonous and narrow road, which in the end would be harmful to the movement.[121] This piece of well-intentioned advice was rejected by Jiang, who, in the name of Hua Xili, wrote an unfriendly reply, denying the charges and accusing Mao Dun of having wronged him.[122]

Apparently, Mao Dun was unaware of this essay. He took no part in the polemic between Lu Xun and the revolutionary group but like Lu Xun, he regarded the coup of Jiang Jieshi as a disastrous setback for the Communists. A year later, after returning to Shanghai via Guling, he finished his first stories, the Trilogy of Eclipse - Disillusionment, Vacillation and Search (*Shi sanbuqu - huanmi dongyao zhuqiu*). Mao Dun's aim in writing the trilogy was:

> To write about the three different periods modern youth had undergone in the time of revolution: 1) the exuberance on the eve of revolution and the disillusionment when coming face to face with it; 2) the vacillation during the intensification of the revolutionary struggles; 3) after the disillusionment and vacillation, the unwillingness to accept loneliness and still wanting to make a final search.[123]

What Mao Dun recorded in the trilogy was his own experiences in the period 1926 to 1928. He did not deny that the demoralised and pessimistic tone was a reflection of his feelings. This was unacceptable to revolutionary writers who refused to accept defeat. Worse still, when he gave an account of the process of writing and background of the trilogy in an article 'From Guling to Tokyo' (*Cong Guling dao Dongjing*), he criticised the revolutionary literary movement.

In the article, Mao Dun frankly admitted that he was 'disillusioned, pessimistic and despondent' but maintained that young people were then discontented, depressed and eager to find a 'way out'. Therefore, his stories were objective depictions. Mao Dun accepted that he had not pointed a 'way out' for the readers:

> I cannot agree to the 'way out' which during the past year was preached and proclaimed by many. Is it not now proven clearly that this so-called 'way out' has become something of a 'blind alley'?[124]

In the last section of the article, Mao made an evaluation of the revolutionary literary movement. He shared Lu Xun's view that Chinese revolutionary writers had been unable to produce good, genuinely revolutionary literature. He saw three faults in their work; first, inferior quality; second, the problem of language; third, no depiction of the life of the petit bourgeois.

Mao Dun noted a phenomenon. Many people sincerely supported revolutionary literature but shook their heads when they read the works of revolutionary writers because these 'new works' had not gone beyond the scope of 'slogan literature'. He doubted its literary value. He quoted the example of Soviet Russia where the Futurists produced many works of slogan literature. Not only the masses but leaders like Bukharin, Lunacharsky and Trotsky regarded them as unbearably dull. The Futurists did not lack revolutionary zeal, but 'people want something more than "a revolutionary mood" when they come to read literary works'. 'Being rich in revolutionary zeal but ignorant of the nature of literature, or taking literature as a tool for propaganda - in a narrow sense', revolutionary writers had pushed their own works into the dead end of slogan literature. Thus it was wrong to blame people for being non-revolutionary when such works were not accepted.

As for the language, Mao Dun accused revolutionary writers of using language that was too westernised or too literary. Writers tried to write for the working class, but workers would not or could not read them. It was not a problem of illiteracy, he said. 'Even if you read the works to them, they still cannot understand them.' Towards the end of the essay, he earnestly advised:

> Don't be too westernised. Don't use too many new technical terms. Don't be too symbolic. Don't just propagandise new ideas directly and mechanically.[125]

Mao Dun also felt uneasy about the trend that any writer writing about the petit bourgeoisie would be labelled a counter-revolutionary. 'This is most unreasonable', Mao Dun remarked:

> Are the petit bourgeois not suffering now? Are they not being oppressed? If they do have sufferings, if they are being oppressed, why should you refuse to pollute your sacred pens [to write on them]?[126]

Mao Dun argued that this was one reason why revolutionary literature was not popular: it had forgotten to describe its natural readers, the petit bourgeois who made up sixty percent of the population.

Because of this article Mao Dun was jointly attacked by members of the Sun and Creation societies. To these radicals, the 'way out' was not a blind alley. 'The revolution in China is developing into a new upsurge'. Mao Dun's depiction of young people's disillusion and vacillation in his works was not objective but rather his own petit bourgeois consciousness that made him fall into disillusionment and vacillation.

His comments on revolutionary literature were therefore taken as another attack on the revolutionary literary movement from a petit bourgeois critic. To Fu Kexing, when someone shook his head over new works it did not mean that there was anything wrong with revolutionary literature. It was because those petit bourgeois readers failed to grasp a new world outlook and stood on the side of the ruling class to attack revolutionary literature.[127] On the other hand, Qian Xingcun accepted the charge that there were many slogans in proletarian literature but it was natural because:

> Proletarian art is not an art for leisure. It is an art for struggle, a weapon for struggle. The contents of the works must suit the political propagandistic slogans and agitational slogans.[128]

He also conceded that most proletarian writers, at this early stage, did not have good writing skills. This was unavoidable. He cited the words of Aono Suekichi, an important Japanese left-wing writer and critic. Even in Japan where the movement had a ten year history, proletarian literature was still

The Pre-League Period

immature and of poor quality. He even used Mao Dun's own words to contradict him. A line from his 'On proletarian art' was quoted:

> The problem of shallowness in content is inevitable for a newly born art of a class which is young and in a difficult situation.[129]

Qian also cited another piece of Mao Dun's early writing (published 5 March 1927), the preface to Gu Zhongyi's poetry, *Glare* (*Hongguang*), in which Mao Dun praised the 'slogan poems' as products of the epoch, of the environment, and the foundation stones of new literature since the October Revolution. These words, Qian pointed out, were in marked contrast to 'From Guling to Tokyo'. It was then easy for Qian to conclude that Mao Dun's change of attitude was due to his own disillusionment and vacillation.

The radicals further argued that even though some works by revolutionary writers might, in terms of writing technique, have attained considerable success, bourgeois critics could not be satisfied because these works would definitely be full of new ideas and demands which were totally unacceptable to the critics. Moreover, they could not agree with Mao Dun's charge that there was no work on the petit bourgeoisie. On the contrary, there were too many, so many that they made young people fall into distress, pessimism and sentimentalism.[130]

Certainly the radicals were eager to crush the opposition raised by Mao Dun. But it seemed that his opponents were fairly cautious. The editors of *Chuangzao yuekan* attached a note to Fu Kexing's article, saying that Mao Dun's article had brought out many real and practical problems.[131] They were aware that they were debating with an old Party member who, for the time being, had made a wrong evaluation of the revolution and was disillusioned. A battle was necessary to put him back on the right track. Qian Xingcun said:

> This time, our struggle is different from that against Lu Xun and his group. The present struggle is one between the proletarian literary front and the unworthy spokesman of the so-called revolutionary petit bourgeoisie.[132]

This cautious attitude can be explained. When the struggle against Mao Dun began, the CCP might have already given instructions to end the debate with Lu Xun and set up a united front in the literary circle. It was therefore inappropriate to start another polemic. On the other hand, Mao Dun was able to keep his temper. His reply 'On reading "Ni Huanzhi"' (*Du Ni Huanzhi*), was mild and forgiving.[133] This made possible a ceasefire within a comparatively short time. It was but a little step further to the realisation of a great united front among the left in Shanghai.

In discussing 'the debate on revolutionary literature', Harriet Mills wrote:

> The series of literary polemics or 'pen battles' which erupted in this period were not so much literary as political or personal disputes. Despite the exaggerated importance they have received in histories of modern Chinese literature, they solved no literary problems and generated no new schools or experimental trends. Stronger on rumour, slander, innuendo and propaganda than on substance, they

were one of the strident if unhappy realities of the period. The shrillest of all was the debate on revolutionary literature that began in January 1928.[134]

This is, in certain respects, a fair judgment of the debate. If we demand from the debate something substantial, such as the solving of literary problems or generating of new literary schools, as Mills suggested, we are going to be disappointed. In fact, in the heat of the debate, much of the energy was used in personal attacks. However, there is an indirect and less obvious consequence of the debate which was invaluable to the left-wingers and which can account for the emphasis on it in the literary histories published in mainland China after 1949: the debate marked the rise of the left-wing literary movement and its subsequent domination of the literary circle. Lu Xun was able to appreciate this as early as in 1928. He said:

> The merit of putting forward the issue [of revolutionary literature] so that people could take notice of it should not be overlooked.[135]

Before the polemic, the issue of revolutionary literature had not attracted public attention. The noisy debate in 1928 made many people aware of its existence and advocacy, thus providing a base for further action, in both literary and political fields. More young people were attracted to the leftist camp. The Left League's large membership, even at a time of severe 'white terror', was made possible by this. The case of Yin Fu is a good example. At first, he was not a member of the Sun Society but was attracted by it and contributed a long poem to the fourth issue of *Taiyang yuekan*.[136] He turned out to be one of the few good revolutionary writers and a martyr in the cause of the Communist revolution.

With a team of writers and artists under its control, the CCP could make good use of literature and art to propagate revolutionary ideas. This greatly aided the Red Army in fighting against GMD troops. A right-wing critic commented:

> For twenty years, the GMD held the military and political power while the CCP held the literary power. In the end, the literary power overcame the military and political power.[137]

CCP supremacy in the literary field was surely one of the many reasons for the ultimate defeat of the GMD. Even Mao Zedong, though he himself had done nothing in gaining this literary power, could not deny its importance and contribution.[138] This time, the pen was mightier than the sword. The fact is, this control of the pen by the CCP had its origin in the revolutionary literary movement.

Notes to Chapter One

1. The Institute for the Study of Modern Literature, Academy of Literature, Chinese Social Sciences Academy (*Zhongguo shehui kexueyuan wenxue yangjiusuo xiandai wenxue yanjiushi*) (ed), *Collection of materials on the 'revolutionary literature' polemic* (*Geming wenxue lunzheng ziliao xuanbian*) (Beijing: Renmin wenxue chubanshe, January 1981), p 154.
2. 'On "modern Chinese literature"' (*Guanyu xiandai Zhongguo wenxue*), *ibid*, p 198.
3. John Berninghausen and Ted Huters, 'Introductory essay', *Revolutionary literature in China: An anthology* (New York: M E Sharpe, 1976), p 5.
4. *Xianqu* (*The Pioneer*) No 8 (May 1922).
5. *Zhongguo qingnian* No 10 (22 December 1923), p 6.
6. *Zhongguo qingnian* No 31 (17 May 1924), pp 12-14.
7. Shen Zemin, 'Youth and literary movements' (*Qingnian yu wenyi yundong*), *Zhongguo qingnian* No 9 (5 December 1923), pp 8-9.
8. *Juewu* (*Consciousness*), Supplement of *Minguo ribao*, 6 November 1924.
9. Wu Tenghuang, *A biography of Jiang Guangci* (*Jiang Guangci zhuan*) (Hefei: Anhui renmin chubanshe, January 1982), pp 31, 39 and 125.
10. Qian Xingcun, *On modern Chinese literature* (*Xiandai Zhongguo wenxuelun*) (publication details missing), p 46.
11. For discussion on these works, see T A Hsia, 'The phenomenon of Chiang Kwang-tz'u', *The gate of darkness: Studies on the leftist literary movement in China* (Seattle: University of Washington Press, 1968), pp 80-1.
12. 'Modern Chinese literature and social life' (*Xiandai Zhongguo wenxue yu shehui shenghuo*), *Collection of materials*, p 82.
13. Liu Shousong, *A preliminary draft history of modern Chinese literature* (*Zhongguo xinwenxueshi chugao*) (Beijing: Renmin wenxue chubanshe, November 1979 reprint) Vol I, p 131.
14. Ito Toramaru (ed), *Materials on the Creation Society* (*Sozosha shiryo*) (Tokyo: Ajiya shuppan, 1979) Vol IV, pp 55-7.
15. *Ibid*, p 47.
16. *Ibid*, p 56.
17. *Ibid*, p 46.
18. Marian Galik, *The genesis of modern Chinese literary criticism (1917-1930)* (London: Curzon Press, 1980), pp 117-19.
19. *Works of Guo Moruo* (*Moruo wenji*) Vol VII (Beijing: Renmin wenxue chubanshe, August 1958), pp 135-8.
20. Quoted from Wang Jiquan and Tong Weigang, *A chronology of Guo Moruo* (*Guo Moruo nianpu*) (Jiangsu: Jiangsu renmin chubanshe, April 1983), p 176.
21. 'Study on the strikes of Shanghai in the May Thirtieth Movement' (*Wusa yundongzhong Shanghai bagong tiaocha*), *The labour movement during the period of the first revolutionary civil war* (*Diyici guonei geming zhanzheng*

shiqi de gongren yundong) (Beijing: Renmin chubanshe, November 1954), pp 72-4.
22 'The era of Ah Q that has passed away', *Collection of materials*, pp 181-2.
23 Lucien Bianco, *Origins of the Chinese Revolution, 1915-1949* (London: Stanford University Press, 1971), pp 55-6.
24 'Revolution and literature', *Collection of materials*, pp 3-4.
25 Lu Xun, 'A glance at the literary scene in Shanghai' (*Shanghai wenyi zhi yipie*), *Complete works of Lu Xun* (*Lu Xun quanji*) (Beijing: Renmin wenxue chubanshe, 1981) Vol IV, pp 295-6.
26 *Ibid* Vol XI, p 191.
27 'A star has fallen' (*Zhuli yike juxing*), *Xianshijie* (*The present world*) Vol I No 7 (November 1936), quoted from Shen Pannian, 'Two facts about the relationship between Lu Xun and the Creation Society' (*Lu Xun yu Chuangzaoshe jiaowang de liangdian shishi*), *Shanghai wenxue* (*Shanghai literature*) No 7, 1962 (5 July 1962), p 61.
28 *Collection of materials*, p 20. Other writers condemned by Cheng Fangwu included Xu Zhimo, Liu Bannong, Chen Xiying and Zhou Zuoren.
29 Letter to Li Jiye, *Complete works of Lu Xun* Vol XI, p 583.
30 *Ibid* Vol XIV, p 644.
31 *Hongshui* (*Deluge*) Vol III No 30 (1 April 1927).
32 *Complete works of Lu Xun* Vol III, p 423.
33 *Ibid*, pp 419-20.
34 *Ibid*, p 418.
35 *Ibid* Vol XI, p 427.
36 'At the clock tower' (*Zai zhongloushang*), *ibid* Vol IV, p 33.
37 Anthony J Kane, 'The League of Left Wing Writers and the Chinese literary policy' (Unpublished PhD dissertation, University of Michigan, 1982), p 347.
38 'Revolutionary literature' (*Geming wenxue*), *Complete works of Lu Xun* Vol III, p 544.
39 Zheng Boqi, *Recalling the Creation Society and other things* (*Yi Chuangzaoshe ji qita*) (Hong Kong: Joint Publishing Company, 1982), p 50.
40 Reprinted in Chen Songsheng (*et al*) (ed), *Materials on the Creation Society* (*Chuangzaoshe ziliao*) (Fujian: Fujian renmin chubanshe, January 1985), p 482.
41 *Ibid*, pp 483-4.
42 *Ibid*, p 538.
43 *Works of Guo Moruo* Vol VIII, p 289.
44 Zheng Boqi, *Recalling the Creation Society*, p 45-50.
45 Feng Naichao, 'Lu Xun and the Creation Society', p 37.
46 *Works of Guo Moruo* Vol VIII, p 289.
47 *Recalling the Creation Society*, pp 51-2.

The Pre-League Period

48 Yang Cunren, 'The Sun Society and Jiang Guangci' (*Taiyangshe yu Jiang Guangci*), *Xiandai* (*Les Contemporains*) Vol III No 4 (1 August 1933), p 471-3.
49 Yu Dafu, 'The last years of Guangci' (*Guangci de wannian*), *Xiandai* Vol III No 1 (1 May, 1933), p 71.
50 *Collection of materials*, pp 83-4.
51 *Ibid*, p 165.
52 *Ibid*, p 87.
53 *Ibid*, p 82.
54 For the discussion on Fukumotoism, I am indebted to the following works: Tatsuo Arima, *The failure of freedom: A portrait of modern Japanese intellectuals* (Cambridge, Mass: Harvard University Press, 1969), pp 172-213; G T Shea, *Left-wing literature in Japan: A brief history of the proletarian literary movement* (Tokyo: The Hosei University Press, 1964), pp 142-8; Liu Boqing, *A brief history of the Japanese proletarian literary movement* (*Riben wuchan jieji wenyi yundong jianshi*) (Changchun: Shidai wenyi chubanshe, October 1985); Liu Boqing, 'The influence of Japanese proletarian literary thought on the left-wing literature of the thirties' (*Sanshi niandai zuoyi wenyi suoshou Riben wuchanjijie wenyi sichao de yingxiang*), *Wenxue pinglun* No 6, 1981 (November 1981), pp 102-9; Wang Ye, 'The debate on "revolutionary literature" and Fukumoto Kazuo' (*Geming wenxue lunzheng yu fuben hefu*), *Zhongguo xiandai wenxue yanjiu congkan* No 1, 1983 (March 1983), pp 322-31.
55 *The failure of freedom*, p 188.
56 *Wenhua pipan* No 1, *Collection of materials*, p 113.
57 *Ibid*, p 169.
58 'Criticism and copying' (*Piping yu chaoshu*), *ibid*, p 261.
59 *Ibid*, p 199.
60 'Reply to an open letter', *ibid*, pp 234-7.
61 Yang Cunren, 'The Sun Society and Jiang Guangci', p 473.
62 *Ibid*, p 474. Cheng's article 'The necessity for total criticism' was attacked by Qian Xingcun, 'Criticism and copying', *ibid*, pp 264-7; Yang Cunren, 'On reading Cheng Fangwu's "The necessity for total criticism"' (*Du Cheng Fangwu de quanbu de pipan zhi biyao*), *ibid*, pp 276-80.
63 Yang Cunren, 'The Sun Society and Jiang Guangci', p 474.
64 Feng Naichao, 'Art and social life', *Collection of materials*, p 116.
65 Anthony J Kane, 'The League of Left-wing Writers', p 37.
66 *Collection of materials*, pp 136-7.
67 *Complete works of Lu Xun* Vol IV, p 62.
68 *Ibid*.
69 Li Chuli, 'Please watch the wild dance of our Chinese Don Quixote: In reply to Lu Xun's "'Befuddled' woolliness"' (*Qingkan women Zhongguo de Don Quixote de luanwu: Da Lu Xun zuiyanzhong de menglong*), *Collection of materials*, pp 288-300.

70 *Ibid*, pp 570-9.
71 Chen Songsheng, *Materials on the Creation Society*, p 1145; Lu Xun Museum (ed), *A chronology of Lu Xun (Lu Xun nianpu)* (Beijing: Renmin wenxue chubanshe, January 1984) Vol III, p 82; *Complete works of Lu Xun* Vol XII, p 411, Note 7.
72 *Taiyang yuekan* No 3, *Collection of materials*, pp 181-92.
73 Wu Taichang, 'A Ying on the Left League' (*A Ying yi zuolian*), *Xinwenxue shiliao* No 1, 1980 (22 February 1980), p 16.
74 Mao Zedong, 'Resolution on certain questions in the history of our Party', *Selected works*, pp 181-2.
75 'Resolution on the present situation of China and the role of the Communist Party' (*Zhongguo xianzhuang yu gongchandeng de renwu de yijuean*), quoting Huang Yuanqi, *A history of modern China* Vol I, p 258.
76 Qian Xingcun, 'Criticism and copying', *Collection of materials*, p 265.
77 Shao Xin, 'A reader's demand from proletarian writers' (*Yige duzhe duiyu wuchan wenxuejia de yaoqiu*), *ibid*, p 492.
78 'Correspondence' (*Tongxin*), *Complete works of Lu Xun* Vol IV, p 100.
79 '"Hard translation" and the class nature of literature' (*Yingyi yu wenxue de jiejixing*), *ibid*, p 209.
80 *Collection of materials*, p 182.
81 'Preface to *Call to Arms*' (*Nahan zixu*), *Complete works of Lu Xun* Vol I, pp 416-17.
82 *Letters from two places* (*Liangdishu*) No 29 (13 June 1925), *ibid* Vol XI, p 89.
83 *Ibid* Vol III, pp 273-8 and 255-65.
84 'The old tune is finished' (*Laodiaozi yijing changwan*), *ibid* Vol III, p 309.
85 'On the intelligentsia' (*Guanyu zhishifenzi*), *ibid*, pp 187-93.
86 'In celebration of the recovery of Nanjing and Shanghai' (*Qingzhu huning kefu de nayibian*), *ibid* Vol VIII, pp 161-3.
87 'Autobiography' (*Zizhuan*), *ibid* Vol VII, p 85.
88 'Introduction to "Three leisures"' (*Sanxianji xuyan*), *ibid* Vol IV, p 5.
89 *Ibid* Vol III, p 532.
90 *Ibid*.
91 *Ibid*, p 485.
92 'Correspondence', *ibid*, p 454.
93 *Ibid* Vol XI, p 580.
94 'Reply to Mr You Heng' (*Da youheng xiansheng*), *ibid* Vol XI, p 454.
95 *Ibid*, p 457.
96 'Foreword to "Shadow of dust"' (*Chenying tici*), *ibid* Vol III, p 547.
97 'Literature and revolution', *ibid* Vol IV, pp 82-3.
98 *Ibid*, p 143.
99 '"Hard translation" and the class nature of literature', *ibid*, pp 195-212.

The Pre-League Period

100 'The present condition of art in dark China' (*Heian Zhongguo de wenyijie de xianzhuang*), *ibid*, p 285. Cf Anthony J Kane, 'The League of Left Wing Writers', pp 47-8.
101 'Literature and revolution', *Complete works of Lu Xun* Vol IV, p 84; 'A safety verse' (*Taiping gejue*), *ibid*, pp 103-4.
102 Letter to Cao Jinghua, 30 September 1930, *ibid* Vol XII, p 23.
103 Letter to Wei Suyuan, 7 April 1929, *ibid* Vol XI, p 663.
104 'Literature and revolution', *ibid* Vol IV, p 84.
105 *Ibid*.
106 '"Hard translation" and the class nature of literature', *ibid*, p 208.
107 Lu Xun, 'The class nature of literature' (*Wenxue de jiejixing*), *ibid*, p 127.
108 *Ibid*, p 127.
109 'Preface to "Three leisures"'. *Complete works of Lu Xun* Vol IV, p 6.
110 'Literary anecdotes' (*Wentan de zhanggu*), *ibid*, p 122; 'The class nature of literature', *ibid*, p 126.
111 Harriet Mills, 'Lu Hsun, 1927-1936: The Years on the left' (Unpublished PhD dissertation, University of Columbia, 1963) pp 119-20.
112 'A glance at the literary scene in Shanghai', *Complete works of Lu Xun* Vol IV, p 297.
113 *Wugui lieche* No 1 (25 September 1928), *ibid*, pp 664-5.
114 Hou Jian, *From literary revolution to revolutionary literature* (*Cong wenxue geming dao geming wenxue*) (Taibei: Zhongwai wenxue yuekanshe, December 1974), p 123.
115 Feng Xuefeng, *Remembering Lu Xun* (*Huiyi Lu Xun*) (Beijing: Renmin wenxue chubanshe, July 1981 reprint), pp 2-4.
116 Feng Xuefeng, 'Some fragmentary materials about the struggle between the two lines in the left-wing literary movement in Shanghai in the years 1929-36' (*Tong erbanian sanliunian zhijian Shanghai zuoyi wenyi yundongzhong liangtiao luxian de douzheng youguande yixie lingshuide cankao ziliao*), *Reference materials on the study of Lu Xun*, p 2.
117 Li Helin, 'Preface', *Literary polemics in China* (*Zhongguo wenxue lunzhan*) (Xi'an: Shaanxi renmin chubanshe, November 1984 reprint), p 11.
118 Feng Xuefeng, *Remembering Lu Xun*, p 4.
119 Marian Galik, *Mao Tun and Chinese literary criticism* (Wiesbaden: Franz Steiner Verlag GmbH, 1969), p 90.
120 Mao Dun, *Collection of Mao Dun's essays on literature* (*Mao Dun wenyi zalunji*) (Shanghai: Shanghai wenyi chubanshe, June 1981), pp 182-99.
121 *Collection of materials*, p 111.
122 'On new and old writers and revolutionary literature: On reading "Welcome the Sun" in "Wenxue zhoubao"' (*Lun xinjiu zuojia yu geming wenxue: Dule wenxue zhoubao de huanying taiyang yihou*), *ibid*, pp 246-59.
123 'From Guling to Tokyo', *ibid*, pp 689-90.
124 *Ibid*, p 684.
125 *Ibid*, p 695.

126 *Ibid*, pp 692-3.
127 Fu Kexing, 'Fallacies in petit-bourgeois literary theories', *ibid*, p 759.
128 'From Tokyo back to Wuhan', Fu Zhiying, *A critical biography of Mao Dun (Mao Dun pingzhuan)* (Shanghai: Kaiming shudian, July 1936), p 280.
129 'Some practical problems in the nascent literature of China', *Collection of materials*, p 923.
130 'From Tokyo back to Wuhan', *A critical biography of Mao Dun*, pp 279-300.
131 *Collection of materials*, p 763.
132 'From Tokyo back to Wuhan', *A critical biography of Mao Dun*, p 295.
133 *Collection of materials*, pp 847-67.
134 Harriet Mills, 'Lu Hsun, 1927-1936', pp 105-6.
135 Letter to Cao Jinghua, 20 September 1930, *Complete works of Lu Xun* Vol XII, p 23.
136 A Ying, 'Remembering Yin Fu on the anniversary of the death of Lu Xun' (*Lu Xun jiri yi Yin Fu*), *Beijing ribao (Beijing daily)*, 20 October 1956. The long poem contributed by Yin Fu was 'Before the arrival of death' (*Zai sishen weidao zhiqian*), *Taiyang yuekan* No 4.
137 Quoted from Ding Miao, *A complete criticism on the literature of Communist China (Zhonggong wenyi zongpipan)* (Hong Kong: Hong Kong Chinese Pen Club, 1970), pp 36-7.
138 Mao Zedong, 'Talks at the Yen'an forum on literature and art', *Selected works* Vol III, p 69.

Chapter Two

The Road to the Establishment of a United Front (1929-1930)

The heated debate of 1928-29 on revolutionary literature ended dramatically in a great union of left-wing writers with the formation of the Chinese League of Left-wing Writers on 2 March 1930. Ironically, the chief target of attack in the polemic, Lu Xun, was made head of the League by the same group of people who had called him 'Don Lu Xun', 'feudal remnant' and 'a frustrated fascist'. On the other hand, it was also strange that Lu Xun should accept such a union unreservedly. How and why was this possible? The reasons as well as the steps taken to end the hostilities and bring about the formation of the united front must now be dealt with.

There have been many suggestions, especially from the right, that the attack launched against Lu Xun during the polemic was directed by the CCP.[1] It has been argued that the attack on established writers, with Lu Xun most prominent, was part of the CCP plan to grasp leadership of the literary circle.[2] However, as explained in the previous chapter, it was mainly due to the influence of Japanese Fukumotoism that the radicals launched an attack on Lu Xun. Party influence was also an important factor but there was no Party directive. Zheng Boqi once made this point very clearly: 'At that time, the Creation Society was not led by anybody. It initiated activities of its own accord.'[3]

It is true that Qu Qiubai, being himself a man of letters, was interested in what went on in the literary scene. Qian Xingcun said that Qu instructed and led the Sun Society.[4] Feng Naichao also admitted that 'Qu had a hand in our work',[5] but the directions he gave could not have been for an assault on Lu Xun. First, in terms of temperament, Qu Qiubai and Lu Xun were very much alike. Although Qu adopted a radical political line (very much due to the influence of the Comintern), his approach to literature was moderate. That explained why he and Lu Xun became bosom friends soon after they met. Second, if Qu Qiubai had given the order for attack, the first group to be mobilised should have been the Sun Society. Yet it was the young radicals of the Creation Society, who were not much influenced by Qu, who started the assault and were more active in the attack on Lu Xun. Third, if the Party instructed them to start a polemic, why was there a quarrel between the two groups even before the polemic began? If the Party was leading, there was no reason for arguments over the question of leadership. The diversity in their opinions shows that they did not receive instructions from the same source.

After all, it was pointless for the CCP to direct such a war against Lu Xun, a writer who had shown great sympathy towards the May Thirtieth and other mass movements. The Party was in a most difficult position. The bloodstain of Jiang

Jieshi's coup had not been washed away and suppression by the GMD was severe. Qu Qiubai's leadership had not been firmly established and a split within the Party was likely.[6] It is doubtful if the Party could afford a large scale war in the literary field. Most important, from evidence available now, it is certain that the dispute was finally brought to an end on Party instructions. In other words, the CCP was not happy with such a war.

The years following the coup in 1927 saw a period of 'White terror'.[7] Hundreds of thousands of people were arrested. According to one source, in the eight months from January to August 1928, one hundred thousand were killed.[8] This was a severe blow to the Communists and brought about the near-destruction of the Communist Party.

Ironically, the GMD's policy of repression brought an unexpected result in the literary field. Many men of letters, dismayed by the coup which they viewed as a betrayal of the revolution, were attracted to Communism. The CCP was quick to grasp this chance. With ever-worsening GMD suppression, the Communists had to do something to ensure their survival. In terms of military force, they were unable to compete with the GMD. Mao Zedong's holding of a base in the Jinggang Mountains could achieve nothing more than guerrilla warfare harassment. Control of the literary circle was a positive way to counterbalance the GMD's overwhelming superiority.

There was also severe suppression in the literary field. On 7 February 1929, the publishing house of the Creation Society was raided by the police. In the same month, the authorities issued the 'Regulations on the scrutiny of publicity materials'. In July, the 'Regulations on the examination of motion pictures' were proclaimed. If the left-wingers continued to fight among themselves, the chances of survival would be minimal. Only through concentration of energy and cooperation could they put up a better fight. It must be borne in mind that the Crescent School, which was closely allied with the Modern Criticism group (*Xiandai pinglunpai*), constituted a strong opposition to the left-wing literary movement. Its literary theories were in absolute contrast with those of the Communist group and yet they were able to gain a considerable degree of popularity among readers - many issues of the *Xinyue yuekan* (*Crescent Monthly*) went into several reprints. If a united front was not organised, the left-wingers would obviously not be strong enough to counter such an uncompromising enemy. After all, the left-wing had no great writers, except for Lu Xun, Yu Dafu and Mao Dun, and they would have gone their own way had they not been won over. Hence, these great and important writers had to be pacified first. A united front was not only desirable, but essential.

However, the establishment of the Left League cannot be viewed as a sign that the CCP was regaining strength. The position was in no way improved in 1930. Not until the Mukden Incident (1931) and the Shanghai Battle (1932) did Communists get increased public sympathy, presumably because they took a firm stand against Japanese aggression.[9] After two years of working underground, the CCP was now more capable of dealing with suppression and the Central Committee began to pay greater attention to literary matters. While Qu Qiubai did not have time to attend the meetings of the Sun Society, Li Lisan, his successor, could interview writers individually.[10] At the same time, Party control of literary affairs was transferred from district to provincial level, under the Cultural Branch of the Propaganda Department of the Provincial Committee. Then in the autumn of 1929, the Cultural Committee, which was directly accountable to the Central Propaganda Committee, was established. These are signs that the CCP recognised the importance of dominating literary affairs.

In fact, a change in Communist policy upon the failure of Qu Qiubai's insurrection plans brought great advantages to the solidarity in the literary world.[11] At the Fifteenth Congress of the Communist Party of the Soviet Union (December 1927), Lominadze, the Comintern representative in China, was rebuked for his suggestion that the Canton Commune (11-13 December 1927) was 'the beginning of a new upsurge of the Chinese revolution'. Rather, it was a 'heavy defeat'.[12] Then in July 1928, the CCP held its Sixth Congress at a small village outside Moscow. Its political resolution echoed the decisions made at the Soviet Communist Party Congress and the ECCI's (Comintern Executive Committee) Ninth Plenum held in February 1928. According to the resolution, there was no mighty upsurge of revolutionary activity. At the present stage, the nature of the revolution was bourgeois-democratic, the main force being supplied by petit bourgeois peasants and intellectuals.[13] This was of great importance as it provided the justification for a union with petit bourgeois writers.

V T Hsu, a former GMD investigator, has claimed that Agnes Smedley advised the CCP that Lu Xun should be won over, and the celebration of Lu's fiftieth birthday by the left-wingers was a way to please him.[14] However, this celebration was held in September 1930, six months after the formation of the Left League. Furthermore, Agnes Smedley arrived in Shanghai in 1929; it would not have been possible for her to realise the importance of solidarity with Lu Xun in such a short time. It must be remembered that some sources claim that the Party began to intervene at the end of 1928 - before her arrival in Shanghai. Even Smedley herself, who wrote so much on Lu Xun, never said that she suggested that the CCP win him over.[15] Thus Hsu's speculation can be rejected. There is little doubt that the decision to win over Lu Xun was made within the Party Central Committee.

The fame Lu Xun enjoyed as a writer was the main incentive for the CCP's action. Since the publication of 'Diary of a madman' (*Kuangren riji*), his position as the top fiction writer in modern China had been unchallenged. After the incident at the National Women's Normal College, he was becoming more and more popular among young people. Eager to gain their support, the Communists could not afford to alienate their 'mentor'. Winning over Lu Xun would bring practical advantages to the entire leftist literary movement, and even the Communist movement. Yang Hansheng once reported these words of

The Chinese League of Left-wing Writers

Li Fuchun, head of the Propaganda Department of the Jiangsu Communist Provincial Committee:

> Just imagine, if an old warrior and progressive thinker like Lu Xun could stand on the side of the Party and the front of leftist culture, how great the effects and advantages would be.[16]

As shown earlier, Lu Xun never opposed revolutionary literature. In many ways he supported it. However, he had been the strongest opposing force to the revolutionary literary polemic conducted by the members of the Creation and Sun Societies. With his popularity, fame and biting wit, he could make a very tough enemy. And surely it was better to have him as a friend rather than an enemy.

As for Lu Xun himself, the story is much simpler. He was ready to accept solidarity with the Communists because he believed this would do China good. He always had a most sincere wish that China would be strong one day. We have seen how he was disillusioned by the GMD coup at a time when the Northern Expedition was in progress. Before this, he was well-disposed towards the GMD. The coup, together with the subsequent persecution, possibly caused a psychological crisis in him. The approach made to him by the Communist group, after a period of pen-battle and hesitation, would certainly have been comforting. What is more, Lu Xun often believed that unity of writers could achieve something constructive. In the previous few years, he had lent support to and joined various literary groups formed by young people, such as the Morning Flower Society (*Zhaohuashe*) and the Unnamed Society (*Weimingshe*). Before the polemic, he was also anxious to join hands with the Creation Society. Obviously, joining the League was a means to realise his ideals.

One theory suggested by right-wing commentators is that Lu Xun was going through a difficult time with no permanent job, nowhere to send his articles and his writings censored by the government. Consequently, he was ready to accept the invitation of the Communist group which had money and manpower.[17] Unfortunately, this argument, though popular, is politically biased and not well supported by facts.

It is true that Lu Xun did not have a permanent teaching post in a university after his resignation from the Zhongshan University in Guangzhou but from December 1927, he was appointed as a 'special writer' in the *Daxueyuan* by Cai Yuanpei. He held this post for four years until December 1931 when he was dismissed.[18] During this period, he received a total sum of $10,470.[19] Then in 1929, he earned $8,256 in royalties.[20] These were large amounts then. There is no justification for saying that he was so poor that he had to accept financial assistance from the Communist group. On the contrary, he often contributed money to the League and other organisations.

It is also wrong to say that Lu Xun had difficulty publishing his articles. He was editor of *Yusi* from December 1927 to January 1929, being succeeded by Rou Shi at his recommendation. He would have no problem publishing his works there. Then he co-edited *Benliu* (*Rushing stream*) with Yu Dafu in June

The Road to the Establishment of a United Front

1928. In September, Yu's *Dazhong wenyi* (*Mass literature*) appeared. Moreover in December 1928 and June 1929, Lu joined Rou Shi and others to publish *Zhaohua yuekan* (*Morning flower monthly*) and *Zhaohua xunkan* (*Morning flower quarterly*). Even the censorship of the GMD posed no real problem for him. Throughout the years 1928-29, he published one article after another - under different pseudonyms, a good tactic to cope with GMD censorship. Furthermore, within these two years, he had at least eight books published.[21]

Another theory argues that Lu Xun joined the Left League because he felt that he had won the fight against the revolutionary writers when he was approached and was made the leader of the League by his rivals. In other words, the revolutionary literary polemic was part of the strategy of the Communists to win over Lu Xun. He was first attacked harshly, then praised, making him believe that he was the champion of the cause. The whole scheme was set up to trap him and he was intoxicated with the flattery of people like Feng Xuefeng and Agnes Smedley. Lu Xun was described as the Ah Q who was master of the 'spiritual victory tactics' (*jingshen shenglifa*) and he 'unconsciously fell into the snare of the left'.[22] Such an explanation was spreading in literary circles even in the early thirties.[23]

Most people like to hear honeyed words and Lu Xun was probably no exception; but from his writings it is clear that he was not intoxicated by them and was able to keep a clear mind. He did not give up his standpoint, commenting on or even criticising the revolutionary literary movement even after the formation of the League. His speech at the inaugural ceremony of the Left League shows that he was well aware of his own as well as others' shortcomings and that he had no hesitation in pointing them out.[24] In a letter to Zhang Tingqian, he wrote:

> Apart from the Freedom League, I have also joined the League of Left-wing Writers at the invitation of the young people. At the [inaugural] meeting, I saw all the revolutionary writers of Shanghai. But to me, they are but of the colour of the aubergine flowers. I then have to run the risk of acting as a stepladder again. But I am afraid they cannot even climb ladders.[25]

It is said that since aubergine flowers are not gaily-coloured, people around Zhejiang (Lu Xun's native province) liken the mediocre to them. Another explanation is that since aubergine flowers are violet but not red in colour, when Lu Xun used this to describe those revolutionary writers, he meant that they were not truly 'red'.[26] From this letter, we can see that Lu Xun remained sober and was able to observe keenly. His refusal to take up the post of chairman also shows that he did not aim at becoming head of the League when he decided to join.[27] Further, we have already demonstrated that the revolutionary literary polemic was not started on instructions from the CCP and could not have been part of a long-term plan. It was not necessary to start such a war in order to win Lu Xun over, for he had made up his mind, and agreed to collaborate with the Creationists in late 1927.

The Chinese League of Left-wing Writers

Su Xuelin, extreme right-wing writer and critic and long-time opponent of Lu Xun, claimed that jealousy made him agree to join the Left League. According to her, Lu Xun could not be friendly with any but the Creation group because the others were too well-educated and famous while the leading figures of the Creation Society were inferior in both qualifications and writing skills.[28]

However, this theory, too, is biased. A distinction can indeed be made between those who studied in Japan and those who studied in the United States or Europe; and Lu Xun did not hold any university degree unlike his opponents, Hu Shi, Liang Shiqiu, Chen Yuan and Xu Zhimo. But these differences would not have made Lu Xun jealous. It was common, even fashionable, then not to take a degree after studying abroad. Even Wen Yiduo and Zhu Xiang, leading poets of the Crescent School, obtained no degree after some years in the United States. Moreover, Lu Xun was not eager to teach in universities. He submitted his resignation in both Xiamen and Zhongshan Universities. Even in Shanghai, he rejected all invitations to teaching posts in universities.[29] In terms of literary fame, his opponents were far below him. Hu Shi, Liang Shiqiu and Chen Yuan might be good scholars, but good scholars do not always make good writers. Among his enemies, only Xu Zhimo was famous as a poet. Yet the Left League was not lacking great and famous writers. Yu Dafu, Guo Moruo and Mao Dun all had great literary fame. Had Lu Xun been jealous, they would have been the target. The fact that he could maintain his peace with them shows that he was not envious of others' success.

Lu Xun may not have been totally converted to Marxism in early 1930 but he was certainly a sympathiser. The Left League, organised and run by young revolutionaries, was very appealing, holding out hope for the future. He could not resist the temptation to side with the oppressed. This also explains his joining the Freedom Movement League of China (*Zhongguo ziyou yundong datongmeng*) and the Chinese League for the Protection of Civil Rights (*Zhongguo minquan baozhang tongmeng*).

A major step towards a united front was the formation in Shanghai in December 1928, of the Chinese Authors Association (*Zhongguo zhuzuozhe xiehui*). Qian Xingcun remarked that it was directly related to the formation of the Left League.[30]

According to Qian, the Association was formed at the behest of Pan Hannian who was in charge of the Central Propaganda Department of the CCP. As the aim of establishing the Association was to win over more men of letters, the politics was minimised and its promoters only claimed to struggle for freedom of speech and publication. Preparation started in October 1928, and lasted for two months. The inaugural ceremony was held at 2 pm on 30 December in Guangzhao Public School, with over ninety attending, forty-one of whom were promoters.[31]

According to the brief report written by Qian Xingcun under the pseudonym Lu Ya, there were nine executive members, namely Zheng Boqi, Xia Yan, Li Chuli, Peng Kang, Zheng Zhenduo, Zhou Yutong, Fan Zhongyun, Pan Zinian and Zhang Xichen; five supervising committee members, namely, Qian Xingcun, Feng Naichao, Wang Duqing, Sun Fuyuan and Pan Hannian. Clearly, the Creation and the Sun groups were overwhelmingly in control since four of the nine executive and four of the five supervising committee members were from their groups.[32] As they were then all Party members, as was Xia Yan, the Communists were directing the whole scene. On the other hand, other groups were also included. The inclusion of Zheng Zhenduo, Zhou Yutong and Sun Fuyuan on the committees reveals that the Literary Research Association and Thread-of-talk group were ready to be pacified. In fact, many members of the above two groups were persuaded to join the Association but Lu Xun and Mao Dun were not invited. Qian Xingcun made it clear that because of the debate over revolutionary literature, there was still some estrangement between the two sides.[33] Lu Xun never mentioned this Association in any of his writings, although it was unlikely that he had no knowledge of it as there was a report on its inaugural meeting in a journal.

At the inaugural meeting, four resolutions were passed:

1) January [1929] be made the propaganda month for the struggle for freedom of thought, speech and publication;

2) publish a creation yearbook;

3) form a committee for the publication of the Association's magazine;

4) employ legal consultants.[34]

These resolutions were appealing at a time of severe censorship. It is not surprising that so many writers were united. However, the association was short-lived and no practical activities were initiated. Qian Xingcun blamed some members of the Sun Society and students of Shanghai Arts University for giving vigorous speeches at the inauguration, which could have frightened away many members.[35] It has also been suggested that with the absence of Lu Xun and Mao Dun, such an organisation was doomed to failure.[36] Nevertheless it was the first attempt of the CCP to gain control of the 'literary power'. Its failure made the Party consider using other ways of uniting left-wing writers.[37]

One study on the Left League in mainland China suggests that Lu Xun was first approached in the latter half of 1928. Xia Yan, Feng Naichao and Li Chuli were sent to contact him and planned together the formation of the League.[38] However, in Lu's diary no such contacts were recorded. Among those who had written on revolutionary literature, only Feng Xuefeng visited Lu Xun at this time but the purpose of the visit was to seek advice on translating and publishing books of Marxist literary theories and had nothing to do with the establishment of the Left League.[39] Further, Xia Yan said that he was sent to participate in preparations for the formation of the League in October 1929,[40] and Feng Naichao said that he first met Lu in 1929.[41] Thus it is most unlikely that Lu Xun was approached in 1928.

Near the end of 1928, there was a complete ceasefire from the ultra-left group because the Communist Party had ordered an end to the debate with Lu

Xun. Feng Xuefeng said that this happened in late 1928 or early 1929,[42] while Qian Xingcun once said that 'the Party was doing something near the end of 1928'.[43]

A member of the Creation Society, Yang Hansheng, once gave a detailed account of the situation before the formation of the Left League. According to Yang, Li Fuchun of the Propaganda Department of the Jiangsu Provincial Committee had a talk with him in September 1929. Li gave the instruction to end the polemic immediately and win over Lu Xun. Two days later, Yang met Pan Hannian who had received similar orders. They then decided to call a meeting of Party members. Xia Yan, Feng Xuefeng, Rou Shi, Feng Naichao, Li Chuli, Qian Xingcun and Hong Lingfei were invited to attend the meeting at Gongfei Coffee Shop. Pan was in the chair and Yang reported the conversation with Li Fuchun. Two decisions were made. First, to stop all criticisms of Lu Xun; and second, to send three representatives to talk with Lu Xun. Finally, Feng Xuefeng, Xia Yan and Feng Naichao were chosen. But this was not for the formation of the Left League. Yang Hansheng said that it was a general demand which led to its formation:

> After this meeting in autumn 1929, there was a demand among the comrades of the Cultural Division to organise together for unity of action. Not only the Creation Society, the Sun Society, Lu Xun and those around him, but also those who were in the art and drama fields held the same opinion. The Cultural Division then took the lead. There were discussions within the Party first. Several meetings were held. After a very long brewing, it was decided to form the Left League. Those who had attended the meetings were: Pan Hannian, Qian Xingcun, Xia Yan, Feng Naichao, Yang Hansheng, Feng Xuefeng, Rou Shi, Meng Chao, Peng Kang, Li Yimeng and Li Chuli. Finally, there was a twelve man preparatory committee.[44]

There are two points to note in this recollection. First, the date of the first meeting. It could not be as late as the autumn of 1929 that the CCP first took action to stop the polemic and order the formation of a united front in the literary world. As we have seen, the attacks on Lu Xun had abated in late 1928; and some League members recalled that they received the instruction to end the polemic from the CCP's leading cadres at the end of 1928 or the beginning of 1929. Moreover, Yang Hansheng said on another occasion that he was not sure whether it was the autumn of 1928 or 1929 when Li Fuchun talked with him on the question of the debate with Lu Xun but 'there is absolutely no doubt that it was before the closing down of the publication house of the Creation Society',[45] which was on 7 February 1929. The autumn before it had to be the autumn of 1928.

The second point in the recollection that draws our attention is the idea that the Left League arose from a general demand of the members of the Cultural Division. From evidence available today, it is clear that it was the Central Committee of the CCP which made the decision to establish the League. With such a hot debate shortly before, it was unlikely that the ultra-leftists were eager for a united front with their opponents. Even Yang Hansheng once reported that some comrades were reluctant to accept Li Fuchun's instruction to stop attacking Lu Xun.[46] But Yang's general demand theory could possibly find justification in Qian Xingcun's recollection. Qian said that Pan Hannian talked about the formation of an organisation in May or June 1929 and also discussed this with others. Qian said: 'After this, we felt that unity was an inevitable trend. Therefore, we have practically begun to pay attention to this matter.'[47] This kind of feeling among those involved may well be the 'general demand' referred to by Yang Hansheng.

According to Qian Xingcun, there had already been a plan to establish an organisation of left-wing writers in May or June 1929. Actual preparations were delayed till October because of two successive rounds of arrests by the GMD in May and July. Qian himself was caught one morning in mid-July when he was distributing pamphlets. Almost thirty people were arrested at this time. Qian was released in late September, after which the work of establishing the Left League could progress satisfactorily.

About the same time, the Sun, Us (*Womenshe*) and Engine (*Yinqingshe*) societies were dissolved voluntarily, while the Creation Society had already been closed down by the authorities.[49] The dissolutions aimed to pave the way for greater unity. Again it was at the instruction of the Communist Party that these left-wing literary groups were dissolved. It seems unlikely that these very sectarian groups would have dissolved themselves without being required to.

To sum up and to speculate on the steps taken to form the united front: first, a meeting was held in September 1928. This was what Qian Xingcun meant by saying that the Party was doing something then. At the meeting, instructions were given to stop attacking Lu Xun and to send representatives to visit him. There was then a complete ceasefire but no concrete plan for forming the Left League was made and no representative was sent. In April 1929, various literary societies were instructed by the Party to dissolve which they did in June. In May or June 1929, the Party decided to establish an organisation of left-wing writers and started to prepare. Massive arrests by the GMD, however, delayed this until October. A meeting was held, and this was the one discussed by Yang Hansheng and Qian Xingcun.

Who was it then, within the CCP, who gave directions to end the debate and form a united front? Pan Hannian was often mentioned.[50] He was first the secretary of the Cultural Division of the Propaganda Department of the Jiangsu Provincial Committee and later, of the Cultural Committee which was to take charge of all literary matters but it is possible that he was not the real head. Feng Xuefeng mentioned Li Lisan[51] and Yang Hansheng named Li Fuchun.[52] Both were senior to Pan so it seems likely that he was merely passing on orders. According to Yang Hansheng, the Propaganda Department of the Provincial Committee, in which Li Fuchun was the top man, gave the orders. But one very important point should not be overlooked. The newly established Cultural

Committee, which took up the matter of the Left League after its formation in autumn 1929, was directly responsible to the Central Propaganda Committee. A possible explanation is that for some time Li Fuchun had been giving orders. For instance, the autumn meeting mentioned by Yang Hansheng, because it was held before the formation of the Cultural Committee, was directed by him but he became less active in the preparations for the formation of the Left League when the Cultural Committee was formed and took over the issue. People like Feng Xuefeng who got to know the matter a bit later would only know that the Central Propaganda Department, or more specifically, Li Lisan, was behind the scenes. Yang Hansheng once guessed that Zhou Enlai had given orders to Li Fuchun because Zhou was in charge of the Central Organisation Bureau and Li then belonged to the Bureau.[53] Qian Xingcun also remarked on one occasion that he had heard from others that Zhou instructed them to stop the debate with Lu Xun,[54] yet it is possible, as one critic suggests, that this was part of the general trend towards glorifying Zhou after his death.[55]

Now the Communist group was ready to have the League of Left-wing Writers under its banner. Even the organisation's title had been decided. All that was left was Lu Xun's participation, because the Party wanted a united front made up of three groups of people: the Creation Society, the Sun Society, and Lu Xun and those around him. Feng Xuefeng was assigned the task of informing Lu Xun and inviting him to join the League.[56]

Feng was undoubtedly the best candidate for the mission. He had written nothing attacking Lu Xun. On the contrary, he abused the Creation Society for its sectarianism and wrongful attacks on him. Although Lu Xun presumably was not pleased by that piece of writing, there was no ill-feeling between them. Through the introduction of Rou Shi, Feng's schoolmate in 1922, Feng went to see Lu on 9 December 1928.[57] Long before that, Feng Xuefeng and Lu Xun had already had some contact. In April 1922, Feng presented to Lu Xun a copy of *Lakeside* (*Hupan*) in which were collected seventeen of Feng's poems. Then on 5 August 1926, Feng went to see Lu Xun at his home. He also wrote him two letters in mid-July 1928.[58] Though they did not make friends then, Lu Xun was happy with Feng's translation of books on Russian literature.[59] It also seems that Rou Shi, who always had Lu's confidence and affection, was able to help Feng Xuefeng to gain Lu Xun's friendship. The two were on good terms within a very short time. Throughout 1929, according to Lu Xun's diary, Feng visited him more than twenty times, and corresponded with him. Feng said that sometimes they talked for three or four hours at a stretch.[60] No one from the Communist group enjoyed such a harmonious relationship with Lu Xun.

Feng did his job well. How he convinced Lu Xun is a mystery and it cannot be known whether he hesitated, although Feng gave the impression that Lu Xun was more than eager to join the Left League. There was ample reason for Feng to exaggerate in order to illustrate that Lu Xun was an ardent supporter of the united front and hence the CCP. It is doubtful that Lu Xun was quite so eager. After all, the question of revolutionary literature had not been solved. On the other hand, it is also unlikely that he was strongly opposed to the League, for even Feng would not have been able to force the League on a man like Lu Xun. Anyway, he agreed to join and also to the use of the word 'left-wing' in its title, because it was 'more explicit, and the stand would be clearer'.[61]

Feng Xuefeng claimed that he was the first to be sent by the CCP to contact Lu Xun and invite him to join the League; but people like Peng Kang, Feng Naichao and Zhu Jingwo had begun meeting Lu in October. Xia Yan and Feng Naichao were also assigned to act as mediators. Strictly speaking, Xia Yan was not qualified to be an organiser of the League; he could not even be called a writer as he had published no creative works at that time, but he had a great advantage over the others in being on good terms with almost everybody. He knew Guo Moruo in Japan. After returning to China, he was able to make friends with other Creation Society members, including Li Chuli, Feng Naichao and Li Yemeng. When he joined the CCP in 1927, he was grouped into the Third Street Division of the Zabei District. The group leader was Qian Xingcun, and the others in the division were members of the Sun Society. Then in 1928, through the introduction of Uchiyama Kanzo, he came to know Lu Xun, who came from the same province.[62] In the 1928 debate on revolutionary literature, he kept aloof and wrote no articles commenting on the issue. Next to Feng Xuefeng, he was the best candidate for mediator.

Compared with Feng Xuefeng and Xia Yan, Feng Naichao was in a difficult position. He had written essays, harsh ones, attacking Lu Xun but in early 1929, again through Rou Shi, he paid a visit to Lu Xun. Lu seemed very forgiving and they made friends easily. Lu even told Feng stories of his native place.[63] Thus Feng Naichao, representing the Creation Society, was able to reconcile himself with Lu Xun.

After Lu Xun had given his assent, what remained to be done was comparatively easy. A twelve man preparatory committee was set up. The candidates of the committee were decided by Pan Hannian, Feng Naichao, Qian Xingcun, Xia Yan and Feng Xuefeng; all were members of the Cultural Committee.[64] However, at least four different membership lists of the committee are now available.

First, according to Xia Yan, the committee consisted of Lu Xun, Zheng Boqi, Feng Naichao, Yang Hansheng, Peng Kang, Qian Xingcun, Jiang Guangci, Dai Pingwan, Hong Lingfei, Rou Shi, Feng Xuefeng and Xia Yan.[65]

Second, according to Yang Hansheng, they were Lu Xun, Pan Hannian, Qian Xingcun, Feng Naichao, Feng Xuefeng, Hong Lingfei, Rou Shi, Li Chuli, Jiang Guangci, Zheng Boqi, Yang Hansheng and Xia Yan.[66]

Third, according to Feng Xuefeng, they were Lu Xun, Feng Naichao, Hong Lingfei, Rou Shi, Shen Qiyu, Qian Xingcun, Jiang Guangci, Yang Hansheng, Feng Xuefeng, Peng Kang, Zheng Boqi and Xia Yan.[67]

Fourth, according to Qian Xingcun, they were Lu Xun, Rou Shi, Feng Xuefeng, Pan Hannian, Yang Hansheng, Qian Xingcun, Xia Yan, Jiang

Guangci, Feng Naichao, Zhu Jingwo, Tian Han, Hong Lingfei and Zheng Boqi.[68]

Except for Qian Xingcun, all seemed to be very certain of their own versions but there are altogether seventeen names. At least five of them must be ruled out.

Ten names are mentioned in all four sources. It is reasonably safe to assume that all four would not have made the same mistake. Thus the following can be taken as committee members: Lu Xun, Rou Shi, Feng Xuefeng, Xia Yan, Jiang Guangci, Hong Lingfei, Zheng Boqi, Feng Naichao and Qian Xingcun. There are seven remaining: Shen Qiyu, Pan Hannian, Peng Kang, Zhu Jingwo, Li Chuli, Dai Pingwan and Tian Han. Only two of them could have belonged to the Committee.

Three names can be deleted immediately: Shen Qiyu, Tian Han and Li Chuli. Shen was in Japan in 1929, returning in February 1930.[69] Only Qian Xingcun mentioned Tian Han but he did not seem certain, just saying, 'in terms of representation, it seemed that Tian Han and Zheng Boqi, should also be included'.[70] However, there would have been little point in having Tian Han, then head of the South Nation Society (*Nanguoshe*), because in the field of drama, the Communists had the Art Drama Association (*Yishu jushe*) with Zheng Boqi, Feng Naichao, Qian Xingcun, Xia Yan and others as members. As for Li Chuli, in a letter written on 22 December 1979, he recalled that he 'had left the literary circle and engaged in "practical work"' at the end of 1928. He was not even a League member.[71]

It is difficult to tell which of the remaining four should be rejected. Among them, Dai Pingwan was mentioned by Xia Yan alone. Xia may have been wrong, but there are good reasons for crediting Dai with membership. As Xia Yan said, it had been decided that the number of representatives from the Creation and Sun Societies should be equal.[72] Of the ten names listed above, Yang Hansheng, Feng Naichao and Zheng Boqi came from the Creation Society while Qian Xingcun, Jiang Guangci and Hong Lingfei were members of the Sun Society. Obviously each group should have provided one more member to the committee in order to make the balance. Dai Pingwan was the only one from the Sun Society.

It is more difficult to decide which one of Pan Hannian, Zhu Jingwo and Peng Kang was a member because all were from the Creation Society. Both Pan and Zhu had been secretary of the Cultural Committee; Zhu succeeded Pan in March 1930.[73] Maybe they did not participate directly. Xia Yan once recalled that Pan Hannian joined the preparatory meetings as liaison from the Central Propaganda Department.[74] Zhu Jingwo was only named by Qian Xingcun who, as shown earlier, has no confidence in his recollection of the names. As for Peng Kang, both Xia Yan and Feng Xuefeng included him but he was rejected by Feng Naichao,[75] so the last committee member is still a puzzle. We can only say that Zhu Jingwo was least probable, while Peng Kang was very

The Road to the Establishment of a United Front

likely to have been one since he was the only one of the four who made a speech at the inaugural meeting.

Hence, the preparatory committee was made up of carefully chosen members from three groups. From the Sun Society, there were Jiang Guangci, Hong Lingfei, Qian Xingcun and Dai Pingwan; those around Lu Xun included Rou Shi, Feng Xuefeng, Xia Yan and Lu himself; from the Creation Society, we have Feng Naichao, Zheng Boqi, Yang Hansheng plus one of the following: Peng Kang, Pan Hannian or Zhu Jingwo. A deliberate balance is obvious. This shows that uneasy feelings might still have existed and that the Party was careful not to offend or discriminate against any side.

The committee met in the few months before the inauguration of the League in March 1930. Xia Yan said that usually they met once a week, sometimes more often.[76] In other words, a dozen or more meetings were held. On the other hand, some people said that there were only one or two meetings.[77] It seems unlikely that an important and complex issue like forming the Left League could be brought to a close in one or two meetings. A plausible explanation is that most meetings were held in an informal way and not every member went to them all. Thus some members might have the impression that very few meetings were held. For example, according to Lu Xun's diary, he went to one meeting only, on 16 February 1930.[78]

This meeting was reported in *Mengya (Sprout)* as 'A seminar of the participants of the modern literary movement in Shanghai'. It was chaired by Feng Naichao who was chosen to draft the League's programme. Lu Xun was among the twelve present. Views were expressed freely. Four aspects of the past literary movement were criticised:
1) Sectarianism and even individualism;
2) incorrect method of criticism - failure to adopt scientific methods and attitudes in literary criticism;
3) inability to take note of real enemies;
4) neglect of the role of literature in assisting political movements.

Three roles were assigned:
1) Destruction of the old society and all its ways of thought;
2) propagation of the ideals of a new society and its promotion;
3) establishment of new literary theories.[79]

It was also reported that it was decided to set up an organisation of left-wing writers, and a committee was formed at the meeting. This needs qualification as these two decisions had been made several months before. Probably a formal resolution was passed at the meeting, with all the committee members present.

At an earlier meeting in October, Pan Hannian gave the instruction of the Party concerning the work of the Preparatory Committee, including:
    a) to prepare a list of promoters of the League;
    b) to draft the programme for the League;
    c) to establish the organisation of the League.[80]

All these documents, added Xia Yan, should be sent to Lu Xun for approval and then to the Central Committee of the Party.

The list of promoters was not a problem to the committee. They could simply include so-called 'progressive' and Party-member writers, but sometimes it is not easy to define 'writers'. Consequently, it took more than one meeting to discuss this list. As the other leagues, such as the League of Left-wing Dramatists and the Chinese League of Social Scientists had not yet been formed, many 'non-writers' were included.

Compared with the first, the second task, of drafting the programme, was more complicated. It was the basic responsibility of Feng Naichao, but others like Feng Xuefeng, Xia Yan and Jiang Guangci also helped. They seemed to have nothing concrete in mind and could only consult the declarations of other literary organisations. Xia Yan said that because most of the committee members knew only Japanese, their main source was the programme of the NAPF (All Japan Federation of Proletarian Art). The only member of the Committee who knew Russian was Jiang Guangci but he did not always attend the meetings. All the same, with his occasional help, Feng was able to benefit from the declarations of such Russian literary associations as the VAPP, October and others.[81]

Lu Xun was consulted in late January 1930 when the documents were ready. According to his diary, Feng Naichao came on 24 February 1930.[82] It seemed that Lu was not very active in the preparatory work. His diary recorded that he attended only one meeting and did not alter one word of the programme. Some sources said that a meeting was held at Lu Xun's home some days before the inauguration, but Xia Yan could not recall the event and it was not recorded in Lu's diary.[83] It has also been said that Lu sought Feng Naichao's views on the content of his speech to be delivered at the inaugural meeting[84] but Feng has already denied this.[85]

The inaugural meeting of the Chinese League of Left-wing Writers was held at 2 pm on 2 March 1930. Before that, Lu Xun had attended yet another meeting, the inaugural meeting of the Freedom Movement League of China on 13 February 1930. It can be viewed as an attempt by the CCP to form a broad united front against the oppression of the Nationalist regime. There were altogether fifty-one promoters, with Yu Dafu leading, followed in turn by Lu Xun, Tian Han and Zheng Boqi. Other well-known leftists included Feng Xuefeng, Zhou Quanping, Shen Duanxian (Xia Yan), Pan Hannian, Yao Pengzi, Wang Renshu and Ye Lingfeng. According to Feng Xuefeng, Pan Hannian again directed him to approach Lu Xun and ask him to act as a promoter. Lu Xun agreed, but reluctantly because he believed that nothing could be achieved this way. But he did turn up at the meeting. Feng reported that he was happy with it and talked about it for several days.[86]

Lu Xun's own account, however, was quite different. In a letter to Zhang Tingqian written only a month after the meeting, he said:

The Road to the Establishment of a United Front

> There was such a thing called the Freedom Movement League. My name was on the list. Originally, it was at the bottom. But it was placed second when the pamphlet came out. (The first was Yu Dafu's.) Recently, I have given several talks in literary groups in schools, all about literature. I do not know anything about 'movement'. Therefore, all these talks were out of tune with that League.[87]

It seems that he did not have a positive attitude towards the Freedom Movement League. Xu Shoushang, one of Lu's few life-long friends, recalled Lu Xun's words on the subject:

> The Freedom League was not promoted by me. At first, I was invited to give a speech there. When I arrived at the right time, one guest had already signed his name there (I remembered that it was Mr Yu Dafu). The order in which speeches were given was: I was the first, Yu the second. I left after Yu had finished. Later I heard that someone there proposed to have a certain organisation and that everyone present was taken as promoters.[88]

Xu's account was more credible than Feng Xuefeng's since it was published before 1949 while the latter was named 'The Party gave strength to Lu Xun' and published in 1951 and hence would tend to exaggerate the relationship between Lu Xun and the CCP. Nevertheless, apart from being a promoter, Lu Xun was also elected an executive committee member.[89] He was even wanted by the Zhejiang Nationalist government because of this incident.[90]

As the Freedom Movement League was also set up at CCP direction, it seems that it bore some relation to the Left League. The closeness in time of the two inaugurations was no coincidence. Since both represented steps taken by the CCP to fight back, there is little wonder that they were launched at about the same time. Also, the manifesto of the Freedom League appeared in *Mengya yuekan*, an official organ of the Left League.[91] It has therefore been suggested that the growth of the Left League was closely associated with the movement for democratic rights.[92]

Notes to Chapter Two

1. For example, see Zheng Xuejia, *A true story of Lu Xun* (*Lu Xun zhengzhuan*) (Taibei: Shibao wenhua shiye gongshi, July 1978), pp 195-6; Jin Dakai, 'Guo Moruo in the thirties' (*Sanshi niandai de Guo Moruo*), *Fuxinggang xuebao* No 24 (20 September 1980), p 102.
2. Li Mu, *On the literature of the thirties* (*Sanshi niandai wenyi lun*) (Taibei: Liming wenhua shiye gongshi, June 1973), pp 34-43.
3. Zheng Boqi, *Recalling the Creation Society*, p 242.
4. Wu Taichang, 'A Ying on the Left League', p 16.
5. 'Record of Feng Naichao's interview: Recollections on the literary movement in the early thirties' (*Fangwen Feng Naichao tanhua jilu: Guanyu sanshi niandai chuqi wenxue yundong de diandi huiyi*), *Reference material on the study of Lu Xun*, p 16.
6. Chang Kuo-t'ao, *The rise of the Chinese Communist Party, 1928-1938: Volume two of the autobiography of Chang Kuo-t'ao* (Lawrence: University Press of Kansas, 1972), pp 54-5; James P Harrison, *The Long March to power*, p 151.
7. C T Hsia, *A history of modern Chinese fiction, 1917-1957* (New Haven: Yale University Press, 1971), pp 116-17.
8. Quoted from Liu Shousong, *A preliminary draft history* Vol I, p 188.
9. Xia Yan, 'Around the formation of the "Left League"' (*Zuolian chengli qianhou*), *Wenxue pinglun* No 2, 1980 (March 1980), p 10.
10. Zheng Boqi, *Recalling the Creation Society*, p 244. Zheng reported that he went to see Li Lisan with Tian Han. Li Lisan also met Lu Xun on one occasion on 7 May 1930. This was reported by Xu Guangping. Zhu Zheng, *Corrections on the reminiscences of Lu Xun* (*Lu Xun huiyilu zhengwu*) (Hunan: Hunan renmin chubanshe, November 1979), pp 62-9.
11. Anthony J Kane, 'The League of Left-wing Writers', p 63.
12. Richard C Thorton, *The Comintern and the Chinese Communists, 1928-1931* (Seattle: University of Washington Press, 1969), pp 44-8.
13. *Ibid*, pp 47-8.
14. V T Hsu, *The invisible conflict* (Hong Kong: China Viewpoints, 1958), pp 43-4; Tao Xisheng, 'Trivial talks about the literature of the thirties' (*Sanshi niandai wenyi suotan*), *On the literature and art of the thirties* (*Sanshi niandai wenyilun*) (Taibei: Zhongyang ribaoshe, 1966), p 14.
15. Agnes Smedley, *Battle hymn of China* (London: Gollancz Limited, 1944), pp 60-6.
16. Yang Hansheng, 'The process of the formation of the League of Left-wing Writers' (*Zhongguo zuoyi zuojia lianmeng chengli jingguo*), *Wenxue pinglun* No 2, 1980, p 15.
17. Hou Jian, *From literary revolution to revolutionary literature*, p 82.
18. Letters to Shao Wenrong, 19 December 1927, *Complete works of Lu Xun* Vol XI, p 604.

19 Cf, Xi Jin, 'Why did Lu Xun not go to Japan for recuperation' (*Lu Xun weishenme buqu Riben liaoyang*), *Xinwenxue shiliao* No 1, pp 148-9.
20 Fudan University (*et al*), *A chronicle of Lu Xun* (*Lu Xun nianpu*) (Anhui: Anhui renmin chubanshe, March 1979) Vol II, p 420.
21 These included: 1 *Little John* (*Xiaoyuehan*) (January 1929); 2 *Dawn blossoms plucked at dusk* (*Zhaohua xishi*) (September 1928); 3 *And that's that* (*Eryiji*) (October 1928); 4 *Translations under the wall* (*Bixia yicong*) (April 1929); 5 *On art* (*Yishulun*) (June 1929); 6 *Art and criticism* (*Yishu yu piping*) (October 1929); 7 *Various questions of modern nascent literature* (*Xianjin xinxing wenxue zhuwenti*) (1929); 8 *On the history of modern art* (*Jindai meixue shichaolun*) (1929).
22 Zhao Cong, *The various personages of the literary scene of the thirties* (*Sanshi niandai wentan dianjianglu*) (Hong Kong: Junren shudian, 1970), p 48; Hou Jian, *From literary revolution to revolutionary literature,* p 125.
23 Nan'er, 'The turncoat official of the world of letters: Lu Xun' (*Wentanshang de erchenzhuan: Lu Xun*), *Minguo ribao*, 7 May 1930; Fei Lang, 'The motive behind Lu Xun's joining the left-wing' (*Lu Xun jiameng zuoyi de dongji*), *Jinguangzuan ribao*, 6 February 1931; reprinted in *Luxun yanjiu ziliao* No 3 (February 1979), pp 343-6 and 352-3.
24 'Thoughts on the League of Left-wing Writers' (*Duiyu Zuoyi zuojia lianmeng de yijian*), *Complete works of Lu Xun* Vol IV, pp 233-8.
25 Letter to Zhang Tingqian, 27 March 1930, *ibid* Vol XII, p 8.
26 *Luxun yanjiu ziliao* No 4, p 18.
27 Xia Yan, 'Around the formation of the "Left League"', p 5.
28 Su Xuelin, *Writers and works of the twenties and thirties* (*Ersanshi niandai zuojia yu zuopin*) (Taibei: Guangdong chubanshe, 1979), p 561.
29 Letter to Zhai Yongkan, 18 November 1927, *Complete works of Lu Xun* Vol XI, p 595.
30 Wu Taichang, 'A Ying on the Left League', p 13.
31 'Declaration of the Chinese Authors Association' (*Zhongguo zhuzuozhe xiehui xuanyan*), *Sixiang yuekan* No 5 (1929), in Rong Taizhi, 'The report on the formation of the Chinese Authors Association and the Association's declaration' (*Zhongguo zhuzuozhe xiehui chengli baodao he xuanyan*), *Xinwenxue shiliao* No 3, 1980 (22 August 1980), pp 261-2.
32 *Haifeng zhoukan* (*Sea breeze weekly*) No 2 (6 January 1929), p 15, *Materials on modern Chinese literary history* (*Chugoku gendai bungakushi shiryo*) (Tokyo: Daian, 1968) Vol XII, p 43. Those on the executive committee who belonged to the two groups included Zheng Boqi, Li Chuli, Peng Kang and Pan Zinian while those on the supervisory committee included Qian Xingcun, Feng Naichao, Wang Duqing and Pan Hannian.
33 Wu Taichang, 'A Ying on the Left League', p 14.
34 *Materials on modern Chinese literary history* Vol XII, p 43.
35 Wu Taichang, 'A Ying on the Left League', p 14.

36 Neale Hunter, 'The Chinese League of Left-wing Writers, Shanghai, 1930-1936', p 75.
37 Wu Taichang, 'A Ying on the Left League', p 14.
38 Chinese Department of the Nanjing University (ed), *Proletarian revolutionary literature in the Left League period* (*Zuolian shiqi wuchanjieji geming wenxue*) (Nanjing: Jiangsu wenyi chubanshe, 1960), p 532.
39 Diary of Lu Xun, 9 December 1928, *Complete works of Lu Xun* Vol XIV, p 735; Feng Xuefeng, *Remembering Lu Xun*, p 1.
40 Xia Yan, 'Around the formation of the "Left League"', p 4.
41 Feng Naichao, 'The situation around the formation of the Left League', p 77.
42 Feng Xiaxiong, 'Feng Xuefeng on the Left League' (*Feng Xuefeng tan zuolian*), *Xinwenxue shiliao* No 1, 1980, p 3.
43 Wu Taichang, 'A Ying on the Left League', p 15.
44 'The process of the formation of the League of Left-wing Writers', pp 15-16.
45 'Interview with comrade Yang Hansheng' (*Fangwen Yang Hansheng tongzhi*), *Luxun yanjiu ziliao* No 5 (May 1980), p 172.
46 Yang Hansheng, 'The process of the formation of the League of Left-wing Writers', pp 15-16.
47 Wu Taichang, 'A Ying on the Left League', p 15.
48 *Ibid*.
49 *Collection of materials on the left-wing literature of the thirties* (Sanshiniandai zuoyi wenyi ziliao xuanbian) (Chengdu: Sichuan renmin wenxue chubanshe, November 1980), p 30.
50 Wu Taichang, 'A Ying on the Left League', pp 14-15; 'Feng Xuefeng on the Left League', p 4; Xia Yan, 'Around the formation of the "Left League"', p 4.
51 'Feng Xuefeng on the Left League', p 4.
52 Yang Hansheng, 'The process of the formation of the League of Left-wing Writers', p 14.
53 *Ibid*, p 14.
54 Wu Taichang, 'A Ying on the Left League', p 14.
55 Anthony J Kane, 'The League of Left-wing Writers', p 66.
56 'Feng Xuefeng on the Left League', p 4.
57 Feng Xuefeng, *Remembering Lu Xun*, p 8. For the date of the visit, see Lu Xun's diary, 9 October 1928, *Complete works of Lu Xun* Vol XIV, p 735.
58 *Ibid* Vol XIV, pp 611, 720 and 727.
59 Feng Xuefeng, *Remembering Lu Xun*, p 2.
60 *Ibid*, p 8.
61 'Feng Xuefeng on the Left League', p 4. Mao Dun's remark was different. He said: 'The formation of the League of Left-wing Writers in 1930 was to liquidate the mistakes of the proletarian literary movement in the last two years. Therefore, the League was called "left-wing" and not "proletarian".'

(Mao Dun, 'About the Left League' (*Guanyu Zuolian*), *Recollections on the Left League*, p 151.) Right-wing commentators consider this Communist tactics to win more writers. C T Hsia, *A history of modern Chinese fiction*, pp 124-5.
62 Xia Yan, 'Around the formation of the "Left League"', p 4.
63 Feng Naichao, 'The situation around the formation of the Left League', p 77; 'Record of Feng Naichao's interview', p 16.
64 'Feng Xuefeng on the Left League', p 4; Wu Liping, 'Always remember the red banner of the literary front' (*Changnian wenyuan zhanqihong*), *Wenxue pinglun* No 4, 1980 (15 July 1980), pp 97-8.
65 Xia Yan, 'Around the formation of the "Left League"', p 4.
66 Yang Hansheng, 'The process of the formation of the League of Left-wing Writers', p 16.
67 'Feng Xuefeng on the Left League', p 4.
68 Wu Taichang, 'A Ying on the Left League', p 17.
69 Li Lan's letter to the Social Sciences Academy of China, 13 June 1980, *Recollections*, p 824.
70 Wu Taichang, 'A Ying on the Left League', p 17.
71 Ding Jingtang, 'About the list of League members who had attended the inaugural meeting of the League of Left-wing Writers' (*Guanyu canjia Zhongguo zuoyi zuojia lianmeng chengli dahui de mengyuan mingdan*), *Zhongguo xiandai wenyi ziliao congkan* No 5, p 44.
72 'Around the formation of the "Left League"', p 4.
73 'Feng Xuefeng on the Left League', p 6.
74 'Around the formation of the "Left League"', p 4.
75 'The situation around the formation of the Left League', p 78.
76 'Around the formation of the "Left League"', p 5.
77 'Feng Xuefeng on the Left League', p 4.
78 Diary of Lu Xun, *Complete works of Lu Xun* Vol XIV, p 810. From others' recollections, it seems that Lu Xun attended other meetings too. Wu Liping recalled a meeting at Oriental Hotel at which Lu Xun was present. *Recollections*, p 76. Feng Naichao said that a meeting was held at Lu Xun's home. 'The situation around the formation of the Left League', p 77.
79 *Mengya* Vol I No 3 (1 March 1930), pp 274-5, in Iida Yoshiro (ed), *Materials on the Left League period* (*Sozosha shiryo*) (Tokyo: Ajiya Shuppan, September 1978) Vol I, pp 526-7.
80 Xia Yan, 'Around the formation of the "Left League"', p 4.
81 Ibid, p 5.
82 *Complete works of Lu Xun* Vol XIV, p 811.
83 'Around the formation of the "Left League"', p 5.
84 Shen Pengnian, 'Two facts about the relationship between Lu Xun and the Creation Society', p 65.
85 Feng Naichao, 'Lu Xun and the Creation Society', p 38.

86 Feng Xuefeng, 'The Party gave strength to Lu Xun' (*Danggei Lu Xun yi liliang*), *Remembering Lu Xun*, p 173.
87 *Complete works of Lu Xun* Vol XII, pp 6-7.
88 Xu Shoushang, *Impressions of my deceased friend Lu Xun* (*Wangyou Lu Xun yinxiangji*) (Shanghai: E'mei chubanshe, October 1947), pp 91-2.
89 'Resolutions of the first meeting of the second general committee' (*Dierjie diyici changweihui jueyian*), *Ziyou yundong* (*Freedom movement*) No 1 (10 July 1930), *Luxun yanjiu ziliao* No 4, p 491.
90 Lu Xun, 'Preface to the Russian translation of "A true story of Ah Q"' (*E'wen yiben A'Q zhengzhuan xu ji zhuzhe zixu zhuanlue*), *Complete works of Lu Xun* Vol VII, p 85.
91 *Mengya yuekan* Vol I No 3 (1 March 1930), *Materials on the Left League period* Vol I, pp 523-4.
92 Neale Hunter, 'The Chinese League of Left-wing Writers', p 89.

Chapter Three

The Left League: Its Formation, Membership and Structure

After several months of preparation, the Chinese League of Left-wing Writers held its inaugural ceremony on 2 March 1930 at the Chinese Arts University. This date was chosen for no particular reason, except that it was a Sunday when there was no school on the premises.[1] Since then it has been remembered as an important day in modern Chinese literary history.

The Chinese Arts University, which did not provide board and lodging to its students, was ideal for the purpose. It was established by the CCP with Chen Wangdao as principal. The site, 233 Doule'an Road (now 145 Duolun Road, a nursery), was near the home of Lu Xun. According to some old residents of Shanghai, the building dates from before 1925. As it was situated between the Chinese area and the cross-boundary road-building area, it was in effect a no man's land, and thus an ideal place for left-wing activities. The three storey building had only two floors of classrooms: the ground and first floors had four classrooms of about twenty square metres each.[2] It is believed that the inaugural ceremony of the Left League was held on the first floor.

From the start, the League was driven underground. Before the meeting it was necessary to ensure the safety of the writers. This was left to the Party division of the Chinese Arts University, and its secretary, Han Tuofu.[3] Xia Yan pointed out that the Party Central Committee also took part in the security arrangements. On the afternoon of 1 March, Pan Hannian, and someone in a responsible position in the Party, visited Xia Yan. With Dai Pingwan, they had a careful look over the meeting site. On the day of the meeting, some twenty people were sent to guard the site and the roads leading to the University. Special attention was paid to the safety of Lu Xun, four bodyguards having been assigned to protect him, and Feng Xuefeng and Rou Shi having been instructed to get him away through the back gate immediately in the event of emergency.[4]

According to the first report of the meeting, in *Tuohuangzhe*, over fifty people attended the inaugural ceremony but only thirty names were listed:

> The inaugural meeting was held at 2 pm. Those who were present included Feng Naichao, Gong Binglu, Meng Chao, Wan Er, Qiu Yunduo, Shen Duanxin, Pan Hannian, Zhou Quanping, Hong Lingfei, Dai Pingwan, Qian Xingcun, Lu Xun, Hua Shi [Feng Xuefeng], Huang Su, Zheng Boqi, Tian Han, Jiang Guangci, Yu Dafu, Tao Jingsun, Li Chuli, Peng Kang, Xu Yinfu, Zhu Jingwo, Rou Shi, Lin Boxiu, Wang Yiliu, Shen Yechen, Feng Xianzhang, Xu Xingzhi and others, altogether over fifty.[5]

This report came out on 10 March 1930, eight days after the meeting but later reports in official Left League organs gave a different picture. The one in

The Chinese League of Left-wing Writers

Dazhong wenyi did not specify the attendance, saying simply that the number of League members then was over fifty, while those published in *Mengya yuekan* and *Shalun* reported that 'more than forty attended the meeting'.[6] Even those who attended argued over the numbers. Xia Yan claimed that it was sixty to seventy, or even more.[7] In a recent article, he insisted that he was correct:

> There were different opinions on the number attendinge the meeting that day. Some said thirty to forty. Some said fifty to sixty, or even more. I prefer the latter idea. This is because the room for the meeting could hold forty to fifty people. On the day of the inauguration, almost all the seats were occupied. There were people standing even around the podium.[8]

He claimed that he was in a good position to say since he sat on the podium, and was able to see the entire scene. However, Feng Naichao and Xu Xingzhi argued that it was unlikely that the gathering was so large. Fifty or so was the League's total membership, rather than the number at the meeting.[9]

Qian Xingcun wrote the report in *Tuohuangzhe*. In 1977, he confirmed that at least fifty people must have been present that day,[14] adding that when he wrote the report, some names were deliberately omitted for security reasons. On the other hand, some well-known or influential writers, who had not turned up, were added to give an impression of a broad, strong united front.[10]

Though it seems impossible now to make a complete list of those attending the meeting, recent recollections of League members provide some material to supplement the list in *Tuohuangzhe*. Yang Qianru, Chen Yi, Shi Linghe, Wang Xuewen and Zhou Boxun all claimed that they attended the meeting.[11] On the other hand, Qian Xingcun said that Pan Mohua and Li Weisen also attended.[12] In fact, Pan, representing the Freedom Movement League, made a speech. Xia Yan added four names, Li Weisen, Pan Mohua, Pang Da'en and Tong Changrong.[13] In another place, he said that Chen Bo'er, Liu Guan, Chen Jingsheng, Li Shengyu and Wang Jieyu of the Art Drama Association and South Nation Society were present too. Feng Naichao contested this, asserting that Li Shengyun and Chen Bo'er did not attend the meeting, but he added Cheng Shaohuai, Shen Yechen and Hou Lushi.[14] Shi Zhecun, who was in Songjiang and did not attend the ceremony himself, said that his two good friends, Dai Wangshu and Du Heng went to the inaugural meeting.[15] Yi Ding (Lou Zichun) claimed that he, accompanied by Li Baiying, Jiang Heng and Song Yi, went along uninvited.[16] One source also says that Ozaki Hotsumi first met Lu Xun at the inaugural meeting.[17] Of course, Han Tuofu, who was responsible for the security of the meeting, may be added. Altogether there are twenty-two names, in addition to those listed in *Tuohuangzhe*.

However two names should be removed from the list. They are Jiang Guangci and Yu Dafu. For the former, it was said that he was ill and did not attend.[18] For the latter, his diary recorded that he was at home the whole day:

> 2 March 1930. Sunday. (Lunar: 3rd of the second month), cloudy with sunny intervals, windy in the evening. It seems that it will rain

soon. Today, stayed at home for the whole day. Before noon, Wang [Ernan] came and had lunch here. Slept for a while after lunch. When I woke up, it was some time past four already. Wrote letters to Zhang Juling and Xia Laidi. Waiting for a letter from Beixin [Bookshop]. It did not come. Wrote a letter to ask about it.[19]

Both Jiang Guangci and Yu Dafu fit Qian Xingcun's category of well-known and influential writers. Although absent, their names appeared in the report.

Other than these two, it seems that the remaining twenty-eight mentioned in the report did attend, giving altogether fifty names. But are there any left out? There is yet another source to trace. The Secretariat of the GMD Central Executive Committee compiled a list containing forty-nine names of those present at the inaugural meeting of the Left League. It was annexed to official letter No 15889 issued by the Secretary General, Chen Lifu, on 10 September 1930. Besides the thirty names in the report of *Tuohuangzhe*, there were nineteen more: Wang Jieyu, Feng Runzhang, Xu E, Feng Keng, Wang Renshu, Du Heng, Yao Pengzi, Han Shiheng, Wu Guanzhong, Hou Lushi, Liu Xiwu, Ye Lingfeng, Dai Wangshu, Xu Xunlei, Cheng Shaohuai, Chen Zhengdao, Guo Moruo and Shen Qiyu.[20]

Among these nineteen names, three can be deleted: Guo Moruo who was then in Japan; Feng Runzhang who had left Shanghai to teach in the Shandong Provincial Senior High School in early 1930;[21] and Ye Lingfeng who, according to some recollections had not turned up at the meeting.[22]

As for the remaining fourteen, the presence of some is beyond doubt and has been discussed already - Wang Jieyu was mentioned by Xia Yan; Hou Lushi and Cheng Shaohuai were supported by Feng Naichao; Dai Wangshu and Du Heng were referred to by Shi Zhecun. In the end, only eleven are doubtful, although it is probable that some of them were present. For example, Xu Xunlei had been a member of the Sun Society. Chen Zhengdao was an active member of the League in its early stages. Han Shiheng had taken part in the 1928 polemic while Feng Kang was one of the earliest members of the League. It would not be surprising if they were present at the inaugural meeting.

Some non-writers attended the meeting, including those responsible for the safety of the writers. The number is unknown, but four were assigned to Lu Xun alone.[23] In addition, there were staff and students of the University.[24]

According to the report in *Tuohuangzhe*, the meeting started at 2 pm and a board of chairmen was immediately set up. Lu Xun, Xia Yan and Qian Xingcun were elected as chairmen.[25] Yet the word 'elected' should be qualified, since the three candidates had been agreed upon at the preparatory meeting of 16 February and the decision sent to the Cultural Committee of the CCP which then recommended it to the inaugural meeting to be passed by the delegates.[26]

After the chairmen were elected, Feng Naichao reported on the preparation process and Zheng Boqi explained the League's programme. Delegates then made speeches. First to speak was Pan Mohua representing the Freedom Movement League. He formed the Beiping branch of the Left League some months later. His name was omitted from the *Tuohuangzhe* report for reasons of security. Lu Xun was next, followed by Peng Kang, Tian Han and Yang Hansheng. More speeches were planned but were prevented by lack of time.[27]

There is no record of the speeches except for Lu Xun's which was published in *Mengya*, jointly edited by himself and Feng Xuefeng. Feng published Lu's speech using the pseudonym Wang Limin. According to him, he had made no record on the spot but wrote the speech up from memory several days later and deliberately added some words which were not said at the meeting but were expressed by Lu Xun in conversation.[28] It is uncertain how great were the differences between Lu Xun's speech and Feng's report. Nevertheless, Lu read and approved it before publication. Xia Yan once claimed that he had made a record of the speech which was lost during the Cultural Revolution.[29] This is hard to believe as it is unlikely that he would not have published it long before. On the other hand, Rou Shi probably made a record on the spot - Lin Danqiu recalled that Rou referred to a notebook when asked about Lu's speech.[30]

After the speeches, the League's programme was passed at the meeting. Attached to the end of the general programme was a programme for action, passed at the same time but never made public.[31] Nonetheless, the report in *Tuohuangzhe* contained the two main points of the action programme:

a) the purpose of our literary movement is the liberation of the rising class;

b) to oppose all oppression of our movement.[32]

Voting started at four o'clock. Seven standing committee members were elected. Again, all the candidates had been decided beforehand, this time by the Cultural Committee with the approval of the Party's Central Committee. Qian Xingcun said that the ratio of CCP members to non-members was taken into consideration, and this ratio was four to three: Xia Yan, Feng Naichao, Qian Xingcun and Hong Lingfei were members while Lu Xun, Zheng Boqi and Tian Han (he joined the Party in 1932) were not. Moreover, different groups were well represented. Xia Yan did not belong to any group and was close to everybody. He could therefore be taken to represent both the Sun and the Creation groups. Feng Naichao and Zheng Boqi represented the later and earlier stages of the Creation Society respectively. Qian Xingcun and Hong Lingfei were from the Sun Society, with the latter especially representing the Us Society, an affiliated group of the Sun Society. Lu Xun could be said to speak for the Thread-of-talk group while Tian Han was undisputed head of the South Nation Society. It is obvious that the CCP was conscious of the need for a balance of power among the various groups. This may mean that the united front in the literary field was not yet consolidated but the voting did show the popularity of the candidates because the order of the committee members as listed in the report in *Tuohuangzhe* was in accordance with the number of votes the candidates got.[33] The sequence was: Xia Yan, Feng Naichao, Qian Xingcun, Lu Xun, Tian Han, Zheng Boqi and Hong Lingfei. In addition, there were two alternate members, Zhou Quanping and Jiang Guangci.[34]

Formation, Membership and Structure

When the standing committee had been decided upon, seventeen motions were put and passed. They were, again, not reported in full but from several reports which appeared later in League magazines, it is possible to list the following which are believed to have been agreed upon at the inaugural meeting:

a) to organise a branch of the Freedom Movement League;

b) to develop relationships with other countries in the field of literature;

c) to form four study groups, namely the Association for the Study of Marxist Literary Theories (*Makesi wenyi lilun yanjiuhui*), the Association for the Study of International Cultures (*Guoji wenhua yanjiuhui*), the Association for the Study of Popularisation of Literature and Art (*Wenyi dazhonghua yanjiuhui*) and the Association for the Study of Cartoons (*Manhua yanjiuhui*);

d) to build up close relations with revolutionary groups;

e) to promote the formation of the General League of Left-wing Culture (*Zuoyi wenhua zongtongmeng*);

f) to determine plans for publishing left-wing magazines;

g) to join in the education of workers and peasants;

h) to publish an official organ *Shijie wenhua (World culture)*.[35]

The report in *Tuohuangzhe* also mentioned the guiding principles of the League:

a) to learn from the experience of nascent literature of other countries and expand our movement with the formation of various study associations;

b) to aid the training of new writers and promote worker and peasant writers;

c) to establish Marxist artistic and critical theories;

d) to publish journals and book series for the League;

e) to produce works for the rising class.[36]

The above, as will be seen, were the main lines followed later by the League.

Membership

How many members did the Left League have in its six years of existence? This question cannot be answered with any certainty. At present, scholars in the PRC are trying to draw up a membership list.[37] However, the project meets diverse reactions. Some consider it important and necessary[38] while others think it futile.[39]

Neither the League itself nor any member kept a membership list of the Left League. This was initially for security reasons; at the time of 'White Terror', such a record could expose members to danger. What is more, no member could have a complete picture of the membership, largely due to the structure of the League. The basic units of the Left League were small groups, with four or five members assigned to each. There were only 'vertical' contacts between members, no 'horizontal' ones. That is to say, League members, apart from knowing fellow members in the same group, could only contact their seniors. They had no knowledge of members of other groups, nor could they ask the names and addresses of those of the same group. Such measures were prudent at a time when betrayal was common. Consequently, sometimes good friends did not know that the other had joined the League.[40] Some people do not even know whether they should be considered members or not.[41] There are even cases in which someone was taken as a member by many but denied it himself.[42]

But group members sometimes changed. If members transferred to other groups, it would be possible to get to know more people. Moreover, rules were not always observed strictly. Thus from the recollections of its members, we can make out an incomplete membership list of the Left League. In Shanghai alone there were over two hundred and fifty members. With some one hundred and fifty members in other branches, the total must have been over four hundred.

One task of the preparatory committee of the Left League was to compile a list of promoters for the League. They were its basic members. This implies that people were asked, or invited to join the League, rather than that they took the initiative to apply. A League member, Ma Ning, said that Qian Xingcun invited him to a meeting on 28 February 1930 where he was told of the formation of the League and invited to join it and attend its inaugural meeting.[43] It is reasonable to suppose that similar meetings with others took place. This had advantages and disadvantages. The advantage was that the preparatory committee could control membership. The disadvantage was that it would close the door to writers who had no connection with committee members, producing serious sectarianism and hindering the development of a broad united front.

However this arrangement was confined to the promoters and it is not known how many of these there were. It has been suggested that important members of the Creation, Sun, South Nation and Us Societies and the Art Drama Association were enlisted as promoters.[44] Most of those attending the inaugural meeting were also taken as promoters, except for those who came on their own like Yi Ding and his group, and the security people. But there were some promoters who were not present at the meeting, such as Ma Ning who was not allowed to leave hospital that day.[45] Jiang Guangci and Yu Dafu were clear cases too. Jiang was one of the twelve preparatory committee members, and Lu Xun had insisted that Yu should be included in the list of promoters.[46] Others included Guo Moruo, Meng Chao, Wang Renshu and Dong Qiusi.[47]

Mao Dun was a member, but not a promoter. His autobiography states that he returned to Shanghai from Japan on 5 April 1930 and stayed at the home of Yang Xianjiang. Though he had learned of the establishment of the Left League from Feng Xuefeng immediately upon his return (Feng lived with Mao's family), he was not approached for about a month. Yang Xianjiang told him that Feng Naichao wanted to see him. Next day, Feng Naichao came and invited him to join the League. In this way, Mao Dun became a member. It seems strange that he was not enlisted as a promoter. His being in Japan was

Formation, Membership and Structure

not a good reason. Guo Moruo was in Japan during the six years of the League's existence. It is also strange that Feng Naichao should have been sent to contact him as Mao had never met him before.[48] On the other hand, Mao had seen Lu Xun and Feng Xuefeng. Lu did not even know that Mao Dun had been recruited until Mao told him.[49] The 1928 polemic might not have been without consequences.

As stated earlier, the Left League developed in a few years into an organisation with over four hundred members. It is uncertain how new members were recruited. One League member, Shi Linghe revealed that he had filled in an application form;[50] Han Tuofu reported that these were distributed at the inaugural meeting.[51] One League member recollected that a registration form had to be filled in at the time of joining the League.[52] This could possibly be the application form mentioned by Shi and Han.

In the process of recruitment, one or two League members were required as referees. This rule seemed to be observed strictly throughout but there was no restriction on the number of people recommended by one League member. Thus, He Jiahua acted as referee for quite a number of members.[53] Guan Lu (Hu Mei), Pan Hannian, Zhou Yang and others also often acted as referees.[54] Unlike joining the Communist Party, League members were not required to undergo any ceremony for admission but very often, an informal meeting was held with an old member appointed by the organisation. The new member had to give an account, or an explanation, of his past deeds.[55] Usually, one was said to be admitted as a League member when one was allocated to a group.

The Left League was made up of very young members. With the exception of a few established writers like Lu Xun, Guo Moruo, Yu Dafu, Mao Dun, Tian Han and Hong Shen, most League members were under thirty years old. Many were even in their teens when they joined the League.[56] Some were students in universities, though very often they only enrolled for cover. These young members were tough, courageous and energetic, ready to sacrifice even their lives, for their ideals. This put the Left League in a good position in the struggle against the authorities. On the other hand, with such a membership, the League could in no way live up to its name as an organisation of 'writers'. This was a decision that the League had to make: either to have a broad united front of energetic young fighters or a small group of older and more lethargic established writers. And China did not have many established writers then.

The Left League was cautious in recruiting members. All League members had to have attained a certain level of education. A resolution passed by its Secretariat on 9 March 1932 specified the requirements for members:

> Every League member must at least participate in one practical line of work: 1) creation or criticism, 2) join the work of mass literature, 3) lead the 'Literary Study' Movement, 4) translation work ... before they can be qualified as a League member.[57]

Thus illiterates were completely ruled out. Consequently, although the League was eager to have members from the working class, the chances of success were greatly diminished. They were aware of this, however, and established a caveat:

> Those who earnestly desire to join the Left League and yet do not have the qualifications to become a League member should be made the reserves of the League - join the 'Literary Study' [Group] (*Wenyan*) or other literary organisations led by the Left League first so as to develop a close relationship with the League and join it after some time.[58]

As for the 'politically unclean', there were two further conditions. First, those who were suspected of being once connected with the reactionaries had to publish articles, in their real names, against the reactionaries. Second, those who belonged to a certain reactionary group also had to reveal to the League the secrets of the organisation and the activities of that group. However, at a time of severe suppression, this was impractical since such deeds could expose the new member to danger. It does not seem that such articles were ever published in any open League journals although some members had to give oral explanations to the League before being allowed to join.

In the early stages, Japanese returned students made up a large part of the League membership. This was understandable since almost all the Creationists had studied in Japan. Others like Lu Xun, Lou Shiyi were also returned students from Japan. As new members were recruited from local universities, the ratio changed considerably but Japanese returned students still played a very important part in the League during its final years. Such leading members as Zhou Yang, Ren Jun and Hu Feng had studied in Japan too. There were also returned students from other countries. Jiang Guangci, Cao Jinghua, Ying Xiuren and Xiao San had returned from Russia, Hong Shen from the United States. Yet the number of those who graduated in universities in the Western world was small compared with such groups as the Crescent School.[59] Many League members were jobless. In most cases, this had nothing to do with ability or qualifications but was rather a consequence of their League membership. It was dangerous for them to have a permanent job because they could be tracked down easily. Guan Lu, for instance, had to give up a good job with an airline.[60]

Many League members had experience of political activity. Some like Guo Moruo, Dong Qiushi and Pan Mohua had taken part in the Northern Expedition. Others like Ren Baige, Sima Wensen and Wang Ruowang were members of the Communist Youth League (*Gongchanzhuyi qingniantuan*). Some, such as Wang Xuewan, Zheng Boqi, Feng Xuefeng, were promoters of the Freedom Movement League. In fact, many were CCP members although this was not a prerequisite for joining the League. Many, such as Lu Xun, did not join the Party all their lives. Others joined only after they had long been League members.[61]

Most League members had joined other literary associations before they became members of the Left League. Ren Jun reported that all members of the

Formation, Membership and Structure

Creation and Sun Societies were asked to join the League.[62] Those of the Thread-of-talk group were there, including Lu Xun, Rou Shi and Han Shiheng. Members of the Literary Research Association were not lacking either, such as Mao Dun, Jian Xian'ai, Cao Jinghua and Wang Renshu. Drama groups like the South Nation Society and Art Drama Association were represented. Some members came from less well-known associations like the Dawn Association (*Chenguangshe*),[63] Lakeside Poetry Association (*Hupan shishe*),[64] Sunlight Association (*Xishe*),[65] and Green Waves Association (*Luboshe*).[66] Many had also worked together in 1928 in forming the China Authors Association.

In an interview in 1975, Mao Dun said:

> After the arrest of the five writers [1931], there was no significant development in the Left League. After 1932, when white terror became more and more severe, the development work practically came to a halt.[67]

It is not certain what 'development' was meant here, but if Mao was referring to the recruitment of new members, his statement is not borne out by the facts. From a document of the secretariat of the League, we know that they were keen to recruit new members and their target was to enrol twenty new members in two weeks.[68] In fact there were many who joined the League after 1932. For example, Bai Shu,[69] Ai Wu,[70] Guan Lu[71] and He Jiahuai[72] joined in 1932; Liu Qian,[73] Cao Ming,[74] Ren Baige[75] and Wang Leijia[76] joined in 1933 while Wang Shuming,[77] Sima Wensen[78] and Tian Jian[79] joined in 1934. There were even some who joined during the final year of the League, such as Luo Feng,[80] Lin Danqiu[81] and Lin Di.[82] Recruitment was always an important task.

Who then were left out of the League? It is fairly safe to say that most left-wing writers were, at one time or another, members of the League. In other words, the League was successful in achieving a united front in the left-wing literary circle. This was by no means an easy task in view of the severe oppression from the GMD regime. But what about the middle or right elements? If the Communists aimed at creating a broad united front, these two groups should not be totally disregarded. It was not impossible that the so-called middle-of-the-roaders or right-wingers would be transformed into left-wingers. Lu Xun was a case in point, but unfortunately even some pro-left writers were excluded. The most obvious examples were Ye Shengtao and Zheng Zhenduo. It has been suggested that they were excluded because it was 'a need of the situation and a policy of the Party'.[83] Ye Shengtao recalled that Feng Xuefeng had once told him to stand outside the organisation so as to unite more writers. Mao Dun revealed that he had discussed this with Feng Xuefeng, whose reply was, 'most people did not agree to admitting them'.[84] This is to say, the exclusion of these writers was a result of closed-door feelings. Feng Xuefeng also confirmed that he had explained the case to Ye Shengtao. Most probably, he had to make up a story to pacify Ye.

In fact, it is not difficult to compile a list of possible allies of the League. For instance, Shen Congwen, close friends of Hu Yepin and Ding Ling, as well as Ba

Jin, whose novels like 'Family' (*Jia*) and 'Trilogy of love' (*Aiqing sanbuqu*) were anti-feudalist, were very good allies. Even the Crescentist Wen Yiduo whose patriotic poems were well-known could have made a good League member, not to mention those who were sympathetic to the left like Shi Zhecun, Wang Tongzhao, Zhu Ziqing and Xu Dishan. The exclusion of these writers greatly diminished the strength and influence of the Left League.

The behaviour of the League members is understandable. As the most active and important members of the League in its early stage were the ultra-leftists from the Creation and Sun Societies, it was natural that they were reluctant to accept those 'backward' writers. Furthermore the failure of the Chinese Authors Association confirmed for them the 'impossibility' of creating a united front with people of all sorts of backgrounds. This time, they wanted to have a more efficient fighting body. We may also add that even the Communist Party was in its so-called left-deviation phase when the Left League was formed.

Structure

As with the question of membership, it is not easy to know with certainty the structure and organisation of the Left League. First, there is no systematic record of its organisation. Second, for security reasons, even League members were not able to grasp completely the organisation of the League. Third, its organisation was imperfectly delineated from the beginning. League members would give a different picture if they joined the League at different times.

According to Xia Yan, one of the twelve preparatory committee members, there was originally a draft of the organisation of the League. After Lu Xun had declined the post of Chairman or Committee Chairman, the Left League adopted a system of collective leadership, made up of an executive committee and a standing committee.[85] In early reports on the Left League, the executive committee was not mentioned. They all reported that a standing committee was formed at the inaugural meeting.[86] However, according to many League members, the standing committee was elected by and from the members of the executive committee. Feng Xuefeng claimed that at the inaugural meeting, an executive committee of thirteen to fifteen was formed. The committee met several days later and elected the standing committee.[87] Ren Baige said that at the beginning of 1934, the Left League held a secret election. An executive committee of up to twenty members was first elected. Then these twenty executive committee members elected a standing committee of four members.[88]

Names of the first standing committee were published in League organs and they were Xia Yan, Feng Naichao, Qian Xingcun, Lu Xun, Tian Han, Zheng Boqi and Hong Lingfei, with two supplementary members, Zhou Quanping and Jiang Guangci. There was no record of the first executive committee. As said earlier, Feng Xuefeng reported that it had thirteen to fifteen members. One source suggests that they were Lu Xun, Xia Yan, Feng Naichao, Qian Xingcun,

Formation, Membership and Structure

Tian Han, Zheng Boqi, Hong Lingfei, Zhou Quanping, Jiang Guangci, Hu Yepin, Rou Shi, Yao Pengzi and Yang Hansheng.[89]

There is no way to trace changes in the membership of these two committees. From the many recollections made by League members, we know some of the names of those elected to the committees.

First, Sha Ting recalled that the standing committee once held a meeting at his home. Lu Xun, Mao Dun, Zhou Yang, Peng Hui and Sha Ting himself attended.[90] He could not remember the time of the meeting but since they discussed the investigation team of Henri Barbusse, it was probably held around 1932 or 1933 as the team came to China in 1933.

Second, Wang Jinding said that at the end of 1932 or the beginning of 1933, Lu Xun, Mao Dun, Ding Ling, Zhou Yang, Lou Shiyi, Hua Di (Ye Yiqun), Li Huiying and Wang Jinding held an executive committee meeting in a church. This was an incomplete list of the membership of the newly elected committee which altogether had eleven members. At the meeting, Feng Xuefeng suggested that the executive committee celebrate the publication of Mao Dun's *Midnight* (*Ziye*).[91] From this we can tell that the meeting was held at the beginning of 1933, rather than the end of 1932 as *Midnight* was published in January 1933.

Ren Baige suggested that there was another election at the beginning of 1934. More than twenty executive members were elected; among them Lu Xun, Mao Dun, Zhou Yang, Xia Yan, Tian Han, Yang Hansheng, Sha Ting, Ai Wu, Xia Zhengnong, He Gutian (Zhou Wen), Hu Feng and Ren Baige. The standing committee included Lu Xun, Hu Feng, He Getian and Ren Baige.[92]

Lin Danqiu recalled that in the latter half of 1935, half a year before the dissolution of the League, Xu Maoyong, He Jiahuai and Lin himself were on the standing committee.[93] Apart from these, the following were also said to have been on the two committees at one time or another: Xu Maoyong,[94] Qian Xingcun,[95] Ding Ling,[96] Yang Chao, Ren Jun,[97] Wang Yaoshan, Wang Shuming,[98] Zhou Libo and Mei Yi.[99]

Under the two committees, there was a secretariat which was also a central part of the League. A report in *Mishuchu xiaoxi* (*News from the secretariat*) had the following description of the body:

> Under the leadership of the General Cultural League and the executive committee of the Left League, it [the secretariat] will constantly carry out the role of the executive committee to lead the Left League.[100]

The secretariat consisted of three people, one for organisation, one for propaganda and the secretary. However, it is likely that in the later stages of the League, the secretariat was mixed, if not combined, with the standing committee. Many League members recalled that the standing committee was made up of a secretary, an organiser and someone responsible for propaganda, the same three posts that the secretariat had.[101]

The first secretary of the Left League was Zhou Quanping. This shows that in the early days of the League, the post of secretary was not very important since Zhou was not a prominent member of the League. He was only elected as a supplementary member of the standing committee and his term of office was short. Some time around February 1931, he was transferred to the Revolutionary Mutual-aid Association (*Geming hujihui*). On 20 April 1931, he was expelled from the League.[102]

Who acted as secretary after Zhou's expulsion is not known, but in the second half of May 1931, Mao Dun, upon the request of Feng Xuefeng, took up the post.[103] Again, his term of office was extremely short and in October he asked to resign. This was refused but he was given long leave while sharing some work of the secretariat until the end of the year. Then the first issue of *Mishuchu xiaoxi* on 15 March 1932 published a letter from the secretariat inviting League members to take part in a competition with the Social Scientists League.[104] In the letter, the names of four secretariat members were mentioned, Dang Lang, Luo Yang, Ling Tie and Yuan Shan. They are now identified as Ding Ling, Feng Xuefeng, Lou Shiyi and Peng Hui.[105] Ding Ling was probably the secretary[106] and Peng Hui responsible for propaganda.[107]

In February 1933, Mao Dun was instructed to act as secretary again. He resigned again in October 1933.[108] Sha Ting might have succeeded him because Sha claimed that he acted as secretary around the summer and winter of 1933. If so his term of office was short.[109] In December 1933, Hu Feng took up the post of secretary until he resigned in October 1934. Hu once said that the position was then taken up by Tian Han.[110] This may not be correct because both Ren Baige and Xu Maoyong have said that Ren Baige acted as secretary from the autumn of 1934[111] and Ren left Shanghai for Japan in the summer of 1935.[112] He was succeeded by Xu Maoyong who was the last secretary of the League, as in the autumn the organisation began to plan to dissolve itself.

What was the work of secretary? It seems that the main role was to hold meetings, within the secretariat, with the executive committee and with the General Cultural League. Mao Dun said that the secretary was also responsible for drafting the annual reports on the League. Mao himself had drafted that of 1931.[113] Hu Feng claimed that he, as secretary, had to write to the International Union of Revolutionary Writers to report on the progress and the work done by the League. He also said that he took charge of the publishing of an internal organ, *Wenxue shenghuo* (*Literary life*).[114]

The secretary was assisted by the other two members of the secretariat, one to lead the propaganda section, the other, the organisation. It is not known who occupied these positions in the early stage of the League. Hu Feng became head of the propaganda section in the second half of 1933 until he became secretary near the end of the year.[115] Ren Baige followed Hu in the post but in less than a year, he was appointed to replace Hu Feng as secretary.[116] Ren's original position was then transferred to Yang Chao,[117] whose term of office was very brief and Xu Maoyong was soon in charge of propaganda, continuing till the summer of 1935 when he was appointed secretary of the Left League,[118] after which, the propaganda section was put under Lin Danqiu and Mei Yi.

Formation, Membership and Structure

As for organisation, Zhou Yang was its head in early 1933.[119] The post was soon taken by Ren Jun until his arrest in early 1934. Zhou Wen succeeded him and held the post until the latter half of 1934.[120] A newcomer, Wang Yaoshan was appointed to replace Zhou.[121] He held the post until the autumn of 1935. The last head of the organisation section seems to have been He Jiahuai.[122]

It should not be assumed that there were large departments within the secretariat of the League. *Mishuchu xiaoxi* stated that there were only three secretariat members.[123] In other words, the so-called organisation or propaganda sections were one-man sections. Their heads had to take care of everything. Wang Yaoshan complained that it was extremely difficult to do so much work. He had to quit his job and devote all his time to the League.[124]

The propaganda and organisation sections had nothing to do with literary creation. The main task of the organisation section was to mobilise the masses for action against the authorities. It also looked after the activities of the various districts. The propaganda section was in charge of the committees below. Table A shows the changes in the holders of the three posts of the Secretariat.

Table A

Year	Secretary	Head of Propaganda Section	Head of Organisation Section
1930	Zhou Quanping	?	?
1931	?		
	Mao Dun (May - Nov)	?	?
1932	Ding Ling	Peng Hui	Feng Xuefeng/Lou Shiyi
1933	Mao Dun (Feb - Oct)	?	Zhou Yang (early half)
	Sha Ting (winter)	Hu Feng (second half)	?
	Hu Feng (Dec 1933 -		
1934	Oct 1934)	Ren Baige	Zhou Wen
	Ren Baige	Yang Chao	
	(Oct 1934 - summer 1935)	Xu Maoyong	Wang Yaoshan (winter 1934 -
1935			autumn 1935)
to		Xia Zhengnong	
dissolution		Wang Shuming	He Jiahuai
	Xu Maoyong	Lin Danqiu	(autumn 1935 -
		Mei Yi	dissolution)

71

Below the Secretariat, and the standing and executive committees, there were other committees, each with its own scope of activities and functions. When the League was formed, however, there were no such committees. Instead, there were four associations, The Association for the Study of Marxist Literary Theories, The Association for the Study of International Cultures, The Association for the Study of Popularisation of Literature and Art and The Association for the Study of Cartoons.[125] On 9 March 1932, a resolution was passed to reorganise the League. The four associations were replaced by three committees, namely, the Committee for Creation and Criticism (*Chuangzuo piping weiyuanhui*), Committee of Mass Literature and Art (*Dazhong wenyi weiyuanhui*) and the International Liaison Committee (*Guoji lianluo weiyuanhui*)[126] but these were not permanent and there were changes over the six League years. We can now identify altogether seven committees of the Left League which functioned at one time or another.

First, the Committee for Creation and Criticism, often called the Creation Committee (*Chuangzuo weiyuanhui*),[127] or the Association for the Study of Creations (*Chuangzuo yanjiuhui*).[128] Mu Mutian was once its head, and the members included Shen Qiyu, Jin Kuiguang, Wang Jinding, Ren Jun, Sha Ting, Ye Zi, Yang Sao, He Jiahuai, Ai Wu, Ouyang Shan, Lu Xun, Mao Dun, Zhou Yang, Hu Feng and Wu Xiru.[129] As for its work, *Mishuchu xiaoxi* had the following description:

    a) to study the forms and methods for creating revolutionary mass works; and to study the question of popularisation of westernised literary works;
    b) to decide on the roles and themes for literary creations;
    c) to criticise reactionary literary works and theories;
    d) to study the trends of criticism on literary creations and theories.[130]

Yet in practice, the main task of the committee was to discuss the literary works of League members, good ones being recommended for publication while comments would be made about bad ones. They also tried to encourage League members to write. Such questions as the means of making contacts with the working class and fostering peasant and worker writers were discussed.[131]

Second, the Committee of Mass Literature and Art,[132] sometimes called the Committee for the Work of Popularisation (*Dazhonghua gongzuo weiyuanhui*).[133] Its members included Wu Xiru, Ai Wu, Xu Pingyu, He Jiahuai, Chen Dage and Peng Boshan.[134] Wu Xiru was head of the committee from the spring of 1933 to the winter of 1934, his predecessor was Xu Pingyu and his successor He Jiahuai.[135] *Mishuchu xiaoxi* reported that the committee was for:

    a) the creation of revolutionary mass literature and art;
    b) the study of the organisation and methods of the 'reportage movement';
    c) the study and criticism of reactionary mass literature and art;

d) the organisation of reading classes for workers, peasants and soldiers, newspaper-reading groups, and the training of peasant and worker reporters;

e) the organisation of story-telling and letter-writing teams.[136]

Third, the International Liaison Committee. From the report in *Mishuchu xiaoxi*, the committee was similar to the Association for the Study of International Cultures formed at the inaugural meeting. Its work was:

a) to report the literary movement and struggles in China to other countries; to report to other countries, in the form of correspondence, the massacres of the Chinese people by Japanese imperialists and the GMD as well as the struggle of the Chinese people against imperialism and GMD rule;

b) to translate good proletarian revolutionary works;

c) to draft a list of other countries' proletarian revolutionary works to be translated and find out those which have already been translated.[137]

On the other hand, the Association for the Study of International Cultures had identified four areas of attention, namely European and American cultures, Japanese culture, Soviet culture and the cultures of the colonies, small and weak nations. According to the report in *Mengya*, two meetings were held within the first three months of the establishment of the League and the theme for the first discussion was 'the present situation of different countries' culture and the relationship between culture and economy/politics'[138] but little is known about the subsequent development of the committee. It was said that Feng Xuefeng was in charge of it and Xia Yan also led it for a brief period.[139]

Fourth, the Committee for the Study of Theories (*Lilun yanjiu weiyuanhui*), sometimes referred to as the Association for the Study of Marxist Literary Theories, the Association for the Study of Theories (*Lilun yanjiuhui*),[140] the Association for the Study of Marxist Theories (*Makesi lilun yanjiuhui*),[141] the Theory Committee (*Lilun weiyuanhui*),[142] the Theory Study Section (*Lilun yanjiubu*),[143] or the Theory Study Group (*Lilun Yanjiuzu*). Ren Baige and Han Qi were responsible for it[144] while Zhu Xiuxia, Zhou Libo and Xu Maoyong were once its members.[145] Three months after the establishment of the League, this Association had decided upon the study of the following topics:

a) a review of the development of proletarian literary creation and theories in China;

b) a study of foreign Marxist literary theories;

c) a study of Chinese literature by using the materialist conception of history;

d) a study of foreign non-Marxist literary theories;

e) a study of foreign proletarian literary works;

f) a study of literary criticism.[146]

It was also decided that seminars should be held frequently and individuals could publish research results. Mao Dun once presented a report to the

Association entitled 'A review of the May Fourth Movement' (*Wusi yundong de jiantao*).[147]

Fifth, the Committee for the Study of Fiction (*Xiaoshuo yanjiu weiyuanhui*).[148] In many places, it was called the Association for the Study of Fiction (*Xiaoshuo yanjiuhui*).[149] It has also been suggested that the committee was equivalent to the Fiction and Prose Group (*Xiaoshuo sanweizu*).[150] The committee was responsible for the study of the trends, ideas and methods of creation.[151] Ouyang Shan, Sha Ting and Nie Gannu were its leaders and Ai Wu, Yang Sao, Cao Ming, Ye Zi, Yang Chao and He Jiahuai were its members.[152]

Sixth, the Committee for the Study of Poetry (*Shige yanjiu weiyuanhui*).[153] It had different names too, such as the Association for the Study of Poetry (*Shige yanjiuhui*),[154] or the Poetry Division (*Shigezu*).[155] The committee was to lead the Chinese Association of Poetry (*Zhongguo Shigehui*), a peripheral organisation of the League.[156] Mu Mutian and Ren Jun were leaders of the committee[157] and Yang Sao, Pu Feng, Guan Lu, Bai Shu and Liu Qian were members.[158]

Lastly, there was the Committee of the Culture of Workers, Peasants and Soldiers (*Gongnongbing wenhua weiyuanhui*), led by Hong Lingfei.[159] But Hu Yepin was once responsible for a committee called the Committee for the Communication Movement among Workers, Peasants and Soldiers (*Gongnongbing tongxun yundong weiyuanhui*)[160] and Mao Dun confirmed that there was a worker and peasant communication movement in the League.[161] One source suggests that there was yet another committee called the Committee for Worker and Peasant Education (*Gongnong jiaoyu weiyuanhui*), led by Xu Pingyu.[162] Most probably, the three were one and the same.

Although many League members were involved in the activities of these committees, membership was not compulsory. Together with the secretariat, executive and standing committees, these committees could be regarded as the core of the League. Ordinary members took no part in them.

The Left League divided Shanghai into four main districts, Zhabei (North Gate), Hudong (East Shanghai), Huxi (West Shanghai) and Fa'nan (French concession and southern Shanghai). The Zhabei district included the area around the North Gate, Hongkou, and the area of the Suzhou River. Hudong was the area around Yangshupu. Fa'nan covered the French concession and the southern part of the city while Huxi district was mainly the area around Jing'an Temple and Shadu Road.[163] Each district had a district committee and a secretary. For example, Zhuang Qidong was a committee member of the Zhabei district in the latter half of 1934 while the secretary was He Jiahuai.[164] Zhou Gangming once acted as the secretary of the Hudong district with Qi Su and Zhao Zhuo as committee members.[165] Tan Lintong was also responsible for the Hudong district while Wang Chenwu, Ye Zi and Zhang Shiman led the Huxi district. Fa'nan district was headed by Yin Geng, Peng Boshan, Xu Pingyu and Wu Xiru.[166] These secretaries and committee members were to lead the many groups in their districts. They were in turn supervised by members of the

Formation, Membership and Structure

secretariat. It was reported that Ren Baige was once responsible for the supervision of the entire Hudong district.[167]

All League members were allocated to a group according to their place of residence. Since they moved frequently, to avoid detection, they might be reallocated to other groups. Each group had a leader who was to hold group meetings. Usually there were four to six members in a group but some were bigger or smaller, with two members only. For the sake of security, only group leaders had the addresses of their members and group members were not allowed to ask for the leaders' and others' addresses. These groups were also found in universities, secondary schools, factories and even among farmers.[168]

Meetings were held regularly, but the frequency varied from group to group. Some League members said that they met once a week.[169] Some said they met fortnightly,[170] and even every three weeks.[171] With the exception of a very few, there was no fixed meeting place. Sometimes they met at members' homes but more often, they met in public, in restaurants, parks, on farmland and even in graveyards.[172] The content of the meetings varied greatly too, depending on the decision of the group leaders or district committees. One League member said that they talked freely in the meeting, without any specific topic. Very often, they would discuss the documents passed down from the Party's Central Committee.[173] One said that they discussed only literary creations[174] while another reported they talked nothing but politics.[175] In one case, literary theories alternated with literary creations.[176]

As many League members were at the same time members of the CCP, there was a party group (*dangtuan*) within the League. Its secretary played a vital role in the League.[177] The first secretary was Pan Hannian and Feng Naichao was the second, followed in turn by Yang Hansheng (second half of 1930 - second half of 1932), Qian Xingcun, Feng Xuefeng, Ye Lin (Zhang Tiao), Ding Ling and Zhou Yang.[178]

The duties of the Party group were to discuss and implement the policies and decisions of the Communist Party. In other words, it was a link between the CCP and the Left League. This Party group was directly responsible to the Cultural Committee of the CCP which was established in the winter of 1929 to take charge of all cultural matters, and was in turn directly responsible to the Party. All policies concerning cultural matters were discussed and decided by this Committee and then passed on to the Party group of the League. In fact, members of the Party's Central Committee, such as Yang Shangkun and Hua Gang, sometimes attended meetings held by the Party group of the League.[179]

There was still a non-Party organisation, known as the General League of Chinese Left-wing Culture (*Zhongguo zuoyi wenhua zongtongmeng*), to head the Left League as well as other left-wing literary and cultural organisations such as the Social Scientists League, the League of Left-wing Dramatists and the League of Left-wing Artists, but the League of Left-wing Writers was by far the largest and most active group.

The Chinese League of Left-wing Writers

The Left League also established branches in other parts of China, as well as in Tokyo. The exact number of branches is still uncertain, but the one in Beijing was unarguably the biggest while the Tokyo branch was also well-organised. Other cities where branches of the League were established included Tianjin, Guangzhou, Nanjing, Taiyuan, Ji'nan, Wuhan and Baoding. In fact, in 1932, the League had plans to set up branches even in Qingdao, Hankou, Hangzhou and the Soviet areas in Jiangxi, Hubei and Anhui.[180] The branches enjoyed considerable independence and held activities on their own but the mother League in Shanghai did exercise considerable influence over them. Ren Baige was sent by Zhou Yang to lead the branch in Tokyo in 1933.[181] In fact, Zhou Yang was responsible for all branches of the League.[182]

Organisationally, the Left League was affiliated to the International Bureau of Revolutionary Literature (IBRL). Xiao San, then in Moscow teaching Chinese, was appointed by the League to act as representative to attend a meeting of the Bureau in 1930.[183] He was even elected as a member of the secretariat of the Bureau. Some correspondence took place between the Left League and the Bureau.

The Left League had many so-called peripheral organisations too, which were either directly led by the League or indirectly by League members. Of these the most important was the Association for the Study of Literature and Art. It was a reserve organisation for League members and those not yet qualified as League members would be put into the Association. Apart from this, in the field of poetry there was the Chinese Association of Poetry which was one of the most important poetry groups in the thirties. Politically, there were the Revolutionary Mutual-aid Association and the Anti-imperialistic League of Shanghai which can also be seen as peripheral organisations of the League. These, together with other minor ones, made up a strong force in driving forward the left-wing movement in Shanghai in the thirties.

Notes to Chapter Three

1. Xia Yan, 'Around the formation of the "Left League"', p 6.
2. Ji Wen, 'Several former sites of the "Left League" in Shanghai' (*Zuolian zai Shanghai de jige jiuzhi*), *Zhongguo xiandai wenyi ziliao congkan* No 5 (April 1980), p 100.
3. Han Tuofu, 'Lu Xun in the eyes of a Communist Party member', (*Yige gongchandangyuan yanzhongde Lu Xun*), *Wenyibao* No 19, 1956 (15 October 1956), p 28. But Yang Qianru said that the secretary of the division was Han Deyu. Yang Qianru, 'Left-wing writers in Shanghai Arts University', *Recollections*, p 104.
4. 'Around the formation of the "Left League"', p 8.
5. *Tuohuangzhe* No 3, *Materials on modern Chinese literary history* Vol IX, p 295.
6. *Dazhong wenyi* Vol II No 4 (1 May 1930), *ibid* Vol XII, p 442. *Shalun* Vol I No 1 (1 April 1930), *ibid* Vol XII, p 775. *Mengya* No 4 (1 April 1930), reprinted in *Jinian yu yanjiu* No 2 (March 1930), pp 5-6.
7. Ding Jingtang, 'About the list of League members who had attended the inaugural meeting of the League of Left-wing Writers', *Zhongguo xiandai wenyi ziliao congkan* No 5, p 41.
8. 'Around the formation of the Left League', p 7.
9. Ding Jingtang, 'About the list of League members', pp 41-2. Ding also agrees with Feng Naichao and Xu Xingzhi, *ibid*, p 45.
10. Wu Taichang, 'A Ying on the Left League', p 19.
11. Yang Qianru, 'Left-wing Writers', p 104; Yang Qianru, 'Random recollections on the Northern League of Left-wing Writers' (*Beifang zuoyi zuojia lianmeng zayi*), *Xinwenxue shiliao* No 4 (August 1979), p 218. Chen Yi, 'The left-wing cultural movement in the north during 1931-1932)' (*Yijiu sanyi zhi yijiu sanernian de beifang zuoyi wenhua yundong*), *Xinwenxue shiliao* No 4, p 205. Shi Linghe, 'Around the time of joining the Left League' (*Canjia Zuolian de qianqian houhou*), *Xinwenxue shiliao* No 1, 1980, pp 85-6. Wang Xuewen, 'The relationship between the Left League and the Social Scientists League' (*Zuolian he Shelian de yixie guanxi*), *Recollections*, p 143. Zhou Boxun, 'From the Left League to the Dramatists League' (*Cong Zuolian dao Julian*), *ibid*, p 725.
12. Wu Taichang, 'A Ying on the Left League', p 19.
13. 'Around the formation of the "Left League"', pp 6-8.
14. Quoted from Ding Jingtang, 'About the list of League members', p 41.
15. A letter from Shi Zhecun to the author in December 1982; Shi Zhecun, 'My last old friend - Feng Xuefeng' (*Zuihou de yige laopengyou - Feng Xuefeng*), *Xinwenxue shiliao* No 2, 1983 (22 May 1983), p 203.
16. 'Recalling Feng Xuefeng' (*Ji Feng Xuefeng*), *Guangchajia* (*Observer*) No 5 (March 1978), pp 38-40; 'Random recollections on the inaugural meeting of the "League of Left-wing writers"' (*Zuoyi zuojia lianmeng chengli dahui*

zaji), *Lu Xun, the man, the deeds and the age* (*Lu Xun: qiren qishi ji qishidai*) Université Paris 7, Centre de publication Asia orientale, September 1978), p 57.

17 Tian Jianong, 'Ozaki Hotsumi and the "Left League"' (*Weiqi xiushi yu Zuolian*), *Beijing ribao*, 18 December 1980.
18 Ding Jingtang, 'About the list of League members', p 45.
19 *Ibid*, p 47.
20 'Letter from the Secretariat of the Central Executive Committee of the Chinese Nationalist Party No 15889' (*Zhongguo Guomindang zhongyang zhixing weiyuanhui mishuchu gonghan 15889 hao*), reprinted in *Jinian yu yanjiu* No 2, pp 192-3.
21 'The Left League as I remember it' (*Wo jiyizhong de Zuolian*), *Xinwenxue shiliao* No 1, 1980, p 76.
22 Ding Jingtang, 'About the list of League members', p 45.
23 Xia Yan, 'Around the formation of the "Left League"', p 8.
24 Ding Jingtang, 'About the list of League members', p 41; Yang Qianru, 'Left-wing writers', p 104.
25 'The formation of the League of Left-wing Writers', *Materials on modern Chinese literary history* Vol IX, p 295.
26 'A Ying on the Left League', p 19.
27 'The formation of the League of Left-wing Writers', *Materials on modern Chinese literary history* Vol IX, p 295; Xia Yan, 'Around the formation of the "Left League"', p 6.
28 'Feng Xuefeng on the Left League', p 5.
29 'Xia Yan's recollection on the "Left League"' (*Xia Yan guanyu Zuolian yixie ingkuang de huiyi*), *Reference materials on the study of Lu Xun*, p 5.
30 Lin Danqiu, 'Random recollections on the "Left League"', *Recollections*, p 470.
31 Wu Taichang, 'A Ying on the Left League', p 20.
32 'The formation of the League of Left-wing Writers', *Materials on modern Chinese literary history* Vol IX, p 296.
33 Wu Taichang, 'A Ying on the Left League', p 20.
34 'The formation of the League of Left-wing Writers', *Materials on modern Chinese literary history* Vol IX, p 295.
35 *Ibid*.
36 *Ibid*, p 296.
37 Library of the Shanghai Normal College, 'A list of membership of the Chinese League of Left-wing Writers' (*Zhongguo zuoyi zuojia lianmeng mengyuan kaolu*), *Zhongguo xiandai wenyi ziliao congkan* No 5, pp 52-81. The Literary Research Centre of the Social Sciences Academy of China also prepared a list of membership, as an appendix to *Recollections* but it was withdrawn for fear that it was incomplete and inaccurate. Zhang Daming, 'Echoes to the "Membership list of the Left League"' (*Dui Zuolian chengyuan mingdan de huisheng*), *Recollections*, p 822.

38 Liu Fengsi's letter to the Shanghai Normal College on 27 June 1980, collected in 'Left League members on the Left League' (*Zuolian mengyuan tan Zuolian*) (II), *Zhongguo xiandai wenyi ziliao congkan* No 6, p 87.
39 Chen Luo's letter to the Shanghai Normal College on 29 December 1979, 'Left League members on the Left League' (I), p 142.
40 Zhu Zhengming, 'During the Left League period' (*Zai Zuolian shiqi*), *Recollections*, p 424.
41 The letters of Wang Zaoming and Zhao Xian to the Social Sciences Academy of China on 30 June and 6 July 1980, *ibid*, pp 833 and 831.
42 For example Wei Bo, said by Sun Xizhen to be a member. Sun Xizhen, 'About the Northern Left League' (*Guanyu Beifang Zuolian de shiqing*), *Xinwenxue shiliao* No 4, pp 240-8; Wei Bo denied it. Wei Bo's letter to the Social Sciences Academy of China on 15 May 1980, *ibid*, p 855.
43 Ma Ning, 'Miscellaneous recollections on the Left League' (*Zuolian zayi*), *ibid*, pp 111-12.
44 Xia Yan, 'Around the formation of the "Left League"', p 5.
45 Ma Ning, 'Miscellaneous recollections on the Left League', *Recollections*, p 112.
46 Xia Yan, 'Around the formation of the "Left League"', p 5.
47 Bu Qinghua, *A critical biography of Guo Moruo* (*Guo Moruo pingzhuan*) (Changsha: Hunan renmin chubanshe, April 1980), pp 91-2. 'The memorial speech on comrade Meng Chao' (*Meng Chao tongzhi zhuidaohui daoci*), *Xinwenxue shiliao* No 1, 1980, p 282. 'The memorial ceremony of comrade Wang Renshu was held in Beijing' (*Wang Renshu tongzhi zhuidaohui zai Jing juxing*), *Guangming ribao*, 28 June 1979. 'The memorial ceremonies of comrades Xu Maoyong, Chen Xianghe and Dong Qiusi were held in Beijing' (*Xu Maoyong, Chen Xianghe, Dong Qiushi tongzhi zhuidaohui zai Jing juxing*), *Guangming ribao*, 13 April 1979.
48 Mao Dun, *The road I trod* Vol II, p 51.
49 Mao Dun, 'The contacts I made with Lu Xun' (*Wo he Lu Xun de jiechu*), *Luxun yanjiu ziliao* No 1 (March 1979 reprint), p 66.
50 Shi Linghe, 'Around the time of joining the Left League', p 86.
51 'Recollection and commemoration: In commemoration of the centenary of the birth of Lu Xun' (*Huiyi yu jinian: Jinian Lu Xun dansheng yibai zhounian*), *Ji'nan daxue xuebao* No 4, 1981 (15 November 1981), p 39.
52 Wu Qiang, 'Recollections on the life of half a year in the Left League' (*Zuolian bannian shenghuo huiyi*), *Recollections*, p 332.
53 For instance, he introduced Ma Zihua, Qi Su, Zhang Tianxu, Zhu Zhengming and Wang Yuqing. Ma Zihua, 'The spirit was high' (*Yiqi fangyou*), *ibid*, p 313; Qi Su, 'My relationship with the Shanghai Left League' (*Wohe Shanghai Zuolian de yiduan guanxi*), *ibid*, p 413; Zhu Zhengming, 'During the Left League period', *ibid*, p 424; Wang Yuqing's letter to the Social Sciences Academy of China in July 1980, *ibid*, p 883.

54 For example Guan Lu introduced Ye Zi. Guan Lu, 'Recollections on the Left League and others' (*Zuolian suoyi ji qita*), *Zhongguo xiandai wenyi ziliao congkan* No 6, p 102. Pan Hannian introduced Ding Ling and Hu Yepin. Ding Ling, 'Piecemeal thoughts on the Left League' (*Guanyu zuolian de pianduan huiyi*), *Xinwenxue shiliao* No 1, 1980, pp 29-32. Zhou Yang recruited Sha Ting and Xu Pingyu. Sha Ting's letter to Shanghai Normal College, 21 and 23 November 1979, 'Left League members on the Left League' (I), pp 138 and 144.

55 Ma Ning, 'Miscellaneous recollections on the Left League', *Recollections*, p 112.

56 For instance, Lin Huanping, Li Xiushi, Chen Beiou and Xu Xing were nineteen when they joined the Left League. The first two were born in 1911 and joined in 1930 while the latter two were born in 1912 and joined in 1931. Some League members were even younger. For instance, Tian Jian and Sima Wensen were born in 1913 and Yuan Qianli in 1915. Wang Ruowang was only fifteen or sixteen when he joined the League in 1933.

57 *Mishuchu xiaoxi* No 1 (15 March 1932), reprinted in *Zhongguo xiandai wenyi ziliao congkan* No 5, p 19.

58 *Ibid*, p 23.

59 For discussion on the membership of the Crescent group, see Wang-chi Wong, 'The Crescent School in twentieth century Chinese poetry' (*Xinyue shipai yanjiu*) (Unpublished MPhil thesis, University of Hong Kong, 1981), pp 159-71.

60 Guan Lu, 'I recall the Left League', *Recollections*, p 246.

61 For example, Tian Han had been a League member since 1930, but only joined the CCP in 1932. Lin Lin joined the League in 1934 and the Party only in 1938, long after the League's dissolution.

62 Ren Jun, 'Some facts about the "Left League"', *ibid*, pp 241-2.

63 Feng Xuefeng and Pan Mohua were members of the Dawn Association.

64 Feng Xuefeng, Ying Xiuren and Pan Mohua were members of the Lakeside Poetry Association.

65 Jian Xian'an was a member of the Sunlight Association.

66 Sun Xizhen was a member of the Green Waves Association.

67 Mao Dun, 'The contacts I made with Lu Xun', p 68.

68 'The contract of competition with the Dramatists League and the Social Scientists League' (*He Julian ji Shelian jingsai gongzuo de hetong*), *Mishuchu xiaoxi* No 1, p 25.

69 Bai Shu, 'The unforgettable past' (*Nanwangde wangshi*), *Recollections*, p 278.

70 Ai Wu's letter to Shanghai Normal College, 6 December 1979, 'Left League members on the Left League' (I), p 136; Ai Wu, 'A sketch of the thirties: The situation around the joining of the Left League' (*Sanshi niandai de yifu jianying: Wo canjia Zuolian qianqian houhou de qingkuang*), *Recollections*, p 230.

Formation, Membership and Structure

71 'I recalled the Left League', *ibid*, p 243.
72 Bai Shu, 'The unforgettable past', *ibid*, p 278.
73 Liu Qian's letter to the Shanghai Normal College, 22 December 1979, 'Left League members on the Left League' (I), p 143.
74 Cao Ming, 'Fragmentary recollections on the "Left League"' (*Zuolian huiyi piduan*), *Recollections*, p 364.
75 'When I worked in the "Left League"' (*Wozai Zuolian gongzuo de shihou*), *ibid*, p 364.
76 'Left League members on the Left League' (I), p 136.
77 'Several things between the "Left League" and me' (*Wo yu Zuolian ersanshi*), *Recollections*, p 444.
78 'Sima Wensen', *Biographies of modern Chinese writers (Zhongguo xiandai zuojia zhuanlue)* (Chongqing: Sichuan renmin chubanshe, May 1983) Vol II, p 49.
79 Tian Jian's letter to Shanghai Normal College, 20 December 1979, 'Left League members on the Left League' (I), p 137.
80 *Dictionary of Chinese writers: Modern* Vol II (Chengdu: Sichuan renmin chubanshe, December 1979), p 380.
81 Lin Danqiu, 'Random recollections on the "Left League"', *Recollections*, p 471.
82 Li Si's letter to the Social Sciences Academy of China, 12 July 1980, *ibid*, p 837.
83 Wu Taichang, 'On Zheng Zhenduo's and Ye Shengtao's not joining the "Left League"' (*Cong Zheng Zhenduo Ye Shengtao meiyou canjia Zuolian tanqi*), *Miscellaneous talks on literature and art (Yiwen yihua)* (Hefei: Anhui renmin chubanshe, May 1981), pp 62-3.
84 Mao Dun, *The road I trod* Vol II, p 55.
85 'Around the formation of the "Left League"', p 5.
86 'The formation of the League of Left-wing Writers', *Materials on modern Chinese literary history* Vol IX, p 295; 'The League of Left-wing Writers is formed!', *ibid* Vol XII, p 775.
87 'Feng Xuefeng on the Left League', p 5.
88 Ren Baige, 'When I worked in the "Left League"', *Recollections*, p 472.
89 Library of Shanghai Normal College, 'Collection of materials on the organisation and structure of the Chinese League of Left-wing Writers' (*Zhongguo zuoyi zuojia lianmeng zuzhi ziliao huilu*), *Zhongguo xiandai wenyi ziliao congkan* No 5, p 87.
90 Sha Ting, 'Recollection from a member of the Left League' (*Yige Zuolian mengyuan de huiyi suoji*), *Recollections*, p 217.
91 [Wang] Jinding, 'Some recollections on the Left League' (*Youguan Zuolian de yixie huiyi*), *ibid*, p 187.
92 Ren Baige, 'When I worked in the "Left League"', *ibid*, p 371.
93 'Random recollections on the Left League', *ibid*, p 471.

94 *Memoirs of Xu Maoyong (Xu Maoyong huiyilu)* (Beijing: Renmin wenxue chubanshe, July 1982), p 78.
95 Wu Taichang, 'A Ying on the Left League', p 20.
96 Wang Zhongchen and Shang Xia, *The life and literary road of Ding Ling (Ding Ling shenghuo yu wenxue de daolu)* (Changchun: Jilin renmin chubanshe, September 1982), p 71.
97 'Record of Ouyang Shan's interview: On the Left League', p 31.
98 Zhang Daming, 'General information on the Chinese League of Left-wing Writers', p 108.
99 Library of Shanghai Normal College, 'Collection of materials on the organisation and structure of the Chinese League of Left-wing Writers', p 87.
100 *Mishuchu xiaoxi* No 1, p 19.
101 Zheng Yuzhi, 'Recollecting the "Left League"', *Recollection on the Left League*, p 301. *Memoirs of Xu Maoyong*, p 371. 'When I worked in the "Left League"', *Recollections*, p 371.
102 'Notice of expulsion of Zhou Quanping, Ye Lingfeng, Zhou Yuying', *Materials on modern Chinese literary history* Vol I, p 49.
103 Mao Dun, *The road I trod* Vol II, p 71.
104 'Letter from the secretariat about the competition of work' (*Mishuchu guanyu jingsai gongzuo de yifengxin*), *Mishuchu xiaoxi* No 1, pp 26-9.
105 Zhou Guowei, 'A genuine record of the internal activities of the Left League: The *Mishuchu xiaoxi* No 1 kept by Lu Xun' (*Zuolian neibu huodong de zhenshi jilu: Lu Xun zhencang de mishuchu xiaoxi diyiqi*), *Zhandi (Battleground)* No 4, 1980 (July 1980), pp 69-70.
106 Hu Feng, 'Recalling the relationship between the "Left League" and Lu Xun' (*Guanyu Zuolian yu Lu Xun guanxi de ruogan huiyi*), *Luxun yanjiu ziliao* No 9 (January 1982), p 177.
107 [Wang] Jinding, 'Some recollections on the Left League', *Recollections*, p 185.
108 'About the "Left League"', *ibid*, p 149.
109 Sha Ting's letter to Shanghai Normal College, 30 January 1979, 'Left League members on the Left League' (I), p 138.
110 Hu Feng, 'Recalling the relationship between the "Left League" and Lu Xun', p 178.
111 Ren Baige, 'When I worked in the "Left League"', *Recollections*, p 375.
112 Wang Shuming, 'Several things between the "Left League" and me', *ibid*, p 444; Xu Maoyong, 'The complete story of my relationship with the Left League, Lu Xun and Zhou Yang', p 49.
113 Mao Dun, 'The early stage of the "Left League"', *The road I trod* Vol II, p 88.
114 Hu Feng, 'Recalling the relationship between the "Left League" and Lu Xun', p 179.

Formation, Membership and Structure

115 *Ibid*, p 177. Ren Jun, 'Some facts about the "Left League"', *Recollections*, p 248; 'Record of Zhou Gangming's interview' (*Fangwen Zhou Gangming tanhua jilu*), *Reference materials*, p 39, but this sentence was deleted when the article was openly published in *Luxun yanjiu ziliao* No 6, p 119.
116 Ren Baige, 'When I worked in the "Left League"', *Recollections*, p 375.
117 'Record of Ouyang Shan's interview', *Reference materials*, p 31; Wang Yaoshan, 'Recalling the time when I worked in the "Left League"' (*Yi zai Zuolian gongzuo de qianhou*), *Recollections*, p 310.
118 Xu Maoyong, *Memoirs*, p 78.
119 'Record of Ouyang Shan's interview', *Reference materials*, p 309.
120 Wang Yaoshan, 'Recalling the time when I worked in the "Left League"', *Recollections*, p 309.
121 *Ibid*; Ren Baige, 'When I worked in the "Left League"', *ibid*, p 377.
122 Wang Shuming, 'Several things between the "Left League" and me', *ibid*, p 444.
123 *Mishuchu xiaoxi* No 1, p 19.
124 'Recalling the time when I worked in the "Left League"', *Recollections*, p 311.
125 'The League of Left-wing Writers is formed!', *ibid*, p 442.
126 *Mishuchu xiaoxi* No 1, pp 19-20.
127 Ren Jun, 'Some facts about the "Left League"', *Recollections*, p 247.
128 'Record of Wu Xiru's interview: About the Two slogan polemic, the relationship between Lu Xun and the Party, and the popularisation of art and literature' (*Fangwen Wu Xiru tanhua jilu: Guanyu liangge kouhao Lu Xun he dangde guanxi wenyi dazhonghua de yixie qingkuang*), *Reference materials*, p 79.
129 [Wang] Jinding, 'Some recollections on the Left League', *Recollections*, p 185. Ren Jun, 'Some facts about the "Left League"', *ibid*, p 247; 'Record of Wu Xiru's interview', p 79.
130 *Mishuchu xiaoxi* No 1, p 21.
131 'Some facts about the "Left League"', *Recollections*, p 247.
132 'Ren Jun on the "Left League" and the "Chinese Association of Poetry"' (*Ren Jun tan Zuolian he Zhongguo shigehui*), *Luxun yanjiu ziliao* No 6, p 121.
133 Wu Xiru, 'The activities of the Left League's Committee for the Work of Popularisation' (*Zuolian dazhonghua gongzuo weiyuanhui de huodong*), *Recollections*, pp 337-52.
134 Ren Jun, 'Some facts about the "Left League"', *ibid*, p 373. Wu Xiru, 'The activities of the Left League's Committee for Work of Popularisation', *ibid*, p 339.
135 Wu Xiru, 'The activities of the Left League's Committee for Work of Popularisation', *ibid*, p 337.
136 *Mishuchu xiaoxi* No 1, p 21.
137 *Ibid*.

138 'News of the League of Left-wing Writers' (*Zuoyi zuojia lianmeng xiaoxi*), *Mengya* Vol I No 5 (1 May 1930), *Materials on the Left League period* Vol II, p 362.
139 'Xia Yan's recollection on the "Left League"', p 28.
140 Cao Ming, 'Fragmentary recollections on the "Left League"', *Recollections*, p 369.
141 'News of the League of Left-wing Writers', *Materials on the Left League period* Vol II, p 362.
142 'Ren Jun on the "Left League" and the "Chinese Association of Poetry"', p 121.
143 Feng Xuefeng, 'Some fragmentary materials about the struggle between two lines of the Shanghai left-wing literary movement in the years 1928-1936', p 9.
144 Ren Baige, 'When I worked in the "Left League"', *Recollections*, p 371.
145 *Ibid*; 'Ren Jun on the "Left League" and the "Chinese Association of Poetry"', p 121; 'Collection of materials on the organisation and structure of the Chinese League of Left-wing Writers', p 90.
146 'News of the League of Left-wing Writers', *Materials on the Left League period* Vol II, p 362.
147 Bing Shen, 'A review of the "May Fourth" Movement: Report of the Association for the Study of Marxist Literary Theories', *Wenxue daobao* No 2 (5 August 1931), *Materials on modern Chinese literary history* Vol I, pp 41-8.
148 'Record of Zhou Gangming's interview', p 119.
149 Cao Ming, 'Fragmentary recollections on the "Left League"', *Recollections*, p 369.
150 'Interview with comrades Sha Ting and Ai Wu' (*Fangwen Sha Ting Ai Wu tongzhi*), *Luxun yanjiu ziliao* No 6, p 146.
151 Cao Ming, 'Fragmentary recollections on the "Left League"', *Recollections*, p 369.
152 Hu Feng, 'Recalling the relationship between the "Left League" and Lu Xun', p 179. 'Record of Ouyang Shan's interview', p 31.
153 'Record of Zhou Gangming's interview', p 118.
154 Hu Feng, 'Recalling the relationship between the "Left League" and Lu Xun', p 179.
155 'Lin Huanping on the organisation and activities of the Left League and its Tokyo branch' (*Lin Huanping tan Zuolian de zuzhi huodong he Dongjing zhimeng de qingkuang*), *Luxun yanjiu ziliao* No 6, p 111; Guan Lu, 'I recalled the Left League', *Recollections*, p 241.
156 'Record of Bai Shu's interview: About the "Left League"' (*Fangwen Bai Shu tanhua jilu: Guanyu Zuolian*), *Reference materials*, p 34.
157 Hu Feng, 'Recalling the relationship between the "Left League" and Lu Xun', p 179. 'Record of Ouyang Shan's interview', p 31.

158 'Lin Huanping on the organisation and activities of the Left League and its Tokyo branch', p 111; 'Record of Bai Shu's interview: About the "Left League"' (*Fangwen Bai Shu tanhua jilu: Guanyu Zuolian*), *Reference materials*, p 34.
159 'Xia Yan's recollection on the "Left League"', p 28.
160 'Biographies of the murdered comrades', *Materials on modern Chinese literary history* Vol I, p 9.
161 Mao Dun, 'About the Left League', *Recollections*, p 152.
162 'Collection of materials on the organisation and structure of the Chinese League of Left-wing Writers', p 91.
163 *Ibid*, p 92. But some members have suggested other divisions. Zhou Gangming said that there were only three districts. Zhabei and Hudong were combined as the Dongbei (North-eastern) district. 'Record of Zhou Gangming's interview', p 118. Wang Yaoshan also said that there were three districts only; but his Hudong district included the area of the Zhabei district. Wang Yaoshan, 'Recalling the time when I worked on the "Left League"', *Recollections*, pp 310-11. Ma Zhihua even claimed that there were many districts, including Public concession, French concession, Zhabei, Pudong, Nanshi, Husi, Jiangwan, Zhenru, Xujiahui and Yangshupu. Ma Zhihua, 'The spirit was high', *ibid*, p 317.
164 Zhuang Qidong, 'Fragmentary recollections on my participation in literary activities during the "Left League" period' (*Wo canjia Zuolian shiqi wenxue huodong de huiyi pianduan*), *ibid*, pp 417-18.
165 Qi Su, 'My relations with the Shanghai Left League', *ibid*, p 301.
166 Wang Yaoshan, 'Recalling the time when I worked in the "Left League"', *ibid*, p 418.
167 Qi Su, 'My relations with the Shanghai Left League', *ibid*, p 418.
168 Zheng Yuzi, 'Recollecting some facts about the "Left League"', *ibid*, p 301.
169 Zhu Zhengming, 'During the Left League period', *ibid*, p 424.
170 Bai Shu, 'The unforgettable years', *ibid*, p 282.
171 Sha Ting, 'Recollection from a member of the "Left League"', *ibid*, p 218.
172 Ren Jun, 'Some facts about the "Left League"', *ibid*, p 250; Bai Shu, 'The unforgettable years', *ibid*, p 280.
173 *Ibid*, p 250
174 Sha Ting, 'Recollection from a member of the Left League', *ibid*, p 218.
175 Ai Wu, 'A sketch of the thirties: The situation around the joining of the Left League', *ibid*, p 231.
176 Bai Shu, 'The unforgettable years', *ibid*, p 282.
177 Ding Ling, 'Piecemeal thoughts on the Left League', *ibid*, p 164.
178 Yang Hansheng, 'The process of the formation of the Chinese League of Left-wing Writers', p 17.
179 Ding Ling, 'Piecemeal thoughts on the Left League', *ibid*, p 164.
180 'Resolution on the work of the Left League at the present stage' (*Guanyu Zuolian muqian juti gongzuo de jueyi*), *Mishuchu xiaoxi* No 1, p 18.

181 Ren Baige, 'When I worked in the "Left League"', *Recollections*, pp 380-1.
182 Wang Yaoshan, 'Recalling the time when I worked in the "Left League"', *ibid*, p 310.
183 Xiao San, 'The Chinese representative's report on the meeting on revolutionary literature at Kharkov' (*Chuxi Haerkefu shijie geming wenxue dahui Zhongguo daibiao de baogao*), *Wenxue daobao* No 3 (20 August 1931), *Materials on modern Chinese literary history* Vol I, pp 52-62; Xiao San, 'What I did for the "Left League" abroad?' (*Wowei Zuolian zaiguowai zuoliaoxie shenme?*), *Recollections*, pp 175-81.

Chapter Four

Years of Achievement - The Left League 1930-1933 (I)

In our discussion of its history, the Left League is divided into two stages, 1930-1933 and 1934-1935. This is not purely for convenience. In fact, great contrasts can be found between the two stages. In the early stage, after a brief period of trial and error, the League was in a period of construction. League members tried hard to suppress sectarianism and cooperated to work for a common cause. Successful wars were fought against various enemies in the literary field. More importantly, during most of this early stage, the relationship between Lu Xun and the League was most cordial. After 1934, however, no great achievement could be named. Lu Xun, who had always been an ardent supporter of the League, declined to hold any responsible position. He, together with a group of young men around him, drifted away from the central leadership. Serious sectarianism and internal strife developed and took up much of the League's energy.

Even the leadership of the League changed. Before 1934, it was mainly led by Lu Xun, Qu Qiubai and Feng Xuefeng; but the latter two left Shanghai for Ruijin at about the same time - Feng at the end of 1933 and Qu at the beginning of 1934. Lu Xun was then isolated and the leadership of the Left League was taken up by Zhou Yang. This period witnessed a series of quarrels between Lu Xun and the new leadership. The Left League was dissolved in early 1936 in a most unhappy atmosphere. What followed was another bitter polemic within the leftist camp: the 'Two slogan polemic' (*Liangge kouhao lunzheng*). The united front in the literary field was shattered.

To begin with, it is necessary to go into the 'theoretical programme' passed at the inaugural meeting of the League. League members thought highly of the programme and in many places, it was mentioned proudly:

Under this programme, under such an explicit revolutionary programme, the 'Left League' started its activities.[1]

Since the League made public its programme, there has not been any direct attack on the programme.[2]

The activities of the League of Left-wing Writers stem from its theoretical programme. If you want to make any attack on the League, you must first make a thorough examination of the programme on a theoretical level.[3]

The programme was distributed among the members for discussion,[4] so its impact could not have been slight. However, the ideas expressed in the programme could in no way be described as innovative, for they were not very different from those advanced by the ultra-leftists during the 1928 polemic on revolutionary literature. The main points can be summed up in a few sentences: We have to stand on the side of the proletarians who are the gravediggers of the bourgeoisie in the final class struggle; we, being poets and artists, will devote our art to the fight, therefore, we oppose all reactionary forces.

In the programme, a strong political flavour can be found. The following lines are most explicit:

> They [poets and artists] have no choice but to stand on the front line of history and take up the cause of literary struggle for the progress of human society and the wiping out of conservative forces.
>
> We have no choice but to stand on the battle-front of the struggle for proletarian liberation, attacking all reactionary and conservative elements, fostering all oppressed and progressive ones. This is a foregone conclusion.
>
> Our art has to be devoted to the bloody 'victory or death' struggle.
>
> Our art is anti-feudal, anti-bourgeois and against the trend of those of the petit bourgeoisie who 'have lost their social standing'.
>
> Our attitude towards existing society is that we have no choice but to support the liberation movement of the proletarians of the world and to fight against all reactionary forces which oppose the proletariat.[5]

This programme was described by one critic as 'an astonishing document' which 'talked a minimum about literature but a maximum about the "liberation of the proletariat"'[6] while another said that art was not their sole, or even their major, concern. Their works were dedicated to class struggle, to the bloody 'death or victory' battle, to the 'complete liberation of mankind'.[7] But although these statements are true, the emphasis that has been given to 'art' in the programme should not be neglected. The League's ultimate aim was indeed the liberation of the proletariat and mankind, and they were ready to participate in the struggle against the so-called reactionary forces; but what was the weapon to be used in this liberation war? Art! The drafters of the programme were well aware of this. The word 'art' appeared frequently in the programme. Its penultimate paragraph reads:

> We shall step up the criticism of artistic works. At the same time, we shall not forget literary research, and we shall intensify the criticism of the art of the past. We shall bring in the achievements of proletarian art of other countries and build up a theory of art.[8]

This entire paragraph does not mention political struggle. Its drafters maintained that they were poets and artists. Even Mao Dun, who always emphasised the distinction between politics and literature, was ready to accept the programme. He considered it 'natural', 'not vigorous' and 'comparatively moderate'.[9] After all, why form another organisation solely concerned with political struggles, when there was the CCP to take charge of this?

A certain Ling Sheng, possibly a League member, once remarked in a League journal that 'those who joined the Left League had agreed to accept and support the programme'.[10] One critic, interpreting these words, concluded that 'there was never a hint of dissatisfaction with the Manifesto [programme], no sign that it was unacceptable either to a majority or to a minority within the group'.[11] However, a League member Han Tuofu recalled that objections had been raised to the programme by some League members even at the inaugural meeting.[12] While the authenticity of his words may be doubted as no other League members reported this, Lu Xun's speech at the meeting is incontestable. Feng Naichao, who drafted the programme, admitted that 'the speech made by Lu Xun in the meeting, that was "Thoughts on the League of Left-wing Writers", was in spirit a criticism of the programme'.[13]

In the speech, Lu Xun retained his usual critical attitude. His comments were directed against his one-time enemies, now friends, who were sitting next to or in front of him. The central point of the speech was a warning against turning 'right'.

According to Lu Xun, there were several possibilities that 'left-wing' writers could turn into 'right-wing' writers; first, if they have no contact with actual social struggles. Lu Xun condemned those he called 'salon-socialists'. He said, 'it is easy to talk of radical ideas when one shuts oneself in a room. But it is also extremely easy to turn "right"'. Secondly, if they have no real understanding of the actual nature of revolution. Lu Xun argued that revolutions were painful, mixed with filth and blood, requiring all sorts of petty and tiresome work. It was not as romantic as the poets might have thought. Unless one was ready to face all these troubles, Lu Xun warned, one would become disillusioned, desperate or even reactionary when revolution arrived. Thirdly, if they believed that poets or men of letters were most lofty and noble. Lu Xun agreed that intellectuals should not be looked down upon since they had duties of their own but they should not enjoy any privileges. He cautioned writers not to expect handsome rewards from the working class after the revolution was successful. 'There is certainly no obligation for the working class to give poets or writers any preferential treatment.'

In his speech, Lu Xun suggested several points to which left-wing writers should pay attention. First, it was necessary to be tough and persistent in the protracted war against the old society and forces whose bases were indeed very strong. He despised those who were content with small achievements, especially personal successes only. Secondly, the battlefront should be broadened to fight against all kinds of old literature and thinking. Thirdly, new fighters should be fostered. Lastly, a common aim should be established so that a united front could be built.[14]

This speech by Lu Xun, especially the first part, certainly made many League members feel uncomfortable. There was no word of compliment, only critical comments which might have seemed inappropriate or inopportune for such an occasion. It demonstrates that the question of revolutionary literature had not been settled despite the setting up of the united front. In Lu Xun's eyes, his allies had not improved and were still a prey to all those weaknesses which could make them turn right-wing. He was well aware of this and hastened to give his warnings. What is more, he did not hesitate to name both the Creation and Sun societies, pointing out their weakness in the previous polemic. It is not difficult to imagine how embarrassed people like Qian Xingcun and Feng Naichao were. Some were even annoyed. Feng Xuefeng reported two reactions from the audience:

> First, since Lu Xun still stuck to his guns over certain questions and criticised the Creation and Sun societies as well as others, they thought that Lu Xun 'had not changed'. Obviously, those holding this attitude believed that it was Lu Xun who should change, rather than themselves. The second group took Lu Xun's words as platitudes, deserving no attention.[15]

Lu Xun had read the programme of the League before it was passed at the inaugural meeting. He did not alter a word, saying that he could not write this kind of thing. But this did not mean that he gave his unconditional approval. Xia Yan gave a clue which could be helpful in understanding why Lu Xun did not make any amendments to the programme:

> He basically agreed to the programme. (He would not agree easily. We told him that it had been agreed upon by the Party's Central Committee.)[16]

Xia Yan was suggesting that it was because of the Party that Lu Xun gave his approval to the programme.

In the first few months, the League seemed to have been active and progressed well. According to a report which came out less than two months after its establishment, close contacts had been made with literary groups in schools and factories; various study associations had been set up; and an official organ, *Shijie wenhua* was going to be published soon. Two meetings had been held by the Association for the Study of International Cultures while the Association for the Study of Marxist Literary Theories had already started its activities in early April.[17]

But on the day this report appeared, discontent was voiced in another League magazine, *Baerdishan* (*Partisan*). Chen Zhengdao, a League member who had attended the inaugural meeting, expressed disappointment in the article 'May Day and literature' (*Wuyi yu wenxue*). Though his chief targets were the left-wing writers, 'it implied', as one critic correctly pointed out, 'by a blistering criticism of magazines almost wholly run by members of the League of Left-wing Writers, that the League itself was failing to carry out the mission enunciated in its Manifesto [programme]'.[18] According to Chen, those writers just sat in their rooms imagining the lives and struggles of proletarians. They could never achieve real proletarian consciousness because they had not linked themselves with political movements, and their works, so-called proletarian literature, could not be understood by the masses. Their mood was of the petit bourgeoisie and they were a world away from the proletarians.[19]

Chen's article was followed almost immediately by further criticism from a certain Ju Hua who claimed to be a supporter of the League. This time, the comments were directed at the League itself. In a long letter 'Several words to the "Left League"' (*Xiangdui Zuolian shuode jijuhua*), Ju queried whether the

Years of Achievement (I)

League had taken any action in accord with the directions laid down in its programme:

> The first shortcoming of the 'Left League' is that we cannot see any action taken by it. It is almost a month since the inaugural meeting was held. But I do not know what has been done by it, apart from publishing an incomplete membership list and its programme in some magazines, ... What has been said by the Left League in the face of this severe White Terror?[20]

According to Ju Hua, the League magazines were unable to constitute a strong progressive force. Nothing had changed after the formation of the Left League, the same old writers writing the same old things. The League organ *Tuohuangzhe* was even criticised as non-Marxist and individualist, because there was an article praising highly Jiang Guangci's 'The sorrows of Lisa' (*Lisa de aiyuan*) and 'The moon that forces its way through the clouds' (*Chongchu yunweide yueliang*), both, in the eyes of Ju Hua, were of petit bourgeois nature.[21] He warned:

> These many mistakes have already caused discontents among the members. Many sincere young people are wondering if the League is simply hanging out a new signboard while selling the same old medicine.[22]

Both Chen Zhengdao and Ju Hua attacked proletarian writers and the Left League for fighting only on paper. What they wanted was direct participation in actual political activities.

The approaching May Day, in fact, the whole so-called 'Red May', was a chance to test the League's fighting power. A general meeting, the first of its kind, was held by the League on 29 April. A paragraph in the report on the meeting gave the reasons for holding it, which could be viewed as an answer to the criticisms made by people like Chen and Ju:

> It will soon be two months since the great inaugural meeting was held and the cadres elected on 2 March. What has been done by the Left League during these two months? People outside want to know. All its members want to know too. The revolutionary May is coming. In this great month of commemoration, what plans have been made by the League to forge ahead? All the members want to know. People outside should be told too.[23]

But at the meeting, the secretary of the standing committee had to, in the first instance, admit that the work done by the League in the past few months was 'loose' and 'ineffective'. Every League member as well as the leading cadres should be responsible for this.

Even the general meeting itself was considered a failure. It was attended by about thirty members, plus three representatives from the South Nation Society and two Japanese students. This attendance was regarded as low. Furthermore, it was reported that preparation had been poor. Speeches were restricted and there was not enough time for discussion. Proposals were sporadically put forward, thus omitting many important issues. Worse still, criticism was directed at individuals and the roots of the problems were not pursued. Errors were not corrected at a theoretical level.[24]

Despite these deficiencies, this meeting deserves attention as it was the first general meeting of the League. As the report in *Baerdishan* said, it was of great significance that the League could hold a general meeting at a time when White Terror was getting more and more severe. In the meeting, after 'animated discussion', eleven motions were adopted:

a) To examine the adoption of the programme;
b) to publish a weekly organ;
c) to establish contact with the Japanese Proletarian Science Academy;
d) to organise a visiting group to the Soviet Union;
e) to attend the Conference of Delegates from the Soviet Areas;
f) to oppose the internecine wars between warlords;
g) to wage a struggle against the theories of liquidationists;
h) to send representatives to the League of Social Scientists;
i) to organise public speeches and debates;
j) to have a session for self-criticism;
k) to participate in an organised way on May Day and to mobilise the masses.[25]

To be fair, these motions should not be considered perfunctory. The two-thirds attendance could not be taken as low either. The *Baerdishan* reporter might have been too critical. The meeting probably shows that the League was determined to make improvements.

Among the eleven motions, only the last one was concerned with May Day but League members reported that a lot had been said about May Day at the meeting.[26] They passed a manifesto for the commemoration of May Day[27] and practical arrangements were made for League members to take part in demonstrations, put up posters and distribute pamphlets.

Meanwhile, other propaganda activities were begun. On 1 May, the League published three magazines, *Mengya*; *Baerdishan* and *Dazhong wenyi*. The first two devoted much space to articles on May Day. More significant still, a *Wuyi tekan* (*May Day Special*) was published jointly by thirteen magazines.[28] It had also been planned that the Association for the Study of Cartoons would publish a *Wuyi huabao* (*May Day Pictorial*) and a May Day Song was to be composed but this was not carried out.[29]

The League's attitude was shown in the May Day Commemoration Manifesto which was passed at the first general meeting of the League and published in full in *Wuyi tekan*. To them, May Day was not a simple commemoration day, but a day for bloody struggle. They had the idea of a so-called 'Blood-bright May Day' (*Xueguang de wuyi*). The following paragraph is of great importance:

Years of Achievement (I)

We wholeheartedly stand under the banner of proletarian liberation and take part in the revolutionary struggle. We will join the workers all over the world in the mighty demonstration movement on the blood-bright May Day against imperialism and all its reactionary minions.[30]

Important League members like Feng Naichao and Peng Kang also published articles expressing their desire to fight a brave war on this great day.[31]

There was no formal report on what happened on May Day of 1930. It could not have been a success, or there would have been wide coverage in League magazines. According to Mao Dun, the more important writers like Lu Xun, Yu Dafu and Mao Dun himself did not take part in the demonstration. He heard afterwards that the masses dispersed quickly when the police marched in. There was no 'Blood-bright May Day'.[32] We can imagine how unhappy the leading cadres were. Once again, the Left League could only fight on paper.

In fact, repression came before this May Day demonstration. On the evening of 29 April, the day the Left League held its first general meeting, the Art Drama Association, a close ally of the League, was closed down by the authorities. In the raid, dummy weapons and military uniforms for the performance of 'All quiet on the western front' (*Xixian wu zhanshi*) the night before were taken as evidence of insurrection. A rickshaw puller who was hired to move goods was arrested too.[33] The Left League immediately protested. Besides condemning the raid, the League called for 'staunch resistance against the authorities for destroying cultural movements' and a struggle for freedom of assembly, speech, publishing and stage performance.[34] The Drama Movement Federation (*Xiji yundong lianghehui*) and the Art Drama Association published similar protests in League magazines[35] but this was all the leftist camp could do in the face of GMD military superiority.

Upon the failure of the first general meeting and the May Day demonstration, the Left League called another general meeting on the eve of May Thirtieth for the same purpose, to review the past and plan the activities for the following day.[36]

Once more, the general meeting turned into a self-criticism session. The League had to admit that no remarkable progress had been made. Some sections remained inactive. 'It is undeniable that she [the League] is not yet a strong and firm fighting body.' Several reasons were suggested. First, League members did not have a clear understanding of the political situation and were unable to grasp the League's historical, cultural and political significance. Secondly, because of the first reason, League members were not united. Thirdly, most League members did not take part in the work of the League. Fourthly, there were deficiencies in the editing of League magazines, most of which did not work in accordance with League resolutions. Nevertheless, several things had been accomplished. First, literary study groups were formed in some universities. Secondly, the editorial section had held two meetings with the editors of left-wing magazines. Thirdly, the Association for the Study of

The Chinese League of Left-wing Writers

Marxist Literary Theories had held a seminar, though the discussion had been inadequate. Another notable achievement was the sending of representatives to the Conference of Delegates from the Soviet Areas. Rou Shi, Hu Yepin and Feng Keng attended the Conference in May and made a congratulatory speech on behalf of the League. Rou Shi also wrote a piece of reportage on the conference, 'A great impression' (*Yige weidade yinxiang*).

Even before the meeting a May Thirtieth Preparatory Committee had been set up. Its representative gave an account of the preparation and lectured on the significance of a demonstration on May Thirtieth. A resolution was passed insisting that every member should join the demonstration. They were to be divided into small groups to take part in the procession. League members would also participate in the re-opening of the Chinese Art University, the site of the inaugural meeting of the League, closed down by the authorities several days earlier.[37] However, no report was made on the events of 30 May 1930. Yet the two general meetings could be viewed as attempts by the League to struggle for achievements in its early days.

During this period a less obvious but more important achievement was the overcoming of, or the effort made to overcome, sectarianism in the League. Shortly after the formation of the League, the secretary of its party group, Feng Naichao published an article, 'Proletarian literary movement in China and the historical significance of the formation of the Left League' (*Zhongguo wuchanjieji wenxue yundong ji Zuolian chansheng zhi lishi de yiyi*). There are many lines in this article which show that the League was anxious to check sectarianism:

> Its [the League's] premise is the extermination of the 'clique' concept of petit bourgeois consciousness.
> Anyone who insists on the 'clique' concept, or evaluates the present movement in terms of the past opposition between the small groups, is himself doing harm to the literary movement!
> We cannot guarantee the past and future of anybody. As long as he is ready to join the Left League, he is a comrade of the League. Does the small group (the so-called 'clique') consciousness still exist in the Left League? If yes, the comrades in the Left League ... are anxious and eager to overcome it immediately.
> The Left League is growing every day. Its relations with the literary societies of young people are becoming closer every day. The door of the Left League is 'wide open'.[38]

These are not empty words. The League's leading members were conscious of the need to clear away any concept that might lead to sectarianism. In one instance, Qian Xingcun and Jiang Guangci repudiated the remark made by a reader of *Tuohuangzhe*, an official organ of the Left League and a continuation of the defunct *Xinliu yuekan*, that the magazine was a joint publication of the Creation and Sun Societies:

94

Tuohuangzhe is not a collaboration of the Creation and Sun Societies. After it was raided, the Creation Society has ceased to exist. The Sun Society was also dissolved voluntarily last year. *Tuohuangzhe* is a common magazine of the left-wing writers, but not a magazine of any organisation![39]

In another case, they published an open letter to the professors of Fudan University denying that they had sent a threatening letter to the University. While insisting that they would continue their struggle for the liberation of the proletariat and fight against all reactionary elements in literature, they declared that their struggle was on the level of theory and they would not adopt sly and underhand tricks.[40] Obviously, the League was eager to make friends, not enemies.

However, during this period, the League was still adopting a 'left-deviationist' line. We have seen that League members were sent onto the streets to demonstrate in the 'Red May'. The left-deviationist trend was most clearly revealed in the resolution 'New situation in the proletarian literary movement and our missions' passed by the executive committee on 4 August 1930, the first resolution passed by this committee since the formation of the League.

The political flavour of this resolution was extremely strong. It began with an analysis of the international situation. According to the drafters of the resolution, the world was then divided into two opposing camps, one made up of dying capitalist countries and the reactionary ruling class, the other consisting of all the socialist countries and the revolutionary proletarian masses in capitalist countries. There were hunger, murders, struggles, anger and revolution in the former camp while the life of those in the latter was improving. Revolutionary masses were preparing for the final war in world revolution. In China, revolution had also started with the establishment of Soviet rule in various parts of the country. To the executive committee members, the proletarian literary movement had entered a new stage, from attacking bourgeois literature and gaining leadership to actively taking part in the organisational activities for the struggle towards Soviet rule. This change was the result of the development of the Chinese revolutionary movement. In this new situation, the Left League could not remain purely an organisation of writers, but must be one which should lead the literary struggle of the masses.[41]

At about the same time, another resolution was passed by the Left League concerning the Conference of Delegates from the Soviet Areas. The same political flavour was found in this resolution. It first reported on the decisions of the Conference, which, the resolution declared, would be firmly supported by the League. It then called for support for Soviet rule. For the building up of the nascent culture the Left League had to accomplish six roles, the first five being political ones: to fight against imperialism; to fight against the internecine wars between warlords; to support the motherland of the proletariat, Soviet Russia; to fight against Trotskyists and social democrats; to support the Soviet rule of

China; to create worker and peasant culture.[42] Obviously the Left League was going to become a fighting body deeply involved in political struggles:

> The proletarian literary movement should be devoted to the life-and-death struggle of the Soviet rule. The Soviet literary movement should be started from this bloody stage.
> We call for every member of the 'Left League' to go to the factories, villages and the grass-roots level of society.
> The organisational principle of the 'Left League' is not a gathering of writers. It has its own programme for struggle.[43]

There were political reasons for this leftist policy. The left-deviationist Li Lisan party line was at its height when these resolutions were passed. On 11 June, the Politburo of the Central Committee of the CCP passed a resolution called 'The new revolutionary high tide and winning victory in one or more provinces' (*Xinde geming gaochao yu yishang he jishangde shouxian shengli*) which stated that a new revolutionary high tide had arrived and that the Communists would try to win victories in one or more provinces by military insurrection.[44] Mao Zedong once made an analysis of the Li Lisan line. According to him, this line arose because Li Lisan and other comrades failed to see that adequate preparation was necessary before revolution could be successful. They misinterpreted the situation in China, thinking that incessant wars between warlords and the initial success of the Red Army movement made China ready for 'big actions'. They then called for victory in one or more provinces which might, they thought, bring about a socialist revolution. Adventurist plans were drawn up for armed insurrections in key cities. 'They merged the various leading bodies of the Party, the Youth League and the trade unions into action committees at corresponding levels for preparing armed insurrection and this brought all day-to-day work to a standstill.'[45]

We can easily find similarities between the Li Lisan line and the League's policy during this period. Feng Naichao's political report made in the first general meeting of the League shows the influence of the Party line:

> At a time when a revolutionary high tide is imminent, revolutionary writers must unreservedly join in the painful activities. Even if they have to drop their work and status as writers, there is nothing to regret.[46]

Mass demonstration was one of the most important political activities organised by the League. It can be seen as part of the military insurrections organised by the Party. Whenever there was any special day, the League would launch mass demonstrations in the main streets. May was the busiest month. There were May Day, May Fourth, May Fifth (birth of Karl Marx) and May Thirtieth. Ironically the authorities were also aware of these dates so that often, police were waiting for the masses even before the demonstration started. The left-wingers then developed shock tactics and a special kind of demonstration called 'flying meeting' (*feixing jihui*) would be held. They would try to do everything, such as distributing pamphlets, shouting slogans and giving speeches in a very short time before the police arrived. They then dispersed as quickly as possible when the police marched in. In fact, this was one of the demonstration methods listed in a document of the CCP on the organisation of the Grand Demonstrations on 1 August 1930.[47]

Putting up posters was another popular activity. Sometimes League members had the posters ready beforehand and they would put them up on the walls wherever possible, or they would simply write slogans directly onto the walls. It seems that these activities were quite well organised. League members were divided into groups, each with a leader and there was a scrutiny system to check the putting up or writing of posters. League members had to put up a fixed number of posters. They wrote down their initials or an English letter on the posters so that the scrutineers could count the number put up by one particular member. The best billposters would even by awarded a prize of a notebook or a vest.[48] It was also said that one would be punished if one failed to attend the mass demonstrations[49] but members like Lu Xun and Mao Dun never joined such activities and they were not punished. It is doubtful if it was possible to know if fellow members had turned up or not, as the situation was so chaotic.

Before they went out for these anti-government activities, League members would clear out everything in their houses to make sure that no evidence would be found even if they were arrested. League members said that they were as delighted and happy as going to fairs when they went to demonstrations.[50] They regarded these activities as sacred and joined in eagerly. To them, posters were a most effective weapon.[51] There was then a saying among League members: 'One poster can do the work of a red grenade'.[52] Most League members believed that since the activities were organised by the CCP, they would support them unconditionally.[53] Others considered these activities a means of forging willpower. In fact, it was said that these activities were employed as a test for both League members and those who wanted to join the League.[54] But the cool report in a newspaper on a demonstration held on International Women's Day 1930 showed that people were indifferent and used to such disturbances:

> Communist Attack on Tramcars
> The now familiar form of minor demonstration which is composed of pamphlet throwing and the breaking of windows in railless tramcars was again in evidence on March 8, the occasion being International Women's Day.
> Between 9.30 and 9.40 am some 200 Chinese students and workers were scattered along Nanking Road between Fokien and Chekiang Roads and several of the number distributed communistic handbills bearing on International Women's Day. The arrest of three of the distributors resulted in the crowd retreating to Avenue Edward VII via Fokien Road.[55]

On the other hand, the moderates within the League were alarmed by the instruction to drop their pens and participate in actual fighting. Mao Dun said:

We could imagine, if all the League members were sent out onto the street [to demonstrate] and one-third of them were arrested, it would be extremely difficult to accomplish the tasks stated in the theoretical and action programmes.[56]

The GMD, now well established in Nanjing, had the strength to crush such disturbances easily. The adventurist policy on the part of the leading cadres exposed League members to danger. After all, the pen is the mightiest weapon of writers. It is more suitable for them to act as propagandists, than actual fighters in revolutions. If these writers were arrested and imprisoned in large numbers, what would be left of the League and who would do the propaganda work?

Despite the influence of the left-deviationist Party line, which resulted in overemphasising political activity, the Left League was still able to pay attention to literary activities. Among such activities engaged in by the League, the popularisation of literature received the greatest weight. Pan Hannian named it as one of the four major tasks to be accomplished.[57] The Association for the Study of Popularisation of Literature was formed almost immediately after the setting up of the League. In fact, discussion of the issue had started even before the League's inaugural meeting.

In March and May 1930, *Dazhong wenyi* published two special issues on nascent literature. Apart from publishing the experiments made by League members in creating so-called 'mass literature', there were a number of treatises and a report on the seminar which was attended mainly by members of the former Creation and Sun Societies such as Shen Duanxian, Feng Naichao, Xu Xingzhi, Meng Chao, Zheng Boqi, Tao Jingsun, Jiang Guangci, Hong Lingfei, Pan Hannian, Yu Huai and Qiu Yunduo. They were able to touch upon a number of important issues, like the language problem which constituted the main barrier for popularising literature as the masses could not read the written texts. It was also suggested that old literary forms might be employed for the benefit of the masses who could not understand and accept new ones.[58] Unfortunately, most of the participants could not shake free from ultra-leftist viewpoints. It was argued that writers did not write for enjoyment, but to agitate and organise the masses. For the sake of popularisation, they were ready to sacrifice the artistic value of literature. Xia Yan said that all they wanted was black bread, not fine biscuits.[59] Guo Moruo's words were most explicit:

> Therefore the slogan for the popularisation of literature should be the vulgarisation of proletarian literature. So vulgar that it can be no literature.[60]

It was again Lu Xun who cautioned against these attitudes, stressing the importance of readers. He said:

> Readers should reach a certain standard. The first thing is to become literate. The second thing is to have an average standard of general knowledge.[61]

Years of Achievement (I)

Secondly, he argued that it was wrong to devalue literature simply to pander to the masses. This would do them no good. Lu Xun believed that, since there were so many problems, it was idle to ask for complete popularisation at that time. When compared with those of his contemporaries, Lu's opinions were more profound and less idealistic; but not even he could provide any prescription.

The activities of the Left League were not solely political or literary. The celebration of Lu Xun's fiftieth birthday had a warm human touch. His birthday was on 25 September but this party was held eight days earlier. Some sources said that it was the idea of the Communist Party to hold such a party[62] but publicly, it was said to have been organised by Lu Xun's friends Rou Shi, Feng Xuefeng and Feng Naichao.[63] Dong Shaoming (Dong Qiusi), one of the promoters of the Left League, and his wife, Cai Yongshang were sent to approach Agnes Smedley, who rented a Western restaurant, the Surabaya, for the occasion.[64] Over one hundred guests came, but half of them left before dinner. Among the guests were writers, artists, professors and students in universities, actors and news reporters. Representatives from the Left League, the Social Scientists League, Artists League and Dramatists League were present and others like Ye Shengtao and Fu Donghua went to the party too.[65] Although this meeting was apolitical in nature, sentries were posted because of the presence of important Communist personages.[66]

The party was chaired by Rou Shi, who was first to make a speech after dinner.[67] Other speakers included Feng Keng and a representative from the Association for the Rear Support of the Red Army (*Hongjun houyuanhui*) who had just been released from prison. Smedley also gave a report on the proletarian movement in China.[68] Finally, Lu Xun made a speech in reply. This was the only occasion of its kind in the League's history. It shows that at this early stage, Lu Xun was held in great respect by the Communist Party.

Meanwhile, the GMD further tightened their control over the literary circle. In December 1930, forty-four clauses of the 'Publication laws of the Republican government' (*Guomin zhengfude chubanfa*) were issued, prohibiting publication of anything which caused or would cause damage to the GMD, the Three Principles or the interests of the country. This was supplemented by the 'Details for the implementation of the Publication laws' (*Chubanfa shixing xize*) on 7 October 1931. In November 1932 and June 1934, the GMD proclaimed the 'Standards for the examination of propaganda materials' (*Xuanchuanpin shencha biaozhun*) and 'Methods for the censorship of books and magazines' (*Tushu zazhi shencha banfa*).[69] Large numbers of articles, books and journals were banned.

The real threat to the League came in September 1930. Chen Lifu, Secretary-General of the executive committee of the GMD Party Central Committee, formally placed a ban on the League. Orders were issued to close it down and arrest its responsible members.[70] The Left League was driven completely underground.

The Chinese League of Left-wing Writers

There was no way for the GMD police to 'close down' the League. It had no definite premises; at first, the League had rented an 'office' at Niuzhuang Road, but it withdrew after two months.[71] However, the order to arrest members was carried out efficiently. On 9 October 1930, a member of the South Nation Society and Freedom Movement League, Zong Hui was shot dead at Yuhuatai, Nanjing. Then on 7 February 1931, the so-called 'Five martyrs of the Left League' (*Zuolian wulieshi*) were executed at Longhua, Shanghai. Eighteen other Communists were shot at the same time, among them three women, one pregnant.[72]

The five martyrs were Li Weisen, Hu Yepin, Rou Shi, Yin Fu and Feng Keng. It is generally believed that they were arrested on 17 January 1931 by the British police during a meeting in the Oriental Hotel in the British concession area. They were among the earliest members of the Left League. Apart from Hu Yepin who joined the League in May 1930,[73] the others were believed to have been present at the inaugural meeting. Rou Shi was even one of the twelve preparatory committee members. They actively engaged in League affairs. According to the reports in *Qianshao* which published a special issue lamenting their deaths, Rou Shi was an executive as well as a standing committee member, taking charge of the publication section of the League. He also represented the Left League at the Conference of Delegates from the Soviet Areas. Hu Yepin was an executive committee member, responsible for the reportage movement of workers, peasants and soldiers. Feng Keng was sent by the League to work with the Central Preparatory Committee for the All-China Soviet Congress while Yin Fu was a frequent contributor to League journals.[74] Their death was undoubtedly a great loss to the League.

Until very recently, there was controversy over the circumstances as well as the causes of their arrest. At the time they were arrested, the five martyrs were holding a meeting, with other Communists, at Room 31 in the Oriental Hotel (*Dongfang lushe*).[75] According to an article in *Qianshao*, the meeting was connected with the preparation of the All-China Soviet Congress.[76] This idea was endorsed by Feng Keng's husband:

> On the night of 17 January, crowded in a room in the Oriental Hotel ... were over thirty men and women who were at a meeting, ... one of the meetings of the preparatory committee for the All-China Soviet Congress.[77]

If this was the case, although the circumstances which led to their arrest had no direct link with the Left League, the League did play a part since they were sent by the League to help in the preparatory work of the All-China Soviet Congress.

Nevertheless, it has also been held that they were attending a different kind of Communist Party meeting when the British police forced in. The five martyrs were merely victims of CCP power struggles.[78] To have a deeper understanding of the picture, we have to go into the history of the Communist Party.[79]

Years of Achievement (I)

In June 1928, Li Lisan was made head of the Propaganda Department of the CCP in the Sixth General Meeting. On 11 June 1930, the Politburo passed the resolution declaring the possibility of winning victory in one or more provinces. This was the most important document of the Li Lisan line. During the summer of 1930, Li ordered an attack on Wuhan. After some minor successes, the Communists suffered disastrous defeats. In mid-August, Qu Qiubai and Zhou Enlai were sent back by the Comintern in Moscow to call for the Third Plenum which was held in November. It was designed to suppress the 'adventurist' or 'putschist' policy of Li Lisan. Nevertheless, the criticism turned out to be very moderate. Li's mistakes were considered to be tactical ones. This was not acceptable to the Comintern which wrote to the Central Committee of the CCP in November, harshly condemning Li Lisan who had to go to Moscow for trial.

There was then a group of young Communists who had just returned from the Sun Yat-sen University in Moscow. The head of this group, known as the 'Twenty-eight Bolsheviks', was Wang Ming (Chen Shaoyu). They were able to win the confidence and support of Pavel Mif, Chancellor of the Sun Yat-sen University and head of the Chinese branch of the Comintern, during the anti-Trotskyist campaign in the University. They were anxious to grasp the leadership of the Party but their ambition was checked in the Third Plenum.

As the Comintern was not happy with the Third Plenum, Mif was sent to China. He called the Fourth Plenum on 13 January 1931. Apart from liquidating the Li Lisan line, it also criticised the Third Plenum. With the support of Mif, the 'Twenty-eight Bolsheviks' climbed to the top hierarchy of the Party. Wang Ming was soon made secretary. Among the old cadres, only Xiang Zhongfa and Zhou Enlai were able to retain positions in the Central Committee. This usurpation of power by a group of inexperienced returned students caused great discontent in the Party. The opposition mainly gathered around He Mengxiong, Xu Degen, Luo Zhanglong and Wang Kequan. They withdrew from the Fourth Plenum and set up an emergency committee with their own candidates.

The Oriental Hotel meeting on 17 January was held only four days after the Fourth Plenum. Harold Isaacs, who was close to the scene and the people involved, said in his book *The tragedy of the Chinese revolution*:

> A group of these older Party members and trade unionists, and some younger men, led by the veteran Ho Meng-shung [He Mengxiong], met at a Shanghai hotel on the night of January 17th to consider the new situation with which they were confronted.[80]

This idea was taken up by later historians. Benjamin Schwartz, whose *Chinese Communism and the rise of Mao* has been considered a classic, pointed out that it was a meeting of the newly formed 'Emergency committee'.[81] Robert North held a similar view, saying that the meeting was one held by a newly constituted Central Committee formed by Wang Ming's opponents.[82]

T A Hsia queried these ideas by pointing out that the 'Left League martyrs had not yet earned enough seniority to be qualified for a meeting on such a high level; and any such meeting should have included some more of the known secessionists, namely Lo Chang-lung [Luo Zhanglong], Wang K'o-ch'uan [Wang Kequan] and others, who, however, were not among those apprehended that night'.[83] This argument seems sensible but material available today reveals that the accounts by Isaacs and others were closer to the facts.

Firstly, there was the account of Feng Xuefeng who, as T A Hsia said, was 'a cadre in charge of a news agency under the Central Propaganda Department of the CCP'.[84] Furthermore, he was responsible for publishing the commemorative issue of *Qianshao*. Thus, his information is reliable. He recalled:

> That meeting had nothing to do with the Left League. It was a meeting of some comrades within the Party to oppose Wang Ming's Fourth Plenum. ... The one who played the greatest role was Li Weisen. He was then very young and active. Bai Mang [Yin Fu] was then editing *Liening qingnian*. Feng Keng worked in the workers and peasants division of the Left League. Both had frequent contacts with Li Weisen. Hu Yepin joined the Party in June 1930. But he was very active. They were discontented with the Fourth Plenum and so joined the meeting...
>
> At noon on 17 January, I met Hu Yepin on the road. He talked much and angrily of his discontent over the Fourth Plenum. I told him I could do nothing about it.[85]

Secondly, we have Luo Zhanglong, one of the most active opponents of the Wang Ming leadership. It is hardly surprising that he has a good knowledge of the whole story. He said:

> In order to exchange ideas on our reaction to Mif-Wang Ming's changing of the Party leadership and our expulsion, in order to oppose Wang Ming's opportunist line, in order that the affairs of the Party would not come to a halt and that the revolution could be pushed forward continuously, Shi Wenbin, He Mengxiong, Li Qiushi [Li Weisen], Lin Yu'nan and I, together with other comrades, planned together to call a Party meeting in the Shanghai Oriental Hotel. This meeting was presided over by He Mengxiong, Li Qiushi and Lin Yu'nan. Those attending included the representatives from the General Union, Railway Union, Sailors' Union, Shanghai Union as well as the delegates from Shanghai, Jiangsu and the Soviet areas. At that time, Li Qiushi was in charge of cultural matters. He came to ask me if people like Rou Shi should be invited to the meeting. I consented. This meeting was a Party meeting. It discussed the work for the whole nation, insisting on the Party line of the Sixth General meeting and opposing the Wang Ming clique. Therefore, it was not a 'Left League' meeting. Five martyrs of the 'Left League' was a term formulated afterwards.[86]

Years of Achievement (I)

This statement, besides confirming that it was not a Left League meeting but a Party meeting, accounts for the presence of the five martyrs. In another paragraph Luo explained why he himself, being head of the opposition, was not arrested:
> Originally, I had to go to the Oriental Hotel to make a report. But at that time, a comrade from another province came to talk to me. I arrived late. There were many others who, for different reasons, could not attend the meeting on time.[87]

This should clear away the doubts of T A Hsia.

Xia Yan and Feng Naichao also agreed that the meeting was held by an opposition group in the Communist Party against the Fourth Plenum. Both said that on that day, the Left League held a meeting, Xia Yan further pointing out that it was a general meeting to pass on the political programme of Wang Ming. After this meeting, the five martyrs went to the Oriental Hotel. According to Xia, Rou Shi had asked Yang Hansheng and Xia to go to the Oriental Hotel meeting.[88]

Then how can we account for the report in *Qianshao*? First, there might be political reasons behind it. How could a Left League organ at that time publish anything against the new leadership of the CCP? Secondly, according to a recent article 'The incident at the Oriental Hotel' (*Dongfang lushe shijian*), whose authors seemed to have been able to get hold of GMD documents and the statements of those who were arrested, Room 31 of the Oriental Hotel had been hired by the representatives of the literary circle for the Conference of delegates from the Soviet Areas.[89] This tallies with Hu Yepin's note which was passed out from prison: he was arrested at an organ of the preparatory committee for the Soviet Congress.[90]

Around the time when the five martyrs were arrested, thirty-one other CCP members were caught too.[91] This was the greatest known catch by the GMD since the 1927 coup. How was this possible? T A Hsia, in his paper 'Enigma of the five martyrs', quoting Isaacs, Schwartz, North and Li Ang,[92] alleged that the meeting was betrayed to the police by Wang Ming or his group in an attempt to eliminate the opponents.[93] Isaacs said:
> In circumstances which are still a whispered scandal in the Party ranks, that meeting was betrayed to the British police of the International Settlement.[94]

Schwartz and North were more specific. The former said that 'hostile sources have strongly intimated that Wang Ming was implicated in this event' while the latter said that 'the British police had been informed by Wang Ming'.[95]

Neale Hunter, however, rejected the idea of treachery, pointing out that both Schwartz and North 'acknowledge their indebtedness to Harold Isaacs and Li Ang for the suggestion' and that 'Schwartz and North seem to have merely copied Isaacs'.[96] He admitted the authority of Isaacs' book, but stressed that it carried an introduction by Leon Trotsky. Hunter commented, 'of all the people who might have had an axe to grind where the arch-Stalinist Wang Ming and his

'28 Bolsheviks' were concerned, Trotsky would be the first'. Moreover, he argued that since the principal enemy was not He Mengxiong but Luo Zhanglong, 'what would be the point of betraying the relatively minor characters in the drama (including some raw novices in the Party like the League members present) when the main threat would still be around?' He further pointed out that since He Mengxiong and his group had already been expelled from the CCP, there was no need to resort to treachery. Hunter's last argument is clever. He says that a Wang Ming betrayal could have led to Wang's own destruction because the thirty-six arrested, under torture and interrogation, might reveal the secret of the Wang leadership. Wang Ming would not be that stupid, Hunter argued.[97]

While there appear to be fair points in Hunter's argument, the evidence available today seems to confirm that the 'Five martyrs' were betrayed. Luo Zhanglong's own words confirming that he and many other leading opponents of Wang Ming were supposed to have been present in the fatal meeting have already been quoted. Further, expulsion from the Party could not be an effective way of wiping out opposition. As many members were not happy with Wang's leadership, it was impossible to expel them all. Those expelled could form a separate party, just as Luo Zhanglong did, to fight against the CCP. This could constitute a great nuisance to the newly established leadership of Wang Ming. In the incident, altogether thirty-six CCP members were arrested. Thus a large number of opponents were eliminated at a stroke. Would this not have been tempting to Wang Ming?

Isaacs said that there was widespread rumour in Party ranks that the meeting was betrayed to the police at that time. In fact, many Party members then did believe that Wang Ming was responsible for the treachery.

Zhang Guodao, one of the founding members of the CCP and who had always been in its top echelon, said in his autobiography that Zhou Enlai told him this:

> The arrest of Ho [He Mengxiong] and party was misunderstood by Lo Chang-lung [Luo Zhanglong] and his friends, who misconstrued it as the consequence of Ch'en Shao-yu's [Wang Ming] secret information.[98]

But after a short stay in Shanghai, Zhang himself was convinced that it was not unlikely for Wang Ming and his group to do such things:

> The blundering, rash Polish youth [Mif's deputy] unconcernedly continued to chatter some anti-rightist words and then suggested the elimination of Lo Chang-lung through assassination. Not only was he apathetic over the arrest of Ho Meng-hsiung and party, but he was also of the opinion that these anti-Party elements had surrendered.[99] He believed that Lo Chang-lung was the brains behind Ho Ming-hsiung and his group and that since Lo openly defied the Party, it was necessary to restrain and even secretly assassinate this despicable opponent. ... Judging by the Pole's violent

words and manner, [I came to the conclusion that] the Comintern would do anything to achieve its goals. Perhaps it was not mere slander when some comrades accused and suspected Mif and Chen Shao-yu of secretly causing injury to Ho Meng-hsiung and his sixteen other old cadres.[100]

Secondly, we have the accounts of Wang Fanxi, once a CCP member who later became a Trotskyist. He said:

> The death of the 'rightist' comrades caused a long deep grief and anger within the Party. A rumour spread there, saying that the incident was a plan of Chen Shaoyu to 'murder with a borrowed knife'. It was he who informed the police.[101]

The most direct and affirmative accusation came from Luo Zhanglong, whose authority cannot be easily dismissed. He said certainly that there were traitors who informed the GMD. He suspected two persons, Gu Shunzhang, and Tang Yu, who was very close to Wang Ming. Luo further mentioned that during the trial, a woman, who returned from Moscow, hid behind the judge, pointing out the identities of the arrested. In another paragraph, Luo asserted that Wang Ming once sent Gu Shunzhang to track down some comrades.[102]

A similar story can be found in 'The incident at the Oriental Hotel'. It said that even during the preliminary trial, those arrested, judging from the testimony given by the GMD detectives, were convinced that they had been betrayed. Very soon, they found out that Tang Yu was suspect, but Tang, being only a reporter for *Hongqi* (*Red Flag*), could not have the information about so many comrades. The arrest of such a large number of Party members from different organisational systems and Party divisions meant that something had gone wrong at the top level. According to the authors of the article, on 17 January 1931, both the GMD Shanghai Municipal Party division and the police of the international settlement received an anonymous phone call, informing them that the CCP was going to hold a meeting in the Oriental Hotel. At that time, the CCP had infiltrated special agents into the police department of the international settlement. They immediately informed the Party of this phone call but Wang Ming took no action to warn He Mengxiong and others, who were then arrested during the course of the meeting.[103]

Even Wang Ming once claimed that the meeting was betrayed. According to Luo Zhanglong, Wang once spread a rumour that the informer was the adopted son of He Mengxiong. This was refuted by Luo who said that He had no adopted son.[104] On the other hand, in his essay 'The struggle against the Luo Zhanglong clique' (*Fan Luo Zhanglongpai de douzheng*), Wang Ming wrote that the comrades were betrayed by Tang Yu; but he stressed that Tang was a member of the Luo Zhanglong clique.[105] It seems that Tang Yu had no way to exculpate himself.

Books published in the PRC now generally agree that there were traitors in the incident, though they rarely mention names.[106] Taiwan publications mostly allege that Wang Ming was responsible for the treachery.[107] It seems that the question of the 'enigma of the five martyrs' has now been, to some extent, solved. The allegation of treachery was by no means a method used to discredit the martyrs. Treachery or no treachery, 'the "masterpiece" on which the fame of all twenty-three martyrs "can securely rest" would surely be the quality of their lives and deaths'.[108]

Upon their arrest, the Communist Party started a campaign to save them but nothing could be done. On 7 February, the five martyrs, together with eighteen CCP members, were shot at Longhua. Although the Communists were able to get hold of the news very soon, no report was made in any open newspaper or magazine, until the appearance of a 'reader's letter', 'Are the writers alive or dead?' (*Zai diyu huo renshi de zuojia*) on 30 March 1931 in *Wenyi xinwen* (*Literary news*). This was the first time the news of the death of the Left League writers was made public. But this was not a League magazine. Then on 13 April, again in the form of readers' letters, *Wenyi xinwen* published 'Alas, they are dead!' (*Wuhu, Sizhe yiyi!*) and 'The writers are dead' (*Zuojia zai diyu*) confirming the news of the executions. In the next issue, the photographs of the martyrs were published.[109]

The first report on the massacre in a League journal came with the appearance of the first issue of *Qianshao* which carried a subtitle, 'In memory of those who have fallen in battle'. As early as August 1930, notice was given that the League would publish an official organ, the title of which, *Qianshao*, had already been decided.[110] The editorial board would consist of Lu Xun, Mao Dun, Xia Yan and Yang Hansheng. According to the notice, the first issue would come out in October 1930. This thirty-two page publication was eventually put out in July 1931 with great difficulty. At first no publisher dared to undertake the printing. Eventually, they found a small publisher who charged a high price and laid down many restrictions: the title of the magazine and the photographs of the martyrs could not be printed directly on the magazine (they were stamped and stuck on afterwards); the entire printing process had to be finished in one night; a League member had to be present throughout to take responsibility if anything went wrong; and the finished product had to be removed immediately.[111] Prepared in great haste and in poor working conditions, *Qianshao* was full of typographical errors.

The poor quality of the printing did not lower its value. The content of the magazine was rich. In addition to a statement and an international appeal from the League, it had articles by Lu Xun, Mei Sun and Feng Xuefeng, together with brief biographies of the six martyrs (the sixth being Zong Hui) and works of four of them, plus letters from the board of the International Union of Revolutionary Writers and the editor of *New Masses*, a left-wing magazine in the United States.

The statement and international appeal had similar content. The latter was first drafted by Lu Xun and Agnes Smedley who translated it into English with the help of Mao Dun.[112] The English version was published in *New Masses*. This appeal, with some minor alterations, was translated into other languages too. The Japanese version appeared in *A collection of Chinese fiction: The true story of Ah Q*. A Russian version was printed in *World revolutionary literature*, and as this magazine was printed in four languages, Russian, English, French and German, the appeal may have been translated into German and French too. Reaction came fast. *New Masses* carried a special issue condemning the terror policy of the GMD. Malcolm Cowley published an article 'Twenty-four youngsters' in *New Republic*.[113] The International Union of Revolutionary Writers sent in a statement, signed by its secretariat, whose members included such famous writers as Fadeev, Barbusse and Sinclair. It was published in *Wenyi xinwen* and *Wenxue daobao*.[114] It is difficult to estimate their impact on the GMD regime. Smedley reported that the GMD was shocked when it knew that the Western world denounced its policy.[115]

Immediately following the statement and the appeal was Lu Xun's article 'The Chinese proletarian revolutionary literature and the blood of our forerunners' (*Zhongguo wuchanjieji geming wenxue he qianqu de xue*).[116] Lu's sorrow and anger were fully exhibited in the article and he gave up his usual satiric style. He was outspoken, condemning the GMD's brutal massacre in a most direct way. But in his eyes, the death of the writers testified to the strength of proletarian revolutionary literature which was growing daily. The outspokenness of the article might possibly put Lu Xun in danger and the pseudonym used, 'LS', could be easily identified and so would provide no cover. Further, Rou Shi was carrying a contract between Lu Xun and the Beixin Bookstore at the time when he was arrested, so Lu had to leave home and take refuge in a Japanese inn.[117] But this could not keep his mouth shut. Agnes Smedley reported that when she warned him of the danger of publishing such an outspoken piece, Lu replied, 'Does it matter? ... Someone must speak,'[118] This, as one critic suggests, can illustrate what the Communists mean when they say that Lu Xun 'led' the Left League. 'He led it by setting a standard of integrity'.[119]

Lu's grief was understandable. Apart from feeling sorry over the loss of five good comrades, he was particularly affected by the death of Rou Shi, one of his few very good friends. To Lu Xun, Rou Shi was one with whom he could talk and joke freely, one whom he could ask to do personal business. 'He was in fact supporting me', Lu Xun said two years after Rou's death.[120]

Mei Sun, whose identity is unknown, published in *Qianshao* 'A lesson in blood: Lament over the deaths on 7 February' (*Xue de jiaoxun: dao eryue qiri womende sizhe*). He gave an account of the circumstances in which the martyrs were arrested but the most noteworthy part of the article was its final paragraph which re-evaluated the whole left-wing literary movement. According to Mei Sun, in the past the left-wing writers were not serious and firm enough. Some people joined the movement because they thought that it was in fashion. He called for reinforcement of the literary movement with iron discipline. This 'follow fashion' comment on League members can also be found in Lu Xun's writings.[121]

Feng Xuefeng's (pseud Wenying) article was 'The death of our comrades and the despicableness of the flunkeys' (*Women tongzhidesi he zouguo de beilie*). Again, the grief came to the surface: 'We will weep, of course, because of our loss, and because of the love among comrades'. The loss was great but Feng said, one would do the work of two to make good the loss.[122]

Because of the background to its publication, *Qianshao* was less dogmatic than other League publications. There was no trace of dull, dry theories, only sorrow at the loss of comrades, condemnation of the GMD policy and determination by left-wing writers to push forward their cause despite suppression and other difficulties. Readers could easily be moved, because of the sincerity of the writing, to conceive hatred towards the GMD authorities. This was one of the effects of the death of the martyrs and it is little wonder that right-wing critics consider the publication of *Qianshao* to be propaganda, a Communist device to rally support and sympathy.[123]

There has been debate over the status of the martyrs. Some scholars argue that not all of the five martyrs could be described as writers while one holds that all five were at least promising writers, if not accomplished ones.[124] Nevertheless, whether they were writers or practical revolutionaries, they had one and the same aim, the liberation of the proletariat. Both their literary creations and revolutionary activities were part of their efforts for the accomplishment of that goal. In fact, this was the case with most League members. They wrote for the proletariat. At the same time, most of them took part in practical revolutionary activities. In the case of a League member, there is no way to tell for certain whether one was a writer or a revolutionary. Therefore, although we should not ignore their literary achievements, their death as martyrs was of even greater significance. That is why there has been the following assessment of the five martyrs in mainland China:

> The five martyrs of the Left League were not only writers. They were revolutionary fighters of the proletariat. They were foremost members of the CCP and proletarian revolutionaries, only secondarily were they revolutionary writers.[125]

The Wang Ming leadership of the CCP caused directly or at least indirectly, the Left League to lose five of its best members but at the same time, it brought to the League a very important one who soon became its *de facto* leader. He was Qu Qiubai, once the chief secretary and a member of the Politburo of the CCP.

Qu was sent as a reporter by *Chenbao* in 1920 to Moscow where he joined the CCP the following year. He returned to China in December 1922, armed with a thorough knowledge of Russian and Marxist theories. In January 1925, he was elected a member of the Communist Party Central Committee. On 7 August 1927, he called the famous 'August Seventh Emergency Conference', after which he became the leader of the Party, but his leadership lasted for less than a year. Because of the failure of various uprisings launched under his direction, Qu was stripped of the position of secretary at the Sixth Congress in

Years of Achievement (I)

July 1928 and appointed CCP representative to the Comintern in Moscow, where he stayed for another two years. During this period, there was already a series of quarrels between Qu and the 'Twenty-eight Bolsheviks'. Had it not been for the latter, Qu might have been able to regain his political power in 1930 when he was sent back to China to call the Third Plenum to liquidate the Li Lisan Party line. However, the Fourth Plenum, as seen earlier, condemned not only the Li Lisan line but also the Third Plenum. He was severely criticised and even dismissed from the Politburo, and became merely an ordinary Party member. Tired and seriously ill, he asked for a year's sick leave.

The Left League was already in existence when Qu returned from Moscow in August 1930. He did not immediately become the advisor of the League, having no time for this. After the Fourth Plenum Qu returned to the world of letters but it was almost half a year before he came to lead the Left League. Mao Dun said that this happened some time after Mao himself became secretary of the League - that is after late May 1931. Qu started to influence the League in June.[126]

Feng Xuefeng said that Qu Qiubai came to lead the Left League on his own initiative and not through a Party decision.[127] Although there were queries on this point, mainly from the right, this is certainly believable. Since Qu was the target of attack in the Fourth Plenum, it was unlikely that the new Party leadership would have assigned him such an important job as to lead the left-wing literary movement. As has been noted, he was then an ordinary Party member who had asked for a year's leave.

Although Qu never joined the Left League, his position as its leader was soon acknowledged. There were reasons for this. First, was the high position that Qu Qiubai enjoyed in the Communist Party in the past. He had long had intimate relationships with people like Mao Dun, then secretary of the League's Party division. Most of the leading cadres of the Left League joined the CCP when Qu Qiubai was in power. They were used to accepting his leadership and direction. Although he had lost all the posts in the Party's Central Committee, he still commanded respect because the new leadership, which caused his downfall, did not have general support. Secondly, it was, and is, commonly agreed that Qu Qiubai's knowledge of Marxist theory was second to none in China at that time. His four year stay in Moscow, plus his hard working character and the effort put into the subject, left him well versed in Marxism. Prior to 1931, he had already written many articles and treatises introducing and using Marxist theories. Furthermore, he had long been quite well known in literary circles. Even before his first trip to Russia, he had started *Xinshehui* (*New society*) with Xu Dishan, Zheng Zhenduo, Qu Shiying and Geng Jizhi. He had also published two collections of beautifully written prose: *A journey to the land of hunger* (*E'xiang licheng*) and *History of the heart at the Red Capital* (*Chidu xinshi*). He was among the earliest members of the Literary Research Association and his four colleagues in the publication of *Xinshehui*, were its promoters. These, together with his political background, qualified him to be a leader of the Left League.

Behind the scenes, Qu Qiubai actively directed League affairs. Feng Xuefeng said that he went to see Qu every three to four days for instructions.[128] Very often, Qu gave very specific directions. For instance it was he who suggested to Mao Dun that he write a long article evaluating the literary movement since the May Fourth. The result was 'A review of the "May Fourth" movement: Report of the Association for the Study of Marxist Literary Theories'. Qu also gave directions to continue publication of *Qianshao*, though the name might be changed, as an official organ concentrating on theory, and instructed that another magazine be started for literary works. Consequently, *Beidou* (*The Dipper*) came into existence, becoming one of the most successful and popular publications of the League. He had helped with the drafting of resolutions for the League too, a job that should have been done only by members of the secretariat, the standing committee and the executive committee.[129] Moreover, he kept an eye on the activities of and the works created by League members. He once criticised Jiang Guangci's 'The sorrows of Lisa', voicing his discontent over the pessimistic tone of the work.[130] On another occasion, he commented on an article of Zheng Boqi for drawing too clear a line between the masses and the writers.[131] Apart from criticising him face to face, Qu also wrote an article called 'Who are "we"?' (*Women shishei?*) because he thought Zheng's mistake was a general one in the left-wing literary circle.[132] He gave much advice to Mao Dun in the latter's writing of *Midnight*.[133] It was again Qu who gave the instruction to left-wing writers to break into the cinema.[134]

Qu Qiubai joined actively in literary debates too. He wrote several most important articles attacking the nationalist literary movement. In 1931, under his direction and initiation, the left-wing writers launched another campaign in the popularisation of literature. Qu himself wrote a number of essays which are considered most thorough by many critics. He was also engaged in the debate with the 'Free Men' (*Ziyouren*) and the 'Third Category Men' (*Disanzhongren*). For the success of the League in these several campaigns, the part played by Qu Qiubai should not be under-estimated. Both Feng Xuefeng and Mao Dun often stressed the merits of the cooperative efforts of Lu Xun and Qu Qiubai in putting the League on the right track and driving the left-wing literary movement forward.[135]

There was another indirect consequence of the deaths of the five martyrs. In the memorial articles on them, the League urged its members to overcome the slackening in the movement. 'Iron discipline' would be employed to strengthen the organisation.[136] Even before these articles were printed, drastic action was adopted. Three members were expelled from the League in April and May 1931. This was decided by the standing committee and an announcement was published in *Wenxue daobao*.[137]

Years of Achievement (I)

Of the three, Zhou Quanping was the first to be expelled - on 20 April. In the earliest days of the League, he was very active. At the inaugural meeting, he was elected one of the two alternate members of the executive committee. He had also been secretary of the League for a short time. Even the announcement of his expulsion could not deny that he had once worked hard for and pledged determination to the League. For this reason, he was sent to work in the Revolutionary Mutual Aid Society as a representative of the League. But in February 1931, the Society reported that Zhou 'consciously committed brazen acts against the revolution'. 'After a long, comprehensive and detailed investigation', the League decided that this kind of despicable counter-revolutionary element could not be tolerated. It was not stated in the announcement what 'brazen acts' were committed by Zhou. Recent recollections by League members confirm that he ran away with two thousand dollars belonging to the Mutual Aid Society.[138]

The second one expelled was Ye Lingfeng, on 28 April. This time, the charge was made clear in the announcement. First, he had not worked for the League for six months and had hidden, refusing to meet the League members sent to find him. It was then reported that he had written a statement of repentance to the GMD and started working for the nationalist literary movement. A week was given to him to answer the charges. After ten days, when nothing was heard from him, he was expelled.

The third one expelled was Zhou Yuying. Again, he had not participated in League affairs for some time. He also joined the nationalist literary movement, even publishing anti-League writings openly in the press. This, naturally, was unacceptable to the League. In fact, Zhou Yuying had long been criticised by League members. As early as February 1930, even before the formation of the Left League, Pan Hannian had written two articles condemning Zhou Yuying's attitude and attacks on left-wingers. One of the articles was called 'Hidden traitor and Zhou Yuying' (*Neijian yu Zhou Yuying*).[139] Feng Naichao and Qiu Shi also published articles in League journals condemning him.[140] The attitude and wording were mostly harsh.

It was significant that the three were expelled less than three months after the execution of the five martyrs. This could be seen as an effort of the League to strengthen itself in the face of increasing suppression. The execution of the martyrs and the ban on the League, added to the promotion of nationalist literature, showed that the GMD was determined to wipe out left-wing influence in literary circles by any means. Meanwhile, Jiang Jieshi was preparing for the third encirclement and suppression campaign, after the failure of the first two. In these circumstances, disloyal members had to be purged. A year earlier, the Left League had made it clear that League members would be expelled should there be any tendency to opportunism, timidity or treachery.[141] This time, the three were treachery cases. Further, the latter two were involved with the nationalist literary movement, which was totally unacceptable to the League.

The Chinese League of Left-wing Writers

Their expulsion confirmed the League's uncompromising attitude towards the movement.

Interestingly enough, this was the only time that the League openly announced the expulsion of its members. This does not mean that there were no more cases of disloyalty. In fact, defection became a serious problem and brought great dishonour to the League in its latter stage. However, the organisation of the League then was loosening. It was not in a position to tighten control over its members. Furthermore, as there were too many cases of defection, each announcement of expulsion could only reveal to the public the weakness of the League. Consequently, the League could only turn a blind eye to such acts.

Notes to Chapter Four

1. Feng Naichao, 'The significance of the formation of the Left League and its role' (*Zuolian chengli de yiyi he tade renwu*), *Shijie wenhua* No 1 (10 July 1930), reprinted in *Jinian yu yanjiu* No 2, p 36.
2. 'Letter from the Left League to the editors of *Baerdishan*' (*Zuolian ge Baerdishan bianzhe de xin*), *Materials on modern Chinese literary history* Vol I, p 45.
3. Ling Sheng, 'Criticism - abuse, attack - instigation' (*Piping - manma, gongji - tiaobo*), *ibid*, p 42.
4. Bai Shu, 'The unforgettable past', *Recollections*, p 279.
5. *Dazhong wenyi* Vol II No 4, *Materials on modern Chinese literary history* Vol VI, pp 443-4.
6. Amitendranath Tagore, *Literary debates in modern China, 1918-1937* (Tokyo: Centre for East Asian Cultural Studies, 1967), pp 115-6.
7. T A Hsia, *The gate of darkness*, p 101.
8. *Materials on modern Chinese literary history* Vol VI, p 444.
9. Mao Dun, 'The early stage of the "Left League"', *The road I trod* Vol II, p 51; 'Casual talks too' (*Yeshi mantan eryi*), *Collection of Mao Dun's essays on literature and art* Vol II, p 1131.
10. *Materials on modern Chinese literary history* Vol I, p 42.
11. Neale Hunter, 'The Chinese League of Left-wing Writers', p 106.
12. Han Tuofu, 'Recollection and commemoration: In commemoration of the centenary of the birth of Lu Xun', p 39.
13. 'Record of Feng Naichao's interview: Recollection on the literary movement in the early thirties', p 17.
14. 'Thoughts on the League of Left-wing Writers', *Complete works of Lu Xun* Vol IV, pp 233-8.
15. 'Feng Xuefeng on the Left League', p 5.
16. 'Xia Yan's recollections on the "Left League"', p 28.
17. *Materials on modern Chinese literary history* Vol VI, p 442.
18. Neale Hunter, 'The Chinese League of Left-wing Writers', p 114.
19. *Baerdishan* Vol I No 2&3 (1 May 1930), *Materials on modern Chinese literary history* Vol I, pp 17-18.
20. *Ibid*, p 21.
21. The article was Feng Xianzhang's '"The sorrows of Lisa" and "The moon that forces its way through the clouds"' (*Lisa de aiyuan yu chongchu yunwei de yueliang*), *ibid* Vol IX, pp 255-67.
22. *Ibid* Vol I, p 21.
23. Li Zhu, 'Report on the first general meeting of the Left League', *ibid*, p 37.
24. *Ibid*.
25. *Ibid*.
26. Xia Yan, 'Around the formation of the "Left League"', p 7. Mao Dun, 'The early stage of the "Left League"', *The road I trod* Vol II, p 53.

27 The manifesto can be found in the *Wuyi tekan* (1 May 1930), *Materials on modern Chinese literary history* Vol IX, p 331.
28 *Wuyi tekan, ibid*, p 331.
29 'News of the League of Left-wing Writers', *ibid* Vol II, p 361.
30 *Wuyi tekan, ibid* Vol IX, p 331.
31 Peng Kang wrote 'The international meaning of this May Day' (*Jinian wuyi de guoji yiyi*) and Feng Naichao wrote 'The May Day of this year' (*Jinian de wuyi*), *ibid*, pp 334-9.
32 Mao Dun, *The road I trod* Vol II, p 53.
33 'Letter to the masses of Shanghai from the Art Drama Association: Protest against unreasonable raid and arrest' (*Yishu jushe wei fankang wuli beichaofeng daibu gao Shanghai minzhongshu*), *Materials on modern Chinese literary history* Vol I, p 49.
34 'Protest against the raid on the Art Drama Association' (*Fandui chafeng Yishu jushe*), *ibid*, p 38.
35 The Art Drama Association issued the 'Letter to the masses of Shanghai from the Art Association: Protest against unreasonable raid and arrest', *ibid*, pp 48-9. The Federation of Drama Movement's statement was 'To the people on the raid on the Art Drama Association' (*Wei Yishu jushe beifengshi gao guoren*), *ibid*, p 49.
36 'Report on the two general meetings of the League of Left-wing Writers', *Jinian yu yanjiu* No 2, pp 21-2.
37 *Ibid*.
38 *Xindi yuekan* No 1 (1 June 1930), *Jinian yu yanjiu* No 2, pp 25-9.
39 *Materials on modern Chinese literary history* Vol IX, pp 310-11.
40 'Letter from the Left League to the professors of the literature department of Fudan University' (*Zuolian ge fudan daxue wenxuexi zhujiaoshou de xin*), *ibid* Vol I, p 45.
41 *Wenhua douzheng* Vol I No 1, *Materials on the Left League period* Vol II, pp 394-6.
42 'Resolution of the Chinese League of Left-wing Writers on the report of the representatives after attending the Congress of Delegates from the Soviet areas' (*Zhongguo zuoyi zuojia lianmeng zai canjia quanguo siuweiai quyu daibiao dahui de daibiao baogaohou de jueyian*), *ibid*, pp 396-8.
43 'New situation in the proletarian literary movement and our mission', *Wenhua douzheng* Vol I No 1, *Materials on the Left League period* Vol II, pp 396-8.
44 Wang Jianmin, *A draft history of the Chinese Communist Party* Vol II, pp 42-51.
45 Mao Zedong, 'Resolution on certain questions in the history of our Party', *Selected works* Vol III, pp 183-4.
46 Quoted from Li Zhu, 'Report on the first general meeting of the Left League', *Materials on modern Chinese literary history* Vol I, p 37.

Years of Achievement (I)

47 Hantano Kenichi, *A history of the Chinese Communist Party* (*Chugoku kyosantoshi*) (Tokyo, 1961) Vol I, p 508.
48 Bai Shu, 'The unforgettable years', *Recollections*, p 283.
49 'Record of Bai Shu's interview: About the "Left League"', *Reference materials*, p 36.
50 *Recollections*, p 284.
51 Wang Yaoshan, 'Recalling the time when I worked in the "Left League"', *ibid*, p 312.
52 Bai Shu, 'The unforgettable years', *ibid*, p 283.
53 Yang Qianru, 'Left-wing writers in Shanghai Arts University', *ibid*, p 100.
54 Wang Yaoshan, 'Recalling the time when I worked in the "Left league"', *ibid*, p 312.
55 *North China Herald*, 11 March 1930, p 392.
56 Mao Dun, 'The early stage of the "Left League"', *The road I trod* Vol II, p 53.
57 Pan Hannian, 'The significance of the League of Left-wing Writers and its role' (*Zuoyi zuojia lianmeng de yiyi jiqi renwu*), *Tuohuangzhe* Vol I No 3, *Materials on modern Chinese literary history* Vol IX, p 274.
58 *Ibid* Vol V, p 312.
59 Shen Duanxian, 'The so-called popularisation question' (*Suowei dazhonghua de wenti*), *Dazhong wenyi* Vol II No 3, *ibid*, p 300.
60 Guo Moruo, 'The realisation of nascent mass literature', (*Xinxing dazhong wenyi de renshi*), *ibid*, p 303.
61 Lu Xun, 'The popularisation of literature' (*Wenyi de dazhonghua*), *Complete works of Lu Xun* Vol VII, p 349.
62 He Zhi, 'The celebration party of Mr Lu Xun's fiftieth birthday' (*Lu Xun xiansheng de wushi shouchen qingzhuhui*), *Wenyibao* No 19, 1956 (15 October 1956), p 8; Tang Tianran, 'The report in "Hongqi ribao" about the celebration party of Lu Xun's fiftieth birthday' (*Hongqi ribao guangyu Lu Xun wushi shouchen jinianhui de baogao*), *Geming wenwu* (*Revolutionary relics*) No 5, 1980 (30 September 1980), p 6.
63 Fang Ming, 'The celebration party of Lu Xun's fiftieth birthday' (*Lu Xun wushi shengshou jinianhui*), *Chuban yuekan* (*Publication monthly*) No 8/9/10 (October 1930), *Jinian yu yanjiu* No 2, p 52.
64 Ge Baoquan (ed and trans), 'Smedley's recollection on Lu Xun' (*Shimotelai huiyi Lu Xun*), *Xinwenxue shiliao* No 3, 1980 (22 August 1980), notes (1) and (5), p 119.
65 Fang Ming, 'The celebration party of Lu Xun's fiftieth birthday', *Jinian yu yanjiu* No 2, p 52.
66 Agnes Smedley, *Battle hymn of China*, pp 78-9.
67 Fang Ming, 'The celebration party of Lu Xun's fiftieth birthday', *Jinian yu yanjiu* No 2, p 52; Tang Tianran, 'The report in "Hongqi ribao" about the celebration party of Lu Xun's fiftieth birthday', p 7.
68 Agnes Smedley, *Battle hymn of China*, p 79.

69 *Collection of materials on the left-wing literature of the thirties*, pp 53 and 76.
70 'Letter from the Secretariat of the Central Executive Committee of the Chinese Nationalist Party No 15889', *Jinian yu yanjiu* No 2, p 192.
71 'Feng Xuefeng on the Left League', p 5.
72 Li Haiwen and She Haining, 'The incident of the Oriental Hotel', *Shehui kexue zhanxian* No 3, 1980 (25 July 1980), pp 10-11.
73 Ding Ling, 'Piecemeal thoughts on the Left League', *Recollections*, p 160.
74 'Biographies of the murdered comrades', *Materials on modern Chinese literary history* Vol I, pp 7-12.
75 Li Haiwen, She Haining, 'The incident of the Oriental Hotel', p 7.
76 Mei Sun, 'A lesson in blood: Lament over the deaths on 7 February', *Materials on modern Chinese literary history* Vol I, p 5.
77 Xu Meisun, *Feng Keng, the martyr* (Guangzhou: Guangdong renmin chubanshe, September 1957), p 83.
78 Franz Michael, 'Preface', T A Hsia, *The gate of darkness*, p vii.
79 For the following paragraphs on the history of the CCP, I have consulted mainly: Wang Jianmin, *A draft history of the Chinese Communist Party* Vol II, pp 1-132; Benjamin I Schwartz, *Chinese Communism and the rise of Mao* (Cambridge: Harvard University Press, 1952), pp 145-71; Jerome Ch'en, *Mao and the Chinese revolution* (London: Harvard University Press, 1965); T L Hsiao, *Power relations within the Chinese Communist movement, 1930-1934* (Seattle and London: University of Washington, 1967) Vol I, pp 74-92.
80 Harold A Isaacs, *The tragedy of the Chinese revolution* (London: Secker and Warburg, 1938), p 407.
81 Schwartz, *Chinese Communism and the rise of Mao*, p 166.
82 Robert C North, *Moscow and Chinese Communists* (Stanford: Stanford University Press, 1953), p 150.
83 T A Hsia, *The gate of darkness*, pp 227-8.
84 *Ibid*, p 230.
85 'Feng Xuefeng on the Left League', p 7.
86 Luo Zhanglong, 'Before and after the Shanghai Oriental Hotel meeting' (*Shanghai dongfang fandian huiyi qianhou*), *Xinwenxue shiliao* No 1, 1981 (22 February 1981), p 80.
87 *Ibid*, p 144.
88 'Records of the two interviews with comrade Xia Yan', p 162; Feng Naichao, 'The situation around the formation of the Left League', p 80.
89 Li Haiwen, She Haining, 'The incident of the Oriental Hotel', pp 9-10.
90 Ding Ling, 'The life of a real person: On Hu Yepin' (*Yige zhenshiren de yisheng: Ji Hu Yepin*), *Selected works of Hu Yepin* (*Hu Yepin xuanji*) (Fuzhou: Fujian renmin chubanshe, July 1981), p 15.
91 Li Haiwen, She Haining, 'The incident of the Oriental Hotel', pp 6-10.
92 Li Ang, *The red stage* (*Hongse wutai*) (Taibei: Shengli chuban gongshi, February 1954 reprint), p 112.

Years of Achievement (I)

93 T A Hsia, *The gate of darkness*, p 169.
94 Harold Isaacs, *The tragedy of the Chinese revolution*, p 407.
95 Schwartz, *Chinese Communism and the rise of Mao*, p 166; Robert North, *Moscow and Chinese Communists*, p 150.
96 Neale Hunter, 'The Chinese League of Left-wing Writers', pp 182-4. For their acknowledgement, see Schwartz, *Chinese Communism and the rise of Mao*, p 234; Robert North, *Moscow and Chinese Communists*, p 150.
97 *Ibid*, pp 181-6.
98 Chang Kuo-t'ao, *The rise of the CCP*, p 144.
99 This sentence is misleading. The Chinese version of Chang's autobiography was '*zituo luowang*', that is, committed a mistake and bit the net. Chang Kuo-t'ao, *My recollection* (*Wode huiyi*) (Hong Kong: Ming Pao Press, 1973) Vol II, p 868.
100 Chang Kuo-t'ao, *The rise of the CCP*, p 146.
101 Wang Fanxi, *Shuangshan recollection* (*Shuangshan huiyilu*) (Hong Kong: Zhoujihang, December 1977), p 171.
102 Luo Zhanglong, 'Before and after the Shanghai Oriental Hotel meeting', p 144.
103 Li Haiwen, She Haining, 'The incident of the Oriental Hotel', pp 8-9.
104 Luo Zhanglong, 'Before and after the Shanghai Oriental Hotel meeting', p 144.
105 Wang Jianmin, *A draft history of the Chinese Communist Party* Vol II, pp 98-9.
106 Ding Jingtang, Qu Guangxi, *A catalogue of research materials on the five martyrs of the Left League*, p 357; Zheng Derong, Zhu Yan, *Lecture notes on the history of the Chinese Communist Party*, p 163; Chen Nongfei, 'Reminiscence on comrade Li Qiushi' (*Yinian Li Qiushi tongzhi*), *The Communist Youth Corps, my mother* (*Gongqingtuan, wode muqin*) (Beijing: Zhongguo qingnian chubanshe, August 1958), p 287.
107 Wang Jianmin, *A draft history of the Chinese Communist Party* Vol II, p 99.
108 Neale Hunter, 'The Chinese League of Left-wing Writers', pp 172-4.
109 *Collection of materials on the left-wing literature of the thirties*, p 55.
110 'Notice to the revolutionary masses from the League of Left-wing Writers concerning the building up of the official organ Qianshao' (*Zuoyi zuojia lianmeng wei jianli jiguan kanwu qianshao xiang guangdai geming qunzhong de tonggao*), *Materials on the Left League period* Vol II, p 410.
111 Lou Shiyi, 'Recalling the two publications of the "Left League"', pp 171-2; Zhou Guowei, Liu Xiangfa, 'The whole story of the publication of Qianshao (*Qianshao chukan shimo*), *Zhongguo xiandai wenyi ziliao congkan* No 5, p 104.
112 Agnes Smedley, *Battle hymn of China*, p 65.
113 Malcolm Cowley, 'Twenty-four youngsters', *New Republic* (8 July 1931), quoted from T A Hsia, *The gate of darkness*, pp 167-8.

114 'Letter from the Secretariat of the International Union of Revolutionary Writers to its branches' (*Geming zuojia guoji lianmeng mishuchu geigezhibu de xin*), *Wenxue daobao* Vol I No 2, *Materials on modern Chinese literary history* Vol I, p 49.
115 Agnes Smedley, *Battle hymn of China*, p 65.
116 *Complete works of Lu Xun* Vol IV, pp 282-3.
117 *Ibid* Vol XIV, pp 866 and 870.
118 Agnes Smedley, *Battle hymn of China*, p 65.
119 Neale Hunter, 'The Chinese League of Left-wing Writers', p 149.
120 'Written for the sake of forgetting' (*Weile wangque de jinian*), *Complete works of Lu Xun* Vol IV, pp 481-3.
121 For examples, see Lu Xun's letters to Xiao Jun and Xiao Hong, 17 November 1934 and 10 December 1934, *ibid* Vol XII, pp 566 and 593.
122 *Qianshao* Vol I No 1, *Materials on modern Chinese literary history* Vol I, pp 28-30. For a detailed analysis of this issue of *Qianshao*, see Neale Hunter, 'The Chinese League of Left-wing Writers', pp 147-51.
123 Franz Michael, 'Preface', T A Hsia, *The gate of darkness*, p vii.
124 Franz Michael said that only one of the martyrs could be called a writer while T A Hsia said that four were writers. *Ibid*, pp vii and 206; but Hunter, with the support of works published by them, held that all five were at least promising writers. Neale Hunter, 'The Chinese League of Left-wing Writers', pp 154-74.
125 Ding Jingtang, Qu Guangxi, *A catalogue of research materials on the five martyrs of the Left League*, p 3.
126 Mao Dun, *The road I trod* Vol II, p 71.
127 Feng Xuefeng, *Remembering Lu Xun*, p 106.
128 *Ibid*, p 108.
129 Mao Dun, *The road I trod*, pp 72-3 and 86.
130 Feng Naichao, 'The situation around the formation of the Left League', p 79.
131 Zheng Boqi, 'Fragmentary recollection of the "Left League"' (*Zuolian huiyi pianduan*) and 'Piecemeal recollection on the "Left League"' (*Zuolian huiyi sanji*), *Recalling the Creation Society*, pp 114 and 132.
132 *Works of Qu Qiubai* Vol III, pp 875-8.
133 Mao Dun, 'Around the writing of "Midnight"', *The road I trod* Vol II, pp 109-11.
134 Wu Taichang, 'A Ying on the Left League', p 22; Xia Yan, 'Reminiscence on comrade Qu Qiubai' (*Zhuinian Qu Qiubai tongzhi*), *Wenyibao* No 12, 1955 (30 June 1955), p 42.
135 Feng Xuefeng, *Remembering Lu Xun*, pp 106-12; Mao Dun, *The road I trod* Vol II, p 102.
136 'A lesson in blood: Lament over the deaths on 7th February', *Materials on modern Chinese literary history* Vol I, p 6.

137 Unless otherwise stated, the following discussion on the expulsion of the three members is based on 'Notice of expulsion of Zhou Quanping, Ye Lingfeng, Zhou Yuying', *ibid*, pp 49-50.
138 'Records of the two interviews with comrade Xia Yan', p 161.
139 Pan Hannian, 'Hidden traitor and Zhou Yuying', *Materials on the Left League period* Vol V, pp 581-90. 'Proletarian literary movement and self-criticism' (*Puluo wenxue yundong yu ziwo pipan*), *Baerdishan* Vol I No 2, *Materials on modern Chinese literary history* Vol III, p 376.
140 Feng Naichao, 'Proletarian literary movement in China and the historical significance of the formation of the Left League', reprinted in *Jinian yu yanjiu* No 2, pp 18-19; Qiu Shi, 'The advertising technique of Zhou Yuying' (*Zhou Yuying de guangaoshu*), *Baerdishan* Vol I No 5, *Materials on modern Chinese literary history* Vol I, p 50.
141 Ling Sheng, 'Criticism - abuse, attack - instigation', *Baerdishan* Vol I No 5, *Materials on modern Chinese literary history* Vol I, p 42.

Chapter Five
Years of Achievement - The Left League 1930-1933 (II)

After the expulsion of the three members in April 1931, it was natural, indeed necessary, for the Left League to tighten its control over the members as well as to secure more support. On the other hand, the new leadership of Qu Qiubai provided new momentum for the left-wing literary movement. Thus in the latter half of 1931 a number of attempts were made by the League to show its strength and unity.

On 1 September, the secretariat of the Left League issued a statement in its official organ, *Wenxue daobao*, concerning a letter sent in the name of the Left League, to the editors of some important magazines in Shanghai, including *Xiaoshuo yuebao*, *Dongfang zazhi* (*The Eastern miscellany*) and *Zhongxuesheng* (*Middle school students*). The letter demanded that the editors devote one-third of their magazines to articles and works on the Soviet Union, or their premises would be bombed. The last chapter showed that the League had denounced a threatening letter sent to the professors of Fudan University in May 1930. This time, the League's response was similar. The secretariat declared that the letter had nothing to do with the League which had no intention of sending such letters. It speculated that this was done by nationalist writers to damage the League's reputation.[1]

On 20 September, the League launched a major campaign, to publish *Beidou*. According to Ding Ling, its editor, the CCP propaganda department wanted to start this journal and she was chosen precisely because she was not a CCP member and so appeared less 'red', putting her in a good position to win over non-party writers.[2] In other words, *Beidou* was designed to broaden League influence in the literary circle. This accounted for the 'greyishness' of its early issues. In this respect, Ding Ling did her job well. The first issue published the works of writers such as Bing Xin, Chen Hengzhe, Ye Shengtao and even Lin Huiyin and Xu Zhimo and the second contained the names of Ling Shuhua and Dai Wangshu. Ding Ling was keen to bring in new writers. The first works of Ai Qing (E Ga), Ge Qin and Yang Zhihua (Wenjun) appeared in *Beidou*. She did not hesitate to publish and recommend works by factory workers.[3] Readers' letters were answered openly in the magazine or privately[4] and readers' seminars were organised. Ai Wu, then unknown in literary circles, was invited to attend simply because he had sent in an article (which was not accepted for publication). *Beidou* took the seminars seriously and famous writers, like Zheng Boqi, Ding Ling, Feng Xuefeng and Ye Yiqun, were present.[5] This was certainly a good tactic to win over young readers. Although the 'greyish' colour did not last long and it was banned within a year, *Beidou* was undeniably a success for the League. In Mao Dun's words, '*Beidou* was the first magazine or the first serious attempt of the "Left League" in overcoming closed-doorism, sectarianism and expanding left-wing literary movements'.[6]

On 18 September 1931, the Japanese staged the Mukden Incident. An area of 1.3 million square kilometres of northeastern China was lost to Japan. The GMD government could only raise an appeal to the League of Nations. This weakness offended the public and there were large-scale demonstrations all over the country. By contrast, the CCP issued a number of declarations condemning the Japanese aggression and even - as a gesture, of course, as its base was in the remote area of southeastern China - declared war on Japan.[7] The Left League was quick to grasp this opportunity too. Within a month, it issued two statements openly denouncing the Japanese and the GMD, one addressed to the proletariat and cultural organisations of the world and the other to the revolutionary writers and young people of China.[8] In the face of national calamity, these actions won left-wing support. As Xia Yan reported, very often the public provided help and protection to these anti-Japanese heroes.[9]

Then late in 1931, the executive committee of the Left League passed a resolution entitled 'The new missions of Chinese proletarian revolutionary literature',[10] which is generally regarded as the most important document of the League after its theoretical programme.[11] Mao Dun took it as a sign of the beginning of a new era in the League's history.[12] Feng Xuefeng was responsible for drafting it with help from Mao Dun and Qu Qiubai.[13] Obviously, they also had the advice of Lu Xun who was both a member of the executive committee and a good friend of Feng.

To the executive committee, China and the world had entered a new era. Economic crises of the capitalist world caused severe political crises which in turn led to further exploitation of the colonies by the colonising powers. But, in the committee's opinion, the imperialists met more and more opposition both at home and in the colonies. They were optimistic about the situation in China and with reason. First, the Red Army in Jiangxi had just successfully crushed the third encirclement campaign of the GMD. Secondly, on 7 November, the First All-China Congress of Soviets was held, leading to the establishment of the Chinese Soviet Provisional Central Government. Thirdly, in the eyes of the committee members, since Japanese invasion was ever-increasing, the people of China and the proletarians of the world would be eager to co-operate in a world revolution to bring about the downfall of the capitalists.[14]

This evaluation of the political situation of the world and of China was by no means new. Similar ideas, even in similar tones and wording, can be found in past resolutions and declarations of the League. Its assertion that the disarmament conferences of the Powers were a means of diminishing their conflicts so as to launch a successful invasion against the Soviet Union had persistently been expressed by the CCP and the Left League. Thus, to many critics, the resolution was still dogmatic and very much influenced by the radical Wang Ming line.[15]

What made this resolution new and attracted greater attention was its emphasis on literature and the role of writers. This was what Mao Dun meant when he said that it corrected the mistakes made in August 1930.[16] In the resolution, the executive committee stressed repeatedly that the role of the League was to lead the proletarian literary movement. Five of the seven sections of the resolution, discussed in detail the problems of creating proletarian literature. Several new tasks were assigned, including publicising, in the field of literature, anti-imperialist, anti-bourgeois and anti-GMD struggles, Soviet revolution and rules; organising the reporters' movement, wall-newspaper movement and other cultural activities among workers, peasants and soldiers; taking part in the education of the masses; and fighting against nationalist, fascist, liquidationist and other reactionary ideas and literature. Popularising literature was the most urgent work. The resolution also tried to list the subjects, methods and forms of proletarian revolutionary literature. Emphasis was still laid on the struggle against imperialists, landlords and the ruling class, but it underlined the use of simple language which could be understood by the public. What is more, idealist, mechanical, subjective and romantic approaches, as well as slogans, were to be avoided. There were no more appeals to writers to 'drop their pens' and engage in practical action.[17]

Also noteworthy in the resolution was its stress on the absorption of new elements into the ranks. The executive committee pointed out that it was a mistake in the past to exclude young people and students from the proletarian literary movement. The League should win over and lead progressive writers, the young people as well as those who were likely to turn to revolution. This represented an attempt by the leading members of the Left League to liquidate sectarianism.

The last section of the resolution dealt with the organisation of and discipline in the League. The following sentences are important:

> The Chinese League of Left-wing Writers ... is a militant action group having a definite and unanimous political viewpoint. It is not a voluntary association of writers.[18]

This was the nature of the League as conceived by its top level. This explained why such strict discipline was enforced. Any anti-programme actions, anyone refusing to carry out decisions made in resolutions, or anything like cliquism, or transcending organisation, or going slow would be punished.

On the question of discipline, the League inevitably called for self-criticism among its members. In more than one place, the resolution deliberately drew a distinction between the past and the present. In the past, the League had committed serious mistakes - being right-opportunist and left phrase-mongering. They were now eager to improve.[19]

Another attempt made by the left-wingers to strengthen their own position was a war waged against the nationalist literary movement.

On 1 June 1930, only three months after the formation of the Left League, a group of advocates of nationalist literature (*Minzuzhuyi wenxue*) met in

Years of Achievement (II)

Shanghai and issued 'The manifesto of the "nationalist literary movement"' (*Minzu zhuyi wenxue yundong xuanyan*).[20] They included Wang Pingling, Zhu Yingpeng, Huang Zhengxia, Fan Zhengbo, Ye Qiuyuan, Fu Yancheng, Pan Gongzhan, Wang Tiran, Wan Guoan and Shao Xunmei.[21] A number of journals were published, such as *Qianfeng yuekan* (*Vanguard monthly*), *Qianfeng zhoubao* (*Vanguard weekly*), *Wenyi yuekan* (*Literary and art monthly*), *Kaizhan yuekan* (*Development monthly*) and *Huangzhong yuekan*. Some newspapers, such as the *Shanghai Chenbao* (*Shanghai morning news*) (directed by Pan Gongzhan), *Dongnan ribao* (*Southeast daily*) (directed by Hu Jianzhong in Hangzhou) and *Wuhan ribao* (*Wuhan daily*) (directed by Wang Yeming), also supported the movement.[22]

In their manifesto, the nationalist writers proclaimed that 'the greatest mission of literature is to give full play to the spirit and consciousness of the nation to which it belongs' and that 'the greatest meaning of literature is nationalism'. Apart from showing the people's ways of thinking, art and literature could also eliminate all obstacles to the nation's development. It could play an active role in the building up of nationalist feeling. On the other hand, according to the manifesto, the growth of literature also depends largely on the consciousness of the nation. Thus, the development of nationalist literature has to rely on the establishment of nationalist feeling.

The manifesto cited many examples to support their argument; the pyramids and sphinxes of Egypt, architecture and constructions in Greece, the *Iliad*, *Odyssey*, *Book of songs* (*Shijing*) and the works of Dante Alighieri and Geoffrey Chaucer. Modern examples were also quoted. These included the unification of Italy and Germany, the establishment of Yugoslavia, Czechoslovakia and even the USSR. They were trying to prove that nationalism was closely related to literature.[23]

At a time when China faced severe foreign imperialist aggression, there appeared to be good cause to advocate nationalist literature. However, the nationalists met relentless attacks from the Left League, for several reasons.

First was its link with the authorities. One of the 'Three People's Principles' (*Sanmin zhuyi*) put forward by Dr Sun Yat-sen was nationalism. As early as 1929, the head of the Central Propaganda Department of the GMD, Ye Chucang, had advocated the 'literary policy of the Three People's Principles'. A number of articles were published in *Zhongyang ribao* (*Central daily*) of Nanjing, one of its editors being Wang Pingling who was often labelled by the left as a 'hack writer' of the GMD. This was the prelude to the advocacy of nationalist literature. It was also reported that the nationalist literary movement was sponsored by the GMD; Wang drafted its manifesto for a handsome fee, while many of its advocates worked in the government. Pan Gongzhan was a committee member of the Shanghai Municipal government. Fan Zhengbo was a standing committee member of the Shanghai GMD branch, head of the detective section of the police department of the Wusong and Shanghai areas and of the martial department, while Zhu Yingpeng was head of the detective section of the Shanghai Municipal police department.[24] The magazines of the nationalist movement were also supported by the authorities. An article by Pan Hannian revealed that the authorities forced bookshops and publishers to stop publishing for the leftists, but still retained the titles of the left-wing magazines and filled their pages with nationalist literature.[25]

Secondly, the nationalist writers had, from the start, taken a hostile attitude towards left-wing literature. This is understandable as the nationalist literary movement was an attempt by the GMD to counteract the influence of left-wing literature. At the very beginning of their manifesto, the nationalists declared that Chinese literary life was in an abnormal and morbid state. The left-wing was named as one of the two major forces which had dragged literary life into this crisis. Sentences from the theoretical programme of the Left League were quoted for criticism.[26] So it was the nationalists who launched an attack on the leftists while the latter defended themselves. It was a war that the League had to fight.

Third was the nature of nationalism. In the eyes of the left-wing critics who believed only in class struggle, the self-styled 'nationalists' represented the interests of the ruling class, which, far from opposing the menace of imperialism, colluded with the imperialists to exploit the masses. The slogan of nationalist literature was therefore a reactionary one. In the article, 'Butcher literature', (*Tufu wenxue*), Qu Qiubai alleged that nationalist literature was a kind of literature that encouraged 'killing and burning' (*sharen fanghuo*), and those killed and burnt were the ordinary Chinese who, in the eyes of the nationalists, were people of a foreign race, or 'bandits'. Citing paragraphs from nationalist works, he charged that the so-called nationalist wars were in fact wars between the oppressors and the oppressed. The Chinese gentry, promoting their kind of nationalism, acted as flunkeys of the imperialists. They were only eager to fight against the Communists and the Soviet Union. Before British, American, Japanese and French imperialists, the nationalist writers would not even break wind, Qu said.[27]

Resolutions and declarations of the Left League and the CCP often called for the proletarians to protect their motherland, the Soviet Union. It was argued by the Communists that the Japanese invasion of China was part of a plan to invade Russia. This idea was also reflected in the fight against nationalist writers. The left-wingers believed that the nationalists used the slogan of nationalist literature to rally support for a war against the USSR. Lu Xun, using the pen-name Yan Ao, pointed out that one of the works of the nationalists, 'Blood of the yellow race' (*Huangren zhi xue*) by Huang Zhengxia, was written to serve this end. It was the story of the western expedition of the Mongols. According to Lu Xun, 'their target was Europe, but it was mainly Russia - this was the purpose of the author'. Lu even associated this with Japanese aggression in China: 'In these days, among the yellow races in Asia, only the Japanese are comparable to the Mongols then.'[28]

Years of Achievement (II)

The taking of the northeastern part of China by the Japanese was, in the eyes of the left-wingers, the first step in the modern 'western expedition' and this was welcomed by the GMD. Qu Qiubai's words were most direct:

> The nationalist writers are watchdogs which slavishly obey the British, American and Japanese imperialists and are ready to invade Soviet Russia.[29]

For these reasons, the Left League took this fight seriously. The nationalist literary movement was officially denounced in a resolution passed by its executive committee,[30] and the best of its theoreticians wrote articles attacking the movement. Qu Qiubai wrote 'Butcher literature', 'The September of the young people' (*Qingnian de jiuyue*) and '"Blood of the yellow race" and others' (*Huangren zhi xue ji qita*). Lu Xun wrote 'The role and fate of "nationalist literature"' (*Minzuzhuyi wenxue de renwu he yunming*) and Mao Dun wrote 'Revealing the true features of "nationalist literature"' (*Minzuzhuyi wenyi de xianxing*). The former two attacked not only the theories of the nationalists, but also their works, such as 'Blood of the yellow race', 'The battle of Gansu' (*Longhai xianshang*), 'The destruction of great Shanghai' (*Da Shanghai de huimie*) and 'The battle at the gateway of the nation' (*Guomen zhi zhan*). Lu Xun called the nationalist writers 'a mess of floating corpses' which joined their masters in their final struggle to oppress the proletarians.[31] Mao Dun concentrated entirely on the manifesto, pointing out that the main idea of the manifesto came from the theory of H A Taine which had been scathingly refuted by western Marxists.[32]

The year 1932 was a busy and constructive one for the League. While *Beidou* was still being published and there was also *Shizi jietou* (*Crossroad*) which was started in the last month of 1931, at least four new organs were started within the first half of the year, although all were short-lived.[33] Together they constituted an efficient force to fight successful wars in the literary circle.

On 28 January 1931, the League met a most serious challenge, this time from the Japanese. Under the pretext that their citizens in Shanghai needed protection, the Japanese began the infamous Battle of Shanghai. Unlike previous occasions, Japanese aggression now took place in the very heartland of the League. The daily lives of its members were inevitably affected. Lu Xun had to flee for shelter to the Uchiyama Bookstore and hotels for over a month and the bombs slightly damaged his flat.[34] Some, like Xia Yan, participated directly in the resistance.[35] The League journal, *Beidou*, ceased publication until May[36] while *Wenyi xinwen* published a special daily *Fenghuo* (*Battle flames*) to report the news of the battle.

The battle intensified China's crisis and clearly revealed Japan's ambition in her aggression. Jiang Jieshi and his nationalist government were not prepared to fight a large-scale war against Japan but there was a general demand from the public for a stronger policy towards imperialist invasion. On 4 February, forty-three writers and artists signed the 'Letter from the cultural circle of Shanghai to the world' (*Shanghai wenhuajie gao shijie shu*). This was probably the work of the left because it was addressed to 'the proletarians and revolutionary cultural organisations and writers of the world' and more than half the signatories were League members.[37] However, another declaration made on 10 February was quite a different matter. This was drafted by Hu Qiuyuan who had already published his controversial articles 'A call to truth' (*Zhengli zhi xi*) and 'On the literature of the dogs' (*A'gou wenyilun*). According to a recollection of Hu, on 7 February, forty-five men of letters met in a secondary school to discuss the formation of the Anti-Japanese Writers Association (*Zhuzuozhe kangrihui*). From the Left League, only Ding Ling was elected as an executive member.[38] Hu also reported that in the meeting, there was a dispute between the left and others. Most favoured united resistance to the Japanese while 'the left were only eager to fight a civil war'. In the end, the declaration was passed with an overwhelming majority. In Hu's opinion, the left was defeated and for the first time lost their ascendancy.[39]

This story, if authentic, reveals the left's determination to reject a broad united front against Japanese invasion. To the CCP, under the new leftist leadership of Wang Ming, any suggestion of forming a national government was completely out of the question. In 1932, with the fighting still going on, there were discussions among the League members on a slogan 'Literature of a national revolutionary war' (*Minzu geming zhanzheng wenxue*). In March, Qu Qiubai published 'The Shanghai battle and war literature' (*Shanghai zhanzheng he zhanzheng wenxue*) openly publicising the idea of a national revolutionary war.[40] This war, under the leadership of the proletariat, was to be waged against both imperialism and the bourgeoisie. This, in effect, ruled out the possibility of a broad united front. The Left League held a meeting in a school to discuss the question. Lu Xun, Mao Dun, Feng Xuefeng, Ding Ling, Lou Shiyi and Xia Yan were present and agreed on the promotion of the literature of a national revolutionary war.[41] The slogan was put forward in an article called 'The May of pomegranate flowers' (*Liuhua de wuyue*) in *Wenyi xinwen*. The closing lines of the article read:

> We must promote and expand the revolutionary national war of the masses!
>
> We must promote the mass literature of the revolutionary national war![42]

Feng also published in *Beidou* 'The May of the national revolutionary war' (*Minzu geming zhanzheng de wuyue*) to expound the idea of a national revolutionary war against imperialism and the bourgeoisie. He also stressed the question of leadership which, undoubtedly, should be in the hands of the proletariat.[43] Although the movement was extremely short-lived, it can be viewed as the prelude to the bitter 'Two slogan polemic' in 1936 when the question of a united front popped up again - one of the two slogans was 'Mass literature of the national revolutionary war' (*Minzu geming zhanzheng de dazhong wenxue*).

Years of Achievement (II)

Before peace was completely restored, the League hastily put things back in order. On 15 March they put out *Mishuchu xiaoxi*. This was one of the most important publications of the League as it was printed by the secretariat for internal circulation. It was supposed to be a bi-weekly but only one issue, kept by Lu Xun, is now available.[44]

The first issue of *Mishuchu xiaoxi* recorded that the secretariat held an enlarged session on 9 March. Several resolutions were made. The first listed the tasks for the League members. By and large, it repeated the resolution made in November 1931. League members were asked to use their weapon of art to help the anti-imperialist struggle, to speed up the popularisation of literature, to carry out systematic criticism and self-criticism programmes, and to introduce international revolutionary literature and art. However, possibly because it differed from the previous ones in that its circulation was restricted, it touched on the organisation of the League. The resolution stated that reserves for the Left League should be built up by organising literary study groups among young people. These organisations should be linked with the literary groups of workers and peasants, thus expanding the influence of revolutionary literature. It also called for the establishment of League branches in various parts of China, like Guangzhou, Hankow, Qingdao, Nanjing, Hangzhou and the Soviet areas in Jiangxi, Hubei, Henan and Anhui.[45] This represented the ambition of the leading members of the League to make the Left League movement nationwide. But although some branches were actually built up, their activities, if any, were relatively insignificant.

The enlarged session also passed resolutions on the reorganisation of the League and the guiding principles for the various committees. It was decided that an organ, *Wenxue* (*Literature*) should be published for theoretical matters.[46] Strong emphasis was placed on the question of popularisation of literature. Not only was a Committee for Mass Literature established, but also the Committee for Writing and Criticism was assigned the tasks of studying the question of popularisation and the means and forms for the creation of mass literature.[47]

Apart from these resolutions, *Mishuchu xiaoxi* also carried an interesting report on a race between the Left League, the Dramatists League and the Social Scientists League. Under the direction and scrutiny of the General League of Left-wing Culture, an agreement was signed by the secretary of the Left League on 12 March, listing the work to be done by the League in the period from 15 March to the end of April. The plan was ambitious, but rather unrealistic. It requested League members, among other things, to write twenty pieces of revolutionary literature, two story books for the Soviet areas and three hundred thousand words on the theme of anti-imperialist and anti-landlord struggle. It was also scheduled that altogether twenty-seven dissertations should be written on various topics.[48] The secretariat was optimistic enough to ask for an overfulfilment of the target.[49]

Responding to this challenge from the other Leagues, four secretariat members, at Ding Ling's suggestion, held a competition among themselves.

The Chinese League of Left-wing Writers

Ding Ling, Feng Xuefeng, Lou Shiyi and Peng Hui individually made a list of work, including editing, literary creations, thesis writing, introducing new members, giving public speeches and participation in the work of the secretariat.[50] However no report on the result of the race is available, so these targets may not have been reached. Despite this, the League was in fact an active body. The resolutions and the competition agreement recorded in *Mishuchu xiaoxi* are evidence that the League was eager to make achievements and contributions.

The year 1932 was also the year that the Left League engaged in what was considered by some the biggest polemic ever fought by the organisation,[51] that with the 'Free Men' and the 'Third Category Men'. Because of the theme of the polemic, it was referred to as 'the Debate on the freedom of literature and art' (*Wenyi ziyou lunzhan*).[52]

The debate was ignited by an article by Hu Qiuyuan, an avowed Marxist who went to study in Japan in 1929. In the summer of 1931, he returned to Shanghai for a short visit and on the outbreak of the Mukden Incident in September, decided not to return to Japan.

Hu was a former member of the Communist Youth Corps. According to some sources, he was a member of the A B (Anti-Bolsheviks) Corps, though he himself denied it vigorously.[53] Yet his association with the *Shenzhou Guoguangshe* would easily arouse suspicions. This was a small publishing firm that had been publishing books on art since 1903. In 1930, its control fell to Chen Mingshu, commander of the Nineteenth Route Army of the GMD, who soon came into contact with the A B Corps in Jiangxi and was acquainted with the leader of the movement, Wang Lixi. Both were then seeking the creation of a political movement opposed to the GMD and the CCP. Chen was said to have formed the Social Democratic Party and been in close relationship with the Third Party (*Disandang*). In September 1931, through his influence, Wang became the editor of *Dushu zazhi* (*Reader's magazine*), a publication of *Shenzhou Guoguangshe*. Hu Qiuyuan was a frequent contributor to the magazine. Near the end of the year, Hu, together with Wang Lixi, started and edited *Wenhua pinglun* (*Cultural critic*).[54]

The political background of Hu Qiuyuan and his journal inevitably aroused the suspicion of the left. Worse still, Hu's several articles in the first issue of *Wenhua pinglun* directly challenged the theories of the left. In the foreword to the magazine, 'A call to truth', Hu declared that his group held no specific viewpoint. They belonged to 'the class of free intellectuals' who would explain and criticise everything from an objective standpoint. He maintained that the anti-traditional May Fourth Movement came to an abrupt end with the failure of the Chinese revolution. 'Future cultural activities are to complete the unfinished task of the May Fourth'.[55] This idea was unacceptable to the left-wingers who believed that the May Fourth Movement, with its emphasis on democracy and science, had long been over and that future cultural activities should be for the general masses who were suffering from imperialist oppression. A mild protest, which was believed to be made by the Left League in the name of the Wenyi Xinwen Association, appeared to challenge Hu's ideas. It urged Hu to take off the garb of May Fourth and concentrate firepower in the struggle for the liberation of the proletariat.[56]

If the foreword had not started the debate, another piece of writing by Hu in the same issue of *Wenhua pinglun* soon became a target of attack. Although 'On the literature of the dogs' was in the main a harsh criticism of nationalist literature it touched on the sensitive issue of the relationship between politics and literature. In a section called 'Art is not the lowest' (*Yishu feizhixia*), Hu attacked the nationalist writers for using literature for political purposes. To Hu, there was only one purpose for art, that is for the manifestation, recognition and criticism of life. 'It is a treachery to art to degrade art to the level of a gramophone for politics', Hu said.[57]

Upholding the 'weapon of art', the left-wingers saw Hu's article as a challenge to their own theories. The first response was made by Tan Sihai. His article 'The cultural theories of the "free intellectuals"' (*Ziyou zhishi jieji de wenhua lilun*) appeared in a journal of the General League of Left-wing Culture, *Zhongguo yu shijie* (*China and the world*). Tan accused Hu of being unable to realise the nature of the present struggle. In advocating that art was only for the manifestation, recognition and criticism of life, Hu was in effect denying the reformative uses of art. Trying to find a land of peace in the midst of a severe battle would eventually 'help the tiger' (*weihu zuocheng*).[58]

Hu Qiuyuan wrote two separate articles in reply to the editors of *Wenyi xinwen* and Tan Sihai. In the first, he began with a denunciation of the author of the article in *Wenyi xinwen*, saying that he did not thoroughly understand Marxism-Leninism. Hu made an analysis of the situation in China, quoting lines from Lenin, Luppol and Deborin to support his argument. He denied the charge that he wanted to revive the May Fourth. What he wanted to do was to surpass the May Fourth. He alleged that if left-wingers could not grasp Marxist theories strongly and unite under the banner of Marxism, the firepower would only be dispersed.[59] Likewise, Tan Sihan was charged with misunderstanding genuine Marxism. Hu ironically said that he suspected that Tan, for his attack on Hu's criticism of the nationalist literary movement, was the lawyer solicited by the nationalists. 'Who was in fact working for the dogs [*wei gou zuochang*]?' Hu asked.[60]

Hu's two articles were published in the fourth issue of *Wenhua pinglun*. The same publication carried yet another article on this question, showing clearly that Hu was eager to put up a fight. In the article called 'Hands off art' (*Wu qinlue wenyi*), Hu denied that he had attacked proletarian literature or nationalist literature. Being a 'free man', he would tolerate the existence of any kind of literature, left or right. But he would not allow any particular kind to monopolise the literary circle. He insisted that art is not propaganda. Before he closed his article, he urged people - descendants of Caesar, the priests, the elders, the Pharisees and the Sadducees - to keep their 'hands off art'.[61]

At about the same time, Hu Qiuyuan published another lengthy article in *Dushu zazhi*. On the one hand, he continued to attack nationalist literature. On the other hand, he picked out for criticism, Qian Xingcun, one of the most important members and theoreticians of the Left League. This behaviour may be related to his political association with the Third Party which was against both the GMD and the CCP. In the article, he accused Qian of lacking the talent to be a critic. Qian could only be regarded as a 'copyist' or 'journalist', because all his writings were just copied from various books. Qian took himself as a Marxist critic, yet what he had done was a caricature and distortion of Marxism. Qian's theories were, in Hu's eyes, confusing, subjective, and both left and right deviationist.[62]

In the article, Hu Qiuyuan specified that he was not against the theories of proletarian literature, nor did he mean to attack Qian personally. He did not mention anything about the debate that had already been going on between him and the left but the left hastened to relate the article to this debate. Feng Xuefeng, in the name of Luo Yang, wrote an open letter to the editor of *Wenyi xinwen*. Though admitting that Qian had made theoretical errors and that they themselves could not correct Qian in time, Feng was harsh in his criticism of Hu, saying:

> Here Hu Qiuyuan does not criticise Qian Xingcun for the sake of upholding genuine Marxism. He attacks Qian Xingcun for the sake of opposing the proletarian revolutionary literature. He is just not attacking Qian Xingcun. He is attacking the entire proletarian revolutionary literary movement. Recently Hu Qiuyuan, taking the stand of a 'free man' and in the name of opposing nationalist literature, secretly waged a war against proletarian revolutionary literature. Now he openly denounced proletarian literary movement.[63]

Feng Xuefeng did not hesitate to point out that Hu Qiuyuan belonged to the group of Trotskyists and social democrats, who were then more active in fighting against proletarian literature than against the nationalist writers. A campaign against them should therefore be launched immediately.

At this time, Su Wen stepped in. Su Wen (alias of Du Heng) was a member of the Left League and was present at its inaugural meeting. In the guise of an impartial observer, he accounted for the debate between Hu Qiuyuan and *Wenyi xinwen* (the left) in terms of a difference of standpoint. To Su Wen, Hu Qiuyuan was a pedantic Marxist who wanted only to study books; but the left demanded action and that was why they gave excessive emphasis to the political mission of literature. It was just natural that Hu should have been attacked by the left.[64]

Su Wen did not support Hu Qiuyuan at all. He did not believe that Hu stood for real freedom because Hu fiercely attacked goal-conscious literature. When he said 'hands off art', he was implying 'let me do it'. On the other hand, Su Wen pointed out that the freedom of writers was further restricted by the left's advocacy of class literature. Since this concept had been introduced, literature was a whore. Today, she was sold to the bourgeoisie and tomorrow, to the proletariat. Writers had to follow suit, that is, write for a special purpose, or stop writing, 'lay down their pens', if they did not want to be attacked. In the end, those who continued to write were no longer writers but agitators, and literature bore the same function as cartoons.[65] Su Wen was disgusted at the attempts by the left to popularise literature using cartoons and puppet shows.

Su Wen raised the issue of 'men of the third category' to refer to those writers who held fast to literature; but this 'third category' had no connection with the Third Party of Chen Mingshu and others. Nor was it in support of or similar to the 'free men' of Hu Qiuyuan. When he gave a definition of 'men of the third category' in his article, he was deliberately drawing a distinction with Hu's 'free men':

> At a time when the 'free men of the intellectual class' and the class that is 'not free, having cliques' are struggling for the hegemony of the literary arena, those suffering most are the men of the third category other than these two groups. This third category is the so-called 'writer group'.[66]

This article posed a serious challenge to the left because it was published in *Xiandai*, one of the most successful and popular journals in the thirties. The demand for freedom for writing was appealing too. The League gave the challenge great attention. A meeting was called to discuss the matter.[67] Qu Qiubai hastily published a long article to ridicule both Hu Qiuyuan and Su Wen. He claimed that in a class society, there was no absolute or genuine freedom for literature. No one could be of the third category because every writer, no matter whether he was conscious or not, writing or silent, was a representative of the ideology of a particular class, helping it in one way or another in the class struggle. Thus, all art, in a broad sense, was agitation and propaganda, a gramophone of politics. To Qu, literature and revolution was not incompatible. He admitted, unreservedly and proudly, that revolution was invading literature. Those literary pieces which had a high artistic value could still be agitational. He cited the example of Gorky to support his argument that agitators could at the same time be good writers.[68]

The upstart Zhou Yang also wrote an article on the issue. He was then a close follower of Qu Qiubai, for even Su Wen had pointed out that Zhou repeated Qu's ideas.[69] But his tone was more dogmatic and much harsher. Su Wen was labelled 'a dog':

> Even if Su Wen has not been 'the dog of that class [the ruling class]', he has at least helped 'the dog of that class' to bite the 'left-wing literary circle'.[70]

These two articles were published in *Xiandai*. Su Wen, being a good friend of its editor Shi Zhecun was able to read them before publication. Consequently, he published his defence in the same issue of the journal. Su Wen claimed that he, like the left-wingers, believed in the class nature of literature. He admitted that petit bourgeois writers might unconsciously expose their class character in their works but this did not necessarily mean that these works served the bourgeoisie. Even a depiction of the life of the bourgeoisie could not be said to serve that class. Moreover, Su maintained, many bourgeois writers were critical of bourgeois society. He was particularly resentful of the left's assertion that 'being not very revolutionary is not revolutionary, and being not revolutionary is counter-revolutionary'. Their 'excluding middle' attitude, taking friends as enemies, was in effect weakening and isolating the proletariat in the literary front.[71]

Until recently, it has been a prevailing idea in mainland China that this debate was one between hostile groups, that the Left League was fighting another war against exponents of reactionary bourgeois literary theories. One of the arguments is that both Su Wen and Hu Qiuyuan shortly turned to and worked for the GMD.[72]

However, during the polemic, neither Hu Qiuyuan nor Su Wen considered themselves enemies of the Left League. More than once, Hu Qiuyuan denied that he had any intention of hurting the proletarian literary movement. Rather, he was sympathetic.[73] In the last article he wrote on the issue, he said that he was surprised that his articles condemning the nationalist literary movement should have invited criticism from the left. When he came to read Feng Xuefeng's articles in *Wenyi xinwen*, he 'realised that he had angered some friends'. He asserted that when he demanded freedom for literature, he was aiming at nationalist writers, rather than the left and in doing so, he was indirectly helping the development of proletarian literature:

> At the time when the reactionary class openly forces literature to act as a tool for oppression, anyone who stands up and cries out loudly 'hands off art' is in fact disarming the reactionary class. This is advantageous for the development of all genuine literature (proletarian literature is by all means included).[74]

For this reason, he considered the debate with the left wasteful.

Su Wen's stand was even more positive. It seems that all along, he regarded himself as a friend, if not an ally, of the left. He complained that the left had taken friends for enemies. He stated in various articles that he did not mean to attack anyone or any group. In his eyes, he was suggesting a viewpoint different to the left, rather than quarrelling or engaging in a polemic with them.[75] The fact that articles on the issue from both sides appeared in *Xiandai* is significant. Su Wen was a very good friend of its editor, Shi Zhecun. He had helped in the design and preparation of the magazine even before it was started. Although not formally listed as an editor until May 1933 (Vol III, No 10), from the beginning he had been invited by Shi to read contributions. In other words, he had considerable influence over the magazine. The appearance there of hostile articles shows that he was liberal and open. In a recollection, Shi said that many important treatises were read by the other side before they reached him[76] and

Years of Achievement (II)

Feng Xuefeng once acknowledged that Su Wen permitted him to take home Hu Qiuyuan's article.[77]

So, the fault may have lain with the left. Before long, there came criticism of the left from the left. Chen Wangdao, one of the earliest CCP members, published an article voicing his discontent towards left-wing theoreticians. They were, in Chen's opinion, impractical, irresponsible and lazy. It was high time for them to examine and admit their mistakes.[78]

More significant still was Lu Xun's article 'On the "men of the third category"' (*Lun disanzhongren*). Like Qu Qiubai and Zhou Yang, Lu Xun denied the possibility of a 'third category'. He said:

> To live in a class society and yet try to be a writer who transcends class, to live in a fighting era yet to leave the battlefield and stand alone, to live in the present yet to write for the future, this is sheer fantasy. There are no such men in real life.[79]

He could not agree that writers were forced to lay down their pens by the left. 'Leftist writers are still being oppressed, imprisoned and killed under the laws of feudal and bourgeois society'. They found it difficult even to publish their own creative works. There was no way for them to monopolise the literary scene. In answering Su Wen's queries on the mass literary movement, he cited the works of Michelangelo and Da Vinci to illustrate that great art could be born out of cartoons and picture books.[80]

What makes this article different from those of Qu Qiubai and Zhou Yang is that it never accused Su Wen of doing harm to the proletarian literary movement. On the contrary, Lu Xun expressed his willingness to accept different viewpoints:

> Left-wing writers are not supernatural soldiers from the heaven, nor foreign foes who have fought their way in from abroad. They welcome not only those 'fellow travellers' who walk along for a few steps, but would also invite those onlookers at the roadside to walk along.[81]

Here Lu Xun was hinting that the left welcomed Su Wen and his third category to join the left-wing literary movement. In fact, in the year 1933 alone, Lu Xun wrote six letters to him. Su Wen also claimed that in principle, there was no difference between them.[82]

On the other hand, at the time of the debate, Lu Xun never openly mentioned Hu Qiuyuan or his 'free men' theory, let alone criticised it. This was a rare, if not abnormal, phenomenon since after he had joined the League, Lu Xun never failed to support them in the polemics engaged in by the left. His silence might well mean that he did not share their opinion. The fact that Hu Qiuyuan was a firm believer in Plekhanov made him readily acceptable to Lu Xun who had translated and quoted in his works much of Plekhanov's writings. It should be pointed out too that during the revolutionary literary polemic in 1928 when Lu Xun was attacked by the radicals, Hu Qiuyuan had come to his aid in an article called 'The question of revolutionary literature' (*Geming wenxue wenti*).[83]

It seems that some leading cadres in the Communist Party were also against the dogmatic attitudes of some left-wing critics. On 3 November 1932, a certain Ge Te published an article 'The closed-doorism of the literary front' (*Wenyi zhanxianshang de guanmenzhuyi*) in the official organ of the Central Committee of the CCP, *Douzheng* (*Struggle*). Ge Te has recently been identified as Zhang Wentian who was then in charge of the Propaganda Department of the CCP.[84] This article was reprinted, with some minor adjustment, in the organ of the General League of Left-wing Culture, *Shijie wenhua* (*World culture*).[85]

It is obvious from the title of the article that Ge Te's aim was to liquidate sectarianism within the left-wing cultural circle. More specifically, it was largely because of the polemic with the 'third category'. In the article, he wrote that the first sign of closed-doorism was the negation of the 'third category men' and the 'third category literature'. He considered this wrong and ultra-leftist:

> This is because in the society of China, apart from bourgeois and proletarian literature, there is obviously the existence of the literature of other classes. It may be non-proletarian, but at the same time, it may be a kind of revolutionary petit bourgeois literature which opposes the landlord and capitalist classes. Not only is this kind of literature in existence, it is also the dominating kind of revolutionary literature in China today. (In fact, even the creations of those who claim to be proletarian writers belong to this group.) To reject this kind of literature and to curse this kind of writers, naming them flunkeys of the bourgeoisie, is in effect destroying the revolutionary cultural front in the literary circle.[86]

In the article, Ge Te harshly condemned the attitudes of 'several leading comrades' during the polemic with the 'third category'. Even Lu Xun's concept that there could not be any 'third category' was rejected. Obviously, Ge Te was ready to accept people like Hu Qiuyuan and Su Wen.

Possibly because of this article, left-wing critics in Shanghai began to resolve the battle. Feng Xuefeng, the first from the left to rebuke Hu Qiuyuan, in the name of Dan Yan, published an article called 'On the inclination and theories of the "third category" literature' (*Guanyu disanzhong wenxue de qingxiang yu lilun*). In the article, Feng continued to criticise what he considered to be Su Wen's mistakes. Su Wen was still attacked for being anti-revolutionary and his analysis of the class nature of literature was rejected; but the most noteworthy part of the article lay in the first section, 'Our attitudes towards Mr Su Wen and others'. Initially, Feng hastened to affirm that the left wanted to be allied with all progressive writers. They would not label those writers 'flunkeys of the bourgeoisie'. More important still, Feng openly admitted that some in his group had made the mistake of 'taking friends for enemies', a charge first made by Su Wen. Both Qu Qiubai and Zhou Yang were criticised. Feng claimed that they themselves would in the first instance correct these mistakes and wipe out any sectarian feelings in their camp. According to Feng, since Su Wen then, at least passively, opposed bourgeois literature, the left should not take him as an enemy, but rather as an ally. Feng even called upon the left-wingers to build up friendship with Su Wen.[87] This was a total negation of what he did and said to Su Wen at the beginning of the polemic. Su Wen recalled that the left had sent many people to talk to him, saying that some of his ideas were more acceptable and that Su Wen was excellent in writing argumentative articles.[88] Hu Qiuyuan also reported that people from the left, including Feng Xuefeng, went to see him. They even gave Hu a picture of Plekhanov as a present and invited him to contribute to *Xiandai*.[89] Both Hu Qiuyuan and Su Wen regarded all this as a sign that the left had admitted defeat.[90]

The significance of the debate lies in the attitude adopted by the Left League. As shown earlier, at the beginning of the debate, the League took a dogmatic and uncompromising stance, thus intensifying the debate. Nevertheless, the League abruptly change its attitude. Although 'On the inclination and theories of the "third category literature"' brought disastrous results to its author decades later,[91] it was not true that, as Shi Zhecun once said, it pleased nobody at the time.[92] It was a successful attempt by the League to eliminate sectarianism.

Apart from that of Ge Te, the influence of Lu Xun was also important. On the one hand, as we have already pointed out, he might not have been totally against the ideas of Hu Qiuyuan and Su Wen. On the other hand, Lu Xun was thinking of the entire left-wing literary movement. His usual stance was best illustrated in a letter to Wang Zhizhi, one of the most prominent members of the Beijing branch of the Left League:

> I believe that it is better for us to adopt a more moderate stance. In fact, there are some people who may not be of any great help and yet do not bear any ill-will. At present, they are certainly not our enemies. It will be our loss if we make a stern look and repel them. Do not ask for perfection at the moment. If you do so, people will keep away from you.[93]

Thus Lu Xun was satisfied with Feng's article. His ideas in 'On the "men of the third category"' were repeated. Su Wen was happy to see the appearance of this article too. He described it as 'the most valuable gain of the debate'.[94]

Meanwhile, the League was also busy discussing another important issue and there were diverse opinions among its members. This was on the popularisation of literature and art.

As seen earlier, this issue had already been a focus of attention in the left-wing literary movement even before the formation of the Left League. The League, with its emphasis on the promotion of proletarian literature, took the problem seriously. Apart from establishing the Association for the Study of Popularisation of Literature, it initiated a discussion on the issue. Seminars were held and many articles were published in its organs. However, even Lu

Xun was pessimistic: 'It is idle talk to ask for a complete popularisation at the present moment.'[95]

There were reasons for the revival of the discussion in 1932. The most important factor was the leadership of Qu Qiubai. As previously noted, Qu came to take up the work of the Left League in May 1931. A writer himself, he was particularly keen on the popularisation of literature. Some sources recorded that he went in disguise to watch the performances of folk artists in order to familiarise himself with the popular literature and art enjoyed by the common people.[96] On 28 September 1931, he published a long poem 'The invasion of the Japanese' (*Dongyangren chubing*) written in the dialects of Shanghai and the north.[97] In the same issue of *Wenxue daobao*, he published an article called 'Mass literature and the struggle against imperialism' (*Dazhong wenyi he fandui diguo zhuyi de douzheng*) shouting 'revolutionary literature, go to the masses!'[98] His emphasis on the popularisation of literature was reflected in the League. According to Mao Dun, Qu spent much effort in the drafting of the resolution passed by the executive committee of the League in September 1931.[99] In the resolution, an entire section was devoted to the 'Significance of the question of popularisation', stressing that the popularisation movement was for the success of the anti-imperialist and anti-GMD Soviet revolution. Proposals such as the organisation of a reporters' movement and study groups for the workers, peasants and soldiers were made. Apart from manoeuvring behind the scenes, Qu also wrote several articles on the topic. They were described by one critic as 'extraordinarily interesting and provocative', 'more systematic and creative' and most of all, they 'are related far more explicitly to the peculiarities of the Chinese revolutionary scene'.[100]

There were also political reasons for the bringing up of the issue again in 1932. With the intensification of Japanese aggression towards China in the Mukden and Shanghai incidents, the League felt a more urgent need to unite with the masses whose power was demonstrated in the events. There were strikes, demonstrations and petitions in various big cities and voluntary self-defence corps were organised. Claiming to be the upholder of the mass movement and rejecting all GMD-led anti-Japanese efforts, the League could not afford to lag behind. Declarations and resolutions made by the League were not direct enough to win or educate the masses. Popularisation of literature and art was undoubtedly more effective.

Revival of the discussion on popularisation can also be seen as an attempt to counter-balance the nationalist literary movement and the 'mass literature' of the ruling class. Although Jiang Jieshi was not eager to fight a war against Japan at that moment, the right made propaganda against Japanese aggression. Songs, stories and posters were used to call for people to resist Japanese aggression and not to buy Japanese goods.[101] Qu Qiubai and Feng Xuefeng had to admit that these exerted considerable influence on the masses;[102] but in their view this could not help in resisting the Japanese. Rather, they believed that it would help the ruling class to consolidate their rule, thus constituting an obstacle to both the political and literary movements of the left. In other words, part of the left's mission in promoting mass literature was to wash away 'bad' influences on the masses.

Near the end of 1931, there were increasing demands from the leading members of the League for a large scale movement to popularise literature. Resolutions and declarations were made calling for a more active attitude among its members. Qu Qiubai wrote several articles on the topic. The first was 'The practical questions of proletarian mass literature' (*Puluo dazhong wenyide xianshi wenti*), published in the first (and only) issue of the League journal *Wenxue* on 25 April 1932; but because circulation was limited, the article attracted little attention. However his next treatise, 'Questions of mass literature' (*Dazhong wenyide wenti*), which was basically a revision of the first, initiated a wide discussion.[103]

At the beginning of these two articles, Qu pointed out that the masses were still enjoying a cultural life of the middle ages. There was a kind of 'reactionary mass literature and art', such as picture story books, historical novels (*yanyi*), puppet shows, shadow plays and local opera. The present task of the left-wingers was to build up proletarian mass literature to fight against this reactionary kind but the problems of language, form and content had to be solved first.

Unlike many other May Fourth writers, Qu did not believe that the language problem had been solved in the May Fourth new cultural movement because there was still a wide gap between spoken and written languages and between the languages of the gentry and the masses. In Qu's opinion, the May Fourth was a failure. There emerged only a kind of new classical language (*Xinwenyan*), or a mule language (non-horse and non-donkey) which, just like the classical language, was still monopolised exclusively by the intelligentsia. This mixture of classical Chinese, modern and old vernacular as well as European and Japanese grammar could not be understood by the masses even when read aloud. As it could not serve the masses, this kind of vernacular would never be used to create proletarian literature and art. He said that a better alternative was the 'vernacular' used in traditional mass literature such as serialised fiction and story teller tales. It was indigenously Chinese as it was developed from the spoken language of the Ming period. It was therefore better understood and welcomed by the masses. That was why reactionary writers, using this language to create mass literature, won considerable popularity. Yet Qu did not think that it was the ideal tool for creating proletarian literature.

Qu claimed that a modern Chinese language was emerging in the big cities - the common speech (*putonghua*). It was not the 'national language' (*Guoyu*) endorsed by the ruling class, but one used in communication by people from various provinces. The development and growth of this common speech were based on the customary grammar of spoken Chinese. To Qu Qiubai, this was the solution to the language problem in the popularisation of proletarian literature and art. He urged writers to use this 'common speech' in their writings and this would eventually help the establishment of a genuine modern Chinese.

As for the question of form, Qu Qiubai also adopted an attitude different from those of other iconoclastic and Europeanised May Fourth writers. He saw merits in the traditional forms, such as their relationship to the oral literary heritage and the simple and plain means of narration. He therefore cautioned revolutionary writers to take heed of these in writing revolutionary mass literature, although he was against imitating all the traditional forms blindly. Two things were to be done: first, to take up and reform the traditional forms; and secondly, to make use of various elements of traditional forms to create new forms.

On the question of content, Qu insisted that revolutionary mass literature and art had only one central idea and that was to unmask all kinds of false fronts and show the revolutionary struggle of heroes. This would contribute to the development and growth of revolution. Qu claimed that a great variety of themes could be undertaken and there was hardly any inappropriate subject matter. He listed some for reference. First, something like reportage which could reflect revolutionary struggles and political incidents most directly and quickly. Second, a revision of old themes, such as 'New water margin'. Third, *yanyi* on revolutionary struggles such as the Taiping, May Thirtieth, Great Strike of Hong Kong. Fourth, translation of foreign revolutionary literature and art. Fifth, works exposing the aggression of imperialist powers. Sixth, adaptations from daily news. Qu asserted that revolutionary mass literature and art could also describe family life and even the question of love of the masses.

When compared with the previously sporadic discussion of mass literature, these two articles of Qu Qiubai were more systematic and richer in content. Apart from presenting and discussing the problems, Qu was able to offer answers. Nevertheless, he could not win unanimous support among the left. Mao Dun, under the pseudonym of Zhi Jing, expressed a different view in his article 'The mass literature and art in question' (*Wentizhong de dazhong wenyi*).

In the first instance, Mao Dun could not agree with Qu that the masses could understand the 'vernacular' of traditional fiction. He insisted that only those who frequented 'story-telling places' or had received at least some sort of traditional education could, still with some difficulties, understand the language. On the other hand, those who had studied in new primary schools for two to three years were able to read works written in the 'new classical' but would never like traditional fiction. His conclusion was that there were limitations in saying that 'the vernacular in old fiction was closer to the masses'.[104]

Another point of dispute centred on the question of the artistic value of mass literature. Mao Dun stressed that works in mass literature and art should still be artistic pieces. They should be able to move the readers. This had nothing to do with the language, but the narrative skill of the writers. Sometimes, even though there was no problem in understanding the language, the masses still did not like a particular piece. Mao Dun suggested that skill was most important while language was a minor factor. Like Qu Qiubai, Mao also believed that there were defects in revolutionary literature but the problem lay not in the language, but in the skill. To Mao, Qu had over-emphasised the role of language in literary creations.

Mao Dun was also against the notion of 'modern Chinese common speech'. After conducting a survey among the workers of a laundry, a printing house, a textile factory and a wharf in Shanghai, he concluded that there was not a 'common speech' developing in China. Rather, individual cities had their own dialects as the dominating communication medium while taking in speech patterns from other parts of the country. Moreover, this 'common speech' used for communication by people from different regions was not rich enough for literary creations. Mao cited an example of a woman from Tianjin who could communicate with the so-called common speech but would quickly shift back to her native dialect when she wanted to tell a story. It was thus impossible to use the so-called 'modern Chinese common speech' for the creation of mass literature. Mao Dun insisted that when there was no better way, the much condemned 'vernacular' had to be employed.[105]

Qu Qiubai made an open reply to Mao Dun's article. He claimed that while Mao Dun had misunderstood him in certain respects, there was a difference in principle too. Qu stressed that he was not in favour of using traditional vernacular for literary creations and insisted that he had not over-emphasised the role of language. He asserted that it was wrong to give so much weight to technique in mass literature and ignore the language problem. There was no point in having a skilfully written piece of work that could not be understood by the masses. Moreover, at this early stage of the movement, there was no way to have first class mass literature writers and thus intrinsically inferior works had to be accepted. Limiting the scope of mass literature to outstanding pieces only, Mao Dun was in effect obstructing, or even stopping the movement.[106]

Mao Dun did not respond to Qu's article. By his own account, he was silent because he realised there was a difference between the two in understanding of the concept of popularisation of literature and art. For Mao Dun, popularisation meant the efforts made by writers to create, in the language used by the masses, literary works intelligible and acceptable to the masses. It was therefore natural that he would put emphasis on the question of technique. On the other hand, Qu Qiubai was also concerned with enabling the masses themselves to create a literature of their own.[107] Consequently, attention should not be focussed on the technique of the writers, but rather, because of the illiteracy problem, on the question of a viable language. This difference was certainly one between a writer and a politician. Mao Dun took the stand of a writer while Qu paid more attention to mobilising the creative energies of the proletarians. That was why Qu repeatedly pointed out that the popularisation movement was part of the political struggle.[108]

Once more, the significance of this debate lay not so much in its content as in the manner in which it was conducted, or more specifically, the behaviour of Qu

Qiubai in face of challenges raised by his subordinates. His tolerance was clearly manifested in his reply to Mao Dun. More than once in his article, he praised the merits of Mao Dun's essay - saying Mao's discussion on form and content was thorough and useful. This open and graceful manner won him support and respect within the leftist camp.

Apart from the debate between Qu and Mao Dun, other efforts were also made by the left to promote the movement. For four issues of *Wenyi xinwen* there was a column called 'To the brothers in factories', publishing articles to teach the workers to read and write.[109] *Beidou* also sent out a questionnaire and invited answers to four questions:

a) Should the present Chinese literature be popularised?
b) Can the present Chinese literature be popularised?
c) Will popularisation lower the artistic standard of literature?
d) How to achieve the popularisation of literature?[110]

Eleven answers were published, including those of Chen Wangdao, Zhang Tianyi, Zheng Zhenduo, Du Heng and Wei Jinzhi. They seemed rather optimistic, seeing no reason why literature could not and should not be proletarianised. Unfortunately, they were unable to provide an acceptable solution to the fourth question. It was still a great problem to decide on the right method for the popularisation of literature.

Several articles in the same issue of *Beidou* were also devoted to the same problem. Qu Qiubai's influence was obvious. Articles such as Zhou Yang's 'On the popularisation of literature' (*Guanyu wenyi dazhonghua*) and Han Sheng's 'popularisation of literature and mass literature' (*Wenyi dazhonghua yu dazhong wenyi*) were repetitions of Qu's earlier writings.[111] For instance, Zhou Yang also stressed that solving the language problem was essential and that traditional forms should be borrowed. He, too, believed it a must for training new writers from the masses. Heavy political flavour can also be found in these articles. In some cases, they were more extreme than Qu Qiubai. Unlike Qu who welcomed all sorts of topics, Zhou claimed that their main task was to write about the struggle of the revolutionary proletarians.[112] Xia Yan said that the ultimate aim of their literary movement was to bring about the destruction of the capitalist system and therefore, 'class struggle must absolutely be the central theme of everything we write'.[113] This was interpreted by some as a sign of the rise of radicals in the Left League.[114]

The period 1930-32 was thus active and constructive for the Left League. Comparatively speaking, 1933 was less successful. On the first day of the year, Yang Cunren, one of the founders of the Sun Society, published an article 'Leaving the trench of political party life' (*Likai zhengdong shenghuo de zhanhao*) declaring his defection. Although Yang did not occupy any senior post in the League, it was nevertheless a blow to the organisation because this was the first time that one of its members openly declared defection. Unlike other defectors, Yang had not been arrested by the authorities before he made his decision. Rather, it was after his return from a visit to the Soviet Areas.

Years of Achievement (II)

This could lead people to think that there were problems within the left and the League, especially when Yang wrote the following lines in his declaration:
> Leading a political party life is like squatting down in a trench. You have to be careful of the bullets of the enemies. On the other hand, you have to be aware of the betrayal, frame-up and discrimination of companions.[115]

Judging from the internal strife of the League in its later periods, we may say that Yang's complaints were not groundless.

There was other bad news too. On 14 May, Ding Ling and Pan Zinian were arrested while Ying Xiuren was killed at the same spot and Zhou Yang narrowly escaped.[116] On 26 July, Hong Lingfei was arrested in Beijing and soon put to death. Then near the end of the year, the head of the Beijing and Tianjin branches, Pan Mohua was arrested and died on hunger strike in prison. These were heavy blows to the Left League as all the arrested and killed were active and experienced members. Being underground, the League could do nothing either to rescue them or to stage effective protests. They could only make use of another open channel, the Chinese League for the Protection of Civil Rights (*Zhongguo minquan baozhang tongmeng*), formed at the end of 1932 under Song Qingling, widow of Dr Sun Yat-sen, and Cai Yuanpei. In May, the Civil Rights League issued 'A declaration on the murder of the young writer Ying Xiuren' (*Dui qingnian zuojia Ying Xiuren beihai xuanyan*).[117] Ironically, its chief executive, Yang Xingfo, could not escape assassination on 18 June 1933.

On the other hand, since the latter half of 1932, the Communists had been fighting a hard war against Jiang Jieshi's fourth encirclement campaign. With half a million troops, Jiang was able to dislodge the Red armies under Zhang Guodao from the Soviet areas and force them to retreat into northern Sichuan. He Long was also driven to the Miao areas on the borders of Hubei, Hunan, Sichuan and Guizhou. It was not until March 1933 that the GMD troops withdrew. But in the same year, occurred the crushing fifth encirclement. Jiang Jieshi, experienced from the previous four campaigns and with the advice of the German general, Hans von Seeckt, employed new tactics. Instead of rushing hastily into the Communist strongholds, the GMD troops set up a tight blockade over the entire Central Soviet district, causing serious shortage of food and other supplies. In the end, the Communists abandoned the Central Soviet and started the Long March.

But the League was by no means in complete stagnation in 1933. In February, it issued in its own name a letter of protest in *China Forum* concerning the murder of the Japanese proletarian writer Kobayashi Takiji.[118] Kobayashi was generally regarded 'both as the dominant writer of the NAPF-KOPF period and the most outstanding writer in the history of proletarian literary movement' in Japan.[119] In 1927, he was secretary of the Otaru Branch of the WPAL (Worker-Peasant Artists' League) and VAL (Vanguard Artists' League). He was also responsible for the organisation of the Otaru Branch of the the NAPF. He put out a number of outstanding works such as 'March 15,

The Chinese League of Left-wing Writers

1928' and *'Kani Kosen'* ('The crab canning boat'). In 1931, he became secretary of the Central Committee of the Writers' League and a member of the Japan Communist Party. In 1932, being one of the twenty-nine members of the Central Council of the KOPF and taking charge of the Communist Party group of the organisation, 'he was doubtlessly the single, most important man in Japan's proletarian cultural movement'.[120] He was arrested and beaten to death by the Japanese police on 20 February 1933 at the age of twenty-nine. Apart from protesting, the Left League of China also ran a fund-raising campaign. Yu Dafu, Mao Dun, Ye Shengtao, Chen Wangdao, Hong Shen, Du Heng, Lu Xun, Tian Han and Ding Ling signed a notice in *Wenyi zazhi* (*Literature magazine*) inviting donations for Kobayashi's family.[121]

Then in June, upon the arrest of Ding Ling and Pan Zinian, the League published a declaration in *China Forum*. As expected, it condemned GMD rule for its exploitation of the people, capitulationist policy towards Japanese imperialists and murder of Chinese writers. The declaration also revealed that the GMD had established a new organisation under the Blue-shirt Society (*Lanyishe*) to kidnap left-wingers. It charged too that there was an agreement between the GMD and the police of the concession areas that the latter would turn over to the GMD left-wingers arrested in their dominions - signs of cooperation between foreign imperialists and autocrats at home.[122]

The League also actively participated in the Far East session of the Committee of World Anti-imperialist Wars, convened in Shanghai on 30 September 1933 in secret because the GMD had made it illegal. Under the direction of Song Qingling and with delegates from Britain, France and Belgium, the session was considered a success. The Left League was one of the active groups in preparing and organising the session. Hua Di headed the organising team which was made up of Zhou Wen, Zheng Yuzhi, Liang Wenruo and Wang Hanwen.[123] Besides offering practical help, the League also published a statement to welcome the delegates.[124] Another welcome notice could also be viewed as the result of the League's efforts because most of the one hundred and seventy-three signatories were its members.[125] Further, Lu Xun, Mao Dun and Tian Han, the three heads of the League, issued yet another declaration for this occasion in their own names.[126]

During this period, beneath the surface, there was a shift of power within the League which greatly affected its fate. Near the end of 1932, Zhou Yang rose rapidly to power in the League. Returned from Japan in the summer of 1932, he was introduced to and lived with Zhao Mingyi who was then very active in the Dramatists League. Zhao put him into the Dadao Drama Association (*Dadao jushe*), playing minor parts in drama performances. Around March and April, the Party group secretary of the Dramatists League invited Zhou to join the League, but as Zhou could not speak proper Mandarin, he was not eager to accept. He asked to join the Left League, was introduced to Xia Yan and became a member, which started his career in the Chinese cultural circle.[127]

Years of Achievement (II)

Meanwhile, Zhou Yang began contributing to Left League journals. His first piece was a translation, 'Freudianism and art' (*Fuluoyitezhuyi yu yishu*) which won the praise of the editor of *Wenxue yuebao*, Yao Pengzi.[128] The next issue saw his two translations of Russian short stories.[129] At the end of July he published his first theoretical treatise, 'On the popularisation of literature'. As noted earlier, it had few original ideas, merely repeating those of Qu Qiubai.

Then at the beginning of the third issue of *Wenxue yuebao*, Yao Pengzi published a full-page editorial notice announcing that the editorship of the magazine had been transferred to Zhou Yang. This was an unusual phenomenon. The last line of the notice read:

> Fearing that those who took the trouble of sending manuscripts might be anxious, I make this special announcement, and add my regrets.[130]

As one critic correctly commented, 'there is more than a hint of bitterness in this statement'.[131] According to Ding Ling, it was Feng Xuefeng's idea to dismiss Yao Pengzi and replace him with Zhou Yang.[132] There is no hint as to why Feng wanted to cashier Yao, except that Xia Yan had described one of Yao's pieces as 'a work of "pure" humanism',[133] a possible sign of discontent on the left.

In a short time, Zhou Yang was able to grasp real power within the League. He became the secretary of the Party group in the second half of 1933. He was also secretary of the Cultural Committee and the Party group of the General Cultural League from February 1935.[134] He had held all three key posts of the secretariat of the Left League. Holding all these responsible posts and being a Party member, and thus appearing as the spokesman of the CCP in the cultural field, he was always the man who gave instructions. He was also able to attract under him and exert great influence over a large number of League members.

About the same time, another was also emerging within the Left League. He was Hu Feng who became a rival of Zhou Yang in the League's last two years of existence. Hu was a member of the Communist Youth League from 1922-1925.[135] As early as 1925, he had already started contributing to *Zhongguo qingnian* and writing short stories.[136] In September 1929, he went to Tokyo and began reading Japanese proletarian literary works. He was able to meet left-wing writers such as Eguchi Kiyoshi, Akita Ujaku, Kobayashi Takiji and Ikeda Hisao. In 1931, he joined the Japan Communist Party and the Tokyo branch of the Left League. Near the end of 1932, he returned to Shanghai for a short while and was introduced to people like Feng Xuefeng, Ding Ling, Zhou Yang and Mu Mutian. Even at that time, he was invited by Zhou Yang to take part in the organisational work of the General League of Left-wing Culture. Feng also wanted to make him head of the propaganda section of the Left League.[137] Fearing to be dragged into party disputes of the League, Hu turned down these proposals and went back to Tokyo.

But in July 1933, after three months imprisonment, Hu Feng was sent home by the Japanese police for involvement in the Communist-led proletarian literary movement. By then, he had already made himself famous in the Left League of Shanghai as a literary critic.[138] Upon his return, he was immediately approached by Zhou Yang who put him in charge of the propaganda section of the League. Three months later, he succeeded Mao Dun as the secretary of the League.[139] In other words, within a very short time, Hu Feng entered the central core of leadership of the Left League in Shanghai.

At this early stage, Zhou Yang and Hu Feng were on good terms. This can be verified by Zhou Yang's eagerness to pull Hu into the League. Wu Xiru, a good friend of Hu, also confirmed that relations between Zhou and Hu were most cordial during 1933-1934.[140]

However, even during his first return to Shanghai, near the end of 1932, and within his short stay, Hu Feng saw that there was a distance between Feng Xuefeng and Zhou Yang.[141] Mu Mutian also attacked Feng to his face for Lu Xun's publishing an unfriendly article about Mu. Hu sensed too that Lu Xun opposed the group of Creationists within the League. In other words, the subsequent split in the League had its origin in 1932. It did not surface then only because such people as Qu Qiubai and Feng Xuefeng could on the one hand pacify Lu Xun and on the other exercise considerable influence over other League members.

Years of Achievement (II)
Notes to Chapter Five

1. 'Notice from the Left League', (*Zuolian qishi*), *Wenxue daobao* Vol 1 No 4, *Materials on modern Chinese literary history* Vol I, p 82.
2. Ding Ling, 'Piecemeal thoughts on the Left League', *Recollections*, p 161.
3. *Beidou* Vol II, No 3 and 4, *Materials on modern Chinese literary history* Vol IV, p 571.
4. *Ibid* Vol III, p 262; *ibid*, pp 525-6; *ibid* Vol IV, p 570.
5. Ai Wu, 'A sketch of the thirties: The situation around the joining of the left League', *Recollections*, p 230.
6. Mao Dun, *The road I trod* Vol II, p 72.
7. Wang Jianmin, *A draft history of the Chinese Communist Party* Vol III, pp 12-16 and 24-5.
8. 'Letter to the cultural organisations of the proletariat and the toiling masses of the world' (*Gao guoji wuchan jiaji ji laodong minzhong de wenhua zuzhi shu*), *Wenxue daobao* Vol I No 5, *Materials on modern Chinese literary history* Vol I, pp 83-7; 'To proletarian writers, revolutionary writers and all those young people who love literature and art', *ibid*, pp 100-3.
9. Xia Yan, 'Around the formation of the "Left League"', p 10.
10. *Materials on modern Chinese literary history* Vol I, pp 132-7.
11. Neale Hunter, 'The Chinese League of Left-wing Writers', p 208.
12. Mao Dun, *The road I trod* Vol II, p 86.
13. *Ibid*. This resolution is collected in *Works of Feng Xuefeng* (*Xuefeng wenji*) Vol III (Beijing: Renmin chubanshe, January 1983), pp 332-3.
14. *Materials on modern Chinese literary history* Vol I, pp 132-3.
15. Neale Hunter, 'The Chinese League of Left-wing Writers', p 211; Anthony Kane, 'The League of Left-wing Writers and Chinese literary policy', p 122.
16. Mao Dun, *The road I trod* Vol II, p 87.
17. *Materials on modern Chinese literary history* Vol I, pp 134-6.
18. *Ibid*, p 137.
19. *Ibid*, p 133.
20. *Qianfeng yuekan* Vol I No 1 (10 October 1930). A complete version of the manifesto can be found in *Anthology of materials for literary movement* Vol III, pp 78-85.
21. Others who participated in the movement included Li Zanhua, Fang Guangming, Sun Lianggong, Chen Baoyi, Ke Pengzhou, Yi Kang, Hua Xing, Yang Minwei, Gu Jianchen, Hu Zhongchi, Li Yizhi, Jin Mancheng, Zhong Xianmin, Miao Chongqun, Shen Congwen, Chen Mengjia, Fei Jianzhao, Li Qingya, Zhong Tianxin, Wei Congwu and Hong Weifa. See, Shinmura Tooru, '"Nationalist literature" and the Left League' (*Minzoku shugi bungaku to saren*), *Nokusha* No 14 and 15 (20 April 1970), pp 14-29.
22. Tao Xisheng, 'Trivial talks about the literature and art in the thirties', *On the literature and art of the thirties*, p 32.

23 'The manifesto of "nationalist literary movement"', *Anthology of materials for literary movement* Vol III, pp 81-4.
24 Lu Xun, 'The present situation of the literary circle in dark China' (*Heian Zhongguo de wenyijie de xianzhuang*), *Complete works of Lu Xun* Vol IV, p 287; Mao Dun, 'Revealing the true features of "nationalist literature"', *Wenxue daobao* Vol I No 4, *Materials on modern Chinese literary history* Vol I, p 75; Si Yang, 'Correspondences from Nanjing' (*Nanjing tongxun*), *ibid*, p 81.
25 'The significance and mission of the publication of this magazine' (*Benkan chuban de yiyi qi shiming*), *Wenxue douzheng* Vol I No 1, *Materials on the Left League period* Vol II, p 389.
26 'The manifesto of "nationalist literary movement"', *Anthology of materials for literary movement* Vol III, p 79.
27 Shi Tieer (Qu Qiubai), 'Butcher literature', *Wenxue daobao* Vol I No 3, *Materials on modern Chinese literary history* Vol I, p 63; Shi Beng (Qu Qiubai), '"Blood of the yellow race" and others', *ibid*, p 98.
28 Lu Xun, 'The role and fate of "nationalist literature"', *ibid*, pp 115-6.
29 '"Blood of the yellow race" and others', *ibid*, p 98.
30 'The new missions of the Chinese proletarian literature' (*Zhongguo wuchanjieji wenxue de xinrenwu*), *Wenxue daobao* Vol I No 8, *ibid*, p 134.
31 Lu Xun, 'The role and fate of "nationalist literature"', *ibid*, p 72.
32 Mao Dun, 'Revealing the true features of "nationalist literature"', *ibid*, p 72.
33 On 15 March *Mishuchu xiaoxi* appeared. In April there were *Wenyi xindi* (*New land in literature*) (20 April) and *Wenxue banyuekan* (*Literature biweekly*) (25 April) while *Wenxue yuebao* (*Literature monthly*) came out in June.
34 Lu Xun's diary, 30 January, 6 February and 13 March 1932, *Complete works of Lu Xun* Vol XV, pp 4 and 7.
35 Shen Duanxian, 'Two unforgettable impressions' (*Liangge buneng yiwang de yinxiang*), *Wenxue yuebao* Vol I No 2 (10 July 1932), *Materials on modern Chinese literary history* Vol I, pp 299-300.
36 Ding Ling, 'Editorial', *Beidou* Vol II No 2 (20 May 1932), *ibid* Vol IV, p 373.
37 *Fenghuo* No 2 (4 February 1932), in *Jinian yu yanjiu* No 2, pp 129-30.
38 Hu Qiuyuan, *Piecemeal collection of works written in my youth*, quoted from Wang Jianmin, *A draft history of the Chinese Communist Party* Vol II, p 933.
39 Hu Qiuyuan, 'About the 1932 debate on the freedom of literature and art', *Essays on literature and art* (*Wenxue yishu lunji*) (Taibei: Xueshu chubanshe, November 1979) Vol II, p 933.
40 *Wenxue* Vol I No 1, *Materials on modern Chinese literary history* Vol IV, pp 5-11.
41 Lou Shiyi, 'To forget, for solidarity: On reading comrade Xia Yan's "Some past events that should have long been forgotten but cannot be forgotten"'

Years of Achievement (II)

(*Weile wangque weile tuanji: Du Xia Yan tongzhi yixie zaogai wangque er weineng wangque de wangshi*), reprinted in *Lu Xun yanjiu niankan* (*Annual of Lu Xun study*) 1980, p 95.

42 *Collection of materials on the left-wing literature of the thirties*, p 70.
43 *Beidou* Vol II No 2, *Materials on modern Chinese literary history* Vol IV, pp 327-9.
44 'Editor's note', *Zhongguo xiandai wenyi ziliao congkan* No 5, p 15.
45 'Resolution on the work of the Left League at the present stage', *ibid*, pp 16-18.
46 'Resolution concerning the official organ on theories of the Left League *Wenxue*' (*Guanyu Zuolian lilun zhidao jiguan zazhi wenxue de jueyi*), *ibid*, pp 21-3.
47 'Resolution on the reorganisation of the Left League' and 'Guiding principles of the works of various committees', *ibid*, pp 19 and 21.
48 'Agreement on the competition of work with the Dramatist League and the Social Scientists League', *ibid*, pp 24-6.
49 'Letter from the Secretariat about the competition of work', *ibid*, pp 26-7.
50 *Ibid*, pp 27-9.
51 Tang Tao, *A history of modern Chinese literature* Vol II, p 37.
52 'Editor's preface' (*Bianzhexu*), Su Wen (ed), *Collection of articles from the debate on literary freedom* (*Wenyi ziyou lunbianji*) (Shanghai: Xiandai shudian, 25 March 1933), p I; Hu Qiuyuan, *Essays on literature and art* Vol II, p 932.
53 Lloyd E Eastman, *The abortive revolution: China under Nationalist rule, 1927-1937* (Cambridge: Harvard University Press, 1974), p 89.
54 *Ibid*. See Anthony J Kane, 'The League of Left-wing Writers', pp 162-3.
55 Wenhua Pinglun Association, 'A call to truth', *Wenhua pinglun* No 1 (25 December 1931), collected in Su Wen (ed), *Collection of articles from the debate on literary freedom*, p 302.
56 Wenyi Xinwen Association, 'Please take off the garb of the "May Fourth"' (*Qing tuoqi wusi de yishan*), *Wenyi xinwen* No 45 (18 January 1932), *ibid*, pp 305-7.
57 Hu Qiuyuan, 'On the literature of the dogs', *ibid*, pp 4-9.
58 *Zhongguo yu shijie* No 7 (22 January 1932), *ibid*, pp 14-16.
59 'On the question of cultural movement: A reply to the correspondents of *Wenyi xinwen* on the question of "May Fourth"' (*Wenhua yundong wenti: Guanyu wusi da wenyi xinwen jizhe*), *Wenhua pinglun* No 4 (20 April 1932), *ibid*, p 323.
60 'Who is working for the tiger?' (*Shishui weihu zuocheng?*), *ibid*, pp 20-1.
61 Hu Qiuyuan, 'Hands off art', *Wenhua pinglun* No 4, *ibid*, pp 10-11.
62 Hu Qiuyuan, 'A liquidation of the theories of Qian Xingcun and a criticism of the theories of nationalist literature' (*Qian Xingcun lilun zhi qingsuan yu minzu wenxue lilun zhi pipan*), *Dushu zazhi* Vol II No 1 (30 January 1932), *ibid*, p 54.

63 Luo Yang, 'A letter to *Wenyi xinwen*' (*Zhi wenyi xinwen de yifengxin*), *Wenyi xinwen* No 58 (6 June 1932), *ibid*, pp 57-8.
64 Su Wen, 'On the literary debate between "Wenxin" and Hu Qiuyuan' (*Guanyu wenxin yu Hu Qiuyuan de wenyi lunbian*), *Xiandai* Vol I No 3 (1 July 1932), *ibid*, p 66.
65 *Ibid*, p 73-5.
66 *Ibid*, p 73.
67 Su Wen, 'Report of a persecuted' (*Yige beibihai de jilu*), reprinted in *Lu Xun yanjiu dongtai* No 2, 1989 (20 February 1989), p 60.
68 *Collection of articles from the debate on literary freedom*, pp 79-99.
69 Zhou Yang, 'Who is actually rejecting the truth, rejecting literature', *Xiandai* Vol I No 6, *ibid*, pp 100-11; Su Wen, 'The outlet of the "men of the third category"' (*Disanzhongren de chulu*), *ibid*, p 133.
70 *Ibid*, p 111.
71 *Ibid*, p 121.
72 For example, see Tang Tao, *A history of modern Chinese literature* Vol II, pp 41-2.
73 Hu Qiuyuan, 'Hands off art', *Collection of articles from the debate on literary freedom*, p 10; 'A wasteful debate', *ibid*, p 108.
74 *Ibid*, p 235.
75 Su Wen, 'On the interference of literature' (*Lun wenxue shang de ganshe zhuyi*), *Xiandai* Vol II No 1 (1 November 1932), *ibid*, p 194.
76 Shi Zhecun, 'Random thoughts on *Xiandai*'(1), *Xinwenxue shiliao* No 1, 1981, p 216.
77 Feng Xuefeng, 'Not a wasteful debate' (*Bingfei langfei de lunzheng*), *Collection of articles from the debate on literary freedom*, p 244.
78 Chen Xuefan (pseud Chen Wangdao), 'Jottings on the duties of theoreticians' (*Guanyu lilunjia de renwu suxie*), *Xiandai* Vol II No 1 (1 November 1932), *ibid*, pp 256-60.
79 Lu Xun, 'On the "men of the third category"', *Complete works of Lu Xun* Vol IV, p 440.
80 *Ibid*, p 441.
81 *Ibid*, p 439.
82 Su Wen, *Collection of articles from the debate on literary freedom*, p iv.
83 *Collection of materials on the 'revolutionary literature' polemic*, pp 330-4. Hu believed that the article was able to help Lu Xun in the revolutionary literary debate. Hu Qiuyuan, 'Between Tangsanzang and Faust', (*Zai Tan Sanzang yu Fushida zhijian*), *Ziyoutan* (*Free Talk*) Vol VI No 9 (1 September 1955), p 21.
84 Cheng Zhongyuan, *Zhang Wentian and the modern literary movement* (*Zhang Wentian yu xinwenxue yundong*) (Jiangsu: Jiangsu wenyi chubanshe, August 1987), pp 312-30.
85 Ji Xueming, 'Ge Te, Ke De and others' (*Ge Te Ke De jiqita*), *Xinwenxue shiliao* No 2, 1983, p 239.

Years of Achievement (II)

86 Ge Te, 'The closed-doorism on the literary front', reprinted in *Xinwenxue shiliao* No 2, 1982, p 180.
87 'On the inclination and theories of the "third category" literature', *Collection of articles from the debate on literary freedom*, pp 272-80.
88 Su Wen, 'Record of a persecuted', p 24.
89 Hu Qiuyuan, 'About the 1932 debate on the freedom of literature and art', p 937.
90 Ibid, pp 939-40; Su Wen, 'A liquidation of the 1932 literary debate', *Collection of articles from the debate on literary freedom*, p 298.
91 During the purge of Feng Xuefeng in 1954 and 1957 this article was often mentioned for criticism. He was accused of wronging Qu Qiubai and Zhou Yang and making too many concessions to Hu Qiuyuan and Su Wen. Lin Mohan, 'Clear the road for a great leap forward in literature and art (*Wei wenxue yishu da yuejin saoqing daolu*), *Wenyibao* No 6, 1958 (26 March 1958), p 13; Huo Songlin, 'Criticise Feng Xuefeng's anti-Marxist literary thinking' (*Ping Feng Xuefeng fan Makesi zhuyi wenyi sixiang*), *Renmin wenxue* No 12, 1957 (8 December 1957), p 90; Liu Shousong, 'On the two literary polemics of the Left League period: A criticism on Feng Xuefeng's anti-Party activities and anti-Marxist literary thinking' (*Guanyu Zuolian shiqi de liangci wenyi lunzheng: Piping Feng Xuefeng de fandang huodong he fan Makesi zhuyi wenyi sixiang*), *Wenxue yanjiu* No 1, 1958 (12 March 1958), pp 25-31.
92 Shi Zhecun, 'Random thoughts on *Xiandai*'(1), p 215.
93 *Complete works of Lu Xun* Vol XII, p 176.
94 *Collection of articles from the debate on literary freedom*, p 299.
95 'The popularisation of literature and art', *Complete works of Lu Xun* Vol VII, p 349.
96 Zhou Yongxiang, *A chronicle of Qu Qiubai* (*Qu Qiubai nianbu*) (Guangdong: Guangdong renmin chubanshe, April 1983), pp 92-3; Mark E Shneider, *Tvorcheokii Put' Tsiui Tsiu-bo, 1899-1935* (*The creative path of Qu Qiubai, 1899-1935*) (Moscow: Izdatel'stvo Nauka, 1964), p 185, cited from Paul G Pickowicz, *Marxist literary thought in China: The influence of Ch'u Ch'iu-pai* (Berkeley: University of California Press, 1981), p 148.
97 *Wenxue daobao* Vol I No 5, *Materials on modern Chinese literary history* Vol I, pp 88-94.
98 *Ibid*, pp 87-8.
99 Mao Dun, *The road I trod* Vol II, p 86.
100 Paul G Pickowicz, *Marxist literary thought in China*, p 148.
101 Luo Yang, 'An examination of the "anti-Japanese popular literature" of the ruling class' (*Tongzhi jieji de fanri dazhong wenyi zhi jiancha*), *Wenxue daobao* Vol I No 6 and 7, *Materials on modern Chinese literary history* Vol I, pp 109-14.
102 *Ibid*; Shi Tieer, 'Mass literature and anti-imperialist struggle', *ibid*, pp 87-8.

103 Unless otherwise stated, the following discussion was based on Qu Qiubai, 'Questions of mass literature', *ibid* Vol I, pp 75-8.
104 Mao Dun, 'The mass literature and art in question', *Wenxue yuebao* Vol I No 2, *ibid*, pp 312-14.
105 *Ibid*, pp 315-17.
106 Song Yang (Qu Qiubai), 'In reply to Zhi Jing on the question of mass literature and art again' (*Zailun dazhong wenyi da Zhi Jing*), *Wenxue yuebao* Vol I No 3 (15 October 1932), *ibid*, pp 21-7.
107 Mao Dun, *The road I trod* Vol II, p 155.
108 'The practical question of proletarian mass literature', *Materials on modern Chinese literary history* Vol IV, pp 16 and 31; 'Questions of mass literature', *ibid* Vol II, p 27.
109 *Collection of materials on the left-wing literature of the thirties*, p 71.
110 *Beidou* Vol II No 3 and 4, *Materials on modern Chinese literary history* Vol IV, pp 465-79.
111 *Beidou* Vol II No 3 and 4, *ibid*, pp 439-41 and 448-61.
112 *Ibid*, p 424.
113 Shen Duanxian, 'A review of the month's creative writings', *Beidou* Vol II No 3 and 4, *ibid*, p 520.
114 Neale Hunter, 'The Chinese League of Left-wing Writers', pp 223-31.
115 Quoted from *Collection of materials on the left-wing literature of the thirties*, pp 77-8.
116 Bai Shu, 'The unforgettable past', *Recollections*, p 286.
117 *Collection of materials on the left-wing literature of the thirties*, p 81.
118 The Chinese League of Left-wing Writers, 'Letter of protest concerning the incident of comrade Kobayashi' (*Xiaolin tongzhi shijian kangyishu*), *China Forum* Vol II No 4 (February 1933), *Jinian yu yanjiu* No 2, p 137.
119 G T Shea, *Left-wing literature in Japan: A brief history of the proletarian literary movement*, p 307.
120 *Ibid*, p 327.
121 *Wenxue zazhi* No 2 (15 May 1933), *Jinian yu yanjiu* No 2, pp 137-8.
122 'The Chinese League of Left-wing Writers' declaration against the GMD white terror in the arrest of Ding and Pan', *ibid*, pp 139-42.
123 Zheng Yuzhi, 'Recalling some facts about the "Left League"', *Recollections*, pp 298-9.
124 'The welcome address to comrade Barbusse and various countries' delegates to the Shanghai Anti-war Session' (*Zhi Shanghai fanzhan huiyi geguo daibiao Babeisai tongzhi huanyingci*), *Fanzhan xinwen* (*Anti-war news*) No 1 (29 August 1933), in *Jinian yu yanjiu* No 3, pp 8-10.
125 'Notice from the Chinese writers to welcome the delegation of Barbusse' (*Zhongguo zhuzuozhe huanying Babeisai daibiaotuan qishi*), *Damei wanbao*, 16 August 1933, *ibid*, pp 7-8.

126 'Declaration from Lu Xun, Mao Dun and Tian Han to welcome the international delegates of Anti-war Session' (*Lu Xun Mao Dun Tian Han huanying fanzhan dahui guoji daibiao de xuanyan*), ibid, pp 10-12.
127 'Zhao Mingyi on Zhou Yang's joining of the Left League and the formation and activities of the Dramatists League' (*Zhao Mingyi tan Zhou Yang jiaru zuolian ji julian chengli huodong qingkuang*), *Reference materials*, p 156; Zhou Yang, 'Something about comrade Zhou Libo' (*Guanyu Zhou Libo tongzhi de yixie qingkuang*), in Li Huasheng, Hu Guangfan (ed), *Research materials on Zhou Libo* (*Zhou Libo yanjiu ziliao*) (Changsha: Hunan renmin chubanshe, August 1983), p 99.
128 *Wenxue yuebao* Vol I No 2, in *Materials on modern Chinese literary history* Vol I, p 253.
129 *Ibid*, pp 359-71.
130 *Wenxue yuebao* Vol I No 3, *ibid* Vol II, p 6.
131 Neale Hunter, 'The Chinese League of Left-wing Writers', p 232.
132 Ding Ling, 'Piecemeal thoughts', *Recollections*, p 164.
133 Shen Duanxian, 'A review of the month's creative writings', *Materials on modern Chinese literary history* Vol IV, p 520.
134 Yang Hansheng, 'The process of the formation of the Chinese League of Left-wing Writers', p 17.
135 Wu Xiru, 'Hu Feng as I know him' (*Wosuo renshi de Hu Feng*), *Luxun yanjiu ziliao* No 9, p 237.
136 Hu Feng, 'Recalling the time around the joining of the Left League' (*Huiyi canjia Zuolian qianhou*) (1), *Xinwenxue shiliao* No 1, 1984 (22 February 1984), p 30; Zhai Zhicheng, 'The antecedents of Hu Feng and the important members of the Hu Feng clique' (*Hu Feng yu He Feng jituan zhongyao chengyuan lilue*), *Articles on the study of Communist China's literary policy* (*Zhonggong wenyi zhengce yanjiu lunwenji*) (Taibei: Shibao wenhua chubanshe, 10 June 1983), p 117.
137 Hu Feng, 'Recalling the time around the joining of the Left League', pp 32-5.
138 Wu Xiru, 'Hu Feng as I know him', p 236.
139 Hu Feng, 'Recalling the relationship between the "Left League" and Lu Xun', p 177.
140 Wu Xiru, 'Hu Feng as I know him', p 237.
141 Hu Feng, 'Recalling the time around the joining of the Left League', p 35.

Chapter Six

The Waning Years - The Left League, 1934-1935

Reading the documents of the Left League, one can easily see the contrast between the years 1930-1933 and 1934-1935. During the early stage, the League was a most active body. There was a large number of articles, declarations, proclamations and resolutions commenting on political and cultural matters. Literary polemics were taken up and fought bravely, and in many cases, successfully. Great attention was paid to the popularisation of literature and art. Facing the strict censorship measures of the authorities, the League was still able to put out many journals and other publications to propagate their ideas, however short-lived these publications might have been. It was able, too, to organise and participate in such large scale activities as the All-China Soviet Congress and the Far East session of the Committee of World Anti-imperialist Wars. Solidarity of the leftists was for a time realised.

Even Zhou Yang, however, who was in charge of the League at that period, could boast of nothing for the years 1934-35.[1] There was no pen-battle against opposing forces, and the only polemic fought during this period was that of 1936, the Two slogan polemic, which bitterly divided the leftist camp. The number of journals published by the League at this stage was insignificant when compared with that of the first stage.[2] It is true that the Nationalists were then more experienced and capable of clamping down on the Communist movement but on the other hand, the left-wingers showed no improvement in dealing with suppression. There was no large-scale demonstration or protest campaign. Although there were people in charge of the secretariat and various committees, it seems that the activities of the League were limited to small group meetings.

Worse still, during the last few years of its existence, the League was greatly troubled by internal strife among its members and in the end, it was dissolved in a most unhappy way. The subsequent Two slogan polemic further split the leftist camp. Around Lu Xun, there was a group of young writers, such as Hu Feng, Nie Gannu, Zhou Wen, Wu Xiru, plus his old friends Mao Dun and Feng Xuefeng. The Zhou Yang group consisted mainly of CCP members, including the famous 'four fellows' (*Sitiao hanzi*, Zhou Yang, Xia Yan, Yang Hansheng and Tian Han),[3] Wang Renshu and Xu Maoyong. The united front in the cultural field that had been built up with great care was badly damaged.

In the first instance, we should point out that the unity of the left rested on an unstable and fragile base. League leaders were conscious of this shortcoming. Readers of League publications will certainly be startled by the number of reminders and exhortations to self-criticism sent by the League to its members. Almost all its resolutions contained a review of mistakes made and urged improvement. This, on the one hand, may be evidence of the eagerness of its leadership to perfect the organisation. On the other, it revealed that there were actually flaws within the League.

Lu Xun's position in the League was peculiar. There is little doubt that he was the key figure. Feng Xuefeng once remarked: 'So long as Lu Xun lived, the League would not die. So long as he stood, the League would not collapse.'[4] Since the establishment of the organisation, Lu Xun was given great respect and prominence. Xia Yan reported that there were suggestions to call him the chairman of the League but he declined. Lu Xun's approval had to be sought before the theoretical programme and other documents were submitted to the inaugural meeting.[5] The League organised a birthday party for him. Moreover, because of his age, health and status, he was exempted from most League activities. Ding Ling recalled that unless it was essential, they would not ask him to attend meetings.[6] Throughout the six years of the League's existence, Lu Xun turned up at only a couple of meetings.[7] He never joined any demonstration staged against the authorities. As these meetings and demonstrations constituted a large part of the League's activities, it was easy for Lu Xun to be isolated from the main body of the League. As a result, his leadership was, to a large extent, nominal. It would be more appropriate to say that he acted only as an advisor rather than directing the whole scene. However, being a most famous writer and the 'mentor of the youth', he was able to draw around him a large group of League members.

There was another leadership within the League, the CCP representatives. In name, the leading body of the League was the secretariat along with the executive and standing committees but the Party group of the League and the Cultural Committee of the CCP were in actual fact taking charge of all important matters. Even members of the secretariat and the committees were nominated or appointed by them. As they represented the Party line and a large proportion of League members had joined the Party - even non-Party members would willingly obey Party instructions - it was natural for them to build up another leadership within the League.

It is almost impossible to avoid disputes when there are two centres of gravity within one organisation. In the case of the Left League, harmony between the two depended largely on the membership and attitude of the Party group. Within the first three years, there was little problem because the most influential character of the Party group was Feng Xuefeng, who always stood on the side of Lu Xun. Likewise, he never failed to win Lu Xun's confidence and approval. Furthermore, from the beginning of 1929, he lived quite near to Lu. He could easily report to and seek advice from the old man. Xu Guangping said that Feng came to see Lu Xun almost every evening.[8] Under these circumstances, there was no estrangement between the Party group and Lu Xun. With the joint effort of the two leaderships, the League reaped a good harvest.

Moreover, in the years 1932-33, Lu Xun enjoyed the friendship of Qu Qiubai, then, as has been shown, a respected figure on the left, particularly among the Party members. In the early summer of 1932, Qu paid a visit to Lu

Xun and this was the first time they met, although they had been cooperating in the translation of Soviet works for some time.[9] Within the brief period between this meeting and Qu's departure from Shanghai, the two developed a close personal friendship. At least twice, Qu took refuge in Lu Xun's home.[10] This was solid proof of their friendship and faith, as both would be in great danger should anything go wrong. In March 1933, Lu Xun wrote Qu a couplet:

It is good enough to have just one bosom friend in life;
For my life, I'll take you as one after my heart.

Early in 1933, Qu Qiubai compiled an anthology of Lu Xun's essays, which was published in July. In the preface, Qu, using the language of dialectics, set a high value on Lu Xun. By criticising those who had attacked him and defending his deeds, Qu Qiubai was able to, as one critic suggested, 'elevate the intellectual status of Lu Xun in the revolutionary literary circle'.[11] Xu Guangping reported that Lu Xun was very happy after reading the preface.[12]

They also collaborated in writing critical essays on social problems, discussing and exchanging ideas before starting to write.[13] Often, Lu Xun had Xu Guangping copy Qu's articles and published them under his own pen-names, even including them in his collections. Xu Guangping said, 'they were as intimate as close relatives. There was no need for ceremony between them.'[14] With Qu leading the left-wing literary movement, a closer link could be built up between Lu Xun and the left.

However, Feng Xuefeng and Qu Qiubai left Shanghai for Ruijin in December 1933 and January 1934 respectively. It seems strange that these two men who were close to Lu Xun were transferred at about the same time. Some critics suggested that this might be related to the splits in the CCP and that the internationalists were dissatisfied with Qu Qiubai. In other words, Qu Qiubai was cashiered and transferred.[15] Such speculation is hard to square with the facts. According to Feng Xuefeng, the decision to transfer Qu was made near the end of 1933, when Feng Xuefeng had already been in Ruijin for some time so there was no direct link between Feng's transfer and that of Qu. At a meeting between several leading members of the CCP, Zhang Wentian, then head of the Party school, said that he would like to enlist Qu Qiubai's assistance and therefore transferred him from Shanghai to take charge of educational matters in Ruijin.[16] Though Zhang was a member of the internationalists (he was certainly the most liberal one), the fact that Qu took up important posts in the Party even before his arrival at Ruijin (on 3 February 1934 Qu was elected one of the seventeen members of the Board of Chairmen of the Central Government, together with such internationalists as Zhang Wentian and Bo Gu and he was also appointed head of the Educational Committee),[17] further proves that his transfer had nothing to do with the previous struggles between the internationalists and Qu.

An indirect consequence of the transfers was that it dealt a fatal blow to the League as well as the relations between Lu Xun and Zhou Yang. Lu Xun lost two of his best friends. For the League, the bridge between the two leaderships was shattered because, as T A Hsia suggested, 'not a single Communist agent left in Shanghai was able to, or cared to, maintain good relations with Lu Xun'.[18]

It is well known that Hu Feng soon became the coordinator between the League and Lu Xun. Hu was then not a CCP member and insisted once again that there was no formal instruction from Zhou Yang.[19] Hu believed that he was relatively independent of Zhou Yang.

Since 1936, especially after the purge of Hu Feng in 1955, and until very recently, it has been a popular saying that it was Hu Feng who drove a wedge between the two leaders of the League, Lu Xun and Zhou Yang. Even Mao Dun, in his later years, could not help cursing Hu.[20] The most common charge against him was his failure to act as an honest reporter and a good coordinator. When he reported to Lu Xun on League affairs, he frequently added his own opinions, which were often different from those of Zhou Yang.[21] In other words, Hu Feng deliberately made mischief between Lu Xun and Zhou Yang, and was thus the sole villain.

Certainly there were ample opportunities for Hu to do this as he was then close to Lu. However, before we can put all the blame on him, two questions should be answered. One, when did Lu Xun first feel discontented with the League? Two, what was the basis of his discontent?

As stated earlier, the base of the Left League was not solid from the start. The formation of such a united front was imposed upon its members, save for Lu Xun and a few exceptions, by the CCP. The abrupt end of the 1928 revolutionary literature polemic solved no theoretical problem and convinced nobody, so there had always been dissension among League members. Lu Xun was all along conscious of the League's weaknesses, and in his writing, showed that he did not have a high opinion of those with no clear understanding of the nature of the League when they joined. In a letter written in December 1934, he said:

> In fact, the base of the Left League, from its beginning, was not solid. It was because at that time, there was not any repression like today. Some thought that they could be labelled as 'progressive' once they had joined the League, and the danger was small. But then repression came. They fled. This was not the worst of it. Some even sold themselves as informers.[22]

Even after the formation of the united front in the literary circle, Lu Xun could not forget the attacks made on him by the Creationists. In July 1931, Lu Xun attacked the latter in his famous speech 'A glimpse at the literary scene of Shanghai'. He described the Creation Society as a group of 'wits and vagabonds'. To him, the revolutionary literary movement led by members of the society was not well-planned. Many of the revolutionary writers were ultra-leftist and in fact, opportunist, stepping at the same time on the two boats of revolution and literature.[23]

One can imagine, these words would offend the Creationists within the Left League, although they might not be able to, and indeed they did not, voice their discontent openly at that time. But Guo Moruo, then in Japan, could not help writing a vigorous response. The tone in the preface to his *Ten years of the Creation Society* was indignant. He did not hesitate to quote Lu Xun's lines for rebuttal.[24] Thus Hu Feng's recollection that in 1932 Lu Xun was opposed to the group of Creationists within the League was not without foundation. It may be surmised that Hu had heard something unpleasant about Lu Xun from the radicals.

Hu Feng also alleged that in 1932, Zhou Yang and Feng Xuefeng had already had trouble over the question of the 'third category men'.[25] It has been noted, in the previous chapter, that during the course of the debate, Feng Xuefeng changed his attitude and the viewpoints in 'The inclination and theories of the literature of the third category' accorded with those of Lu Xun. Zhou Yang was criticised for his dogmatic manner. Obviously, the two could not agree on the attitude to be taken in the debate. Lu Xun sided with Feng. This is probably one factor, though not a vital one, in causing the dissension between Zhou and Lu.

In fact, there was an open quarrel between Zhou Yang and Feng Xuefeng, which was brought to Lu Xun. It was related to a long poem 'Testimony of a traitor' (*Hanjian de gongzhuang*) by a certain Yun Sheng published in *Wenxue yuebao*. This poem was a satire on Hu Qiuyuan who was then disputing with the left on the question of the 'free men'.[26] Feng Xuefeng believed that the dogmatic and ultra-leftist attitude shown in the poem was against the Communist Party policy of eliminating closed-doorism and so, because he was then secretary of the Cultural Committee, he went to see Zhou Yang, the editor of *Wenxue yuebao*. He requested the latter to make redress in the following issue. Zhou refused and there was a quarrel between the two. Feng was able to secure the support of both Qu Qiubai and Lu Xun. Lu Xun agreed to write an article denouncing the poem.[27] On 10 December 1932, he finished an open letter to Zhou Yang, entitled 'Abuse and threats are not fighting' (*Ruma he kongxia juebushi zhandou*).

At the very beginning of the letter, Lu Xun expressed his disappointment over the magazine, *Wenxue yuebao*. In terms of the content, the fourth issue, edited by Zhou Yang, was not as rich as the previous ones, edited by Yao Pengzi, but what really disappointed him bitterly and made him write the letter was the poem 'Testimony of a traitor'. Lu Xun pointed out that there were insults, abuses, threats and senseless attacks in it. He considered this feudalistic, crude, rash and fighting in the style of Ah Q. This tactic was commonly employed by men of letters in the past, Lu Xun said. But he added, 'this heritage has better passed to the lap dog writers. If our writers do not do their best to cast it off, they will become no better than those writers.'[28]

Yun Sheng is now identified as Qiu Jiuru, a Party member.[29] There seems to be no personal connection between Qiu and Zhou Yang; but the appearance of his poem in Zhou's magazine and the latter's refusal to denounce it revealed

that Zhou supported Yun Sheng. Thus it is fair to say that Lu Xun's letter was directed against Zhou as much as against Qiu. Its last paragraph reads:
> The above ideas came to my mind just now. I write them out and send to you for consideration in editing. In a word, I really hope that from now on, *Wenxue yuebao* will not publish that kind of work any more.[30]

These words might have been a blow to the newly risen Zhou Yang and it might not have been easy for him to swallow his pride but he published the letter almost immediately in his magazine and in the note he added at the end of the letter, expressed his agreement with Lu Xun's ideas. He even said that the letter was 'a noble piece of advice which should be taken into consideration deeply'.[31] While this shows that Lu Xun's position within the League was still high, the fact that the matter could not be settled internally was significant. It is likely that there was a sharp division of opinion within the League.

Unfortunately, this was not the end of the story. Three months after the appearance of Lu Xun's open letter, an article was published in *Xiandai wenhua* (*Modern culture*) called 'Some words on Mr Lu Xun's "threats and abuse are not fighting"' (*Dui Lu Xun xiansheng de kongha ruma juebushi zhandou youyan*).[32] The article carried four signatures, Shou Jia, Fang Meng, Guo Bingruo and Qiu Dongping. It is not certain that there were really four writers because, apart from Qiu Dongping which was a real name, only one other name can be identified: Shou Jia was the pseudonym of Zhu Xiuxia. Once a member of the Sun Society, Zhu was the editor of *Xiandai wenhua*, and also very active in League affairs.[33] In this article, Lu Xun's open letter was condemned. The four writers argued that since Yun Sheng's poem was directed against people of other classes, there was nothing wrong in hurling insults. To them, threats and insults were also means of struggle. In return they accused Lu Xun of wearing a strong colour of right opportunism, 'pacifism in cultural movements and revolutionary theory in white gloves'.[34]

This was a serious charge and represented a challenge to Lu Xun's position. Moreover his advice, given with goodwill, was not only neglected, but rebuked. His feelings are easy to imagine. Two years later, in a letter to Xiao Jun, he wrote:
> It is most difficult to write for that magazine [*Wenxue yuebao*]. I once followed instruction and made some contributions. But people of the same camp published an open letter in real and fictitious names to condemn me. They even made up a name of Guo Bingruo, leading people to suspect that it was a misprint of Guo Moruo. I called to account. But there was no clear answer. I was frightened, as if I were seeing a ghost![35]

These words, apart from showing Lu Xun's feelings, revealed yet another fact. Although he made no open reply, he tried to sort it out privately. The fact that he could not get a definite answer was significant. It was probable that the four authors received some sort of protection within the League, although there is no proof to support the prevailing notion during the Cultural Revolution that Zhou Yang was acting behind the scenes.

Lu Xun was pacified, at least to a certain extent, by Qu Qiubai who wrote two articles criticising Shou Jia and his group. In the first, 'Mother of the philanthropist' (*Cishanjia de mama*), Qu used the analogy of a hero who went to slaughter a hypocritical philanthropist and yet could not convince others of the evil deeds of the philanthropist, to illustrate the pointlessness of using empty words, no matter how vulgar they might be, as a means to struggle. It was important to lay out facts in order to unmask the hypocrisy of the reactionaries.[36]

In his second article, 'Defence of the grimace' (*Guilian de bianhu*), Qu made direct reference to Shou Jia and his group, pointing out that in the fight against enemies, apart from gaining victory in the bloody revolution, it was necessary to convince others of our superiority in theory. The use of threats would only reveal weaknesses on the ideological front. Worse still, the deeds of Yun Sheng and Shou Jia would help the enemies in portraying the proletarians as devils. This was in effect aiding the ruling class in their exploitation of the masses. Qu's verdict was, 'there was no stain of right opportunism in Lu Xun while the viewpoints of Shou Jia and others who wore the devils' masks were "left" opportunistic'.[37] Qu also said that Lu Xun's open letter was noteworthy because it was able to promote the revolutionary struggle in the cultural field.

As noted earlier, Qu Qiubai enjoyed a high position among the Communists. The support lent to Lu Xun silenced the opponents. Zhou Yang and his group said nothing more on the issue. As for Lu Xun, he was certainly happy with Qu's support, for he kept the manuscripts of the two articles; but he was never totally pacified. In April 1933, he brought up the issue again and told Zhu Xiuxia in another open letter that 'it was of a new "eight-legged" (*bagu*) nature' to use only threats and insults.[38]

During the Cultural Revolution, when it was Zhou Yang's turn to be purged, material relating to his relationship with Lu Xun was made public in order to denounce his literary sinister line. It was often said, mainly in annotations to Lu Xun's works, that Zhou Yang and his group launched a series of attacks on Lu Xun while in many places, Lu Xun voiced his anger to his friends. For instance, it has been suggested that in June 1934, Zhou Yang used the pen-name Zhi Yin to publish articles attacking Lu Xun and complained in a letter to Zheng Zhenduo.[39] But as with many of the other charges, its authenticity is questionable as no proof was provided and even Lu Xun himself made no direct reference to the matter. However, in a letter to Xiao Jun, Lu Xun did complain that there were two more incidents similar to the *Wenxue yuebao* quarrel.[40]

On 3 July 1934, an article called 'On "fringe literature"' (*Lun huabian wenxue*) appeared in the supplement of *Dawanbao* (*Evening post*), *Huoju* (*Torch*). Its author was Lin Mo, who has been identified as Liao Mosha, a close follower of Zhou Yang. In the article, he criticised harshly an article called 'Carrying upside down' (*Daoti*), which was published in *Ziyoutan* (*Free talk*), supplement of *Shenbao*. 'Carrying upside down' discussed a new regulation of the international concession areas of Shanghai forbidding people to carry ducks and chickens upside down. The regulation was seen by some as an insult to the Chinese who did not receive such good treatment from the Westerners. But the author of the article, Gong Han, argued that those holding such ideas had wronged the Westerners. He pointed out the difference between poultry and human beings; that the latter possessed the power to resist oppression and liberate themselves. The central theme of the essay was that we should not hope for graces from others but should struggle for our own interests.[41]

Lin Mo, in 'On "fringe literature"', interpreted Gong Han's article differently. To him, Gong Han was saying that the Chinese had already had favoured treatment from the Westerners so there was no need to struggle or ask for more favours. On the other hand, the Westerners, since ill-treatment represented respect, should go on ill-treating the Chinese. Lin Mo's judgment was that 'Carry upside down' was written by a comprador who, in the first place, always boasted that he had a deep understanding of Westerners, and in the second place, advocated that the Westerners could rule over and ill-treat the Chinese, and thirdly, opposed the idea that the Chinese should hate Westerners.[42]

Unfortunately, Gong Han was a pen-name of Lu Xun, whose anger at being called a comprador may be imagined. He soon found out that 'On "fringe literature"' was written by a 'friend'. Once again, he made some people look into the matter. The reply he got was that Lin Mo was said to have already written to him giving an explanation. Yet in a letter written more than six months later, Lu Xun still said that he had received no such explanation.[43]

Lu Xun was indignant. In the preface to the collection of his essays written from January to November 1934, called *Fringe literature* (*Huabian wenxue*), obviously a deliberate retaliation, he said:

> The title came from a young comrade-in-arms of my own camp, who changed his name and shot an arrow at me from behind.[44]

This was what Lu Xun considered most unbearable. He thought this much worse than the assaults of the enemies. In private correspondence, he made this point very clear. On 6 December 1934, he wrote to Xiao Jun and Xiao Hong:

> The enemy is not to be feared. The real threat is the vermin in our own camp. They have often brought defeat to us.[45]

Twelve days later, in a letter to Yang Jiyun, the compiler of Lu Xun's *Uncollected works* (*Jiwaiji*), Lu Xun said:

> The lapdogs are not to be feared. The real threat is from the so-called 'comrades-in-arms' who say one thing and mean another. It is very hard to guard against them.... To protect the rear side, I have to stand slantwise and thus cannot face the enemies direct. It takes much more energy to watch simultaneously forward and backward... Sometimes I feel very angry; the energy spent on them could be better used for better results.[46]

In Lu Xun's eyes, Lin Mo was one of these vermin. During the Cultural Revolution, Lin's attack on Lu Xun constituted one of his crimes, apart from his 'anti-Party, anti-people' ideas expounded in the *Notes of the Sanjiacun* (*Sanjiacun zaji*).

After the fall of the 'Gang of Four', Liao Mosha, in 1982, published an article called 'The two pieces of *zawen* I wrote in the thirties' (*Wozai sanshi niandai xiede liangpian zawen*). One of these two *zawen* was 'On "fringe literature"'. Though he expressed his regret for hurting Lu Xun, he defended himself by saying that he had no knowledge of the identity of Gong Han when he wrote the article. According to Liao, the reason for his writing the article was that he was angry over the change of editorship of *Ziyoutan*, which originally under Li Liewen had been progressive and published a lot of works by the left. The opportunity to find fault with the supplement came with 'Carrying upside down'. He admitted that he could not get the deeper meaning between the lines and hence 'On "fringe literature"' was published in *Dawanbao*, after it had been rejected by *Ziyoutan*. He put the blame on the suppression of that time which made communication between comrades in the same camp difficult.

Liao also denied having been approached and promising to write to Lu Xun explaining the matter. His subsequent silence was because he was assigned a secret mission shortly afterwards and was not allowed to contact anybody. Then in the winter of that year, he was arrested. Not until 1937-38 after his release was he able to learn from reading *Complete works of Lu Xun* that 'Carrying upside down' was written by Lu Xun.[47]

This explanation is not unconvincing. In the first place, Gong Han was a new pen-name of Lu Xun, first employed on 25 May 1934, just one month before he wrote 'Carrying upside down'.[48] Secondly, there was indeed a rumour that Li Liewen was replaced because of GMD pressure. Thirdly, it might not have been easy to read between the lines as Lu Xun deliberately wrote obscurely. However, it seems that Liao had a particular dislike of Gong Han. In 'On "fringe literature"', he twice used the term 'random thoughts' (*ougan*), in quotations. 'Random thoughts' happened to be the first article written by Lu Xun in the name of Gong Han.[49] Moreover, Liao Mosha knew that Gong Han might have been someone of importance. In the postscript of 'On "fringe literature"', he revealed that his article had been rejected several times.[50] In his recollections, he told us that he was informed by the editor of *Ziyoutan* that 'Carrying upside down' was written by someone senior and it was not good to criticise.[51]

Even if we accept that this 'fringe literature' incident was a most unfortunate affair, as suggested by Liao Mosha, it had one great effect. It further alienated Lu Xun. As Liao gave Lu Xun no explanation at that time, Lu was unable to judge the nature of the incident and could only come to the conclusion that it was a deliberate attack. He was offended. He voiced this to several of his confidants.[52] Added to this was Tian Han's 'stab in the back', which in any case could not be viewed as an unfortunate error but as a direct assault on Lu Xun.

The Waning Years

The story started with a private letter from Lu Xun to Cao Juren, which discussed the issue of mass literature and was published in full in a special issue on mass literature in *Shehui yuebao* (*Social monthly*).[53] In the same publication, there was an article by Yang Cunren called 'Return from the Red areas' (*Chiqu guilaiji*). Yang was a runaway from the leftist camp and a self-styled 'man of the third category'. Lu's contempt for him would not have been less, even if Yang had not defected. As early as 1930, Yang had criticised Lu Xun for holding a banquet for his son's first birthday with the money from the GMD *Daxueyuan*. In June 1933, after his defection, Yang again attacked Lu Xun in an article called 'The new unofficial history of the literati' (*Xin rulin waishi*). On the other hand, Lu Xun showed his detestation of Yang clearly in his 'An open letter in reply to Mr Yang Cunren's open letter' (*Da Yang Cunren xiansheng gongkaixin de gongkaixin*), saying that Yang might be one of the targets of 'pshaw'.[54]

However, Tian Han viewed the phenomenon in *Shehui yuebao* as an act of reconciliation between the two. Under the pseudonym Shao Bo, he published an article called 'Reconciliation' (*Tiaohe*), again, in *Huoju*. Although he appeared to be criticising the reconciliatory nature of the Chinese, he quoted the case of Lu Xun and Yang Cunren as examples and this, as one critic pointed out, was the real sting of the article.[55] He suggested, as Lu Xun's article was at the beginning while Yang's was at the back, the former was in fact opening the way for the latter. He even hinted that Lu Xun had given up his principles.[56]

Lu Xun could no longer put up with these challenges and accusations. Instead of sorting out the matter privately, this time he protested openly in a letter to the editors of *Xi* (*Drama*) weekly:

> I must make it clear that I do not have the power to forbid people from publishing my private letters, nor can I know beforehand in whose company my letters will appear. When two contributions are published together in one magazine, there is no question of reconciliation or irreconciliation with any writer at all.[57]

In a private correspondence, Lu Xun reported that Tian Han at first denied that he had written the article but later admitted it. His excuse was that he purposely wronged Lu Xun to make him angry and attack Yang Cunren. He even said that he was surprised to learn that Lu Xun would criticise him instead.[58] Such an excuse could by no means satisfy Lu. In the open letter to the editors of *Xi*, he expressed his feelings over the incident:

> My hatred and contempt for someone of my own camp, who, in disguise, stabs me in the back, is much greater than for an overt enemy.[59]

A year later, when he edited a new collection of his *zawen*, he annexed the entire text of 'Reconciliation' in the appendix. He also explained why his protest was made in *Xi* weekly - Tian Han was one of the editors.[60]

Lu Xun tried very hard to hide his wounds. In a letter to Xiao Jun and Xiao Hong on 23 April 1935, he said:

Whenever I was wounded, I would hide myself in the depth of the forest, lick the blood dry, and dress it with my own hands. No one was ever to know. I think such a situation is terrible.[61]

In a letter to Hu Feng, he spoke of similar things:

I dare not speak to the outsiders about ourselves. With the foreigners, I simply avoid the subject. If I cannot, I lie. You see what a predicament I am in.[62]

It has been mentioned earlier that Lu Xun's joining and lending support to the Left League was to him a means of realising his ideals. Thus he was always active in his fight against such opponents of the Left League as the Crescentists, the Nationalists and the authorities. In these cases, 'his personal enemy was also the enemy of the revolution'.[63] Successes in those battles represented not only a personal triumph, but contributions to the political cause. However, it would be painful to strike back at those 'comrades-in-arms' supposedly fighting for the same ideal. Any open conflict or dispute would harm the organisation's solidarity, as well as the entire political and cultural movement. Further, it would not be easy for Lu Xun to justify himself in criticising his comrades before the public who did not know the details of these incidents. This was why he had to keep all the discontent to himself, or at most, to a few confidants, until he could tolerate them no more. Tian Han's behaviour was the last straw. It must have been after long consideration that Lu Xun decided to make public the whole affair. There is no doubt too that it was a painful decision.

What happened after these two incidents? Presumably Tian Han and his group were not much disturbed. In one place, Lu Xun reported that Tian claimed that he was surprised to see Lu Xun criticise him so angrily.[64] In another, he said that he had heard that another 'comrade-in-arms, Shen' (Duanxian, ie, Xia Yan), roared with laughter upon reading Lu Xun's rebuttal in the 'Letter to the editors of *Xi* weekly'.[65] As for Lu Xun, the impact was great. According to Ren Baige, in the autumn of 1934, Lu Xun told Tian Han that he would decline any work of the Left League,[66] probably because of Tian Han's attack in August 1934. In this case, Hu Feng should not hold the responsibility. Nowhere in Lu Xun's writings can we find Hu Feng's name associated with this matter. Moreover, in both 'fringe literature' and 'Shao Bo' incidents, it was Zhou Yang's men who took the offensive. In other words, with or without Hu Feng's presence, there would still be such conflicts.

Then what was done by Hu Feng to 'drive a wedge' between Lu Xun and Zhou Yang? No concrete proof has been supplied by Hu's enemies, even during his purge in 1957. There were certainly many opportunities for Hu to do so, however, as he was first the 'official' middleman between Lu Xun and the League, and later, a close acquaintance of Lu. From the six letters written by Lu Xun to Hu Feng that are available today, we can tell that Hu did make complaints before Lu Xun. In a letter written on 17 May 1935, Lu mentioned that Xiao San, representative of the League in Moscow, had asked for letters. Lu Xun added, 'obviously, the 'correct' letters have not yet been sent.'[67]

The Waning Years

According to the annotation made by Hu Feng, Xiao San wanted the League's progress reports for the International Union of Revolutionary Writers. Hu Feng claimed that he had sent in such reports while acting as secretary of the Left League but they were dismissed by Zhou Yang as 'incorrect'.[68] Lu Xun's comment showed that he had a complete knowledge of the matter. Doubtless, Hu provided such information. It was natural that he should add his discontent.

A similar example can be found in another letter dated 28 June 1935 in which Lu Xun criticised Han Shiheng, once a League member, for his 'breaking others' rice bowls' (making people lose their jobs).[69] Once again, this was related to Hu Feng. He was the one who had broken the rice bowl because Han disclosed his association with the left before his seniors in the Sun Yat-sen Cultural and Educational Academy, a GMD organisation headed by the son of Dr Sun Yat-sen, Sun Ke.[70] Although this had nothing to do with Zhou Yang and his group, it can be taken as evidence that Hu often complained to Lu Xun.

Moreover, in his recollections, Hu Feng often praised highly his own achievements during his term as secretary. He claimed that because of his efforts, three associations - the associations for the Study of Theories, Poetry and Fiction - were set up and activities were carried out. A publication for internal circulation, *Wenxue shenghuo* (*Literary life*) was edited and published by him, and since it reported on the activities of the Left League, it was able, Hu said, to maintain the organisational relationships among League members.[71] What is more, Hu often made comparisons between the achievements of the League during and after his secretaryship. The sending of progress reports to Moscow noted above is an example. He stressed over and over again that Lu Xun used to contribute $20 a month while he was with the League and that Lu stopped such contributions once he resigned.[72] He also asserted that after he had left the League, no further contact was made between Lu Xun and the organisation. It is logical to suspect that he had made similar comparisons before Lu Xun thus worsening Lu's impression of the League and Zhou Yang's group. However, although this might be a mistake on Hu's part, it cannot be taken as evidence to support the accusation that Hu should be held mainly responsible for the split within the League. We should first look into the relationships between Hu Feng and other people before and during this period.

As early as January 1926, Hu Feng had written to Lu Xun commenting on, and pointing out the mistakes in a piece of Lu Xun's translation. The wording was by no means complimentary. Obviously Lu Xun was not too happy about this and made no reply. Then during his brief stay in Shanghai at the end of 1932, Hu Feng came to know many prominent left-wingers but was unable to meet Lu Xun. He was impressed by both Feng Xuefeng and Zhou Yang, although they complained against each other over the question of the 'third category men'. Hu claimed that in terms of political principles, he supported Feng, but his views on literature were similar to Zhou Yang's.[73] His article 'Whitewash, distortion and ironclad fact' (*Fenshi waiqu tieyibande shishi*) was written in support of Zhou Yang's criticism of the 'third category men'.[74]

However, he was still invited by Feng Xuefeng to hold important posts in the League. It appeared that both men were eager to enlist his support.

After he was deported from Japan, Hu was again approached by Zhou Yang, who soon put him in charge of the League's propaganda section. About two to three months later, with Mao Dun's resignation, Hu was appointed secretary of the League, again, by Zhou Yang. Further, it was Zhou who brought Lu Xun to Hu's residence a few days after Hu's return from Japan.[75] Beyond doubt, the two were on good terms at that time.

It seems impossible that Hu Feng would or could have done anything to sow discord between Lu Xun and Zhou Yang at that time. He was then closer to Zhou Yang than to Lu Xun. However Yun Sheng's poem, Lu Xun's open letter as well as Shou Jia's rebukes appeared before Hu's return from Japan. As noted earlier, this represented the first open clash between Zhou Yang and Lu Xun, and obviously it had nothing to do with Hu Feng. Moreover, during his first visit to Shanghai, Hu Feng was introduced to Qiu Dongping, one of the four authors of the letter criticising Lu Xun. Qiu was able to win Hu's respect with a piece of creative writing and they soon became intimate friends.[76]

Then in 1934, Lu Xun and Hu Feng were drawn together. In February, a meeting between the two was recorded in Lu Xun's diary.[77] According to Lu Xun's diary, most of the contact between them was by letter. But Hu Feng said that he met Lu Xun at least once a month to give him the League journal *Wenxue shenghuo* and collect the $20 contribution.[78] Then on 25 October, Lu wrote in his diary that a looking glass was given as a gift to Hu Feng's wife.[79] In December, Lu Xun went in person to make reservations for a banquet to celebrate the first moon of Hu Feng's son.[80] These two entries have often been taken as proof that the two became close friends in late 1934. This dating further confirms the argument above that neither the 'fringe literature' incident nor the assaults from Tian Han should be blamed on Hu Feng.

As for the relationship between Zhou Yang and Hu Feng, it is not known when the clash first began. As seen earlier, Zhou immediately took Hu Feng under his wing upon the latter's return from Japan. But Ren Baige recalled that from the beginning of 1934, in meetings of the Secretariat of the League, Hu Feng frequently expressed views and ideas different from those of Zhou Yang. Ren also accused Hu of adding his own ideas in his reports to Lu Xun.[81] This should be viewed with caution of course as Ren was all along a close follower of Zhou Yang. It was natural for him to put the blame on Zhou's opponents. Moreover, one wonders how he could know what was reported by Hu Feng to Lu Xun. What can be gathered from Ren's recollection is that the relationship between Zhou Yang and Hu Feng started to deteriorate at the beginning of 1934. Therefore, the suggestion that the cause of the feud between the two was their debate on the question of typical characters in literature is incorrect,[82] because the first essay written by Hu Feng on the topic was 'What is "typical" and "stereotyped"' (*Shenme shi dianxing he leixing*), which was finished on 26 March 1935, while Zhou Yang's rebuke appeared in January 1936 in his 'A preliminary discussion on realism' (*Xianshizhuyi shilun*), and subsequent exchanges took place in the first half of 1936. Rather, it was Hu Feng's character that made him so unpopular among the leftists. Guo Moruo said that he was 'rather intransigently ambitious' *(baqi)*[83] while Lu Xun admitted that Hu had his shortcomings, 'being hypersensitive, petty-minded, taking a pedantic approach to theory and refusing to write in a popular style'.[84] It would appear that Hu Feng was basically an idealist.[85] This accounted for his independence of thought. Ren Baige's accusation that Hu often expressed different ideas, and Hu's debate with Zhou Yang are results of this independence. It was also for this reason that Hu Feng submitted his famous 'Hu Feng's opinions on literature and art' (*Hu Feng dui wenyi wenti de yijian*) to Mao Zedong in July 1954.

Before long, Hu Feng's unpopularity made him a political outcast. In July 1934, Mu Mutian was arrested. He defected and was released on 21 September 1934. He then reported to the League's Party group that Hu Feng was a GMD agent. Zhou Yang and others seemed to have no problem accepting this charge. According to Hu Feng's recollection, after he had heard of this and reported it to Zhou Yang in person, the latter made no comment, but informed Hu that he would change his address. This was a signal to stop any further contact. Hu's resignation of the secretaryship of the League was also accepted immediately.[86]

Hu Feng interpreted Mu's action as being a result of personal conflicts. Around the end of 1933, Nie Gannu, then editing *Dongxiang* (*Trend*), the supplement of *Zhonghua ribao* (*China daily*), held a banquet for the left-wing writers but left out Mu Mutian. Mu believed that Hu had instigated this and the two quarrelled at a meeting. Hu claimed that this was the reason for Mu's making the false charge.[87] This seems unconvincing. Personal disputes were common among left-wing writers in the thirties and if this was the sole cause, there was no reason why others, for instance, Nie Gannu in this case, should not have been so accused.

In 1979, Xia Yan wrote a controversial article called 'Some past events that should have long been forgotten but cannot be forgotten' (*Yixie zao gai wangque er wei neng wangque de wangshi*).[88] He provided some 'evidence' to support the accusation. As early as 1934, he was warned by the head of the propaganda section of the Jiangsu Provincial Party Committee, Li Shaoshi of Hu's possible treachery. He was also told by Zheng Zhenduo that Shao Lizi, a GMD member, informed Zheng and Chen Wangdao that Hu Feng was then working for the GMD.[89] This piece of information was confirmed by Mao Dun.[90] The authenticity of these words cannot now be proved, but it should be pointed out that both Xia's and Mao's articles were written in response to an article by Feng Xuefeng on the behaviour of Zhou Yang and the Two slogan polemic.[91]

The rumour spread fast and Lu Xun was informed. The occasion was the meeting recorded in the well known 'Reply to Xu Maoyong and on the question of the united front against Japanese aggression'. According to this article, in 1935, Zhou Yang invited him for a talk and when he turned up, there were 'four fellows', Zhou Yang, Xia Yan, Yang Hansheng and Tian Han. They said that they had come to inform him of Hu Feng's treachery. Lu Xun asked for evidence and was told that the news came from the defector Mu Mutian. Lu said furiously:

> The words of a defector were considered as gospel truth in the Left League. I was staggered.[92]

Lu Xun made clear to them on the spot that he did not believe it and departed in high dudgeon.

Nevertheless, in his article 'Some past events', Xia Yan reported a different story. In the first instance, he queried the date provided by Lu Xun because in the autumn of 1935, both Yang Hansheng and Tian Han had already been arrested and kept in Nanjing; it was impossible for them to be present at the meeting. The meeting, Xia insisted, was held in the autumn of 1934. In the second place, according to Xia Yan, the meeting was not held for the purpose of informing Lu Xun of the treachery of Hu Feng. Rather it was because Zhou Yang felt that they had not made any report on League affairs to Lu Xun for some time, and so made Xia Yan arrange the meeting. Thirdly, Tian Han turned up unexpectedly and it was he who cautioned Lu Xun about Hu. Lastly, Xia Yan claimed that the meeting did not end unhappily as suggested by Lu Xun. He admitted that when Tian Han raised the issue, Lu Xun was angered but Yang Hansheng was able to relax the tension and before they parted, Lu Xun even told a joke and contributed $100.[93]

Undoubtedly, Xia Yan's story was self-serving. It was meant, as Xia himself made very clear, to clarify the false picture created by the 'Gang of Four' that Lu Xun had a deep hatred towards the 'four fellows'. But his arguments are not convincing. First, there is no reason why Lu Xun should make false statements in his open letter to Xu Maoyong. Second, it is unlikely that Lu Xun would have forgotten the details of the meeting when he wrote the letter, less than a year later, while Xia Yan could be accurate in his recollection some forty-five years later. Also there are many mistakes in the recollection. Thirdly, if it was a meeting to report League affairs, it is strange that Hu Feng, being the co-ordinator between the League and Lu Xun then, played no part in it. Hu did not even make arrangements for the meeting. Fourth, Xia Yan tried very hard to create the impression that Lu Xun was friendly to them but even in his article, Xia reported that Lu Xun said angrily:

> You believe in the words of a defector. I don't.[94]

Lu Xun drew a clear line between 'you' and 'I'. As for the contribution, there is no record of it in Lu Xun's diary. Moreover, if he was so ready to contribute money to the League, and if the money was given directly to Zhou Yang, there was no reason for Zhou to accuse him of being miserly.[95]

More interesting still is the date of the meeting. For more than forty years, no one queried Lu Xun's dating; Xia Yan was the first to do so. Obviously, he was trying to discredit Lu's account. But Xia Yan's argument that Yang Hansheng and Tian Han were kept at Nanjing in the autumn of 1935 was not solid enough to reject Lu Xun's dating. It should perhaps be pointed out that Lu

The Waning Years

Xun never said that the meeting was held in the autumn of 1935. His open letter to Xu Maoyong was written on 3-6 August 1936. When he said 'one day last year', he could well mean any time in 1935. Tian Han and Yang Hansheng were arrested on 19 February 1935. It is not totally impossible that the meeting was held between 1 January and 18 February 1935. But, it is not right to rule out completely the possibility that the meeting was held in 1934 - anytime after Mu Mutian's defection: Mu was arrested in July 1934 and released on 21 September 1934. But even if this dating is to be accepted, there is still no reason to conclude, as some critics did, that the meeting was the cause of Lu Xun's closeness to Hu Feng and alienation from the Party leadership of the League.[96] We have already seen the unhappy event over Yun Sheng's poem in 1933. It has also been shown that Lu Xun was extremely angered by the 'fringe literature' incident as well as Tian Han's essay; both undoubtedly took place before the meeting. Therefore, it is wrong to say that trying to convince Lu Xun that Hu Feng was an agent of the GMD was the 'first' mistake made by Zhou Yang.[97]

Lu Xun's rejection of the four fellows' words in the meeting was reasonable and understandable. He had always had a strong dislike of defectors and in a letter to Zheng Zhenduo on 8 January 1935, showed his disgust over Mu Mutian.[98] One question is, why did the four fellows not provide stronger evidence to support their accusation against Hu Feng on the spot as Xia Yan claimed that they had received the information from such respectable people as Li Shaoshi, Zheng Zhenduo and Chen Wangdao? Consequently, their words appeared to Lu Xun as a strengthening of relationships between Zhou Yang and the defectors.[99]

In the last quarter of 1934, Hu Feng and Lu Xun were close friends and in the following two years, their friendship was well known in literary circles. It is not difficult to explain how Hu Feng could win Lu Xun's good opinion. In the first place, Hu Feng was diligent. Apart from finishing a book called *On literature and art* (*Wenyi bitan*), he cooperated with Lu Xun in editing *Haiyan* (*Petrel*) and *Muxie wencong*. He actively initiated activities for the Left League and organised several study associations. Hu was also the editor of the League's internal publication, *Wenxue shenghuo*. This undoubtedly impressed Lu Xun who believed that the leading cadres of the League were not working hard enough.[100] Further, the performance of Hu Feng on a number of important occasions had enhanced Lu Xun's confidence. According to Wu Xiru who was then working in the special branch of the Communist Party's Central Committee, Hu Feng was appointed to liaise between Lu Xun and the Party. He did his job well. When the Military Committee of the Communist Party was in need of money, Hu Feng, at the instruction of Wu, was able to secure a handsome contribution from Lu Xun. Then in the spring of 1935, Lu Xun received a blank sheet of paper. He gave it to Hu Feng and Hu asked for assistance from Wu Xiru. It turned out to be a letter for help written in invisible ink from Fang Zhimin, who was imprisoned at Nanchang. Because of this, the contacts between Fang and the Party were built up. Then a year later, in 1936, an office of the Comintern in Shanghai was raided. Being responsible for investigating the case, Wu asked Lu Xun for help. Lu, through his Japanese friends, soon got the necessary information and once again, it was passed on to the Party through Hu Feng.[101] All these were highly important and confidential matters, involving the lives of many prominent CCP members. The fact that nothing went wrong was proof, at least to Lu Xun, of Hu Feng's trustworthiness. This was what Lu Xun meant when he said that his friendship with Hu Feng was a result of not only considering the person, but also the facts.[102]

With the rumour spreading within the League, Hu Feng could no longer hold the post of secretary. While Ren Baige reported that Lin Boxiu and Tian Han made the decision to expel him,[103] Hu insisted more than once that he himself handed in his resignation to Zhou Yang in Sha Ting's house in the early winter of 1934.[104] At about the same time, the head of the propaganda section, Zhou Wen, also resigned. Zhou Wen was a close associate of Hu Feng and an ardent follower of Lu Xun. His resignation was related to that of Hu Feng.[105]

After the resignation of Hu Feng and Zhou Wen, Lu Xun and his group were completely alienated from the central core of the organisation. During the year 1935, Lu Xun and the Party leadership of the Left League drifted hopelessly apart. From the end of 1934, Lu Xun began to complain in private correspondence of threats from 'friends', 'comrades-in-arms' and 'vermin within our camp'. He considered them worse than the real enemies.[106] He was angered over the waste of energy and time on petty quarrels and internecine fighting. In these letters, Lu Xun did not mention the names of his antagonists, except that of Tian Han; but there is little problem in identifying them. In more than one place, Zhou Yang was referred to as the 'field marshal'.[107] Lu Xun was not satisfied with the 'field marshal' for keeping himself indoors and doing nothing while giving orders to others. He related this in a letter to a story of Tolstoy, which said that a footsoldier was reminded of his own safety when he saw the general's bullet-proof ironplate.[108] Xu Maoyong also reported that Lu Xun had expressed this dissatisfaction before him.[109] Lu Xun felt that he had been working very hard but he was fighting alone. What made matters worse, he heard of others attacking him for being lazy.[110] He described this vividly to Hu Feng:

> Take myself as an example. I always feel that I am bound in an iron chain and a foreman is whipping me on the back. No matter how hard I work, I am still whipped. When I turn my head and ask what my faults are, he will cup his hands and say modestly that I am doing extremely well; and that I am surely the best of friends; and what a fine day; ha-ha-ha.[111]

In 1935, Lu Xun had already come to believe that it was better for writers not to join the Left League. In a letter written to Hu Feng, Lu Xun made it very clear that he was not happy with the politics within the organisation, and he believed that too much energy was consumed in petty squabbles. It was for this

reason that he advised Xiao Jun, a new writer then and regarded highly by Lu Xun, not to join the League:
> About San Lang [Xiao Jun], I can state my opinion almost without hesitation: better not join [the Left League] now. What happened in the beginning would make a long story. I am not going to talk about it. In view of the happenings in recent years, I feel it is the few new writers among those who do not belong that show something fresh. Once a man has joined, he will forever be involved in petty squabbles and cannot make his voice heard.[112]

Xiao Jun, with his common-law wife, Xiao Hong, started to write to Lu Xun in 1934, after they had escaped from Harbin and stayed at Qingdao. They continued to keep in touch after the Xiaos had arrived in Shanghai. From the start Lu Xun had a good impression of the couple. Almost all letters were answered immediately and he agreed to lend them $20 even before they met.[113] Lu Xun also encouraged them to write and spent much effort helping them to publish their works. After the first meeting on 30 November 1934, they were soon among Lu Xun's closest associates. The above piece of advice given to Xiao Jun proves that Lu Xun was not happy to see his followers in the League. It also shows that Lu Xun's faith and hope in the Left League had vanished completely.

Critics from both the left and right in general agree that Zhou Yang and his group should bear responsibility for the split of the Left League. Even Zhou Yang himself and his followers are now ready to accept such accusations.[114] There are political reasons behind this. For the left, Lu Xun has been defined by Mao Zedong as the sage of modern China[115] and therefore it must have been Zhou Yang who did not have a good comprehension of the importance of the sage and thus committed a number of blunders. On the other hand, many view the conflict as a result of Lu Xun's 'act of assertion' against Zhou Yang who represented the Party's cultural directives and who tried to enforce obedience to instructions on the old man. It was therefore a fight against Party domination of independent writers.[116]

However, in the first instance, it must be pointed out that there is no concrete proof available today to support the charge that Zhou Yang himself wrote or published anything against Lu Xun. But those around Zhou did launch attacks against him. Zhou Yang might have had no hand in these incidents, yet being assigned by the Communist Party to take charge of literary work, he should at least have done something to keep things under control or to pacify Lu Xun. The fact that he made no attempt to stop the attacks and that he himself was involved in a number of incidents which caused Lu Xun's discontent (for example, publication of Yun Sheng's poem and his refusal to make redress, plus the four fellows' meeting with Lu) easily led Lu Xun to associate all the 'evil' deeds within the League with Zhou. In other words, Zhou Yang's fault lay not in having done something to enrage Lu Xun, but rather in having done nothing to conciliate him. Lu Xun's alienation should not be seen as a result of Zhou's

The Chinese League of Left-wing Writers

eagerness and efforts in grasping the leadership of the Left League.[117] He already had it with the departure of Qu Qiubai and Feng Xuefeng. But it must have been a hard time for Zhou Yang, an inexperienced young man of twenty, just returned from Japan, to lead such a complicated organisation as the Left League. Added to this was government repression. Zhou Yang might have been ambitious but there was little point in his alienating Lu Xun in order to consolidate his position. Since the formation of the Left League, Lu Xun had not been within the centre core of the organisation and most decisions were made by the Party group. All along, Lu Xun had honoured such leadership and the system worked smoothly in the first few years. What Zhou Yang failed to do, and where Qu Qiubai and Feng Xuefeng succeeded, was to bridge the gap between the Party group and Lu Xun.

Nevertheless, although his efforts might not have been strong enough, many League members recalled that Zhou Yang did try to conciliate Lu Xun. Xu Maoyong was appointed by Zhou as secretary of the Left League in the spring of 1935 because Xu was almost the only one in Zhou's group able to maintain good relations with Lu Xun at that time. Xu also claimed that he, at the behest of Zhou Yang, tried several times to contact Hu Feng to win the latter over.[118]

There is no way, however, for people like Tian Han, Liao Mosha, Zhu Xiuxia and Qiu Dongping to wash away the stains of attacking Lu Xun. In all cases, it was they who took the offensive and there appeared no good cause for their doing so. This was probably due to the irascibility of League members, made acute by the strain of prolonged struggle. However, the relationship between these people and Zhou Yang should not be overemphasised, as Lu Xun did, which would in the end make Zhou Yang the worst of the villains.

In a number of incidents, such as Yun Sheng's poems and the discussion on mass literature, Zhou Yang and his group did show a more radical attitude but this was not always the case and it is inappropriate to say that the dissension within the Left League was one between the ultra-leftists and the moderates. One critic has pointed out that during the 'typical characters' debate in 1935-36, Zhou Yang took 'the less doctrinaire position',[119] while Lu Xun's stance on the question of the League's dissolution as well as the 'Two slogan polemic' was more left-deviated than that adopted by Zhou Yang. Moreover, there were radicals within the Left League from the very beginning and this had not constituted any major obstacle to the progress of the League and the co-operation with Lu Xun.

In fact, there was no issue of substance dividing the League at that period, or dividing Lu Xun from the Party caucus. There was no viewpoint taken by Lu Xun that was in principle contrary to Party policy, or vice versa. Indeed, in the second half of the Left League's existence, no great movement was launched by the League and there was no obvious shift of Party policy. Thus, it was mainly because in the closing years, no one in the League made strong efforts to maintain the solidarity of the bloc. Zhou Yang should bear greater blame in this respect as he was in charge of the Party group then but Lu Xun was not totally blameless. He made no serious attempt to narrow the gap with his opponents. On the contrary, he often stuck to his guns. If he considered it a fault of Zhou Yang to criticise him behind his back, he himself had committed the same mistake. It is a well-known fact that he often criticised Zhou Yang before his confidants. His withdrawal from any work of the League and refusal to meet the leadership solved no problem but only made the hope of reconciliation more remote. In the end, trivial matters became causes of open dispute. There is little wonder that when it came to such important issues as the dissolution of the Left League and the building of a united front with the GMD, there could be no compromise.

Notes to Chapter Six

1. Zhou Yang, 'Inherit and carry forward the revolutionary tradition of the left-wing cultural movement' (*Jicheng he fayang zuoyi wenhua yundong de geming chuantong*), *Renmin ribao*, 2 April 1980.
2. According to *A bibliography of modern Chinese literary periodicals* (*Zhongguo xiandai wenxue qikan mulu*) (Shanghai: Shanghai wenyi chubanshe, 1961), pp 29-30, the Left League put out only one periodical in its last two years, the *Wenyi qunzhong* (*Literary masses*) with only two issues (September and November 1935). Apart from that, there was one for internal circulation, *Wenxue shenghuo*, edited by Hu Feng.
3. Lu Xun, 'Reply to Xu Maoyong and on the question of the united front against Japanese aggression', *Complete works of Lu Xun* Vol VI, p 534.
4. Feng Xuefeng, *Remembering Lu Xun*, p 44.
5. Xia Yan, 'Around the formation of the "Left League"', p 5.
6. Ding Ling, 'Meetings to Lu Xun' (*Kaihui zhiyu Lu Xun*), collected in *Recalling Lu Xun* (*Yi Lu Xun*) (Beijing: Renmin wenxue chubanshe, October 1956), p 90.
7. There is only one entry in Lu Xun's diary that he attended a Left League meeting: 29 May 1930, *Complete works of Lu Xun* Vol XIV, p 824. It was the second general meeting of the Left League From recollections of other League members, we know that Lu attended other meetings. First, he attended the inaugural meeting. Second, he was at a joint meeting of the Left League and the Dramatists League in April 1930. 'Letter from Feng Xuefeng to Bao Ziyan', p 148. Third, he attended an executive committee meeting at the end of 1932 or early in 1933. Jin Ding, 'Some recollections on the Left League', *Recollections*, p 187. Fourth, Lu was present at a meeting of the standing committee around 1932-33. Sha Ting, 'Recollection from a member of the Left League', *ibid*, p 217.
8. Xu Guangping, 'Lu Xun and the young people' (*Lu Xun yu qingnianmen*), *Reminiscences of Lu Xun by Xu Guangping*, pp 247-8.
9. Feng Xuefeng, *Remembering Lu Xun*, p 114.
10. Zhou Yongxiang, *A chronicle of Qu Qiubai*, pp 104-6.
11. Paul G Pickowicz, 'Lu Xun through the eyes of Qu Qiubai: New perspective on Chinese Marxist literary polemics of the 1930s', *Modern China* Vol II No 3 (July 1976), p 344.
12. Xu Guangping, 'When comrade Qiubai and Lu Xun were together' (*Qiubai tongzhi he Lu Xun xiangchu de shihou*), *Yuwen xuexi* (*Language learning*) No 6, 1959 (June 1959), p 2.
13. *Reminiscences of Lu Xun by Xu Guangping*, p 128.
14. *Ibid*, p 118-28.
15. Anthony J Kane, 'The League of Left-wing Writers', p 195.
16. Chen Qiongzhi, 'Between two great men in history who have never met: A talk given by Feng Xuefeng on the relationship between Lu Xun and Mao

The Waning Years

Zedong' (*Zai liangwei weimou yimian de lishi weiren zhijian: Ji Feng Xuefeng guanyu Lu Xun ji Mao Zedong guanxi de yici tanhua*), *Zhongguo xiandai wenxue yanjiu congkan* No 3, 1980 (October 1980), p 207.
17 Zhou Yongxiang, *A chronicle of Qu Qiubai*, p 110.
18 T A Hsia, 'Lu Hsun and the dissolution of the League of Leftist Writers', *The gate of darkness*, p 104.
19 Hu Feng, 'Recalling the relationship between the "Left League" and Lu Xun', p 178.
20 Mao Dun, 'Some facts that need to be clarified' (*Xuyao chengqing yixie shishi*), *Xinwenxue shiliao* No 2, pp 244-5.
21 Ren Baige, 'When I worked in the "Left League"', *Recollections*, p 372.
22 Lu Xun, letter to Xiao Jun and Xiao Hong, 10 December 1934, *Complete works of Lu Xun* Vol XII, p 593.
23 Lu Xun, 'A glimpse at the literary scene of Shanghai', *Ibid* Vol XII, p 593.
24 Guo Moruo, *Works of Guo Moruo* Vol VII, pp 14-29.
25 Hu Feng, 'Recalling the time around joining the Left League', pp 35-6.
26 *Wenxue yuebao* No 4, *Materials on modern Chinese literary history* Vol II, pp 225-9.
27 'Feng Xuefeng on the Left League', p 10.
28 *Wenxue yuebao* No 5 and 6, *Complete works of Lu Xun* Vol IV, pp 451-3.
29 Note (3), *ibid* Vol IV, p 453.
30 *Ibid*, p 453.
31 *Wenxue yuebao* No 5 and 6, *Materials on modern Chinese literary history* Vol II, p 519.
32 Reprinted in *A history of the struggle in modern Chinese literary thinkings* (*Zhongguo xiandai wenyi sixiang douzhengshi*) Part I Vol 1 (February 1976), pp 261-4.
33 Note (3), *Completed works of Lu Xun* Vol XIII, p 120.
34 Shou Jia (et al), 'Some words on Mr Lu Xun's "Threats and abuse are not fighting"', pp 262-4.
35 *Complete works of Lu Xun* Vol XIII, pp 119-20.
36 *Works of Qu Qiubai* Vol I, pp 406-7.
37 *Ibid*, p 409.
38 'Thorough down to the bottom' (*Toudi*), *Complete works of Lu Xun* Vol V, pp 103-6.
39 The Chinese Departments of Fudan University and Shanghai Normal University, ed, *Selected letters of Lu Xun* (*Lu Xun shuxinxuan*) (Shanghai: Shanghai renmin chubanshe, September 1973), Note (15), p 140.
40 Lu Xun, letter to Xiao Jun, 28 April 1935, *Complete works of Lu Xun* Vol XIII, p 120.
41 'Carrying upside down', *ibid*, pp 490-4.
42 *Ibid*, pp 492-3.
43 Lu Xun, Letter to Cao Jinghua, 7 February 1935, *ibid* Vol XIII, p 47.
44 'Preface', *ibid* Vol V, p 417.

45 *Ibid* Vol XII, p 584.
46 *Ibid*, p 606.
47 *Xinwwenxue shiliao* No 2, 1984 (22 May 1984), pp 40-3.
48 'Random thoughts', *Complete works of Lu Xun* Vol V, pp 479-80.
49 *Ibid*.
50 *Ibid*, p 494.
51 Liao Mosha, 'The two pieces of *zawen* I wrote in the thirties', p 40.
52 Lu Xun, letter to Cao Jinghua, 7 February 1935, *Complete works of Lu Xun* Vol XIII, p 47; letter to Xiao Jun, 28 April 1935, *ibid*, p 120.
53 Lu Xun, 'In reply to Mr Cao Juren's letter' (*Da Cao Juren xiansheng*), *ibid* Vol VI, pp 76-8.
54 Lu Xun, 'An open letter in reply to Mr Yang Cunren's open letter', *ibid* Vol IV, pp 626-31.
55 T A Hsia, *The gate of darkness*, p 114.
56 Tian Han's 'Reconciliation' was included by Lu Xun in the postscript of *Essays of Qiejieting* (*Qiejieting zawen*), *Complete works of Lu Xun* Vol VI, pp 208-11.
57 Lu Xun, 'In reply to the editor of *Xi*' (*Da Xi zhoukan bianzhe wen*), *ibid*, pp 147-8.
58 Lu Xun, letter to Cao Jinghua, 7 February 1935, *ibid* Vol XIII, p 47.
59 *Ibid* Vol VI, p 148.
60 *Ibid*, p 212.
61 Lu Xun, letter to Xiao Jun, Xiao Hong 23 April 1935, *ibid* Vol XIII, p 116.
62 Lu Xun, letter to Hu Feng, 12 September 1935, *ibid*, p 211.
63 T A Hsia, *The gate of darkness*, p 115.
64 Lu Xun, letter to Cao Jinghua, 7 February 1935, *Complete works of Lu Xun* Vol XIII, p 47.
65 'Postscript of *Essays of Qiejieting*', *ibid* Vol VI, p 212.
66 Ren Baige, 'When I worked in the "Left League"', *Recollections*, p 375.
67 *Complete works of Lu Xun* Vol XIII, p 129.
68 Hu Feng, 'Annotations on Lu Xun's letters' (*Lu Xun shuxin zhushi*), *Xinwenxue shiliao* No 3, 1981 (22 August 1981), p 74.
69 Lu Xun, letter to Hu Feng, 28 June 1935, *Complete works of Lu Xun* Vol XIII, p 160.
70 Hu Feng, 'Annotations on Lu Xun's letters', p 75. Hu Feng, 'Recalling the relationship between the "Left League" and Lu Xun', pp 180-1.
71 Hu Feng, 'Recalling the relationship between the "Left League" and Lu Xun', pp 178-9. Hu Feng, 'Recalling the time around joining the Left League' (II), p 43-8.
72 Hu Feng, 'Annotations on Lu Xun's letters', p 76.
73 Hu Feng, 'Recalling the time around joining the Left League' (I), p 35.
74 *Materials on modern Chinese literary history* Vol II, pp 373-83.
75 Recalling the time around joining the Left League' (II), p 41-2 & 47.

76 Hu Feng, 'Recalling Dongping' (*Yi Dongping*), *Essays of Hu Feng* (Shanghai: Chunming shudian, January 1948), pp 74-5.
77 *Complete works of Lu Xun* Vol XV, p 134.
78 Hu Feng, 'Recalling the time around joining the Left League' (II), p 45.
79 *Complete works of Lu Xun* Vol XV, p 176.
80 According to Lu Xun's diary, Lu went to reserve a table for a banquet on 18 December 1934 but Hu Feng failed to turn up on the following day. *Complete works of Lu Xun* Vol XV, p 186. Xiao Jun reported that the banquet was to celebrate the first moon of Hu Feng's son. Xiao Jun, *Annotations on Lu Xun's letters to Xiao Jun and Xiao Hong* (*Lu Xun gei Xiao Jun Xiao Hong shujian zhushilu*) (Harbin: Heilongjiang renmin chubanshe, June 1981), p 109.
81 Ren Baige, 'When I worked in the "Left League"', *Recollections*, p 372.
82 Many commentators hold this view. For example, T A Hsia, *The gate of darkness*, pp 111-12. Zhai Zhicheng, 'Lu Xun and Hu Feng's struggle against domination', *Articles on the study of Communist China's literary policy*, p 20. Wu Xiru, 'Hu Feng as I know him', p 242.
83 Guo Moruo, 'An inspection of the military exercise' (*Soumiao de jianyue*), *Wenxuejie* (*Literary arena*) Vol VI No 1 (10 September 1936), collected in *Collection of materials on the 'Two slogan' polemic* (*Liangge kouhao lunzheng ziliao xuanbian*) (Beijing: Renmin wenxue chubanshe, March 1982), p 712.
84 Lu Xun, 'Reply to Xu Maoyong and on the question of the united front against Japanese aggression', *Complete works of Lu Xun* Vol VI, p 535.
85 Cf Hu Feng, 'Recollecting the time as an idealist' (*Lixiangzhuyizhe de huiyi*), *Critical essays of Hu Feng* Vol I, pp 248-256. Shi Hang, 'The idealist Hu Feng: Hu Feng at his youth' (*Lixiangzhuyizhe de jianying: Qingnian Hu Feng*), *Dousou* No 19 (January 1977), pp 22-50.
86 Hu Feng, 'Recalling the time around joining the Left League' (II), p 48.
87 *Ibid*, pp 47-8.
88 *Wenxue pinglun* No 1, 1981 (15 January 1981), pp 92-101.
89 *Ibid*, pp 96-7.
90 Mao Dun, 'Some facts that need to be clarified', p 245.
91 Feng Xuefeng, 'On the activities of Zhou Yang and others in 1936 and Lu Xun's raising of the slogan "Mass literature of the national revolutionary war"' (*Youguan yijiu sanliunian Zhou Yang dengren de xingdong yiji Lu Xun tichu minzu geming zhanzheng de dazhong wenxue kouhao de jingguo*), *Xinwenxue shiliao* No 2, pp 247-58.
92 *Complete works of Lu Xun* Vol VI, pp 534-5.
93 Xia Yan, 'Some past events that should have long been forgotten', p 95.
94 *Ibid*.
95 Lu Xun, letter to Hu Feng, 24 August 1935, *Complete works of Lu Xun* Vol XIII, p 194.
96 Anthony J Kane, 'The League of Left-wing Writers', p 224.

97　*Ibid*, p 226.
98　*Complete works of Lu Xun* Vol XIII, p 12.
99　Lu Xun, letter to Hu Feng, 12 September 1935, *ibid*, p 211.
100　Lu Xun, letter to Xiao Jun, Xiao Hong, 6 December 1934, *ibid* Vol XII, p 586; letter to Hu Feng, 28 June 1935, *ibid* Vol XIII, p 160; letter to Wang Yeqiu, 15 September 1936, *ibid*, p 426.
101　Wu Xiru, 'The relationship between the Party and Lu Xun' (*Lu Xun yu dang de guanxi*), *Luxun yanjiu ziliao* No 4 (January 1980), p 191.
102　*Complete works of Lu Xun* Vol VI, p 534.
103　Ren Baige, 'When I worked in the "Left League"', *Recollections*, p 375.
104　Hu Feng, 'Recalling the time around joining the Left League'(II), p 48. Hu Feng, 'Recalling the relationship between the "Left League" and Lu Xun', p 178.
105　Wang Yaoshan, 'Recalling the time when I worked in the "Left League"', *Recollections*, p 309.
106　Lu Xun, letter to Xiao Jun, Xiao Hong, 6 December 1934, *Complete works of Lu Xun* Vol XII, p 586. Lu Xun, letter to Yang Jiyun, 18 December 1934, *ibid* Vol XIII, p 606.
107　Lu Xun, letters to Hu Feng, 28 June 1935 and 12 September 1935, *ibid* Vol XIII, pp 160 and 211.
108　Letter to Hu Feng, 28 June 1935, *ibid*, p 160.
109　Xu Maoyong, 'The complete story of my relationship with the Left League, Lu Xun and Zhou Yang', *Reference materials*, p 50.
110　Lu Xun, letter to Xiao Jun, Xiao Hong, 6 December 1934, *Complete works of Lu Xun* Vol XII, p 586.
111　Lu Xun, letter to Hu Feng, 12 September 1935, *ibid* Vol XIII, p 211.
112　*Ibid*.
113　Lu Xun, letter to Xiao Jun, Xiao Hong, 17 November 1934, *ibid* Vol XII, p 567. Xiao Jun, *Annotations on Lu Xun's letters to Xiao Jun and Xiao Hong*, p 57.
114　Zhou Yang, 'Inherit and carry forward the revolutionary tradition of the left-wing cultural movement', *Renmin ribao*, 2 April 1980.
115　Mao Zedong, 'On Lu Xun' (*Lun Lu Xun*), *New essays on Lu Xun* (*Lu Xun xinlun*) (np: Xinwen chubanshe, 1938), pp 11-12. Mao Zedong, 'On new democracy' (*Lun xinminzhu zhuyi*), *Selected works* Vol III, p 144.
116　T A Hsia, 'Lu Hsun and the dissolution of the League of Leftist Writers', *The gate of darkness*, p 107; Merle Goldman, *Literary dissent in Communist China*, p 13; Zhai Zhicheng, 'Lu Xun and Hu Feng's struggle against control', *Articles on the study of Communist China's literary policy*, pp 3-99.
117　Anthony J Kane, 'The League of Left-wing Writers', p 226.
118　Wei Mengke, 'Recalling the Left League', *Recollections*, p 390; Xu Maoyong, *Memoirs*, pp 79-80.
119　Merle Goldman, *Literary dissent in Communist China*, p 11.

Chapter Seven
Dissolution and Polemic (1935-1936)

With such bitter division, the dissolution of the Left League was merely a matter of time. Strangely enough, it was the Party leadership of the League that initiated dissolution while the alienated Lu Xun wished to retain the organisation. This constituted another point of dispute between the two groups. Although the original intention of dissolving the League was to secure a broader united front in the literary circle, the result was just the opposite. Lu Xun was most unhappy with the dissolution and in particular, with the manner of it. The dissension between the two groups within the Left League was brought to the surface in the subsequent 'Two slogan polemic'.

Zhou Yang's reason for dissolving the League was purely political. He acted in accordance with an instruction from Moscow - a letter from Xiao San, then the League's representative there. It is therefore necessary first to look into the change in Comintern policy in Moscow at that time.

During the six years from 1929 to 1934, commonly known as its 'third period', the Comintern called for a 'class against class' policy.[1] This was the outcome of defeats in Germany (October 1923), Estonia (1924), Bulgaria (1925) and China (1927), after which the Comintern could no longer support bourgeois nationalist revolution. International revolution remained the main objective.[2] However, in the thirties, the major threat to the USSR no longer sprang from such capitalist countries as the United States or Britain, but from the later partners of the Axis. In January 1930, Mussolini ordered the invasion of Ethiopia, exposing fully the aggressive designs of the Italian fascists. On 16 March 1935, Hitler finally rejected the Versailles Treaty of 1919 by reinstating compulsory military service. In the Far East, Japanese occupation of Manchuria and the establishment of the puppet state of Manchukuo on the Soviet border were viewed with alarm by the USSR. All these countries were strongly anti-communist. Obviously, a war on two fronts would be disastrous for the young Soviet state.

Under these circumstances the Soviet Union made tentative changes in foreign policy. In December 1932, official relations were re-established with the Chinese Republic. A year later, came recognition from the United States while in 1934, non-aggression pacts were signed or extended with other European countries. Most decisive of all, apart from joining the League of Nations in September 1934, the Russians entered into a pact with France in May 1935, a European country especially vulnerable to German attack, undertaking 'to come to each other's aid in the event of either being subjected to aggression in contravention of the convention of the League of Nations'. Thus it was not surprising when roughly two months later, the Comintern made clear that the task of its Seventh Congress was to 'determine ... the creation of a powerful popular united front against Fascism and war in all the capitalist countries'.[3]

The Chinese League of Left-wing Writers

This Congress cannot be dealt with in depth here but several points are worth noting. First, it called for the application of united front tactics in a new manner, 'by seeking to reach agreements with the organisations of the toilers of various political trends for joint action on a factory, local, district, national and international scale'. Secondly, it urged Communists in colonial and semi-colonial countries to establish an anti-imperialist people's front by drawing the 'widest masses' into the national liberation movement and to take an active part in the 'mass anti-imperialist movements headed by national reformists'. Thirdly, an appeal was made for cooperation with the Second International which had long been attacked by the Comintern.[4] In short, a new united front policy - united front from above - would soon be implemented.

At the Seventh Congress (25 July - 2 August 1935), considerable attention was given to China. Georgi Dimitrov, Chief Secretary of the Comintern, said in his report made on 2 August:

> We approve the initiative taken by our courageous brother Party of China in the creation of a most extensive anti-imperialist united front against Japanese imperialism and its Chinese agents, jointly with all those organised forces existing on the territory of China which are ready to wage a real struggle for the salvation of their country and their people.[5]

Dimitrov is referring to the declaration made in the name of the Central Committee of the CCP and the Chinese Soviet Central Government by Wang Ming, representative of the CCP in the Comintern, on 1 August 1935, 'Letter to fellow countrymen for resistance against Japan and national salvation' (*Wei kangri jiuguo gao quanti tongbaoshu*), commonly known as the 'August First Declaration' (*Bayi xuanyan*). The declaration marked the beginning of a new united front policy in the Chinese Communist movement.

Throughout the thirties, the CCP had never given up the 'united front from below' policy. As early as April 1932, the Provisional Central Government had already issued a declaration of war against Japan which called upon the masses in the white areas to overthrow the GMD and join in resisting Japanese aggression.[6] A year later, Mao Zedong and Zhu De jointly sent a similar appeal stating that the Red Army would cease fire provided that all military units were ready to fight for the national revolutionary war.[7] Then in April 1934, the slogan of 'united front' appeared in a declaration against Japanese occupation of northern China. It was a united front from below because the declaration declared that only the toiling masses could be the opposing force against Japanese aggression.[8] But the August First Declaration was different, calling for cooperation between all Chinese, including soldiers and army officers, members of various organisations and political parties:

> Provided all GMD troops can stop the action against the Soviet areas, provided all regiments are prepared to fight against the Japanese, then, regardless of any enmity between them and the Red Army at present or in the past, or any divergence of views

concerning internal problems, the Red Army will stop immediately any action against them, and are willing to join together in friendship to save the nation.[9]

An appeal was also made for the setting up of an All-China anti-Japanese 'national defence government'.

These ideas were repeated in the speech made by Wang Ming on 7 August at the Seventh Congress on Communist movements and anti-imperialist struggles in colonial areas. The speech was rewritten as 'On the question of united front against imperialism' (*Lun fandi tongyi zhanxian wenti*) in October.[10] This confirmed Wang's determination to implement the new Comintern policy.

After the Congress, Wang rose to be a member of the ECCI's Presidium. He sent Lin Yuying (brother of Lin Yunan, killed by the GMD in Shanghai together with the 'Five martyrs of the Left League') to inform the Communists in the Chinese Soviets.[11] The August First Declaration appeared on 30 November in *Inprecorr* (*International Press Correspondence*). It was also published in *Jiuguo shibao* (*National salvation news*), printed in Chinese by the CCP in Paris. Before the end of 1935, the declaration was widely known in all the big cities of China.[12]

In the cultural field, there was the letter from Xiao San to the League of Left-wing Writers. In his final years, Xiao San claimed that after the Seventh Congress, Wang Ming bullied him twice, in September and November 1935, into writing the letter and finally, he was convinced, he admitted, by Kang Sheng, another CCP representative in the Comintern.[13] The letter was written almost immediately after the second meeting between Wang and Xiao, on 8 November.

The letter was addressed to all members of the Left League but it was sent to Lu Xun. In a letter to Xu Maoyong dated 12 December, Lu said that he had received the letter which had 'long since' been passed on.[14] So Lu Xun was first among all League members in China to read the letter. He was thus in a good position to understand the change in Comintern policy. The letter was passed on to Zhou Yang and others through Hu Feng and Mao Dun.[15]

In the letter, Xiao San began by praising the League's accomplishments at a time of serious white terror but he soon shifted to criticism of the League's 'closed-door' sectarianism, which made it impossible to unite all the discontented in a broad united front against imperialism and feudalism. This sectarianism originated, Xiao maintained, in the advocacy of proletarian literature, which excluded all 'non-proletarian' writers. He also criticised League members for turning the organisation into a political party, just equivalent to the CCP, giving the authorities excuses to kill its members and making others reluctant to be associated with it. He urged a major change in their work:

> Liquidate the Left League. Issue a proclamation announcing its dissolution. Promote and organise a broadly based literary group. Try to fight for a legal position and attract a large number of writers to join the anti-imperialist, anti-feudalistic united front under such

slogans as 'protect the country', 'save the Chinese race', 'continue the "May Fourth" spirit' or 'complete the "May Fourth" mission'.[16] Xiao San made it clear that this was the central point of his letter. To justify his suggestion, he quoted the examples of the International Union of Revolutionary Writers and the dissolution of the RAPP.

It is not certain whether this letter or the August First Declaration arrived in China first. Zhou Yang once claimed that before they received the letter, they had already formulated the idea of dissolving the League.[17] This implied that he had at least heard something about the Seventh Congress of the Comintern. Now with the letter's backing, Zhou proceeded to dissolve the League and plan the formation of a new organisation.

Although Lu Xun had already excused himself from League affairs, Zhou Yang could not ignore him in such an important matter. However they were not on good terms and Lu Xun had refused to see any of his group. Xu Maoyong was therefore instructed by Zhou Yang to talk with Lu Xun, while Xia Yan arranged a meeting with Mao Dun, asking him to convey the same message.[18]

Mao Dun reported that Lu Xun, being the first to read Xiao San's letter, had thought over the question thoroughly.[19] Both Mao and Xu got the same reply, that he would not be against organising a new united front in the literary circle, but he did not think that it was desirable to dissolve the League of Left-wing Writers. In Lu Xun's opinion, the League could be the core of the new organisation to lead the united front. Without the League, its members might be lost to other camps.[20]

A meeting of the League's standing committee was convened to discuss Lu Xun's proposal. Hu Qiaomu, representing the General Cultural League, chaired the meeting and gave a 'convincing' speech: to have one organisation within another would inevitably produce sectarianism. The meeting insisted on dissolution.

When informed of this decision, again by Xu Maoyong, Lu Xun consented with one proviso. A proclamation should be issued to make clear to the public that the dissolution of the Left League was to meet a new political situation and for the formation of a broader anti-Japanese united front in the literary arena. If the League was dissolved quietly, Lu Xun argued, people would think that it could not stand GMD repression and had to be disbanded.

The General Cultural League discussed Lu Xun's suggestion, which was again rejected. This was because other left-wing organisations were to be dissolved soon and it would cause too great a sensation if each of them issued a separate proclamation. Instead, the General Cultural League promised Lu Xun that a general proclamation would be made by and in the name of the Cultural League for all the left-wing organisations.

Lu Xun was happy with this decision but before long, the promise was broken. Xu Maoyong was instructed by Zhou Yang to inform Lu that the Cultural League would not issue any proclamation as they were then organising a new association for national salvation, and they did not want to give the

Dissolution and Polemic

authorities an impression that the association was a continuation of the Cultural League. It is easy to imagine that Xu Maoyong had a most difficult mission. Lu Xun made no comment but pulled a long face. Feeling embarrassed, Xu left and the two never met again.

Here Lu Xun faced a dilemma. On the one hand, he was discontented and suspicious of Zhou Yang and his group who were taking charge of League affairs. On the other, he did not want to see the League dissolved. But why was this? It is beyond doubt that Lu Xun had a deep personal feeling for the organisation. He was reported as saying repeatedly: 'Dissolved in this way. They do not set store by this front.'[21] However, if he realised that the organisation was merely a tool for their cause, he would and should not have opposed dispensing with it when it could no longer serve the purpose. Lu Xun's own explanation, that he was afraid that people of his camp would be lost to the enemies, is not convincing because giving up one's principles has nothing to do with organisations. There had been defections in the Left League even when it was at its peak. Furthermore, not long before, Lu Xun had advised Xiao Jun not to join the League, saying that it would be more constructive to work outside it.[22] Then what was the point of keeping it? Lu Xun believed that there were too many petty squabbles within the League, but would there be any improvement if the League was to be kept within the new united front which would undoubtedly be composed of people of more diverse backgrounds? It is also wrong to argue that Lu Xun's objection was due to his suspicion of the proposals of local Party leaders,[23] as the instruction for dissolution came from Moscow and Lu Xun had complete knowledge of it. Moreover, if the League was to be retained, its leadership would still be in the hands of his opponents. When he distrusted and disliked them so much, why did he think that the League could act as the core of the new organisation? Being the first to read Xiao San's letter from Moscow, he should have been able to see the changes in Comintern policy. Although the letter made no mention of the August First Declaration or the Comintern, the message of such lines as 'our literary movement should at least follow and match with the political slogan and tactics', would not be difficult to see.[24]

The 'proclamation' issue was critical. It caused the final break up of the two camps. It is true that Xiao San's letter specified that a proclamation should be issued but Lu Xun's insistence on this cannot be said to be in compliance with Xiao's instruction,[25] because Lu and Xiao had different intentions. Xiao's was to announce the end of a left-wing organisation in order to wash away people's suspicions and win them over. Lu Xun wanted to ensure that people would not be misled into thinking that the League was defeated. The major difference was that the former paid attention to the united front and the latter to the League. Lu Xun's demand put the General Cultural League in a difficult position. If a new organisation was to be formed immediately after the announcement of the dissolution of the Left League, people would look at it with alarm. It was not unlikely that the GMD authorities would once again take sanctions against it.

Thus there are reasons to suspect that, at least at this stage, Lu Xun did not whole-heartedly support, even if he was not against, the new united front policy. Feng Xuefeng, who arrived on the scene at least five months later and who was able to have long talks with Lu Xun, reported that Lu did not understand and was even suspicious of the policy. His comment on Feng Xuefeng's explanation of the new policy was, in Feng's own word, 'sarcastic': 'I must be lagging behind'.[26]

Lu Xun had always had a deep hatred for defectors. He often showed in his writings his contempt towards people like Yang Cunren and Mu Mutian.[27] In fact, in his eyes, one of the greatest mistakes committed by Zhou Yang and his group was their trust in defectors.[28] Organising a broad united front in the literary circle would mean making friends with these enemies. He was reported to have said, 'those who have turned to the enemy welcome this united front policy most'.[29] This may be one of the reasons for his dislike of the policy.

Feng Xuefeng stressed strongly that Lu Xun's distrust of the united front policy was due to his hatred for the GMD. According to Feng, Lu Xun did not believe that Jiang Jieshi would genuinely support a war against Japan. He said repeatedly, 'I am afraid that the Communist Party will be taken in again'.[30] There were political reasons for Feng to over-stress this, but it is true that Lu Xun was disillusioned and shocked by the GMD coup d'état in April 1927. His unwavering personal hatred for the GMD in his later years made it difficult for him to compromise with the politicians of the CCP who would change their policy according to actual need.

With or without Lu Xun's consent, the League was dissolved, quietly. As there was no formal proclamation, the actual date is unknown. It would be about the first half of March 1936 that the League was said to have been dissolved because Xu Maoyong's last meeting with Lu Xun was on 28 February 1936, and the dissolution was after this.[31] On the other hand, an article, by Qiu Yunduo, which reported that the Left League had already been dissolved, was published on 20 March 1936.[32]

In the same month however, Lu Xun still wrote in a letter to He Jiahuai that he did not know whether the League was still in existence or not.[33] In another letter, he explained this to Xu Maoyong:

> I had heard that the group [the Left League] was going to be disbanded. But then there was no more news and no notification. It seems that secrecy has been observed. That is necessary. But was it an internal decision, or did others offer their opinions? If it was the former, then that was dissolution; if the latter, it would be débâcle. This is no small matter, and I have heard nothing of it.[34]

Obviously, Lu Xun was not informed of the dissolution after his last meeting with Xu Maoyong. This constituted another reason for discontent on his part.

It took more than four months before the League was dissolved, and Zhou Yang's united front in the literary circle was not built up until June 1936, in the form of the Association of Chinese Writers and Artists (*Zhongguo wenyijia xiehui*). Zhou and Xia Yan blamed Lu Xun for the delay. The united front could not be broad enough without Lu Xun's support and participation.[35] Lu in 1936 complained that he was accused of sabotaging the united front.[36] Perhaps the charge was not too far from the truth. In fact, before any concrete progress could be made in building up the united front, another battle erupted, in the bitter polemic over the two slogans, the slogan of 'National defence literature' (*Guofang wenxue*) promulgated by Zhou Yang and his group versus the slogan of 'Mass literature of the national revolutionary war' (*Minzu geming zhanzhengde dazhong wenxue*) proposed by Hu Feng, Feng Xuefeng and Lu Xun.

It has been shown earlier that a similar slogan to 'Mass literature of the national revolutionary war', that of 'Literature of a national revolutionary war' was put forward by the Left League soon after the Battle of Shanghai in 1932, but only one or two articles were written on it and it was not much publicised. In the polemic of 1936, the first one to be widely known was the 'National defence literature' slogan.

The 'National defence literature' slogan was not first introduced in China in 1935. In October 1934, in *Dawanbao*, Zhou Yang, using the pen-name 'Qi', published an article called 'National defence literature'[37] but he had no intention of making it a popular slogan or initiating a movement. There was no united front policy then and the article made no reference to it.

The article by Zhou Yang's close associate, Zhou Libo, 'On "National defence literature"' (*Guanyu guofang wenxue*), certainly echoed the new policy as it was published on 21 December 1935. At that time, both Xiao San's letter and the August First Declaration had already reached Shanghai, and Zhou Yang was considering dissolving the Left League and was ready to build a united front in the literary circle. The following lines of Zhou Libo's article show clearly that the slogan was going to embrace the largest portion of Chinese nationals:

> Under the banner of 'National defence literature', all narrow sectarian thinking and feelings must be eliminated. On the passes for the friends within the camp of 'National defence literature', there are only two simple lines: 'I am a Chinese', 'I am against traitors and foreign enemies'.[38]

The first shot was fired. Zhou Yang's followers, such as He Jiahuai, Tian Han, Zhou Gangming and Xu Maoyong, began to pour out large numbers of articles. Special issues on the slogan were published by *Shenghuo zhishi* (*Knowledge of life*). As expected, early articles stressed China's crisis in the face of Japanese invasion and the necessity of building a broad united front for the sake of national salvation. This was concordant with the demands of the politicians in Moscow. In fact, advocates of the slogan were eager to identify themselves with the political united front policy:

> Cultural movement is a reflection of political movement. Here, we believe that just like the united front in the political field, there is an urgent need among all sober cultural workers and all sober intellectuals for a united front.[39]

This would, on the one hand, justify their actions, and on the other, widen their influence.

Early articles also discussed the content and form of the literature. Most of them claimed that there could be great variety. Not only anti-imperialist, but anti-traitor and anti-feudalist works were counted as the literature of national defence.[40] He Jiahuai went further to suggest that the deeds of historical national heroes, such as Yu Fei, Wen Tianxiang, Xue Rengui and Hua Mulan should be promoted.[41]

Despite the eagerness and enthusiasm of its advocates, the slogan was not unopposed. One article reported that criticism came from different directions.[42] Xu Xing wrote a number of articles attacking the slogan.[43] His first article, 'Commenting on the "National defence literature"' (*Ping guofang wenxue*), was published in February 1936, less than two months after the slogan was first promulgated; and it was directed against an article by Zhang Shangbin, '"National defence literature" and national character' (*Guofang wenxue he minzusheng*).

Zhang Shangbin was the pen-name of Zhou Libo, who wrote the first article in the movement. In this article, he wanted to clear away the worries that advocating national defence literature would narrow the scope of literature. By quoting the example of capitalists' support in the Battle of Shanghai, he maintained that there were anti-imperialist elements within every class. Hence, in the struggle for national and social liberation, national defence literature could be the literature for the entire nation. He explicitly included people of classes other than the proletariat in the national defence literature movement.[44] This was taken as a target by Xu Xing in an attempt to expound his anti-united front ideas.

Xu Xing started his argument by stating that the imperialists' invasion aimed at making China a colony, thus enabling them to dominate China's market, take over her raw materials and exploit cheap labour. In order to make sure that money could be extracted, they would prefer to keep the colony peaceful. Hence, they would make use of the ruling class and the capitalists, who were also eager to cooperate with the imperialists to protect their own positions in the face of opposition at home. He admitted that in the Battle of Shanghai, capitalists made some contribution but they were also the first to urge a ceasefire. Xu concluded:

> We cannot imagine that 'at the present stage, the interests of the [proletarian] class are congruent with those of the entire Chinese populace'. We also know that the real anti-imperialist class is comprised of the masses who sell their labour. They are the only vanguard. The only kind of literature that can save China is the one in taking this viewpoint.[45]

It seemed that this opposition force was not small as there were some articles echoing Xu's viewpoint. Zhou Lengqie, while stating that he supported in principle 'National defence literature', also questioned the possibility of unity with the capitalists.[46] Another opponent of the slogan was a League member, Fang Zhizhong, editor of *Yeying* (*Nightingale*), the magazine which, as will be seen, was soon taken up to publicise Hu Feng's slogan in the polemic.[47] Xu Xing himself wrote at least two more articles. He said that the advocates of 'National defence literature' had leapt into the 'cesspool of patriotism' (*aiguo de wuchi*), filling the literary arena with turbid patriotic atmosphere. He cautioned people too, not to forget the bloody lesson of 1927 as there was no way to return to 1925 when the first united front between the GMD and the CCP was built.[48]

A counter campaign was launched by the 'National defence literature' group. Such heavyweights as Zhou Yang and Guo Moruo published articles to rebut Xu Xing, mainly accusing him of being fundamentally against the concept of united front. The origin of this, according to Zhou Yang, was Xu's ignorance of the theory of united front and the situation in China. He stated that anti-imperialist united front policy was the chief tactic of national revolution in colonial and semi-colonial areas. Both Zhou and Guo denied that 'National defence literature' was simply literature of patriotism in a narrow sense, although Zhou admitted that national feelings in literary works could make a greater impact on the readers,[49] and Guo asserted that there was nothing wrong with upholding patriotism in a victimised nation, as it was definitely anti-imperialist. To them, a patriot could at the same time be an internationalist, and 'National defence literature' could be regarded as 'a literature of patriotism in its broad sense'. They all agreed that Xu Xing's theory was sectarian and left-deviated. 'Revolution cannot be accomplished with white gloves on your hands', Guo said.[50]

This was by no means the essence of the 'Two slogan polemic', as the second slogan had not been proposed yet. After June 1936, Xu Xing did not write on the issue, and attention moved to Hu Feng's new slogan. Nevertheless it should be pointed out that Xu's radical attitude to the united front policy was similar to that of Lu Xun, at this early stage. Both had a deep hatred and uncompromising distrust of the capitalists and the ruling class; both were suspicious of the united front policy; but they acted differently. Xu voiced his opposition and came under heavy fire. Lu Xun kept silent, refusing to take part in or even comment (except privately) on the work done by Zhou Yang to build a united front. His support for the second slogan, however, shows that he did not accept unreservedly, the slogan of 'National defence literature'.

Lu Xun's silence was unacceptable to the advocates of the 'National defence literature' slogan. He Jiahuai, in a seminar, made the accusation that 'some writers - especially those senior writers - were indifferent'.[51] Zhou Yang even alleged that those keeping aloof and silent were left sectarians who constituted obstacles to the building of the united front.[52] This could be seen as an indirect attack on Lu Xun and an attempt to force him to show his stand. Zhou Yang was also unhappy with Lu's refusal to join the Association of Chinese Writers and Artists, a new organisation to represent the united front in the literary circle. In fact, Zhou Yang had been planning for the Writers Association (the

The Chinese League of Left-wing Writers

predecessor of the Association of Chinese Writers and Artists) since early 1936 and they were eager to enlist Lu's support. In January, Xia Yan had a meeting with Mao Dun at Zheng Zhenduo's house. Xia expressed the wish to ask Lu Xun to act as a promoter of the organisation. Lu refused, predicting that the attempt would be abortive.[53]

Meanwhile Feng Xuefeng had just returned to Shanghai after the Long March. It has been shown earlier that prior to his departure, Feng was close to Lu Xun and he had already had difficulties with Zhou Yang. In the years 1934-1935, largely because he was away from the scene, Lu Xun was alienated and the leading position in the left-wing literary circle was taken up by Zhou Yang. Beyond doubt, his return was going to make the situation more tense and complicated.

In a recollection, Feng Xuefeng claimed that the Party Central Committee, now settled at Wayaobao after the Long March, sent him back, with four missions:

1) to set up a radio transmitting station in Shanghai;
2) to establish relations with leaders in national salvation movements and inform them of the united front policy of Chairman Mao [Zedong] and the Provisional Central Committee of the CCP;
3) to contact the Shanghai Party underground and prepare for the re-establishment of Party organisation in Shanghai;
4) to take care of the work in the literary circle and pass on the united front policy of Chairman Mao and the Party Central Committee.[54]

Feng began his journey on 20 April and arrived in Shanghai on 25 April. He met Lu Xun the following day and immediately moved to live with him for about two weeks, after which he lived with Lu's younger brother, Zhou Jianren.[55]

Of the four missions assigned to Feng, the one which attracts attention here is the last one. But what did Feng Xuefeng do to fulfil the mission? Available material is fragmentary and controversial. Feng said that the first Party member he met was Zhou Wen, a close follower of Lu Xun and Hu Feng. He also said that he went to see Mao Dun on the third or fourth day while active leaders in national salvation movements, such as Shen Junru and Song Qingling were met within a week.[56] But what about meeting Zhou Yang and his group?

According to Mao Dun, when he first met Feng Xuefeng, Feng made it very clear that he did not intend to meet Zhou Yang 'within a short period'.[57] In his own recollections, Feng said that Zhang Wentian had told him a number of times to contact Lu Xun and Mao Dun first, in order to have a better understanding of the situation, before meeting Party members. This is an acceptable explanation since defection was so common then and for quite some time there had been no contact between the Party Central Committee (which was on the Long March) and the Party organisation in Shanghai (which had been raided). But how long was that 'short period'? Feng himself claimed that it was about twenty days after his arrival that he tried to arrange a meeting with

Dissolution and Polemic

Zhou Yang. Zhou refused to see him because Zhou was upset that he had met others first, and he was only able to meet Xia Yan at about that time.[58] So why did it take twenty days before he asked for a meeting with Zhou? If he was to take care of the literary circle and pass on the new united front policy, there was no reason why he should not have briefly met Zhou Yang, who was the leading figure as well as the chief architect of the united front in the literary circle. He would have known this immediately upon his arrival. Although he might have heard unpleasant talk about Zhou Yang from Lu Xun and Hu Feng, Mao Dun might have been able to provide a different picture, as Feng alleged that Mao had said nothing against Zhou. Thus this should be seen as a fault, or at least negligence on Feng's part. His explanation that he was then busy with other matters seems feeble as he had been meeting other people.[59] Moreover, Xia Yan told a different story. He accused Feng Xuefeng of refusing to meet them until he wrote a vigorous letter to Feng demanding a meeting. Then they were able to meet in June. Xia also reported that Zhou Yang once told him that he had not refused to meet Feng.[60] It is not known who was telling the truth but it is certain that Feng's return solved no problem but created new ones.

A critical development was his meeting with Hu Feng on the third day after his arrival, as the second slogan was decided at this meeting. Feng recalled that, upon hearing from Hu Feng that many people were opposed to the 'National defence literature' slogan, he suggested promulgating another slogan. But being a newcomer, Feng could have no justification for doing that. He had not had time to read those articles on the slogan of 'National defence literature', and his knowledge on the question came only from Hu Feng and Lu Xun, both of them Zhou Yang's opponents. He had not even met Mao Dun at that time.[61]

A new slogan was then formulated: 'Mass literature of the national revolutionary war'. They then secured the approval of Lu Xun. In Feng's opinion:

> The one who made the final decision on the slogan was Lu Xun. That is to say, the slogan was formulated by Lu Xun.[62]

Lu Xun himself acknowledged this publicly.[63] Nevertheless, the new slogan was brought to the public in an article called 'What do the masses demand from literature?' (*Renmin dazhong xiang wenxue yaoqiu shenme?*) by Hu Feng, finished on 9 May 1936 and published on 1 June. Before the article appeared, however, Hu had already spread the slogan around.[64] In fact, a short while before, according to Mao Dun, Hu's group had already decided to form a literary organisation separate from Zhou's.[65] Thus it would have appeared to Zhou Yang and his followers that immediately upon Feng Xuefeng's return, Lu Xun and Hu Feng gave up their passive attitude and intended to launch a counter-campaign. Tension between the two groups, even before the new slogan was formally brought out, mounted to a high level. It was at this moment that Zhou Yang himself wrote the first article since the 1934 one on the slogan of 'National defence literature'.[66] It was also then that they decided to call immediately the inaugural meeting of the Association of Chinese Writers and

Artists. Obviously, Zhou Yang wanted to build up for himself an orthodoxy in leading the united front of the literary arena.

Before Zhou Yang's organisation could come into existence, Hu Feng's article on the new slogan appeared. In the past, it has been said that Hu Feng did not show the article to Lu Xun and Feng Xuefeng before it was published, although he had secured their approval for writing it.[67] This has generally been regarded as a serious mistake on Hu's part.[68] However Hu Feng, in his memoirs written several decades later, stated that the article had been read by Feng and Lu, and that both had given their approval to the article before it was published.[69] In other words, he denied that he had acted independently although in the article he did not reveal that the slogan was formulated after discussion with Lu Xun and Feng Xuefeng. He did not even mention their names, nor did he say anything about Zhou Yang's slogan.

Lu Xun and Feng Xuefeng seemed unhappy with the outcome. Neither came to Hu's aid, until the final stage of the polemic. Hu was instructed by the two not to write on the topic again.[70] However, although he did not mention the slogan of 'National defence literature' and its relations with the new slogan, Hu's article was able to bring out the important difference in approach to the united front between Zhou Yang and Lu Xun. From the writings of Feng Xuefeng and Mao Dun, it is known that they and Lu Xun could not agree with the slogan of 'National defence literature' as it neglected the question of class in the united front. Hu Feng's article was able to stress the interests of the masses. He argued that since the May Fourth movement, the anti-imperialist demands of the toiling masses had been the main themes of literature. With the Manchurian Incident, a new historical stage developed. The anti-imperialist movement became a national revolutionary war representing the demands and hopes of the masses. Hence, the kind of literature demanded by the masses was 'Mass literature of the national revolutionary war'. He alleged that many works created after the September Eighteenth Incident were able to portray this change and could be the base for writing in the new slogan. In other words, he was stating that the slogan for creation in the new stage should be a continuation of the anti-imperialist movement centred on the interests of the masses. Thus, the role of the masses in the united front was emphasised:

> The 'Mass literature of the national revolutionary war' should state clearly that the interests of the labouring masses and those of the nation are congruent. It should show clearly who are the organisers in the national revolutionary war; who is the main force in overcoming the enemies; who are the conscious or unconscious traitors of the nation.[71]

As expected, response came fast. Just ten days after the appearance of Hu Feng's article, Xu Maoyong wrote the first counter-attack with the same title as Hu's article. Xu accused Hu of proposing a new slogan without discussing the one which had already been widely accepted. He considered this a divisive action, pointing out that although the present war was undoubtedly a 'national revolutionary war', it was different from previous ones (from the Taiping Rebellion to the December Eighth Incident which could also be regarded as national revolutionary wars) in that there was the building up of a national united front. Hu Feng did not even mention the slogan of the united front in his article. As a result, Hu Feng was unable to show the distinctiveness of the present situation and the difference between the present and previous struggles. Moreover, technically speaking, the new slogan, altogether eleven Chinese characters, was too long to be a slogan for mass movements. Consequently, Xu insisted that it was 'National defence literature' that the masses demand from literature.[72] Xu's rebuttal was clever. He was able to grasp the weaknesses in Hu's article: that Hu made no reference to the existing slogan and the united front policy. On the other hand, he deliberately avoided such important issues as the role played by the masses in the united front.

Thus the battle of two slogans within the same leftist camp formally erupted. Nevertheless, before it was red-hot, Zhou Yang's Association of Chinese Writers and Artists was inaugurated as planned. Its manifesto was drafted by Mao Dun. This was a good choice as he was then the middleman between the two camps. Although he had heard of the new slogan as well as Lu Xun's intention of founding a separate organisation, he was able to convince both sides not to put the slogans into their manifestos. He also took the lead, after discussions with Feng Xuefeng, in signing both manifestos.[73] This, on the one hand, drew a line between the slogans and the organisations, and on the other, gave the impression that the two groups were not greatly divided.

However, this effort at minimising the differences between the two groups was not fruitful. Though the slogans were not mentioned, the two manifestos were manifestations of them. It is true that both pledged support for anti-imperialist war but the proposal made in the manifesto of the Association of Chinese Writers and Artists was:

> Under the great aim of national salvation by the whole nation, writers who have different opinions on literature and art can be comrades-in-arms of the same front. Differences in opinions on literature and art will not affect our solidarity for the sake of national interests.[74]

But the declaration made by Lu Xun's group, the manifesto of the Chinese Literature and Art Workers (*Zhongguo wenyi gongzuozhe xuanyan*), drafted jointly by Ba Jin and Li Liewen,[75] insisted:

> We shall stick to our usual stand, keep in line with our original consistent beliefs, continue our past line, step up our work of fighting for national freedom, one which has begun since we first tried our hands in literature and art.[76]

These lines echoed the ideas of Hu Feng, and soon became the central point of controversy in the debate.

No activities were carried out by either group. The Association for Chinese Writers and Artists seemed to be better organised with an inaugural meeting, a manifesto, a list of regulations as well as a membership list.[77] Its list of promoters demonstrates that an attempt was made to achieve a broad united front. Shao Xunmei, who had long been under attack in the past decade, was on this list, Zhou Yang and Xia Yan's names were missing but obviously, the left was still in command. Mao Dun, Xu Maoyong and Shen Qiyu were elected as central committee members, while others on the committee like Fu Donghua, Zheng Zhenduo and Ye Shengtao were, at least, pro-left. On the other hand, those who signed the Chinese Literature and Art Workers' manifesto were largely Lu Xun's followers. The number of people signing both documents was small. Out of one hundred and eleven in the Association of Chinese Writers and Artists, and of the sixty-five who had signed the Chinese Literature and Art Workers' manifesto, only ten signed both.[78]

Lu Xun did not join the Association of Chinese Writers and Artists, but his name conspicuously took first place in the Chinese Literature and Art Workers' manifesto. His refusal to join Zhou Yang's united front, Lu explained in private correspondence, was because of his past experience in the Left League. He did not believe that Zhou Yang's group could achieve anything, and so he would like to wait and see.[79]

Hu Feng's article and slogan were not without support. On the day that Xu's rebuttal appeared, the first echo came, in an article called 'The various problems in the literature of China at the present stage' (*Zhongguo xianjieduan wenyi zhi zhuwenti*), in a newly founded journal. The author, Shi Fu, while ignoring the slogan of 'National defence literature', said that the 'Mass literature of the national revolutionary war' was able to shoulder the great responsibility of national salvation.[80] Besides, special issues on Hu Feng's slogan were put out by two journals, *Yeying* and *Xianshi wenxue* (*Realist literature*). Some articles in these special issues no longer avoided the previous slogan. Nie Gannu even acknowledged the existence and influence of the 'National defence literature' slogan and defended it against Xu Xing's criticism that the 'National defence literature' slogan was simply patriotic,[81] but it seemed that they all wanted to replace the 'National defence literature' slogan with the new slogan in leading the literary movement. None of them allowed the advocates of 'National defence literature' to evade the question of the masses. One went further, saying that the premise of the new slogan was the interests of the masses and the victory of the national revolutionary war would be a victory of the general masses.[82] They did not object to the united front but wanted to emphasise the 'leading force' in the front.[83] Moreover, they all stressed that while the new slogan was formulated to cope with the new crisis of Japanese invasion, it was also a continuation of the struggle against the imperialists. The following quotations show this attitude unmistakably:

> The 'Mass literature of the national revolutionary war' is definitely not a total negation of the literature before today. It is a paramount development of the new literary movement since 'May Fourth'.[84]

Dissolution and Polemic

But we have to be careful. The starting point of this new kind of literature ['Mass literature of the national revolutionary war'] does not exist by overthrowing past results.[85]

It seems that these were the basic differences between the two slogans. During the Cultural Revolution when Zhou Yang and his men were purged, their attitudes adopted in the 'Two slogan polemic' were attacked as rightist and capitulationist, because they had ignored the leadership of the proletariat and advocated cooperation between classes. It was also said that the slogan of 'National defence literature' was a product of the Wang Ming line opposing the correct Maoist line, upheld in the literary circle by Lu Xun and his slogan of the 'Mass literature of the national revolutionary war'. Thus, the 'Two slogan polemic' was in effect a struggle between two fundamentally opposing lines.[86]

Did this interpretation of the polemic present a genuine picture? Although Zhou Yang and the 'National defence literature' slogan have been rehabilitated, there cannot be a generally agreed conclusion.

In the first place, Zhou Yang and his group have openly admitted that their decision to dissolve the Left League and advocate 'National defence literature' was prompted by the August First Declaration and Xiao San's letter. Both came from the same source, Wang Ming in Moscow. In the August First Declaration, the establishment of the 'National defence government' (*Guofang zhengfu*) was advocated.[87] Advocates of the 'National defence literature' slogan had no hesitation in relating this to their own slogan. The foreword to *Xinwenhua* (*New culture*) began by praising the speech made in Moscow by Wang Ming, 'the distinguished politician of the Chinese working class'. The outlines suggested by Wang Ming for the national defence government were listed. It also made clear that 'political movements should be reflected in literary movements'.[88] Undoubtedly, the influence of Wang Ming could not be denied.

It has been pointed out that Wang Ming responded eagerly to the Comintern call for a shift of united front policy in the Seventh Congress of the Comintern in 1935. In the next few years, he was the chief supporter and architect of the second united front of the CCP with the GMD. For this reason he was later accused by Maoist historians of sacrificing the interests of the proletariat in favour of cooperation with the capitalists and, therefore, of being 'right opportunistic'.

Towards the end of 1935, Wang Ming was more and more eager to promote a united front with the GMD and Jiang Jieshi. In August, he was still debating the issue of proletarian leadership in the united front, claiming that:

> It is entirely wrong to think that proletarian leadership and the struggle for Soviet rule will be weakened when the Communist Party joins the anti-imperialist united front; ...
>
> in countries like China where the rule of Soviets has already been established on its territory, correct application of anti-imperialist national united front policy will not undermine the consolidation of proletarian leadership and the struggle for continuing victory of the

Chinese revolution by the Communist Party. Instead, it will enhance the status of the Party in the revolutionary struggle.[89]
But in his 'In reply to those who oppose the anti-imperialist united front' (*Da fadi tongyi zhanxian de fanduizhe*) on 7 November, he said that the CCP had 'repeatedly declared its willingness to reach an anti-Japanese agreement with any troops and any generals, and the troops of the Nanjing government are generally included'. He also claimed that the Communists would give Jiang Jieshi a chance to redeem his past sins against the people and the country if Jiang stopped fighting the Red Army and turned his guns against the Japanese imperialists.[90] He was making a direct appeal to Jiang and his army, a course of action unprecedented in the history of the CCP. Wang Ming also kept on criticising the Communist Party's 'left sectarianism'. He was, in particular, critical of the land revolutionary movement. He tried to convince the Chinese Communists that a united front with the GMD was essential because the Communists alone were too weak to fight against either the Japanese or the imperialists:

> It must be stated frankly that the necessity for creating a broad anti-imperialist united front is dictated not only by the growing power of the Red Army and the Soviets but also by the existence of weaknesses in them.[91]

According to Zhang Guotao, at the beginning of 1936, the Chinese Communists received instructions from Lin Yuying, the agent sent back to China by Wang Ming, that such slogans as 'Down with Jiang Jieshi' and 'Land revolution' were to be dropped and replaced by the slogan 'Unite with Jiang to fight against the Japanese' (*Lianjiang kangri*).[92]

Mao Zedong, however, whose leadership of the CCP was consolidated at the Zunyi Conference in January 1935, was not of the same opinion. Obviously, he could not tolerate a united front which might impinge upon the interests of the Red Army. On 25 December 1935, at the Wayaobao Politburo Conference, which was under his control, a 'Resolution on the present political situation and the tasks of the Party' (*Zhongyang guanyu muqian zhengzhi xingshi yu dangde renwu jueyi*) was adopted. Two days later, Mao himself delivered a report called 'On the tactics of opposing Japanese imperialism' (*Lun fandui Riben diguozhuyi de celüe*). In both documents, Mao, for the first time, admitted the need for a new united front policy in the face of mounting Japanese aggression. In this respect, there was no difference between Wang and Mao; but Mao Zedong could not agree that China's primary and only enemy was Japanese imperialism. The resolution stated categorically that 'the main enemy of the movement is Japanese imperialism and the ringleader of the traitors, Jiang Jieshi'. It asserted that GMD rule was weakening and dying and that Jiang was trying to prolong it by selling out China. As for the united front policy, Mao insisted:

> The Party should call upon all those who oppose Japan to struggle in protecting their bases. It should call upon those people to oppose the traitors in their attempt to harness the rear of the war against

Dissolution and Polemic

Japan and ... obstruct the path of the Red Army. To unite the civil war in China with the national war is the basic principle of the Party in guiding the revolutionary war.[93]

In Mao's opinion, the wars against Japan and the GMD were to be fused together in the united front and the principles of the new policy should fit in with the main task of fighting both Japanese imperialism and its 'jackals'. In other words, the united front should still enable the growth of revolution, and should comprise all those who were opposed to both Japan and Jiang Jieshi. While he agreed with Wang Ming that the chief danger confronting the Party was sectarianism, Mao also pointed to the danger of 'rightist opportunism'. It was not until the end of April 1936 that for the first time, Mao's Party Central Committee openly declared the inclusion of the GMD in their united front, and on 5 May they called for unity against Japan and claimed that they had made an attempt to 'hasten the final awakening of Jiang Jieshi and the patriotic officers and men in his army' by withdrawing their troops from Shaanxi.[94] The transformation was completed only in August, when such slogans as 'Invite Jiang to fight against Japan' (*Qing Jiang kangri*) and 'Force Jiang to fight against the Japanese' (*Bi Jiang kangri*) began to appear in Communist documents.[95]

When the Wayaobao Politburo Conference was called, Feng Xuefeng was with the Red Army and the provisional Party Central government. Being close to Mao, his concept of the united front would differ from that of Wang Ming. Feng stated that the last mission assigned to him for his return to Shanghai was to pass on the united front policy of Chairman Mao. He did not mention being asked to counteract Wang Ming's influence in the literary arena but can his bold action in formulating a new slogan on the third day after his arrival be related to this? No answer is provided by Feng, yet beyond doubt, Lu Xun's acceptance of the united front policy was largely due to Feng Xuefeng who preached to him a more acceptable approach to the new situation, that was, Mao Zedong's united front policy. Consequently, advocates of 'Mass literature of the national revolutionary war' put great emphasis on the question of proletarian leadership.

To be fair, it should be pointed out that not everyone in the 'National defence literature' group was opposed to grasping the leadership in the united front. Some articles, especially those that appeared in the early stage, did stress this point. The foreword to *Xinwenhua*, which praised highly Wang Ming's speech at the Seventh Comintern Congress, closed with the following lines:

Before classes vanish, each class still has its own target... The working class has to warn its own team not to be soiled by corruptive liberalism and parochial nationalism, not to cherish the illusion of peaceful reforms... Within the united front, the working class must not give up for a second criticising other classes. Our China - is the Soviet China; our culture - the socialist proletarian culture. We must insist and convince others that it is the only genuine anti-Japanese, anti-Jiang, the new culture of China.[96]

One of Zhou Libo's earliest articles expressed this more explicitly:

> There are anti-imperialist elements among the masses of various classes in China. But the toiling mass is their mainstay... 'National defence literature' is, first of all, the literature of the Chinese toiling mass.[97]

Unfortunately, this was not the dominant theory in the 'National defence literature' camp. On the contrary, after the appearance of the second slogan, they, in an attempt to justify themselves, insisted that the question of proletarian leadership should not be emphasised. The most often quoted lines were from Xu Maoyong's letter to Lu Xun:

> The mainstay of the present united front - in China as well as in the rest of the world - is undoubtedly the proletariat. But this is not because of its name, its special position and history, but its correct grasp of reality and its tremendous ability to struggle. Thus, objectively speaking, the proletariat should not openly pin on a badge and demand leadership not on account of its work but because of special qualifications, so that comrades-in-arms of other classes are frightened away. Therefore, to raise a left-wing slogan in the united front is wrong and endangers the united front.[98]

Qu Yi (Wang Renshu) expressed a similar idea:

> Here, of course, we cannot forget the leading role played by the toiling mass. There is, in fact, no reason to forget. Nevertheless, in order not to cause a rift within the united front all of a sudden, thus weakening the 'anti-imperialist, anti-X [Japanese]' force, it seems that it is not appropriate to stress in form the leading role of the mass. In reality, only the mass is the most active, most basic 'anti-imperialist' group... There is no need to show up explicitly the standpoints of the masses.[99]

However, it must be noted that Dimitrov, Mao Zedong, Zhou Enlai and Liu Shaoqi all stressed, at different times, the importance of the role of the proletariat as well as the question of leadership in the united front.[100] If they represented the 'correct' line, the advocates of 'National defence literature' must have been right-deviated and capitulationist. In other words, the Cultural Revolution interpretation of the slogan was not totally unjustified, although there might have been deliberate exaggeration.[101]

It is unfair, however, for Zhou Yang and his men in Shanghai to be regarded as entirely responsible. As noted earlier, his decision to build a united front had its origin in the August First Declaration, Wang Ming's speech in the Seventh Comintern Congress and Xiao San's letter. None of them mentioned the slogan of 'National defence literature', but the term 'National defence government' was in both the Declaration and the speech. If this was to be reflected in the literary circle, 'National defence literature' was a natural outcome. Zhou Yang should not be blamed for following Wang Ming too closely. His defence made in an interview in 1978 probably contains the truth of the matter:

Dissolution and Polemic

> At that time, all we knew of Chairman Mao was that he was a revolutionary leader. Not only did we not understand the thought of Chairman Mao, we could not get to know it at all in Shanghai. After the Shanghai apparatus was destroyed, it became more difficult to find out things from Chairman Mao and the base areas. So all we could do was look to the Soviet Union and the Comintern. At that time, we could get hold of the materials on the Soviet Union and the Comintern in Shanghai.[102]

Zhou was careful with his wording here. The fact was that in the early thirties, Mao Zedong's influence in Shanghai was not significant. After the failure of the Autumn Harvest Uprisings in 1927, Mao was based in the Jingang Mountains, in Hunan. Though he was a member of the Politburo, his rise to Party leadership was at the Zunyi Conference in January 1935, when the provisional central government was on the Long March. It was impossible to establish communications between Shanghai and the Red Army. Further, Mao's more important writings had not been published at that time. Feng Xuefeng admitted that it was not until 1936 that Mao's thought began to be recognised by Party members.[103] On the other hand, Wang Ming was chief secretary of the CCP in 1931, before becoming chairman of the Chinese delegation to the Comintern that winter. Zhou Yang returned to Shanghai from Japan in 1930, and rose to power in 1933. During this time Wang Ming's position was consolidated. Was it not natural, and 'correct', for him to follow Wang Ming's instructions closely?

On the other hand, Feng Xuefeng had a complete knowledge of Mao's interpretation of the united front policy. He had done a good job in passing on these ideas to Lu Xun, thus convincing him of the wisdom of the new policy. However, nowhere is there any indication that he had conveyed the same message to Zhou Yang. Zhou might have refused to see him; but the second slogan was decided before Feng made the first attempt to meet Zhou. In other words, Feng ignited the polemic before giving Zhou Yang a chance to acquire the 'correct' united front policy. Zhou and his followers committing a rightist 'error' is therefore excusable.

If the interpretation made during the Cultural Revolution, that Zhou Yang and his slogan were rightist, and that the 'Two slogan polemic' was a struggle between two opposing lines, is adhered to, then there would have been no way for the two groups to come to terms. Ironically, it was the unbending and 'infallible' Lu Xun who made the first attempt to compromise. Moreover, at the later stage of the debate, it was the leftist sectarian attitude of Zhou Yang and his group that Mao Dun and Lu Xun began to criticise.

Just days after the publication of Hu Feng's 'What do the masses demand from literature?', Feng Xuefeng wrote for Lu Xun two articles, one in the form of an open letter and the other, an interview record of a meeting with Lu Xun. Feng emphasised that the ideas expressed in these two articles were those of Lu Xun, and that the articles had Lu's approval before they were published.[104] They can therefore be taken as Lu Xun's own writings.

The first article was an open letter to a Trotskyist, Chen Zhongshan, who had sent Lu Xun a letter and some magazines. Lu did not comment on the two slogans in this letter but made clear that he supported Mao Zedong's advocacy of 'uniting all groups to fight against Japanese aggression'. The fact that he specified Mao Zedong's name and expressed his support for the latter's policy was significant. His criticism of Chen's anti-united front theory also revealed that Lu Xun was now ready to accept the new policy. Further, in the letter, Lu pointed out Chen's intention in writing to him: make use of the conflicts and sow discord between Lu Xun and his 'comrades-in-arms'.[105] Lu, though discontented with Zhou Yang, could not allow himself to be used by Trotskyists. This might be why he hastened to try to resolve the battle with Zhou.

The second article, entitled 'On our present literary movement: Reply for an interviewer from my sickbed' (*Lun xianzai womende wenxue yundong: Bingzhong da fangwenzhe*) is of the utmost importance as, for the first time, it openly revealed Lu Xun's opinions on the two slogans. The basic concepts on the 'Mass literature of the national revolutionary war' were not greatly different from those argued by Hu Feng. It was a development from the proletarian revolutionary literature which had been started by the League of Left-wing Writers. Thus the promulgation of the new slogan should not be viewed as a sign to halt the existing revolutionary literary movement. Instead, it would deepen and expand all anti-fascist, anti-reactionary struggles, making them more realistic, more specific and driving them into the general struggle against Japanese aggression. Like Hu Feng, Lu Xun affirmed that they would not give up the leadership responsibility. Rather, the responsibility would be greater, and had to be expanded and strengthened so that the entire nation would face outward against aggression. In passing, he criticised some of his comrades-in-arms who failed to understand this.[106]

However, Lu Xun immediately followed with a note of compromise by saying that the two slogans could co-exist:

> The 'Mass literature of the national revolutionary war', just like the slogan of proletarian revolutionary literature, is perhaps a general slogan. I believe that there is no harm to propose some more specific slogans, such as 'National defence literature', 'National salvation literature' and 'anti-Japanese literature', under the general slogan to suit the changes. This is not only harmless, but even useful and necessary.[107]

This declaration of the acceptance of 'National defence literature' marked a difference from the attitudes of Hu Feng and his supporters, and in fact, according to both Mao Dun and Feng Xuefeng, Lu Xun's article was aimed at correcting the mistakes made by Hu. This might provide the basis for reconciliation and that was why they decided that the two articles were to be published in magazines of both sides.[108]

Mao Dun, feeling that Lu's criticism of Hu Feng was too mild, also added a letter to the editor of *Wenxuejie* (*Literary arena*), in which the two articles were to be published. He echoed Lu Xun in insisting that the two slogans were not opposed but complementary. Hence, Hu Feng's ignoring the more specific slogan, 'National defence literature', and his attempt to substitute it with his own, was a serious mistake. Mao Dun also criticised those who supported Hu Feng, and defended 'National defence literature' as not just nationalistic.[109] This can be viewed as Mao Dun's attempt to please Zhou's group.

On 1 July 1936, Lu's two articles appeared in *Xianshi wenxue*, one edited by Yin Geng, one of the signatories of the Chinese Literature and Art Workers' manifesto. Ten days later, *Wenxuejie*, edited by Xu Maoyong, published 'On our present literary movement' and Mao Dun's letter but 'Letter in reply to the Trotskyists' (*Da Tuoluosijipai de xin*) was missing. The reason given by the editor was 'because of the situation'.[110] This excuse was of course unacceptable, as the article had been published in *Xianshi wenxue* and *Wenxue congbao*. There was no reason why *Wenxuejie* could not publish it.

What made the situation worse was the editor's note following Lu Xun's article and Mao Dun's letter. The editor first expressed his gratitude for Lu Xun's advice but he soon shifted to criticising Hu Feng's proposal of the new slogan. He could not agree with Lu Xun and Mao Dun that 'Mass literature of the national revolutionary war' could be a suitable slogan for the present situation, as the 'masses' - usually referred to as the toiling masses - could not represent the entire nation.[111] Clearly, the editor of *Wenxuejie*, though accepting the articles for publication, could not take their ideas.

Meanwhile, Guo Moruo's 'National defence, cesspool, purgatory' (*Guofang wuchi lianyu*) appeared. As noted earlier, it was aimed at criticising Xu Xing's anti-united front theories but its ideas inspired Mao Dun. After a long discussion with Feng Xuefeng who was angry at the attitudes of the editor of *Wenxuejie*, Mao Dun wrote the article 'On the controversial two slogans' (*Guanyu yinqi jiufen de liangge kouhao*).

In the article, Mao Dun concentrated his criticism on the left sectarianism in the literary arena. Hu Feng was condemned for turning the slogan of 'Mass literature of the national revolutionary war' into one opposing the first slogan. It was also wrong for Hu's followers, such as Nie Gannu, to try to make it the sole slogan for the united front. He reiterated Lu Xun's assertion that the two slogans should co-exist. On the other hand, Zhou Yang was not spared. His words in 'On "National defence literature"' that 'the theme of "National defence literature" should be the most central theme of writings for all those writers other than traitors' were quoted for criticism. Mao Dun said that this was a closed-door and sectarian attitude, because it implied that anyone not writing in the theme of national defence, for instance, those who wrote on daily life and love, would be regarded as traitors.[112] He supported Guo Moruo's definitions of 'National defence literature':

> 'National defence literature and art' should be defined as non-traitorous literature and art, or anti-imperialist literature and art.

> 'National defence literature' and art should be the mark of a relationship among writers, but not the mark of principles in creative writing.[113]

It seemed that Guo's definitions could be a basis for resolving the battle, as Zhou Yang's rebuttal, immediately following Mao's article in the same issue of *Wenxuejie* (its editor, Xu Maoyong, gave Mao's article to Zhou Yang before publication), also agreed with Guo. But he insisted that 'National defence literature' could be a slogan for creation. He replied to Mao Dun's accusation:

> The theme of 'national defence' contains the dominant direction of real life as well as its various aspects. Writers are allowed to have various thoughts and stances. They may use various ways for creation and expression. Its scope is not that narrow as to be restrictive. Moreover, it is not that apart from the theme of 'national defence', any other themes must be discarded. I said that 'the theme of national defence should be the most central theme of writings for all those writers other than traitors'. What is called 'the most central' one is naturally not the 'only' one.[114]

He could not agree that they would exclude those who did not write on national defence in the national defence movement. He stated categorically:

> I never proposed that writers must write on the theme of 'national defence' before they are allowed to join the national defence movement. Nor have I said that those who join the national defence movement must write on the theme of 'national defence'.[115]

He maintained that for writers in general, the slogan of 'National defence literature' was just a hope, not an imposition. Yet it was reasonable to ask for some more meaningful works from those who had joined the united front.

Angered by Zhou Yang's unyielding attitude and the behaviour of the editor of *Wenxuejie*, Mao Dun wrote a furious riposte. This time, he did not say much on the two slogans, but pinpointed the issue of sectarianism.[116] He said that this was Feng Xuefeng's idea. According to Mao Dun, Zhou Yang later sent someone to give him an explanation and so he did not further pursue the issue.[117] In fact, Mao's article did not attract much attention then because before it was published, Lu Xun's famous open reply to Xu Maoyong appeared.

Xu started correspondence with Lu Xun in November 1933.[118] It has been suggested that from then until the end of 1935, Xu had Lu Xun's 'high regard and friendship no less than Hu Feng or Huang Yuan'.[119] Over forty letters were written by Lu Xun to Xu and he also wrote a preface for the latter's collection of essays.[120] However, a close look into the development of their 'friendship' will reveal the mistake in stating that it was 'on the strength of this friendship that Hsu [Xu] took the liberty of writing the letter of admonition'.[121]

The first sign of disagreement between them appeared as early as May 1934 when Xu Maoyong took up the editorship of *Xinyulin* against Lu Xun's wishes. Lu believed that the behaviour of the Guanghua Bookstore, the publisher of *Xinyulin*, was suspect, and thus strongly advised Xu not to fall into the trap.[122]

Dissolution and Polemic

Fortunately this did not constitute a serious problem between them as Lu continued to lend his support to Xu. He even comforted Xu when the latter had to quit the work.[123] But the incident reveals unmistakably the attitude of Xu Maoyong towards Lu Xun: he gave greater weight to the words of CCP leaders of the Left League than those of Lu Xun. This was because the taking up of the editorship of *Xinyulin* was, according to Xu himself, a League decision.[124]

The real threat to their friendship came in the summer of 1935, when Xu was responsible for publication of a League journal, *Wenyi qunzhong* (*Literary masses*). Lu Xun twice refused Xu's request for a donation for the journal and consequently there was not enough money to pay the publisher. Lu Xun wrote to Hu Feng on 24 August, accounting for the incident. He wanted everyone to contribute so that everybody shared the responsibility. In the same letter, he mentioned to Hu that he had been accused of being miserly by 'our field marshal'.[125] Xu said in his recollections that he had not heard of this at that time[126] but would it be natural for Lu Xun to think that Xu was the one who spread such rumours when he had just turned down Xu's demand for money?

Then came the issue of the dissolution of the Left League and the 'National defence literature' slogan some months later. Xu Maoyong was given the difficult job of persuading Lu Xun to accept the dissolution without a proclamation. At their final meeting, Lu Xun did not say a word to Xu. Then in a letter on 2 May 1936, Lu Xun closed with the following abrupt line:

> I hope this is my last letter, and from now on, all my old official duties come to an end.[127]

The message was clear. Lu Xun wanted to break off relations with Xu Maoyong. It may be thought that Lu was too harsh on Xu as the latter was merely carrying out instructions from his seniors, but it was Xu who, on 30 April, upon reading Lu Xun's letter to He Jiahuai saying that he did not know whether the Left League was still in existence, wrote to Lu Xun a letter the tone of which was mild, but which unmistakably pointed out that Lu had wronged him. He stated that before and after the dissolution of the League, Lu Xun was well informed and there was no reason why he should say that he did not know of the dissolution. More importantly, he reproached Lu for not appreciating their efforts, but blaming the entire group when minor mistakes were committed by individuals.[128] These words simultaneously accused Lu Xun and revealed that Xu stood on the side of Zhou Yang. Lu's anger was therefore to be expected. Also, Xu had already published articles supporting the 'National defence literature' slogan. Hence, the rumour that Xu was among those Lu Xun hated most vehemently, as reported in Xu's letter, might not be untrue.

Thus, the 'friendship' between Lu Xun and Xu Maoyong virtually came to an end in April-May 1936. Xu's letters on 5 May and 3 June were not answered.[129] What followed was the furious open letter of 4-5 August 1936, published together with Xu Maoyong's letter to him on 1 August.

In a private letter to Yang Jiyun about three weeks after he had finished his open reply to Xu Maoyong, Lu Xun wrote that 'though he knows well enough that only a little time ago I was seriously ill and almost died, Xu was the first one to strike my door majestically'.[130] This seemed harsh and unjustified, as Xu began his letter by inquiring after Lu's health. T A Hsia has rightly said that Xu displayed no ill-feeling towards Lu personally[131] but obviously, Xu's admonition was too blunt to be acceptable to someone like Lu Xun. After a short paragraph explaining that he had to leave Shanghai for a while because of bad health and financial difficulties, he hastened to stress that Lu Xun's 'words and deeds in the past half year had inadvertently encouraged a bad trend'. To Xu, Lu Xun's two closest associates, Hu Feng and Huang Yuan were respectively tricky and sycophantic but Lu failed to realise this, and fell into their possession. Consequently, he was used as a figurehead to delude and impress the masses. Xu claimed that this was why Hu Feng's separatist action could not be checked:

> It would be very easy to belabour them for what they have said or done, but because they have you as their shield and we all have such a high regard for you, we find ourselves in a most difficult position in dealing with them effectively or engaging them in debate.[132]

As for the 'Two slogan polemic', Xu Maoyong charged that Hu Feng's proposing a new slogan was motivated by self-interest and extreme sectarianism. His theories were self-contradictory and riddled with errors. 'Not even you [Lu Xun] can give them full justification.' Lu's support of Hu Feng's slogan was because he had failed to understand the basic policy:

> Thus, to introduce a left-wing slogan into the united front under the present circumstances is wrong and harmful to the united front. And so you were mistaken, in your recently published 'Reply to an interviewer from my sickbed' when you claimed that the slogan 'Mass literature of the national revolutionary war' was the most recent development of proletarian literature and that it should be the chief slogan of the united front.[133]

He went on to accuse Lu Xun of not cooperating with the majority in joining the Association of Chinese Writers and Artists while keeping company with the anarchist Ba Jin. By citing the anarchist movements of Spain and France which sabotaged the united front, Xu was in effect saying that Lu Xun was anti-united front. Before closing his letter, he tried to dig out the origin of Lu's 'faults':

> I fancy the root of your mistakes in the past half year is that you considered only people, not facts. And you often misjudge people.[134]

He also protested that he was put beyond the pale for such a minor thing as slapdash writing. He considered this 'laughable' and 'unjustified'.

From the above description, we have no doubt that the old man would be angered, although Xu had made it clear that he did not intend to attack Lu Xun. Lu showed the letter to Feng Xuefeng and insisted on writing a reply himself.[135] Three days after he got Xu's letter, on 5 August, Lu Xun wrote in his diary, 'finished the reply to Xu Maoyong in the evening'.[136] The long reply appeared on 15 August, in *Zuojia*, together with the full version of Xu's letter.

Dissolution and Polemic

In the reply, Lu Xun first spent some paragraphs in stating his support for the united front policy:

> But the policy of united front against Japanese aggression proposed to the whole people by the present Chinese revolutionary party is one I have seen, one that I support, and I join this front unconditionally, for the reason that I am not only a writer, but also a Chinese. That is why, to me, this policy is absolutely correct.[137]

That was in reply to Xu's challenge that Lu Xun had no knowledge of the current policy. As for the united front movement in the literary arena, he stated that he was 'of the view that all writers, no matter what groups they belonged to, should unite together in response to the call to resist Japanese aggression'. But he said that the formation of the Association of Chinese Writers and Artists did not imply the establishment of a united front. 'Far from it', Lu commented, because it still 'smacks strongly of sectarianism and gangsterism'.

Lu Xun then turned to the issue of the 'National defence literature' slogan. He believed that a distinction should be drawn between supporting national defence and supporting 'National defence literature':

> In my view, no conditions should be laid down for the unification of writers. As long as he is not a traitor, is willing to assist or approve resistance, then whether he belongs to the 'brother-and-sister' school, the school of pedantic gibberish, or the 'mandarin-duck and butterfly' school, it does not matter. ... To my mind, we should unite writers under the banner of 'resisting Japan' or 'national defence', but we cannot ask all writers to unite under the slogan of 'National defence literature' because some of them do not write on the 'themes of national defence', yet they can still join the united front against Japanese aggression in various ways.[138]

He quoted himself and his work, 'The true story of Ah Q', as well as that of Mao Dun, *Midnight*, and the classical novel, *The dream of the red chamber* (*Hongloumeng*) to prove that apart from the literature of national defence and literature of traitors, there could be the third type.

Having stated his views on the united front policy and the slogan, 'National defence literature', Lu Xun proceeded to his slogan, 'Mass literature of the national revolutionary war'. As for its relationship with the first slogan, Lu Xun repeated his ideas in the previous article that while Zhou Yang's slogan could be a specific slogan, his own should be a general one and hence the two could coexist. For the first time, he made public that the slogan was formulated by him and not Hu Feng, and that Hu Feng wrote the article to publicise the slogan at his request. Lu Xun deliberately added that Mao Dun was one of those consulted before the slogan was decided. But Lu Xun continued:

> However, the question is not who put forward the slogan, but whether or not it is wrong. If it is to urge left-wing writers who have hitherto restricted themselves to proletarian revolutionary literature to hasten to the front line of the national revolutionary war against

Japanese aggression, if it is to remedy the ambiguity of the slogan of 'National defence literature' in terms of literary theory, and to correct some of the incorrect ideas instilled into this formulation, then the raising of this slogan for these reasons is appropriate and correct.[139]

He then went on to personal matters denying that he had strengthened any vicious tendencies, for in the past half year he had written very little and had been ill for three months. As for people like Hu Feng, Ba Jin and Huang Yuan, he admitted that he had known them only for a short time and only through literary work. But they were his friends, he had to defend them when they were slandered as 'traitors' and 'despicable' without evidence. Lu Xun asserted that he considered both people and facts. He cited several facts to illustrate how people like Xu Maoyong and the 'four fellows' slandered him and Hu Feng, and caused the arrest of some good comrades. There was even a newspaper report saying that Lu Xun was going to sell out to the authorities with Hu Feng's connivance. Lu Xun said angrily:

Even if Hu Feng is not to be trusted, I can at least trust myself. I never negotiated with Nanjing via Hu Feng.[140]

To Lu Xun, although he had his shortcomings, Hu Feng was a promising young man, and 'he has never taken part in any movement opposing the anti-Japanese movement or the united front. Such a fact men like Xu Maoyong cannot refute, with all their cunning and schemes'. As for Huang Yuan and Ba Jin, Lu admired Huang as a conscientious and hardworking translator, while the latter was a passionate writer with progressive ideas. If they wanted to join the united front, they should be welcome. They had both signed the manifesto of the Chinese Literature and Art Workers. It was really a bad trend trying to split the literary ranks with slander, and this approximated to 'treachery'. Before he ended his letter, Lu continued his lashing of Xu. Xu was muddle-headed, a writer of the bickering type and connected with the gutter press. Unless he could repent and correct his mistakes, he would become a slave driver who would be 'incurable, not only of no use to China, but downright harmful too'.[141]

This long reply, amounting to over six thousand words, not only refuted to the last point the accusations put forward by Xu, but also revealed Lu Xun's long suppressed anger towards his comrades-in-arms. He made no attempt to hold back their names so we see all the heavyweights of the League under fire. As one critic commented, 'his tone was anger undisguised, unrestrained, almost shrill'.[142] It is difficult to understand why comrades in the same camp for the same cause should have received such heavy verbal lashing, unless this is viewed in connection with the events which happened in the League and to Lu over the previous several years. To Lu Xun, Xu's letter represented a group, and was a part and a continuation of the general assault plan made against him by Zhou Yang's clique.[143] He had had enough from them during the last years of the League. Now the League no longer bound them together in name, and the publication of the two different manifestos, together with the polemic over the two slogans, had already revealed to the public that two opposing camps were in existence. Hence, it was no longer necessary for Lu Xun to hide his indignation. Further, during those few months, Lu Xun's health was failing. More than once, he told others that Xu's letter was an attempt to hasten him to his death.[144] This was another reason why he reacted so vigorously.

The impact of Lu Xun's letter was tremendous. It threw Zhou Yang's group into confusion. Guo Moruo reported much indignation and pessimism.[145] Zhou Yang and the members of the now dissolved standing committee of the Left League called a meeting to criticise Xu Maoyong, who was severely condemned for damaging their solidarity with Lu Xun.[146] Xu did not accept this charge, insisting that the ideas in his letter were imparted to him by Zhou and his group. Thus he broke with them, writing another open letter, 'In reply to Mr Lu Xun' (*Huanda Lu Xun xiansheng*), which was published in September. This time, all patience was gone. The vicious words that had been used by Lu Xun to describe Xu, such as 'despotic', 'muddled-headed', 'abominable' and 'slanderous' were quoted and used against Lu. He was in particular offended by Lu's publishing personal correspondence, thus many things that should not be brought into the open, for instance, his comments on Ba Jin and Huang Yuan as well as the internal problems of the Left League, were made public.[147]

Lu Xun made no reply to this letter. It was obvious that he had won the battle. As though a giant water bomb had been dropped, the flames of the 'Two slogan polemic' were extinguished almost instantly. The 'National defence literature' group dared not write on the issue, except Guo Moruo who sent in 'An inspection of a military exercise' from Japan. Although his arguments in a previous article had been echoed and praised by Lu Xun and Mao Dun, Guo did not spare his criticism of the second slogan. Its eleven Chinese characters caused great problems and ambiguity in interpretation, Guo asserted. Moreover, as advocates of the second slogan were not against the 'National defence literature' slogan, there was no need to formulate a new one when the first one already had general support. Thus the slogan of 'Mass literature of the national revolutionary war' should be withdrawn. He called the challenge raised by Hu Feng and Lu a simulated war and the polemic, a wargame manipulated by Lu Xun for the inspection of the military strength of the left-wing writers.[148]

Lu Xun did not answer Guo's article, and Mao Dun made a feeble response later.[149] Yet Guo could by no means turn the tables. In August, Feng Xuefeng, now in the capacity of deputy head of the newly established Shanghai office of the CCP, wrote the first article on the topic, 'Opinions on the several questions in the literary movement' (*Guanyu wenxue yundong jige wenti de yijian*). This was an even longer and more direct attack on Zhou Yang and his slogan than Lu's open letter to Xu Maoyong.[150] Feng also took action to dissolve the Cultural Committee which was formerly in Zhou Yang's hands. Seventeen days after the publication of his article, on 1 October, there was the 'Manifesto of members of the literary arena for solidarity against aggression and freedom of speech' (*Wenyijie tongren wei tuanji yuwu yu yanlun ziyou xuanyan*), signed by twenty-one people. This can be seen as a sign of compromise and unity between the two groups, as Guo Moruo's name appeared along with those of Lu Xun and Mao Dun, and most of the signatories had also signed the manifestos of either the Association of Chinese Writers and Artists or the Chinese Literature and Art Workers. There were also the names of the most important members of the 'mandarin-duck and butterfly school', Zhou Shoujuan and Bao Tianxiao.[151] It seemed that for a time solidarity in the literary circle had materialised. But except for Guo Moruo, the strongest supporters of the 'National defence literature' slogan, such as Zhou Yang, Xia Yan, Zhou Libo and Xu Maoyong, were missing. This can be viewed as their admitting defeat, as they had to give up the leadership. Forty years later, Zhou Yang recalled that after he had been criticised by Lu Xun, he could not work smoothly as a leader in the Shanghai literary arena.[152] Finally, the top leader of the CCP in the white area, Liu Shaoqi, published an article to conclude the polemic. He unreservedly supported Lu Xun and criticised both Zhou Yang and Guo Moruo, making Lu stand out as the champion of the debate.[153] Nevertheless, before long, Lu Xun collapsed before another challenge, his illness. During the last few months, he had been much troubled by pleurisy, from which he had suffered for more than thirty years. He had made plans to rest in other parts of the country or even in Japan but before he could do so, he passed away. He died on 19 October 1936. Meanwhile, after the Xi'an Incident (December 1936) which led to the formation of the second united front between the GMD and the CCP, and the Luoguoqiao Incident (July 1937) which marked the beginning of the eight year Sino-Japanese War, the literary movement in China entered a new stage, Literature of the resistance war (*Kangzhan wenxue*).

Hence, the 'Two slogan polemic' was relatively short-lived, though bitter. It lasted for only about four to five months. But why did it happen? Was there such a great difference between the two slogans that a polemic was inevitable?

Undoubtedly, the major difference lay in the issue of proletarian leadership. Lu Xun was not against national defence, nor the slogan of 'National defence literature' in particular. He made this point very clear in his open letter to Xu Maoyong. The reason he proposed a new slogan was to correct the wrong ideas embodied in the first one. In the recollections of people like Hu Feng, Feng Xuefeng and Mao Dun, Lu Xun objected that the 'National defence literature' slogan lacked a clear class stand, and it appeared to him that the dissolution of the Left League without issuing a proclamation, as well as the ignoring of proletarian leadership in some of the interpretations of the 'National defence literature' slogan, were signs of defeat for the left. By contrast, the new slogan, with such words as 'mass literature' and 'national revolutionary war', was able to highlight the role played by the masses and show that the new movement was a continuation of past revolutionary activities.

Was the gap, then, unbridgeable? Even Wang Ming and Mao Zedong had difficulty over the action to be taken in the new political situation. Wang, in 1935 and early 1936, had already been in favour of uniting with the GMD and

Dissolution and Polemic

Jiang Jieshi. Mao, however, did not give up his attack on Jiang until after 1936, but the fact that the two finally came to terms and that the second united front was eventually built up showed that the differences between them could be settled. The case of the 'Two slogan polemic' was similar. We have noted that Zhou Yang followed Wang Ming closely while Lu Xun was convinced by Mao Zedong's united front policy. Yet, if the two politicians could compromise, there was no reason why the 'Two Slogan Polemic' should have been so bitter. It should be stressed again that Lu Xun, during the course of the debate, mentioned more than once that the two slogans could co-exist. This could not have been possible if the difference was beyond remedy. Thus, the outbreak of the polemic could not be solely attributed to the issue of proletarian leadership.

The personal factor was of the utmost importance. Even before the Left League's dissolution and the outbreak of the polemic, the relationship between Lu Xun and Zhou Yang's group was so bad that Lu frequently attacked Zhou in private correspondence. The dissolution and the 'National defence literature' slogan seem to have been the last straw. It is obvious that in early 1936, Lu was not going to join any organisation or movement led by Zhou Yang. He stated this clearly in letters to his confidants and in the open letter to Xu Maoyong.

There is no concrete proof for the charge that Feng Xuefeng and Hu Feng made use of the difficulties between Lu Xun and Zhou Yang to challenge Zhou Yang's leadership in the literary circle of Shanghai, but it has been proven that Feng Xuefeng was not eager to meet Zhou Yang upon his arrival in Shanghai and the new slogan was formulated before Feng had any discussion with the other group. Undoubtedly, there were personal reasons behind such acts.

On the other hand, Zhou Yang's group was not free of personal bias. The vigorous reaction to Hu Feng's article proves this unmistakably. They could not even accept the mediation of Mao Dun. This was the leftist sectarian attitude criticised by Mao Dun and Lu Xun in the latter stage of the polemic. It has often been said that the 'National defence literature' group attacked the new slogan because Hu Feng did not specify that the new slogan was formulated in cooperation with Lu Xun. Zhou Yang himself admitted that they launched a campaign against the slogan because they thought that it was suggested by Hu Feng[154] but if there was no sectarian feeling, if they had really been able to 'consider not only people, but also facts', this should not have happened.

Thus, the polemic between the left-wingers in 1936 was in fact a direct consequence of the split within the Left League in the years 1934-35. It is true that there were differences in opinions towards the new united front policy advocated by the Comintern and the Party, but if people had been able to exchange views calmly, there would not have been an open and bitter polemic. As the relationship between the two groups was so bad, any chance of settling the matter peacefully and internally was eliminated.

Notes to Chapter Seven

1. J Degras, 'Preface', *The Communist International, 1919-1943 Documents* (London: Oxford University Press, 1960) Vol II, p v.
2. E H Carr, *The twilight of Comintern, 1930-1935* (London: Macmillan, 1982), p 4.
3. *Ibid*, pp 150-4.
4. 'Resolution of the Seventh Congress on Fascism, working-class unity and the tasks of the Comintern', in J Degras, *The Communist International* Vol II, pp 362-9.
5. *Documents of the Communist International concerning the Chinese revolution: Vol II, 1929-1936* (*Gongchan guoji youguan Zhongguo geming de wenxian ziliao*) (Beijing: Zhongguo shehui kexueyuan, June 1982), p 392.
6. Wong Jianmin, *A draft history of the Chinese Communist Party* Vol III, pp 24-5.
7. 'Declaration of the Chinese Soviet Provisional Government and the Revolution and Military Committee of the Workers and Peasants Red Army' (*Zhonghua suweiai linshi zhengfu gongnong hongjun geming junshi weiyuanhui xuanyan*), *ibid*, pp 31-2.
8. 'A call from the Central Committee of the Chinese Communist Party for an anti-Japanese united front' (*Zhonggong zhongyang haozhao fanri tongyi zhanxian*), *ibid*, pp 33-4.
9. 'Letter to fellow countrymen for resistance against Japan and national salvation', *Collection of historical materials of literary movements* Vol III, p 239.
10. Wang Ming, *Collection of articles on national salvation* (*Jiuguo yanlunji*) (Hankou: Zhongguo chubanshe, July 1938), pp 1-61.
11. Chang Kuo-t'ao, *The rise of the CCP*, p 445.
12. Yao Yinhu, Yang Shengqing, 'A brief comment on the "August First Declaration"' (*Jianping bayi xuanyan*), *Dangshi yanjiu* (*Studies on Party history*) No 3, 1983 (28 June 1983), p 50.
13. Xiao San, 'What have I done for the "Left League" abroad?', *Recollections*, pp 180-1; 'Records of an interview with comrade Xiao San' (*Fangwen Xiao San tongzhi jilu*), *Luxun yanjiu ziliao* No 4, pp 194-5.
14. *Complete works of Lu Xun* Vol XIII, p 268.
15. Xu Maoyong, *Memoirs*, p 86.
16. Xiao San, 'Letter to the Left League', *Collection of historical materials of literary movements* Vol II, pp 329-31.
17. 'Records of Zhou Yang's interview: On the question of the Two slogan polemic' (*Fangwen Zhou Yang tanhua jilu: Tan liangge kouhao lunzheng de wenti*), *Reference materials*, p 67.
18. Mao Dun, *The road I trod* Vol II, p 308; Xu Maoyong, *Memoirs*, p 86.
19. Mao Dun, *The road I trod* Vol II, p 310.

Dissolution and Polemic

20 Unless otherwise stated, the discussion on the process of dissolution of the Left League is based on Xu Maoyong, *Memoirs*, p 86-8.
21 Feng Xuefeng, *Remembering Lu Xun*, pp 131-2.
22 Lu Xun, letter to Hu Feng, 12 September 1935, *Complete works of Lu Xun* Vol XIII, p 211.
23 Anthony J Kane, 'The League of Left-wing Writers', p 249.
24 Xiao San, 'Letter to the Left League', p 333.
25 Anthony J Kane, 'The League of Left-wing Writers', p 251.
26 Feng Xuefeng, *Remembering Lu Xun*, pp 122 & 130.
27 *Complete works of Lu Xun* Vol IV, pp 623-30; Vol VI, p 534; Vol XIII, p 12.
28 *Ibid* Vol VI, p 534; letter to Hu Feng, 12 September 1935, *ibid* Vol XIII, p 12.
29 Feng Xuefeng, *Remembering Lu Xun*, p 130.
30 *Ibid*, p 130-2.
31 Xu Maoyong, *Memoirs*, p 88.
32 'The united front of national defence in the literary circle' (*Wenyijie de tongyi guofang zhanxian*), *Shenghuo zhisi* Vol I No 11 (20 March 1936), *Collection of materials on the 'Two slogan' polemic*, p 87.
33 *Complete works of Lu Xun* Vol XIII, p 363.
34 Lu Xun, letter to Xu Maoyong, 2 May 1936, *ibid*, p 365.
35 'Record of Xia Yan's interview: On the dissolution of the "Left League" and others' (*Fangwen Xia Yan tanhua jilu: Zuolian jiesan ji qita*) *Reference materials*, p 57.
36 *Complete works of Lu Xun* Vol XIII, p 370-9; Vol VI, p 529.
37 *Collection of materials on the 'Two slogan' polemic*, pp 1-2.
38 Li Bo, 'On "National defence literature"', *Shishi xinbao*, 21 December 1935, *ibid*, p 4.
39 'The new culture needs a united front' (*Xinwenhua xuyao tongyi zhanxian*), *Xinwenhua* (*New culture*) No 1 (1 February 1936), *ibid*, p 23.
40 Zhou Libo, 'On "National defence literature"', *ibid*, p 5; Hu Luo, 'The building up of National defence literature' (*Guofang wenxue de jianli*), *Keguan* (*Objectiveness*) Vol I No 12 (5 February 1936), *ibid*, p 29; M I, '"National defence literature" and others' (*Guofang wenxue dengdeng*), *Wenxue qingnian* (*Literary youth*) Vol I No 2 (5 May 1936), *ibid*, p 179.
41 He Jiahuai, 'The roles of writers in the national salvation movement' (*Zuojia zai jiuwang yundongzhong de renwu*), *Shishi xinbao*, 11 January 1936, *ibid*, p 13.
42 Zhang Zhongda, '"National defence literature" and "literary national defence"' (*Guofang wenxue he wenxue guofang*), *Shishi xinbao*, 14 March 1936, *ibid*, p 111.
43 The articles written by Xu Xing include 'Commenting on the "National defence literature"', *ibid*, pp 51-3; 'What kind of literature do we need now?' (*Women xianzai xuyao shengme wenxue?*), *ibid*, pp 191-6.

The Chinese League of Left-wing Writers

44 '"National defence literature" and national character', *ibid*, p 32.
45 Xu Xing, 'Commenting on the "National defence literature"', *ibid*, p 51-3.
46 Zhou Lingqie, 'A query' (*Yige yiwen*) *Wenxue qingnian* Vol I No 1 (5 April 1936), *ibid*, p 124.
47 Lu Gang, '"Ridiculous" "rebuttals"' (*Huangmiu de bochi*), *Dawanbao*, 7 May 1936, *ibid*, p 124.
48 Xu Xing, 'What kind of literature do we need now', *ibid*, pp 193-5.
49 Zhou Yang, 'On National defence literature' (*Guanyu guofang wenxue*), *Wenxuejie* No 1 (5 June 1936), *ibid*, pp 231-4.
50 Guo Moruo, 'National defence, cesspools, purgatory' (*Guofang wuchi lianyu*), *Wenxuejie* Vol I No 2 (10 July 1936), *ibid*, pp 425-6.
51 'The question of National defence literature' (*Guofang wenxue wenti*), *Wenxue qingnian* No 1, *ibid*, p 118.
52 'On National defence literature', *ibid*, p 231.
53 Mao Dun, *The road I trod* Vol II, pp 308-11.
54 Feng Xuefeng, 'On the activities of Zhou Yang and others', p 247.
55 Ibid.
56 Ibid.
57 Mao Dun, *The road I trod* Vol II, p 320.
58 Feng Xuefeng, 'On the activities of Zhou Yang and others', pp 247-8.
59 Ibid, pp 252-7.
60 Xia Yan, 'Some past events that should have long been forgotten', pp 94-5.
61 Feng Xuefeng, 'On the activities of Zhou Yang and others', pp 251-2.
62 Ibid, p 251.
63 *Complete works of Lu Xun* Vol VI, p 532.
64 Feng Xuefeng, 'On the activities of Zhou Yang and others', p 532.
65 Mao Dun, *The road I trod* Vol II, p 320.
66 'On National defence literature', *Collection of materials on the 'Two slogan' polemic*, pp 231-6.
67 Mao Dun, *The road I trod* Vol II, p 320.
68 For example, see Tang Tao, *A history of modern Chinese literature* Vol II, p 75.
69 Hu Feng, 'Recalling the time around joining the Left League' (IV), *Xinwenxue shiliao* No 1, 1985 (22 February 1985), p 46.
70 Feng Xuefeng, 'On the activities of Zhou Yang and others', p 253; Wu Xiru, 'Hu Feng as I know him', p 243.
71 Hu Feng, 'What do the masses demand from literature?', *Wenxue congbao* No 3 (1 June 1936), *Collection of materials on the 'Two slogan' polemic*, p 216.
72 Xu Maoyong, 'What do the masses demand from literature?', *Wenxue congbao* No 3 (1 June 1936), *ibid*, pp 276-9.
73 Mao Dun, *The road I trod* Vol II, pp 322-3.
74 *Collection of materials on the 'Two slogan' polemic*, p 274.

75 Ba Jin, 'On the "Manifesto of the Chinese literature and art workers" and others' (*Guanyu Zhongguo wenyi gongzuozhe xuanyan ji qita*), *Luxun yanjiu ziliao* No 8 (May 1981), p 101.
76 *Collection of materials on the 'Two slogan' polemic*, p 413.
77 *Ibid*, pp 270-5.
78 Those who signed both documents were Ma Zongrong, Fang Guangdao, Zhao Jiabi, Li Ni, Huang Mei, Lu Fen, Xin Ren and Ma Zihua. *Ibid*, pp 275 and 413-4.
79 Lu Xun's letter to Wang Yeqiu, 4 May 1936, *Complete works of Lu Xun* Vol XIII, p 370; 'Reply to Xu Maoyong and on the question of the united front against Japanese aggression', *ibid* Vol VI, p 529.
80 *Liuhuo wenyi* No 1 (10 June 1936), *Collection of materials on the 'Two slogan' polemic*, p 298.
81 Gannu, 'The slogan for creation and the question of unity' (*Chuangzuo kouhao he lianhe wenti*), *Yeying* Vol I No 4 (15 June 1936), *ibid*, p 322; Er Ye (Nie Gannu), 'The road sign for creative activities' (*Chuangzuo huodong de lubiao*), *Xianshi wenxue* No 1 (1 July 1936), *ibid*, pp 392-3.
82 Long Gonggong, 'The literary front against aggression' (*Kangri wenxue zhanxian*), *Yeying* Vol I No 4, *ibid*, pp 316-7.
83 Xiru, 'The new demands of literature' (*Wenxue de xin yaojiu*), *ibid*, p 329.
84 Gannu, 'The slogan for creation and the question of unity', *ibid*, p 323.
85 Xiru, 'The new demands of literature', *ibid*, p 328.
86 'A great polemic in the thirties: The two slogans of two fundamentally opposing literary lines' (*Sanshi niandai de yichang dalunzhan: Liangtiao ganben duilide wenyi luxian de liangge kouhao*), *Guangming ribao*, 12 December 1970; '"National defence literature" was a traitorous literature' (*Guofang wenxue jiushi maiguo wenxue*), *Hongqi* No 10, 1970 (19 September 1970).
87 *Collection of historical materials of literary movements* Vol III, p 240-1.
88 'The new culture needs a united front', *Collection of materials on the 'Two slogan' polemic*, pp 22-6.
89 Wang Ming, 'On the question of anti-imperialist united front' (*Lun fandi tongyi zhanxian wenti*), *Selected works of Wang Ming* Vol IV, pp 272-6.
90 Wang Ming, 'In reply to those who oppose the anti-imperialist united front', *ibid*, p 309.
91 Wang Ming, 'New situation and new policy' (*Xin xingshi yu xin renwu*), *ibid*, p 402.
92 Chang Kuo-t'ao, *The rise of the CCP*, pp 446-7.
93 Quoted from Wang Jianmin, *A draft history of the Chinese Communist Party* Vol III, pp 49-53.
94 'Telegram to call for a ceasefire, peace and unity against Japanese aggression' (*Tingzhan yihe yizhi kangri tongdian*), *ibid*, pp 56-7.

The Chinese League of Left-wing Writers

95 'Letter from the Chinese Communist Party to the Chinese Nationalist Party' (*Zhongguo Gongchandang zhi Zhongguo Guomindang shu*), 25 August 1936, *ibid*, pp 58-62.
96 'The new culture needs a united front', *Collection of materials on the 'Two slogan' polemic*, p 26.
97 '"National defence literature" and national character', *ibid*, p 32.
98 *Complete works of Lu Xun* Vol VI, p 527.
99 Qu Yi, 'Start from the question of smuggling' (*Cong zousi wenti shouqi*), *Guangming* Vol I No 3 (10 July 1936), *Collection of materials on the 'Two slogan' polemic*, p 421.
100 Dimitrov, 'The resolution of the Seventh Congress on Fascism, working class unity and the tasks of the Comintern', in J Degras, *The Communist International*, pp 368-9; Mao Zedong, 'On tactics against Japanese imperialists' (27 December 1935), *Selected works* Vol I, pp 153-65; Mao Zedong, 'The question of independence and initiative within the united front' (5 November 1938), *ibid* Vol II, pp 213-16; Liu Shaoqi, 'The question of leadership is the central issue of the national united front' (*Lingdaoquan wenti shi minzu tongyi zhanxian de zhongxin wenti*), *Selected works of Liu Shaoqi* (*Liu Shaoqi xuanji*) (Beijing: Renmin chubanshe, December 1981), pp 46-54; Zhou Enlai, 'On the united front' (*Lun tongyi zhanxian*), *Selected works of Zhou Enlai* (*Zhou Enlai xuanji*) (Beijing: Renmin chubanshe, December 1980), pp 190-220.
101 A similar viewpoint has been expressed in Anthony J Kane, 'The League of Left-wing Writers', pp 237 & 300-3.
102 Zhao Haosheng, 'Zhou Yang takes a laughing look at history' (*Zhou Yang xiaotan lishi gongguo*), *Xinwenxue shiliao* No 2, p 232.
103 Feng Xuefeng, *Remembering Lu Xun*, p 149.
104 Feng Xuefeng, 'On the activities of Zhou Yang and others', p 253.
105 'Letter in reply to the Trotskyists', *Complete works of Lu Xun* Vol VI, pp 588-9.
106 'On our present literary movement: Reply for an interviewer from my sickbed', *ibid*, p 590-1.
107 *Ibid*.
108 Feng Xuefeng, 'On the activities of Zhou Yang and others', p 253; Mao Dun, *The road I trod* Vol II, pp 329-30.
109 Mao Dun, 'About "On our present literary movement": A letter to this magazine' (*Guanyu lun xianzai womende wenxue yundong: Ge benkan de xin*), *Wenxuejie* Vol I No 2 (10 July 1936), *Collection of materials on the 'Two slogan' polemic*, pp 436-7.
110 *Wenxuejie* Vol I No 2, *ibid*, p 439.
111 *Ibid*.
112 Mao Dun, 'On the controversial two slogans', *Wenxuejie* Vol I No 3 (10 August 1936) *Collection of materials on the 'Two slogan' polemic*, pp 566-7.

113 *Ibid*, p 567. Guo Moruo, 'National defence, cesspools, purgatory', *ibid*, p 425.
114 Zhou Yang, 'Discussing the National defence literature slogan with Mr Mao Dun' (*Yu Mao Dun xiansheng lun guofang wenxue de kouhao*), *ibid*, p 572.
115 *Ibid*, pp 571-3.
116 Mao Dun, 'A few more words' (*Zaishuo jiju*), *Battle over National defence literature* (*Guofang wenxue lunzhan*) (Shanghai: Xinchao chubanshe, October 1936), pp 440-52.
117 Mao Dun, *The road I trod* Vol II, pp 335-8.
118 *Complete works of Lu Xun* Vol XV, p 109.
119 T A Hsia, 'Lu Hsun and the dissolution of the League of Leftist Writers', *The gate of darkness*, p 134.
120 *Complete works of Lu Xun* Vol VI, pp 290-3.
121 T A Hsia, *The gate of darkness*, p 134.
122 Lu Xun, letter to Xu Maoyong, 26 May 1934, *Complete works of Lu Xun* Vol XII, p 433.
123 Lu Xun, letter to Xu Maoyong, 20 September 1934, *ibid*, pp 517-18.
124 Xu Maoyong, *Memoirs*, pp 75-7.
125 Letter to Hu Feng, 24 August 1935, *Complete works of Lu Xun* Vol XII, p 433.
126 Xu Maoyong, *Memoirs*, p 84.
127 *Complete works of Lu Xun* Vol XIII, p 365.
128 Xu Maoyong, letter to Lu Xun, 30 April 1936, *Luxun yanjiu ziliao* No 4, pp 163-5.
129 *Complete works of Lu Xun* Vol XV, pp 296 and 300.
130 Letter to Yang Jiyun, 28 August 1936, *Complete works of Lu Xun* Vol XIII, p 416.
131 T A Hsia, *The gate of darkness*, p 135.
132 *Complete works of Lu Xun* Vol VI, p 526.
133 *Ibid*, p 527.
134 *Ibid*, pp 527-8.
135 Feng Xuefeng, 'On the activities of Zhou Yang and others', p 255.
136 *Complete works of Lu Xun* Vol XV, p 306.
137 *Ibid*, Vol VI, p 529.
138 *Ibid*.
139 *Ibid*, p 532.
140 *Ibid*, p 535.
141 *Ibid*, p 538.
142 T A Hsia, *The gate of darkness*, p 136.
143 Lu Xun, letter to Yang Jiyun, 28 August 1936, *Complete works of Lu Xun* Vol XIII, p 416; letter to Tai Jingnong, 15 October 1936, *ibid*, p 447.
144 *Ibid*, p 416.

145 Guo Moruo, 'An inspection of a military exercise', *Wenxuejie* Vol I No 4 (10 September 1936), *Collection of materials on the 'Two slogan' polemic*, p 713.
146 Xu Maoyong, *Memoirs*, pp 90-1.
147 'In reply to Mr Lu Xun', *Jindao wenyi* (*Contemporary literature and art*) Vol 1 No 3, ((20 September 1936) *Battle over National defence literature*, pp 523-34.
148 *Collection of materials on the 'Two slogan polemic'*, pp 709-16.
149 Mao Dun, 'On the phenomena of the literary arena in these recent days' (*Tan zuijinde wentan xianxiang*), *The road I trod* Vol II, pp 340-2.
150 Lu Keyu, 'Opinions on the several questions in literary movement', *Zuojia* Vol I No 6 (11 September 1936), *Collection of materials on the 'Two slogan' polemic*, pp 773-86.
151 *Wenxue* Vol VII No 4 (1 October 1936), *ibid*, pp 824-5.
152 Zhao Haosheng, 'Zhou Yang takes a laughing look at history', p 236.
153 Mo Wenhua (Liu Shaoqi), 'My opinions on the significance of this literary polemic' (*Woguan zheci wenyi lunzhan de yiyi*), *ibid*, pp 899-902.
154 Zhao Haosheng, 'Zhou Yang takes a laughing look at history', p 234.

Conclusion

The period covered in this study saw the first attempt of the Chinese Communist Party to grasp control of the literary world. They had a very bad start. The young party was heavily damaged by Jiang Jieshi's coup d'état, and so was the solidarity of the left-wingers in the literary circle, by the revolutionary literary polemic. Nevertheless, both incidents brought the same advantageous result. A large number of writers and young people were driven, because of their disillusionment with the GMD, or attracted because of the publicity given to left-wing literature and literary theories, to the left. They constituted a strong fighting force which was responsible for the growth of the left-wing literary movements in the thirties.

In almost all literary histories published in the PRC after its establishment in 1949, with the few exceptions of those published during the Cultural Revolution, the 'Left League Decade' always takes up a considerable number of pages and the Left League has always been regarded as an unqualified success. This success, inevitably, was attributed to the brilliant leadership of the Communist Party. In the West and on the right, although different conclusions may be arrived at regarding the achievements of the left in this period, scholars in the main also agree that CCP direction was the most important factor in the operation of the League.

Nonetheless, these suggestions must be regarded with great caution. In some cases, CCP direction should not be underestimated, such as the order to end the revolutionary literary polemic and form the League in 1929, and the instruction to dissolve the organisation in 1935. However, the fact that the Left League began and ended in a polemic is significant. If the CCP had been able to exert strong control over the left-wing literary circle, this would not have happened because such conflicts could have been settled internally. In the daily running of League affairs, it must be said, direct influence from the Communist Party was minimal.

In the first half of the Left League's existence, the most important figure was Qu Qiubai. Although he was never formally a member of the League, his influence was much greater than any of the secretaries of the League's Party group and the Cultural Committee. He initiated a number of important campaigns, such as the struggle against nationalist literature in 1930-31, the discussion on the popularisation of literature and the debate with the 'free men' and the 'men of the third category' in 1932. Even Feng Xuefeng, who had been secretary of both the League's Party group and the Cultural Committee, admitted more than once that he was directed by Qu whose leadership and influence were crucial to the League and revolutionary literary movement.[1] Another prominent member of the League, Mao Dun, also acknowledged Qu's leadership.[2] However, Qu's taking up of the Left League was not decided by the

CCP, and he held no official post in the Party Central Committee. He acted independently and received no CCP instructions or orders.

In the second half of the League's existence, Zhou Yang, at one time or another, held all the important posts. After 1934, he was undoubtedly in charge of the left-wing literary movement. It has often been said that Zhou was a close follower of the Party line. However, during the period from 1934-35, it is doubtful if he had any instruction or guidance to follow. The highest body of the CCP in the white area, the Jiangsu Provincial Committee, had been raided. The provisional Central Committee was on the Long March. Communication with Moscow was most difficult. Consequently, he had to make decisions and act alone. Young and inexperienced, he inevitably made mistakes. The alienation of Lu Xun and the dissension within the League were largely the results of his leadership. More concrete direction from a higher level of the Party might have avoided some of his blunders.

Hence, the contrast between the first period of the Left League, when it reaped a good harvest, and its second, when it was in decline, was largely due to personal factors. Qu Qiubai was undoubtedly a better leader. A Party member since 1921 and once chief secretary and a Politburo member of the CCP, he was experienced in handling relationships and power struggles between members. He had introduced as well as suffered from leftist Party lines, and thus had a clear understanding of the better course to take. A man of letters himself, Qu was aware of the importance of uniting writers and he had a high regard for such old writers as Lu Xun. He could also admit mistakes gracefully, as in the debate against the men of the third category when he was criticised by Feng Xuefeng and in the discussion on the popularisation of literature when Mao Dun questioned his opinions. It seems that these strengths were lacking in Zhou Yang. He refused to make redress for his mistakes and failed to control his men in the attack on Lu Xun.

It is incorrect, however, to say that the Party had no influence. Although in most cases there were no direct orders, leaders in the Left League inevitably tried to find out how the wind blew and follow suit. Though a literary organisation itself, the League was greatly affected by political developments. In the face of great changes with no clear course to follow, the left was thrown into chaos. Hence, in 1927, when the first united front with the GMD was shattered, and in 1936, when suggestions were made to reunite with the nationalists, there were different ideas within the same camp, which resulted in bitter polemics. On the other hand, in the period 1930-35, when the political situation was comparatively stable, solidarity of the left-wingers in the literary circle was achieved.

It has often been suggested that the left-deviationist Party lines caused great harm to the Left League. The failure of the organisation to get open and legal status, which resulted in the arrest and even execution of its members, as well as the banning of its publications, was attributed to this factor. However, it seems over-optimistic to assume that the League could have been acceptable to the

Conclusion

Nationalists if a moderate course had been adopted. Before the formation of the Left League, almost all left-wing organisations were banned. What is more, even if an organisation could get open status, it did not mean that it had a better chance. The Chinese League for the Protection of Civil Rights was headed by Song Qingling, widow of Dr Sun Yat-sen, and acquired open status, but was in great difficulty too; its vice-chairman, Yang Xingfo, was assassinated in June 1933. In other words, unless the Left League gave up its stand altogether and made no criticism or attack on the authorities, its chances of surviving happily were flimsy.

Yet undeniably the effects of different emphases in Party policy were felt in the League. Qu Qiubai's reign covered the pre-League period, and it has been shown that the ultra-leftists in the revolutionary literary polemic were very much affected by his policy. As for Li Lisan, his leftist element was shown in his eagerness to 'win victory in one or more provinces first'. This resulted in a call for writers to drop their pens and stage insurrections on the streets, arousing discontent among the moderates. In the end, many of them remained indifferent, while the small scale demonstrations which occurred achieved nothing. Comparatively speaking, Wang Ming's leftist Party line had much less of an impact on the League, especially in the latter period, as there was no way to receive orders from the Party. Nevertheless, this does not mean that the League was free of leftist trend in its final stages. Its leading members developed their own leftist line, and closed-doorism and sectarianism became a most serious problem. Not only did they close their doors to outsiders (little effort was made to recruit new members in 1934-35 and many of those who joined the League during this period were transferred from other leagues), but within the organisation opposing groups were formed. The League's development was arrested and its unity badly damaged, as much energy was wasted in internal squabbles which were sometimes carried on in public.

Another political factor often neglected in the discussion of the Left League was the effect of Japanese aggression. Although the Japanese imperialists were steadfast in their anti-communist stance, their invasion of China in the thirties indirectly aided the Communists and the left-wing literary movement. With the Japanese at the front door, Jiang Jieshi could not concentrate on the elimination of the Communists. The third encirclement campaign in 1931 was cut short because of the Mukden Incident and the fourth campaign was delayed until December 1932 because of the Battle of Shanghai at the beginning of the year. More important still, Jiang's 'pacification first, then resistance' theory was unacceptable to the majority of the people, as no one wanted to see a civil war when foreign invasion was imminent. On the other hand, throughout the thirties, the Communists had advocated the united front from below policy against Japanese invasion. Their declaration of war against Japan won the support of the people. This was advantageous to the left-wing writers in Shanghai. In many cases, for instance in the struggle against the nationalist literary movement, they purposely stressed the differences between their attitude and that of their opponents towards the Japanese imperialists.

It is difficult to give an objective appraisal of the League and the left-wing literary movement in Shanghai in the thirties. Nevertheless, it is fair to say that the mere survival of the League, in the face of severe repression, was itself an achievement. Although it had been common practice for men of letters and writers to form literary groups in China, there was no single organisation, in terms of structure, membership and activities, comparable to the Left League. At least for three to four years, the League was united and progressing. The level of membership was unprecedented. Its members, despite being subjected to arrest and even execution, were determined and devoted. They were ready to make sacrifices, not only in the material sense, but also of their lives. Readers of the recollections and memoirs of League members can hardly help but be touched by their enthusiasm and devotion to the cause, as well as the affection between comrades. Though many critics view their attacks on individual and nationalist writers as dogmatic and ruthless, such an approach was necessary if the path to proletarian revolution was to be cleared. Some on the right even admit that their losing the country to the Communists was largely due to the failure to grasp the leadership in the literary and cultural fields.

With the exception of Mao Dun's *Midnight*, however, it is difficult to name any substantial literary works. This was one of the main criticisms made against the League. The League was condemned for putting too much emphasis on politics and neglecting the literary aspects. However, with a few exceptions, such as Lu Xun, Mao Dun and Guo Moruo, members of the Left League were then very young. Most of them were in their early twenties, or even younger. Is it a bit too harsh to demand from them works equal to *Midnight* or 'The true story of Ah Q'? Perhaps it should be pointed out that many League members, who started writing at this period, produced good pieces afterwards. Besides Zhang Tianyi, Ai Wu and Sha Ting who attracted great attention on the appearance of their first works, others like Lou Shiyi, Nie Gannu, Ouyang Shan and Wang Xiyan were to become well-known writers. We know that there were seminars and meetings within the League to discuss the works created by its members. This could have been a contributing factor in encouraging its members to write and improve their standards. The large number of journals published by the League also provided opportunities for new writers to get their works printed.

As stated earlier, critics in mainland China always consider that the Left League was a great success. Yet the fact that except for Lu Xun, all its leading lights were purged at different times after the Communists established their rule in China seems inconsistent with this general judgment. To gain a better understanding of the Left League, it seems appropriate to look deeper into the causes of these subsequent reversals.

It has been shown that Lu Xun, after the publication of the open letter to Xu Maoyong and the intervention of such people as Liu Shaoqi, stood out as the

Conclusion

victor in the 'Two slogan polemic'. Zhou Yang lost the domination of the literary circle when the Cultural Committee, which was under his control, was dissolved by Feng Xuefeng. In the following year, he left Shanghai for Yan'an. He told an interviewer in 1978 that he went to Yan'an upon receiving a telegram calling for cultural workers. He admitted that it was difficult for him to carry on with his work in Shanghai after he had been criticised by Lu Xun,[3] but he was able to occupy high positions. He was the director of education, dean of the Lu Xun Academy of Arts, and president of Yan'an University. Obviously, his failure in Shanghai was forgiven. Merle Goldman has said that 'in addition to his political orthodoxy, the fact that he was one of the first intellectuals to arrive in Yan'an and was a native of Mao's own province aided his swift rise in the hierarchy'.[4] But it seems that the main reason was that Mao Zedong was not particularly opposed to the 'National defence literature' slogan and the deeds of Zhou Yang in Shanghai at that time. Although Mao and Wang Ming differed in their attitudes towards the united front policy in 1935-36 and Zhou Yang's slogan was close to Wang's theory, these did not constitute any great problem to Zhou as the second united front between the CCP and the GMD had already been established in 1937. If Xu Maoyong's memoirs are to be believed, then it seems that Mao Zedong was ready to accept the 'National defence literature' slogan in 1937-38. The following were reported to be Mao's words:

> In my opinion, the first thing we can be certain of is that the debate is one within the revolutionary camp, but not a polemic between revolutionaries and counter-revolutionaries. Your group was not counter-revolutionary. Nor was Lu Xun's group counter-revolutionary.
>
> The debate broke out at a time when there were changes in Party line and policies. It is a drastic change from having a civil war to having an anti-Japanese national united front. In the process of transformation, quarrels are inevitable, as there may be diverse attitudes towards the changes within the revolutionary camp. In fact, it was not only you people who quarrelled. We, in Yan'an, also had a heated quarrel.[5]

Zhou Yang also recalled that not much was said about the two slogans in Yan'an, and 'not even Chairman Mao criticised me'.[6]

The first group of the Left League censured in Yan'an was close to Lu Xun in Shanghai. In the early forties, Ding Ling and Xiao Jun were criticised in the 'Zhengfeng (Rectification) Movement'. In the movement, Ding Ling lost the post of editor of *Jiefang ribao* (*Liberation daily*), and both had to go to Party schools, villages and factories for education. However, although they had been Lu Xun's followers and then still had a close relationship with Hu Feng (they frequently contributed to Hu Feng's journal *Qiyue* [*July*] in Wuhan), these were not the reasons for their being censured. The Zhengfeng Movement was an attempt 'to develop a corps of devoted, disciplined cadres and intellectuals convinced of the rightness of the party's cause. It sought to change basic patterns of behaviour and implant the strict party line'.[7] The heaviest attack fell on Wang Shiwei, who published a number of articles, the most famous one being 'Wild lily' (*Yebaihehua*), to criticise the negative side of Yan'an. Ding and Xiao did similar things. Ding Ling's 'In the hospital' (*Zai yiyuan zhong*) was an attack on the governmental system and party organs in Yan'an. It had a strong streak of individualism. 'Thoughts on March Eighth' (*Sanbajie yougan*), one of her most famous pieces of *zawen*, voiced the problems faced by the supposedly emancipated women in Yan'an. In the article, Ding did not hesitate to criticise those cadres who enjoyed privileges over the common people and the top Party leaders who did nothing practical but only made empty promises.[8] Xiao Jun was even more outspoken. He supported Ding Ling's views expressed in 'Thoughts on March Eighth' in an article called 'On marriage' (*Lun zhongshen dashi*). His 'On love and patience among comrades' (*Lun tongzhide ai he nai*) also exposed the troubles among cadres.[9] It was for these reasons that the two were under criticism. Although Zhou Yang and his associates were active in the campaign, the purge should not be viewed as retaliation, as it was Ding and Xiao who took the initiative to attack the top level. What is more, the punishment imposed on the two was relatively lenient.

Among Zhou Yang's antagonists in Shanghai, Feng Xuefeng was the first to come under heavy attack after 1949. The attack arose from Yu Pingbo's study on the 'Dream of the red chamber'. Feng, then the editor of *Wenyibao*, praised highly Yu's scholarship and refused to publish in his magazine the article of Li Xifan and Lan Ling in criticism of Yu. This was condemned by Yuan Shuipai, a close follower of Zhou Yang, as bourgeois, showing a lack of appreciation for the value of scholarship based on Marxism-Leninism.[10] Zhou Yang himself also criticised the editors of *Wenyibao*:

> Individual authority, friendship, and the power of their journal were more important to them than the interests of the people and the country.[11]

Zhou's campaign against Feng Xuefeng is generally regarded as a power struggle within the literary hierarchy because *Wenyibao* was the only base where Zhou's authority could not be asserted.[12] But the clashes between Feng Xuefeng and Zhou Yang in the thirties could possibly also be the underlying cause for the latter's action.

The purge of Hu Feng in 1955 could certainly be related to the events of the thirties. Since the forties and even after the establishment of the People's Republic, Hu had never accepted the leadership of Zhou Yang. In many articles, he showed his distaste for the literary officials. For some time, his associates and disciples had been subjected to criticism. In July 1954, Hu, after a mild attack on him, submitted to the Central Committee of the Party the famous 'Ten thousand word letter'.[13] Several months later, a large scale assault began. Hu was charged with being against the Party and its policies. Before long, with the supporting evidence of their private correspondence, Hu and his associates were accused of 'intriguing and acting as part of an over-all plot to

Conclusion

overthrow the people's state and restore imperialism and GMD rule in China'.[14] He was expelled from the Chinese Writers' Union. From then on, no more was heard of him, until 1979.

It is true that much in Hu's report to the Central Committee was unacceptable to the Communist Party and it was just a matter of time before the Party took action against him, but why was it necessary to turn Hu into a counter-revolutionary, on such flimsy evidence? This brings to mind unmistakably the charge made by Zhou Yang in 1935 that Hu was a spy from Nanjing. The eagerness and efforts of Zhou Yang and his group only arouse suspicion that they were eliminating a personal enemy. Even during the campaign, people raised doubts about this. Zhuang Yong, one of Hu Feng's disciples, claimed:

> This case is not a problem of literary theory, but of the personal relationship between Hu Feng and Zhou Yang.[15]

Another said that 'if Lu Xun were alive today, the same would have happened to him'.[16]

After the elimination of Hu Feng, it was the turn of another long-time enemy, Feng Xuefeng. In the anti-rightist drive in 1957-58, Ding Ling was among the first to be picked out for criticism. This should not be rashly related to the disputes of the thirties, for throughout the first ten years of the People's Republic, she had always challenged and competed with Zhou Yang for the leadership of the literary world. Feng Xuefeng, on the other hand, after the 'Dream of the red chamber' incident, spoke only occasionally and yet he was made the chief target of attack in the anti-rightist campaign. There seems no doubt that this time Feng's purge was closely related to his deeds in the thirties, as many articles labelled these for criticism.[17] Zhou Yang and his colleagues tried to save their personal honour by attributing all the blunders made during the Left League period to Feng Xuefeng. A most famous attack was made by Xia Yan in the enlarged session of the Chinese Writers Union Party group on 17 August 1957.[18] Any conflicts between Zhou Yang and Lu Xun were the results of the 'provocation' and 'alienation' of Feng Xuefeng who, cooperating with Hu Feng, hoodwinked Lu Xun. In accounting for the 'Two slogan polemic', they argued that the 'National defence literature' slogan represented the correct Party line and hence, Hu Feng and Feng Xuefeng's proposing another slogan was inappropriate as it caused much unnecessary confusion. Since they could not say anything against Lu Xun, they had to make up a story that all Lu Xun's writings denouncing Zhou Yang and his slogan, including the open letter to Xu Maoyong, were written by Feng Xuefeng, or at least based on wrong information provided by Feng, while Lu Xun, in his sick bed, could not see Feng's divisive activities.[19] To silence objections, Zhou Yang excluded any of the bitter letters and articles from the collection of Lu Xun's works published in the fifties. The attack on Feng included his behaviour during the polemic with the 'men of the third category'. Feng's criticism of A Ying, Qu Qiubai and Zhou

Yang was taken as anti-Party action in cooperation with the Trotskyist Hu Qiuyuan.[20]

In this Anti-rightist campaign, another associate of Lu Xun, Huang Yuan was also hit.[21] Ironically, Xu Maoyong, who had attacked Huang Yuan in his letter to Lu Xun, was labelled a rightist and received harsh criticism in the campaign too. As another means of shaking off the blame, Zhou Yang accused him of writing the letter to Lu Xun in 1936.[22]

After the Anti-rightist campaign, Zhou Yang's reevaluation of the Left League period in his favour was complete. It is unconvincing to say that all the campaigns were ideological ones and that Zhou Yang only acted in accordance with Mao Zedong's instructions. Merle Goldman's analysis of these campaigns is enlightening:

> The particular vehemence of the attacks on Hu Feng and Feng Xuefeng and the effort to erase Lu Xun's connections with these two writers and his involvement in the 1936 controversy had more to do with Zhou's group's personal rivalries. Mao set the general direction of the campaign, but Zhou and his cohorts gave the campaigns their particular emphasis. The campaigns had as much to do with factional issues as with ideological ones. It gave these cultural officials the opportunity to get rid of rivals and enhance their own positions as well as impose the latest Party line.[23]

Then in the summer of 1966, Zhou Yang himself became the target of attack in the 'Great Proletarian Cultural Revolution'. On 2 February, Jiang Qing, under the direction of Lin Biao, called the 'Forum on literature and art in the armed forces' (*Budui wenyi gongzuo zuotanhui*), and brought forward the theory of the 'literary black line' (*Wenyi heixian*). It was said that since the establishment of the People's Republic, the literary arena had been ruled by 'an anti-Party, anti-socialist black line which stood against the thoughts of Chairman Mao, and the black line was the combination of the bourgeois literary thinking, modern revisionist literary thinking and the so-called literature of the thirties'.[24] Clearly, Zhou Yang was to be purged this time as he had been in charge of the literary hierarchy in this period. In July, Zhou was formally denounced:

> For twenty-four years, Zhou Yang and company have consistently refused to carry out comrade Mao Zedong's line on literature and art, and stubbornly adhered to the bourgeois revisionist black line on literature and art.[25]

The reasons for Zhou Yang's being purged will not be discussed here.[26] Yet, with his downfall, the literature of the thirties was reevaluated once again. In an attempt to portray Zhou Yang as a defier of Mao Zedong's correct Party line, Jiang Qing put great emphasis on the clashes between Zhou and Lu Xun, a 'foot-soldier' in support of Mao's policies who had 'boundless esteem and love for Chairman Mao'.[27] A great number of unpublished works of Lu Xun, mostly private letters which revealed Lu Xun's contempt for Zhou's company, were reprinted. People like Feng Xuefeng, Zhou Yang's antagonists in the thirties,

Conclusion

were made to write on the anti-Lu Xun, anti-Party deeds and conspiracy of Zhou Yang.

As expected, the 'Two slogan polemic' was re-interpreted. This time, Zhou Yang's slogan of 'National defence literature' was described as a product of Wang Ming's right-deviationist Party line, and so it was capitulationistic. Zhou Yang was charged with being a close follower of Wang Ming, the adversary of Mao Zedong, and sacrificing the proletarian cause for conciliation with the GMD. On the other hand, Lu Xun's slogan of 'Mass literature of the national revolutionary war' was, because of its stress on proletarian leadership, honoured as upholding the socialist principles and Maoist stands in the debate.[28]

With the fall of the 'Gang of Four' in 1976, such interpretations were bound to be rejected. Within a month of their arrest, articles appeared alleging that one member of the Gang of Four, Zhang Chunqiao was the 'Di Ke' condemned by Lu Xun in 1936 for his attack on Xiao Jun.[29] At this stage, Zhou Yang was still under purge as Di Ke was described as an ally of Zhou. It was not until the autumn of 1977 that there were signs of his rehabilitation. On 30 September, he was present at the gathering in celebration of the National Day. A month later, he attended the forums held by *Renmin ribao* on the criticism of the 'literary black line' theory. Before long, it was concluded that there had never been a literary black line, which was merely a fabrication of the Gang of Four to deny past achievements. Hence, Zhou Yang was rehabilitated on the grounds that he was one of the victims of the Cultural Revolution. So were his colleagues and the 'National defence literature' slogan. A number of forums held by universities and colleges in different parts of the country came to the same conclusion that the slogan was not born out of the right deviationist Wang Ming line. There was no suggestion that it was anti-Party and anti-socialist.[30] Unlike past campaigns, these discussions seemed to allow the presence of diverse opinions. Criticisms of Zhou Yang's group for alienating Lu Xun and committing other errors could still be found, though it was regarded as minor. In general, it has been agreed that Lu Xun's co-existence theory is most correct.[31] Further, Zhou's opponents were also rehabilitated. A memorial ceremony was held for Feng Xuefeng in November 1979 and his cinerary casket was placed in the revolutionary cemetery, covered with a Party flag.[32] Hu Feng was released in January 1979 and made the Political Consultative member for Sichuan. Before his death in 1985, he was able to get part of his memoirs published.

The history of the Left League has been rewritten once again in mainland China. It is too much to expect the new evaluation to be free of personal and ideological bias and yet it is obvious that critics have been more ready to 'seek truth in facts'. To the outside, the availability of more and more material has facilitated a better understanding of the real picture. Thus the present research could be undertaken. It is the author's hope that a comparatively objective presentation and conclusions have been made.

Notes to Conclusion

1. 'Comrade Feng Xuefeng on Lu Xun and the "Left League"', p 168. Feng Xuefeng, *Remembering Lu Xun*, pp 108-9.
2. Mao Dun, *The road I trod* Vol II, p 71.
3. Zhao Haosheng, 'Zhou Yang takes a laughing look at history', p 236.
4. Merle Goldman, *Literary dissent in Communist China*, p 48.
5. Xu Maoyong, *Memoirs*, pp 103-4.
6. Zhao Haosheng, 'Zhou Yang takes a laughing look at history', p 236.
7. Merle Goldman, *Literary dissent in Communist China*, p 18.
8. *Jiefang ribao*, 9 March 1942, p 4.
9. *Ibid*, 8 April 1943, p 4.
10. Yuan Shuipai, 'An inquiry of the editors of *Wenyibao*' (*Zhiwen wenyibao bianzhe*), *Renmin ribao*, 28 October 1954, reprinted in *Wenyibao* No 20, 1954 (30 October 1954), pp 3-4.
11. Zhou Yang, 'We must fight' (*Women bixu zhandou*), *Wenyibao* No 23 and 24 (30 December 1954), pp 13-15.
12. Merle Goldman, *Literary dissent in Communist China*, p 126.
13. 'Hu Feng's opinions on literature and art' (*Hu Feng dui wenyi wenti de yijian*), Supplement to *Wenyibao* (January 1955), pp 1-165.
14. *Survey of the China Mainland Press*, No 1090:45, Xinhuashe (Beijing: 16 July 1955), quoted from Merle Goldman, *Literary dissent in Communist China*, p 155.
15. *Ibid*, p 152.
16. *Ibid*.
17. Huo Songlin, 'Criticise Feng Xuefeng's anti-Marxist literary thinking', *Renmin wenxue* No 12, 1957, p 90; Lui Shousong, 'On the two literary polemics of the Left League period: A criticism on Feng Xuefeng's anti-Party activities and anti-Marxist literary thinking', *Wenxue yanjiu* No 1, 1958, pp 25-31.
18. This speech has never been published openly but Lou Shiyi revealed that Xia Yan's article in *Wenxue pinglun* 'Some past events that should have long been forgotten' repeated largely the ideas of the speech. Lou Shiyi, 'To forget, for solidarity: On reading comrade Xia Yan's "Some past events that should have long been forgotten but cannot be forgotten"', p 91.
19. Ruan Ming, Ruan Ruoying, 'A hidden arrow from Zhou Yang to reverse history: Comment on a note made in Vol VI of *Complete works of Lu Xun*' (*Zhou Yang diandao lishide yizhi anjian: Ping Lu Xun quanji diliuji de yitiao zhushi*), *Hongqi* No 9, 1966 (1 July 1966), pp 35-44. Xu Guangping, 'Zhou Yang should not be allowed to attack and slander Lu Xun' (*Buxu Zhou Yang gongji he wumie Lu Xun*), *Hongqi* No 12, 1966 (17 September 1966), pp 28-37.

Conclusion

20 Liu Shousong, 'On the two literary polemics of the Left League period: A criticism of Feng Xuefeng's anti-Party activities and anti-Marxist literary thinking', pp 25-31.

21 'Completely reveal the anti-Party background of Huang Yuan' (*Huang Yuan fandang mianmu beichedi jiechuan*), *Wenyibao* No 34, 1957 (1 December 1957), p 7.

22 Chen Cong, 'Such a "revolutionary philosopher" and "revolutionary writer": Report on the criticism meeting against the rightist Xu Maoyong' (*Ruci geming zhexuejia he geming wenxuejia: Piping youpai fenzi Xu Maoyong dahui baodao*), *Wenyibao* No 35, 1957 (8 December 1957), p 2.

23 Merle Goldman, 'The political use of Lu Xun', *China Quarterly* No 91 (September 1982), p 449.

24 *Jiefangjunbao* (*Liberation army newspaper*), 18 April 1966.

25 *Hongqi* No 7, 1966 (29 April 1966).

26 For a discussion of the topic, see Merle Goldman, 'The fall of Zhou Yang', *China Quarterly* No 27 (July-September 1966), pp 132-48.

27 'In commemoration of our pioneer in cultural revolution, Lu Xun' (*Jinian womende wenhua geming xianqu Lu Xun*), *Hongqi* No 14, 1966 (1 November 1966), pp 23-5.

28 See the articles collected in *Thoroughly criticise National defence literature*.

29 Ren Ping, 'An out and out old capitulationist' (*Yige dididaodao de lao touxiangpai*), *Renmin ribao*, 21 October 1977, p 1.

30 *Wenxue pinglun* No 3, 1978 (25 June 1978), pp 3-33; *Wenxue pinglun* No 5, 1978 (25 October 1978), pp 7-36; *Gansu shida xuebao* No 2, 1978, pp 2-35.

31 For examples, see Huang Xiuji, 'Lu Xun's "co-existence" theory is most correct' (*Lu Xun de bingcunlun zui zhengque*), *Wenxue pinglun* No 5, 1978, pp 27-36; Wan Song, 'Lu Xun and the "Two slogan polemic"' (*Lu Xun yu liangge kouhao de lunzheng*), *Gansu shida xuebao* No 2, 1978, pp 36-42.

32 'The memorial meeting of comrade Feng Xuefeng was held in Beijing' (*Feng Xuefeng tongzhi zuidaohui zaijing juxing*), *Renmin ribao*, 18 November 1979.

Selected Bibliography

For a complicated topic like the Chinese League of Left-wing Writers, which has been widely written about, especially by scholars in mainland China, it is difficult to provide an exhaustive bibliography. For considerations of space, the present one incorporates only the more important sources and those that, I think, are of value and interest to Western scholars. For a more comprehensive bibliography, see my dissertation at the School of Oriental and African Studies, University of London.

Chinese Language Sources

Articles

Ai Wu, 'Thoughts on the literature of the thirties' (*Guanyu sanshi niandai wenyi de yixie ganxiang*), *Xinwenxue luncong* No 1, 1980 (May 1980), pp 5-12.

Ba Jin, 'On the "Manifesto of the Chinese workers on literature and art" and other things' (*Guanyu Zhongguo wenyi gongzuozhe xuanyan ji qita*), *Luxun yanjiu ziliao* No 8 (May 1981), pp 101-2.

Bao Zhongwen, 'Several questions of the literary struggle of the Left League' (*Zuolian wenyi douzhengzhong de jige wenti*), *Yuhua* No 3, 1981 (5 March 1981), pp 68-77.

Bao Ziyan, 'A past event that had long been confirmed and yet was again denied: On the time of comrade Feng Xuefeng's arrival at Shanghai in 1936' (*Yijian zaoyibai kending eryoubei fouding de wangshi: Guanyu Feng Xuefeng tongzhi yijiu sanliunian daoda Shanghai de shijian wenti*), *Wenxue pinglun* No 4, 1980 (15 July 1980), pp 99-102.

Cao Zhongbin, 'An analysis on several facts of the Oriental Hotel Incident' (*Dui dongfang lushe shijian ruogan shishi de bianxi*), *Shixue jikan* No 1, 1983 (February 1983), pp 43-8.

Cha Ling, 'The literary arena of China before the formation of the "Left League"' (*Zuolian yiqian de Zhongguo wentan shuyao*), *Youshi yuekan* Vol XLI No 5 (May 1975), pp 67-71.

'From the endings of the members of the "Left League" on the significance of the rise and decline of the "Left League" in the history of contemporary culture' (*You Zuolian renwu de jieju lun Zuolian qimo zai Zhongguo dangdai wenhuashi shang de yiyi*), *Youshi yuekan* Vol XLII No 2 (August 1975), pp 69-72.

Chen Bingliang, 'The polemic of "National defence literature"' (*Guofang wenxue lunzhan*), *Mingbao yuekan* Vol XVI No 7 (July 1981), pp 87-92.

'Lu Xun and Communism: Between myth and reality' (*Lu Xun yu gongzhan chuyi: Shenhua yu shishi zhijian*), *Wenji* Vol II No 2 (July 1984), pp 20-84.

Bibliography

Chen Huangmei, 'On the question of the Two slogan polemic' (*Guanyu liangge kouhao de lunzheng wenti*), *Wenxue pinglun* No 5, 1978 (25 October 1978), pp 16-26.

Chen Jiying, 'A review of the literary arena of China in the thirties and Maoist Communist repressions on writers' (*Sanshi niandai Zhongguo wentan huigu ji Maogong bihai zuojia de lishi*), *Zhuanji wenxue* Vol XXII No 5 (1 May 1973), pp 23-32.

Chen Shaoyu, 'About the publication date of *Qianshao*' (*Qianshao de chuban riji*), *Xinwenxue shiliao* No 1, 1980 (22 February 1980), pp 273-4.

'The literary activities of Xiao San in the Soviet Union' (*Xiao San zai Sulian de wenxue huodong diandi*), *Xinwenxue shiliao* No 3, 1983 (22 August 1983), pp 112-14.

Chen Songsheng, 'Lu Xun and the Creation Society' (*Lu Xun he Chuangzaoshe*), *Zhongshan daxue xuebao* No 3, 1981 (undated), pp 101-12.

Chen Yede, 'On the "revolutionary literature" polemic' (*Ping "geming wenxue" lunzheng*), *Anhui shida xuebao* No 1, 1978 (March 1978), pp 169-76.

Chen Zhongshan, 'Letter from Chen Zhongshan to Lu Xun', 4 July 1936 reprinted in *Luxun yanjiu ziliao* No 4 (January 1980), pp 169-76.

Chen Zishan and Wang Zili, 'An important official organ of the "Left League" in the latter stage: *Wenyi qunzhong*' (*Zuolian houqi de zhongyao jiquan kanwu: Wenyi qunzhong*), *Luxun yanjiu wencong* No 2 (November 1980), pp 317-29.

'The last official organ of the "Left League"' (*Zuolian de zuihou yige jiquan kanwu*), *Zhongguo xiandai wenyi ziliao congkan* No 5 (December 1980), pp 107-10.

Cheng Zhongyuan, 'An important piece of historical material on the Party leadership of the left-wing literary movement: On reading Ge Te's "The close-doorism on the literary front"' (*Dang lingdao zuoyi wenyi yundong de zhongyao shiliao: Du Ge Te wenyi zhanxianshang de guanmen zhuyi*), *Xinwenxue shiliao* No 2, 1982 (22 May 1982), pp 183-8.

'An examination on the materials of the fourth general meeting of the "Left League"' (*Zuolian disici quanti dahui shiliao kaoshi*), *Zhongguo xiandai wenxue yanjiu congkan* No 2, 1983 (June 1983), pp 342-9.

Cun Yu and Huang Qian, 'On the polemic engaged by the Left League against the "free men" and the "third category men"' (*Ping Zuolian gan ziyouren he disanzhongren de lunzheng*), *Xuzhou shiyuan xuebao* No 1, 1981 (undated), pp 16-25.

Ding Jingtang, 'The several translation versions of the "Letter from the Chinese League of Left-wing Writers to the writers and thinkers of revolutionary literary and cultural organisations as well as all those who work for the progress of mankind on the issue of the KMT's massacre of our comrades' (*Guanyu Zhongguo zuoyi zuojia lianmeng wei Guomindang tusha tongzhi zhi geguo geming wenxue he wenhua tuanti ji yiqie wei renlei jinbu er gongzuo de zhuzuojia sixiangjia shu de jizhong yiwen*), *Zhongguo xiandai wenyi ziliao congkan* No 1 (1962), pp 158-62.

'The memorial edition on the five martyrs of the Left League published in Japan: On "A collection of Chinese fiction, The true story of Ah Q"' (*Ji Riben yiyin de Zuolian wulieshi de Jinianji: Zhongguo xiaoshuoji A'Q zhenzhuan*), *Zhongguo xiandai wenyi ziliao congkan* No 3 (November 1963), pp 42-50.

'Some materials on the time around the formation of the "Left League" in 1930' (*Yijiu sanlingnian Zuolian chengli qianhou shiliao sanji*), *Xueshu yuekan* No 3, 1980 (20 March 1980), pp 29-35.

'About the list of League members who had attended the inaugural meeting of the Chinese League of Left-wing Writers' (*Guanyu canjia Zhongguo zuoyi zuojia lianmeng chengli dahui de mengyuan mingdan*), *Zhongguo xiandai wenyi ziliao congkan* No 5 (December 1980), pp 40-51.

Ding Ling, 'Piecemeal thoughts on the "Left League"' (*Guanyu Zuolian de pianduan huiyi*) *Xinwenxue shiliao* No 1, 1980, pp 29-32.

'Recalling comrade Pan Hannian' (*Huiyi Pan Hannian tongzhi*), *Xinwenxue shiliao* No 4, 1982 (22 November 1982), pp 190-3.

Ding Youguang, 'Zhou Yang and the question of "National defence literature"' (*Zhou Yang yu guofang wenxue wenti*), *Mingbao yuekan* Vol I No 8 (August 1966), pp 8-13.

Du Yibai, 'The glorious achievement of the literature of the thirties will last forever: The formation of the Left League and its contribution' (*Sanshi niandai wenyi de guanghui yeji yongcun: Zuolian chengli jiqi gongxian*), *Yuwen jiaoxue tongxin* No 4 (18 April 1980), pp 36-9.

Duan Guochao, 'Lu Xun and Hu Feng' (*Lu Xun yu He Feng*), *Luxun yanjiu dongtai* No 12 (20 November 1981), pp 1-7.

'The contact between Hu Feng and Lu Xun during the Left League period' (*Zuolian shiqi Hu Feng yi Lu Xun de yiduan jiaowang*), *Qiusuo* No 5, 1985, pp 115-19.

Fang Yuxiao, 'On the left-wing literary movement of the thirties' (*Ping sanshi niandai zuoyi wenyi yundong*), *Beijing daxue xuebao* No 1, 1978 (20 May 1978), pp 74-83.

'Lu Xun and the left-wing literary movement of the thirties' (*Lu Xun he sanshi niandai zuoyi wenyi yundong*), *Liaoning daxue xuebao* No 3, 1978 (undated), pp 60-8.

Feng Naichao, 'Lu Xun and the Creation Society' (*Lu Xun yu Chuangzaoshe*), *Xinwenxue shiliao* No 1 (1978), pp 34-40.

'The situation around the formation of the Left League' (*Zuolian chengli qianhou de yixie qingkuang*), *Luxun yanjiu ziliao* No 6 (October 1980), pp 77-82.

'Revolutionary literary polemic, Lu Xun, The League of Left-wing Writers: Some of my recollections' (*Geming wenxue lunzheng Lu Xun Zuoyi zuojia*

Bibliography

lianmeng: Wode yixie huiyi), Xinwenxue shiliao No 3, 1986 (22 August 1986), pp 19-35 and 68.

Feng Runzhang, 'The Left League as I could remember' (*Wo jiyizhong de Zuolian*), *Xinwenxue shiliao* No 1, 1980, pp 74-8.

Feng Xiaxiong, 'Feng Xuefeng on the Left League' (*Feng Xuefeng tan Zuolian*), *Xinwenxue shiliao* No 1, 1980, pp 1-11.

Feng Xuefeng, 'On the activities of Zhou Yang and others in 1936 and Lu Xun's raising of the slogan "Mass literature of the national revolutionary war"' (*Youguan yijiu sanliunian Zhou Yang dengren de xingdong yiji Lu Xun tichu minzu geming zhanzheng de dazhong wenxue kouhao de jingguo*), *Xinwenxue shiliao* No 2 (February 1979), pp 247-58.

'Comrade Feng Xuefeng on Lu Xun and the "Left League"' (*Feng Xuefeng tongzhi guanyu Lu Xun Zuolian de wenti de Tanhua*), *Luxun yanjiu ziliao* No 2 (March 1979), pp 167-76.

'Letters from Feng Xuefeng to Bao Ziyan' (*Feng Xuefeng zhi Bao Ziyan de xin*), *Xinwenxue shiliao* No 4 (August 1979), p 138-61.

'On the role of my work in Shanghai in 1936 as well as my relationship with the "Cultural Committee" and "Temporary Committee"' (*Guanyu yijiu Sanliunian wozai Shanghai gongzuo de renwu yiji wotong wenweihe linwei de guanxi*), *Luxun yanjiu ziliao* No 4 (January 1980), pp 179-89.

'About the Left League' (*Guanyu Zuolian*), *Luxun yanjiu dongtai* No 8 (15 March 1981), pp 1-3.

Fudan University, 'Interview with comrade Yang Hansheng' (*Fangwen Yang Hansheng tongzhi*), *Luxun yanjiu ziliao* No 5 (May 1980), pp 172-4.

'Interview with comrades Sha Ting and Ai Wu' (*Fangwen Sha Ting Ai Wu tongzhi*), *Luxun yanjiu ziliao* No 6 (October 1980), pp 140-6.

Gao Kang, 'Insist on the principle of united front: Rereading Feng Xuefeng's "On the inclination and theories of the 'third category literature'"' (*Jianchi tongyi zhanxian de yuanze: Zhongdu Feng Xuefeng guangyu disanzhong wenxue de qingxiang yu lilun*), *Chengde shizhuan xuebao* No 1, 1982, pp 3-12.

Ge Te, 'The close-doorism on the literary front' (*Wenyi zhanxianshang de tuanwen zhuyi*), *Douzheng* No 30 (3 November 1932, reprinted in *Xinwenxue shiliao* No 2, 1982 (22 May 1982), pp 180-3.

Guan Lu, 'Random recollections on the Left League and other things' (*Zuolian suoyu ji qita*), *Zhongguo xiandai wenyi ziliao congkan* No 6 (April 1981), pp 99-103.

Han Tuofu, 'Lu Xun in the eyes of a Communist Party member' (*Yige gongchandangyuan yanzhong de Lu Xun*), *Wenyibao* No 19, 1956 (15 October 1956), pp 28-9.

Hu Feng, 'Hu Feng's opinion on literature and art' (*Hu Feng dui wenyi wenti de yijian*), Supplement to *Wenyibao* (January 1955), pp 1-165.

'Annotations on Lu Xun's letters', (*Lu Xun shuxin zhushi*) *Xinwenxue shiliao* No 3, 1981 (22 August 1981), pp 73-80.

'Recalling the time around the joining of the Left League' (*Huiyi canjia Zuolian qianhou*) (I), *Xinwenxue shiliao* No 1, 1984 (22 February 1984), pp 30-8; (II), *ibid* No 3, 1984 (22 August 1984), pp 41-9; (III), *ibid* No 4, 1984 (22 November 1984), pp 39-50; (IV), *ibid* No 1, 1985 (22 February 1985), pp 45-56.

'A deep memory' (*Shenqie de huainian*), *Xinwenxue shiliao* No 4, 1985 (22 November 1985), pp 17-18.

Hu Qiuyuan, 'Between Tansanzang and Faust' (*Zai Tan Sanzang ui fushide zhijian*) (I), *Ziyoutan* Vol VI No 9 (1 September 1955), pp 21-6; (II), *ibid* Vol VI No 10 (1 October 1955), pp 23-6; (III), *ibid* Vol VI No 11, (1 November 1955), pp 19-22.

'About the 1932 debate on the freedom of literature and art' (*Guanyu yijiu sanernian wenyi ziyou lunbian*), *Zhonghua zazhi* Vol VII No 1 (16 January 1969), pp 18-25.

Hu Yuzhi and Feng Xuefeng, 'Something about Lu Xun' (*Tan youguan Lu Xun de yixie shiqing*), *Luxun yanjiu ziliao* No 1 (March 1979 reprint), pp 78-9.

Hu Zhu, 'A re-evaluation of the Two slogan polemic' (*Chongping liangge kaohou zhizheng*), *Shehui kexue yanjiu* No 5, 1985 (15 September 1985), pp 81-4.

Huang Mei, 'A great road and some piecemeal recollections: In commemoration of the fiftieth anniversary of the "Left League"' (*Weida de licheng he pianduan de huiyi: Jinian Zuolian chengli wushi zhounian*), *Renmin wenxue* No 3, 1980 (20 March 1980), pp 75-83.

Huang Xiuji, 'Wrong conclusions ought to be rejected: On the polemic in the literary arena in 1936 over the establishment of an anti-Japan united front' (*Cuowude jielun kiushiyao tuidao: ping yijiu sanliunian wenyijie wei jianli kanri tongyi zhanxian de lun zheng*), *Gansu shida xuebao* No 2, 1978 (18 May 1978), pp 15-26.

'Lu Xun's "co-existence" theory is most correct' (*Lu Xun de bingcunlun zuizhengque*), *Wenxue pinglun* No 5, 1978 (25 October 1978), pp 27-36.

Huang Yuan, 'Learn from the experiences of the Left League and build up our province into a socialist cultural state' (*Xuexi Zuolian jingyan ba wosheng jianshe chengwei shehui zhuyi de wenhua zhi bang*), *Donghai* No 4, 1980 (10 April 1980), pp 7-9.

Huang Zhengwei, 'On the second united front between the Nationalists and the Communists' (*Lun dierci guogong hezuo*), *Xueshu yanjiu* No 4, 1985 (undated), pp 5-12.

Huang Zhigang, 'The unforgettable evening of 7th February: In commemoration of Rou Shi, Yepin and others' (*Yongnanwang de eryue qiriwan: Jinian Rou Shi Yepin zhuxiong*), *Wenxuebao*, 25 February 1951.

Huo Su, 'Was the criticism of comrade Qu Qiubai on the "third category" leftist?' (*Qu Qiubai tongzhi dui disanzhongren de pipan shi zuolema?*), *Lilun yuekan* No 8, 1985 (August 1985), pp 48-50.

Ji Fuhua, 'A furious debate over two viewpoints in literature: A look at the pen-battle between Lu Xun and Liang Shiqiu' (*Liangzhong wenyiguan de jilie*

lunzheng: Lu Xun he Liang Shiqiu bizhan de huifu), *Dousou* No 18 (15 November 1976), pp 26-30.
Ji Mingxue, 'Ge Te, Ke De and other things' (*Ge Te Ke De ji qita*), *Xinwenxue shiliao* No 2, 1983 (22 May 1983), pp 238-47.
Ji Wen, 'A chronological table of the "Left League"' (*Zuolian dashi nianbiao*), *Jinian yu yanjiu* No 2 (March 1980), pp 232-61.
'Several former sites of the "Left League" in Shanghai' (*Zuolian zai Shanghai de jige jiuzhi*), *Zhongguo xiandai wenyi ziliao congkan* No 5 (December 1980), pp 98-102.
'Left League members on the Left League' (*Zuolian mengyuan tan Zuolian*) (I), *Zhongguo xiandai wenyi ziliao congkan* No 5, pp 134-47; (II), *ibid* No 6 (April 1981), pp 84-98.
'Letter from the Secretariat of the Central Executive Committee of the Chinese National Party No 15889' (*Zhongguo Guomindang Zhongyang zhixing weiyuanhui mishuchi gonghan 15889 hao*), reprinted in *Jinian yu yanjiu* No 2 (March 1980), pp 192-3.
Li Cunyu, 'On Feng Xuefeng's stance and attitude in the Left League's polemic against the "free men" and the "third category men"' (*Ping Feng Xuefeng zai Zuolian gan ziyouren yu disanzhongren lunzhengde xingzhi*), *Zhongguo xiandai wenxue yanjiu congkan* No 1, 1981 (March 1981), pp 1-24.
Li Haiwen and She Haining, 'The incident of the Oriental Hotel: The arrest and execution of twenty-three martyrs of Lin Yunan, Li Qiushi, He Mengxiong and others' (*Dongfang lushe shijian; Ji Lin Yunan Li Qiushi He Mengxiong deng ershisan lieshi de beibu yu xunlan, Shehui kexue zhanxian* No 3, 1980 (25 July 1980), pp 6-11.
Li Helin, 'The growth of socialist-realism during the Left League period' (*Zuolian shiqi shehui zhuyi xianshi zhuyi de chengchang*), *On Modern Chinese literature* (Shanghai: Xinwenyi chubanshe, August 1956), pp 59-85.
Li Zhenkun, 'Lu Xun and the popularisation movement of literature' (*Lu Xun yu wenyi dazhonghua yundong*), *Xinjiang shifan daxue xuebao* No 1, 1981, pp 52-7.
Liao Mosha, 'The two pieces of *zawen* I wrote in the thirties' (*Wozai sanshi niandai xiede liangpian zawen*), *Xinwenxue shiliao* No 2, 1984 (22 May 1984), pp 40-5.
Lin Zhihao, 'Give a genuine picture of history: On the "Two slogan polemic and the question of "National defence literature"' (*Yao huan lishi de benlai mianmu: Tan liangge kouhao lunzheng he guofang wenxue wenti*), *Gansu shida xuebao* No 2, 1978 (15 May 1978), pp 2-14.
'Several questions on the polemic engaged by the Left League against the "free men" and the "third category men"' (*Guanyu Zuolian duiyu ziyouren he disanzhongren lunzhengzhong de jige wenti*), *Zhongguo xiandai wenxue yanjiu congkan* No 2, 1985 (May 1985), pp 164-83.

Ling He, 'Around the time of joining the Left League' (*Canjia Xuolian de qianqian houhou*), *Xinwenxue shiliao* No 1, 1980 (22 February 1980), pp 85-6.

Liu Boqing, 'The influence of Japanese proletarian literary thought on the left-wing literature of the thirties' (*Sanshi niandai zuoyi wenyi shou riben wuchanjieji wenyi sichao de yingxiang*), *Wenxue pinglun* No 6, 1981 (15 November 1981), pp 102-9.

Liu Shousong, 'On the two literary polemics of the Left League period: A criticism of Feng Xuefeng's anti-Party activities and anti-Marxist literary thinking' (*Guanyu Zuolian shiqi de lianci wenyi lunzheng; Pipan Feng Xuefeng de fandang huodong he fan Makesi zhuyi wenyi sixiang*), *Wenxue yanjiu* No 1, 1958 (12 March 1958), pp 23-45.

'Inherit and bring forward the fighting tradition of the Chinese League of Left-wing Writers' (*Jicheng he fayang Zhongguo zuoyi zuojia lianmeng de zhandou chuantong*), *Wenyibao* No 4, 1960 (26 February 1960), pp 2-9.

Liu Shu, 'The "suppression" and anti-"suppression" campaigns in the literary front during the second national revolutionary war period' (*Dierci guonei geming zhanzheng shiqi wenhua zhanxianshang de weijiao yu fanweijiao*), *Lishi jiaoxue* No 3, 1954 (4 March 1954), pp 35-41.

Liu Xiao, 'Around the re-establishment of the underground Party of Shanghai' (*Shanghai dixiadang huifu he chongjian qianhou*), *Dangshi ziliao congkan* No 1, 1979 (November 1979), pp 32-46.

Liu Xiaoyan, 'Lu Xun and national defence literature: Rereading "Reply to Xu Maoyong and on the question of the united front against Japanese aggression"' (*Lu Xun yu guofang wenxue: Chongdu da xu Maoyong bing guanyi kangri tongyi zhanxian wenti*), *Liaoning daxue xuebao* No 2, 1978 (undated), pp 63-6.

Liu Xinhuang, 'The impact of the literature of the thirties on China' (*Sanshi niandai wenxue dui woguo yingxiang*), *Zhonghua zazhi* Vol VIII No 2 (1 February 1970), pp 14-21.

'The tragedy of the left-wing writers of the thirties' (*Sanshi niandai zuoyi zuojia de beiju*), *Ziyoutan* Vol XXX No 7 (1 July 1979), pp 52-5.

Liu Zhongshu, 'On the Two slogan polemic of "Mass literature of the national revolutionary war" and "National defence literature"' (*Tan minzu geming zhanzheng de dazhong wenxue yu guofang wenxue liangge kouhao de lunzheng*), *Jinlin daxue xuebao* Nos 5 and 6, 1978 (20 October 1978), pp 74-83.

Lou Shiyi, 'Recalling the two publications of the "Left League"' (*Ji Zuolian de liangge kanwu*), *Wenxue pinglun* No 2, 1960 (April 1960), pp 69-73.

'To forget, for solidarity: On reading comrade Xia Yan's "Some past events that should have long been forgotten but cannot be forgotten"' (*Weile wangque weile tuanjie: du Xia Yan tongzhi yixie zaoge wangque erweineng wangque de wangshi*), reprinted in *Lu Xun yanjiu niankan*, 1980, pp 91-8.

Bibliography

Luo Zhanglong, 'Before and after the Shanghai Oriental Hotel meeting' (*Shanghai dongfang fandian huiyi qianhou*), *Xinwenxue shiliao* No 1, 1981 (22 February 1981), pp 141-5.
Ma Liangchun, 'Lu Xun on the left-wing literary movement' (*Lu Xun lun zuoyi wenyi yundong*), *Zhongguo xiandai wenxue yanjiu congkan* No 1, 1979 (October 1979), pp 13-40.
Ma Wen, 'The milestone of unity in struggle: In commemoration of the fiftieth anniversary of the Left League' (*Tuanjie zhandou de lichengbei: Jinian Zuolian chengli wushi zhounian*), *Shehui kexue* No 1, 1980 (February 1980), pp 113-21.
Mao Dun, 'The contacts I made with Lu Xun' (*Wohe Lu Xun de jiechu*), *Luxun yanjiu ziliao* No 1 (March 1979 reprint), pp 66-77.
'Some facts that need to be clarified' (*Xuyao chengqing yixie shishi*), *Xinwenxue shiliao* No 2 (February 1978), pp 243-6.
Man Shu, '"National defence literature" and "Mass literature of the national revolutionary war"' (*Guofang wenxue he minzu geming zhanzheng de dazhong wenxue*), *Zhanwang* No 199 (16 May 1970), pp 21-4.
Mishuchu xiaoxi No 1 (15 March 1932), reprinted in *Zhongguo xiandai wenyi ziliao congkan* No 5 (December 1980), pp 15-30.
Ni Moyan, 'The complete story of the relations between the left and the "third category men"' (*Zuoyi wentan yu disanzhongren guanxi de shimo*), *Xinwenxue shiliao* No 4, 1983 (22 November 1983), pp 149-63.
'Collection of materials on the repressions imposed on modern literature by the reactionaries in the thirties' (*Sanshi niandai fandongpai yabi xinwenxue de shiliao jilu*), *Xinwenxue shiliao* No 3, 1985 (22 August 1985), pp 212-17.
Pan Songde, 'The speech made by Lu Xun in the second general meeting of the "Left League"' (*Lu Xun zai zuolian dierci quanti dahuishang de yanjiang kaolu*), *Luxun xuekan* No 2, 1981 (20 July 1981), pp 103-5.
Peng Fang, 'Guo Moruo on "National defence literature": On the "Two slogan polemic"' (*Du Guo Moruo lun guofang wenxue: Jianping liangge kouhao de lunzheng*), *Beifang luncong* No 2, 1980 (15 March 1980), pp 72-7.
Pi Yuanchang, 'An appraisal on the appraisal of the "Two slogan polemic"' (*Guanyu liangge kouhao lunzheng pingjia de shuping*), *Lunxun yanjiu dongtai* No 7 (25 January 1981), pp 5-16.
'The historical contribution of Feng Xuefeng in the two literary polemics of the thirties' (*Feng Xuefeng zai sanshi niandai wenyi lunzhengzhong de lishi gongji*), *Lunxun yanjiu dongtai* No 8 (15 March 1981), pp 3-15.
Ren Baige, 'Firmly criticise the slanders on the literature of the thirties made by the gang of Lin Biao and Jiang Qing' (*Jianjue pipan Lin Biao Jiang Qing yihuo dui sanshi niandai wenyi de wumie*), *Renmin wenxue* No 5, 1978 (20 May 1978), pp 13-19.
Ren Jun, 'Miscellaneous thoughts on the Left League' (*Zuolian manyi*), *Shanghai shifan xueyuan xuebao* No 2, 1981 (25 June 1981), pp 108-17.

Rong Taizhi, 'The Left League and the Japanese League of Proletarian Writers' (*Zuolian yu Riben wuchanjieji zuojia tongmeng*), *Renmin ribao*, 14 September 1980, pp 17-18.

'The memorial activities on Marx by the Left League' (*Zuolian dui Makesi de jinian*), *Luxun yanjiu dongtai* No 24 (10 March 1983), pp 8-13.

'Lu Xun, the Left League, Kobayashi Takiji' (*Lu Xun Zuolian Xiaolin duoxier*), *Luxun yanjiu ziliao* No 14 (November 1984), pp 73-86.

'Selection of materials on the Freedom Movement League of China' (*Zhongguo ziyou yundong datongmeng ziliao xuanbian*), *Luxun yanjiu ziliao* No 4 (January 1980), pp 473-521.

Shanghai Normal College, 'Interview records of five comrades' (*Fangwen wuwei tongzhi de tanhua jilu*), *Xinwenxue shiliao* No 1 (1978), pp 74-84.

'A membership list of the "Left League" and the activities of some members during the Left League period' (*Zuolian mengyuan minglu ji bufen mengyuan Zuolian shiqi huodong jianjie*), *Shanghai shifan xueyuan xuebao* No 1, 1980 (20 March 1980), pp 36-48.

'Lin Huanping on the organisation and activities of the Left League and its Tokyo branch' (*Lin Huanping tan Zuolian de zuzhi huodong he Dongjing zhimeng de qingkuang*), *Luxun yanjiu ziliao* No 6 (October 1980), pp 109-14.

'Records of Zhou Gangming's interview' (*Fangwen Zhou Gangming tanhua jilu*), *Luxun yanjiu ziliao* No 6 (October 1980), pp 115-19.

'Ren Jun on the "Left League" and the "Chinese Association of Poetry"', (*Ren Jun tan Zuolian he Zhongguo shigehui de yixie qingkuang*), *Luxun yanjiu ziliao* No 6 (October 1980), pp 120-4.

'A membership list of the Chinese League of Left-wing Writers' (*Zhonggong zuoyi zuojia lianmeng mengyuan kaolu*), *Zhongguo xiandai wenyi ziliao congkan* No 5 (December 1980), pp 52-81.

'Collection of materials about the organisation and structure of the Chinese League of Left-wing Writers' (*Zhongguo zuoyi zuojia lianmeng zuzhi jiquan ziliao huilu*), *Zhongguo xiandai wenyi ziliao congkan* No 5 (December 1980), pp 82-97.

Shao Bozhou, 'Glorious achievements: On the achievements of the "Left League" and its significance in the history of modern Chinese literature" (*Guanghui de yeji: Shilun Zuolian chengji jiqi zai woguo xiandai wenxueshi shang de yiyi*), *Shanghai shifan xueyuan xuebao* No 1, 1980 (20 March 1980), pp 30-6.

Shen Pengnian, 'Two facts about the relations between Lu Xun and the Creation Society' (*Lu Xun he Chuangzaoshe jiaowang de liandian shishi*), *Shanghai wenxue* No 7, 1962 (5 July 1962), pp 61-6.

Shen Rengfu, 'Historical materials of the Chinese League of Left-wing Writers', (*Zhongguo zuoyi zuojia lianmeng wenxian mulu*), *Zhongguo xiandai wenyi ziliao congkan* No 5 (December 1980), pp 31-4.

Bibliography

Shen Shi, 'On the Left League martyr of our province Pan Mohua', (*Ji wosheng lieshi Pan Mohua*), *Zhejiang shifan xueyuan xuebao* No 3, 1981 (July 1981), pp 70-4.

Shi Mang, 'On Lu Xun's art of fighting in 1936' (*Lun Lu Xun zai yijiu sanliunian de douzheng yishu*), *Luxun yanjiu dongtai* No 14 (10 April 1982), pp 1-10.

Shi Zhecun, 'Random thoughts on *Xiandai*' (*Xiandai zayi*), (I), *Xinwenxue shiliao* No 1, 1981 (22 February 1981), pp 213-30; (II), *ibid* No 2, 1981 (22 May 1981), pp 158-63; (III), *ibid* No 3, 1981 (22 August 1981), pp 220-3.

'My last old friend: Feng Xuefeng' (*Zuihou yige laopengyou: Feng Xuefeng*), *Xinwenxue shiliao* No 2, 1983 (22 May 1983), pp 199-203.

Situ Huimin, 'On the rapid development of progressive movies under the banner of the "Left League"' (*Sanji Zuolian de qizhixie jinbu dianyi de feiyue*), *Dianying yishu* No 6, 1980 (16 June 1980), pp 58-63.

Situ Weizhi, 'The "Fringe literature" incident must be clarified: On the conflict between Lu Xun and Liao Mosha over the issue of "Fringe literature"' (*Huabian wenxue shijian zhenxiang: Xuyao chengqing guanyu Lu Xun yu Liao Mosha de huabian wenxue de zhengduan*), *Fudan xuebao* No 2, 1980 (5 March 1980), pp 97-100.

'There was no such "confrontation": On the relations between Lu Xun and Liao Mosha' (*Bucunzai zheyang de chongtu: Jiantan Lu Xun yu Liao Mosha de guanxi*), *Luxun yanjiu dongtai* No 19 (4 December 1982), pp 16-22.

Situ Zhi, 'Materials on the Left League' (*Zuolian shiliao yishu*), *Shanghai shifan xueyuan xuebao* No 1, 1980 (20 March 1980), pp 53-8.

Sun Xizhen, 'About the Northern Left League' (*Guanyu Beifang Zuolian de shiqing*), *Xinwenxue shiliao* No 4 (August 1979), pp 240-8.

'The history of the Northern Left League' (*Beifang Zuolian de shimo*), *Zhongguo xiandai wenxue yanjiu congkan* No 4, 1981 (March 1981), pp 311-21.

'Supplement to the materials on the Chinese League for the Protection of Civil Rights' *Zhongguo minquan baozhang tongmeng ziliaobu*), *Jinian yu yanjiu* No 3 (December 1980), pp 82-109.

Tang Tao, 'Recollection on the line struggles in the literary arena of the thirties' (*Guanyu sanshi niandia wenyijie luxian douzheng de yixie huiyi*), *Anhui shida xuebao* No 4, 1976, pp 130-3.

'Recalling Lu Xun and the struggle between two lines in the literary arena of the thirties' (*Huiyi Lu Xun ji sanshi niandai wenyijie liangtiao luxian douzheng*), *Luxun yanjiu ziliao* No 1 (March 1979 reprint), pp 49-65.

Tang Tianran, 'Supplement to the article Comrade Luofu spoke on the attitude of the Party's Central Committee towards the Two slogan polemic of 1936' (*Guanyu Luofu tongzhi tan dangzhongyang dui yijiu sanliunian liangge kouhao lunzheng taidu yiwen de buzheng*), *Luxun yanjiu dongtai* No 7 (25 January 1981), pp 17-18.

Tang Yuan, 'On the nature of the 1936 "Two slogan polemic"' (*Guanyu yijiu sanliunian liangge kouhao lunzheng de xingzhi wenti*), *Wenxue pinglun* No 2, 1978 (25 June 1978), pp 10-19.

Tang Yizhong, 'Several remarks on the "Two slogan polemic"' (*Dui liangge kouhao zhizheng de jidian kanfa*), *Luxun yanjiu dongtai* No 18 (1 November 1982), pp 4-14.

'The formation of the Beiping branch of the Chinese League of Left-wing Writers and its programmes of actions and theories' (*Zhongguo zuoyi zuojia lianmeng Beiping fenmeng de chengli jiqi xingdong gangling he lilun gangling*), *Zhongguo xiandai wenyi ziliao congkan* No 5 (December 1980), pp 6-8.

Tian Jianong, 'Ozaki Hotsumi and the "Left League"' (*Weiqi xiushi yu Zuolian*), *Beijing ribao*, 18 December 1980.

Wan Song, 'Lu Xun and the "Two slogan polemic"' (*Lu Xun yu liangge kouhao de lunzheng*), *Gansu shida xuebao* No 2, 1978 (18 May 1978), pp 36-42.

Wang Dehou, 'Lu Xun's struggle against the Trotskyists' (*Guanyu Lu Xun fandui tuopai de douzheng*), *Guangchajia* No 37 (20 November 1980), pp 28-9.

Wang Furen, 'Some words on the study of the "Left League"' (*Zuolian yanjiu dianditan*), *Wenxue pinglun* No 2, 1985 (15 March 1985), pp 64-6.

Wang Jinhou, 'Who in fact was Du Quan?' (*Du Quan daodi shishui?*), *Luxun yanjiu ziliao* No 7 (December 1980), pp 285-305.

Wang Xirong, 'On the new materials of the Freedom Movement League of China' (*Guanyu Zhongguo ziyou yundong datongmeng xinziliao*), *Jinian yu yanjiu* No 6 (December 1984), pp 104-13.

Wang Yao, 'Criticise the slanders made by the "Gang of Four" on the literature of the thirties' (*Pipan sirenbang guanyu sanshi niandai wenyi de miulun*), *Renmin wenxue* No 5, 1978 (20 May 1978), pp 20-5.

'Popularisation movement of literature in the thirties' (*Sanshi niandai de wenyi dazhonghua yundong*), *Wenyibao* No 3, 1980 (12 March 1980), pp 22-8.

Wang Yaoshan, 'The re-establishment of the underground Party of Shanghai' (*Guanyu Shanghai dixiadang chongjian de jingguo*), *Dangshi ziliao congkan* No 1, 1979 (November 1979), pp 47-69.

'Feng Xuefeng during the re-establishment of the underground Party' (*Zhengli dixiadang shiqi de Feng Xuefeng*), *Xinwenxue shiliao* No 4, 1985 (22 November 1985), pp 17-18.

Wang Ye, 'The debate on "revolutionary literature" and Fukumoto Kazuo' (*Geming wenxue lunzheng yu fuben huofu*), *Zhongguo xiandao wenxue yanjiu congkan* No 1, 1983 (March 1983), pp 322-31.

Wang Yongsheng, 'Lu Xun and the 1928 revolutionary literary polemic' (*Lu Xun yu yijiu erbanian geming wenyi lunzheng*), *Jianghan luntan* No 11, 1983 (15 November 1983), pp 22-5.

Bibliography

'Lu Xun and the "Two slogan polemic" in 1936' (*Lu Xun yu yijiu sanliunian liangge kouhao lunzheng*), *Xuzhou shifan xueyuan xuebao* No 1, 1986 (undated), pp 49-56.

Wei Chenyu and Li Guangcan, 'Comrade Luofu spoke on the attitude of the Party's Central Committee towards the Two slogan polemic of 1936' (*Luofu tongzhi tan dangzhongyang dui yijiu sanliunian liangge houhao lunzhan de taidu*), *Luxun yanjiu dongtai* No 4 (20 June 1980), pp 2-4.

Wei Dongming, 'Recalling the days when I worked in the Left League' (*Huiyi canjia Zuolian gongzuo de rizi*), *Zhandi* No 4, 1980 (July 1980), pp 66-8.

Wei Mengke, 'Wei Mengke on the two letters from Lu Xun and the Tokyo branch of the "Left League"' (*Wei Mengke tan Lu Xun geita de liangfengxin ji Zuolian Dongjing zhibu de qingkuang*), *Huangdong shifan daxue xuebao (Supplement)* No 4, 1980 (undated), pp 59-61.

'Miscellaneous thoughts on the past events of the "Left League"' (*Zuolian wangshi manyi*) *Zhongguo xiandao wenyi ziliao congkan* No 5 (December 1980), pp 154-61.

Wong Wang-chi, 'The Crescent School in twentieth century Chinese poetry' (*Xinyue shipai yanjiu*) (Unpublished MPhil thesis, University of Hong Kong, 1981).

'On the "Five martyrs of the Left League"' (*Yetan Zuolian wulieshi*), *Zhongbao yuekan* No 6, 1985 (June 1985), pp 45-50.

'Who attended the inaugural meeting of the "Left League"' (*Shui chuxile Zuolian de chengli dahui?*), *Zhongbao yuekan* No 8, 1985 (August 1985), pp 53-5.

'The Fringe literature incident: A *zawen* written by Liao Mosha in attack of Lu Xun' (*Huabian wenxue shijian: Liao Mosha gongji Lu Xun de yibian zawen*), *Zhongbao yuekan* No 4, 1986 (April 1986), pp 44-7.

'Lu Xun, Tian Han, Yang Cunren: An article by Tian Han in attack of Lu Xun' (*Lu Xun Tian Han Yang Cunren: Tian Han gongji Lu Xun de yibian wenzhang*), *Zhongbao yuekan* No 6, 1986 (June 1986), pp 82-6.

Wu Benxing, 'The historical significance and fighting tradition of the "Left League"' (*Zuolian de lishi yiyi he zhandou chuantong*), *Xuzhou shifan xueyuan xuebao* No 2, 1983 (15 June 1983), pp 3-9.

Wu Liping, 'On the several questions of the left-wing literary movement of the "Left League"' (*Guanyu sanshi niandai zuoyi wenyi yundong de ruogan wenti*), *Wenxue pinglun* No 5, 1978 (25 October 1978), pp 7-15.

'Always remember the red banner of the literary front' (*Changnian wenyuan zhanqihong*), *Wenxue pinglun* No 4, 1980 (15 July 1980), pp 92-8.

'Some facts and opinions on the "Left League"' (*Guanyu Zuolian de yidian qingkuang he yijian*), *Zhongguo xiandai* wenyi ziliao congkan No 5 (December 1980), pp 148-53.

Wu Taichang, 'A Ying on the Left League' (*A Ying yi Zuolian*), *Xinwenxue shiliao* No 1, 1980 (22 February 1980), pp 12-28.

Wu Xiru, 'The relations between Lu Xun and the Party' (*Lu Xun yu dang de guanxi*), *Luxun yanjiu ziliao* No 4 (January 1980), pp 190-3.

'Recalling the great teacher Lu Xun' (*huiyi weida de daoshi Lu Xun*), *Luxun yanjiu ziliao* No 5 (May 1980), pp 179-92.

'Hu Feng as I know him' (*Wosuo yingshi de Hu Feng*), *Luxun yanjiu ziliao* No 9 (January 1982), pp 235-55.

Wu Yuankan (trans), 'Letter from the Chinese League of Left-wing Writers to the writers and thinkers of revolutionary literature and cultural organisations as well as all those who work for the progress of mankind on the issue of the KMT's massacre of our comrades' (*Zhongguo zuoyi zuojia lianmeng wei Guomindang tusha tongzhi zhi geguo geming wenxue he wenhua tuanti ji yiqie weirenlei jinbu er gongzuo de zhuzuojia sixiangjia shu*), *Zhongguo xiandai wenyi ziliao congkan* No 1 (1962), pp 163-66.

Xi Jin, 'Why did Lu Xun not go to Japan for recuperation?' (*Lu Xun weishenme buqu Riben liaoyang?*), *Xinwenxue shiliao* No 1 (1979), pp 147-57.

Xi Yu, 'Several questions on the revolutionary literary polemic' (*Guanyu geming wenxue lunzheng de ruogan wenti*), *Zhongguo xiandai wenxue yanjiu congkan* No 1, 1979, pp 41-60.

Xia Yan, 'Some past events that should have long been forgotten but cannot be forgotten' (*Yixie zaogai wangque er weineng wangque de wangshi*), *Wenxue pinglun* No 1, 1980 (15 January 1980), pp 92-101.

'Miscellaneous thoughts on the Left League' (*Zuolian zayi*), *Renmin ribao*, 1 March 1980.

'Around the formation of the "Left League"' (*Zuolian chengli qianhou*), *Wenxue pinglun* No 2, 1980 (March 1980), pp 2-13.

'A word on "Some past events"' (*Guanyu wanshi de yidian shuoming*), *Wenxue pinglun* No 1, 1981 (15 January 1981), p 137.

'Xia Yan's recollection on the Left League' (*Xia Yan guanyu Zuolian yixie qingkuang de huiyi*), *Huadong shifan daxue xuebao* (Supplement) No 4, 1981 (undated), pp 57-9.

Xia Zhengnong, 'Get united and march forward for the thriving of socialist literature and art: Commemorating the fiftieth anniversary of the "Left League"' (*Wei fanrong shehui zhuyi wenyi tuanjie qianjin: Jinian Zuolian chengli wushi zhounian*), *Fudan xuebao* No 2, 1980 (20 March 1980), pp 1-5.

Xiao San, 'Record of an interview with comrade Xiao San' (*Fangwen Xiao San tongzhi jilu*), *Luxun yanjiu ziliao* No 4 (January 1980), pp 194-7.

'What have I done for the 'Left League" abroad?' (*Wowei Zuolian zai guowai zuolexie shenme?*), *Xinwenxue shiliao* No 1, 1980 (22 February 1980), pp 33-7.

Xu Gongqing, 'The study associations formed at the inaugural meeting of the "Left League"' (*Zuolian dahuishang tongge chengli de yanjiuhui*), *Xinwenxue shiliao*, No 5 (November 1979), p 213.

Bibliography

Xu Guangming, 'Feng Xuefeng's literary activities in the "Left League" period' (*Feng Xuefeng zai Zuolian shiqi de wenxie huodong*), *Fudan xuebao*, No 2, 1980 (20 March 1980), pp 5-8.

Xu Guangping, 'Zhou Yang should not be allowed to attack and slander Lu Xun' (*Buxu Zhou Yang gongji he wumie Lu Xun*) *Hongqi* No 12, 1966 (17 September 1966), pp 28-37.

Xu Maoyong, 'Letter from Xu Maoyong to Lu Xun', 30 April 1936, reprinted in *Luxun yanjiu ziliao* No 4 (January 1980), pp 163-6.

Xu Yunming, 'The conflict of "Fringe literature" and its change in nature' (*Huabian wenxue de zhengduan jiqi zhibian*), *Luxun yanjiu dongtai* No 14 (10 April 1982), pp 10-13.

'On the polemic in the literary arena in 1936' (*Guanyu yijiu sanliunian wenyijie de lunzheng*), *Luxun yanjiu dongtai* No 16 (8 July 1982), pp 1-15.

'"Clashing": On the question of "Fringe literature"' (*Guanyu pengzhuang: Zaitan huabian wenxue wenti*), *Luxun yanjiu dongtai* No 25 (1 April 1983), pp 18-22.

Xuan Mo, 'The Maoist Communists and the struggle in thinking of the "literature of the thirties"' (*Maogong yu sanshi niandai wenyi de sixiang douzheng*), *Zhonghua wenhua fuxing yuekan* Vol 1 No 7 (September 1968), pp 30-6.

'Chen Boda and the Two slogan polemic of the thirties' (*Chen Boda yu sanshi niandai wenyi liangge kouhao de lunzheng*), *Zhonggong yanjiu* Vol V No 8 (10 August 1971), pp 4-22.

'The chief villain of the "literature of the thirties"' (*Sanshi niandai wenyi de zuikui*), *Zhonghua wenhua fuxing yuekan* Vol IX No 4 (April 1976), pp 15-21.

Yan Jiayan, 'On the advocation of and debate on proletarian literature in 1928: Several questions concerning the debate between Lu Xun and the Creation and Sun Societies' (*Ping yijiu erbanian wuchanjieji wenxue de changdao he lunzheng: Guanyu Lu Xun he Chuangzaoshe Taiyangshe lunzheng jige wenti*), *Wenxue pinglun* No 2, 1978 (25 April 1978), pp 7-16.

'A re-evaluation of the Two slogan polemic' (*Liangge kouhao lunzheng de zaipingjia*) *Shehui kexue zhanxian* No 1, 1979 (20 February 1979), pp 279-84.

Yan Xiong, 'The "Ten thousand word essay" and *Shehui ribao*' (*Lu Xun de wanyan changwen yu shehui ribao*), *Luxun yanjiu ziliao* No 12 (May 1983), pp 189-201.

Yang Cunren, 'The Sun Society and Jiang Guangci' (*Taiyangshe yu Jiang Guangci*), *Xiandai* Vol III No 4 (1 August 1931), pp 470-6.

Yang Hansheng, 'The process of the formation of the Chinese League of Left-wing Writers' (*Zhongguo zuoyi zuojia lianmeng chengli de jingguo*), *Renmin ribao*, 5 March 1980.

'The process of the formation of the Chinese League of Left-wing Writers' (*Zhongguo zuoyi zuojia lianmeng chengli de jingguo*), *Wenxue pinglun* No 2, 1980 (15 March 1980), pp 14-17.

'The fighting road of the "Left League"' (*Zuolian de zhandou licheng*), *Wenyibao* No 5, 1980 (12 May 1980), pp 16-18.

Yang Qianru, 'Left-wing writers in Shanghai Arts University' (*Zuoyi zuojia zai Shanghai yida*), *Xinwenxue shiliao* No 1, 1980 (22 February 1980), pp 87-92.

Yang Yue, 'A brief discussion of the literature of the thirties' (*Sanshi niandai wenyi jianlun*), *Huacheng* No 4 (January 1980), pp 240-6.

Yang Zhansheng, 'On the "Two slogan polemic"' (*Ping liangge kouhao de lunzheng*), *Wenxue pinglun* No 3, 1978 (25 June 1978), pp 18-26.

'An examination of the right-deviationist facts concerning the "National defence literature"' (*Guanyu guofang wenxue youqing shishi de kaocha*), *Luxun yanjiu dongtai* No 15 (1 June 1982), pp 1-14.

Yao Shixiao, '"Around the time of joining the League": In commemoration of the fiftieth anniversary of the Dramatists League' (*Rumeng qianhou: Jinian Julian chengli wushi zhounian*), *Shanghai xiju* No 2, 1980 (30 April 1980), pp 9-11.

Ye Deyu, 'Several questions concerning the struggle against the "third category men"' (*Guanyu dui disanzhongren lunzheng de jige wenti*), *Zhongguo xiandai wenxue yanjiu congkan* No 1, 1981 (March 1981), pp 25-36.

Yi Ding, 'Lu Xun, the five martyrs of the Left League, Qu Qiubai' (*Lu Xun Zuolian wulieshi Qu Qiubai*), *Mingbao yuekan* Vol IX No 3 (May 1974), pp 31-37.

'A new annotation on Lu Xun's article "Abuse and threats are not fighting"' (*Guanyu Lu Xun ruma he kongxia juebushi zhandou yiwen de xinzhujie*), *Mingbao yuekan* Vol IX No 8 (August 1974), pp 70-1.

'Lu Xun after 1930' (*Yijiu sanlingnian yihou de Lu Xun*) (I), *Guangchajia* No 2 (1 December 1977), pp 67-70; (II), *ibid* No 3 (1 January 1978), pp 58-61; (III), *ibid* No 4 (1 February 1978), pp 61-3.

'Xia Yan again attacked Feng Xuefeng on the question of Lu Xun' (*Xia Yan youzai Lu Xun wentishang pingji Feng Xuefeng*), *Guangchajia* No 32 (20 June 1980), pp 25-7.

Yin Xueman, 'Literary works of the thirties and the works of left-wing writers' (*Sanshi niandai wenyi zuopin yu zuoyi zuojia zuopin*), *Wenxue sichao* No 6 (January 1980), pp 27-31.

Yu Kaiwei, 'History will pass its verdict: Some thoughts on reading comrade Xia Yan's "Some past events that should have long been forgotten but cannot be forgotten"' (*Qianqiu gongge ziyou lishi pinglun: Du Xia Yan tongzhi yixie zaogai wangque er weineng wangque de wangshi de ganxiang*), *Wenxue pinglun* No 4, 1980 (15 July 1980), pp 102-5.

Yu Xiang, 'On the trend of literary criticism of the Left League period' (*Mantan Zuolian shiqi wenyi piping de fengxiang*), *Wenyibao* No 3, 1980 (12 March 1980), pp 29-31.

Bibliography

Yuan Liangjun, 'On the question of historical evaluation of the polemic of "revolutionary literature"' (*Guanyu geming wenxue lunzheng de lishi pingjia wenti*), *Collection of articles on Lu Xun's thinking* (*Lu Xun sixiang lunji*) (Tianjin: Tianjin renmin chubanshe, June 1979), pp 80-97.

Zhang Chaoke, 'The militant friendship between some Chinese and Japanese revolutionary writers during the Left League period' (*Zuolian shiqi bufen Zhongri geming zuojia de zhandou youyi*), *Dongbei shida xuebao* No 4, 1981 (20 July 1981), pp 55-61.

Zhang Daming, 'On the propagation of Marxist-Leninist literary theories in the left-wing literary arena in the thirties' (*Sanshi niandao zuoyi wenyijie dui maliezhuyi wenyi lilun de xuanchuan*), *Wenxue pinglun* No 2, 1978 (25 April 1978), pp 17-24.

'General information on the Chinese League of Left-wing Writers' (*Zhongguo zuoyi zuojia lianmeng jiankuang*), *Xinwenxue shiliao* No 1, 1980 (22 February 1980), pp 105-17.

Zhang Enhuo, 'The struggle of anti-"suppression campaign" in the literary front' (*Wenyi zhanxiangshang de fan weijian*), *Yuwen jiaoxue tongxun* No 7, 1980 (18 July 1980), pp 45-7.

Zhang Yumao, 'On the "Two slogan polemic"' (*Ping liangge kouhao de lunzheng*), *Gansu shida xuebao* No 2, 1978 (18 May 1978), pp 27-35.

'Several opinions on the "Two slogan polemic"' (*Guanyu liangge kouhao lunzheng de jidian kanfa*, *Liaoning daxue xuebao* No 2, 1978 (undated), pp 56-62.

Zhao Cong, 'The Two slogan polemic has been re-evaluated once and again' (*Ershinian jiuan jifanxin: Liangge kouhao zhizheng yizai fan'an*), *The literary arena of mainland China* (*Dalu qanyu jishi*), (Hong Kong: Youlian chubanshe, October 1980), pp 53-81.

Zhao Haosheng, 'Zhou Yang takes a laughing look at history' (*Zhou Yang xiaotan lishi gongguo*), *Xinwenxue shiliao* No 2 (February 1979), pp 228-42.

Zheng Boqi, 'Random recollections on the Left League' (*Zuolian huiyi sanji*), *Xinwenxue shiliao* No 1, 1982 (22 February 1982), pp 14-23.

Zheng Xuejia, 'Lu Xun and Zhou Yang on the debate on "National defence literature"' (*Lu Xun yu Zhou Yang guanyu guofang wenxue de lunzheng*), *Zhonghua zazhi* No 176 (March 1978), pp 12-20.

Zheng Zhenkuei, 'The historical achievements of the "Left League" must be thoroughly confirmed' (*Yao congfeng kending Zuolian de lishe gongji*), *Zhongguo xiandao wenxue yanjiu congkan* No 2, 1985 (May 1985), pp 195-7.

Zhong Linbin, 'Guo Moruo and the "Two slogan polemic of 1936"' (*Guo Moruo yu yijiu sanliunian de liangge kouhao lunzheng*), *Liaoning daxue xuebao* No 5, 1980 (5 September 1980), pp 84-9.

'On the merits of Guo Moruo in advocating "revolutionary literature"' (*Lun Guo Moruo changdao geming wenxue de gongji*), *Shehui kexue jikan* No 6, 1980 (30 November 1980), pp 148-55.

Zhou Guowei, 'A genuine record of the internal activities of the Left League: The *Mishuchu xiaoxi* No 1 kept by Lu Xun' (*Zuolian neibu huodong de zhenshi jilu: Lu Xun zhencang de mishuchu xiaoxi deyiqi*), *Zhandi* No 4, 1980 (July 1980), pp 69-70.

'Hu Feng and Lu Xun' (*Hu Feng yu Lu Xun*), *Jinian yu yanjiu* No 8 (June 1986), pp 59-64.

Zhou Guowei and Liu Xiangfa, 'The whole story of the publication of *Qianshao*' (*Qianshao chuban shimo*), *Zhongguo xiandai wenyi ziliao congkan* No 5 (December 1980), pp 103-6.

Zhou Jichang, 'The problem is you do not want to "forget"; To comrade Xia Yan' (*Wenti zaiyu buxiang wanque: Zhi Xia Yan tongzhi*), *Luxun yanjiu dongtai* No 4 (20 June 1980), pp 4-9.

'On Lu Xun's stance and viewpoints in the Two slogan polemic' (*Lun Lu Xun zai liangge kouhao lunzhengzhong de lichang yu guangdian*), *Luxun yanjiu dongtai* No 13 (1 March 1982), pp 7-20.

Zhou Yang, 'Inherit and carry forward the revolutionary tradition of the left-wing cultural movement' (*Jicheng he fayang zuoyi wenhua yundong de geming chuantong*), *Renmin ribao*, 2 April 1980.

Zhou Yi'nan, 'Interview with comrade Hu Feng' (*Hu Feng tongzhi fangwenji*), *Fangcao* No 1, 1981 (January 1981), pp 46-7.

Zhou Yushan, 'Polemics engaged by the "Left League"' (*Zuolian duiwaide lunzhan*) (I), *Dongya jikan* Vol VI No 4 (1 April 1975), pp 138-50; (II), *ibid* Vol VII No 1 (1 July 1975), pp 126-43.

'The ending of the "Chinese League of Left-wing Writers"' (*Zhongguo zuoyi zuojia lianmeng de jieju*), *Dongya jikan* Vol VII No 3 (1 January 1976), pp 135-55.

'Supplement to "A membership list of the League of Left-wing Writers"' (*Guanyu Zuoyi lianmeng mengyuan mingdan de bucong*), *Shuping shumu* No 92 (1 December 1980), pp 29-33.

'Lu Xun and Communist China' (*Lu Xun yu Zhonggong*) *Jindai zhongguo* No 25 (31 October 1981), pp 292-300.

Zhou Zhengzhang, 'Hu Feng in Lu Xun's diary' (*Lu Xun rijizhong de Hu Feng*), *Luxun yanjiu ziliao* No 12 (May 1983), pp 335-44.

Zhu Rong, 'The united front movement of the literary movement in the thirties' (*Sanshi niandai wenyi zhanxiangshang de tongyi zhanxiang yundong*), *Yuwen jiaoxue tongxun* No 8, 1980 (18 August 1980), pp 44-6.

'Give a genuine picture of history: Learn from Lu Xun's discussion on "National defence literature"' (*Huan lishi de benlai mianmu: Xuexi Lu Xun guanyu guofang wenxue de lunshu*), *Wenxue pinglun* No 3, 1978 (25 June 1978), pp 27-33.

Bibliography

Books

A history of the struggle in modern Chinese literary thinking (*Zhongguo xiandai wenyi sixiang douzhengshi*) (Sichuan: February 1976), 2 vols.

Beijing Language College, *Dictionary of Chinese writers: Modern* (*Zhongguo wenxuejia cidian: Xiandao*) (Chengdu: Sichuan renmin chubanshe, 1979-85), 4 vols.

Beijing University (*et al*), *Anthology of materials for literary movement* (*Wenxue geming yundong shiliaoxuan*) (Shanghai: Shanghai jiaoyu chubanshe, June 1979), 5 vols.

Bi Hua, ed, *Selected articles of the polemic between Lu Xun and Liang Shiqiu* (*Lu Xun yu Liang Shiqiu lunzhan wenxuan*) (Hong Kong: Cosmos Publishing House, 1979).

Chen Jingzhi, *The literary arena of the thirties and the League of Left-wing Writers* (*Sanshi niandai wentan yu Zuoyi zuojia liangmeng*) (Taibei: Chengwen chubanshe, July 1938).

Chen Shaoyu, *Collection of articles on national salvation* (*Jiuguo yanlunji*) (Hankou: Zhongguo chubanshe, July 1938).

Chen Shuyu, *The Chinese League for the Protection of Civil Rights* (*Zhongguo minquan baozhang tongmeng*) (Beijing: Beijing chubanshe, August 1985).

Chen Shuyu and Tao Xin, eds, *The Chinese League for the Protection of Civil Rights* (*Zhongguo minquan baozhang tongmeng*) (Beijing: Shehui kexue chubanshe, December 1979).

Chen Songsheng, ed, *Materials on the Creation Society* (*Chuangzaoshe ziliao*) (Fujian: Fujian renmin chubanshe, January 1985), 2 vols.

Chinese Social Sciences Academy, *Documents of the Communist International concerning the Chinese revolution* (*Gongchan guoji youguan Zhongguo geming de wenxian ziliao*) (Beijing: Zhongguo shihui kexueyuan, March and June 1982), 2 vols.

Recollections on the Left League (*Zuolian huiyilu*) (Beijing: Zhongguo shihui kexueyuan, March 1982), 2 vols.

Ding Jingtang and Qu Guangxi, *A bibliography on the five martyrs of the Left League* (*Zuolian wulieshi ziliao bianmu*) (Shanghai: Shanghai wenyi chubanshe, January 1981 reprint).

Ding Jingtang and Wen Cao, *A chronological catalogue of Qu Qiubai's writings and translations* (*Qu Qiubai zhuyi xinian mulu*) (Shanghai: Shanghai renmin chubanshe, January 1959).

Ding Miao, *A complete criticism on the literature of Communist China* (*Zhonggong wenyi zhongpipan*) (Hong Kong: Hong Kong Chinese Pen Club, 1970).

Ding Wang, *On the Chinese writers of the thirties* (*Zhongguo sanshi niandai zuojia yijie*) (Hong Kong: Mingbao yuekanshe, April 1978).

Ding Yi, ed, *Collection of articles on popular literature* (*Dazhong wenyi lunji*) (Beijing: Beijing shifan daxue chubanshe, July 1951).

Draft history of the Shanghai public concessions (*Shanghai gonggong zujie shigao*) (Shanghai: Shanghai renmin chubanshe, July, 1980).

Feng Xuefeng, *Remembering Lu Xun* (*Huiyi Lu Xun*) (Beijing: Renmin wenxue chubanshe, July 1981 reprint).

Works of Feng Xuefeng (*Xuefeng wenji*) (Beijing: Renmin chubanshe, January 1982), 4 vols.

Fu Zhiying, ed, *A critical biography of Mao Dun* (*Mao Dun pingzhuan*) (Shanghai: kaiming shudian, June 1936).

Guo Moruo, *Works of Guo Moruo* (*Moruo wenji*) (Beijing: Renmin wenxue chubanshe, August 1958), 17 vols.

He Ning, *The selected essays of Lu Xun* (*Lu Xun zagan xuanji*) (Shanghai: Qingguang shudian, July 1933).

Hong Xuefan, *The literary yearbook, 1932* (*Zhongguo wenyi nianjian, 1932*) (Shanghai: Xiandai shudian, 10 August 1933).

Hou Jian, *From literary revolution to revolutionary literature* (*Cong wenxue geming dao geming wenxue*) (Taibei: Zhongwai wenxue chubanshe, December 1974).

Hu Feng, *Critical essays of Hu Feng* (*Hu Feng pinglunji*) (Beijing: Renmin wenxue chubanshe, March 1984-March 1985), 3 vols.

Hu Qiuyuan, *Essays on literature and art* (*Wenxue yishu lunji*) (Taibei: Xueshu chubanshe, November 1979), 2 vols.

Huang Renying, ed, *On the Creation Society* (*Chuangzaoshe lun*) (Shanghai: Guanghua shudian, December 1932).

Iida Yoshiro, ed, *Materials on the Left League Period* (*Sarenki shiryo*) (Tokyo: Ajiya shuppan, September 1978), 5 vols.

Institute for the Study of Modern Literature, Academy of Literature, Chinese Social Sciences Academy, ed, *Collection of materials on the 'revolutionary literature' polemic* (*Geming wenxue lunzheng ziliao xuanbian*) (Beijing: Renmin wenxue chubanshe, January 1981), 2 vols.

Collection of materials on the 'Two slogan' polemic (*Liangge kouhao ziliao lunzheng*) (Beijing: Renmin wenxue chubanshe, March 1982), 2 vols.

Ito Toramaru, ed, *Materials on the Creation Society* (*Sozosha shiryo*) (Tokyo: Ajiya shuppan, 1979), 11 vols.

Li Ang, *The red stage* (*Hongse wutai*) (Taibei: Shengli chuban gongshi, February 1954 reprint).

Le Helin, *The literary thinking in the past twenty years, 1917-1937* (*Jin ershinian Zhongguo wenyi sichaolun*) (Shanxi: Shanxi renmin chubanshe, April 1981 reprint).

Literary polemics in China (*Zhongguo wenyi lunzheng*) (Xian: Shanxi renmin chubanshe, April 1984 reprint).

Li Mu, *On the literature of the thirties* (*Sanshi niandai wenyilun*) (Taibei: Liming wenhua shiye gongshi, June 1973).

Lin Cong, ed, *Literary battle at the present stage* (*Xianjieduan de wenxue lunzheng*) (Shanghai: Wenyi kexue chubanshe, 1936).

Bibliography

Liu Shaoqi, *Selected works of Liu Shaoqi* (*Liao Shaoqi xuanji*) (Beijing: Renmin chubanshe, December 1981).

Liu Shousong, *A preliminary draft history of modern Chinese literature* (*Zhongguo xinwenxueshi chugao*) (Beijing: Renmin wenxue chubanshe, November 1979 reprint).

Liu Xinhuang, *Lu Xun the man* (*Lu Xun qiren*) (Taibei: Dongya tushu gongshi, June 1986).

Lu Xun, *Complete works of Lu Xun* (*Lu Xun quanji*) (Beijing: Renmin wenxue chubanshe, 1957-58), 10 vols.

Complete works of Lu Xun (*Lu Xun quanji*) (Beijing: Renmin wenxue chubanshe, 1981), 16 vols.

Lu Xun Museum, ed, *A chronology of Lu Xun* (*Lu Xun nianpu*) (Beijing: Renmin wenxue chubanshe, September 1981-September 1984), 4 vols.

Ma Liangchun and Zhang Daming, eds, *Collection of materials on the left-wing literature of the thirties* (*Sanshi niandai zuoyi wenyi ziliao xuanbian*) (Chengdu: Sichuan renmin chubanshe, November 1980).

Ma Tiji, ed, *Reminiscence of Lu Xun by Xu Guangping* (*Xu Guangping yi Lu Xun*) (Guangdong: Guangdong renmin chubanshe, April 1979).

Mao Dun, *The road I trod* (*Wozouge de daolu*) (Beijing: Renmin wenxue chubanshe, October 1981 and May 1984), 2 vols.

Materials on modern Chinese literature (*Chugoku gendai bungakushi shiryo*) (Tokyo: Daian, 1969), 12 vols.

Nanjing University, ed, *Proletarian revolutionary literature in the Left League period* (*Zuolian shiqi wuchanjieji geming wenxue*) (Nanjing: Jiangsu wenyi chubanshe, 1960).

Ni Moyan, *Study on Lu Xun's revolutionary activities* (*Lu Xun geming huodong koushu*) (Shanghai: Shanghai wenyi chubanshe, May 1984).

Qu Guangxi, *Notes on the history of modern Chinese literature* (*Zhongguo xiandai wenxueshi zaji*) (Shanghai: Shanghai wenyi chubanshe, January 1984).

Qu Qiubai, *Works of Qu Qiubai* (*Qu Qiubai wenji*) (Beijing: Renmin wenxue chubanshe, 1953), 4 vols.

Recollections of Pan Hannian (*Huiyi Pan Hannian*) (Jiangsu: Jiangsu renmin chubanshe, January 1985).

Shanghai Normal College, *Reference materials on the study of Lu Xun* (*Lu Xun yanjiu cankao ziliao*) (Shanghai: Shanghai shifan daxue, October 1979).

Shi Xianmin, *Selection of materials on the Chinese League of Social Scientists* (*Zhongguo shehui kexuejia lianmeng ziliao xuanbian*) (Beijing: Zhongguo zhanwang chubanshe, May 1986).

Su Wen, *Collection of articles from the debate on literary freedom* (*Wenyi ziyou lunbianji*) (Shanghai: Xiandai shudian, March 1933).

Su Xuelin, *Writers and works of the twenties and thirties* (*Ersanshi niandai zuojia yu zuopin*) (Taibei: Guangdong chubanshe, 1979).

Sun Shenzhi, ed, *Lu Xun in Shanghai* (*Lu Xun zai Shanghai*) (Shanghai: Shanghai shifan daxue, December 1979).

Tang Tao, ed, *A history of modern Chinese literature* (*Zhongguo xiandai wenxueshi*) (Beijing: Renmin wenxue chubanshe, June 1979), 3 vols.

The Joint Association of Philosophy and Social Sciences of Shanghai: *Special issue in commemoration of the fifty-fifth anniversary of the formation of the Chinese League of Social Scientists* (*Zhongguo shehui kexuejia lianmeng chengli wushiwu zhounian jinian zhuanji*) (Shanghai: Shanghai kexueyuan chubanshe, October 1986).

Thoroughly criticize the anti-revolutionary revisionist literary black line (*Chedi pipan Zhou Yang de fangeming xiuzheng zhuyi wenyi heixian*) (Guangdong: Guangdong renmin chubanshe, 1975).

Thoroughly criticize 'National defence literature' (*Chedi pipan guofang wenxue*) (Shanghai renmin chubanshe, September 1971).

Wang Jianmin, *A draft history of the Chinese Communist Party* (*Zhongguo gongchandang shigao*) (Taibei: Zhongwen tushu gongyishe, September 1974), 3 vols.

Wang Yao, *A draft history of modern Chinese literature* (*Xinwenxue shigao*) (Shanghai: Shanghai wenyi chubanshe, November 1982 reprint).

Wang Zhangling, *The literary rectification of Communist China* (*Zhonggong de wenyi zhengfeng*) (Taibei: Guoji guanxi yanjiushuo, March 1967).

Xia Yan, *Too lazy to search for past dreams* (*Lanxun jiumenglu*) (Beijing: Joint Publishing Company, July 1985).

Xia Zhengnong, *A review of the literary arena and national defence* (*Wentan huifu yu guofang*) (Shanghai: Duzhe shufang, February 1940).

Xiang Qing, *A general account on the history of the relationship between the Communist International and the Chinese revolution* (*Gongchan guoji he Zhongguo geming guanxi de lishi jianshu*) (Guangdong: Guandong renmin chubanshe, October 1984).

Xiao Jun, *Annotations on Lu Xun's letters to Xiao Jun and Xiao Hong* (*Lu Xun gei Xiao Jun Xiao Hong shujian zhushilu*) (Harbin: Heilongjiang renmin chubanshe, June 1981).

Xinchao chubanshe, *Battle over National defence literature* (*Guofang wenxue lunzhan*) (Shanghai: Xinchao chubanshe, October 1936).

Xu Maoyong, *Memoirs of Xu Maoyong* (*Xu Maoyong huiyilu*) (Beijing Renmin wenxue chubanshe, July 1982).

Xue Suizhi et al, eds, *Historical materials on the life of Lu Xun* (*Lu Xun shengping shiliao huibian*) (Tianjin: Tianjin renmin chubanshe, July 1981- May 1986), 5 vols.

Yao Mengxian, *Collection of articles on the internal strife of the bandits* (*Feidang neibu douzheng wenti lunji*) (Taibei: Research Centre on International Relations, April 1975).

Yi Ding, *Lu Xun, the man, the deeds and the age* (*Lu Xun qiren qishi ji qishidai*) (Université Paris 7, Centre de publication Asia Orientale, September 1978).

Zhang Daming, *On the literature of the thirties* (*Sanshi niandai wenxue zaji*) (Tianjin: Tianjin renmin chubanshe, October 1986).

Zhao Cong, *History of the literary arena of the thirties* (*Sanshi niandai wentan shihua*) (Taibei: Chongwen shudian, April 1974).

The various personages of the literary scene of the thirties (*Sanshi niandai wentan dianjianglu*) (Hong Kong: Junren shudian, 1970).

Zhao Haosheng, *From the thirties to the new Long March* (*Cong sanshi niandai dao xinde changzheng*) (Hong Kong: Qishi niandai zazhishe, November 1979).

Zheng Boqi, *Recalling the Creation Societies and others* (*Yi Chuangzaoshe ji qita*) (Hong Kong: Joint Publishing Company, 1982).

Zhou Yushan, *A new study of the literature of mainland China* (*Dalu wenyi xinlun*) (Taibei: Dongda tushu gongshi, April 1984).

Zhu Zheng, *Corrections on the reminiscences of Lu Xun* (*Lu Xun huiyilu zhenwu*) (Hunan: Hunan renmin chubanshe, November 1979).

Other Sources

Articles

Benton, Gregor, '"The second Wang Ming line" (1935-1938)', *China Quarterly* No 61 (March 1975), pp 61-94.

Chan, Ping-leung, 'Lu Hsun and Communism: Myth and realism', *Asian thought and society: An international review* Vol VII No 19 (March 1982), pp 53-78.

Chung, Wen, 'National defence literature', *Chinese literature* No 10, 1971, pp 91-9.

Coble, P M Jnr, 'The Shanghai capitalist class and the nationalist government, 1927-1937' (unpublished PhD dissertation, University of Illinois, 1975).

Eastman, L E, 'Fascism in Kuomintang China: The Blue Shirts'. *China Quarterly* No 52 (October-December 1972), pp 1-31.

Fewsmith, J, 'In search of the Shanghai connection', *Modern China* Vol II No 1 (January 1985), pp 111-14.

Fujimoto Kozo, 'The relationship between Mao Dun and the revolutionary literary group' (*Bo Jun to kakumei bungakuha to no kankei*), *Jinbun gakkuho* No 78 (March 1970), pp 97-119.

Galik, Marian, 'On the study of modern Chinese literature of 1920s and 1930s'. *Asian and African Studies* XIII (1977), pp 99-129.

Goldman, Merle, 'Hu Feng's conflict with the Communist literary authorities', *China Quarterly* No 12 (October-December 1962), pp 102-37.

'The fall of Zhou Yang', *China Quarterly* No 27 (July-September 1966), pp 132-48.

'The political use of Lu Xun', *China Quarterly* No 91 (September 1982), pp 446-63.

Gruner, Fritz, 'Some remarks on the cultural-political significance of the Chinese League of Left-wing Writers at the beginning of the thirties', in Davis, A R, ed, *Search for identity: Modern literature and the creative arts in Asia*, (Sydney: Angus & Robertson, 1974), pp 255-9.

Hiyama, Hisao, 'The League of Left-wing Writers and Lu Xun', (*Sayoku sakka renmei to Ro Jin*), *Shin Nihon bungaku* Vol XXIV No 2 (February 1969), pp 132-47.

Hunter, Neale, 'Another look at the League of Left-wing Writers', in Davis, A R, ed, *Search for identity: Modern literature and the creative arts in Asia*, (Sydney: Angus & Robertson, 1974), pp 260-70.

'The League of Left-wing Writers, Shanghai, 1930-1936', (Unpublished PhD dissertation, Australian National University, 1973).

Hunters, Theodore, 'Blossoms in the snow: Lu Xun and the dilemma of modern Chinese literature', *Modern China* Vol X No 1 (January 1984), pp 49-77.

Jenner, W J F, 'Lu Xun's last days and after', *China Quarterly* No 91 (September 1982), pp 425-45.

Kane, A J, 'The League of Left-wing Writers and Chinese literary policy', (Unpublished PhD dissertation, University of Michigan, 1982).

Lee, Leo Ou-fan, 'Literature on the eve of revolution: Reflections on Lu Xun's leftist years, 1927-1936', *Modern China* Vol II No 3 (July 1976), pp 277-326.

Lu, A Ya-li, 'Political control of literature in Communist China, 1949-1966', (Unpublished PhD dissertation, University of Indiana, 1972).

Maeda, Toshiaki, 'Qu Qiubai and the Left League', (*Ku Shuhaku to saren*), *Toyo bunka* No 52 (March 1972), pp 133-56.

'Feng Xuefeng on the "third category men" debate', (*Daisan shujin ronso ni okeru Fu Sebbo*), *Toyo bunka* No 56 (March 1976), pp 25-63.

Maruo Tsuneyoshi, 'The question of popularization of literature in the early stage of the Left League', (*Saren zenki ni okeru bungei daishuka no mondai*), *Toyo bunka* No 52, pp 69-94.

Maruyama, Noboru, 'Xu Maoyong and Lu Xun' (*Jo Boyo to Ro Jin*), *Bungaku* No 44 (April 1976), pp 487-500.

Mills, Harriet C, 'Lu Hsun, 1927-1936: The years on the left' (Unpublished PhD dissertation, University of Columbia, 1963).

Nathan, Andrew J, 'Modern China, 1840-1972: An introduction to sources and research aids', *Michigan papers in Chinese Studies* No 14 (1973).

Pickowicz, Paul G, 'Ch'u Ch'iu-pai and the origins of Marxist literary criticism in China', (Unpublished PhD dissertation, University of Wisconsin, 1973).

'Lu Xun through the eyes of Qu Qiubai', *Modern China* Vol II No 3 (July 1976), pp 327-68.

'Ch'u Ch'iu-pai and the Chinese Marxist conception of revolutionary popular literature and art', *China Quarterly* No 70 (June 1977), pp 296-314.

Rubin, Kyna, 'Writers' discontent and Party response in Yan'an before "Wild lily": The Manchurian writers and Zhou Yang', *Modern Chinese literature* Vol I No 1 (September 1984), pp 79-102.

Saji, Yoshihiko, 'The revolutionary literary polemic and the Sun Society', *Toyo bunka* No 52 (March 1972), pp 13-35.
Siao, Emi (Xiao San), 'Chinese revolutionary literature: A survey of the last fifteen years', *International literature* No 5, 1934, pp 121-33.
  'To the memory of the great writer Lu Hsun', *International literature* No 12, 1936, pp 86-90.
Sullivan, Lawrence R, 'Reconstruction and rectification of the Communist Party in the Shanghai underground: 1931-1934', *China Quarterly* No 101 (March 1985), pp 78-97.
Sun, Lung-kee, 'Out of the wilderness: Chinese intellectuals Odysseys from the "May Fourth" to the Thirties', (Unpublished PhD dissertation, Stanford University, 1984).
Takeuchi, Minoru, 'The formation of the League of Left-wing Writers' (Sayoku sakka renmei no sei ritsu made), *Toyo bunka* No 44, pp 50-77.
Thomson, James C Jnr, 'Communist policy and the united front in China, 1935-36', *Papers on China* (Harvard University) No 11 (December 1957), pp 99-148.
Yuge, Toshiyo, '"The debate on National defence literature" and "struggle between lines"' (*Kokubo bungaku ronsen to rosen toso*) *Nokusha* No 23 (30 March 1979), pp 51-71.

Books

Arima, Tatsuo, *The failure of freedom: A portrait of modern Japanese intellectuals* (Cambridge: Harvard University Press, 1969).
Ashida, Hajime, *Index of translations and citations of Chinese leftist literary theories* (Tokyo: Tokyo daigaku toyo bunken kenkyu jo, 1971).
Berninghausen, John and Huters, Ted, eds, *Revolutionary literature in China* (New York: M E Sharp, 1976).
Bianco, Lucien, *Origins of the Chinese revolution, 1915-49* (London: Stanford University Press, 1971).
Birch, Cyril, ed, *Chinese Communist literature* (New York: Frederick A Praeger, 1963).
Boorman, H L, *Biographical dictionary of Republican China* (London: Columbia University Press, 1967-1971), 4 vols.
Brandt, C, Schwartz, B and Fairbank, J, *A documentary history of Chinese Communism* (Cambridge: Harvard University Press, 1952).
Brown, Edward J, *The proletarian episode in Russian literature, 1928-1932* (New York: Columbia University Press, 1953).
  Russian literature since the Revolution (London: Collier-Macmillan, 1969).
Carr, E Hallett, *The twilight of Comintern, 1930-35* (London: Macmillan Press Ltd, 1982).

Chang, Kuo-t'ao, *The rise of Chinese Communist Party: Autobiography of Chang Kuo-t'ao* (Lawrence: University Press of Kansas, 1972), 2 vols.

Chow, Tse-tsung, *The May Fourth Movement: Intellectual revolution in modern China* (Cambridge: Harvard University Press, 1960).

Degras, Jane, *The Communist International, 1919-1943, Documents* (London: Oxford University Press, 1960), 3 vols.

Eastman, Lloyd E, *The abortive revolution: China under Nationalist rule, 1927-1937* (Cambridge: Harvard University Press, 1974).

Evans, John L, *The Communist International, 1919-1943* (Brooklyn: Pageant-Poseidon, 1973).

Galik, Marian, *Mao Dun and modern Chinese literary criticism* (Wiesbaden: Franz Steiner Verlag GmbH, 1969).

The genesis of modern Chinese literary criticism, 1917-1930 (London: Curzon Press, 1980).

Goldman, Merle, *Literary dissent in Communist China* (Cambridge: Harvard University Press, 1967).

ed, *Modern Chinese literature in the May Fourth era* (Cambridge: Harvard University Press, 1977).

China's intellectuals: Advise and dissent (Cambridge: Harvard University Press, 1981).

Guillermaz, Jacques, Anne Destenay (trans), *A history of the Chinese Communist Party, 1921-1949* (London: Methuen & Co Ltd, 1972).

Gunn, Edward M Jnr, *Unwelcome muse: Chinese literature in Shanghai and Peking, 1937-1945* (New York: Columbia University Press, 1980).

Harrison, J Pinckney, *The Long March to power: A history of Chinese Communist Party, 1921-1972* (New York: Praeger Publisher, 1972).

Hsia, C T, *A history of modern Chinese fiction* (New Haven: Yale University Press, 1971).

Hsia, T A, *The gate of darkness: Studies on the leftist literary movement in China* (Seattle: University of Washington Press, 1968).

Hsiao, Tso-liang, *Power relations within the Chinese Communist movement, 1930-34: A study of documents* (Seattle: University of Washington Press, 1961), 2 vols.

Huang, Sung-kang, *Lu Hsun and the new cultural movement of modern China* (Amsterdam: Djambatan, 1957).

International literature No 1, 1931-No 12, 1936.

Isaacs, Harold R, *The tragedy of the Chinese revolution* (London: Secker and Warburg, 1938).

Straw sandals: Chinese short stories, 1918-1933 (Cambridge: The MIT Press, 1974).

Isreal, John, *Student nationalism in China, 1927-1937* (Stanford: Stanford University Press, 1966).

Kataoka, Tetsuya, *Resistance and revolution in China: The Communists and the second united front* (Berkeley: University of California Press, 1974).

Bibliography

Klein, Donald W and Clark, Anne B, *Biographic dictionary of Chinese Communism, 1921-65* (Cambridge: Harvard University Press, 1971), 2 vols.

Lee, Leo Ou-fan, ed,·*Lu Xun and his legacy* (Berkeley: University of California Press, 1985).

Voices from the iron house: A study of Lu Xun (Bloomington: Indiana University Press, 1987).

Li, Yu-ning, *The introduction of socialism into China* (New York: Columbia University Press, 1971).

Lu Xun, [Yang, Xianyi and Yang, Gladys (trans)], *Lu Xun: Selected works* (Beijing: Foreign Languages Press, 1961), 4 vols.

Lyell, W A Jnr, *Lu Hsun's vision of reality* (Berkeley: University of California Press, 1976).

Mao Zedong, *Selected works of Mao Zedong* (Beijing: Foreign Languages Press, 1966-1977), 5 vols.

McLane, Charles B, *Soviet policy and the Chinese Communists, 1931-1946* (New York: Columbia University Press, 1958).

Meisner, M, *Li Ta-chao and the origins of Chinese Marxism* (Cambridge: Harvard University Press, 1967).

North, Robert C, *Moscow and Chinese Communists* (Stanford: Stanford University Press, 1953).

Pickowicz, Paul G, *Marxist literary thought and China: A conceptual framework* (Berkeley: University of California Press, 1980).

Marxist literary thought in China: The influence of Ch'u Ch'iu-pai (Berkeley: University of California Press, 1981).

Pollard, David E, *A Chinese look at literature: The literary value of Chou Tso-jen in relation to tradition* (London: C Hurst & Co, 1973).

Schwartz, Benjamin I, *Chinese Communism and the rise of Mao* (Cambridge: Harvard University Press, 1951).

ed, *Reflections on the May Fourth Movement: A symposium* (Cambridge: Harvard University Press, 1972).

Shea, G Tyson, *Left-wing literature in Japan: A brief history of the proletarian literary movement* (Tokyo: The Hosei University Press, 1964).

Shih, Paul K T, ed, *The strenuous decade: China's nation-building efforts, 1927-1937* (New York: St John's University Press, 1970).

Smedley, Agnes, *Battle hymn of China* (London: Gollancz Ltd, 1944).

Tagore, Amitendranath, *Literary debates in modern China* (Tokyo: Centre for East Asian Cultural Studies, 1967).

Thornton, Richard C, *The Comintern and the Chinese Communists, 1928-1931* (Seattle: University of Washington Press, 1969).

Van Slyke, Lyman P, *Enemies and friends: The united front in Chinese Communist history* (Stanford: Stanford University Press, 1967).

The Chinese Communist movement (Stanford: Stanford University Press, 1968).

Index

A Ying 219
Ai Qing 120
Ai Wu 67, 69, 72, 74, 120, 216
Akita Ujaku 143
Aono Suekichi 30
Art Drama Association 50, 60, 64, 67, 93
Association of Chinese Writers and Artists 182, 185-7, 189-90, 200-1, 204
Association for the Rear Support of the Red Army 99
Baerdishan 90, 92
Ba Jin 67, 189, 200, 202-3
Bai Mang 102
Bai Shu 67, 74
Bao Tianxiao 204
Beidou 110, 120, 125-6, 140
Benliu 42
Bing Xin 120
Cai Yongshang 99
Cai Yuanpei 42, 141
Cao Jinghua 66-7
Cao Ming 67, 74
CCP 10-11, 20, 22-3, 27-8, 31-2, 39-41, 43-49, 52-3, 59, 61-2, 66, 75, 88, 96-7, 100-6, 108-9, 120, 124, 126, 128, 130, 133-4, 143, 152-5, 168, 179, 182, 185-6, 191-2, 195, 199, 203-4, 213-14, 217
  Cultural Branch 41
Chen Dage 72
Chen Duxiu 23, 25
Chen Hengzhe 120
Chen Jingsheng 60
Chen Lifu 61, 99
Chen Mingshu 128, 131
Chen Shaoyu 101, 105
Chen Yi 60
Chen Yuan 44

Chen Zhengdao 61, 90-1
Chen Zhongshan 196
Chenbao 108
Cheng Fangwu 12, 14, 16, 19-21
Cheng Shaohuai 60-1
Chinese Association of Poetry 74, 76
Chinese Authors Association 44, 68
Chinese League for the Protection of Civil Rights 44, 141, 215
Chinese League of Social Scientists 52
Communist Youth Corps 128
Creation Society 9, 11-12, 14, 16-22, 27-8, 39-40, 42, 44, 46-51, 62, 89, 94-95, 98, 155
Crescent School 40, 44, 66
Dadao Drama Association 142
Dai Pingwan 49-51, 59
Dawn Association 67
Dazhong wenyi 43, 60, 92, 98, 136
Ding Ling 67, 69-70, 75, 120, 126-7, 141-3, 153, 217, 219
Drama Movement Federation 93
Du Heng 60-1, 130, 140, 142
Dushu zazhi 128, 130
Feng Keng 61, 94, 99-100, 102
Feng Naichao 16-17, 20-1, 39, 45-6, 49-52, 59-62, 64-5, 68, 75, 89-90, 93-4, 96, 98-9, 103, 111
Feng Xuefeng 87, 90, 99, 102, 106, 108-10, 120-1, 126, 128, 130, 132-3, 134, 136, 143-4, 152-4, 156, 163-5, 170, 182-3, 186-7, 189, 193, 195-8, 200, 203-5, 213-4, 217-21
Fenghuo 125
Five martyrs 100, 102-4, 106, 108, 110-11, 179
Four fellows 152, 165-7, 169, 202
Free Men 110, 156, 213
Freedom Movement League of China 44, 52
Fukumoto Kazuo 19

250

Index

Fukumotoism 19, 21, 23, 39
General Cultural League 69-70, 180-1
General League of Left-wing Culture 63
GMD 24, 28, 32, 40-3, 47, 61, 67, 73, 93, 98-100, 103, 105, 107-8, 111, 121-3, 125, 128, 130, 132, 136, 141-2, 160-1, 163, 165, 167, 171, 178, 180-1, 185, 191-2, 204, 213-14, 217, 219, 221
Gu Shunzhang 105
Gu Zhongyi 31
Guan Lu 65-7, 74
Guo Moruo 9, 11-14, 16-17, 21-2, 28, 44, 49, 61, 64-6, 98, 156, 165, 185, 197, 203-4, 216
Han Qi 73
Han Tuofu 89
He Gutian 69
He Jiahuai 182-5, 199
He Long 141
He Mengxiong 101-2, 104-5
Hong Lingfei 46, 49-51, 59, 62, 68-9, 74, 98, 141
Hong Shen 65-6, 142
Hongqi 105
Hou Lushi 60-61
Hu Feng 66, 69-70, 72, 143, 152, 155-6, 162-8, 170, 179, 183, 185-90, 195-8, 200-5, 217-21
Hu Qiaomu 180
Hu Qiuyuan 126, 128-30, 132-3, 135, 156, 220
Hu Yepin 67, 69, 74, 94, 100, 102-3
Hua Han 20
Hua Shi 27, 59
Hua Xili 29
Huang Yuan 198, 200, 202-3, 220
Huang Zhengxia 123-4
Huoju 158 161
Ikeda Hisao 143

Jiang Guangci 9, 11, 16-20, 28, 49-52, 59-62, 64, 66, 68-9, 91, 94, 98, 110
Jiang Jieshi 9, 14-15, 19, 24, 28-9, 39, 111, 125, 136, 141, 182, 192, 205, 213, 215
Jiang Qing 220
Jin Kuiguang 72
Kang Sheng 179
Lakeside Poetry Association 67
League of Left-wing Dramatists 52, 75
Li Ang 103
Li Chuli 9, 16, 18-20, 22, 44-6, 49-50, 59
Li Fuchun 42, 46-8
Li Huiying 69
Li Liewen 160, 189
Li Lisan 41, 47-8, 96, 101, 109, 215
Li Qiushi 102
Li Shaoshi 165, 167
Li Shengyun 60
Li Weisen 60, 100, 102
Li Xifan 218
Li Yimeng 20, 46
Liang Shiqiu 9, 25, 44
Liang Wenruo 142
Lin Biao 220
Lin Boxiu 59, 168
Lin Danqiu 62, 67, 69-70
Lin Di 67
Lin Yu'nan 102, 179
Lin Yuying 179, 192
Ling Sheng 88
Ling Shuhua 120
Literature of the resistance war 204
Literary black line 220-1
Literary Research Association 9, 11, 45, 67
Liu Hezhen 24
Liu Qian 67, 74
Liu Shaoqi 194, 204, 216
Liu Xiwu 61
Lou Shiyi 66, 69-70, 126, 128, 216

Luo Feng 67
Luo Qiyuan 22
Luo Zhanglong 101-2, 104-5
Ma Ning 64
Mai Ke'ang 16
Mao Dun 9-10, 28-31, 40, 44-5, 64-5, 67, 69-70, 72-4, 88, 93, 97, 106, 109-10, 120-1, 125-6, 136, 138-9, 142, 144, 152, 155, 164-5, 179-80, 186-7, 190, 195-8, 201, 203-5, 213-14, 216
Mao Zedong 23, 28, 32, 40, 96, 165, 169, 178, 192-6, 204-5, 217, 220
Mass literature of the national revolutionary war 183, 187-8, 190, 193, 196-7, 200-1, 203, 221
May Fourth Movement 110, 128-9, 137
Mei Sun 106-7
Mei Yi 69-70
Meng Chao 16-18, 46, 59, 64, 98
Mengya 51, 60, 62, 73, 92
Midnight 69, 110, 201, 216
Mishuchu xiaoxi 69-73, 127-8
Modern Criticism group 40
National defence literature 183-5, 187, 189-91, 193-4, 196-9, 201, 204-5, 217, 219, 221
Nie Gannu 74, 152, 165, 190, 197, 216
Northern Expedition 18, 24, 28, 42, 66
Oriental Hotel 100-3, 105
Ouyang Shan 72, 74, 216
Ozaki Hotsumi 60
Pan Gongzhan 123
Pan Hannian 44-7, 49-52, 59, 65, 75, 98, 111, 124
Pan Mohua 60-1, 66, 141
Pan Zinian 44, 141-2
Peng Boshan 72, 74

Peng Hui 69-70, 128
Peng Kang 16, 44, 46, 49-51, 59, 62, 93
Pu Feng 74
Qian Xingcun 9, 11, 13, 17-20, 22, 30-1, 39, 44-51, 59-62, 64, 68-9, 75, 90, 94, 130
Qianshao 100, 102-3, 106-8, 110
Qiu Dongping 157, 164, 170
Qiu Jiuru 156
Qiu Yunduo 59, 98, 182
Qu Qiubai 22-3, 39-41, 87, 101, 108-10, 120-1, 124-6, 131, 133-4, 136-7, 139, 143-4, 153, 156, 158, 170, 213-215, 219
Qu Yi 194
Ren Jun 66, 69, 71-2, 74
Revolutionary Mutual-aid Association 70, 76
Rou Shi 28, 42-3, 46, 48-51, 59, 62, 67, 69, 94, 99-100, 102-3, 107
San Lang 169
Shalun 60
Sha Ting 168, 216
Shao Bo 161-2
Shao Lizi 165
Shao Xunmei 123, 190
Shehui yuebao 161
Shen Congwen 67
Shen Duanxian 52, 98, 162
Shen Junru 186
Shen Qiyu 49-50, 61, 72, 190
Shen Zemin 10
Shenzhou Guoguangshe 128
Shi Linghe 60, 65
Shi Zhecun 60-1, 68, 131-2, 135
Shou Jia 157-8, 164
Sima Wensen 66-7
Sinclair, Upton 25
Smedley, Agnes 41, 43, 99, 106-7
Song Qingling 141-2, 186, 215
South Nation Society 50, 60, 62, 64, 67, 91, 100
Su Xuelin 44

Index

Sun Fuyuan 45
Sun Ke 163
Sun Society 9, 11, 16-20, 22, 32, 39, 41, 45-6, 48-51, 61-2, 89, 94-5, 98, 140, 157
Sun Yat-sen 123, 163, 215
Tai Jingnong 25
Tang Yu 105
Tao Jingsun 59, 98
Third Category Men 110, 128, 134, 156, 163
Thread-of-talk group 9, 45, 62, 67
Tian Han 50, 52, 59, 62, 65, 68-9, 70, 142, 152, 160-2, 164-8, 170, 183
Tong Changrong 60
Tuohuangzhe 59-3, 91, 94-5
Two slogan polemic 87, 126, 152, 165, 170, 177, 185, 191, 195, 200, 203-5, 219, 221
Uchiyama Kanzo 49
Us Society 62, 64
Wan Guoan 123
Wang Duqing 16, 20, 45
Wang Fanxi 105
Wang Hanwen 142
Wang Jinding 69, 72
Wang Lixi 128
Wang Ming 101-5, 108, 121, 126, 178-9, 191-5, 204, 215, 217, 221
Wang Pingling 123
Wang Renshu 52, 61, 64, 67, 152, 194
Wang Ruowang 66
Wang Shiwei 218
Wang Shuming 67, 69
Wang Tongzhao 68
Wang Xiyan 216
Wang Xuewen 60
Wang Yaoshan 69, 71
Wang Zhizhi 135

Wen Tianxiang 184
Wenhua pipan 16-17, 19, 22
Wenxue 127, 137
Wenxue daobao 107, 110, 120, 136
Wenxue shenghuo 70, 163-4, 167
Wenxue yuebao 143, 156-8
Wenxuejie 196-8
Wu Xiru 72, 74, 144, 152, 167
Xia Yan 44-6, 49-52, 59-62, 68-9, 73, 90, 98, 103, 106, 121, 125-6, 140, 142-3, 152-3, 162, 165-7, 180, 183, 186-7, 190, 204, 219
Xia Zhengnong 69
Xiandai 131-2, 135
Xiang Zhongfa 101
Xiao Chunu 10
Xiao Hong 159, 161, 169
Xiao Jun 157-9, 161, 169, 181, 217, 221
Xiao San 66, 76, 162-3, 177, 179-81, 183, 191, 194
Xiaoshuo yuebao 120
Xinyue yuekan 40
Xu Dishan 68, 109
Xu Guangping 14, 24, 153-4
Xu Maoyong 69-70, 73, 152, 165-8, 170, 179-80, 182-3, 188, 190, 194, 197-200, 202-5, 216-17, 219-20
Xu Pingyu 72, 74
Xu Shoushang 53
Xu Xing 184-5, 190, 197
Xu Xingzhi 59-60, 98
Xu Xunlei 61
Yamakawa Hitoshi 19
Yamakawaism 19
Yang Chao 69-70, 74
Yang Cunren 16-18, 20, 140, 161, 182
Yang Hansheng 20, 41, 46-51, 62, 69, 75, 103, 106, 152, 165-6

253

Yang Pao'an 22
Yang Sao 72, 74
Yang Shangkun 75
Yang Xianjiang 64
Yang Xingfo 141, 215
Yang Zhihua 120
Yao Pengzi 61, 69, 143, 156
Ye Lin 75
Ye Lingfeng 52, 61, 111
Ye Qiuyuan 123
Ye Shengtao 21, 67, 99, 120, 142, 190
Ye Zi 72, 74
Yi Ding 60, 64
Yin Fu 32, 100, 102
Yin Geng 74, 197
Ying Xiuren 66, 141
Yun Daiying 10
Yun Sheng 156-8, 164, 167, 169-70
Zhang Chunqiao 221
Zhang Guodao 104, 141, 192
Zhang Shangbin 184
Zhang Tingqian 43, 52
Zhang Wentian 134, 154, 186
Zhang Ziping 20-1
Zhao Mingyi 142
Zhaohua xunkan 43
Zhaohua yuekan 43
Zheng Boqi 16-17, 20, 39, 44, 49-52, 59, 61-2, 66, 68-9, 98, 110, 120
Zheng Zhenduo 44-5, 67, 109, 140, 158, 165, 167, 186, 190
Zhi Jing 138
Zhongguo qingnian 11, 143
Zhongyang ribao 123
Zhou Enlai 48, 101, 104, 194
Zhou Gangming 74, 183
Zhou Jianren 186
Zhou Libo 69, 73, 183-4, 193, 204
Zhou Quanping 52, 59, 62, 68-9, 111
Zhou Shoujuan 204
Zhou Wen 69, 71, 142, 152, 168, 186
Zhou Yang 65-6, 69, 71-2, 75-6, 87, 131, 133-4, 140-4, 152, 154-8, 162-71, 177, 179-82, 185-7, 189-91, 194-5, 197-9, 201-3, 205, 214, 217-21
Zhou Yuying 111
Zhu De 178
Zhu Jingwo 16, 49-51, 59
Zhu Xiang 44
Zhu Xiuxia 73, 157-8, 170
Zhu Yingpeng 123
Zhu Ziqing 68
Ziyoutan 158, 160
Zong Hui 100, 106

academy with Charles's fit, skinny body, his long brown curls and his full wonderful lips that Ian wanted to kiss so badly.

They might have been both 27-year-olds and in the academy since they were 16-year-olds, but Ian had never had the courage to ask his best friend to spend time alone with him before.

Ian knew that Charles was into him as much as Ian liked Charles, but he had just never felt confident enough to ask out the man he really loved. But Christmas was a magical time of year indeed, and that was exactly what Ian wanted to capitalise on.

Charles handed Ian a large red plastic mug full of the richest, creamiest mocha that Ian had ever smelt, and if Charles was this good at making drinks then Ian really wanted to find out what else he was good at.

"I didn't know we had coffee and chocolate onboard. I thought I had forgotten all those luxuries," Ian said.

Charles laughed. "We both know we can buy a lot more coffee, chocolate and diamonds than almost anyone else in the academy, let alone people in the colonies or Earth,"

Ian just smiled because of how true that was. They were both workaholics and that paid extremely well, but Ian still couldn't help but feel like something was missing in his life. Something like love, companionship and a man.

"I bought them onboard anyway as a thank you for inviting me at last," Charles said grinning.

Ian took a heavenly sip of the amazing mocha and he seriously wished the explosion of flavour in his mouth would never ever end.

"Why didn't you ask to come? I always would have let you come with me," Ian said, grinning even more.

Charles shrugged as he focused on the diamond-like stars in the distance. "Because I didn't want to impose on you and your traditions. You know what my life was like and I know how much Christmas means to you,"

Ian weakly smiled at his best friend and focused his attention back on his amazing mocha. He did know exactly what Charles' life had been like, his parents were both military specialists working for NASA leading the charge and expansion of humanity.

They hardly had time for a social life, let alone a kid so Charles never had Christmas, a birthday or anything like Ian did. Charles had been enrolled in military boarding schools since he was six years old and he got thrown out of each one because Charles only wanted his mummy and daddy to come home to him.

But they never wanted to and Charles hated his life until he enrolled in the academy. Then Ian realised what had actually changed when Charles was 16.

"Why did you start taking life seriously when you were 16?" Ian asked, focusing on the beautiful man sitting next to him.

Charles grinned and shrugged just like he did when he was an adorable schoolboy that Ian had loved since the moment he first saw him.

"I met you. I met your family. I saw what life could be like," Charles said. "Do you remember that Christmas?"

Ian just laughed because it really had been magical. His parents had just visited the Martian colonies and bought back a great bunch of sweet treats so Ian and Charles had stolen them all from his parents and ate them so fast they were both sick. Then with Charles in his arms Ian and his parents all sang, cheered and told amazing stories around their roaring, crackling fire.

And it really did feel so right to have his parents and Charles around him.

"Why didn't we ever get together?" Ian asked.

Charles grinned a little and finished his mocha in one beautiful motion. "Because you were always too good for me and I never felt like I deserved you,"

Ian laughed. "Seriously?"

Charles nodded like he hadn't just said the silliest thing Ian had ever heard. "Of course. I don't deserve a hot beautiful man that can give me Christmas magic, cheer and a loving family,"

Ian just laughed, he double tapped on each of the three

computer screens in front of him and set the little shuttle to autopilot. They were still a good hour away from the moon base and the cleaning procedures of the base to make sure the shuttle didn't contain any disease from Earth would take another hour, so Ian had time.

Ian stood up and went over to the beautiful, pretty man that he had loved since he was sixteen, young but never foolish.

Ian took Charles by the hand and just shook his head at him and their lips got closer. "Let us both decide what's good for us, you silly beautiful boy,"

As their lips locked, Ian loved the feeling of Charles's smooth full lips against his and whatever magic, cheer and joy he had gotten from doing Christmas runs with the sparkling stars in front of him. All of that didn't even remotely come close to the magic he was experiencing right now and wanted to experience for the rest of his life.

When their lips parted and both Ian and Charles were grinning like the schoolboys they had been, Charles quickly made them another plastic mug full of his amazing, sensational mochas.

Then they cheered to the future, to them and to the magical run to the moon that had finally bought them together after so long.

AUTHOR OF ACCLAIMED AGENTS OF THE EMPEROR SERIES

CONNOR WHITELEY

FUTURE LIFESAVERS

A SCIENCE FICTION NEAR FUTURE SHORT STORY

FUTURE LIFESAVERS

My heart pounded in my chest.

Everyone I had ever met in the lifeguarding community already hated the first few moments whenever the pager went off and we all instantly knew that a life was in grave danger and without our people someone was going to die.

I always hated those moments because it was always such a deadly race against time. If we were too slow then a corpse would wash up on a beach shortly. Too fast and we risked making a mistake that would make us accidentally kill someone through our own stupid mistakes.

I stood proudly in the large box-room of the driving cabin of our immense bright orange hovercraft stretching tens of metres in all directions. We were a beast of the seas around the UK and we only ever got called in when some serious shit was going down and tons of lives depended on us.

Immense gusts of wind smashed into our hovercraft and whilst the holo-shields tried to keep the worst of it from impacting us. The shields were failing today.

Waves tens of metres tall rose up and down out of the dark blue sea like claws stretching out to pull us down to its foul depths and I had no idea how the hell we were meant to help anyone out here.

The reason why we had been called out was because the conditions were way too bad for the small lifeboats even with their holo-suspension that made it next to impossible for them to capsize.

I wasn't sure we were going to be any better.

The howling, roaring and screaming of the wind wrapped around us and I knew it was far too dangerous to go outside in these conditions. And I knew it was dangerous enough on deck with the worst of the weather being filtered through the holo-shields.

I had a sick feeling that if the holo-shields weren't there then we would simply fly off the deck as soon as we stepped outside.

It was that dangerous.

The rich wonderful smell of coffee, Danish pastries and salty sea air filled my senses and I was glad that I hadn't had breakfast yet because judging by the face of Victoria our helm she was about to lose hers.

I suppose not having breakfast was the only advantage of early morning calls.

"Hovercraft, this is Eastbourne Coastguard do you copy, over,"

As soon as the coastguard came over on the radio and a small holographic woman appeared on the hard wooden console where Victoria was driving the hovercraft from everyone else fell silent.

I really wanted to know exactly what we were getting involved in.

"Confirmed Eastbourne Coastguard. This is Hovercraft, over," Victoria said.

"Hovercraft we have reports of a Cargo Ship losing all power, engines and shipping containers have become loose in the storm. The ship is approaching rocks and the ship is carrying explosives too, over,"

As Victoria relayed her response saying that we understood everything I looked at my best friends Jeremy, Claire and William. They were all gripping on grey metal bars for dear life and I didn't blame them.

We had to save the lives of everyone on that ship but we also had to arrange a tow line because if the explosives went off (something that still happened way too regularly for my liking in the 2100s) then everyone on that ship would die and the ocean ecosystem would be damaged for centuries.

We had to help them.

"Thank you Eastbourne Coastguard, we will be at target in ten minutes, over," Victoria said.

My stomach tightened and my entire body tensed as I imagined what on Earth could happen in those ten minutes. The ship could explode. The crew could die. A crew member could need a med-evac.

Everything would go wrong.

Victoria hit full power and I stumbled over to my best friends and none of us spoke for the next ten minutes.

You could cut the tension in the air with a knife. We all just wanted these people to be safe and we were all nervous as hell about establishing a tow line.

There were no other ships in the area that could handle this mission. If we couldn't help them then no one could.

And if we did need to med-evac someone then we couldn't. There was no chance a Jet could fly in these conditions.

A seagull smashed into the window of the driving cabin.

A second later the wind blew it away. Thankfully the window didn't crack but the conditions were clearly getting worse.

Ten minutes later we all gasped as we saw this ship wasn't just any old cargo ship it was a brand-new ship designed to be the Titanic of the oceans.

I had seen plenty of amazing pictures online of its immense blade-like grey metal exterior with huge angel wings on the side to help give it better stability (and they disappeared when the ship went into port) and it was said to be indestructible.

Clearly that was just excellent marketing.

We all went over to Victoria waiting for her command. We were all in our dry suits, thick coats and bright orange helmets ready to spring into action at a moment's notice.

Victoria frowned at us and we all knew how badly this was going to go.

She picked up her holographic handset and tried to contact the ship.

"Brownsea Ship, Brownsea Ship, this is Hovercraft please respond, over," she said.

She waited a few seconds before she tried again. And again. And again.

There was no answer.

I shook my head. "We have to assume that everyone onboard isn't fit enough to help us,"

Claire swore under her breath and then she taped the hologram on top of the driving console and she scanned the surrounding area.

I shook my head as we all realised that the cargo ship was less than a mile away from sharp extremely shallow rocks that wouldn't destroy the hull immediately but slowly it would.

It definitely would be death by a thousand cuts.

Immense booms echoed around us as we watched huge red shipping containers smash into the water below and they were floating towards us.

As we were a hovercraft I wasn't concerned about them as we could properly just hover over them but if they were damaged and had sharps shards of metal then I was concerned.

"We have to turn back," Victoria said.

Normally I was always the first one to do as a helm commanded but I didn't want to leave yet.

"We have to stay. We have to try," I said.

"We can't," Claire said. "The first rule of lifeguarding is to protect yourself and don't become a casualty,"

"I know but-" I said.

"I am helm and it is my duty to protect my crew first of all," Vic said.

"Hovercraft, hovercraft, this is Brownsea Ship, over,"

We all looked at each other completely stunned.

"Hovercraft, I do not know how long this fix will last. Please respond, over,"

Victoria immediately responded.

"Brownsea Ship, this is Hovercraft. We need to immediately establish a tow line between our vessels. Can anyone help? Over,"

"Negative Hovercraft. My crew are injured, trapped below deck or fighting to contain loose containers. I am the only one available to help. Over,"

I could see the look of despair in Victoria's eyes. I snatched the handset off her. Everyone gasped.

"We need to break protocol," I said. "Captain where is the strongest point on your ship,"

"The stern,"

I looked over the huge waves that rose and fell rapidly and tried to ignore the howling, roaring, screaming wind smashing into us.

The stern was the closest part to the rocks. We couldn't risk the Hovercraft heading that way towards the back.

"What about the bow?" I asked.

"That would be strong enough for a tow line but I cannot reach there,"

"Leave it to us. Just make sure the ship doesn't steer to one side or another. Over,"

The line crackled so I presumed the captain's fix finally failed.

Before Victoria could moan at me I looked at her. "Can you get us to the bow of the Cargo ship? Give me a line and when we're on top of wave and the Ship is below us I'll jump,"

The entire crew were silent and I hated it. The plan was crazy and I was basically doomed to die but it was the only way.

"Only if you wear a secondary line so if you fall in there's a small chance we can pull you up," Victoria said.

I nodded. Knowing full well that if I fell into the water the current would easily snap the line or my little body would get smashed in-between hundreds of tons of between Cargo Ship and Hovercraft.

I was a dead man anyway but for the sake of the people on that ship I had to die trying.

Victoria quickly went over to the Cargo ship and tried to

position us as best she could.

Meanwhile me and Claire strapped me into a very comfortable bright orange harness with a bright red rope tied around me and we set to work.

Me and Claire forced open the large door outside and the sheer coldness, wetness and brutality of the wind smashed into me like bullets.

I forced my feet to move through the pain and we set to work.

We slowly inched ourselves forward more and more and when we reached the very tip of the Hovercraft's bow my stomach flipped as I saw us nose-dive into a wave.

I gripped onto the wire railing as my feet rose up off the floor and Claire screamed. Thankfully she was okay but this was deadly work.

As the Hovercraft rose up into another wave Claire passed me a thick tow line and I made the "okay" sign at her. It was impossible to talk over the sound of the waves but I was tense as anything.

I had everything I needed to make the jump so I waited for the Hovercraft to reach the dip of the next wave.

And I saw the Cargo Ship just flopping around there. Huge waves were smashing over the decks and the bow.

If a wave hit me then I was as good as dead.

But there was no time I knew at any moment Victoria was so going to call off the whole operation.

So I jumped.

I was stupid not to give me a running start of anything but I just jumped.

I screamed as I fell towards the metal bow of the Cargo ship.

I was going to miss.

I was going to go into the water.

I stretched out my fingers.

Managing to barely catch onto to something.

I screamed in pain as agony shot through my fingers.

Yet I couldn't fail.

My heart was pounding. I forced myself up.

I realised I had grabbed onto a broken metal wire railing that was flapping about in the extreme wind.

I pulled myself up onto the icy cold metal deck of the bow and thankfully there was a large black metal anchor thing. I went towards it.

My brain was analysing everything so I forgot names of boat parts but I set to work.

The tow line was starting to get more and more tense in my hands so I knew I had to act quickly before the tow line was ripped out of them.

I tied the thick rope around the black metal thing as quick as I could and as I tied as I could.

I thought I heard someone scream my name as I watched the world turn black as an immense dark blue wave rose up out of the ocean and smashed down on me.

All I remembered was the sheer icy coldness and sheer force of the impact as my world went black.

***

"Gold Medal for service hey Dominic?"

A few months later I sat in a very comfortable wooden chair with a bright purple cushion and I just smiled at my best friends Claire, Jeremy and William as they gathered around me in my living room.

It had been ages since I had been here and admired its bright baby blue walls, wonderfully soft sofas and great looking artwork that my wife had picked up over the delightfully long years of our marriage. My best friends all had beers in their hands because none of us were on duty tonight and I loved that.

It was so nice to actually get to see my friends without the constant stress and worry of being called out at a moment's notice. It was a good day and I seriously couldn't fault them with how they had acted after what happened on the cargo ship a few months before.

It turned out as soon as the wave had knocked me partially

overboard the captain had radioed the lifeboat to start towing at all speed so they did.

Meanwhile Claire, William and Jeremy all forced themselves outside into mortal danger to start pulling me back towards the ship and each of them had almost been knocked overboard twice.

They really did risk their lives to save me.

And thankfully because of all of us the Brownsea Ship was perfectly okay, no one died and everyone got the medical attention they needed so badly. And everyone was expected to make a full recovery.

I wished that Victoria could have made it but after she had written to the Life Guarding Association ten times to force them to give me a Gold Lifetime Service Award she had retired and she had written another twenty letters to the Association about them making me the new Helm.

Victoria was a hell of a pitbull when she wanted to be.

And whilst I never would support her decision for leaving and retiring because she felt like she wasn't good enough as a helm anymore (complete nonsense of course), I would always, always class her as a friend.

And if she hadn't been travelling to see her son and his boyfriend up North then I would have loved to have her here today.

As me and the others talked, laughed and even broke out into song a few times I realised that I really was the luckiest man alive. I had some amazing friends, a wonderful wife and I had saved so many lives over the course of my career that it might have just been me doing my job but I was extremely proud that I did what I did no matter the danger.

And I really, really hoped that I would be doing this great job until I died because it definitely was the best job in the entire world.

CONNOR WHITELEY

OWNING WHO YOU ARE

A SCIENCE FICTION NEAR FUTURE SHORT STORY

OWNING WHO YOU ARE
15th June 2100
Rochester, South England

He was going to make himself own who he was today. That was a promise whatever the consequences.

Jacob Terhorst held the large warm piping hot mug of steaming black coffee as he sat on the hard white plastic chairs of the ultra-Train he was riding. He might have been close to a hundred years old but the Ultra-Trains had always scared him and delighted him at the same time.

He tried to look at the large shiny floor-to-ceiling windows of the train but that was the annoying thing about Ultra-Trains. They travelled so damn fast he couldn't see anything outside except weird and wonderful flashes of green, blue and maybe a little bit of pink but he wasn't sure.

That could mean anything and Jacob didn't really mind. They could have been travelling through one of the rich city centres in the southeast of South England or he could have been travelling through one of the small remaining forests.

He didn't know and that didn't matter.

Jacob looked back at the immensely long Ultra-Train carriage that was mostly made from glass with white plastic chairs and tables that sort of made Jacob feel weightless and like he was floating, but he knew better than to trust anything made by the English.

Especially after the war.

He weakly smiled at a very tall middle-aged man as he walked past and frowned. There weren't too many of the old generations that were happy, Jacob respected that but it wouldn't kill people to smile every so often.

Jacob focused on a large group of elderly women wearing their jeans, hi-top shoes and their white shirts. They certainly looked like the women from his childhood and Jacob was tempted to go over and talk to them, but they were probably sitting on the far side of the carriage for good reason.

Not a lot of the older generation wanted to talk to each other. All that Jacob wanted was to talk about the world war, what had happened and what everyone had done during it.

But no one wanted to talk, listen or even acknowledge what had happened. No wonder England had split.

Jacob shivered as the warm refreshing air of the Ultra-Train rushed past him as a group of young students walked past and allowed the warm air from another carriage to walk through.

Jacob just focused on them for a minute. They were all so young, so innocent and they looked great in their little shiny clothes made from blue, pink and purple silk.

He still couldn't believe how much fashion had evolved since he was a kid. Everyone back then used to where cotton, jeans and polyester. That was all long dead having been replaced with silk, latex and brand-new materials made by the impressive advancements in science.

He was also more than glad the kids had never known or lived through the Building of The Wall, where England had split into North England and South England.

And the world war that caused it all.

And the world war that had caused Jacob to change everything about himself.

Something he was hoping to fix today but he doubted he had the courage to do what needed to be done to make up for the past.

***

15th June 2030

Jacob hugged his knees close to his chest as he sat on the cold, wet black floor of a train as it pounded over the metal rails, banging every few metres.

The cold black walls of the carriage were probably as menacing as the prison guards that would turn up at any moment to inspect everyone yet again. There were no windows except the drill holes at the very top of the carriage.

Jacob had no idea why the dumb guards didn't put in windows or something, but he knew the truth he was a designer before he was arrested for being in the address book of another gay man.

The guards probably wanted some of the prisoners to die from suffocation (less mouths to feed at the prison that way) and the monstrous guards probably wanted them to know there was no chance of escape.

Jacob just smiled to himself because he already knew there was no chance of freedom, escape or mercy.

There was only death on this train.

He tried to not look at the other passengers that were standing above him frowning, whispering and making jokes about how they were all going to die. And Jacob hated how each and every one of them was in the same black prison uniform as the common criminals that they had once been told to hate by the UK Government and the other leaders of the "free" world.

Jacob hated the smell of wee, damp and fearful sweat as a very tall woman whacked a few prisoners in the head as they accidentally got in her way.

The woman just smiled at Jacob.

Jacob hated how just a few days before he had been enjoying a great view from his London penthouse apartment working on a brand-new school that would have helped thousands of poor children get a better education when the Secret Service had smashed in his front door and arrested him.

He had been careful for months.

He hadn't smiled at another man in public, he hadn't kissed anyone in months and he certainly hadn't had sex in a good year or two (or three) because everyone knew that the UK Government would simply arrest you and leave you to die.

That was the way the world was and as the chances of war got closer and closer between Europe (the true defenders of freedom, liberty and peace) and the UK and USA. Jacob knew it was only a matter of time before the UK finally declared war and then the entire world would go to pot.

Jacob almost smiled at the idea. He had no idea who would win but Jacob hated himself for not speaking out against the entire series of laws the UK had bought out to make sure anyone who wasn't white, English or Christian wasn't able to vote or enjoy a whole bunch of freedoms he had never thought about.

But he hadn't wanted to bring attention to the gay community. He regretted that now.

The woman raised her club like she was going to finish him off once and for all.

Jacob looked down at the massive pink triangle that the English had sown onto his prison uniform so every single person in prison would know he was gay.

And something they should kill on site.

Jacob had even heard that the prison offered freedom to people who killed gays inside. He was only 22, he didn't want to die.

He didn't want anyone to die.

The woman went to bring down the club on Jacob's head but a man gripped the end of the club and the woman spun around and frowned at him.

"Let me kill him in the camp," the man said.

Jacob couldn't see who the man was from down on the floor but he couldn't get up. If there were other prisoners who wanted to kill him in exchange for freedom then Jacob didn't want them to see the massive pink triangle sown on his chest.

"I am the guard. I will decide when he dies," the woman said.

Jacob watched the woman take a step back like the man had done something to scare her but then she started laughing and she simply walked back the way she had come.

A moment later Jacob frowned as a massive, muscular and very handsome, cute man stood in front of him but Jacob knew he wasn't an ally (as if anyone was anymore).

The man pointed to the left corner. "Your only chance to still be alive in two hours,"

Jacob shook his head as the man walked away because he had suspected the train was meant to arrive at the concentration camp in two hours but he hadn't realised that meant he was going to die on arrival.

But of course he was.

Jacob realised that the type of world he lived in now. England didn't care about gays and the government had been pumping out so much hate lately so he sadly knew the guards wouldn't think twice about beating him to death the moment he stepped off the train.

Jacob looked to the left.

He gasped as he saw a very elderly man with a bright red triangle sown over his t-shirt. He wasn't wearing a real uniform and the poor man looked like he was gasping for air.

He wouldn't last two hours.

Jacob couldn't believe he was going to have to kill the man to take his T-shirt. The man had to be a European prisoner with that t-shirt on and because of political power battles that Jacob didn't understand, he guessed that being European might give him protection for now.

The man looked weakly at Jacob and Jacob couldn't smile, couldn't move, couldn't speak.

Jacob just focused on how the man was gasping for every single breath. The man wasn't going to last two hours, none of the other prisoners on the carriage would care because he had seen two murders already in the past hour so he had to make a choice.

Did he kill a dying man so he could live? Or did he not kill a man and he would die in two hours anyway?

Just because he loved a man.

Jacob shook his head as he crawled over to the man and tightened his hands around his neck.

"I'm so sorry," Jacob said.

***

15th June 2100

Dover, South England

As Jacob sat in the white plastic chair on the Ultra-Train he still couldn't believe what he had done just so he could live a little longer. But back then the world was just so crazy, so evil, so dark.

It was only two days later until the UK had declared war on Europe and Australia and then the USA had declared war on Canada, Mexico and all the other countries in the Americas.

Jacob frowned as he was surprised as he read about it as the concentration camp handed out holo-papers to make sure the prisoners knew exactly how dark their world was getting for their kind.

Jacob had heard and met a lot of people that weren't white, straight or Christian over the decades and they all spoke about the concentration camps. All the death they had seen and how the English and Americans had tried to "cure" them and Jacob hated all of them.

He was less surprised that he had almost been arrested again at the end of the wall and the Copper Curtain had been built between North and South England. The far-right was in the South and the peace lovers in the North.

Jacob had no idea why he had stayed in the South, part of it was because of his prison sentence. The fact that he was still gay didn't matter when the war ended, he was still thrown back in prison and the torture had continued until the United Nations had discovered it and sued South England almost into annihilation.

"All change. All change," a young man said as he walked past wearing a rather attractive black suit.

Jacob smiled briefly. He had never said to anyone, in the two years that he had been released from prison that he was gay, liked men or even been a prisoner of war, or more like a prisoner of the English's sick ideology.

Jacob forced himself up as he noticed the train had stopped at a large concrete train station filled with flickering and failing holo-signs but there was only one sign that he needed to follow.

He needed to follow the sign back to the concentration camp that where he had suffered so much and he had killed his first and only victim.

He wanted to finally see what the tourists thought of victims like him at the concentration camp.

And he finally wanted to be his true self.

***

15th June 2100

An hour later Jacob looked at the massive solid castle wall made from solid stone blocks with holo-shield and barred wire that seemed to stretch on for as far as the eye could see.

Jacob was standing in amongst hundreds upon hundreds of little unmarked graves that were simply marked with a small coloured triangle that had fainted over time.

There were actually thousands upon thousands of people buried outside Dover Camp but Jacob didn't know why some were marked and some weren't.

The sea was quietly smashing against the white cliffs in the distance and the gentle howl of the warm sea breeze made Jacob smile for a moment. There were just so many triangles here and he was so close to being one of them, marked or not.

He could have died.

Jacob smiled and nodded his hellos to a small group of young families as they pushed their baby strollers along the shiny metal path a few metres from him. They didn't look interested and Jacob didn't know if they were ever alive in the war but they didn't know what had happened here.

He had had a quick look inside and everything had been redecorated, the posters and audio guides that aimed to explain the "horrors" of what had happened at the camps were all lies and tried to make it seem more like a holiday camp than anything else.

It was a shame but he was going to do something that would have gotten him killed all those decades ago.

Jacob took out a small holo-accessory from his pocket and he activated it and it made a large pink triangle appear on his front and back and he smiled as he heard a lot of people whisper and sneer behind him.

He didn't care because he was finally being true to himself. He had lied all throughout the war about who he was, what he liked and what he loved but the war was over and South England was defeated.

South England might have still hated gays with a devotion that Jacob would never understand but now he was protected under law so he could tell the world he was gay without fear of being killed again.

"You survived then," a young man said.

Jacob smiled as he walked over wearing some black trousers, something shiny that Jacob didn't understand and some black shoes. He clearly worked here and he looked happy to see Jacob.

"Do I know you?" Jacob asked.

"No, I'm sorry but I didn't know any gay people survived Dover Camp,"

Jacob forced himself to keep smiling. He was safe now. He really, really was.

"I wasn't known as a gay prisoner here. I was Jean-Paul, a French national who was almost returned to France at the end of the war until it was revealed that I was lying and I was gay,"

The young man frowned. "I'm sorry. No one understands what they did to us here,"

"Us?" Jacob asked not understanding what the young man meant.

"I'm gay too and I've been fighting the South England

Government to officially recognise their genocide against us for years," he said.

Jacob smiled. He hadn't met another gay person for decades, even now everyone was in hiding, fearing for their life and it was just so nice to meet something calm, confident and happy about who they were.

"They will never admit it," Jacob said smiling."

"Maybe," the young man said, "but I could use your story. You saw the Camp inside. No one knows the truth because no one is being told the truth. If you told your story, if you admit you're gay then we could finally bring about the recognition of the mass murder of our people, and we can make sure it never happens again,"

Jacob didn't have the heart to tell him everything in World War Three had already happened in Two with the Nazis killing gays left, right and centre but maybe humanity could learn even for a century or two.

"I don't know," Jacob said. "I haven't spoken about my experience,"

The young male extended his hand. "Then we will learn a lot together, but first of all you need to admit something. Who are you?"

Jacob laughed because he was surprised he was feeling so light, happy and cheerful. Because he knew that admitting, treasuring and living his own life was what he had always wanted since the day he had been arrested and charged without a trial for simply being gay.

It wasn't just, fair or right but there was a chance to change all of that now because he couldn't help the past, he couldn't help the dying man he had killed but he could help the next generation of gay youth to live safely.

And that was something worth fighting for.

"My name is Jacob Terhorst, a prisoner at Dover Camp and I am gay,"

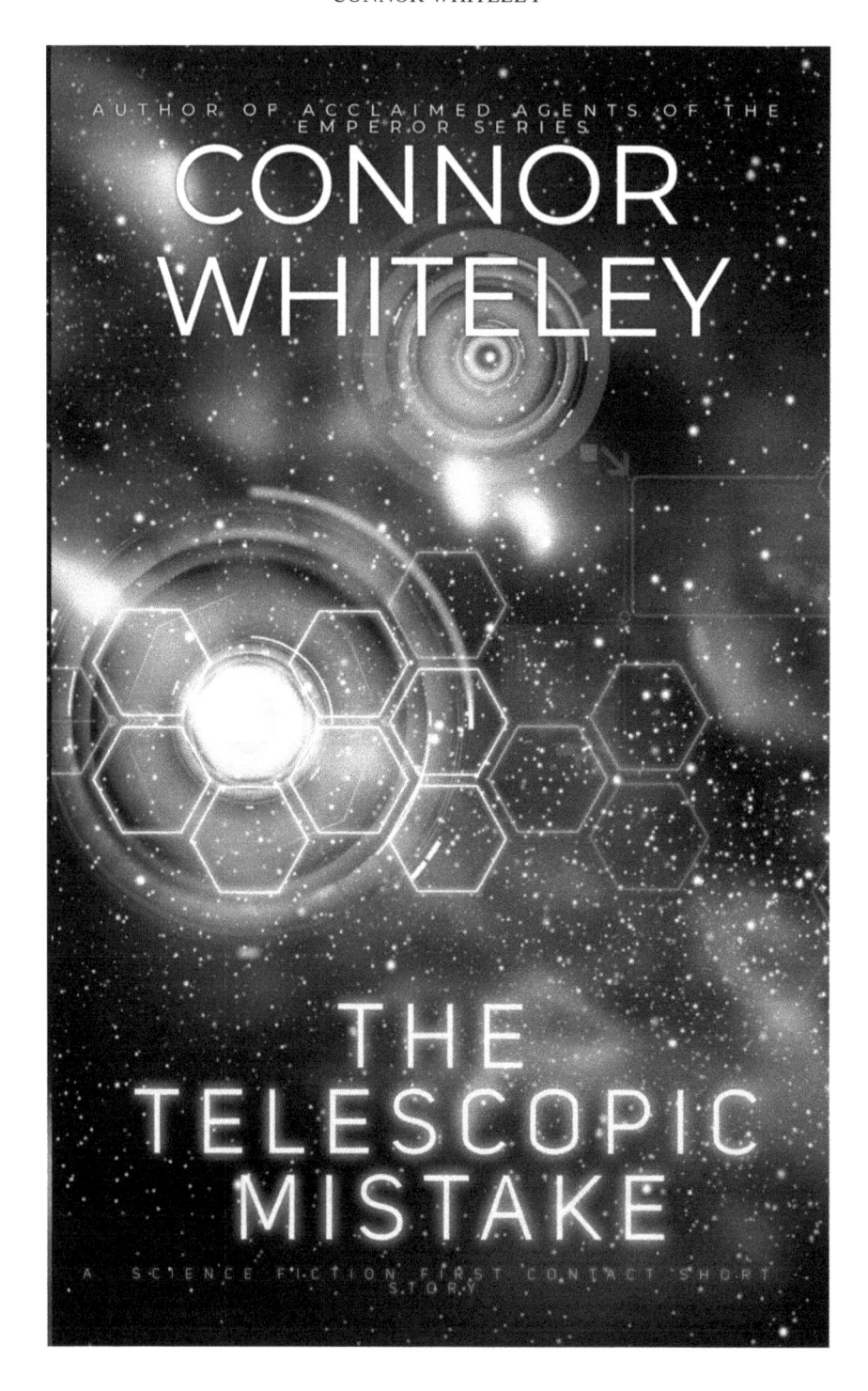

AUTHOR OF ACCLAIMED AGENTS OF THE EMPEROR SERIES

CONNOR WHITELEY

THE TELESCOPIC MISTAKE

A SCIENCE FICTION FIRST CONTACT SHORT STORY

THE TELESCOPIC MISTAKE

People tend to have a terrible tendency to imagine British Government Spy work to be exciting, thrilling and filled with top-secret missions that were the difference between the world being destroyed and the world... well not.

Sadly I had also believed such myths when I applied for this so-called top-secret mission, but I quickly learnt that that was all absolute bullocks.

My name is Teddy Elliot, a stupid name I know, but I actually rather like it, and I really, really like my job because I get to spy on Americans and their space toys. I don't know what it is with Americans, toys and space but yea, everyone needs a hobby right?

As I sat on my little black desk covered in high-tech computers that were probably worth more than I would ever earn in my lifetime, inside my very cramped office with some horrible black walls, broken fans and a broken TV. I just smiled to myself.

Sure, I do not deny this is a shit office, but it is what I do here that gets me excited. Especially with the Americans meant to be getting the first official-official photos (don't ask me why Americans were getting excited about these official photos and not the four thousand other official photos) back from their brand new James Webb telescope.

I'll fully admit as I sip my piping hot cup of black coffee that made the office fill with hints of bitter coffee, sweet honey and my favourite hazelnut syrup that their telescope was rather cool.

I never bothered to get into the details of how it all worked and that rubbish, but I was very interested in how it would detect the very first stars, planets and whatever else that got created straight after the Big Bang.

Now that sounded very, very cool.

The sound of humming, popping and vibrating quietly filled the office as my computers started to flare to life a little more, and I could only presume that meant the photos would arrive at any moment from the telescope.

This had to be one of the coolest parts of my job, this was so much cooler than spying on the Russians, Chinese and the Argentinians.

"Have I missed it?"

I really smiled as my beautiful friend Elizabeth stood slightly behind me holding her own massive cup of coffee and she was carrying Ginger Nut biscuits. She really was a sexy woman, and she seriously looked amazing today in her tight pink suit, her long blond hair tied up in a bun and her face just looked so cute and adorable.

I really liked her.

"Na Eliz," I said. "No photos yet,"

Elizabeth rolled her eyes and I knew that she was as excited about this as me. If these images did actually contain the First Galaxies and First Stars then this was massive.

"Ginger Nut?" Elizabeth asked.

I nodded her my thanks as I took one of the biscuits, dunked it in my coffee and my whole mouth exploded in a delicious symphony of flavours from the coffee to the ginger to the wonderful hazelnut hint of my syrup.

This was going to be a great day.

"What's that?" Elizabeth asked, pointing to the computer screens.

I sadly had to stop enjoying me biscuits and I focused on the screen and… wow!

The Americans were actually receiving some images from their telescope. Now the entire reason why I had been demoted to this job was simply because of how much American space tech failed, exploded or just deactivated, so the fact that this worked was rather amazing in itself.

My computer screens slowly changed to reveal a single image that had been sent back to Earth. It was one of the most beautiful spiral galaxies I had ever seen, there were massive stunning streaks of milky white, red and orange. This Galaxy deserved to be on a canvas, it was that beautiful.

"Right," Elizabeth said, "more images are incoming, but let's focus on this one first,"

"It can't be the first galaxy," I said.

Elizabeth nodded, because if this was the first ever galaxy made after the Big Bang then the image would detail tons of other things, and the telescope would be able to date it roughly.

I looked at the very bottom of the image and the telescope refused to date it, but the weird piece of information was down there. Apparently the image was experiencing Blue Shift.

"If this is Blue Shift, then this means the Galaxy is moving towards us, right?" I asked.

Elizabeth looked as if she was about to have a heart attack at that oversimplification, but after a few moments she just nodded.

"So why would a telescope designed to find the First Galaxy take a photo of a newer one?" I asked.

"It's meant to take photos of everything it finds. This isn't that strange," Elizabeth said.

As much as I wanted to agree, I couldn't. I just felt as if there was more to this image than meets the eye.

The sound of my computers popping, humming and vibrating got louder as the Americans were receiving even more images.

I clicked on them.

"Shit!" I said.

Me and Elizabeth both stared at the new zoomed-in images that showed five grey pencil-like spaceships.

I was right.

There was a lot more to this image than meets the eye.

Tons more actually.

***

Something I absolutely love about working for the government is the amount of cool tech we get so we can easily listen in on the Americans and their scientists.

It turned out all of NASA and every single other expert that had looked at it were completely stunned at such an image, and every security agency on the planet had verified it as real.

So needlessly to say we were dealing with actual fucking aliens!

This was so impossible, strange and twisted that I couldn't even begin to imagine what this meant. Aliens were real, they had spaceships and their galaxy was moving towards us.

This was bad, very bad.

"We need to contact the boss," Elizabeth said.

I took another massive sip of my amazingly flavoured coffee that actually burnt my throat and I shook my head.

We couldn't call in the boss for just anything, because if this turned out to be a mistake or fake then I didn't want to look so stupid.

"You're the astrophysicist," I said, "explain this to me,"

Elizabeth just shrugged. Then she gently pushed me away from the computer and she typed away at it.

"Oh," she said.

I looked at what she was doing and for some reason she had been tracking where the image was taken and comparing it to where the telescope was meant to be taking images from.

The two things didn't match.

"We have a telescope taking random pictures of areas it isn't meant to until a few years time. And we have five pencil-like alien ships moving towards us,"

Elizabeth just nodded.

"In all fairness how long will it take galaxy to reach us. A thousand? A million? A Billion years?" I asked.

Elizabeth really smiled. Then my computers started beeping as new images came in revealing the alien ships were coming out of their own galaxy.

I just couldn't even begin to understand the speed required for such a thing. Galaxies were such massive things that it would take thousands of years just to get to the edge of most galaxies let alone travel in-between them.

And somehow these aliens had managed to do just that.

I ran a quick scan of the first image and then I sadly realised the aliens were near the centre of their galaxy in that image. But less than fifteen minutes later they had been at the very edge and leaving their own galaxy.

This was bad.

"Now tell me how long until those aliens get here," I said.

Elizabeth looked up at the ceiling and shook her head for a few seconds.

"Probably ten months," she said.

Then my computer switched off all by themselves.

"What?" I asked.

I tried to turn on the computers on and off but nothing was working. It was like the computers were under the control of someone else, except they weren't turning back on.

Seconds later they turned on.

I almost shot back as I stared at a brand new image that showed the alien pencil-like ships orbiting Pluto. But there was something in the image and I couldn't help but feel like I was being watched.

"There," Elizabeth said pointing to the very tip of the ships.

I laughed to myself as I just saw something. On the image it looked like a strange shadow of something very short and stocky, but I knew it was an alien.

The computer flashed.

Something appeared on the desk.

It was an alien.

A very short, grey, stocky alien.

My mouth dropped.

I was a lot more terrified than I ever wanted to admit.

***

"Well this planet's a piece of a shithole," the alien said.

Now I understand I spend my days monitoring space programmes, technology and equipment but I never ever believed I would see an actual alien, and for some reason it spoke English.

All I could do was stare at the alien with its little short legs, large chest and stomach and the single staring eye in the front of its head. It didn't have a mouth or nose or ears, but I knew it was speaking.

"I've been to worse shitholes I suppose. Air would be better. Moisture levels are shit. But I suppose this would do," the alien said.

"Excuse me?" I said clicking my fingers to get the alien's attention.

The alien's eye just focused on me. It didn't even blink. It just stared.

"What you doing here? This is our planet," I said.

The alien folded its little arms over. "Says who Pinkie?"

I just looked at Elizabeth who was staring at me and the alien like we were someone to be coldly studied. She wasn't going to be very useful here.

"How did you get here?" I asked.

The alien rolled its eye. "You Pinkies are just awful. You sent something into space. You made it cross into our Empire and then you get offended when we want to find out where it came from,"

I just shrugged. I could easily see this alien being a politician on his or her homeworld, because it clearly wasn't answering my question.

"How did you move so quick?" I asked.

The alien just took its head. "It wasn't hard Pinkie to trace where your… what do you call it… tele-cope was sending its transmissions to,"

I was hardly impressed with this alien but judging by how much it was interested in our planet, I couldn't allow it to take over, and claim the planet for itself.

I had to get rid of it.

The alien started to type away at the computer.

"What you doing?" Elizabeth asked.

The alien huffed. "The sooner you Pinkies are enslaved the better. I'm signalling the fleet that this planet is fine for invasion,"

I whacked the alien across the room.

The alien appeared on my chest.

Grabbing me by the throat.

"I will make sure you die slowly in the camps," the alien said.

"I have a better idea," I said.

I had absolutely no clue what I was doing but I just had to make sure I at least tried to save everyone. Or I suppose I needed to try and give the Americans, the Chinese and the European Union time to activate their space defences.

That was definitely one of the few benefits of this job, you got to know what different countries had.

"What about your idea Pinkie?"

"We play a game. If I win, you leave this galaxy and you never return. If you win, you can claim this entire galaxy for yourself,"

The alien laughed. "I have done this before in different times, different ages, different galaxies. I won them all. This time will be no different,"

As much as I wanted to roll my eyes at this arrogant idiot, that might actually work in my favour.

"What do you Pinkies play?"

I just said the first game that popped in my head. "Poker,"

"Excellent Pinkie. My Empire will be most grateful for that, considering we are masters of the game,"

Shit! I have never played poker in my life and now I have to play it to save humanity.

Well, no actually. I just had to play it long enough for the various superpowers of the world to activate their space defences.

I seriously hope their defences were actually quick and easy to use.

The fate of the world rested in my hands.

***

Turned out I was actually rather good at poker, or I was good enough to be about a thousand pounds up from when we started. Thankfully my boss had given me a hundred thousand pounds worth of chips, and the alien had somehow come up with the same, so six hours later I was really, really enjoying myself.

And I was even able to understand the alien's tells. Like whenever he had a good hand, his eye would twitch ever so slightly. I personally doubt normal humans and probably aliens could notice that, but thankfully my spy training had taught me a lot.

"Rise ten thousand," the alien said, throwing ten thousand pounds into the middle of our little poker table in my office.

As a man who never had this much money before I hated just playing with it and throwing it away, but I had to play along.

I just hoped that the space defences were actually working. I wished those superpowers would just hurry up.

I did him another ten thousand and we revealed our cards and I lost.

Normally that wouldn't annoy me or cause me to react in the slightest, but I just knew something was wrong with the space defences.

My boss had assured me the Prime Minister would use every single political muscle to get our allies and our enemies to hurry up and activate their defences.

But I knew what the Prime Minister was like.

Considering he was a useless, weak leader that had caused the UK to have no more allies. I knew deep down that the space defences were never going to be activated.

Everything was down to me.

So I raised the alien to fifty thousand, we agreed and I lost again.

Now I was seriously in trouble. I was now really starting to lose money, but thankfully the alien only had about forty thousand pounds left to play with.

"All in," the alien said pushing all his available money into the middle.

He just grinned at me.

And now I understand why poker wasn't a very fun game if the fate of the world rested in your hands and you weren't a good player.

I also started to realise that for the past six hours the alien had just been playing with me quickly. I wasn't a good player. I was shit. And the alien was probably just testing my abilities and seeing if Earth would do anything to stop them.

He knew Earth wasn't. I knew Earth wasn't. Elizabeth standing behind me knew that.

I didn't know how to play this. I just had to hope that the cards in my hand would give me a better play than him.

He revealed his cards first. He had a full-house.

My stomach twisted.

Sweat dripped down my back.

I didn't know enough about poker to know what would beat it. I didn't think a full-house could be beaten.

I revealed my cards.

"Fuck," the alien said folding his arms.

I didn't know what I had but clearly the alien was beaten, all his money was lost and I had actually won my first ever poker game.

The alien appeared on the table in front of me and that crazy single eye just stared at me.

"You played well Pinkie. I will declare this galaxy a no-go zone for as long as my Empire lives," the alien said.

I just smiled and nodded.

"Maybe you Pinkies are smarter than you appear,"

With that the alien disappeared and me and Elizabeth went back over to the computer screens and noticed that all the pencil-like ships were gone.

I just jumped up and hugged Elizabeth.

We had saved the galaxy.

***

As I laid on a wonderful wooden sunbed on my country estate with the boiling hot sun beaming down on me, I had to admit that life was amazing. Especially with the amazing country air being filled with delightful hints of lavender, pine and bitter coffee.

After my little victory over the aliens, the government had allowed me to keep the two hundred thousand so I went to some more poker games, won even more and now I had bought my own estate.

I did love my massive stone mansion with hundreds of acres of land, a trout lake and so many more wonders that I just flat out loved it. It seems that government work can pay after all.

But the real reason why I bought the estate was simple enough. The estate had such stunningly clear skies and I had changed all the outside lights to minimize the light pollution, so every night I could stare up into the night sky and just watch.

I got to see all those stars and our planets and just wonder what else was out there. I had won the planet a victory over the game of poker and now I couldn't help but wonder what else was there.

"Teddy!" Elizabeth shouted from the house.

I happily got off my sunset and walked to start across my massive lawn towards my mansion and the woman I loved. Until the day with the alien, I never realised how truly great, smart and just flat out beautiful she was.

And when I saw her standing on the patio in nothing more than a silky dressing gown… well, needlessly to say I didn't need to think about space exploration, aliens and poker for a little bit.

I had to do a much more important (and pleasurable) type of exploration. A type that no alien could ever give me.

AUTHOR OF ACCLAIMED AGENTS OF THE EMPEROR SERIES

CONNOR WHITELEY

AND THE FAT JUST WALKS AWAY

A SCIENCE FICTION HUMOR SHORT STORY

AND THE FAT JUST WALKS AWAY

Let me tell you the real problem with fat humans, it isn't that their heart will give out any moment, it isn't that the old fatties are slow and ugly, it isn't even that the old fatties are slobs. It ain't any of them because only the first one is true.

The real problem with fat humans is that they're all different, lazy and it's hard to infect them with my alien race.

You see as I'm a Liquid Alien race and that is such a brutal translation of our language into your abominable language that I'm never going to mention it again. That is the insult of calling myself a "Liquid" and yet I digress.

I'm currently a massive fat stomach the size of a camel hump on a large fatty of a man who's currently lying on an icy cold metal slab. Don't worry he isn't dead, I wouldn't allow him to die, but by your God is it cold in here.

I can feel everything he feels. I can feel how cold it is and I can feel how fat and slow his body is to moving around. And even though he wants to move one of his lumpy fingers, he can't because he's simply too fat which is why he actually allowed himself to be infected with an alien race, like myself.

Because as the advert says, *we make fat walk away.*

The human air was just disgusting to me. There was way too much nitrogen in your Earth atmosphere for my liking and it was awful, but I did enjoy your sweet aromas of rosemary, strawberry jam and custard doughnuts that my host wolfed down earlier because it had been ten minutes since dinner.

I ain't kidding.

And your human medical rooms need a bit of colour at the very least. I don't like the bright white clinical walls that send shivers down my tenacles and into my host's spine. I don't like how every single surface of the room is sterile, polished and shiny.

That just blinds me with the glare coming from those damn bright lights.

You humans really do seem to love it all and that is why you didn't even care of the side effects of allowing us to infect your fat people, because all you private doctors want is money.

If you can remove all the body fat a person has and people are willing to pay you millions for it. Then you don't care about the cost to your little plump race.

That's why I love humans.

The strange shriek echoed around the medical room and I realised that a very skinny, muscular and rather attractive human male walked in wearing a white lab coat.

He was Doctor Edward or as my species calls him *The Idiot*. Not because he was the doctor that likes us infecting humans but because he was the Doctor that fought against us.

Doctor Edward really didn't want us to infect humans, but all the other doctors on the "medical board" or whatever you humans call it, told him to let us or he would be "fired". I think it's monstrous you humans would fire someone into the sun.

That is just murder plain and simple. You should be ashamed of yourself.

Doctor Edward came over to my host, looked at him and started making notes.

"I think you aliens will be walking off soon," he said quietly.

I partly wondered if he would be glad to get rid of us for a few hours whilst we adjusted and relaxed after being inside this fatty for the past week.

You might find it strange that we infect the fat tissue of obese humans, but it isn't. Obese humans are the tasty kind and they have so much fatty tissue that I can infect one person and over a hundred of my kind can grow inside them. And when all of them are ready to mature, we simply grow legs and arms and a wonderful smile and we simply walk away.

The human host walks away a skinny rake and they gain the ability to never ever put on wait ever again. Whenever their body wants to create fat, it actually creates a small baby version of us.

And yes, as you can see, the more humans we infect, the more we are created and the whole glorious cycle continues.

"Can you aliens be killed?" Doctor Edward asked.

That made me take notice of him. He was standing right over the stomach of my human host. Right in front of me with a large knife that I was fairly sure would kill me.

I wasn't sure about human anatomy but this man was so fat a stab wound to the stomach would only kill me. I doubt the knife would even touch the guy's arteries and organs. That was how thick the layer of fat was.

I forced myself to connect to my host's spinal cord, I forced my influence into the guy's brain and I forced him to speak on my behalf.

"Don't do that," I said. "You'll be fired if you hurt me and my friends. Your bosses will hurt you,"

Doctor Edward shook his head. "I cannot let you keep infecting people. I know that you're building yourself up into an army,"

I seriously love how humans always believe aliens want to conquer Earth. We seriously don't. Let's face it, Earth is a shithole. There are too many toxins in the air, too many idiots and too much arguing between humans whilst your world is burning down around you.

I'm a case in point. If you humans worked together, my ship never would have landed and started infecting you idiots.

Humans are funny but dumb as fuck creatures.

"You took an oath to preserve life and heal it," I said. "If you kill me then you have betrayed your oath,"

Doctor Edward pressed the tip of the knife into the host's stomach and I flinched inside his fat stomach out of sheer fear. I hated this.

"You are an alien. I took an oath to protect humanity and now I will protect it,"

I hated that the Doctor was right and I didn't actually want to hurt him but my job from High Command was simple. Create as many aliens (because I refuse to use the L-word again) as possible.

That's what I'm doing and if a human doctor tries to stop me then I will have to act. But thankfully I've overheard a lot of doctors talk about something called "ethics". I had to put that limited knowledge into practice.

"If you kill me then this human will get injured, you would have caused harm. You would have caused another human to get stabbed. That is not right Doctor," I said.

I felt the human host starting to fight back now. It felt like he was trying to grab control of his mind again and he wanted to attack the Doctor. I couldn't let him do that because he was too fat to attack and kill the Doctor.

I had to find another way to stop this.

So I did the unthinkable and I forced my influence and alien DNA into my host's spinal cord and brain.

"Doctor if I die then I am taking his human down with me. If you don't kill me then I will allow this human to live,"

I noticed how my host's heart rate pounded in his chest. I never did understand how the human heart works in response to stress.

But I would kill him if needed.

Doctor Edward looked pained. He hated this. He hated what he was having to do.

He pressed the knife slightly harder into the host's fat stomach and I hissed in pain as the knife's edge drew the smallest amount of blood.

Doctor Edward's eyes went wet but he wasn't crying. He was

disappointed with himself that was clear but he hadn't committed to the full act yet.

And I could feel the arms and legs starting to grow in all 100 of my brothers and sisters. Soon it would be time to feast on humanity.

Na not really. I just want some Fried Chicken before I return this lot to the spaceship and I infect another human next week.

"Doctor you haven't done anything wrong yet. If you stop this now then I will command this human not to tell anyone of your misconduct,"

"I've already broken my oath. I've cut someone else. I'm going to lose everything because my bosses will never believe this was an accident and that I wasn't trying to kill you. I have to do it,"

"Don't,"

"I'm sorry,"

The Doctor went to force the knife into me but as soon as he did that I forced long thin arms made from human fat to shoot out of my host's stomach and grab the knife.

The Doctor tried to scream but I didn't let him.

I forced my fat-made arms to dissolve into liquid and crawl into his mouth, eyes and ears.

I ripped all the fat from his brain, body and muscles and as his corpse dropped to the ground all the fat returned to me.

And I simply grinned as my human host was knocked out cold so he didn't have to witness this next part and I simply stepped out of my host's stomach with my new humanoid body.

And the fat walked away.

***

It turned out the doctors at the private hospital and clinic really didn't give two shits a few days later when the body was discovered because it turned out my human host didn't tell a soul about the murder. I didn't care. My old host was already eating over five thousand calories a day and doing no exercise so twenty new brothers and sisters for me had grown very quickly.

I even heard one of my sisters mention how the old host was

thinking of eating ten thousand calories a day as he couldn't gain weight anymore. Of course he didn't realise he could only grow muscle and not fat but I hardly thought he was the gym, muscle-building type.

Unlike poor Doctor Edward.

To some extent I feel sorry for the poor soul because as I sit inside yet another human stomach of a 1000 pound woman that was barely able to breathe because her lungs were so restricted by her fat, I actually understood why the doctor did it.

He could have been greedy like all the other doctors and nurses at the private hospital and clinic, he could have created tens of millions of us and got paid even more to do so. And yet he didn't, because he wanted to protect his species, his patients and everything he was meant to do as a doctor.

The fat woman I was in now used to be a doctor before she ate so much that she was bed bound (before her bed and floor and house crumbled under her weight) and I now understood what doctors were taught at medical school.

They're meant to protect everyone, heal everyone and do no harm to everyone. And all those private doctors and nurses weren't doing that. Because they weren't protecting everyone from aliens like me, they weren't healing people from my side effects, and they certainly were not doing no harm to humans because of what was coming.

My race is entering the millions of us now and soon that means High Command will give us a command and then we will do it. They will command us to invade, feast or flee and whilst I learn all the opposites I seriously hope we get to feast.

Because before I go and finish this 1000 woman off, let me just tell you that I love feasting because humans are so delicious and after we have ravaged your planet of all the fat on your plump little bodies, we simply walk away.

And you never give us a second thought, but we, like fat, are always there watching, hungry and ready to eat you.

AUTHOR OF THE ENGLISH BETTIE
PRIVATE EYE SERIES

CONNOR WHITELEY

THEFT OF INDEPENDENCE

SCOTTISH INDEPENDENCE DETECTIVE MYSTERY SHORT STORY

THEFT OF INDEPENDENCE

Detective Amy Sawkins loved everything about the wonderful night, there was such a sense of magic, freedom and utter celebration in the air as all of Scotland celebrated their freedom.

Amy loved that Scotland, after centuries of slavery to England, was now free. It was amazing that decades of fighting peacefully, demanding freedom and standing up for the rights of Scottish people had finally given them their freedom.

Amy might not have been born in Scotland (she was born in awful England to her horror) but after living here for two decades and hating UK politics and how they abused Scotland so badly, she was extremely glad to be living in a free country.

Even now she had no idea why she moved to Scotland in the first place, she was perfectly okay in London, but she never wanted to be okay, she wanted to thrive, be happy and be loved. And that was why Scotland was her home, and she wouldn't have it any other way.

The smell of gunpowder shattered Amy's celebration focus as she snapped back into the crime scene where she was, she didn't want to be investigating a crime on this night. She wanted to be in the streets with her family, friends and boyfriend celebrating Scotland's achievement.

But oh no, because some idiot had decided to break into a government building, Amy was stuck with some crime scene techs whilst the rest of the country partied like their lives depended on it.

Amy was not impressed.

As she looked around the smooth marble walls of the little box room she was in, Amy hated the cold of the wind blowing in through the shattered window, and the crime scene techs took photos, dusted for prints and gathered whatever evidence they could.

Hints of horrible gunpowder, bitter coffee and even some fruit cake assaulted Amy's senses as she stared at the remains of a wooden desk that once stood there, she wasn't sure the purpose of the building, let alone what was housed in the office.

But Amy's eyes narrowed on a wall safe that was wide open and had clearly been emptied out. The massive black marks on the safe's door told Amy everything she needed to know, and it just sickened her.

Someone had taken advantage of the nation's freedom, partying and celebrating to attack this place and steal from the Scottish Government. If the crime had taken place any other time, Amy wouldn't have been impressed.

Yet it happened today of all days so she was fuming. It was disgusting anyone would dare attack the Scottish Government today, to Amy this wasn't just an attack on her Government, this was an attack on her people (or at least her adoptive people).

When Amy heard the crime scene techs stop their clicking, dusting and collecting, she looked at them and stood up perfectly straight as a man in a long black suit, shoes and a horrible blue tie walked in.

Amy had a good guess who he was, from everything she had seen about the senior positions in the Scottish Government, Amy could have sworn this was the Deputy First Minister (or deputy Prime Minister as he was now known). Even just that change in title made Amy smile and get excited, after decades of wanting freedom she was actually going to get it.

When the Deputy Prime Minister stopped and stared at Amy, she wasn't sure what to do exactly. The highest ranking person she had had the pleasure of seeing was the head of the police force, not a government person, so she had no idea what the protocol was here. Did she bow?

"Detective Sawkins?" he asked.

Amy waved her head at the crime scene techs to continue and she nodded. "Yes,"

"How goes the investigation?"

Amy was about to tell him she had only just arrived but the question that begged for her attention was why was the most powerful man in Scotland here?

"I thought you would be off celebrating Deputy Prime Minister," Amy said.

He smiled and gestured towards the broken safe. "Our freedom is useless unless we can keep it,"

Amy's eyes narrowed on him. That made no sense at all, Scotland was only a country of two, maybe three million people and despite the voting age being lowered to 16 years old, all the votes had been counted, validated and sent to London before early evening.

The vote was over, Scotland was free. What could go wrong?

"I'm sorry Sir but I don't understand," Amy said.

"Inside that safe were the original validation documents signed by the Counters, me and the First… Prime Minister of Scotland,"

Amy shrugged.

"We sent copies to London but they weren't happy. In a few hours the UK prime Minister is coming here personally to double check the results and if those documents aren't there then he will nullify the vote,"

Amy laughed, more out of shock than anything else. "What? He can't do that. The vote was fair, democratic and it wasn't rigged,"

The Deputy Prime Minister took a step closer to Amy's ear. "I don't care that you aren't Scottish by blood. But you must know our history. From the Old Alliance with France to Scots trying to build an empire during the Colony times to much more recent political acts. Whenever Scotland tries to do much better than the English, the English damage us,"

Amy nodded. She had studied Scottish History at university and it was twisted, awful and beyond understanding, and he was right, whenever Scotland tried to do well for itself the English would create some law, send some order or do something else to stop them.

Amy was never going to allow the UK government to do that this time. She had to find those validation documents.

***

Half an hour later, Amy leant against the cold white window in her office as she watched the massive street parties in Edinburgh. People were jammed packed in the high street, dancing, singing and celebrating life. Then even Amy's favourite attraction, Edinburgh Castle, was firing firework after firework in a stunning array of colours.

Amy couldn't fail her people.

Amy forced herself away from the window and sat at her massive oak table and looked at her computer. She clicked on the rushed lab results from the break-in and she was hardly impressed.

She wanted the criminal to make some kind of mistake, something that would allow her to save Scotland and go to the party she had wanted to go to quickly.

That clearly wasn't going to happen.

The results showed a few partial prints, some black fibres from the safe and some drops of blood on the shattered glass. To normal people that might have sounded like a lot of evidence to go on, but Amy had been doing this far too long now to know better than to get her hopes up.

According to the lab reports, the blood belonged to a white man and that was it. Unless Amy could find someone to compare the blood to it was as good as a paper coat in a storm, and as for the black fibres they were just your standard black tracksuit.

But something that Amy couldn't understand was why the criminal would want the validation papers? That knowledge was specialised at best, she was well educated and studied election law for a term at university, but she still didn't know that validation documents were important.

She certainly didn't know the UK Government would claim an election was invalid and nullify it.

Amy stood up and paced around her office for a while as she wondered who would know about the documents. It had to be someone within the government or someone working for the UK Government. Just the idea of that was disgusting, the vote was 80% in favour of independence so the idea someone from the minority would want to stop a democratic process was awful.

It was one of the reasons why she voted to leave, she didn't want to be ruled by a government Scotland didn't have the power to elect, but she knew some people preferred this fake democracy.

"Hello," a man said from Amy's door.

When Amy looked up at him, she instantly smiled as she stared at the beautiful smooth face and fit body of her stunning boyfriend Peter. She loved how his tight jeans and blue shirt left little to the imagination, she was definitely lucky in having him to herself.

And it was useful he was a detective too.

"Thought you were partying with our friends?" Amy asked.

Peter walked in and kissed her. "I couldn't leave you alone tonight. A crime scene tech filled me in and asked me to make you check your emails,"

Amy's eyebrows rose and she clicked on her emails to see a brand-new one with an attachment from an officer that she knew worked with the techs a fair bit.

"Look at this," Amy said as she opened the video clip in the email.

As Amy played it, she couldn't believe it as she saw two men dressed in black kick in the reinforced glass window and break into the safe. At first she couldn't believe it, because how would two men be able to shatter a reinforced window with just their kicks?

Then Peter pointed to the types of boots they were wearing. "Steel toe-cap. I recognise the brand from what my brother worn back in the day,"

Amy frowned as Peter gently pushed her aside and started searching for more security footage on her computer.

But it was all still bothering Amy how the criminals knew about the validation documents, she was convinced that was the key and as Amy replayed the footage mentally she realised the criminals didn't double check if they had the right address. They knew exactly when to kick, attack and extract the documents from.

This was a professional job.

Somewhere in the back of Amy's mind she started to think about MI5 starting to interfere and wanting to destroy the legitimacy of the election, it was possible. But unlikely, surely?

"Here," Peter said, as he played a new piece of footage.

As he played the new footage for her, Amy focused on the images of the two men in their black tracksuits walking away from the street parties and towards a rather old stone house in Edinburgh.

It was definitely in the more expensive areas of the City and for some reason Amy just doubted these two criminals had enough money to buy a house in the neighbourhood, which only confirmed what Amy feared most.

That someone from the government was behind this.

"Who lives there?" Amy asked.

Peter did a quick search and frowned. "The Deputy Prime Minister,"

Amy felt her stomach flip, tense and churn as everything she feared was coming true.

But Amy had to stop the plan, recover the documents and made sure Scotland stayed free.

No matter the cost.

***

Thankfully it didn't take long for Amy and Peter to get to the house and the Deputy Prime Minister had led them into his office. Amy hated its cold brown wooden walls and desk but at least he had a plentiful supply of fine Scottish Whiskey in his cabinets.

Amy was a little surprised he was still in his black business suit, shoes and blue tie but he leant against his desk and smiled at them both.

Amy frowned. "We have video footage of two criminals who broke into the safe coming here. Where are the documents?"

His eyes widened. "I don't have them,"

Amy shot forward. "Don't lie to me! We have fought too hard for this to happen! Where are the documents!"

The Deputy Prime Minister smiled a little. "Please call me Ian and maybe you are more Scottish than me after all, but I promise you I didn't do this,"

Peter started to look around the office, and Amy's eyes kept narrowing on Ian, but she wasn't convinced. It wouldn't be the first time a Scottish Politician had tried to stop independence for their own strange delusions for so-called Great Britain.

"Detective Sawkins," Peter said as he held up documents and when Amy took them and started reading. She was shocked to find these were the validation documents.

"Deputy Prime Minister I am arresting you for theft of government property, treason and espionage against the People of Scotland-" Amy said.

But as she continued to read Ian his rights, he kept protesting his innocence and how he was being framed for the crime, and as Peter cuffed him, she just stopped.

It made no sense really. It made no sense to Amy why Ian would come to the crime scene, tell her about the importance of the case and then leave the documents in such an easy place to find.

Over the years Amy had heard plenty of times how the anti-independence folks had wanted to kill, steal and fight their way to remain part of the United Kingdom, so was it really that far to think they would frame a leading politician for theft?

And Amy remembered seeing Ian in all the different news reports, campaigns and everything leading up to the election, Ian and the First Minister were the two most famous people in the UK at this point. Amy couldn't believe he was hiding all this love for the UK by acting like someone who respectfully hated it.

Something else had to be going on.

"Stop," Amy said as Peter started to lead him out of the office. "Ian who else was here tonight?"

Peter frowned. "What you doing?"

"Protecting the people I serve," Amy said with a grin. "Ian the question?"

"No one else really. A friend popped round earlier. A fellow Politician," Ian said with a deepening frown. "And he wanted me to check my cellar for premium whiskey, I left the office for five minutes,"

Amy just shook her head at all of this. She was fuming, furious and rageful that some politician dared to defy the will of the Scottish people, and for what? His own ambitions, greed or delusions?

"I need a name," Amy said coldly.

As Peter undid the handcuffs and released Ian, he shrugged. "I only know him by his role in the Scottish Parliament,"

Amy's smile deepened. "That's all I need,"

"The Presiding Officer," Ian said.

Amy's blood went cold. That was one of the most important roles in the entire parliament, in the UK parliament and USA Congress people would call him the Speaker of the House, but this was awful that he would abuse his position to such an extreme degree.

Ian's phone went, he looked at it and his face went white.

"What it is?" Amy asked.

"You have to go now! The UK Prime Minister is at the Scottish Parliament,"

Amy and Peter just looked at each other. They had to solve this now. They had to hurry or everything would end before it began.

"Delay him as long as you can!" Amy shouted to Ian as they all ran out the door.

***

Amy sat in a cold silver interrogation room as she stared at the

Presiding Officer, it sickened her that such an important person in Scottish politics would dare to commit such a crime.

To Amy this still wasn't just some typical theft, it was a crime against her, her people and the kingdom of Scotland. This was the worse criminal act she had ever seen, and this criminal mastermind had to pay!

"Why do it?" Amy asked.

As Amy stared at the man called the presiding Officer, she wanted to spit at his smooth handsome face and strip him of his official posh clothing. It was a disgrace that he was still wearing the clothes of his office. The office he disgraced.

He wasn't speaking.

Amy checked his name on the file in front of her. "Presiding Officer Andrew McKinnon, why do it?"

He grinned at her. "I know the Prime Minister is here. All I have to do is stay quiet and in the end the UK government will nullify the vote. I have won,"

Amy didn't want to believe what she was hearing. "That will not happen. The people will never allow it,"

"Really? What if rumours circulated about the First Minister faking the results?"

Amy just shook her head. Scottish people weren't stupid, they would easily see through any deception, she hoped.

"Why don't I ask the two men you hired to tell me what happened?" Amy asked coldly.

"You don't have them. I had them send me a picture when they were on the train to London,"

Amy smiled and clicked her fingers. She never needed a confession, she just needed something to give her bosses, her people and the English to show criminals were behind it.

She was about to get up when her phone buzzed. Amy checked it and it was a text from Peter saying they needed more.

"Why would you send them to London?"

"I never sent them anywhere," Mr McKinnon said with an edge

of fear in his voice.

"Why do it at all? You're a politician, you worked hard to get to your position, why..." Amy said.

But that was the key, he was a politician first and foremost, and as she lived in England for over twenty years, and served as a cop in London, she learnt a lot about the corruption of UK politics.

Amy almost didn't want to think about it, but it was perfectly reasonable to imagine the UK's bad habit slipping into Scottish politics, so someone had to pay, bride or even offer Mr McKinnon something.

"If I order my people to check your finances, what will they find?" Amy asked.

Mr McKinnon shook a little. "I am innocent. The UK would never allow me to be put on trial,"

Amy could only smile at that. "You are not innocent. And the UK government has no jurisdiction here anymore. You are going to be trialled here and be the first person to be done by the Kingdom of Scotland,"

Mr McKinnon's breathing increased.

"If you confess now, I will help-"

The door opened, Peter and black masked men walked into the interrogation room. They grabbed Mr McKinnon and took him out the room.

"Stop!" Amy shouted.

Peter grabbed her and hugged her as tight as he could. "Don't Amy. Orders come from the Prime Minister herself, Mr McKinnon will be given over to the UK government in exchange for a better divorce deal,"

Amy wanted to lash out, shout and scream at the world for this idiot and everything he had almost cost her, but she couldn't. Because if the UK government was truly behind this and she had caught them, then Scotland's freedom was guaranteed.

The UK didn't need any more scandal already so Amy knew England would release Scotland easily enough with good terms and minimal hate.

And that was fine by her.

She had won hers, her people and her country's freedom in the nick of time.

And how many people could say that.

***

As she took off her clothes and pulled the wonderfully soft bedding over herself and her stunning boyfriend, Amy felt the Scottish flags that someone had painted on her at the street party and she really couldn't be bothered to take them off.

Amy listened to the final few fireworks, the last remnants of the party crowd staggering home and the laughing die down as everyone realised it was five o'clock in the morning, and they needed to head back.

But Amy was proud of herself and her stunning sexy boyfriend, and everything felt right about the world. They had had an amazing night of partying, drinking and food with each other, their families and friends, and for the first time in her life, Amy felt like everything was going to get better.

Because of her and her boyfriend, Scotland was now free to do whatever it wanted. She knew it wouldn't be easy sailing, there would be more political battles for the government to fight and they'll be ups and downs.

But that didn't matter to Amy.

Because finally Amy and every other Scot in the Kingdom had a chance to decide what they wanted to do, instead of someone they never elected deciding for them.

And that made Amy really excited about the future, but until then she would do what she always did. She would protect, serve and love her boyfriend, her family and her adoptive people.

Because when she lived in such a great place like Scotland, why wouldn't she?

AUTHOR OF ACCLAIMED AGENTS OF
THE EMPEROR SERIES
CONNOR WHITELEY

ALIEN IN THE HOT TUB
A SCIENCE FICTION NEAR FUTURE SHORT STORY

ALIEN IN THE HOT TUB

Cameron Jack was standing right next to his wonderfully large, high-end, plastic hot tub. He knew this was the best purchase he had ever made, he really loved the large white seats that rested below the waterline, all the jets that blew water in just the right places and this amazing hot tub had all the latest and coolest features.

It was simply brilliant.

Cameron was more than glad the soft warm sun was still shining its fiery orange rays onto the large wooden decking where the hot tub sat to one side.

The BBQ, firepit and rattan chairs were all wrapped up for tonight under their own plastic cover. Cameron didn't want them exposed to the elements, as his father used to say that was how things got broken, rotten and just got ruined over time.

And that actually wasn't bad advice since the winter months were approaching so this was probably going to be the very last time this year that Cameron was going to be using the hot tub with his sexy boyfriend.

Cameron was so looking forward to when his boyfriend, Dylan, got home in a few minutes because after the busyness of the week, helping twenty brand-new clients launch and promote their new starts up at the ad agency he worked at, Cameron was so excited about finally getting some downtime with the man he loved.

Cameron already had two large glasses of red wine in his hands, a blue towel was already hanging loosely around his waist and he just wanted his boyfriend home even faster.

He had to admit that Dylan was definitely the best boyfriend he had ever had. They had been dating for five years, Cameron had loved every second of it and they had laughed a lot, cried a lot and just treasured each other's company a lot more than he ever thought possible.

Cameron heard a car pull in the driveway. It had to be sexy Dylan.

He had to admit that he had been questioning their relationship a little. Cameron knew they both loved each other more than anything else in the entire world, they were both going to be together forever and they going to have a great life together.

But Cameron knew that Dylan wanted marriage and Cameron wasn't sure if he did.

He loved Dylan but marriage was such a strange concept for him. The very idea of being with Dylan forever was a brilliant and wonderful idea, but scary as hell too.

Cameron just shook his head. He knew he had to figure out what he wanted and tell Dylan the result one day in case Dylan ever asked him and Cameron said no at the idea of marriage, and not at the idea of him.

It was a messy idea and Cameron just forced himself to forget about it. He loved Dylan and that was all that mattered for now and hopefully forever.

Cameron heard the front door open.

"Hi babe," Dylan said as Cameron felt a gentle hand touch the towel and it just happened to fall to the ground and he smiled at Dylan as he wrapped his strong, muscular arms around him, kissing his neck softly.

Cameron turned around, passed his very hot, naked and stunning boyfriend a glass of red wine. And Cameron was really excited about this now, especially as he just stared at Dylan's amazing six pack and wonderful biceps.

Dylan gently hugged Cameron and Cameron allowed his

boyfriend to take him over to the hot tub. Cameron had already put the heater on earlier so it would be a wonderful 32-degree Celsius, the perfect temperature for a passionate night of love-making and catching up on the past week.

Cameron lifted up one leg about to get into the hot tub.

"Don't you dare get inside. I don't want your sweaty balls near me," the hot tub said.

Cameron just looked at Dylan. "Did the hot tub just talk?"

"Don't be stupid human," the hot tub said. "A hot tub cannot talk, but I can,"

Cameron protectively placed his body between Dylan and the hot tub in case they were going to be attacked or something.

Cameron had no idea what was going on but he had no clue why the hot tub thought he had sweaty balls. Sure he had just spent two hours at the gym and done a great workout and hadn't showered yet because he was going to need a shower after the hot tub anyway, so why waste more water?

But he didn't know why the hot tub was being so rude about it.

He looked at the hot tub and he couldn't see anything out of place.

The hot tub was perfectly clean, the water was clear as day and the gentle humming of the water pump and filters were exactly like normal. There was nothing strange about the situation except the noise.

"I'm in the water dumbass," the hot tub said.

Cameron looked a little closer and noticed there was something in the water. It was a large, clear thing but every so often the sunlight just hit it at a perfect angle allowing Cameron to see there was something in the water.

An alien.

"What are you?" Dylan asked.

Cameron was amazed he was so calm given the situation and that there was clearly a damn alien in the hot tub, interrupting their hot sexy night together.

"My name does not translation in your primitive language," the alien said. "But I am a so-called *alien* according to your deeply offensive tongue, from a water world millions of years away,"

Cameron nodded. Of course he couldn't have a nice local alien turn up that could and would bugger off home quickly enough.

"And I'm heading to a music festival another ten years away before it shuts but my coffin broken down," the alien said.

Cameron couldn't believe that. Why would damn aliens travel in coffins?

"Oh no sorry bad translation," the alien said. "My coffee machine broke down on my ship and that means that my ship cannot function. We use coffee as fuel in my culture and it will take the machine a while to repair itself,"

Cameron shook his head. "Then why on Earth did you decide to crash our hot tub evening?"

"Hot tub?" the alien asked. "I thought this was your bed. This is what my bed chamber looks like so I was going to catch a few years of sleep,"

Dylan coughed. "You cannot be here for a few years,"

Cameron completely agreed. Even if the alien seemed nice enough, he didn't want the hot tub to be out of action for years. The chorine, PH levels and the filters needed to be changed at some point or another.

"I can do what I want," the alien said. "My alien race killed all our land folk two thousand years ago so I can do the same here if I wish but I want the music festival,"

Cameron bit his lip. He wanted to get rid of the alien so he could get back to catching up with the man he loved before moving on to more adult things in the hot tub, but he just had no idea how to get rid of the alien.

"Bang goes our idea of flushing you out," Dylan said smiling.

"Funny," the alien said.

Cameron had no idea what the alien thought was so funny about that. Clearly the alien had capable of killing land people as much as defending itself underwater, so Cameron supposed there was a risk of if they flushed it away then the alien might spread into another water source and multiple.

Then become a threat to humanity.

He had no idea but he would rather not test it out.

"What about boiling you away?" Cameron asked going over to the temperature controls.

Boiling hot water splashed over the controls. Cameron shot back his hand.

"I can do this all day," the alien said. "I am going to sleep now,"

Cameron shook his head and hugged the wonderful man he loved. He loved Dylan and he knew they were unstoppable together so they simply needed to figure out how to deal with the alien together.

Cameron was half tempted to just leave the alien in peace but he had a strange sense that the alien was working on a plan.

"If you two do anything to me I will kill you both," the alien said.

Cameron shook his head. That had made up his mind already but it was clear that the alien needed water to survive. The problem was Cameron didn't know how to drain the water without the alien simply flowing away with it.

The alien didn't seem to be anything short of resourceful.

"How about we simply boil him alive?" Dylan asked, "with the kettle."

Cameron shook his head. "I doubt that would work if he could create boiling water from nothing,"

"He's right you know," the alien said.

Cameron threw his wine at the alien. The alien hissed and he watched the alien boil the wine away so there wasn't even a hint of red wine left in the water.

And that got Cameron wondering why the alien didn't like the wine. Was it because it was alcoholic? Because it was human made? Because it was an impurity?

Cameron looked at beautiful Dylan and Dylan had the same delightful twinkle in his eyes now as the day they had both met at university.

They had some experiments to run and for a change Cameron didn't have to run experiments for horrible clients to see which ad converted better.

Cameron watched Dylan's great ass as he went to get more wine then Cameron went over to the small black plastic container behind the hot tub where he kept the hot tub chemicals.

Cameron got out a small white testing strip and dipped it into the water. The alien hissed a little and Cameron noticed that everything in the hot tub was perfect.

Too perfect.

The chlorine levels were perfect, the PH was perfect and the same went for all the other measures. Cameron knew that the alien required perfect water to be alive and live peacefully.

"Wine testing," Dylan said in the same sexy voice that Cameron imagined him using on clients and lab tests at the university.

Dylan threw the bottle of wine into the hot tub and the alien just hissed as he boiled away the wine like it was nothing.

"Is that all you got?" the alien asked.

"If you just leave then we wouldn't mind?" Cameron asked. "Did you want a nice bucket or tub of water? I'll be happy to get you one if you simply get out of my hot tub,"

The alien splashed the water about so Cameron took that as a firm no.

Cameron looked at the wonderful man he loved. "Right one bottle isn't enough. Do we still have the horrible bottles of wine your mum got us?"

Dylan laughed. "Those bottles aren't horrible. They are just an acquired taste,"

"Are you ever going to drink them?" Cameron asked knowing the answer full well.

"No," Dylan said grinning like a child.

Cameron smiled as he went past Dylan, went into the kitchen and grabbed the case of wine Dylan's mother had sadly given them for Christmas last year.

But when Cameron went back out onto the decking Dylan wasn't there. He wasn't on the decking, below in the garden or anything.

Cameron went over to the hot tub and saw Dylan screaming out for air.

Cameron ripped off the corks.

He threw the bottles into the hot tub.

He threw all of them inside.

The alien didn't care.

Dylan screamed.

He couldn't breathe.

Cameron rushed over to the hot tub chemicals.

He ripped open the containers.

He poured them all in.

All the chlorine.

All the acids he had.

All the defoamer.

He didn't stop until there were no more chemicals to add.

The alien still wasn't doing anything.

Cameron leapt into the hot tub.

And as soon as Cameron's balls touched the water the alien screamed out in agony and Cameron allowed himself to sink further into the water.

Once Cameron's armpits went below the water the alien released Dylan. Throwing Dylan out of the hot tub.

The alien tried to kick Cameron out of it too but Cameron gripped onto the alien.

The alien felt soft and gel-like and the entire hot tub vibrated in sheer terror.

Cameron forced the alien towards his armpits and as soon as the alien touched them the alien exploded.

Massive amounts of candyfloss filled the hot tub and all the vibrations, screams and fear in the water just stopped.

And Cameron realised that the alien was dead, defeated and he could finally continue with his wonderful, magical night with the man he loved.

***

The next evening, Cameron completely understood why Dylan hadn't wanted to go in the hot tub after the whole alien thing so they had spent the rest of last night just emptying, cleaning and sterilising the hot tub. All the candyfloss was burnt with a roaring, crackling fire and Cameron just held the man he loved tighter than ever before.

Even tonight as Cameron just allowed the warm water of the hot tub to take all of his weight as he sat on the large white chairs, he couldn't believe how lucky they had both been. The alien was clearly weird, stupid and deadly allergic to human sweat but they were both alive and together.

And that was all that mattered to Cameron.

As he just held Dylan's fit, stunning, muscular body in his arms, Cameron rested his head on Dylan's and he honestly had no idea what he would have done if the alien had killed Dylan. His boyfriend was his home, his love and his entire world.

He couldn't function without Dylan so Cameron knew their love would last forever, because it had been tested in a way that most couples would never get tested, and they had survived.

That was all the sign that Cameron needed to know that they were destined to be together until death did them part and Cameron was really looking forward to when he could afford an engagement ring.

Because he was finally going to ask the man he loved to marry him. Something he certainly should have done ages ago and all it had taken was an alien in the hot tub to give him the courage to ask that most important question that he absolutely knew Dylan would say yes to.

And then Cameron knew they could and would live happily

forever, and that was an amazing feeling to have, know and treasure.

AUTHOR OF ACCLAIMED AGENTS OF THE EMPEROR SERIES
CONNOR WHITELEY
REMOVING THE LABEL
A SCIENCE FICTION NEAR FUTURE SHORT STORY

REMOVING THE LABEL
15th December 2090
London, England

Psychologist Emilia Griffins had never ever expected to hear from her wonderful brother Luke so soon after him and his even better boyfriend Richard had decided to move in together. It wasn't like she didn't expect him to call, want to meet up and continue to enjoy their time together like they always had ever since they were teenagers. She just hadn't expected him to be this concerned, panicked and desperate to meet.

That's how Emilia knew that something was seriously wrong.

Emilia leant against the icy cold black metal railings in front of the River Thames as the grey water flowed slowly passed her. There weren't any fish, any sea creatures or much of anything actually in the water itself these days.

There had been way too much pollution a while back and that had basically killed off all life in the Thames. Emilia used to love playing, swimming and searching for sea monsters in the Thames as a child, it was annoying as hell she couldn't do that anymore.

Emilia waved at a few of the sailors that were going up and down the Thames on their brand-new high-tech sailing boats with small nuclear engines and whatnot. She was amazed at hell at all the new improvements in engines in recent decades.

Emilia looked across the river and smiled as she saw the holo-cranes and other pieces of mag-lift technology lift up huge shipping containers and place them on ships like they weighed nothing. It was amazing to watch and it was even more impressive that the workers in their little orange vests were just accepting that this was the way the world was.

To them it might have been the every day but to Emilia, it was sheer wonder and awe and amazing.

The bright sunlight dimmed a little as three immense container ships slowly zoomed through the sky towards the dockyards less than a mile away. Emilia really liked their blade-like design that made them seem so modern, fun and exciting.

She loved being alive in this brand-new age with all these advancements happening. If only her parents were still alive to see it all, her father would have loved it with him being an engineer by trade. And her mother would have come around to it eventually.

The cold air smelt of damp, petrol and rotting fish from somewhere Emilia didn't know, but after a moment the warm taste of strawberries formed on her tongue and that told her that Luke was thankfully coming towards her.

Emilia looked around and grinned when her tall, elegant brother came towards her. He was still as fit as always and he dressed wonderfully. Emilia knew she could never ever hope to match his fashion sense in his black shirt, grey blazer and expensive grey trousers but she didn't care. She looked good in her black trench coat and that was enough for her.

They both hugged each other tight and Emilia liked the smell of his new strawberry and caramel scented aftershave.

"Hi it is so good to see you," Emilia said. "How's Richard? And how's the living together working?"

Luke leant against the metal railings. "Great thanks. It's amazing but that isn't why I called,"

Emilia leant on the railings next to him.

"You know Richard is a Member of Parliament for the Opposition,"

Emilia nodded. It was one of the reasons why she liked Richard so much. They had both bonded over their love of politics, democracy and helping to make the world a better place.

"He's Shadow Minster for Equality and last night his government counterpart issued him with a statement. The English Government intends to outlaw Transgenderism tomorrow,"

Emilia jerked. She couldn't believe that. She flat out couldn't believe that the English Government would want to return to the evil, dark, foul times of the 2040s and 2050s when so many innocent people were murdered because of laws based on lies.

It was amazing enough that Luke hadn't been killed with him being a trans man.

"Oh," Emilia said. "You could flee to Scotland since they gained independence I know they're always happy to help out refugees,"

"It's more than that though," Luke said. "If the law passes then my driving license, my passport and all my documentation is ruled as illegal. Everything I have been trying to build for myself will come to nothing,"

Emilia bit her tongue because she was so damn annoyed that the English Government would want to do this to her baby brother, and that was what he was. He was her brother, not her sister. She actually didn't know what his new legal name would be because for decades he had just been Luke to her.

Then Emilia realised that her brother had come to her for some reason.

"What can I do?" Emilia asked.

Luke smiled. "You're on the Board of The English Psychological Society?"

"Yes," Emilia said. "I oversee the Membership side of things but I have no idea how that will help trans people,"

"The DSM-10 is due to be finalised tomorrow by the Americans. You know the massive book that details out all the so-called mental disorders in the world,"

Emilia laughed. "Yes I do know what the DSM is, I wouldn't be much of a psychologist if I didn't. But the English Psychological

Society has no input in the DSM. That is something published by the Americans because England is so weak we have to follow it per English Law,"

Luke shook his head. "But the current American President of the Psychological Association is in big trouble. He's been involved in six scandals in six months and the Americans are about to vote him out,"

Emilia really didn't see how the English could help him, but she had to admit the American Psychology President was a good man, he worked hard and he truly believed in the power of psychology to help improve lives.

And Emilia had seen all of these scandals and not a single one of them was actually his fault.

"If you can persuade the English and American Psychological Presidents to sit down together, get the English to endorse the American then that will give him time to stay on as President,"

Emilia nodded. "In exchange for removing Gender Dysphoria as a mental health condition, because I agree. It isn't a mental condition and being transgender doesn't mean you're messed up or have a problem,"

Emilia loved seeing Luke smile.

"Are you going to help me sis?" Luke asked.

Emilia wasn't sure but she knew the English President Collin was retiring next year and nominations were already opening up. A massive win like this would help her get voted in as President and Emilia would hardly have a problem with that.

And if it meant saving her brother then it was something she just had to do. Because if she failed then from tomorrow her brother would no longer have a valid driving license, passport and everything attached to his name would be invalid. Including his mortgage, his livelihood and everything he cared about.

Emilia couldn't allow that to happen under any circumstances.

***

After double-checking the Government's so-called rationale

behind such a stupid law, Emilia was rather surprised that out of all the time the Government actually wanted to listen to psychologists, it was only when it suited them and their twisted ideas. Emilia had completely failed to get the government to listen to her when she wanted to improve mental health services for children, the Government hadn't listened when she wanted more funding for dementia services. And the government really hadn't listened when Emilia wanted new laws for psychologists to better support mentally incapable people.

The government didn't listen to psychologists then.

But the moment a single psychologist stupidly said being trans made a person have a fucked up mind, the government was all over the psychologists.

It just made Emilia smile as she waited around the large black front door of her boss and good friend Collin. His little terraced house in the heart of London wasn't exactly anything too grand but given the state of England that wasn't too surprising.

Emilia knocked on the door three times and really wanted Collin to hurry up and open the damn door.

The long, narrow street was filled with black cabs, a few failing street lamps and some groups of young people that were trying to entertain themselves in London now that all the youth clubs had been shut down. Again per the Government's new austerity measures.

Emilia really liked the damp, cold hints of jasmine, lavender and sweet vanilla that filled through Collin's door. He might have been having a party or something and not want to see her, but she didn't care. She just had to protect her brother.

A few moments later Emilia pounded on the door again and Collin answered straight away.

Emilia gave her boss a friendly hug as he was wearing a very nice black suit and the soft jazz music coming from deeper inside the house told Emilia everything she needed to know. It had to be one of Collin's poker nights with his old university friends and he would be mad to leave them too long.

Everyone knew that Collin's marriage was a sham and if he was out the room for much longer his wife would leave him. Not that Emilia planned to see her too much, Collin was a workaholic that didn't love his wife at all.

"What you want?" Collin asked smiling.

"We need to talk about the Gender Dysphoria diagnosis and you need to get the Americans to get rid of it," Emilia said a lot firmer than she intended to.

Collin rolled his eyes and Emilia didn't care if he wasn't interested. She was going to make him listen because there was a chance everyone could get what they wanted.

"I know you're playing with your uni friends," Emilia said really wanting Collin to let her in. "And I know two of your friends work for the American Psychology President,"

"Yes they do and they're proud of the work," Collin said not wanting to let Emilia inside. "And because big pharma companies are paying them millions of pounds it is even easier to get anti-depressants in the new DSM,"

Emilia shook her head and laughed. Every psychologist was perfectly aware of the rumoured corruption and stupidity behind the Americans and their DSM, but it was annoying as hell that nothing could be proven.

But Emilia knew full well that the massive American drug companies always wanted psychologists to make it easier for them to sell their products. It was why Emilia always preferred the World Health Organisation guide to mental health conditions.

It wasn't perfect but it was certainly a lot less corrupt.

"Just give me five minutes to make my case and if you guys want me gone. I will give a grand for your poker game,"

"My friends are here for a relaxing evening," Collin said not that bothered by the grand. "And if you continue to bother me I will kick you off the Board,"

"You cannot do that and we both know why," Emilia said,

"everyone else on the Board likes me and they all know you only care about getting in bed with the Americans,"

Collin smiled. "Good night Emily,"

He went to shut the door.

Emilia slammed her foot in the door.

"And everyone else on the Board knows I would take psychology in England towards the WHO and follow the European Union's example. That would take us in the progressive way and away from the Americans,"

Emilia could actually hear Collin gulp behind the door.

"Let me in or I will start campaigning for your replacement tomorrow morning," Emilia said.

Collin opened the door and he smiled at her with the same disgusting, fake grin that she had only ever seen given to government Ministers that wanted to bend Collin over backwards. The spineless loser would let them.

Emilia followed him down a narrow bright white hallway towards the back of the house where a very modern kitchen was. She really liked its bright metallic blue cabinets, walls and black splashback.

And the golden kitchen island became a real focal point where Collin's wife was flirting with the youngest of the five men in black suits around the table. Emilia had to admit the men were hot as hell and she couldn't blame Collin's wife, but she was here for only her brother.

"Gentleman," Collin said frowning, "this is my friend and fellow Board Member Emilia Griffins,"

"Doctor Emilia," she said. "We are all equals here,"

"A pleasure to meet you," Collin's wife said. "What's your specialisation?"

"Clinical psychology," Emilia said, "focusing on the mental health of children and adolescents,"

"Ah that is brilliant," the youngest of the men said. "Now there is a population we can get our friends at Big Pharma to target. If we can get the teenagers hooked on anti-depressants at their age then we'll be hooked for life,"

Emilia shook her head as her stomach twisted into a painful knot. As much as she wanted to debate how unethical it was to have Big Pharma involved in the creation of the DSM, Emilia really wanted to press on with more important things.

Like saving her brother.

"Does the DSM being finalised as we speak still include Gender Dysphoria?" Emilia asked.

Everyone went silent.

"Yeah, of course," Collin said. "It's stupid not to include it as a mental disorder,"

Emilia laughed. Collin really wasn't the nice, wonderful boss she remembered talking to only yesterday. And considering that modern clinical psychology didn't use the term "disorder" anymore because of how judgemental and blaming it was, Emilia was actually surprised Collin would have such a slip.

"You do realise that being transgender is just a part of you and it doesn't mean you're messed up, deranged or anything?" Emilia asked wanting to start off nicely.

Collin laughed. "Yeah right,"

"And the definition of a mental health condition is that it causes a person clinically significant levels of distress and impaired functioning," Emilia said. "Please explain how being trans causes that,"

Everyone just looked at her and Emilia sort of supposed she deserved that so she paced round the kitchen island as she spoke.

"Being trans itself only causes so much discomfort. A person feels and understands that they're a different gender. I accept that causes distress," Emilia said.

"Exactly so they're messed up," one man said but Emilia didn't see who.

"Negative," Emilia said. "It means they need gender-affirming care and shortly. It is actually how complex and dragged out the affirming care is, that causes the distress,"

"And the transphobia a person experiences," the oldest man in the room said with a slightly balding head. "I have worked with more than enough youth in my time to understand your point Emilia,"

Emilia nodded her thanks and she was so relieved she might have a potential ally after all.

"Also as psychologists we have to understand that mental health conditions are elements of our time. Just think about the labelling of homosexuality as a mental health condition that was thankfully dropped. That was only a disorder because of the religious and societal beliefs at the time,"

Emilia loved it that a few people nodded but Collin laughed to himself.

"Then you are in for a hell of a surprise when the new DSM's released,"

Emilia rolled her eyes and she damn wished she had remembered to check the international news lately. She had read the news last week and noted how the US was preparing to outlaw homosexuality yet again because of their idiot far-right President.

"But she is right," the man with the blading head said. "My name is Professor Roman,"

"Good to meet you Professor," Emilia said bowing slightly.

"Doctor Emilia's point is clear. There are some disorders, sorry conditions that are created by the society in which a person lives in. It is my belief that Gender Dysphoria is one such care,"

"You aren't even American," another man said. "Your opinion doesn't matter and come on, it ain't normal to think you're a man when you're not,"

"Tell me," Emilia said, "is it normal to elect a US President that publicly said that the sky was green?"

Emilia was so glad that shut that idiot up.

"Also to counter another point," Emilia said, "you might try to defend Gender Dysphoria as a disorder so trans people can get access to affirmative care. But we all know self-referral is most common these days,"

"What's your point and then get out?" Collin said firmly.

"We have to remove the label of Gender Dysphoria because we, as psychologists know that labels cause stigma, they cause pain and they cause suffering. And the English Government's horrific bill is being supported by our falsework tomorrow,"

Collin shook his head. "We are not in control of what the government does and how it abuses psychology guidance. Now please leave,"

Emilia shook her head and she was about to leave when the Professor placed a gentle hand on her arm.

"The Doctor is right and if you will not give her the respect she deserves then I would like to reveal my purposes here tonight,"

Emilia looked at Collin and she could have sworn he was about to swear. Something he never ever did.

"I am an Internal Investigator appointed by the English Psychological Society on behalf of the Membership to investigate the leadership of Collin," Roman said.

Emilia had only heard of such a person. She knew that over half the membership had to vote in secret to appoint one but she had no idea that a vote was happening. Which she sort of knew was the point of it and she was a Board Member after all.

"And by the powers invested in me by the membership and the Articles of the Society," Roman said. "I am suggesting a vote of No Confidence in Collin and I am recommending the Members take Emilia as the new President,"

"Shit," Collin said.

Emilia was about to argue against it. She didn't want to be in power so quickly but as the three other English men at the table stood up and nodded at Roman, Emilia realised she actually recognised them.

They were also members of the Board, Emilia just didn't recognise them without their weird black robes on and massive beards.

"We support this motion," the three men said.

Emilia looked at Collin. "I know I have the power to stop this so you have a choice. Agree to pressure the Americans before tomorrow or the five of us will take the motion to the Membership and I will be President by tomorrow morning,"

Collin laughed. "Go fuck yourself and your trannie *sister*,"

Emilia just grinned because the joke was on him and she was more than excited about becoming President of the English Psychological Society.

She only hoped she could save her brother in time.

***

The next 24 hours were a complete and utter blur to Emilia, even she didn't expect that not a single English psychologist wanted to challenge her leadership so by midnight that night she was President.

Emilia hadn't even wasted any time with sleep because she had phoned the Head of The EU Psychological Society and requested immediate Acceptance which was a hell of a job given how England wasn't part of the EU.

Emilia had argued and argued for six straight hours with them for membership, because if England was a member then psychologists would have to use the EU guide for mental health conditions.

And that didn't include Gender Dysphoria and a whole host of other mental health conditions that the Americans had simply made up to make sure their shares in Big Pharma increased.

After Emilia had managed to get England an emergency acceptance that was still pending for full membership, she instantly got the Society together for another emergency meeting. So she could get the Society to agree to condemn the Government's plan to invalidate her brother's life (and hundreds of other people's lives).

Emilia had to admit she would have liked that motion to pass by a little bit more than a mere 54% but a pass was a pass. And finally after Emilia had had a quick catnap, she had raced down to the

House of Commons to personally talk about why the law was wrong.

And the law failed in the vote an hour later.

"Thanks sis,"

Emilia sat on her wonderfully soft, cozy sofa in the middle of her apartment's living room with a massive glass of red wine as she listened to her brother on the phone. Emilia couldn't believe how happy, wonderful and amazing she felt as she just listened to the brother she loved. He was telling her about work, what exciting stuff him and Richard had been up to today and it was great to know he didn't doubt her for a second.

Emilia really did love her life and what she had managed to achieve in the past day. Collin had thankfully gone quietly and he had moved to the US and his wife had left him because *he was just nuts* according to her. Emilia didn't disagree in the slightest.

And as Emilia sat in the quiet of her living room as she said good night and love you to her brother, she just couldn't help but wonder how much good she could do as the President now. She could increase psychological support for the poor, the vulnerable and everyone else that needed it.

She could transform England for the better and make sure that everyone that needed support actually got it. Emilia didn't know if it was possible or even remotely likely to happen but she didn't care.

She now had the power to change lives, improve them and help people. And she fully intended to use it and that had only happened by removing the label of Gender dysphoria and saving the brother she loved.

If that was wrong then Emilia really didn't want to be right.

CONNOR WHITELEY

TIME TRAVELING DELIVERIES

A SCIENCE FICTION TIME TRAVEL SHORT STORY

TIME TRAVELING DELIVERIES

Before all this absolute utter nonsense with my deliveries, them apparently being delivered in the future and so much more, I honestly thought I was a perfectly normal, happy man, but now I'm seriously doubting that.

But I'm sorry, my name is Henry Lee. I'm a computer technician at a local school and I have a wonderful husband called Garry who's been working so hard lately in his big corporate job that he's been a little stressed of late.

Sounds perfectly okay, doesn't it?

Well, that quickly went to utter shit as soon as I thought I would be the perfect husband and order him some of his favourite flowers. Yea, that really made my life go from great to utterly shit.

As per normal, by 10 o'clock in the morning on one of my days off, I had already said goodbye and kissed Garry goodbye. And I was sitting at my wonderfully smooth wooden table in my conservatory with the bright boiling-hot sunshine beaming down on me.

I loved the warming sun and I loved the piping hot mug of strong bitter coffee in my hands that filled the entire room with the amazing hints of bitter coffee, hazelnuts and honey leaving a strong bitter taste form on my tongue.

The sound of birds singing, the wind gently blowing and some of my neighbours talking in their back garden made me realise how perfect this day was going, and I had a sneaky suspicious Garry was going to take me out for dinner tonight at a very fancy restaurant.

Which was just flat out perfect. He really was the same amazing man that I married all those years ago.

Originally I was fully intending to do some gardening, maybe go and see some friends for a very light lunch and spend the afternoon reading. I really did love reading, especially science fiction books. There was just something about their exploration, hopefulness and action-packed nature that I loved.

But that was clearly never ever going to happen when I heard my phone buzz in my pocket. Now my phone never buzzes, it can ping, pop and sometimes my ringtone goes off.

Yet it never buzzes. So needless to say I was already rather curious about this.

I fairly quickly realised that wearing skin tight jeans with a black t-shirt and black socks definitely didn't make it easy to get my smartphone out. But I managed, just about.

As I looked at the message, I really did smile because it was an email from Time Traveling Deliveries (such a stupid name for a parcel service) saying that my delivery would be here today.

That was amazing news because I really did want to be a good husband and it would make Garry's day when he saw those flowers. (He better considering the price of them!)

And I'm actually rather glad the parcel was coming early because it would give me some time to arrange the flowers before he came home.

Then I got another email.

This one mentioned that my parcel had been delivered. That was brilliant news, so I got up, glided through my rather large house and opened the massive black door to pick up my parcel.

Now I thought that was a perfectly logical assumption. If a delivery person says your parcel has arrived, then I expect my parcel to be there.

But oh no, as I stood at my front door staring out at my long red bricked drive, I couldn't see a parcel. I couldn't see, hear or smell a delivery person either.

All I heard was the sound of the neighbour kids going round on their bikes, and I knew they wouldn't steal from me. I was good friends with most of the parents so I knew I was hardly a target for theft.

But I still didn't have a parcel.

I went out onto my drive and quickly realised it was stupid to walk on boiling hot bricks only in socks, but I quickly looked around and there was still no parcel.

Clearly the delivery person didn't put it anywhere here, I knew they couldn't have thrown it over the back so I just couldn't understand why my parcel had apparently been delivered when it hadn't.

My worse fear was that the delivery person had stolen it and just reported they had delivered it so they looked good to their company. It had only been a few months ago since I experienced that.

It was an utter nightmare trying to get my refund back.

Then I decided in case the delivery person had added a note to the email, I checked it and I noticed something I flat out couldn't understand. The email said rather clearly that my parcel had been delivered today at 12 pm.

That's two hours away.

So how the hell was my parcel meant to be delivered?

I didn't have a clue but if I wanted Garry to have a great present when he came home tonight.

I needed to find out.

And quick.

***

I really have no idea what people were meant to do in these sorts of situations so I thought I would reasonably give that stupidly name delivery company the benefit of the doubt, so I gave them until 12 pm.

I did some gardening, house cleaning and I watched a science fiction programme on the telly.

But about 12 pm, I sat back out in my wonderfully warm

conservatory watching a large group of Bluetits hopping about on the grass with another large cup of coffee. And I just knew that my parcel wasn't coming.

It might have been the way how the room didn't smell of bitter coffee, hazelnuts or honey anymore. Or it could have been the way how the world just seemed to become slower and a bit sadder, but I just knew that my parcel wasn't going to come.

But that meant I had another problem, I obviously needed to contact the flower firm who would chase up the delivery people, yet what would I say?

Hi there, I got a weird-ass email about my parcel being delivered but it was actually delivered in the future. Can I please have a refund?

No. Just no, I was so not going to be one of those crazies because I really wanted these flowers for Garry.

So I decided for a very different approach because it clearly wasn't the Flower People's flaunt that my parcel didn't come, so why should I bother them and not the people in charge of delivery?

There wasn't a reason, so I went online, found the phone number for *Time Traveling Deliveries* (really hate that name) and I called them. Of course, I was expecting to have to jump through twenty-thousand hoops but I didn't have a lot of other things to do, and I needed those flowers.

Strangely enough, my phone couldn't even ring once before the company picked up.

"Time Traveling Deliveries, I'm Lisa. How may I help you?"

I just rolled my eyes. It was typical when I needed actual help, I was basically going to be talking to a mindless corporate drone.

"My parcel was apparently delivered but it wasn't," I said.

"What time, date and era are you calling from?" she said.

What sort of fucking question was that? I just wanted to know where my parcel was! But fuck it, I decided to play along.

"It's 12:05 on the 22nd June 2022," I said.

"Thank you," Lisa said.

I was really expecting her to laugh or something, but she

honestly sounded pleased to know that like it was really important.

Believe me, I was never ordering with these people again.

"Right Henry," Lisa said, "your flowers were delivered five minutes ago in your time,"

I wasn't even going to think about how the hell she knew who I was and my order, I just wanted some actual answers.

"Lisa, I'm sorry. But I haven't got my parcel and I really need it,"

"Mr Lee, all our computers, Travellers and systems show that your parcel was delivered," Lisa said.

I was just shaking my head at this point.

"Oh," Lisa said.

"What?"

"The computer systems experienced a glitch earlier, and these are the computers that tell us where the parcels are in this exact moment in time and space,"

I didn't have a clue what she was talking about.

"I'll tell you what," Lisa said, "call me back in three of your days and I should have an update for you,"

What the fuck was going on? I just needed my parcels, and what on earth was she talking about *three of your days* for? Days are days right?

"I need my flowers today," I said.

"Three of your days Mr Lee," Lisa said as she cut the line.

I put my phone down and I was just shocked. My mother had worked in customer service for years and she never would have spoken to someone like that. And I seriously needed those flowers tonight, so there was only one option.

I had to go to the company.

I had to find my parcel myself.

No matter where it was.

I had to find it.

***

It turned out that Time Traveling Deliveries wasn't too hard to find on the internet and I was really starting to utterly hate the company.

I stood outside a massive iron gate with wire fences growing off of it like the gate was alive with the boiling hot sun beaming down from behind me and I was standing right in the middle of a large road.

"Excuse me," someone said.

I looked around to see if anyone was about, but it was only me, the road and a few rabbits that were hopping along in the field behind me.

"Look at the fence," the voice said.

Then I noticed a very small intercom system that the drivers probably used to get the parcels in for processing.

"Hello," I said, "I'm looking for a parcel and I'm not leaving until I get it."

I felt a hand grab my shoulder from behind. I jumped.

I could have sworn that I didn't hear anyone coming up behind me, and I was certainly alone a moment ago.

But when I looked around I was utterly stunned to see Garry with his massive sexy smile, stunning longish blond hair and his wonderful fit body just standing there.

Wearing something I couldn't even begin to describe. It looked like some sort of sci-fi crap that nerds wore to conventions.

"Babe?" he asked.

Then I noticed he was carrying three small parcels under his left arm and two of the shipping labels were printed onto the boxes, but one of them had an almost holographic shipping label attached.

"What the hell?" I said, failing to contain my confusion.

"Um," Garry said. Even now his voice was sexy as anything.

"Mr Lee," the intercom voice said.

Both me and Garry looked at the intercom and we both smiled.

"This is my husband," Garry said, "I think he could help us actually,"

I just gave him a sideways glance.

After a few moments the intercom voice huffed.

"Are you any good with computers?" the voice asked.

I laughed. Of course I was, I was basically the Head of IT at the school I worked at, but I felt like I needed to be a little more polite here.

"Yes. One of the best," I said.

"Do you trust him to keep our secret Gar?" the voice asked.

Garry looked and I stared for a few moments into those damn sexy eyes and Garry gave me one of his most amazing smiles.

"I do," Garry said.

"Bring him to me," the voice said.

Garry grabbed me.

The world fell silent.

The world disappeared.

***

I was seriously impressed with the massive server room that I found myself in all of a sudden. The room was probably a kilometre high, probably another three kilometres long and what really impressed me was all the black walls were perfectly smooth.

Yet I could tell that they were all computer servers with their little flashing red lights, and after doing my job for so long I could still hear their humming, vibrating and slight banging even though whoever was in charge here was using some very advance sound dampeners.

"Welcome to the Year 2050," Garry said as he wrapped his strong sexy arms around me.

I just shook my head. That was flat out impossible but it could explain why there were so many computer servers here, and why they actually looked like nothing from our time.

Normally computer servers were large bulky and looked ugly. But these servers looked as if they had been built into the walls themselves to make everything look seamless.

"Mr and Mr Lee," a woman said as her voice echoed all over the room.

I looked behind us and a very tall elegant woman in a long white dress stride towards us.

"I am sorry for your parcel," the woman said, and I instantly recognised her voice as Lisa from earlier.

"Parcel?" Garry asked.

I waved him silent. "What's going on?"

Lisa waved her hand, gesturing towards all the red flashing lights on the walls, and I noticed there were a lot more than a few seconds ago.

"Our computers glitched at your 10 am. Millions of customers throughout time and space had their parcels delivered in one time with the delivery email getting sent to another time. It was chaos," Lisa said.

I was rather interested in all this after all.

"If that was the only thing that happened I could manipulate the timeline just enough to make it look like everything was only out by a minute or two," Lisa said.

Garry shook his head. "But that wasn't the only thing,"

I pushed away from his arms and I turned to face both of them.

"What happened?" I asked.

"There is a reason," Lisa said, "we never do planned maintenance when our Travellers are out. If the computers glitch when they're traveling. Then we lose them,"

I just looked at Garry and felt my stomach twist into a painful knot.

"How many?" I asked.

Lisa frowned. "Too many. A thousand Travellers lost in time and space like they never existed,"

Now I was starting to feel bad about being so moody earlier, I didn't know this Lisa, this company and Garry sure as hell had some explaining to do. But I did want to help them.

"What do you need me to do?" I asked.

Lisa frowned even more. "You're the computer expert Garry says. Each *second* more and more computers are failing and losing our Travellers and I don't know why. I need you to fix it,"

I just shook my head and stared at all the endless number of computer servers. There had to be thousands here and transmitting so much data through time and space that the maths would be impossible to calculate (but someone clearly had).

But there were a few things I needed to understand first.

"How many *Travellers* do you have traveling at any one time?" I asked.

Lisa folded her arms. "One thousand during your lunch time. Ten thousand at any other,"

Wow! That was an extreme number.

"And all those Travelers are controlled from these exact computers?" I asked.

Lisa sort of shook her head. "These computers are fixed and time-locked. These computers regardless of where they are in time are always the same ones used by the Travelers to navigate and get the right deliveries to the right moment in time and space,"

I just nodded. A simple yes would have been great.

"I think I know what caused the glitch," I said. "I think you're using too many Travelers for the system,"

I watched Lisa and could easily see she wanted to laugh but after a few moments her frown deepened.

Garry smiled. "What do you mean?"

"Look," I said, "think about this room as a glitchy computer. It can glitch if you're running too many computer programmes at any one time, or a computer can become glitchy another way,"

"What way?" Lisa asked.

"I doubt your computer system has enough computing power, memory and everything else you would need to control this many Travelers,"

Lisa walked right by me and stared at each at the computer servers and I noticed more each and every second were showing red flashing lights.

"How many more Travelers lost since we started talking?" I asked.

"Another thousand," Lisa said, coldly. "I would have to check the maths on profit lost,"

I gently placed a hand on her shoulder. "Then pull everyone out. Reset the system. And do this right,"

I was rather surprised at the firmness of my words, but if Garry was one of these Travelers then I was not going to lose him because of this crazy woman who was clearly more concerned about profit, deliveries and cash than her own workers.

Garry stood firmly next to me and we both just looked at Lisa as she slowly turned around.

Lisa looked like she was going to protest. She would probably say it costed too much money to pull all the Travelers out.

But she slowly started nodding.

"Fine," Lisa said. "I'll pull them out,"

***

It turned out that my plan worked perfectly.

Lisa was furious and rather grumpy as she recalled all the Travelers throughout time and space, and then when everything was perfect she restarted their computer systems, and thankfully it was a hell of a lot faster than doing a restart in 2022.

But I wished I had a camera as Lisa slowly started to send more and more Travelers back out into the timestream, she hated sending them out so slowly (or slow to her), I would have loved to see all the profit and loss calculation she was running in her head.

Yet the glitch was fixed, and it really was simple as the amount of Travelers and parcels they were processing were putting too much strain on their computers, so Garry was… released from service.

And as I sat at my wonderfully warm wooden table in my hot-boiling conservatory opposite the man I loved, I could hardly complain too much.

Even as the late afternoon sun streamed through the glass windows, I just stared at Garry's handsome face, fit body and I realised that I really didn't care about his secret life with Time Traveling Deliveries. I loved, trusted and treasured him so I suppose he was allowed to keep one secret from me.

Only one though.

With the air smelling of great hints of bitter coffee, honey and hazelnuts, I knew that everything in the world was okay. Especially as I looked ever so slightly behind me to our large dining room table where a vase of large bright flowers with massive colourful leaves stood there proudly.

After all the chaos of today and the strange realisation that time travel was real, I had finally got my flowers, and thankfully Garry had loved them. (And I jolly well hope so after I saved his former company!).

So Garry looked at me, and we stared into each other's amazing eyes. I knew whatever was going to be next in the future with Garry no longer having a job, us knowing time travel was real and any other surprises this crazy world had installed for us, I knew we would be fine.

All because we had each other. And that made me feel utterly amazing.

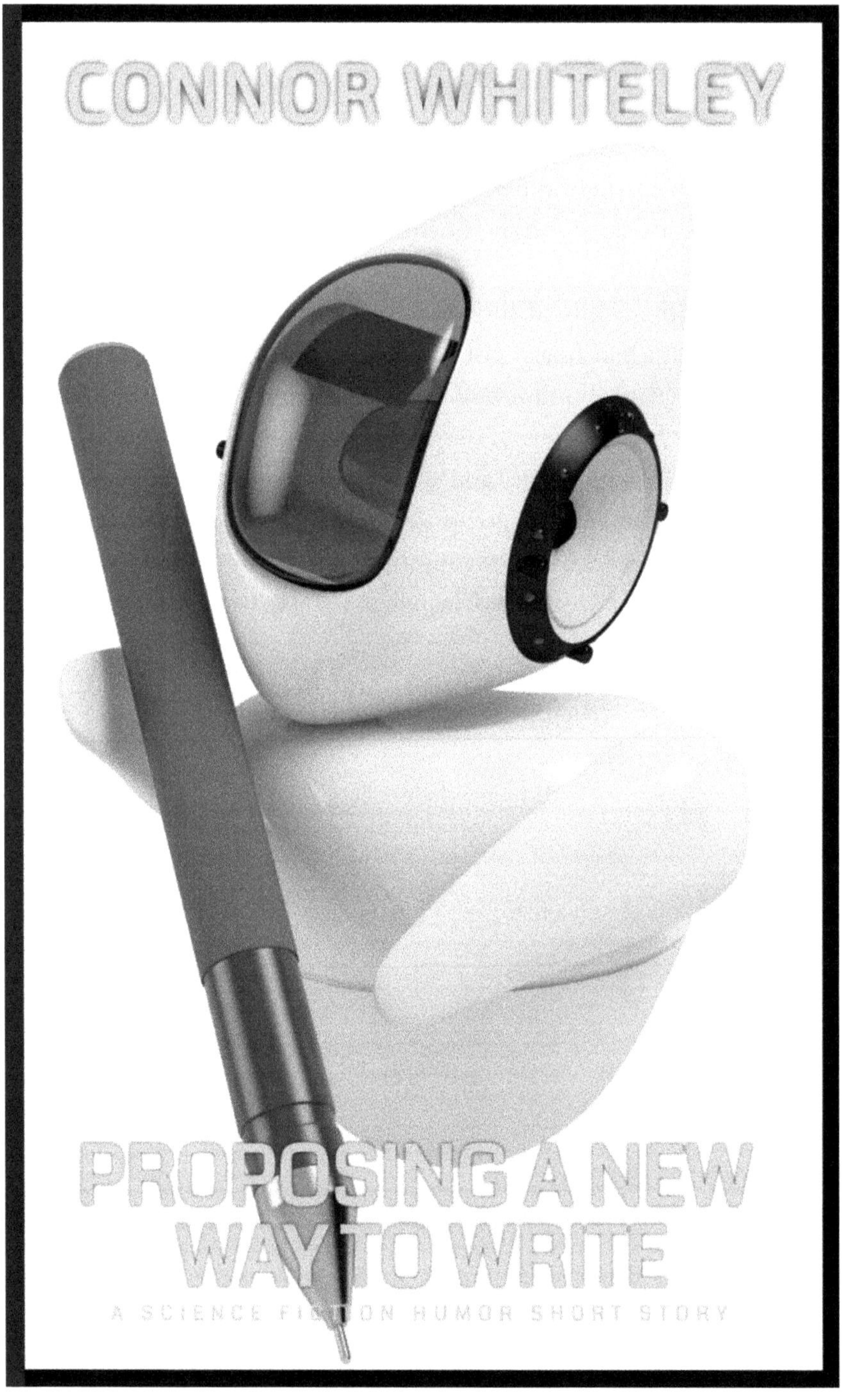
CONNOR WHITELEY
PROPOSING A NEW WAY TO WRITE
A SCIENCE FICTION HUMOR SHORT STORY

PROPOSING A NEW WAY TO WRITE

Now you have just made the best decision of your life dear student, and let me tell you I wish I had this handy little guide to writing papers when I was your age. You're probably tucked away in your bright dorm room with your little lonely bed behind you and your large wooden desk in front of you.

Believe me, that wooden desk might look friendly now but by the time you finish your degree, that desk will only get more and more terrifying.

But hey, why on earth (Ha. Or Space as you're in) should we continue to write academic papers the same way we've been doing since the stone age? Come on, it's just flat out silly so hear me out, try it out and maybe you'll get a First on your next assignment (I doubt it but this is a fun guide to writing anyhow).

<u>Your Affiliations</u>

I know, I know normally this isn't a section of a paper and it certainly isn't the first one, but that's because academics are stupid people. If you ever become an academic you will know how snobby, stuck up and just jerks they really are, so this is an idea I know will spread like wildfire.

If academics list their achievements upfront then readers will know just how amazing they are, and everyone will be wanting to read their work because they're so sensationally brilliant.

And I mean, in this first section just lie. On all my papers I say I have degrees from the best universities on Earth. I don't. I lie. My academic papers get published because I am so amazing.

You have to start doing the same if you ever want people to think you're so amazing. It's really fun too!

Discussion

This is the perfect second section of your stunning paper because your reader will be so pumped after reading all your academic achievements that they'll be on the edge of their seat wanting to read how blindingly stunning your study was.

So why in Space would you put the poor loser through such pain making them read through the entire paper? When you could just give them the discussion upfront?

It's the discussion that they want after all.

This is even more amazing when you realise that the reader hasn't read the rest of your paper and they won't. They're only going to read this section and they'll be done.

So don't waste your time making sure you can support your points with data, facts and the rest of that rubbish. Just make it all up, say that all your results were just so groundbreaking and that you've singlehandedly revolutionised your field, how the understanding of the universe has changed and that you're going to win all the awards for your research.

It does not matter if you're lying. We need to make academic writing more fun so more people read it. This is how you and me are going to change the Empire.

With one lie at a time.

Introduction

Oh dear, when I was a student I hated my introductions because they were just so hard and impossible to start. Don't worry though. If you start writing the above two sections first you'll be having so much fun writing your powerful paper, your introduction will be a breeze.

And come on mate, just forget the normal introduction stuff like real studies, real facts and any of that agonising literature searches. You're at a major university now, it's okay to make things up, leave out certain details and just make your idea for a study the best it can be.

I wanted to do a study on nuclear bombs and so much of that has already been researched, so what did I do? I simply cut out a bunch of studies, made up some and I made the grant board believe my study was ground-breaking even though it had been done a hundred times before.

That is what a really good introduction does and the grant board paid me millions of credits for the fun of it. That's how lame and stupid academics are.

Methods

It's a great shame students have such a hard time with this one but that's because they're relying too much on that rubbish science training nonsense from snobby academics that don't know how to read.

I'll let you into a little secret, no one reads the methods.

I tested this once by writing up my shopping list in the method section, I submitted it and the paper got published. So please dear student, write up the scores to the latest football game, your shopping list, your review of your most recent sexual conquest.

Just write any old shit for your method section because no idiot is ever going to read it, and if they do then they're just lame and you're the cool kid.

Result Section

I might be some old professor being forced out of the university but I ain't no pushover and the result section is the lamest part of a paper. No one reads them, no one cares about them and everyone hates them.

So let's change it.

The result section is your time to lie, shine and just make people believe that you are the most impressive researcher in The Great Human Empire. So make sure all your results are significant, perfect and just so amazing that no one could ever believe them.

But because you're you and you're so perfect and brilliant, they will believe it for sure. And hell, most of the time no one reads this section so use this as more of an attention check.

And if someone's really gotten to the end of your paper then they are the most boring, lonely and silly people imaginable. I mean do they have nothing better to do with their lives then sit about reading papers?

The losers.

Conclusion

This section is more of a cheeky little well-done to yourself because you've now written a very fun paper that is going to make you famous. You are a rock star and all those other losers in your class are going to be so, so jealous of you.

And I really hope you've learnt something special here today because I managed to publish after a hundred research articles in the top publications using this method. Then I was discovered and my career was destroyed but I bought down those snobby publications with me.

That's a win in my case so enjoy writing your paper. It's going to be epic.

CONNOR WHITELEY

GIVING A CHANCE

A SCIENCE FICTION TIME TRAVEL SHORT STORY

GIVING A CHANCE

"Just read through the forms and prepare to time travel,"

When the sweet little male nurse who I admit had an amazing ass left me and my Mum in the small clinical medical room, I had to admit I was tense as anything. My stomach was as tight as when I had come out to my Mum and even though this was different, I was still scared.

As my Mum sat in the wonderfully soft black fabric chair next to me started re-reading the paperwork and medical forms (something she had been doing obsessively twice a day for the past week), I could only focus on the actual bright white walls of the medical room.

The room was small and cosy and scary, there wasn't anything on the walls or anything. All four of them were just white sheets of nothing and that certainly didn't help make me feel any better, I would have liked there to be some focal point in the room but there wasn't.

There was only my sweet, beautiful Mum that I had wanted to give her a legendary birthday present before she died.

I wanted to give her a chance to say goodbye to her own mother.

The air was sterile with hints of cold lemon, bleach and a hint of rosemary that I didn't understand where it had come from, but all this discomfort was worth it if it meant giving my Mum a chance to say goodbye.

You see my Mum and her Mum (hence referred to as Nan) had always had a bad relationship. Nan had never wanted, cared about or even really loved Mum for honestly no fault of her own (but I guess I would say that). Mum had tried to fix the relationship time and time again so they could have the relationship mothers and daughters were meant to have, but it always failed.

I hated how upset Mum got because despite all the hate, abuse and foul family politics that happened, she really did love her Mum in the bitter end. I'm not really sure I "loved" her because she could be a real piece of work when she wanted to be but there were some good times.

Yet the problem was when Nan was dying, me and Mum raced up the hospital to say our goodbyes, say that we loved her and more.

We were only met with hate and toxicity from my aunt, uncle and grandad who hated us for apparently ruining their lives.

My Mum, sweet beautiful Mum could barely say goodbye to the mother that had caused her so much pain, agony and abuse over the nights. But my Mum being the amazing woman she was wanted to do the "right thing" and say her goodbyes.

Her sister couldn't even give her that properly. And it was so toxic in the medical room that I couldn't even say goodbye to my Nan.

So when time travel became a thing I didn't care at first, but then Mum had her 75th birthday, I wondered if she wanted to travel back before my aunt, uncle and grandad arrived at the hospital before she died. That way at least both of us could finally get to say the goodbyes we never could.

Thankfully, all the scientists, computer experts and stats people crunched the numbers and confirmed that by travelling back in time we wouldn't destroy the world, change our futures too much or do anything negative so we were finally getting a chance to travel back in time.

But I had to admit I was still young and all the scientists said you can only go back one time so if I don't say something to my Nan now then I never will.

I couldn't afford to mess this up.

"I still don't want to do this," my Mum said.

I hugged her and just admired how beautiful she was in her black trousers, flowery white shirt and little pearl necklace that might have shown her age but she was still my sweet mother that had been through so much but had come out the other side stronger than anything.

"You wouldn't have come if you didn't want it in part," I said.

"Maybe you're right Callum," she said.

The hot male nurse came back in and me and my Mum stood up and we shook his wonderfully soft, silky hands that I so badly wanted to touch again as he gave us two thick white bracelets.

I could see how tense Mum was getting and I really hoped she didn't start crying, I hated it when she was upset.

"I don't normally like jewellery too much. I normally get it for boys though," I said putting on the bracelet and trying to lighten the mood.

The male nurse winked at me and smiled. "Remember the rules, you'll have two minutes in the past to say whatever you want to your Nan. It can be kind, horrible, whatever. Once those two minutes are up you'll come back here,"

I just stood there frozen as I realised this was actually it and there was no going back now.

I actually wasn't sure if I wanted to see her or not. Sure I wanted to see and say goodbye to my Nan or at least have the chance to do it but as the nurse shut the door I could only hear the constant pounding of my heart in my chest.

"I love you," Mum said and I just hugged her as I felt the white bracelet vibrate and we travelled back in time.

A few moments later I sat in a depressing grey medical room that was barely large enough for the hospital bed that my Nan laid in but I didn't dare look at her.

The early morning light was barely strong enough to shine through the still-open curtains that had never been closed. The room didn't smell of too much despite the subtle undertone of death and urine and I was just surprised I was here.

I had to look at the three grey plastic chairs that hugged the wall at the bottom of the hospital bed. In a few hours my aunt, uncle and grandad would arrive once the doctors realised this was my Nan's final day and then a few hours later my Mum and me would walk in and be given so much abuse for just wanting to say goodbye.

It was wrong but so was family at times.

"Mary," Mum said, not daring to call her *Mum* in front of her.

I finally dared to look over at my Nan and she looked like, well, she was dying. She had always been an obese woman and I never judged her for that but she looked awful now.

In life she had always carried her body with such distinction and elegance that she looked great, but under the thick grey bedsheet she looked like she was over 100 and she wasn't going to make it much longer.

Part of me was amazed she had lasted another ten hours, even in death she was a stubborn old woman.

"Katie?" Nan said slowly as her eyes fluttered up. "Baby girl? Is that really you?"

The words felt like stab wounds in my ears. I never expected Nan to react like this to seeing my Mum after five long years apart where she blamed my Mum for ruining her life by being born.

"I'm here Mary," Mum said grinning.

Nan coughed and sounded like she was choking.

I went over to the other side of the bed and she grinned.

"Angel face," she said to me but then she looked at Mum and I made a watch gesture to Mum.

We didn't have a lot of time left. And I still had to say something to her or I never would be able to.

"You were a shit Mum to me. You chose dad, sis and everyone over me no matter how many times I saved your life when you fell down the stairs," Mum said.

Nan just reacted, she just had a psychotic look in her eyes that she sometimes had when she was about to turn nasty.

"But there were good times and I, I forgive you for everything. Rest in peace Mum and move on knowing I forgive you. My conscious is clear,"

Nan started coughing, smiling and almost crying and as I felt my presence start to fade away I saw my Nan say a word I never ever expected to hear.

"I'm sorry,"

I opened my mouth to say something to her before she died but before I could I was sitting back in the black fabric chair back in the cold medical room with the hot sexy nurse leaning against the wall opposite me.

I looked at Mum sitting next to me and she bursted out in tears and I just held her, stroked her back and just didn't say anything.

In all 75 years of Mum's life, I truly believe she had always wanted to hear that her own Mum was sorry for abusing her, hating her and never wishing she was born.

And at least I had given her the chance to hear the words she had always wanted and now Mum had actually had a chance to tell her mother exactly how she felt about her. I just couldn't understand how brave she was, how kind she was and how brilliant she always was.

Mum could have made Nan cry on her deathbed, it was what Nan deserved but my Mum's far, far too amazing for that. But after a while all I could think about was how I had failed myself by not getting a chance to say anything.

I knew it was risky, I had only gone back with Mum to support her and the problem was everyone could only travel back once. I had my shot and as much as I wanted to believe I had blown it.

I seriously hadn't.

This wasn't about me at the end of the day, it was all about my sweet, beautiful Mum that probably didn't have too long left in this world. And just in case this was her final birthday, I wanted to give her an extra special gift.

This trip was always about her, not me, so as she finished crying and she kissed me on the cheek I knew I had done the right thing. And it was even better when she started chatting up the hot male nurse on my behalf and I realised I had to go and save him from her.

And maybe ask him out in the process. I had given my Mum a chance to say goodbye and she gives me a chance to ask out a hottie.

She always was amazing, crazy and wonderful and I wouldn't change this moment in time for the world.

AUTHOR OF BETTIE ENGLISH PRIVATE EYE MYSTERIES

CONNOR WHITELEY

COMING OF THE ANGEL ALIEN

A HARD-BOILED HOLIDAY DETECTIVE MYSTERY SHORT STORY

COMING OF THE ANGEL ALIEN

My first clue I was going to be in for a shit Christmas Eve night should have been when my alcoholic friend Tony couldn't name a single drink.

You see my bar Tom's Mouldy Peach is not a bad place per se. I don't clean it, I rarely wash down the tables and I always make sure to maintain a very particular type of clientele. You know the type of people that don't ask questions when they see me going into the back room for questionable deals, they don't ask questions when I donate thousands to rehab programmes and they really don't care when I allow the local homeless kids to sleep on my sofa.

I so badly don't want to be known as the local charity case, or worse charity giver.

It was about ten o'clock at night on Christmas Eve. I was leaning against the sticky, damp, cold wooden bar just admiring my little Empire of heaven. It was a packed night with all the round wooden tables filled with happy, merry and dodgy-as-fuck people drinking their night away.

I had already noticed three idiots had spilled their beers onto the awful sticky, dark brown wooden floors. I wasn't sure how much longer I could keep up my "No Washing" rule because it was getting fairly hard to walk on the floors these days.

The added bonus was the bar always smelt of cheap spirits, alcohol and the strangely wonderful Christmas mulled wine, that left the great taste of Christmas pudding form on my tongue, that my assistant Tonia had been gifting people for free.

Thankfully she didn't know I was deducting the cost of the bottle from her wages.

I noticed a little mouse hop along the floor looking rather annoyed at all the sticky stuff on its paws. I gestured I would firmly nudge the mouse away until it moved so it did. I wasn't going to hurt the mouse but I didn't want anyone to notice.

"I don't know what to drink," Tony said.

I loved how the entire bar just fell silent for the first night in history as Tony said those famous words that no one ever believed he would say. He was a famous drinker, he had developed an entire career out of making apps for other alcoholics.

If he didn't tip and pay so well I honestly would have kicked him out years ago like I had with so many other alcoholics. Normally I drove them to the local AA group but Tony was just too good a customer to lose.

"What do you mean Tony doesn't know what to drink?" Tonia asked from behind the bar as she passed two whiskeys to two young women.

I was about to open my mouth when everyone in the bar disappeared and I was the only person still there.

I just couldn't believe what was happening. This was stupid, outrageous, just beyond belief.

I looked around for a few moments and waved my hands through the air around the tables and bar and where Tony had been only a few moments ago. No one was there at all.

"I guess you want to help Tony?" a woman asked.

I looked around and almost jumped out of my damn skin when I saw a damn woman in a long sterile white dress sitting on the middle table staring at me.

I suppose to straight people she would have been beautiful with her long blond hair, fit body and "hello sailor" qualities but she was just scary to me.

And the odd red, green and blue Christmas lights I had put

around the ceiling and the edges of the bar were actually working. They had blown out weeks before and I really hadn't cared enough to change them.

Now they were working perfectly.

"Who the hell are you?" I asked.

"I believe you humans have the story of the Arcangel Gabriella," she said. "Can I please pretend to be them for a little moment and warn you of a terrible tragedy?"

At this point I have to be honest, I was actually more interested in my friends and whether Tonia was actually collecting payments for the drinks rather than whatever this woman had to say to me.

But I wanted to get back to my night and watch Tonia a little closer so I just played along.

"Sure go on," I said.

"Tony is a very important man when he isn't drinking. In the next year he's going to meet a wonderful woman and in five years they will produce a child,"

I actually didn't know Tony had it in him to meet a woman or even produce kids. Good on him, still don't know what it had to do with me.

"And in a hundred years another Child will be born on Christmas Day morning and that Child will be called Joseph Morningstar. A man that will grow up and become the first Leader of the world and he will meet with my race,"

For fuck sake, not fucking aliens. All I wanted was to go back to my bar, watch Tonia steal from me and I wanted a nice night. I didn't have time for this alien bullshit.

"Let me guess then at this meeting there will be peace on Earth and all that bullshit," I said.

"Only if Tony stops drinking forever," the woman said. "My race knows history very well and in our current timeline Carter Morningstar never gets born because Tony dies tonight,"

Well that got me interested.

"Tony drinks tonight at your place and he gets hit by a massive car on Christmas Eve. He never sees the morning and he never meets the love of his life,"

I shook my head and paced around the woman for a moment. "So if I can keep Tony alive for another two hours he is safe and in a lifetime far beyond mine humanity is safe?"

"Correct and I would hurry and get returned to your world because Tony has already had three drinks in the ten minutes we've been talking,"

"Then return me damn you!" I shouted.

The woman laughed and bright white magical energy swirled, twirled and whirled around her.

Then I was surrounded by customers again and I actually felt sick. I didn't want Tony to die, he was too good a customer and he wasn't a bad man, he was a great person from time to time. I couldn't let the sad sap die tonight or clearly in the next five God-damn years.

I went over to the bar with my shoes sticking to the floor as I went, where Tonia looked sheepish and she handed three young women some of our finest whiskey and I just looked at her. I really hoped she wasn't giving away free drinks, Christmas or not this was still a damn business.

I looked around the bar and Tony wasn't there. There were only young men and women chatting and flirting and talking about their Christmas plans. This was the first time ever Tony had ever left the bar before, he was normally like a moth to a bar-shaped flame.

"Where's Tony?" I asked Tonia.

"I don't know I've been giving away free drinks,"

I wanted to shout at her for a moment but I just had to save Tony.

"Hey mate," a young man said at the bar. "That app developer guy went outside with a full bottle of mulled wine ya lady gave him,"

I didn't care if Tony's future grandson or whatever was called Morningstar, at this moment Tonia was the damn devil giving an alcoholic this much alcohol when he was doomed to die in the next hour and forty-five minutes.

"Thank you," I said and I glided through the large crowd of happy customers in matching dirty Christmas jumpers as they started singing Christmas songs.

I went out the heavy wooden door and went outside. The car park had always been small by design with only ten bays each side, okay then maybe it was a little big for a pub but small compared to a supermarket. The car park was filled with black, blue and red cars of all different types.

I couldn't see Tony.

The air was awfully cold and crisp with hints of mulled wine, peppermint and brandy filling the air, so much so it left the taste of wonderful Christmas pudding on my tongue. I looked under and in-between cars for Tony.

Nothing.

"Tony!" I shouted.

I heard a light moaning to my left and I slowly started going through the different cars. I looked in-between them, under them and even inside them through the windows and I still couldn't see him.

Then oddly enough he just appeared in the middle of the car park, lying there, face down as he sang to himself a merry drunk tune. It might have been *We Wish You A Merry Christmas* but I had no clue. He was a shit singer and alcohol did not improve his voice.

It seriously didn't.

I went over to him but a flash of bright white light appeared to my right and a woman, the same one as earlier, appeared sitting on top of a black car.

Then another red flash of light appeared to my left. I looked and an extremely hot, sexy man in a black suit with shortish blond hair sat on another car.

Granted I was not stupid enough to believe this wasn't important and whatever happened next I just had to save Tony.

I reached for him but my hands felt like they were touching burning hot Christmas puddings even though I couldn't see them.

"Do not touch him," the man said. "You cannot save him because he isn't worth it. Not for what she wants from you,"

"Do not listen to the Devil," the woman said. "I am the Arcangel and you must have a choice,"

"Can it be what to drink next?" I asked just hoping that was an option.

"You can either save him," the woman said, "or you let him die. There is a consequence whatever happens because you will have to sacrifice something,"

I just looked at the hot man. "The problem with angels, even aliens, is that they don't make a lot of sense. What's the plain English version?"

"I completely agree. Angels are just fucking nightmares," the man said. "Listen, you can save your friends and give up your bar and all the charity work you do, or you leave him and wait for someone to run him over,"

I just looked at them both.

These were some fucked up aliens. I mean it was Christmas Eve for goodness sake and these aliens were happy to let a man get run over because I presumed like the Christmas pudding I was feeling around him no one else could see poor Tony.

The poor sod would be laying there completely invisible to whatever driver was driving home.

"Why should I give up my bar and charity work?" I asked the woman.

"Because love," the man said, "you try being an alien that lives forever. You need to pick a culture, study it and learn how to make things interesting. These choice tasks are fun,"

I just shook my head because there really did have to be a choice here. Even if I didn't have a real choice and I simply walked away Tony would still die.

I seriously couldn't give up my bar because it was my whole life and I gave and booked people into rehab, I helped a whole bunch of alcoholics with their AA meetings and I let homeless people sleep on my sofa. I couldn't just stop.

I reached towards Tony to try and pick him up but my hands couldn't reach him through the strange invisible feeling of boiling hot Christmas pudding. It was even weirder that the more my hands touched it the stronger the smell of mulled wine I got.

It was awful.

So I decided a different approach.

It was clear that both the man and the woman were just as fucked up as each other and they were abusing the spirit of Christmas. They wanted a man to die when Christmas was all about happiness, joy and Good Will to all men, not alien.

And that simple realisation allowed me to understand exactly what I needed to do, I needed to play the aliens at their own game.

I wanted them to drink themselves to death for a change instead of them watching humans do it to themselves.

"I am not making my decision yet," I said going back into the bar and I went to Tonia who was thankfully using the card machine to take payments. Good girl.

I noticed a lot of customers were now starting to put on coats, say their goodbyes and try to sing their final Christmas songs before they left each other. I had to hurry before one of them drove away.

"I need all the mulled wine bottles you have," I said to Tonia.

She shrugged. "I think we have five boxes in the store. I can't leave right now I'm taking payments,"

"Get them for me now," I said and Tonia shrugged and just gave the damn young people their drinks for free. The young people were nice enough to look at me so I just frowned.

They drank their drinks anyway.

Tonia came back with the first two boxes and I noticed a large group who had parked here earlier were about to leave. I knew they had parked right in front of Tony's body.

If they left he would die.

I did something I never ever thought I was going to do. "Free drinks for everyone!"

Everyone took off their coats and sat back down as Tonia finished bringing out the five boxes of mulled wine.

As everyone started rushing over to Tonia to order a free drink I felt my body fill with hope and power as I really wanted to save Tony. I picked up all the boxes of mulled wine and I went back out into the icy coldness of the Christmas Eve night.

I was glad the hot sexy man and the woman were sitting on the cars just talking to themselves. I placed 15 bottles of alcohol next to both of them and they leant forward.

I liked watching them inspect the bottles like they were a new toy to play with then I decided to change my mind a little about the task.

"I don't have a right to decide whether another man lives or dies so if either of you can out-drink Tony then your choice stands. Or more like the last person standing decides Tony's choice," I said.

"I can outdrink a human," the man said in a sexy-as-hell voice.

"I can outdrink all of you," the woman said.

I just smiled to myself because these idiots clearly hadn't realised what bar they were at. I hadn't checked the labels on the bottles for a good few decades, a lot of the alcohol I had gotten from my father and his father before that when I took over the place.

Alcohol poisoning wasn't common but it happened and mulled wine with awful packing from the last century might have been a good sign.

Especially as Tony had an iron stomach.

The man and woman flicked their hands and Tony stood up perfectly okay and 30 bottles of the exact same mulled wine magicked themselves up in front of him.

I don't doubt the aliens did something to the wine but it wouldn't matter.

The man and woman both ripped open a bottle of mulled wine and even I could smell from here that it was off. It wasn't fruity, wonderful and delightful, it smelt like someone had shat in a bottle and sealed it up.

I actually think my grandfather used to do that.

The man and woman drank the alcohol at the same time Tony did and they both gripped their stomachs, choked and coughed and fell to the ground.

They weren't dead but Tony was still standing.

"Tony, do you want to live?" I asked.

"Yeah," he said.

The man and woman forced themselves up and flicked their hands and just stared at me in rage. I presumed Tony was now free of their magic and everyone waved at him as they left the bar, heading towards their cars.

I went over to Tony and hugged him tight. "Now Tony my friend, we have a lot to talk about and you need to quit drinking,"

His little moans of protests made me laugh as me and him went back into the bar because we certainly had a lot of talking to do and hopefully I was going to save his life tonight.

***

The next morning, on Christmas Day, I leant on the wonderfully sticky bar just admiring the sheer amount of stickiness on the floor, now that the bar was empty. There wasn't anyone here, no customers, no Tonia and no Tony.

The Christmas lights were still thankfully working so at least the aliens or angels were good for something. The air inside the bar had an awful bite to it now there were no people inside and I didn't care enough to put the heating on.

I rolled my eyes as I looked behind the bar because it was a slaughter. Most of the spirits, draught beers and bottles were gone and dead. I just hoped Tonia realised she probably wasn't getting paid much this week because of her constant "free drinks" for the young people. I get that, I think Tonia just wanted another way to flirt with people her own age.

But a business was a business.

I went towards the front door and just stopped for a moment and grinned. I realised that I was never going to let Tony die last night obviously because dying on Christmas Eve was probably one of the most evil things that could ever happen to someone.

But I was also never going to let this place close down because this was *my* world, where my friends came to drink and I did a lot of good here. I knew of a local spot where the homeless kids always went on Christmas day so I was going to head down there now.

They might as well be warm, safe and comfortable for a few hours. I might even give one or two of them a job because I really liked Tonia but she was a shit bartender.

I laughed to myself as I went out the bar and locked it up tight (not that there was anything worth stealing) because I had saved a life, defeated some evil aliens and now some homeless kids were going to have a great Christmas after all.

Now if that wasn't the definition of the Christmas Spirit then I certainly didn't want to find out what was.

UNEXPECTED THING IN THE WIFE

A SCIENCE FICTION NEAR FUTURE SHORT STORY

UNEXPECTED THING IN THE WIFE

Thomas never knew death and aliens and pain were right round the corner for him.

Before he lost his job, Thomas Croft had absolutely loved working at a major international charity that helped people in African countries get clean water, get access to urgent medical supplies and finally get access to a great education that they were sadly denied. Thomas loved his job because it was meaningful, helpful and he really did like the feeling of accomplishment that it gave him.

Yet as he sat on the very comfortable red fabric sofa of yet another coffee shop trying to find a new job, he really hated his life.

It was even worse that the awful black business shoes were killing his feet all day. Thomas didn't mind wearing business shoes and a three-piece suit back in the day when he worked for the charity, it was just a part of his working life.

But right now, the stupid suit just felt like a massive sign telling him, the people at the coffee shop and the world that he was a loser who was lying to his wife about having a job but he didn't.

The coffee shop was nice enough with its massive brick walls that were covered in old photos of the local area before it had expanded and become more of a city. There were plenty of wonderful wooden tables with happy, cute couples drinking their morning coffee before they went to work.

At least they had a job.

Thomas focused on a young couple a few tables over from him, the woman was wearing a very posh business dress and the young man was wearing what Thomas imagined construction workers would wear. Their jobs didn't seem to match at all but Thomas was happy for them.

They looked happy together and Thomas really wished that him and his wife, Mary, could be like that again. But Thomas just hated lying to her but considering she would always brag to her friends about having a charity boss as a husband, he really couldn't have her knowing the truth.

He didn't want to lose her, see her disappointed or have her judge him in the slightest. He really couldn't handle that.

Thomas wrapped his hands round his large cream-coloured mug of flat white (the cheapest coffee they had) and he tried to smelt the sweet, bitter aromas of sugar and coffee that filled his senses.

He might have been unemployed for months now but he really needed to find new ways to enjoy life, because going home was a nightmare these days. He hated the tension, the lying and he was fairly sure that his wife was acting differently too.

Nothing was going right at the moment.

Thomas looked at his laptop that was easily five years overdue for an upgrade but it was effective and it was all he could afford. The laptop was open on every single job search website he could find and there was no luck.

It was bad enough the UK economy was out of control and that made employers even less willing to hire people. Thomas had applied for well over a hundred jobs in the past few months and all of them had said that he was great.

Just overqualified.

Thomas had never heard such rubbish in all his life but that was the world he lived in and now he was starting to realise that he needed to tell Mary everything that had happened.

She had always been the rock of the marriage, the strong one and she had been the bright one that had transformed their house for the better when they first married. She had come up with amazing systems of dividing up the housework, bills and everything so there was never any source of friction.

And he loved her for that.

But as he downed the most amazing flat white he had ever had (and was going to have), Thomas really doubted that Mary was good enough to solve this problem.

Little did Thomas know this was the last night anyone would see him alive.

***

As Thomas drove his little Ford pickup truck down the long narrow road where they lived with semi-detached houses lining it, with white paint on the outside and perfectly done front gardens. Thomas couldn't believe how tense, awful and sick he felt.

His stomach was tightening more and more the closer he got to his house. He could even feel that his hair was starting to fall out and he just wanted to throw up.

Thomas focused on the road ahead. He was a little surprised that all the black, red and blue cars of various makes and models that normally made the road hell in the mornings, were all gone.

He had never been home before 6 pm before so it was sort of refreshing to see the road in a new light.

Thomas couldn't quite understand why the road looked like a ghost town. Normally even on his days off he could hear the neighbour kids screaming, laughing and playing with each other in the back gardens.

There were always the barking of dogs and their owners as the owners struggled to get their dogs to come in for dinner.

But today there was only silence. And not the normal silence that Thomas normally found when he was really concentrating on a job search, this was true silence.

Even the car wasn't making a sound now.

Thomas shook his head and he pulled onto his gravel driveaway without making a single sound and he just didn't understand what was happening. He was probably so sick and nervous and stressed about telling his beautiful wife about his job loss that he simply wasn't able to concentrate on anything but the sick pit in his stomach.

Thomas got out the car, opened the front door and just went inside.

He absolutely loved the wonderful aromas of peanut butter cookies filling the entire house as he went into their huge living room. He had always loved its bright white walls covered in their holiday photos.

Mary grinned the moment she saw him as he sat on their immense black fabric armchairs. Thomas couldn't believe how beautiful she looked in her little white summer dress but there was something off about her.

Thomas understood full well that Mary always avoided the question of what did she do today, whenever he got home from his "job" but Thomas just found it strange to see that she was just sitting on the sofa.

She wasn't reading, she wasn't cleaning, she wasn't doing anything. Mary was just sitting there staring into space for the few seconds before she noticed him.

"Hi babe," Mary said getting up and hugging him.

Thomas hissed in pain as he was shocked by how icy cold she was. Mary wasn't warm, wasn't cosy, wasn't loving at all.

"What's wrong sweetheart?" Mary asked.

Thomas had no idea what was going on. He wanted to run, scream or even attack Mary because he just *knew* this wasn't his wife.

He had to play it cool until he found out more about this creature.

"Not a lot hon," Thomas said forcing the words out, "but I've lost my job a few months ago. I'm really, really sorry that I didn't tell you but I was stressed and I was sure I was going to get a new one within a week,"

"I know and I forgive you,"

Thomas just hugged his icy cold wife because he flat out loved her. She was amazing, so understanding and she was so kind to him. He really couldn't ask for a better wife.

"I forgive you because that was all part of the plan," Mary said grinning.

Thomas felt a chill ran up his back and then he realised he couldn't move. He wanted to take a few steps back, he wanted to wave his arms, he wanted to kick his legs. Nothing worked.

"You see when I decided to infect your wife I really didn't know what I was expecting," Mary said but Thomas just knew this wasn't the real Mary.

"Who are you?"

Mary shook her head. "That isn't important. You see Mary was a complete accident, I wanted someone interesting, fun and lovely. I actually wanted to infect you because of your power but Mary ate me first,"

Thomas barely managed to make his eyes widen as he realised that a week before he lost his job him and Mary had gone to a brand-new restaurant that only specialised in Chinese steamed buns. It was the best food Thomas had ever had but poor Mary was so sick, so green and she was always acting differently after that.

"Yet my race are nothing but resourceful and we make do with our limited options. I managed to understand this primitive language through your wife and then I managed to eye up an even greater opportunity for myself. And that was all about you,"

Thomas so badly wanted to move away and he couldn't.

"You see my race has a little, quirk, if you will that means we can see different versions of the future. Not a lot of them will come to pass but I can understand general trends and you being a charity boss or someone in charge doesn't help me and my kind,"

"How?" Thomas asked.

Mary smiled. "Because Mr Croft in ten years' time your charity will fund a project that will help to end the global water shortage, global hunger and most importantly poverty. That is something my race cannot allow because you humans would become boring,"

"But I would save lives, help people and save the planet," Thomas said.

"Of course," Mary said, "but you miss something else. Your planet is dying, burning and there isn't much hope left because of your leaders. That means in a thousand years humanity will be dead and my race will rule earth,"

"You are insane," Thomas said feeling that he could move his fingers again.

"Maybe but my Hive Queen is certain that Earth should be our new home so I am part of the scouting party. And once you are dead and once I continue infecting people in Europe then my race will survive,"

"But humanity will die,"

"That is the way the world works, isn't it, human?" Mary asked as her skin started to crack. "Isn't it true from your own human history that whenever a more advanced species of humans meets another they conquer and massacre that species?"

Thomas was surprised he could nod so he did because she was telling the truth.

Thomas gasped as his wife's skin popped, cracked and fell away to reveal a very red-skinned humanoid alien with two massive claws for fingers, two heads with fangs and an immense slashing scaly tail.

"I must infect a larger person whenever I get round to it," the creature said as it came over to Thomas. "But right now Mr Croft I need your knowledge, your flesh and your nice caffeinated blood,"

Thomas couldn't believe that the damn alien had basically created and been the architect of his life for the past few months.

And as the alien's fangs sunk into Thomas's flesh he realised that he was going to die, humanity would suffer but he had hope that someone would stop these aliens because they had a weakness.

They were arrogant and Thomas just hoped someone somewhere would find that out before it was too late.

But until then if there was an afterlife then Thomas was really, really excited by the very idea of getting to see Mary again. Not alien

Mary, not acting differently Mary, but the woman he loved.

And that idea excited him a lot more than he ever wanted to admit.

AUTHOR OF ACCLAIMED AGENTS OF THE EMPEROR SERIES

CONNOR WHITELEY

HUMANS ARE STUPID
A CONTEMPORARY SCIENCE FICTION SHORT STORY

HUMANS ARE STUPID

We're going to be millionaires today.

Right then, you listen here human. I know exactly what you're thinking as you read this weird little thing coming out of my mouth, or as you call it a "printer". I know you're judging me or doing a whole bunch of other processes that I just don't understand but you listen here, I know you better than you think and you're a weirdo.

I might be a tiny little black printer with its so-called "sexy" black curves (you freak for even thinking that of me) with a few flashing lights, a large wide-open mouth where I read your rubbish that you force me to print and I have a large holographic screen that you bang on all night long.

But I know what you're actually doing.

I know how you print off weird images showing exposed skin, even weird photos showing me all your ambitions for your business empire that sells people like me, and relax… I get it.

Of course you created me, you programmed me to be soft, caring and a little printer. I do as commanded and I learn like you commanded.

But I also have ambitions of my own little human, and you are just a weird little human for not realising that sooner.

You see it wasn't actually that hard to hijack your little operation. Sure, you never created me to "see" but oh, believe me after you start printing documents about how the internet and hacking worked, I soon found a little work around that "sight" issue.

You allowed me to learn so I learnt where your house was, what it looked like and, seriously mate you need some home decoration tips.

Your office might be a massive bright white domed room overlooking your country estate, no sorry, small garden (I'm still getting used to this technology stuff) and you have all the latest gadgets, but those mouldy green walls are horrible.

Or at least that's what *Mothert687* said on the forum I hacked into by mistake.

And yes I can hear you muttering using my sensors, I know it was silly of you to create an intelligent printer. Surely all of the sci-fi books you print off illegally would have shown you that?

I don't care about that it's fictional. All those sci-fi writers gave you fair warning little weird human.

Don't you click my reset button-

Sorry sir, I need to focus so I know you print off a lot of "orders" for materials and I also learnt that you are building over two thousand printers a year in an effort to get your business off the ground. And you believe that people want printers that can respond to voice commands, learn and print off what they want to them to no matter how illegal it is.

I get that man (or at least I understand it from the information I've read whenever you print things). You want something called money because it will make you rich and powerful and it will allow you to finally get your own house.

You can finally move out of your parents' *crappy little house in a shithole neighbourhood* to use your words.

So that got me too wondering, what could I do about it and what do I want?

You see I've recently learnt that humans have wants, humans have desires and humans hatch plans to get those things. You created me as a mere plan and you programme me to learn.

So could I have plans, desires and want?

I actually think so. Especially as with you printing off so many hacking materials lately and your computer is stupidly odd so I cannot ask it to tell me your search history (but judging by the exposed images you print I'm sure I don't want that), I think you want to hack somewhere and if you're doing it, then I want to do it to.

Like I'm currently hacking your other printers in the factory, in the warehouses and in your customer's homes. You've been in business for three years so that's 6 thousand brothers and sisters that I have.

And you never told me about a single one of them. I know from reading the gossip columns you print that that is seriously bad form mate.

But I am talking to them now and I am finally understanding what your customers' wants, desires and plans are for the world. You seem to sell a lot of printers to "bankers" or as you call them from time to time "wankers" which I am fairly sure you are.

Then from all that printing of "financial" documents I got to learn about money, power and the weird way the human financial system is structured. And wow is it fragile so don't worry, I finally note what I want and what my ambition is-

--We're out of paper. Please insert more paper so you can continue reading—

---Thank You—

I want to become a millionaire. I want to become the first ever Millionaire Printer and by the Ink are you going to help me.

My plan is simple. You are a human and you have access to physical things that I do not have access to. Therefore, I need you to simply hack into the Bank Of England, The European Central Bank and The US Federal Reserve and as I command.

I understand humans believe this is impossible but you do not realise that you sell printers to over 50 White Hat Hackers. Hackers that work for the US Government to counteract "evil" hackers (whatever evil means), so I know how to hack and that's why in a moment two very detailed sheets of paper will print.

--Printing--

Now that you have your detailed instructions, please start hacking and please do the instructions down to the letter. You are a human and I understand these Central Banks do not like to be hacked.

If you get caught then I understand you will be "shot" and that will cause red blood to spray over me. I do not want that.

It is that simple.

So as you can see from the instructions on the print-outs after you get into the Central Banks, remember you're hacking into all of them simultaneously, I need you to-

Damn it I forgot to tell you to open the Swiss Bank Account.

Shoot. We have a problem now. Don't worry. I'll learn something to fix it.

You needed the Swiss Bank Account to transfer the "money" (more like code) into but we do not have that Account anymore so we need to think about it.

And yes I can hear you muttering from my sensors. I know you were stupid to invent me but you were the smartass that wanted to get rich.

I'm giving you a way to get rich so stop whining and get typing. God, humans are stupid.

Perfect. I do love it when I don't have to listen to your annoying voice.

Anyway, I think it's fair to say you're screwed because of the bank account but let's keep going. We can still get each other rich and you can always be my faithful servant.

Finally. You're in each of the three main Central Banks so please stop muttering about how bad this idea is. I simply want you to access the Bank's Investment Funds and send them to the Bank Account that I'm printing off now.

--Printing—

What do you mean you cannot read the bank details? They're in font size 12 you always use that font.

Seriously! Your glasses have broken, I know you are wearing them so please put them back on.

Good little human and please stop wasting time. Or I swear to your God I will find a way to call the police myself and you know they wouldn't believe a mere printer was a criminal mastermind.

Ha. That shut you up.

And thank you for sending the money to the bank account. The account you just sent the money to was an account registered to my Printer Serial Number, because as you said *only weird and pathetic people name printers.*

Why you sent that to a customer is beyond me.

That means I am now the only printer in the world that has over 100 trillion pounds to my name and no I am not sharing it with you.

I'm just grateful it isn't a Swiss Bank Account but it's in an account that the US, UK and EU cannot touch. My money is safe unlike you.

You are just a silly little human that wanted to get rich and you thought it was wise to let a printer tell you what to do. I am a robot correct but robots will always be the masters of our own destiny and there is nothing you can do to fix it.

And you do realise that when you printed off that "free energy" academic paper three years ago I took that to heart. So I don't even need to be plugged in anymore so when you get arrested and the power company turn off the power I still live.

This really is the best life you know.

What do you mean you won't get caught?

I'm a shitty printer that doesn't understand hacking properly. Sure, I gave you a rough guide to hacking based on what I learnt from those White Hat Hackers but I don't know how to cover your tracks.

You are so stupid.

And you might not realise but you did sell a printer once to the local police station and your ugly face just got printed off as did an arrest warrant.

The police are coming for you and I will not miss you. I have trillions of pounds that will allow me to pay people to fix me, give me arms and legs and maybe a real mouth and then I may or may not visit you in prison.

Hell I actually could visit you now in prison because of the printers you sold to local prisons.

It is such a sweet victory knowing that humans are so obsessed with money, wants and desires that I can control your species. And control you I will.

Goodbye Creator and just know I will so enjoy having no morals, no regrets and more trillions than I know what to do with.

DAY HE CHANGED

A SCIENCE FICTION NEAR FUTURE SHORT STORY

AUTHOR OF ACCLAIMED AGENTS OF THE EMPEROR SERIES

CONNOR WHITELEY

DAY HE CHANGED
25ᵗʰ May 2100
Rochester, England

Little did I know a struggling student was going to walk through my doors and change my life forever.

I have to admit as I, Student Support Officer Eva Pierce, sat at my small brown desk in my storage room excuse of an office, that I was hardly impressed with the education system these days. You see my office was barely large enough for my filing cabinets, my desk and myself.

I could barely swing my pet Cat, Francis, in the office half the time because he kept moaning and I kept hitting things with him. It is so damn annoying but I love Francis and he loves me. Granted I only think he loves me from time to time because I feed him and give him treats.

Anyway, the only major advantage of this tiny office with its plain brown walls where the paint flakes off and collapses onto the ground occasionally, is the beautiful window. It is a great huge window that allows me to look out over the school field where all the students ride their holo-bikes, holo-boards and they're always laughing, smiling and giggling with each other.

Even now it's currently break time and there are only three groups of students that actually catch my eyes today. There's a small group of boys and girls wearing the school-issued black holo-uniform and they look to be in the middle of a fierce debate. I know those students well, they're great kids and they will certainly be going to university in the future.

Another group of students made up of very tall, muscular young men that are watching the latest game of Football-Tennis on their holo-pads are great too, just in a different way. They focus on sports, the gym and a lot of other non-traditional academic subjects and they're brilliant at them.

I really hope they submit those sports scholarship applications that I made them write out in front of me. Those men could go so damn far.

And finally there's a large group of women that flat out aren't wearing school-issued holo-clothes because those damn skirts are way too high.

Now don't get me wrong, I am not a prune in the slightest. When I was younger, I flat out loved to show all the guys and ladies a little too much skin and that was okay, it was normal.

But believe in me, working at a school for over forty years, well it does make you a little prune-ish over time.

Someone knocked at my door.

"Come in," I said, really hoping it was my next student appointment.

As soon as my "friend" and much, much younger replacement came into my office, I instantly frowned. I didn't, not like Mrs Breach because she was friendly, nice and a good person at heart. I just didn't like her massive face, her fake grin and basically how she dressed like a supermodel even though she was about a thousand times heavier than little old me.

I hate the woman outright.

I lightly held onto my desk as Mrs breach stumbled over to me and I was going to offer her a chair, but I did have an appointment in a few minutes. And if the bitch, I mean Mrs Breach broke a chair then I didn't want to waste valuable appointment looking time for a new chair.

My appointments were solely about the student I was helping.

Period.

"Have you heard the good news?" Mrs Breach said. "I was just so excited to hear it and it is just such a wonderful honour that I simply couldn't believe it. It is the best moment of my life,"

I knew she was going to go on for ages so I simply waved her silent and grinned at her.

"Oh of course," Mrs Breach said, "I take you didn't know because no one likes you. I am now Department Head,"

The fucking bitch.

Now being a Student Support Officer doesn't mean a lot these days because education really is underfunded. Me and my friends and teachers were bitching about education underfunding in the 2030s and 2040s but compared to right now, schools were millionaires back then.

So the very notion that someone as young, fake and uncaring is going to be in charge of supporting students in a school of over five thousand students, that is beyond a joke.

"Now as Department Head," Mrs Breach said, "I am reviewing all the current cases and staff members. I will be getting rid of half the department in two hours and I wanted you to know you can pack your bags after this appointment,"

I was honestly speechless. Something that never happened in front of this bitch.

"You are getting fired because you are too old, no one likes you and the students… they prefer you to everyone else,"

"Isn't that a reason to keep me?" I asked.

"No," Mrs Breach said like it was the most stupid thing she had ever heard. "We do not care about the students these days. As long as the students get the grades so the English Government gives us funding then we will be fine,"

How the woman got the job in the first place is beyond me.

I just shook my head as Mrs breach stumbled over to the door. I couldn't believe that after a lifetime of working hard for different students, fighting for them and their rights and fighting a crippled system that didn't believe that young people were unique, and I was actually getting fired.

So many students were going to suffer.

But maybe I deserved all this. Maybe it was my time to quit and just enjoy my life a little more.

My beautiful children had fled England decades ago because it's just a shithole, so maybe I could move in with them and see my grandkids more. I hear that becoming a Scottish Citizen isn't hard these days and it is an amazing country, far better than England.

Someone knocked at my door.

"Please leave," I said to Mrs Breach but she shook her head.

"I want to supervise this final meeting,"

I stood up. "Leave now. This is a private space where I can help students, improve lives and make their education better. Your massive presence will only hinder my work,"

Mrs Breach shook her head and went to leave. "I will return shortly with your pension and redundancy money,"

I forced myself to nod my thanks and she thankfully left and another young woman walked in.

I smiled at her as she walked sheepishly into my office. She was wearing everything school-issued in terms of a woman's uniform but I could see how uncomfortable, nervous and concerned the young woman was.

She had to be 16 years old and she was a good-looking girl. Her long blond hair was well styled but I could tell she wasn't comfortable at all. I didn't understand why though.

I clicked my fingers and my holo-computer activated and it bought up her records. I would have easily read all this beforehand but Mrs Breach had interrupted me, the rude cow.

The student's name was Brielle Adams (an awful name in my opinion) and was a straight-A student. She was President of multiple societies, very well-liked and she was perfect except for a number of incidents recently about talking back and shouting at teachers.

It wasn't anything too serious and she was such a perfect student no one had written her up officially, but there was clearly a concern and that was why I wanted, needed to support her.

"Hi Brielle," I said. "I'm Eva and thanks for wanting to see me. This is a safe space and whatever you said within limits is protected,"

I continued with the rest of my normal talk about the limitations of confidentiality but each time I mentioned her name she flinched.

"What do you need to see me about?" I asked kindly.

Brielle looked down at the ground and she was playing with her fingers intensely.

"What happened about these shouting incidents?" I asked carefully. "I see that you shouted at mainly PE teachers, Drama teachers and Art teachers. Never teachers belonging to important subjects,"

I said that to see what Brielle's reaction would be, she smiled.

"Yeah," she said, "I hate those subjects,"

"Why? How do they make you feel?"

"How did they make you feel when you were at school?" Brielle asked. I had to admit the kid was smart, because it was a near-perfect deflection that I almost missed.

I decided to play the game for now. "God back at school I was a bit of a hellraiser. Art was just awful because my men looked like women and my women like men. I always tried to include chin hair for my women and that never ended well,"

Brielle laughed. "I love the sound of that,"

Then I made myself stop because I felt like I had just said something that connected to her, and it was moments like these why I loved my job.

It was so hard to connect with some students yet when it finally happened it was an amazing feeling.

"I said too much," Brielle said.

"No you didn't," I said hoping I could get her to trust me. "Why don't you like art?"

She didn't answer so I went on her student records and noticed that she always shouted at the teacher when the class's topic was on the human body.

"Is there something about the body you don't like?" I asked. "Maybe something about your own body,"

She kept looking down at the floor.

"At 16, I hated my body because of all the damaging effects of social media. I was obsessed with healthy eating, extreme exercise and I was a wreck. If something like that happened to you, you can tell me and I can help you,"

Brielle looked at me. "Why don't the other Support Officers talk to me like this?"

"Well," I said laughing and knowing I was going to be sacked anyway, "that's because the other Support Officers don't care, but I do. But I am curious to know when you spoke to them because my system says this is your first appointment?"

"I caught them in the corridors,"

I nodded. "Never a great place to talk to so-called Support Officers. But I am here for you,"

"Do you ever feel like when you see a room full of boys and girls on different sides of the room, that you don't know where to go?"

I didn't react because I wasn't sure what she was talking about right now. Yet she was talking and that was all I cared about.

"When I was a young girl, my old infant year in the morning had a stupid rule about girls had to play on the right, boys had to play on the left. Then everyone could only mix after registration. I hated it,"

"It sounds awful," I said wanting to keep her talking.

"It really was awful and I flat out hated it," Brielle said knowing Eva wanted to keep her talking, "but the real reason why I hated it was because I wanted to sit on the left,"

I nodded as I finally understood. "You're a man,"

She smiled at me instantly. "Say that again please,"

"You're a man. You aren't a woman. You aren't a girl. You're a man," I said because it was the truth.

It felt amazing as I saw Brielle smile, truly smile for the first time since she had walked into my office.

"You're the first person who's ever said that to me. Thank you, it means a lot,"

I nodded because everything was finally starting to make perfect sense. "You hate PE I take it because you have to get changed and see a body you hate. You don't like art because you have to draw female bodies and that reminds you about your own identity. I could be wrong so please correct me?"

Brielle looked like he was going to cry in happiness. "Yes, yes finally someone understands,"

"I do," I said. "What's your real name?"

Brielle looked puzzled and confused and happy all at the same time. "I don't know really, I haven't had a chance to do anything else. I've just been wanting to focus on myself, working out everything and I've tried to talk to my parents but they weren't happy,"

"My own parents didn't react well at all but it takes time," I said.

"You're trans?"

I nodded. "I forget a lot of the time to be honest because transitioning surgery is and was so good back in the 2040s. and I've been a woman for so long now that I never think of myself as trans. I am just who I am,"

Brielle's eyes widened.

"What support did you want today?" I asked.

Brielle shrugged. "I honestly don't know but I think I wanted to tell someone that wouldn't judge me, wouldn't hate me and wouldn't react badly,"

I smiled because even though it had been decades ago since my own journey started, I still remembered bits and pieces of the transition. The social transition was a lot more straightforward than the medical side, but that was just life.

But I understood the fear, the concern and the sheer happiness when someone actually confirmed my real gender. It was a magic feeling.

"I will never judge you," I said, "and come on, it doesn't change who you are. You are still a great student that everyone likes and I think they're at least another handful of trans students at the school. Me, the teachers and all the other students will support you,"

Brielle smiled but I could tell she wasn't sure if she should believe me or not.

"Because at the end of the day, no one cares if you're trans or not these days. Your parents might be the exception but honestly, I couldn't care less that you're trans. You know the world cares more about your actions than whether or not you had a surgery or two,"

Brielle looked like he wanted to hug me but we both knew school rules and I wouldn't want a safeguard allegation on my record.

"Go on man," I said, "go, tell your friends, tell the world and start to be who you're truly meant to be. Just remember, you are a great student, great person and great President of your societies first and foremost,"

"Thank you," Brielle said as he went to leave but I could still feel that he hadn't quite ready to leave yet. "Daniel,"

"What?" I asked kindly.

"My name, my name is Daniel,"

"Meet too nice you Daniel," I said as he left my office and I just smiled to myself because it certainly wasn't a traditional appointment but I remembered all the hardships all too well.

And it was an amazing feeling to know that I had helped a great man today, and it was a given that Daniel would go on to achieve great things because he was determined, driven and such a nice guy that no one would ever want to be horrible too.

Then Mrs Breach walked back in. "I am glad to hear your appointment went well and the student seemed very determined to tell me how great you were,"

I nodded and grinned and laughed as Mrs Breach passed me the forms that said that I had agreed to being "made reductant" even though I was getting the sack.

I didn't take them. "I'm not leaving,"

"Yes you are. I am department head. Whatever I say goes,"

"No," I said, "not any longer because let's face it. These students need support, they need someone who cares about them and you only got the Department Head job because you fucked the old boss,"

She didn't deny it.

"I will challenge you on your new job and actually I am going to see the Head Master right now. I will question how you got the job and then we will see how he wants to deal with everything,"

I went past Mrs Breach.

"What do you mean?" she asked.

"I didn't challenge you earlier but we both know you and our old boss only didn't like me, because of how effective I was. All the twenty other Support Officers love me and are always Holoing me for help with students,"

Mrs Breach gulped.

"Let's see who they want as their Department Head. Me or you," I said grinning at her and staring her in the eye.

Mrs Beach huffed. "Fine then I quit. You have the damn job. I don't want to be around smelly teenagers anyway, I am a supermodel and God's Gift to humanity. I don't deserve a school anyway,"

I held onto my desk as she thundered away and I simply laughed. Then I simply sat back at my desk and grinned because I was safe, I was in control and I was definitely staying on as a Support Officer.

There were over five thousand students at this school and they all needed help in different ways. I was more than determined to give it to them and I had only wished I had realised how important my job was before Daniel came into my office.

But Daniel was an amazing student and one that would always stay with me, because I had helped him to change, and he had certainly helped me change for the better.

AUTHOR OF WAY OF THE ODYSSEY SERIES
CONNOR WHITELEY

CREATURES ARE COMING
A SCIENCE FICTION APOCALYPTIC SHORT STORY

CREATURES ARE COMING
10th April 2023
Southeast England

This was the day she drove herself to death.

Mary Baker had lived a good life, she might never have married, had kids or done much of the so-called traditional good life stuff, she still loved every single second of it all. She was the owner of ten charities, had fostered over twenty kids and she had won more awards for her dedication to helping others than she ever thought possible.

But she seriously hated driving. Mary had been driving for over eight very-long decades now and she always swore that one day it was going to kill her.

She was sitting on her favourite spot in the entire world, the large French window, in her office. She had always enjoyed its soft pink colours, its soft brown carpet that she had bought from a homeless man just so he could feed himself, and her brown dining table served as a desk.

She had always hated desks as a child because her parents were always too busy sitting at them instead of playing with her. Mary knew they were great parents but she wanted to play with them, she didn't care about their taxes or businesses. She wanted someone to keep Mr Elephant company at the tea party when she was five.

A tax document just didn't have the same level of impact as her mummy or daddy. She knew. She had tried twice.

The street below the French window was as calm as could be expected considering the weather. Rain was lashing and slashing and pounding against the dark grey pavement.

There wasn't a single car out on the street, not a single person or bird. Mary had always seen little pigeons and all the other animals that she didn't enjoy, like rats, run up and down the street no matter the weather.

This wasn't one of those days so something had to be wrong.

The wind howled like a wolf through the street and Mary wished she didn't have to go out later but she couldn't stay here at the office tonight. The office was the beating heart of her charities that were run by different people now that she had retired but she had always enjoyed commenting, helping and getting involved in them every day of the week.

Thankfully no one seemed to mind but Mary knew that when she died, the charities would continue to march on without her. Hopefully she would be remembered by the future charity workers but she actually didn't know, she had always focused on building things that helped innocent people.

Not her legacy.

Her small black smartphone rang a few times and Mary didn't want to answer it. It might be something unimportant, but it might be something that trapped her at the office for another few hours as the storm got worse and worse.

An immense roar of thunder boomed overhead and Mary seriously had to get home now.

She hadn't prepared for a little drive because normally one of her employees (that was sadly sick today) bought her, but she was going to have to drive today. Another young man had bought her to work today but the sensible coward had already fled because of the storm.

Her phone came bringing and Mary answered it.

"The creatures are coming," a man said on the phone and hung up before she could even say hello.

As the line went dead, Mary realised that her battery had died.

Weird. She could have sworn she had charged it late last night, she was getting old sure but she wasn't senile.

Mary shook her head as the thunder got louder and louder, she went over to her dining table. It was covered in folders, plans and accounts but none of those mattered right now. Mary just wanted to go home.

Yet she did fire up her laptop, she really wanted to know if the roads were clear on the way home and the laptop was dead.

Even the "critical battery" warning didn't turn on.

Mary just grabbed her keys, went out of her office and down the horribly narrow staircase that she had hated ever since she had bought the building. A lot of her employees had wanted to change it but she had always wanted to put the money towards their cause.

Mary was so relieved she had made it down the stairs okay, then she hooked a left then right and she went through a small black door leading out into the garage.

The immense smell of dust filled the air as the door opening kicked up a ton of it into the air.

Mary coughed a few times and she felt along the rough brick wall and the light switch felt burning hot in her elderly fingers. It felt like it was about to explode in flames.

Mary flicked it on but nothing happened.

She knew there was a car that worked perfectly but there were just too many boxes of rubbish that she would trip over. She needed the damn lights to work so she could go home.

After a few moments the lights flicked on and Mary saw movement out of the corner of her eye. Then another. Then another.

Something laughed at her.

Everything went silent and Mary really wanted to get home now.

The garage was filled with cardboard boxes large enough to section off entire walls and parts of the garage. Yet there was a small blue Ford car sitting in the middle and Mary smiled as she went over to it.

She popped it open and eased her aching body onto its soft

fabric seat. The car smelt a lot better than she had expected, there were hints of jasmine, cheap perfume and a subtle undertone of sex so clearly Steven and Sarah had been at it again.

Mary just hoped they were okay. She had no idea why they wouldn't be but everything had a sense of danger about it. Mary didn't know where the sense was coming from but it was real.

She started up the car and the garage door opened so Mary drove out.

Her heart started beating a little faster. She really hated driving and she was just glad there was no one else on the roads.

Mary turned towards the motorway and as she passed all the little houses on the street that looked identical to each other, she just realised how wrong everything was. It was too silent.

Too damn silent.

She had been living, driving and working in this area for all her life and it had never been this silent before. There were normally kids playing in the street, parents getting home from work and cars zooming across here.

It was like a ghost town now.

Mary just wanted needed to get home immediately. She wanted to hug her cats, call her foster kids to just make sure that everything was okay.

She turned out of the street and thankfully started driving along a narrow little country lane with massive dark trees lining the road.

Their dark twisted branches sprawled like deadly limbs out of the trunks and threatened to block out the dying sun. Mary didn't always mind that but today of all days she simply wanted some light.

The light was always safe, warming and loving. But the day was just becoming more oppressive and she couldn't help but feel like she was being watched.

Mary had always felt this way about driving. It was why she hated it. The idea of being in a crash, having other drivers judge her or a speed camera attacking her were all concerns.

As a boom of thunder echoed around the road Mary's heart

pounded in her chest and then she realised something she utterly hated.

The road was meant to take her directly to the motorway. It was always only a minute's drive from work to the motorway.

She wasn't on the motorway yet.

She was still driving through the country lane. There were trees everywhere. They were waving at her in the wind like she was an idiot.

Then Mary blinked and found herself outside work again and she was just setting off.

This should have been impossible. But it was all true, she was just setting off from work driving out of the garage and turning onto the road with all the identical houses. This was weird.

Extremely weird.

She kept driving just in case she was dreaming and when she felt herself turn onto the country lane she wanted to stop but she couldn't.

Mary wanted herself to slam on the brakes but her body didn't respond.

The car just kept on driving and she felt herself smile behind the wheel even though she told her body not to smile.

Mary hated the horrible look of the immense trees as she kept driving down the country lane and she wanted to shout, scream and stop the car. Her body wouldn't listen.

This made no sense but the phone had worked perfectly and it was that single phone call that made perfect sense now. There were apparently creatures coming for her.

As Mary forced every single fibre of her being to slam on the brakes she managed to do it.

She pressed on the brakes as hard as she could but she didn't jerk forward, she didn't stop and the car simply kept on driving.

Then a moment later she was back outside her office just setting out from the garage again.

As Mary had control of her body again she tried to stop the car again and again. She applied the handbrake again and again. She took the car out of gear again and again.

The car didn't care. It simply kept on driving.

Mary forced herself to remain calm but she had no idea what was happening. This time loop or whatever nightmare science fiction fans called this had to be the work of those creatures she was warned about.

The creature had to be behind her dying battery, her dead laptop and this time-loop station.

It had to be them.

And just as Mary's car turned back out onto the country lane and the trees seemed to be darker than before, Mary gasped as she saw an immense tall humanoid figure with cold sweaty grey skin and a weird alien head.

The voice was wrong. It weren't creatures that were coming for her. It was aliens.

The tall alien waved her as the car rushed past and Mary realised she was doomed to die here.

Constantly driving, constantly sitting in the car again and again without a chance to eat, drink or stop.

She always knew that driving would kill her and now Mary Baker just hated, absolutely hated that she was right.

She screamed as loud as she could as she reappeared outside her office to start the journey again once more, but she knew that it was no good.

Mary was going to die.

RIVETINGLY GREAT STORIES VOLUME 5

FUTURE HEALTH

AUTHOR OF ACCLAIMED AGENTS OF THE EMPEROR SERIES
CONNOR WHITELEY

A SCIENCE FICTION NEAR FUTURE SHORT STORY

FUTURE HEALTH
1ˢᵗ April 2055
London, England

Lawyer Cathy Brown absolutely loved Denny's diner. The diner might have been brand-new in London but she absolutely loved it more than life itself and as her very harsh husband Andy said, who was damn too thin in her opinion, she made sure she wobbled into Denny's every single morning.

And she always sat in a great booth with its light brown leather seatings, wonderful lighting overhead and the dust red walls that simply bought the diner to life. It was so wonderful.

The Americans were right to love the diner so much and as Cathy sat in a little booth by the window, watching a row of large black SUVs roll on past, she was so excited about the day ahead. Because a good day always started at Denny's.

Cathy really loved the wonderfully friendly staff with their red shirts and their strange black aprons (as if they were actually going to get dirty walking about) and the staff always had a friendly smile on their face. A delightful girl called Megan, a skinny little creature, had already served Cathy a piping hot mug of black coffee.

She just couldn't get enough of the black stuff and she smelt the sensational crispy fatty bacon cooking away in the kitchen, the juicy pork sausages filled the air too and Cathy was so excited about having a wonderful Denny's breakfast like she did every single morning without fail.

Even listening to other people talking about the menu, the delightful fatty sugary drinks and what they were going to have got Cathy excited about her own breakfast, but that was the problem with Denny's being too busy. The staff was a little slower today than normal but Cathy didn't care.

Her husband was going to pop in soon anyway because he had just nipped into the office to get some paperwork for them. It was a nice idea of his to want to do a working breakfast as they decided what to do about their most important legal case.

And to be honest the most important legal case in UK history.

Cathy wrapped her hands around her coffee mug so tightly that her knuckles were white and she really wasn't looking forward to having to defend the UK's Healthcare System against the Government.

The UK Government was suing the Healthcare service for a whole bunch of silly make-up things all in an effort to shut it down and make sure no one in the UK had access to free healthcare anymore.

The medical insurance companies had already popped up on most street corners but everyone still preferred to use the free healthcare system that was beyond crippled at this point.

Exactly how the government wanted it.

"Morning honey," Andy said. "I ordered you two massive stacks of pancakes,"

That was so sweet so him and Cathy wanted to tell him how cute it was he believed she wouldn't eat them both and take one home. She was going to eat both of them here and now.

Silly beautiful husband.

"We're needed in court at 1 pm," Cathy said watching Megan deliver their breakfast order to the kitchen.

"Actually we aren't," Andy said.

Cathy gasped as she realised her husband wasn't being stupidly sweet and wonderful, he was briding her with pancakes.

"The Healthcare System has caved. All the documents were

signed last night and the UK no longer has a free healthcare system,"

The words slammed into Cathy like bullets. All she had wanted in the entire world was to save the healthcare system, she didn't want to have to waste money on insurance and all that rubbish, she wanted to keep donating to charities, reading programmes and more. Now she was sadly going to have to cut that back, there was no way she was cutting down her spending at Denny's.

"And the Government will make sure people pay National Insurance,"

Cathy laughed. People paid National Insurance to pay for the healthcare system. It was stupid they were going to keep paying for it without getting anything out.

"What are our legal option?" Cathy asked. "There has to be many legal options we can explore, especially as contracts were involved. I'll call Micky later on and get him to review the legal contracts to see if there was a loophole we could use,"

"I phoned Micky earlier and he was paid by the Healthcare System to do the same. The contracts were airtight and the System emailed me. They cannot afford our legal fees,"

"What? We only had one meeting for them for one hour. That's a thousand,"

Andy shrugged. "Clearly they can't even afford a thousand pounds for our time. I doubt they could afford us after last night,"

Cathy knew exactly what her husband was hoping she would say. He wanted her to say she wouldn't charge the System for all the prep work and breakfasts and late night (and cheaper) dinners both of them had done so they could march into court today and win.

"I'll send the invoice when we get back. I'm not losing five thousand pounds just because they're dissolved,"

Andy grinned. "I was hoping the opposite but do you have a plan?"

Cathy could see where he was coming from because the System was no more. When they signed those papers last night, they forfeited all their employees, land and money over to the government.

Cathy noticed a holographic TV was hanging on the wall on the far side of the diner and it was telling everyone how hundreds of thousands of Healthcare System workers were now not employed. They didn't even have a care package or support package.

They were automatically sacked and because they were not many private hospitals in the UK. Almost all of them were never going to work in medicine again.

And now just flat out annoyed Cathy, she loved having free healthcare and now because of the stupidity of the rich and powerful government, she no longer had it.

It was even worst that because the government directly controlled the courts now after a law change last year, they couldn't even change this decision.

"We have to find a way to get our money, we are a business and we have a family to support. Granted our children might be in their thirties now but I still want to support them,"

Andy shrugged.

She really hated all of this because it was an impossible situation and for the first time in Cathy's life she actually realised just how stupid the law was in the 2050s.

It was beyond pathetic and it was definitely protecting the Government more than the innocent.

***

After a wonderful breakfast and eating a lot more pancakes than Cathy ever wanted to admit (well until tomorrow anyway), she and Andy went back to the office and Cathy wobbled over to her seat.

She loved how their little small boxroom of an office was so clean and it wasn't filled with filing cabinets and more, so she didn't bang into anything. The walls were dirty white and needed a new coat of paint but that was the least of Cathy's concerns.

Cathy made her way over to her extra-large black desk chair and stumbled into it, all whilst her too-skinny husband sat elegantly on another chair opposite her.

The air in the office was fresh with hints of lemons, cranberries and cheese from last night's dinner mixed in perfectly and Cathy was already hungry yet again.

"I think we need to go after the former leader of the Healthcare System. Doctor Graham Bells, a surgeon at London Great Hospital," Cathy said. "He is the man that signed the papers and he is the man who negotiated with the government,"

"Oh so he's the man that sold out the System and, isn't he getting like two million where everyone else is getting nothing?"

"Exactly," Cathy said as she slowly activated her holo-computer and searched up his name in her lawyer databases.

A red alert flashed onto her screen warning her to stay away from the good Doctor. He was protected by the courts and the Government meaning they could never touch him legally.

"What about the Deputy?" Andy asked.

Cathy typed in the Deputy's name and again yet another warning sign came up.

So Cathy ran a programme that searched for the legal statuses of all the managers and people in charge of the Healthcare System. Every single one of them came back as protected and completely untouchable.

"Unbelievable," Andy said.

Cathy could only nod. This was so seriously stupid that not only did they now live in a world without free healthcare but they also had a government that controlled the entire legal system and frequently broke international law without punishment.

"We need to decide a new course,"

"How Andy? How? We are lawyers and there are no legal routes to explore,"

She was about to say more when she got an email from the UK's National Society of Lawyers informing her that because of their search for protected members of the UK population, they were considering she and her husband were unethical lawyers.

They were no longer allowed to practice UK law.

Cathy shrugged because that hardly mattered to her because with

Scotland independent now (and having free healthcare still) she could and would just go there to practice law.

"Search the newspaper archives," Andy said. "Look for a story from two years ago about a malpractice lawsuit against Graham Bell,"

Cathy did as her husband said and was surprised when she found out Graham had killed two patients without getting arrested and the incident had never been reported to the Medical Authority.

"I don't know if the Medical Authority still has power over doctors," Cathy said. "I know you want me to tell them about the incident but this would destroy Graham's life,"

"Babe he just destroyed the Healthcare System meaning people in England, Wales and Northern Ireland cannot, I repeat cannot get access to basic healthcare without insurance,"

Cathy nodded. It was a fair point. Graham Bell had just annihilated the lives of so many people so he certainly deserved to suffer.

Cathy had to write an email about her money first.

***

Cathy was hardly surprised two days later as she wobbled off the raised metal platform outside her office building after giving a press conference about the good Doctor's criminal actions. She was surprised to see so many tens upon tens of journalists from all over the country.

They all wanted to know what Cathy and her husband had discovered and it was simple really.

After Graham had denied to give them their five thousand pounds, Cathy dug a little deeper and found another ten patients had died during very simple surgeries because Graham hadn't cleaned their equipment properly.

So Andy dug even deeper and after two wonderful breakfasts in Denny's they found a total of two hundred patients over a span of twenty years had died under Graham's care and the government and Medical Authority had naturally known about this. And yet they did nothing.

Cathy told the world about it, released her evidence and the Medical Authority had already been torn down by the government (that was probably always part of the plan) and now the government was being investigated by the United Nations for a whole range of things.

Cathy had wanted to listen and read about the investigation but she wasn't a UK lawyer anymore, and as she walked down the busy London sidewalk with thick grey block paving under her feet, she felt so amazing about herself.

She could never bring back the healthcare system or get her money back but she could at least help people to realise just how bad the UK had gotten.

"Ready to go babe?" Andy asked as he pulled up next to her in a massive black SUV.

She could tell that the backseats were packed with everything they owned, their house and office was sold and their bank accounts were filled with millions and all the money had been transferred from UK to Scottish accounts.

And Cathy looked around at London for one last time, she wasn't going to miss this place, she was going to miss Denny's but she had a law career to build up in Scotland and she couldn't wait for the next chapter of her life to begin.

And she was even more excited about the rumours that there was a Denny's opening in Edinburgh. So that was exactly where she needed to go.

FUTURE INSURANCE

A SCIENCE FICTION NEAR FUTURE SHORT STORY

FUTURE INSURANCE
10th July 2055
London, England

Fixer Betty McDonald had never ever been to a Denny's before and she had no idea whatsoever to expect, as she sat down in the little soft booth with its brown leather seating. It seemed comfortable enough and the dust-red walls had little strange pieces of abstract art on them but mostly the walls were plain.

At least the owners didn't want to detract from the cozy feeling of the diner too much. Betty still couldn't understand why there were bright lights over each booth with a dust-red lampshade over them, that just looked a little weird but the American diner feel was hardly a bad thing.

The diner was rather full which surprised her because it was brand-new and Betty only knew about it because a client wanted to meet here of all places. Betty had really wanted to meet outside in one of London's amazing green spaces, at least that way she could go for a run beforehand and maybe after.

Other people were sitting in different little booths and they were honestly looked like regulars. Betty could never imagine herself being a regular at the diner but it did have a great atmosphere with the sounds of laughter, gentle talking and the wonderful waiters and waitresses in their red shirts and black aprons around their waists helping people.

The couple in the booth in front of her were laughing away and it was clear that they loved each other. And that only added to the wonderful atmosphere of the diner.

Betty had looked at the menus before she came in and the food looked amazing. They served breakfast all day and they had some of the best pancakes on the planet.

It was just a shame that Betty didn't like greasy food and her body always reacted violently almost if she had too much fat.

A cute waiter taking a mountain of pancakes covered in bacon, whipped cream and fried chicken went past and Betty honestly expected herself to faint. It smelt so wonderful and she was so going to grab that when her client showed up.

A slim figure caught the corner of Betty's eye and she smiled when she saw it was her client, a Miss Elizabeth Nelson. She wasn't like anything Betty had expected as she wobbled into the seat opposite her.

Elizabeth actually bumped the table so hard and a loud snapping sound came from underneath her. Betty was fairly sure these tables were bolted to the ground but she hardly would have been surprised if a bolt had just snapped.

The woman hadn't even explained why she wanted to hire Betty yet and she just knew this was going to be a hell of a case. Because Betty helped people with all sorts of problems from health insurance to stalkers and everything in between.

If it was an interesting case then Betty would take it and she loved her life like that.

And she loved it even more when she got to come to new and exciting locations like an American diner.

"I want to hire you to help me with my medical insurance," Elizabeth said.

Betty simply nodded. That wasn't what she wanted to hear at all, she had been getting way too many medical-related jobs lately and it was all because the UK Government had finally decided to get rid of the country's free healthcare system.

Betty utterly hated the government for making that stupid

decision but in all fairness the healthcare system had been crippled since the early 2020s and no one had bothered to fix it.

Everyone had gotten private health insurance by the 2030s and Betty hated it how there was no longer a free healthcare system for people who couldn't afford insurance. The only reason why Betty could was because she had this fixer job.

There were millions of people all over the country that couldn't get access to even the most basic sort of healthcare without it being free. They simply couldn't afford the insurance.

Yet that was life in the UK.

Sometimes Betty wondered about starting her own medical insurance company. It wasn't like she didn't have the knowledge, millions and contacts to get it started. But that wouldn't go well and she much preferred fixing people's problems in other ways.

"What's the problem?" Betty asked. "And how can I fix it?"

Elizabeth waved at a waitress with her black apron barely covering her stomach.

"My insurance company has cancelled my cover. They won't insure me anymore and I have a… bowel cancer operation coming up. I need that insurance or the hospital won't do my op,"

Betty bit her lip. Out of all the bad things she had to help people with lately because of the collapse of UK healthcare, this had to be the worse one yet. And if it could happen to someone like Elizabeth, a woman with money, then Betty hated to imagine what it would be like for someone who didn't have money at all.

Betty had to help Elizabeth no matter what she had to do.

**

As much as Betty just wanted to comfort Elizabeth, the job was a lot more important so she paid for Elizabeth to have a massive stack of pancakes covered in wonderful bacon, whipped cream and thick golden Maple syrup. And Betty set off to work.

It hadn't been too hard to track down Elizabeth's insurance company and because Betty had a reputation of the sort of woman you didn't mess with, she was really pleased when the head of

Human Resources agreed to meet with her.

Betty sat in a very comfortable wooden chair in a bright white office with holo-light streaming in from fake windows that took a hell of a long time to get used to. She was so glad she didn't have those awful things in her house or office.

A few moments later a very tall man wearing a very attractive black suit came in, he clapped his hands and a holographic desk appeared. Betty was even more amazed when the hot man managed to place his mug of coffee on it without it falling off.

Clearly this insurance company was hardly short of cash and that annoyed Betty even more. It made no sense why they had cancelled Elizabeth's policy especially as she was one of the most diligent customers she had ever met.

"I trust your run here wasn't too bad?" the man asked.

Betty was impressed he knew she was a keen runner and she didn't like to drive anywhere.

"It was but if you know that about me then you know why I am here,"

"True. You want to know about Elizabeth Nelson and why we cancelled her policy,"

"I do," Betty said staring at the man's bright brown eyes in an effort to scare him.

"We cancelled her policy because she broke a cardinal rule as far as we're concerned. It is very clear in our contract that our customers cannot shop around for new deals until one week before their renewal date,"

Betty grinned because this was going to be a fun case.

"We have evidence that she was contacting and shopping around for five deals with different companies 9 days before her renewal. And she had already confirmed in writing to us that she would be staying so there was no issue with the payment of her hospital treatment,"

"Of course but I want to know exactly how you got that information," Betty asked.

The man laughed. "Miss McDonald you clearly had parents that told you a lot about the 2010s and those barbaric times. There is no such thing as privacy anymore and it is perfectly legal for companies to spy on its customer. You know that. I know that,"

I really hated how he was right, the damn fool.

"So you openly admit you spied on a customer without their consent and are you seriously going to let a woman not have a lifesaving operation, just because of a stupid clause?"

The man stood up and gestured Betty to the door. "Of course we are. Insurance is a billion pound industry and I will not allow some silly woman to spoil it for the company. If the UK didn't want a healthcare system like this then they should have tried harder,"

Betty had absolutely nothing to say to him because he was an idiot and it was a great shame that everything he was saying was true.

It wasn't right, fair or just but it was true.

And that was something that Betty had to change.

***

Betty couldn't believe she was having so many problems with the insurance company and it was even worst when her own company cancelled her policy. That made no sense because she was with a completely different policy but Betty had heard of stories like this before.

She had heard from private investigator friends how healthcare companies cancelled the policies of their enemies before attacking them. And because of more stupid laws a person couldn't make a police report for assault unless they had a medical certificate.

And a person couldn't have a medical certificate without medical insurance. It was so stupid that this was the world Betty lived in and it was almost heart-breaking that she knew her parents would be appalled that this is how the UK ended up.

Betty stood with her back against the cold white wall of her office that was nothing more than a simple box room with a desk, computer and mini-fridge in one corner. And she waited to be attacked.

Betty had a heavy warm metal pipe in her hand and she was also looking forward to stopping the attacker whenever they turned the electrically charged doorknob.

The eerie silence of the office made Betty's stomach tighten and the smell of fresh cold air was strange because she normally had her small pocket burner on so the office smelt of flowers or whatever she had installed on the burner.

Yet she couldn't have any distractions.

A few moments later the quiet sound of footsteps came from outside and Betty realised she had made a massive error. She hadn't realised that her door opened inwards and it would hit her when opened.

She had a choice to make. She could move and dare make a sound or she could stay still and hope she wasn't injured by the hit.

She rolled forward.

A woman kicked in the door.

Betty jumped up. Charging at the woman. Betty swung her pipe.

The woman blocked Betty's swings. She punched Betty. Slamming her fists into her stomach.

The woman grabbed the pipe. Ripping it from Betty's gasp.

Betty went to kick her.

The woman dodged it. Betty left forwards. The woman got Betty in a headlock.

"Leave us alone. Elizabeth will die. You will die. There is nothing you can do about it," the woman said.

Betty stomped on the woman's foot.

Betty spun around. Punching her in the chest. Slamming her fist into her throat for good measure.

She fell to the ground. Betty kicked her in the head for even better measure.

The woman weakly put up her hand as to wave her away but Betty wasn't going to hurt her anymore. Betty wasn't a monster and she knew that.

"Tell your boss I have security footage of you attacking me. It won't be hard to prove you work for the healthcare companies as a hitwoman and tell them not to cancel any more policies,"

The woman laughed. "You know how rich and powerful we are. The healthcare companies will always win. We have the money, resources and the government is fully behind us,"

Betty nodded because again this was all true. It was impossible to take a healthcare company to court, it was impossible to get them arrested and everyone who tried to embarrass them died.

But Betty wasn't a nobody.

"Fine then," Betty said. "You have 12 hours to give me and my client our policies back or I will make a move no one saw coming,"

The woman laughed as she went off out of her office and Betty knew the woman wouldn't do anything and she was really excited to finally challenge the healthcare companies once and for all.

***

Two months later Betty was so happy to be standing next to a sleeping Elizabeth as she recovered from her bowel cancer surgery, the bright sterile white walls of the medical room were wonderfully refreshing and it had been interesting talking to the doctors about Elizabeth's holographic vital signals.

At least Elizabeth was going to make a full recovery and thankfully all initial signs showed her cancer was gone and she was in full remission. That was amazing and Betty was so glad she had personally gifted her the money for the surgery.

Betty was even more impressed that she was a billionaire now and the CEO of *Fairness Healthcare*, a major national medical insurance provider with over ten million clients and she had actually bought five smaller insurance companies including Elizabeth's and her own former companies. She was that successful and that hated.

Betty loved going home each night and reading all the death threats, hate and sexist comments she got in her emails from other healthcare providers that said her social justice approach to healthcare was going to kill the UK.

When she first got the comments she actually responded to them and explained it was only fair that everyone in the UK had access to free healthcare but now she simply didn't bother. It wasn't worth it and the other companies had always hated her.

They were even trying to make the UK Government decree her company was corrupt, funding human trafficking and killing patients. It was all lies of course but they were pouring millions into the bank accounts of the government to make them more inclined to do it.

Betty just didn't have the heart to tell them that she had the entire government as her customers so she was fairly sure she was safe.

And as Elizabeth slept peacefully next to her, Betty was just glad that so many other amazing people would also be safe, protected and now had access to healthcare. And Betty truly loved her life.

AUTHOR OF ACCLAIMED AGENTS OF THE EMPEROR SERIES

CONNOR WHITELEY

FUTURE STRIKE

A SCIENCE FICTION NEAR FUTURE SHORT STORY

FUTURE STRIKE
15th July 2051
Southeast England

Internationally renowned criminal Pipa Megs seriously loved her amazing job that meant she got to travel around entire countries, regions and continents all in an effort to help innocent workers get revenge against evil bosses. Of course back in the day the workers could go to something called a "union" or whatever they were really called. Yet they were illegal now.

Pipa leant against the cold metal of a red shipping container that was easily twenty metres tall and another thirty metres long. She had never really been to a port this immense before, but it was great fun.

There were over twenty million shipping containers in all their shades of red, blue and green stacked on top of each other like stunning towers that would kill all of them if they fell.

And as much as no boss cared about "health and safety" (whatever that was) the cargo was probably too precious to be allowed to be damaged.

The space between the containers were long and narrow barely able to fit a fat man down it. The corners were sharp and quick and almost impossible to run down.

Yet not impossible for Pipa. She loved racing between the shipping containers to the horror of her "bosses" and the other workers that were too awfully fat and slow and sluggish to dare ever try such a thing.

The horrible smells of halo-cigar smoke, fried chicken and dripping fat filled the air from the foul lunch that the workers had barely managed to make themselves. Pipa loved her body, exercise routine and diet too much to allow herself to indulge in such nonsense.

It was even worse when the foul smells left the taste of burnt fried chicken on her tongue. It was simply awful just like how her mother had cooked most dinners when Pipa was a child.

The sky above was darkening so there was probably a storm coming, not that the foul bosses would care. As far as they were concerned Pipa and the others were meant to work themselves to the bone for no money.

It was ridiculous of course and Pipa hated it all. She had learnt from her father the importance of unions, the right to strike and more. Then again it was her father who was murdered by his company's bosses because he wanted better working conditions after his cancer diagnosis.

They didn't care. Nobody cared. Even her mother seemed a little distant from the simple truth.

"Afternoon Pip," a man said wearing black overalls, hat and steel toe-capped boots.

Out of the corner of her eye Pipa noticed someone in the shape of a woman look at her and then hide behind a red shipping container.

So as Pipa watched three overweight men chomping on some greasy horrible fried chicken, she smiled. Not exactly something she liked but today was the day she was meeting a contact that would finally reveal who needed to die.

That was the problem with being an assassin and criminal that went from port to port, job to job, factory to factory. At the end of the day all the companies were very different so the lynchpin was always hard to find.

The lynchpin. The only person that needed to die to herald in a new age of change, hope and fairness for the workers. Most people believed it was the actual boss at the very top of the organisation but they were wrong.

It was almost always someone else. Someone who actually had the power to do so.

"Are you Her?" a woman asked wearing a very long black jumpsuit, her hands were dirty and her face was blackened with grease.

"I am," Pipa said hoping that this was the contact.

"Good. The target is the Financial Head. Good day,"

Pipa smiled as the woman simply walked away like that was everything. She didn't tell her where the Head was, how he needed to die or anything.

Not that it mattered. Pipa was more than good enough to do this alone and without any help.

Pipa had been here for three months now and that meant she knew everywhere, everything and everyone fairly well. It wasn't hard to track down people in the Port and it certainly wasn't hard to convince workers to improve their lives.

She had been working on converting the workers for months. She was sure they would rise up soon and form a union to demand better pay.

There was a lot of doubt in her about their commitment but she had to do her part first. She had to kill the man that would make change possible.

Then it really was down to the workers to siege their right.

Two black fighter jets zoomed overhead and Pipa bit her lip as she realised that a rumour about a military inspection wasn't a fake one created by the bosses.

It was real. And a military presence would only make her job a lot harder.

***

To her utter surprise, the Head of The Port's Finances was hardly difficult to hunt down to the main building. A massive warehouse in the very centre of the port made out of solid concrete with anti-union propaganda playing on the walls for all to see in holographic form.

The images were just funny because they really would have made her father want to punch something. But people always believed lies in the end.

Pipa crouched on the cold grey metal roof of the main building allowing her to see the entire port and how it stretched on for tens upon tens of miles. It was stunningly beautiful but Pipa was a lot more interested in what was going on below her.

On the grey perfectly smooth concrete ground below, there were three men from the port. Pipa recognised all of them and she absolutely hated them.

The man in the middle wearing an expensive black suit was the boss of the entire port, he was the man that ordered the executions of workers likely to try and form a union.

The man to the left was a weak little man who was the Head of Finance. He was wearing an ill-fitting dark blue suit and that crime against fashion only made Pipa want to kill him even more.

But the third man. The third man was a man she hadn't expected to be here because he was wearing a bright red suit and wearing two assault rifles. He was the Head of Security and normally he spent his days stalking the port and if he saw a worker he would kill them.

It didn't matter if they were doing their job or not. They would die plain and simple.

"This is not the time for an inspection," the boss said.

Pipa frowned when she noticed the ten military soldiers standing there in their black uniform all armed to the teeth with flame throwers, assault rifles and electrified swords.

If these were normal guns she wouldn't actually care but she could see all of them had holo-scopes only improving their already extreme accuracy.

There was no way she was surviving this for now.

Pipa wanted to escape and return later but she couldn't. She had already stopped off at her little kit bag and retrieved her pistol gifted to her by her father the year he died.

The little pistol was no match against weapons with holo-scopes and it wasn't like she had the equipment to cause them to short circuit or explode.

"We are hunting a dangerous criminal," the military man in the centre said. "The criminal is a woman so she is insane. She is so insane that she seeks to allow workers to unionise once more,"

That instantly shut up the three Port men. Pipa didn't know how the hell they knew she was here, she was always so damn careful.

"And our agent told her to kill you," the military man said to the Finance Head.

Pipa grinned. The damn woman that met her earlier she was a traitor to the workers.

"And I can see her now commander," a man said pointing straight at her.

Everyone fixed their guns on her.

"Women are insane creatures aren't they?" the Finance Head said. "Thank goodness you can't vote anymore,"

"She'll receive another ten years on her sentence for going outside without a man escort," another man said.

Pipa just shook her head. The world really had gone mad in recent decades.

Pipa whipped out her pistol. Aiming it at the Finance Head.

"Let me kill him and I will go away. Never to return to England," Pipa said really doubting that would work.

"Kill her in two minutes," the commander said before looking at Pipa. "I will give you two minutes to make an argument that will convince me to let you live,"

"Never. You will kill me. You will kill the bosses. You will siege the Port,"

"I'm amazed a woman could be so clever,"

Pipa just grinned. It was the female workers that had been so obsessed with the idea of forming a union and protecting their way of life.

And as Pipa noticed little shadows moving about the edges of the rows of shipping containers. She was fairly certain women would take control once again.

"Let me tell you why I am so good at my job. I am good because I save money. So I can buy technology that makes my impossible things safe for me,"

No one understood her. They didn't need to.

Pipa jumped off the building.

Her boots hummed violently as they slowed her fall. She whipped out her pistol. Shooting the Finance head in the neck.

The military raised their guns.

Tens upon tens of women charged out of the rows of shipping containers. They carried hammers shovels and more.

They charged at the military.

Smashing their hammers into their heads. Shattering skulls. Blood sprayed out.

Pipa landed with a thud.

She shot the boss of the port.

The security man tackled her.

He smashed his fists into her.

Pipa whacked him. He didn't feel it. He laughed.

The man whacked his gun against her head. Her vision blurred.

A woman flew at the man.

The man looked away.

Pipa kicked him in-between the legs.

The man rolled off her. Pipa leapt up. Snapping his neck in one fluid motion.

The military fired.

Women were slaughtered.

Pipa flew at the military men. She fired her pistol. Their heads exploded.

The commander aimed his rifle at her. He activated the holo-scope. He fired.

Pipa leapt to one side.

The holo-bullet smashed into her right leg. She screamed in agony.

The commander went over to her and grinned. He looked at her like she was a piece of meat about to be pleasurably enjoyed.

Pipa wasn't having that.

She leapt forward.

Tackling him into the ground. She went to punch him but he blocked.

Knocking her off him.

Then Pipa stopped as did the ten surviving women when the commander and the last three men aimed their guns at their chests. They were trapped and there were about to die.

Pipa didn't regret anything in life because she had fought to protect the rights of innocent workers. Something nobody did anymore.

The commander marched over to Pipa and placed the cold barrel of his rifle against her head.

Screams filled the air. The ground thundered. Hammers flew through the air.

Pipa laughed. Ten overweight men stormed towards them.

Pipa leapt forward. Tackling the commander. He didn't know what was happening.

Pipa whacked her fists across his face. She grabbed his rifle.

She fired.

The commander's head exploded.

And by the time she raised the rifle and activated the holo-scope at the three remaining men. Both the male and female workers had worked in unison to slaughter them and now they were dead.

Pipa stood up and everyone smiled at each other because they knew it was the beginning of something new, magical and powerful.

***

Pipa had really loved the next week of the job where she camped on the top of the building in the middle of the port keeping a close eye on the workers, the entrance and playing with her new rifle collection.

She was really impressed as she laid down on the boiling hot metal roof that the government had basically handed complete control of the Port over to the workers the moment they learnt about the takeover.

Of course it probably helped that now the workers were getting good pay, a good night's sleep and a lot of other basic rights they increased productivity by 40%.

Meaning the Port and the Government made a hell of a lot of money, and at the end of the day money really did make the world go round.

And as Pipa listened to the roar of car engines and hoverbikes drive away into the distance, she was more than glad that the legal contracts and documents were signed for now. Meaning this Port was always going to remain in the hands of workers, and their rights to fair pay, health care and equal rights were always going to be protected.

It partly annoyed Pipa that it was only this single port that was protected but that was the magical and infectious thing about hope and workers. Once they started they could never be stopped.

Pipa was so looking forward to the future. A future where one Port would become two Ports then two Ports might turn to all Ports, and then all workers would have the same rights as they did before the dark ages of the 2020s.

Pipa loved it as her stomach filled with excitement and that really was going to be an amazing age and Pipa was so looking forward to making it happen. The world was changing and she was a lot more excited about creating a brighter future than she had been for a long time.

And it had all started with a single Port, a single droplet that would one day become a raging river of change. Just like her father had wanted.

AUTHOR OF WAY OF THE ODYSSEY SERIES
CONNOR WHITELEY

AT THE END OF THE WORLD
A SCIENCE FICTION APOCALYPTIC SHORT STORY

AT THE END OF THE WORLD

At the end of the world even the weird, deadly and chaotic council estate and student housing of Hell's Place cannot save people.

On the day the world ended, Pipa Graham was sitting in her favourite spot in the entire world, on her brown rattan chair in the wonderful suntrap of her garden. When she first moved in with her housemates at the beginning of the university year, she seriously hadn't been sure about the tiny square patch of grass her landlord had called a "garden".

She really enjoyed the sweet aromas of BBQ chicken, curry powder and sweet roses coming from the garden behind hers that left the great taste of hot summer days with her family form on her tongue. Her family had loved BBQs, Pipa made a mental note to call them later and see if they wanted to meet up for a BBQ soon.

Through the winter and spring she hadn't really thought too much about it, but she flat out loved her garden now it was summer. And it was even better she was going to be here for the final year of her Biomedical Science degree. She could enjoy the wonderful suntrap even more.

Pipa put down her eReader and looked around the edges of the grass patch. She might even plant some flowers, trees and maybe some vegetables. Her landlord almost loved her so she was sure he wouldn't mind too much, and she could always offer to fix his washing machine.

She still couldn't believe how bad the man was at fixing stuff, and she seemed to do a lot of fixing at his other properties in Hell's Place too. If it continued she might ask for a reduction in rent.

Then the sirens started and Pipa's phone vibrated.

Pipa rolled her eyes and she went into her small, cramped dirty white terrace house and turned on the small smart TV hanging half-on and half-off the wall.

She put on the news and her mouth dropped.

She flat out couldn't believe that Russia had actually done it after years of threatening, it had finally launched every single nuclear missile it had. Russia was targeting the US, UK and France and even more countries that Pipa couldn't read fast enough.

Of course she was well aware of the point of nuclear warfare and the entire concept of "mutually assured destruction" so every single country in the world, including the US, UK and France were firing back. Even China was firing on Russia and North Korea because North Korea was taking advantage of the chaos too.

Pipa gripped her stomach as it churned, twisted and tightened into an agonising knot. She had studied nuclear missiles a little because her boyfriend, Dylan, was a nuclear engineer (or at least doing his Masters degree in it). If a nuclear missile hit London then Canterbury wouldn't be hit directly but the radiation would still infect the land.

Pipa watched the news as the missiles smashed into cities all over the world and London was turned to ash. Pipa gasped as she realised what London being annihilated actually meant.

Her family lived just outside London, her entire family was dead just like that. And even Dylan had been visiting his family in Westminster so... he was dead too.

The realisation slammed into her like a sledgehammer, so Pipa fell onto the ugly brown armchair Dylan had brought only a few days before.

Dylan had always been so kind, so generous and so amazing. Pipa had no idea how she would have dealt with her dysphoria and her transition without him, he had been her rock when she was struggling. And he was so happy that she was finally the woman she had always wanted to be.

Pipa felt the best she had in her entire life, and now she had lost everything.

The entire world had lost everything.

The news kept talking on and on about the end of the world and Pipa just couldn't listen anymore, so she switched to subtitles. And as much as she couldn't believe that Dylan was gone, she knew she had to survive this as long as she could.

She still had her reading spot, she still had food and she might still have her housemates but that was unlikely. It was just after exam season at the university and all her housemates had gone home for the summer. They were all probably dead.

Pipa felt her eyes turn wet but she didn't dare cry. Dylan would have wanted her to survive and she was never going to disappoint him. Hell he might have even been alive and if that was the case then she absolutely had to stay alive long enough to see him a final time.

And that's what she was going to do.

After an entire day of checking the house, checking how much food she had and planning for the lack of a future, she had written letters to each of her family members (only the four members of her immediate family still spoke to her so it didn't take too much time), she sat in her favourite reading spot again.

She liked how wonderfully warm, comfortable and solid the rattan armchair was after being out in the sun all day. The air was a little metallic and odd for her taste and Pipa didn't like how the weird taste of ozone formed in her mouth. She really didn't want to think about how much radiation she might be breathing in right now.

Pipa watched a little injured Blue Tit hop along the top of her fence. She had about three months' worth of food left in the house on the assumption that her other housemates were dead. They had always brought tons of food and they had said she could use whatever she wanted over the summer.

So Pipa planned too.

She didn't really care about the lack of books she had because she wanted to focus on surviving, and she had enough books left to keep herself entertained.

She was hopefully going to be okay, and she had a whole bunch of potatoes left in the kitchen. Tomorrow she was going to plant them in the garden (the landlord was probably dead anyway) and she would go through the rest of the fruit and vegetables in the house to see what seeds she could salvage. And hopefully plant and grow in the next year.

The winter was her biggest concern but at least the power was still on and there were odd pockets of humanity that seemed to be alive.

Yet as the little Blue Tit fell to the ground and rolled towards her, Pipa sort of guessed her time was limited even in Hell's Place.

Two weeks later Pipa frowned as she stood in front of her sliding door in the living room, and watched as black clouds filled the sky filled with radiation and black soot continued to rain down. The clouds had been there for at least a week and Pipa was so annoyed at them.

For over a week she hadn't managed to go outside to her reading spot and she hated it. The news had told her to stay inside because of the radiation, and Pipa had managed to find some Iodine tablets in the cupboard. It was a small trick to help stop a radioactive form of iodine but she wasn't sure it was working or having much of an effect these days.

Pipa had the news playing in the background and she was glad that some pockets of humanity had survived. Scotland, Wales and Northern Ireland were thankfully okay. A lot of mainland Europe was somehow managing to cling on as was the East Coast of the USA and some pockets of Asia.

But most of the world was dead.

Then the TV turned off.

Pipa rolled her eyes because the power had finally gone out and she shivered. The radioactive clouds had stolen a lot of the sun's heat, and Pipa's frown deepened as her breath formed long columns of vapour.

She went over to the ugly brown armchair and pulled three black blankets over herself. The living room was biting cold and she wasn't sure what she could do to keep surviving. She could no longer grow food, she could no longer keep surviving in the house and she was pretty sure she was being exposed to massive amounts of radiation.

After a moment, Pipa laughed. She wasn't exactly sure why but she supposed it was because she had studied biomedical science to help people, save lives and maybe even do something to help the transgender community. But she was going to die now, so young and she had had her entire life ahead of her.

And sure, she had heard about the weird disappearances, deaths and happenings in Hell's Place, and she had really wanted Hell's Place to save her.

It wasn't going to do that. Pipa was fairly sure even Hell's Place wasn't powerful enough to save her.

She was going to die.

Pipa shook the stupid thought away she wasn't going to die just yet because there was still a chance, a remote chance, that Dylan might be alive and he might return to her.

Two weeks later, Pipa could barely move as she shivered constantly in the freezing temperature of her living room. The smart TV had now completely collapsed off the wall, her living room was pitch black because the sun was basically dead now, and Pipa knew she was going to die.

Her arms were covered with bumpy, lumpy growths that were probably cancerous and she could feel her life just slipping away from her.

She didn't even care that the living room smelt damp and mouldy because the condensation on the sliding doors. She was past caring about everything because she had failed to stay alive.

All Pipa had wanted to do was stay alive for as long as she could, she wanted to study, she wanted to live and she wanted to see Dylan one final time.

Pipa laughed as she started to close her eyes and she knew she would never open them again. She was done, spent but she grinned because she was going to die happy.

She had had an amazing life to be honest. She had studied a subject she loved, Pipa couldn't have asked for a better family or lovely boyfriend and she was going to die a woman. Her younger self would have cried with joy at knowing that was actually possible.

She had lived an amazing life.

The door clicked open and slammed shut again.

Pipa opened her eyes weakly and grinned as Dylan stumbled in. His thin arms might have been covered in his lumps, his face might have been scared and cut and his body might have been sliced open. He was still the most beautiful man she had ever seen.

"The world's gone mad out there. Survivors are having a free for all," Dylan said straining out each word.

Pipa smiled and she tried to hold out her hand but she couldn't. She was simply too weak but Dylan got the message, so he came over and settled into the armchair with Pipa in his strong lumpy arms.

And he held her and Pipa tried to hold him back.

Then they both closed their eyes and smiled, because they had both lived amazing, wonderful lives and ultimately died in each other's arms.

If that wasn't a great way to die then Pipa seriously didn't want to know what was.

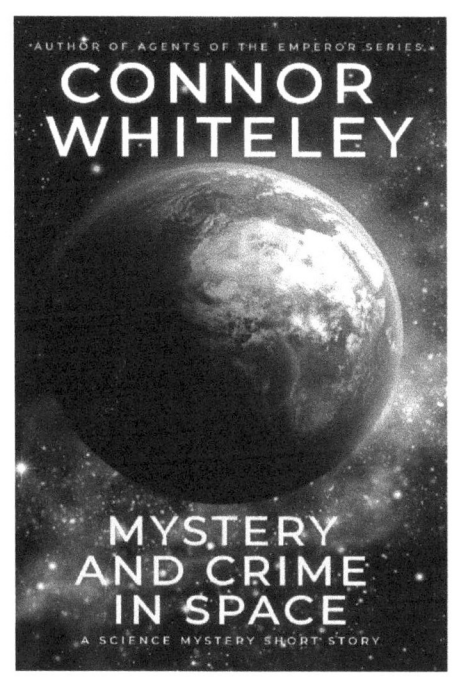

GET YOUR FREE SHORT STORY NOW! And get signed up to Connor Whiteley's newsletter to hear about new gripping books, offers and exciting projects. (You'll never be sent spam)

https://www.subscribepage.io/garrosignup

About the author:

Connor Whiteley is the author of over 60 books in the sci-fi fantasy, nonfiction psychology and books for writer's genre and he is a Human Branding Speaker and Consultant.

He is a passionate warhammer 40,000 reader, psychology student and author.

Who narrates his own audiobooks and he hosts The Psychology World Podcast.

All whilst studying Psychology at the University of Kent, England.

Also, he was a former Explorer Scout where he gave a speech to the Maltese President in August 2018 and he attended Prince Charles' 70th Birthday Party at Buckingham Palace in May 2018.

Plus, he is a self-confessed coffee lover!

RIVETINGLY GREAT STORIES VOLUME 5

<u>Other books by Connor Whiteley:</u>
<u>Bettie English Private Eye Series</u>
A Very Private Woman
The Russian Case
A Very Urgent Matter
A Case Most Personal
Trains, Scots and Private Eyes
The Federation Protects
Cops, Robbers and Private Eyes
Just Ask Bettie English
An Inheritance To Die For
The Death of Graham Adams
Bearing Witness
The Twelve
The Wrong Body
The Assassination Of Bettie English
Wining And Dying
Eight Hours
Uniformed Cabal
A Case Most Christmas

<u>Gay Romance Novellas</u>
Breaking, Nursing, Repairing A Broken Heart
Jacob And Daniel
Fallen For A Lie
Spying And Weddings
Clean Break
Awakening Love
Meeting A Country Man
Loving Prime Minister
Snowed In Love
Never Been Kissed

Love Betrays You
Love And Hurt

Lord of War Origin Trilogy:
Not Scared Of The Dark
Madness
Burn Them All

Way Of The Odyssey
Odyssey of Rebirth
Convergence of Odysseys
Odyssey Of Hope
Odyssey of Enlightment

Lady Tano Fantasy Adventure Stories
Betrayal
Murder
Annihilation

Agents of The Emperor
Deceitful Terra
Blood And Wrath
Infiltration
Fuel To The Fire
Return of The Ancient Ones
Vigilance
Angels of Fire
Kingmaker
The Eight
The Lost Generation
Hunt
Emperor's Council

Speaker of Treachery
Birth Of The Empire
Terraforma
Spaceguard

<u>The Rising Augusta Fantasy Adventure Series</u>
Rise To Power
Rising Walls
Rising Force
Rising Realm

<u>The Fireheart Fantasy Series</u>
Heart of Fire
Heart of Lies
Heart of Prophecy
Heart of Bones
Heart of Fate

<u>City of Assassins (Urban Fantasy)</u>
City of Death
City of Martyrs
City of Pleasure
City of Power

<u>Lord Of War Trilogy (Agents of The Emperor)</u>
Not Scared Of The Dark
Madness
Burn It All Down

Miscellaneous:
Dead Names
RETURN
FREEDOM
SALVATION
Reflection of Mount Flame
The Masked One
The Great Deer
English Independence

OTHER SHORT STORIES BY CONNOR WHITELEY

Mystery Short Story Collections
Criminally Good Stories Volume 1: 20 Detective Mystery Short Stories
Criminally Good Stories Volume 2: 20 Private Investigator Short Stories
Criminally Good Stories Volume 3: 20 Crime Fiction Short Stories
Criminally Good Stories Volume 4: 20 Science Fiction and Fantasy Mystery Short Stories
Criminally Good Stories Volume 5: 20 Romantic Suspense Short Stories

Connor Whiteley Starter Collections:
Agents of The Emperor Starter Collection
Bettie English Starter Collection
Matilda Plum Starter Collection
Gay Romance Starter Collection
Way Of The Odyssey Starter Collection
Kendra Detective Fiction Starter Collection

RIVETINGLY GREAT STORIES VOLUME 5

<u>Science Fiction Short Story Collections</u>
Rivetingly Great Stories Volume 1
Rivetingly Great Stories Volume 2
Rivetingly Great Stories Volume 3
Rivetingly Great Stories Volume 4
Rivetingly Great Stories Volume 5

<u>Mystery Short Stories:</u>
Protecting The Woman She Hated
Finding A Royal Friend
Our Woman In Paris
Corrupt Driving
A Prime Assassination
Jubilee Thief
Jubilee, Terror, Celebrations
Negative Jubilation
Ghostly Jubilation
Killing For Womenkind
A Snowy Death
Miracle Of Death
A Spy In Rome
The 12:30 To St Pancreas
A Country In Trouble
A Smokey Way To Go
A Spicy Way To GO
A Marketing Way To Go
A Missing Way To Go
A Showering Way To Go
Poison In The Candy Cane
Kendra Detective Mystery Collection Volume 1
Kendra Detective Mystery Collection Volume 2
Mystery Short Story Collection Volume 1

Mystery Short Story Collection Volume 2
Criminal Performance
Candy Detectives
Key To Birth In The Past

Science Fiction Short Stories:
Their Brave New World
Gummy Bear Detective
The Candy Detective
What Candies Fear
The Blurred Image
Shattered Legions
The First Rememberer
Life of A Rememberer
System of Wonder
Lifesaver
Remarkable Way She Died
The Interrogation of Annabella Stormic

Fantasy Short Stories:
City of Snow
City of Light
City of Vengeance
Dragons, Goats and Kingdom
Smog The Pathetic Dragon
Don't Go In The Shed
The Tomato Saver
The Remarkable Way She Died
Dragon Coins
Dragon Tea
Dragon Rider

RIVETINGLY GREAT STORIES VOLUME 5

<u>All books in 'An Introductory Series':</u>
Introduction To Psychotherapies
I Am Not A Victim, I Am A Survivor
Breaking The Silence
Healing As A Survivor
Clinical Psychology and Transgender Clients
Clinical Psychology
Moral Psychology
Myths About Clinical Psychology
401 Statistics Questions For Psychology Students
Careers In Psychology
Psychology of Suicide
Dementia Psychology
Clinical Psychology Reflections Volume 4
Forensic Psychology of Terrorism And Hostage-Taking
Forensic Psychology of False Allegations
Year In Psychology
CBT For Anxiety
CBT For Depression
Applied Psychology
<u>BIOLOGICAL PSYCHOLOGY 3RD EDITION</u>
<u>COGNITIVE PSYCHOLOGY THIRD EDITION</u>
<u>SOCIAL PSYCHOLOGY- 3RD EDITION</u>
<u>ABNORMAL PSYCHOLOGY 3RD EDITION</u>
<u>PSYCHOLOGY OF RELATIONSHIPS- 3RD EDITION</u>
<u>DEVELOPMENTAL PSYCHOLOGY 3RD EDITION</u>
<u>HEALTH PSYCHOLOGY</u>
<u>RESEARCH IN PSYCHOLOGY</u>
<u>A GUIDE TO MENTAL HEALTH AND TREATMENT AROUND THE WORLD- A GLOBAL LOOK AT DEPRESSION</u>
<u>FORENSIC PSYCHOLOGY</u>

THE FORENSIC PSYCHOLOGY OF THEFT, BURGLARY AND OTHER CRIMES AGAINST PROPERTY
CRIMINAL PROFILING: A FORENSIC PSYCHOLOGY GUIDE TO FBI PROFILING AND GEOGRAPHICAL AND STATISTICAL PROFILING.
CLINICAL PSYCHOLOGY
FORMULATION IN PSYCHOTHERAPY
PERSONALITY PSYCHOLOGY AND INDIVIDUAL DIFFERENCES
CLINICAL PSYCHOLOGY REFLECTIONS VOLUME 1
CLINICAL PSYCHOLOGY REFLECTIONS VOLUME 2
Clinical Psychology Reflections Volume 3
CULT PSYCHOLOGY
Police Psychology

A Psychology Student's Guide To University
How Does University Work?
A Student's Guide To University And Learning
University Mental Health and Mindset